WESTERN ARABIA AND THE RED SEA

T0314625

Produced during the Second World War for the use of commanding officers, this work is a complete guide to the lands of Western Arabia. Sections on geology, geography, the coasts, climate, vegetation, history, administration, people, public health, agriculture, economy, ports and towns offer readers a unique military perspective on this important region. Supplemented with hundreds of maps, photographs and figures, this book will be of great use to anyone with an interest in Arabia.

1. *The Centre of Islam*

WESTERN ARABIA AND THE RED SEA

BY

THE NAVAL INTELLIGENCE DIVISION

Routledge
Taylor & Francis Group

LONDON AND NEW YORK

First published in 1946 by Naval Intelligence Division.

This edition first published in 2009 by
Routledge
2 Park Square, Milton Park, Abingdon, Oxon, OX14 4RN

Simultaneously published in the USA and Canada
by Routledge
711 Third Avenue, New York, NY 10017

Routledge is an imprint of the Taylor & Francis Group, an informa business

© Naval Intelligence Division 1946

First issued in paperback 2012

British Library Cataloguing in Publication Data
A catalogue record for this book is available from the British Library

ISBN13: 978-0-415-65321-3 (PBK)
ISBN13: 978-0-710-31034-7 (HBK)

Publisher's Note
The publisher has gone to great lengths to ensure the quality of this reprint
but points out that some imperfections in the original copies may be
apparent. The publisher has made every effort to contact original copyright
holders and would welcome correspondence from those they have been
unable to trace.

PREFACE

IN 1915 a Geographical Section was formed in the Naval Intelligence Division of the Admiralty to write Geographical Handbooks on various parts of the world. The purpose of these Handbooks was to supply, by scientific research and skilled arrangement, material for the discussion of naval, military, and political problems, as distinct from the examination of the problems themselves. Many distinguished collaborators assisted in their production, and by the end of 1918 upwards of fifty volumes had been produced in Handbook and Manual form, as well as numerous short-term geographical reports. The demand for these books increased rapidly with each new issue, and they acquired a high reputation for accuracy and impartiality. They are now to be found in Service Establishments and Embassies throughout the world, and in the early years after the last war were much used by the League of Nations.

The old Handbooks have been extensively used in the present war, and experience has disclosed both their value and their limitations. On the one hand they have proved, beyond all question, how greatly the work of the fighting services and of Government Departments is facilitated if countries of strategic or political importance are covered by handbooks which deal, in a convenient and easily digested form, with their geography, ethnology, administration, and resources. On the other hand it has become apparent that something more is required to meet present-day requirements. The old series does not cover many of the countries closely affected by the present war (e.g. Germany, France, Poland, Spain, Portugal, to name only a few); its books are somewhat uneven in quality, and they are inadequately equipped with maps, diagrams, and photographic illustrations.

The present series of Handbooks, while owing its inspiration largely to the former series, is in no sense an attempt to revise or re-edit that series. It is an entirely new set of books, produced in the Naval Intelligence Division by trained geographers drawn largely from the Universities, and working at sub-centres established at Oxford and Cambridge, and is printed by the Oxford and Cambridge University Presses. The books follow, in general, a uniform scheme, though minor modifications will be found in particular cases; and they are illustrated by numerous maps and photographs.

The purpose of the books is primarily naval. They are designed first to provide, for the use of Commanding Officers, information in a comprehensive and convenient form about countries which they may be called upon to visit, not only in war but in peace-time; secondly, to maintain the high standard of education in the Navy and, by supplying officers with material for lectures to naval personnel ashore and afloat, to ensure for all ranks that visits to a new country shall be both interesting and profitable.

Their contents are, however, by no means confined to matters of purely naval interest. For many purposes (e.g. history, administration, resources, communications, &c.) countries must necessarily be treated as a whole, and no attempt is made to limit their treatment exclusively to coastal zones. It is hoped therefore that the Army, the Royal Air Force, and other Government Departments (many of whom have given great assistance in the production of the series) will find these Handbooks even more valuable than their predecessors proved to be both during and after the last war.

J. H. GODFREY
Director of Naval Intelligence
1942

The foregoing preface has appeared from the beginning of this series of Geographical Handbooks. It describes so effectively their origin and purpose that I have decided to retain it in its original form.

This volume has been prepared by the Oxford sub-centre of the Naval Intelligence Division under the direction of Lieut.-Colonel K. Mason, M.C., M.A., R.E., Professor of Geography in the University of Oxford, and is the work of a number of contributors, whose names are given on page 619.

E. G. N. RUSHBROOKE
Director of Naval Intelligence
JUNE 1946

CONTENTS

TEXT-FIGURES AND MAPS

LIST OF ILLUSTRATIONS

CHAPTER I

INTRODUCTION

TRAVELLERS approaching Arabia by the Suez Canal and the Red Sea first sight the north-western part of the vast peninsula. Here, the granite peaks of the desert ranges, in reddish-yellow and violet shades, look over steely dark-blue waters from which leap countless flying-fish. Farther south, the silhouettes of the south-western highlands, tawny or buff or silver-grey in different lights, are seen from afar across a low, arid coastal belt. Often the outlines of those mighty ramparts are softened by morning mist, while, in the late afternoons and evenings of the summer monsoon, huge mountains of cumulus cloud float above the terrestrial ranges. In the sunshine of midday all may be shrouded by an atmosphere filled with fine dust, or distorted in the hot trembling air. Probably few who pass up and down the Red Sea highway think of the ancient caravan route and the age-old cities lying but a few days' or even a few hours' journey from those coral-bound coasts: Mecca, holy city of a ninth part of the human race; Al Madina, guarding the Prophet's tomb; San'ā, itself centuries old, heir to a succession of civilizations extending back long before the birth of Muhammad or Christ; and the modern Arab skyscrapers of Shibām and other towns of the Hadhramaut.

Limits, Shape, Size, and Population

In this volume, which deals principally with *Western Arabia and the Red Sea*, the area to be described has no definite geographical or political boundaries. Arbitrary lines must therefore be taken to serve as general limits. An irregular line may be drawn roughly from the point where the old Hejaz railway crosses the Sa'ūdi Arabian frontier near Qal'at al Mudauwara, east of 'Aqaba in the north, to Ras Dhurbat 'Ali, which marks the frontier on the south coast of Arabia between the Aden Protectorate and the Sultanate of 'Omān. Of the modern states and territories composing Arabia, a great part of the Sa'ūdi Kingdom, the whole of the Kingdom of the Yemen, and the Aden Protectorate lie west of this line; consideration of these three, therefore, forms a large part of this volume. The Sultanate of Kuweit and the Sheikhdom of Bahrein, with the chieftaincies of the Trucial

Coast, have been dealt with in *Iraq and the Persian Gulf* (B.R. 524, Chap. III, 1944). As for the remaining State, the Sultanate of 'Omān, detailed accounts of its history, administration, and towns are perforce omitted, though its physical geography, geology, climate, vegetation, and ethnology are included with those of Arabia as a whole.

So far as possible the Red Sea, with the gulfs of Suez and 'Aqaba, and their coasts, are treated as a single entity in regard to the general subjects just mentioned, as well as in some phases of their history. To-day these coasts touch seven separate states and territories, as detailed on pp. 58–59. The wedge of Sinai, politically part of Egypt, is described in Chapter II, and the Red Sea coasts of Egypt, the Sudan, and Eritrea are dealt with in Chapter III.

It is, indeed, impossible to describe the land and its people within the limits laid down without some account of the Arabian peninsula as a whole, that huge rectangular block broken off the African continent and separated from it by the Red Sea rift. Its long axis is inclined considerably east of south; the longer sides are roughly parallel in the north, where the mean width is about 700 miles. In the south the peninsula broadens in a north-easterly direction to include 'Omān. The western side of the Arabian block measures over 1,250 miles in a straight line from 'Aqaba to Ras al 'Āra, the southernmost point of the peninsula, about 30 miles east of the strait of Bab al Mandeb; the distance from Ras al 'Āra to Ras al Hadd, the most easterly point, is almost as great; from Ras al Hadd to Ras Masandam, at the entrance to the Persian Gulf in the strait of Hormuz, the distance is nearly 350 miles.

The exact area of the peninsula is difficult to assess, because it is hard to define the northern limit. A line drawn from 'Aqaba to the head of the Persian Gulf lies close to the 30th parallel, but cannot be taken as the northern boundary, either politically or geographically, since the borders of Sa'ūdi Arabia reach 32° N., and the deserts of Arabia continue into the Hamād of Syria and into the Jazira of 'Iraq.

The areas of the component parts of Arabia in square miles are, however, roughly estimated as follows: Sa'ūdi Arabia 927,000 (made up of Nejd and dependencies 800,000; the Hejaz 113,000; 'Asir 14,000); the Yemen 74,000; Aden Colony 75 (plus its dependencies, Perim island 5 and the Kuria Muria islands 30); Aden Protectorate 112,000; Kamarān island (p. 59) 22; Kuweit 2,000; Bahrein 200; Qatar 8,000; 'Omān (Sultanate) 82,000. These figures amount to 1,205,332, so that, with certain indeterminate areas, the total may reach the usually accepted figure of over a million and a quarter, or rather larger than peninsular India. But whereas the latter has hundreds of millions of inhabitants, Arabia supports only about six million people, of whom roughly half inhabit the fertile south-western corner; the rest of the country consists of restricted settled oases, steppes roamed over by a sparse nomad population, and pure sand-deserts.

Land of Contrasts

Few people realize how great is the diversity of land-forms composing Arabia. The whole is not occupied by sand-deserts or semi-desert steppes. The sand-deserts, comprising the northern and western *nafūds*, the long curving strip of the Dahana, and the vast southern expanse of the Rub' al Khali (the 'Empty Quarter'), form a nearly complete girdle round the central steppe-country of Nejd. In parts of the deserts crescentic dunes rise to 400 or 600 feet or even higher. The Northern or Great Nafūd alone, by no means the largest sand-expanse, is at its widest 200 miles each way, 30,000 square miles of wind-blown sand lying in a vast depression, yet piled high above the surrounding steppe, so that it forms a carmine band on the eastern horizon when approached at early morning from the west. So sharply defined are its margins that in many places a single pace will lead from hard stony desert on to fine, deep sand. But this and all other sand-deserts of Arabia, excepting a great part of the Rub' al Khali, which is utterly lifeless, are not devoid of life. They hold the secret of nomad existence, for after even slight rains the sides of the great parallel wave-like dunes are flushed with rich green pasture. More desolate are the dreary expanses of waterless steppe-desert or hard, barren, gravelly steppe, or the monotonous, open, smooth, black expanse of the Desert of Flint, the Ardh as Sawwān (photos. 36, 50.)

Even in Desert Arabia, the grim stony steppes hold perennial sources of water, supplying cities of immemorial antiquity or comparatively recent settlements. Thus Riyādh, the central capital of Sa'ūdi Arabia, a great walled city of clay, forms with other settlements, embowered in date-palms, a single oasis standing back from the flood-level of Wadi Hanīfa, where that watercourse emerges from a cliff-bound channel in the long crescentic plateau of Jebel Tuweiq. At Teima—Tema of the Old Testament and of even more ancient times—throughout history the great caravan junction of the north-west, is the great well-pit of Haddaj, from which sixty to a hundred camels can draw at the same time, so that 100,000 gallons daily may be lifted in 20-gallon buckets of hide. This copious supply of the main oasis, and the twenty smaller wells of two subsidiary settlements, fill a network of irrigation-channels and reservoirs, so that Teima produces not only dates but cereals and fruit. But Nejrān, perhaps, excels all other palm-oases of Arabia in beauty; a broad valley of date-palms bounded on either side by lofty granite cliffs topped by strangely shaped sandstone ranges. A centre of ancient astral worship, and later of Christianity, now the focus of one of the most remote settlements of south Arabian Jews, Nejrān produces wheat and other crops, besides its famous dates. Far to the east, Al Hasa, with the important commercial centre of Hofūf, consists of two broad parallel belts of palms separated by a wide strip of bare, stony plain. Here, on the gentle eastward slope of the limestone steppe, are swamps and rice-fields, fed by perennial waters which percolate underground from higher land far away in central Arabia. Again, in Trucial 'Omān, at the base of the horn running north to the strait of Hormuz, lies the oasis of Bareimi, comprising ten separate villages in a circular oasis 6 miles in diameter, supporting a population of about 5,000, having some 60,000 date-palms, and producing cereals, lucerne, and many kinds of fruit and vegetables, sub-tropical and tropical. The surrounding country is mountainous on the east and south, a mixture of sand-desert and acacia scrub elsewhere. These examples are chosen as representative, but not necessarily the largest, oases.

On the south coast, more than midway from Bab al Mandeb to Ras al Hadd, Dhufār is the most tropical enclave of Arabia. Shut in on the north by the bow of the Qara mountains, the first obstacle causing precipitation from the moisture-laden south-west monsoon, its long crescentic maritime plain, dotted with remains of ancient cities, probably the biblical Ophir, is fringed with coconut-palms. The limestone Qara mountains, rising to 3,000 feet, bear patches of thick forest on their lower slopes and rolling pastures supporting rich herds of cattle above (photos. 63, 124).

Farther west, the Wadi Hadhramaut with its tributaries is formed by canyons between high bare plateaux. On the slopes at the foot of the canyon walls several skyscraper cities stand back from the flat wadi-bed and above the level of sudden floods. The general direction of the main wadi is from west to east, with table-lands to the north reaching 3,500 feet, and to the south 6,000 feet (photos. 23, 58).

Lastly, the south-western corner of the peninsula is the largest part to be classed with the monsoon-lands. Here the long block of the 'Asīr–Yemen highlands runs more than 400 miles from north-north-

west to south-south-east. At its southern end the Kaur ranges project
eastwards towards the high plateaux south of Wadi Hadhramaut. In
the main block, behind the arid coastal belt of the Tihama, consisting
of alluvial and wind-blown deposits 30 to 60 miles wide, the land
rises in successive steps to the high plateaux, 7,000 to 9,000 feet above
sea-level. Many parts of the land-steps, especially at the southern
end, are broken into wild jagged ranges or small isolated plateaux
separated by deep, steep-sided valleys. Once past the barren foothills
the steep mountain-sides are intensively cultivated, with soil built up
into stone-faced terraces rising one above the other for hundreds of
feet. Here are countless terraced fields of *dhura*, and, in some districts, the coffee still named from the decayed port of Mocha, and
many other tropical products. The hot, steamy, malarious valleys
hold an exuberant vegetation, with patches of wild-fig and leguminous
trees of forest-size. In the middle altitudes, drier and more stony
places are dotted with scrub of flat-topped thorny acacias, or covered
with succulent cactus-like euphorbias. These lowlands and medium
altitudes of the south-west form another extensive tropical enclave,
strikingly reminiscent of east Africa. (Photos. 242, 259.)

The terraces of the hill-sides and the plantations in the valley-
bottoms depend on innumerable wells, or on perennial streams and
rivers, which descend the ranges forming the tilted outer margin of
the high table-lands, westwards to the Red Sea lowland, and southwards towards the hinterland of Aden, but rarely reach the sea. The
high plateaux consist of large expanses of plain cultivated with *dhura*,
wheat, barley, lucerne, and pulses. Little of this land is permanently
irrigated; most depends on the direct summer rainfall. Rain-water,
collected in ancient masonry cisterns, or drawn from deep wells sunk
in the porous soil, supplies the needs of man and livestock, but during
the dry winter months most of the land lies fallow or is under the
plough. Streams, however, flow from the eastern side of the watershed, into great wadi-systems extending far across the peninsula,
though in historical times these 'rivers' have been normally dry, and
the waters are lost in the arid interior. But the valleys where the
eastward-flowing streams rise contain irrigated fields where green
crops succeed one another even in the dry months. In such spots lie
the orchards supplying with early fruit the numerous cities and
villages studding these fertile highlands.

From these high plateaux soar peaks and ranges reaching 10,000
and 11,000 feet, especially in the unexplored country of northern
Yemen. In parts of these highlands minerals have been worked for

centuries, iron, sulphur, and probably some lead and gold; but it is doubtful whether they are present in great quantity. The inner slopes of the high table-lands, facing to the deserts of the interior, are much less abrupt than the huge mountain escarpments facing seawards, but they can be striking enough. A traveller of more than seventy years ago has described dramatically the culminating point of the Yemen plateau, north-east of San'ā, on the way to the district of the Yemen Jauf. He felt as though he were hanging over an immense abyss with notched margins, while beneath his feet innumerable summits forming an amphitheatre became gradually lower in succeeding ranges till they faded into sandy desert.

In the heart of the peninsula the 700-mile long crescentic plateau of Jebel Tuweiq, sandstone-built and thinly capped with limestone, rises precipitously from its base at 2,000 feet above sea-level to a mean altitude of 3,000 feet. Near the eastern escarpment of Jebel Tuweiq is a small lake (Umm al Jebel, 'the Mother of the Mountain') three-quarters of a mile long, with broad reedy fringes; it is the only tarn known in Arabia, far different from the salt lagoons inland of the Qatar peninsula near the Persian Gulf. The largest of these salt-lakes, Sabkhet al 'Amra, is about 7 miles long by 1½ miles wide, bordered in parts by a 20-foot belt of rock-salt. Other salt-marshes in the same region may become lakes after heavy rains or exceptionally high tides; for the whole of this area is below sea-level, including probably the low-lying strips of salt-desert, known as 'jaubs' (*jibān*).

Manifestations of dead or dying volcanic activity, such as volcanic craters, lava-flows, and *harras*, surfaces of corrugated and fissured scoriae, often forming large districts, lie almost entirely in western and south-western Arabia, where are such relics as the Aden peninsula itself, several islands in the Red Sea, and grim cones and craters rising from the high plateaux to altitudes of between 9,000 and 10,000 feet. One at least of these craters still emits sulphurous vapour, while in the south-western corner of the Aden Protectorate and parts of the Yemen are found many hot springs. In the north, volcanic action has left ruins of other kinds, such as the fantastic scenery of the Tubeiq hills, a sandstone range with lava outcrops; there, the sandstone has been mainly worn away, leaving lava-capped, blackened, sandstone table-mountains, or black cores of basalt watching over denuded sandstone slopes, an extremely desolate scene. (Photos. 7–12.)

Last in this sketch of strange and varied features may be mentioned Al Hadida, in the eastern part of the 'Empty Quarter', where the impact of meteorites on the desert sands has formed a group of craters on which is based the tradition of an ancient city, Wabar, destroyed by fire (p. 50).

Climate

Arabia falls within the trade-wind desert zone which stretches from the Sahara to Central Asia, but its climate is modified by the troughs of the Red Sea and the Persian Gulf, and by the mountain rims along the western and southern sides. As yet it is impossible to give a systematic and detailed account of the climate of Arabia, because of the lack of detailed observations, but in Chapter IV an attempt is made to bring together all that is known.

The People and their History

Arabia has few historical records before the rise of Islam, but glimpses of the remote past are gained from rock inscriptions, from contacts with the empires of Egypt, Babylon, and Assyria, from the Bible, and from Greek and Roman writings. The same theme runs throughout the centuries: most of the people collected in the more favoured south-western corner, Arabia Felix and the incense country of classical times, the Aden Protectorate, the Yemen, and 'Asīr of to-day. But even here the hard struggle for existence has precluded a peaceful way of life, and internal strife has been constant. Prolonged drought and occasionally violent flood have driven settled peoples to migrate, the general tendency being to move northwards to the 'fertile crescent' along the foothills of Syria and 'Iraq. The inhabitants of Arabia have therefore always included nomadic tribes and settled peoples, and there has always been strife between 'the desert' and 'the sown'. Periods of prosperity have generally been brought about by outside and artificial influences: by the spice and incense trade of the south with Egypt and Syria in ancient times, by the entrepot traffic of the Persian Gulf and Red Sea ports between East and West in medieval times; by political and trade contacts with East Africa, India, and the Far East more recently; and by the great pilgrimage to Mecca ever since the rise of Islam. Thus, while the internal history is often a turmoil of faction and strife, the external contacts, to which considerable space is devoted in Chapter V, have often brought most benefit to the land.

Though internal strife has never permitted Arabia to become a united land, no foreign Power has ever completely dominated it.

Judaism and Christianity, penetrating the country before Muhammad's time, had prepared the way for the unifying religious force of Islam. But neither Muhammad nor his successors, the Omeiyad and Abbasid Caliphs, ever united Arabia politically. The sectarian strife resulting from the growth of the Arab Empire and its break-up into provincial and antagonistic caliphates acted as a separating rather than a unifying force. Only in most recent times has a commanding figure emerged to unite a large part of the peninsula into Sa'ūdi Arabia, leaving but the south-western and southern fringe—the Yemen, Aden and the Aden Protectorate, and 'Omān—independent of his rule.

Administration and Economic Geography

A general account of the administration of these different political divisions excepting the Sultanate of 'Omān is given in Chapter VI. Each part of the country needs administering differently from the rest; to understand the varying administrations it is essential to bear in mind the different ways of life forced on the various peoples by their environment, climate, history, and development. Thus the Hejaz is more sophisticated and more developed than Nejd; the Yemen retains more of its Turkish background than the Hejaz; Aden and the Aden Protectorate have been influenced more by Indian than by Turkish contacts. And, except in the Aden hinterland, European penetration has had extraordinarily little influence on administrative and economic development.

The rapidity of the changes taking place in some parts of Arabia in social conditions and administration should be clearly borne in mind. Such processes as the institution of the non-tribal settlements of *Ikhwān* (p. 286) in Sa'ūdi Arabia, the scarcely completed drastic recasting of the old administrative divisions of the Yemen (p. 331), and the partial disintegration of certain tribal confederations in the Aden Protectorate, render it difficult to keep information up to date.

Aden is the only port of call for large trading-vessels and liners; most of the other ports are used only by Arab dhows and occasional small steamships. Inland, with very few exceptions, roads are still unmetalled and primitive, used almost entirely by pack-animals, the camel and the ass. The only railway, the old Turkish pilgrim line to Al Madina, has long been derelict, and King Ibn Sa'ūd is unlikely to rebuild it. The War of 1939–1945 has seen considerable development in air communications, mostly along the coastal fringes; among the Wahhabis such modern contrivances as the aeroplane are still likely to be looked upon as contraptions of the devil.

Transliteration of Arabic Words

It has been found impossible to follow a consistent system, representing the Arabic letters always by the same Latin characters. In some obscure place-names, and tribal names of plants and other objects, no example of the name in Arabic characters has been available, and the English forms adopted by various authors have had to be used. Authorities differ, largely according to whether their main interests lie in Egypt, Syria, 'Iraq, or India, all of which adopt different systems. On the 1 : 1,000,000 map including Sinai, the letter G appears where J or Q would be used in the sheets covering Arabia proper; even *Jebel* appears as *Gebel*, though the more familiar spelling of the word is used throughout this book. Moreover, writers on Arabia proper differ widely according to their date, personal opinions, and nationality; for example, some words, especially in the Ruwalla dialect, transliterated by Musil, cannot easily be changed to the English system, even with that author's key to the Arabic characters.

The First and Second Lists of Place-Names in Arabia (respectively NW. and SW., and NE. and SE.), issued by the Permanent Committee on Geographical Names in 1931 and 1937, have been followed in the main. The principal deviation is the use of E and EI instead of A and AI in some names, a usage also adopted in the lists of names in south-west Arabia issued at Aden in 1937. By the use of EI as well as AI, an unpractised reader is enabled to distinguish between the vowel-sound in such names as *Hais* (nearly as in 'rye is') and *Seiyūn* (as in 'obey'), both of which are spelt with AI in the official lists. (Incidentally *Yemen* and *Seiyūn* are spelt with E and EI respectively on their postage-stamps, but Kuweit and Bahrein stamps have AI, having been overprinted in India.) Though it might have been simpler to use A and AI throughout, nearness to the correct sound seemed more important than rigid adherence to rule.

The sound represented by AU (Arabic diphthong *fat-ha wau*) also varies. Normally it is as in 'cow', but in the south-west more frequently a long O or even U. Thus, the northern *Jauf* is 'jowf', but the Yemen *Jauf* usually rhymes with 'loaf'; in the south-west *Naubat* is sounded 'no bat', and *Laudar* is 'loader' not 'louder'. The last syllable of *Hadhramaut* is often nearly like 'moot' in that country.

The aspirate or choking sound represented by the letter *ain*, ع, is indicated by '. However difficult to pronounce, its position in a word may be important; for instance, *San'ā* is a large city, *Sāna'* a small village to the south of it. The *hamza* and other diacritical marks are omitted. The Arabic *qāf*, ق, is transliterated Q in accordance with modern English practice, but in parts of Arabia it is sounded like G or confused with K, and in this volume G has been retained in some vernacular or dialect words. The long Ā, Ō, and Ū do not necessarily represent particular Arabic vowels or diphthongs, but are meant simply to aid pronunciation, e.g. the *jōls* of south Arabia rhyme with 'goals', not 'dolls'. Some conventional spellings are employed, such as *Moslem, Mecca, Aden,* instead of *Muslim, Makka, 'Adan,* while *beduin* is used to indicate a single nomad or more than one, rather than *badāwi* (plur. *badu*) or other forms which, incidentally, are not usually applied by the true beduin to themselves (p. 397).

Finally, readers are warned that the spelling of names on the coloured map at the end of the volume may not always agree with that adopted in the text; and on this map the political boundaries are not up to date. These boundaries are shown more correctly on figs. 7, 8, 10, and 11, though they have not been demarcated on the ground.

CHAPTER II

GEOLOGY AND PHYSICAL GEOGRAPHY

As the area under detailed review has no clear natural or political boundaries, it is necessary to consider the geology and physical geography of peninsular Arabia as a whole, before concentrating attention on the parts west of the line laid down. The great rifts or 'trough-faults' bounding the peninsula on the west and south must also be outlined, for they have an important bearing on the coasts described in Chapter III.

The Arabian peninsula owes its existence as a separate land-mass to faulting in the earth's crust. The rifts may therefore be briefly discussed first, then the geology and physiography of the peninsula itself. The principal divisions of this chapter, some of which are further subdivided, are:

(i) The rifts.

(ii) Structure and relief.

(iii) Geology (p. 16).

(iv) Drainage (p. 22).

(v) Chief physiographic divisions of the peninsula (p. 37).

(i) THE RIFTS

Not only are the Red Sea and the Gulf of Aden, with their coasts, the results of an immense system of faults in the earth's crust, but the eastern part of the south Arabian coast is also probably due to extensive faulting. As remarked in Chapter I, the southern coast of Arabia from Bab al Mandeb runs in a general direction north of east for more than half its course. Then, from about Marbāt, at the eastern extremity of Dhufār in 'Omān, to Ras al Hadd the general trend is from south-west to north-east. Here the coast is in almost direct line with that south-westwards from Cape Gardafui at the horn of Africa, suggesting control by the same system of faults. The faulting is probably geologically recent (Pliocene or Post-Pliocene) and may be part of a net of faults developed round the northern part of the Arabian Sea.

Faults of the Red Sea and Gulf of Aden group are part of one vast system which can be traced south from near the Syrian border (fig. 12). Thence a narrow trough-fault extends from north to south along the

Jordan valley, the Dead Sea, and the Wadi 'Araba to the Gulf of 'Aqaba. At the mouth of the gulf, near the southern tip of the Sinai peninsula, the Palestinian rift joins the wide 'Eritrean trough-fault', in which lie the shallow Gulf of Suez (200 miles) and the deep Red Sea (1,180 miles), giving a total length from Suez to Bab al Mandeb of some 1,380 miles; its direction is from north-north-west to south-south-east. At Bab al Mandeb it is joined by the broad Gulf of Aden and appears to connect with the great east African rifts which extend south-west and then south for hundreds of miles through Abyssinia, Kenya, and Tanganyika Territory.

The Gulf of Aden series of faults runs nearly west-south-west to east-north-east, at right angles to the Red Sea, and may connect with a depression in the floor of the Indian Ocean, running parallel to the submerged 'Carlsberg Ridge'.

(ii) Structure and Relief

Though separated from Africa by the great rifts, Arabia has with north-east Africa a common basement of very ancient crystalline rocks, comprising schist, gneiss, and granite. Before the rifts were formed the history of Arabia and north-east Africa is that of a single continental block with relatively slight elevations and depressions, where desert conditions prevailed until Middle Cretaceous times. Sometimes the sea encroached on parts of its rim. After the separation of Arabia from Africa the Arabian land-mass assumed a form best pictured from the diagrammatic cross-sections shown in fig. 3.

Arabia is a block of the earth's crust tilted so that its western edge is raised high, the elevation being greatest towards its south-western corner, while eastwards the surface slopes gradually to the lowlands of 'Iraq in the north-east and to the Persian Gulf farther south. The Mesopotamian lowlands are contiguous with the mountains of Persia, especially with the foreland formed by the Zagros mountains; thus the Arabian block abuts on the great belt of mountains extending from the Alps through south-eastern Europe, Asia Minor, Persia, and Afghanistan to the Himalayas.

The peninsula rises in a succession of precipitous submarine steps from the deep central trough of the Red Sea. The outer margin of the shallowest submerged step is fringed with coral reefs; above sea-level this step continues as a slightly sloping coastal plain of varying width, but usually narrow, and behind this plain the last steps rise more or less abruptly to the great tablelands of the interior. In the northern half the ranges forming the western margin of these table-

4. *View south-west from near Kirsh, Western Aden Protectorate*

5. *Looking west down the Wadi Masna, in the central Yemen*

6. *Zibb al Hamudh, a rock obelisk near the western scarp of the Tuweiq range*

7. *Table mountains in Jebel Tubeiq*

lands are irregular and tend to form separate massifs; they attain heights of from 3,000 to 7,000 feet (in the north-west corner, north-east of Muweilih, Jebel Debbagh even reaches about 7,700 ft.). In the southern half the long block of the 'Asīr–Yemen highlands faces the coastal plain in an almost unbroken series of huge escarpments, rising in mighty steps to the western marginal ranges of the high plateaux, among which the greatest heights in the entire peninsula (10,000–12,000 ft.) are reached. The 'Asīr–Yemen highlands are an uplifted block, with escarpments along fault-lines on their eastern edge as well as seawards, though the eastern slopes, falling to the desert interior, are much lower. The highest point in 'Asīr itself, Jebel Suda (west of Abhā), is about 9,250 feet; nearly 250 miles north-north-west the peaks around Tāif reach heights between 7,200 and 8,300 feet; some 260 miles farther, and almost exactly midway between the Tāif peaks and Jebel Debbagh, Jebel Radhwa, north-east of Yenbo', just touches 6,000 feet.

The many traces of dead or dying volcanic activity, relics of successive eruptions, lie almost wholly on the west of the peninsula and in its south-western corner. These craters, lava-flows, and *harras* are discussed in more detail below (p. 20).

In about the middle third of the length of the peninsula ancient crystalline rocks continuous with the western ranges form a broad expanse of steppe-lands, with mean elevation from 3,000 to 4,500 feet. Harder masses rise to 5,000 feet or more: such are Jebel Hajar and Jebel Abyadh (where 6,000 ft. is recorded at one point), respectively north and east of Kheibar, and other massifs north-west and south-east of Hāil in Jebel Shammar (photos. 38, 39).

The crystalline shield is bounded on the east by a broken and irregular band of sand-desert, which connects the northern Nafūd with the Nafūd Dāhi, and eventually with the north-western corner of the great southern desert (fig. 4). The sand originated from the disintegration of sandstones which appear in the lower part of the western escarpment of the Jebel Tuweiq range. It forms the western side of the girdle of sand-deserts encircling the central highlands of Nejd, the western edge of which consists of the long crescentic range of Jebel Tuweiq, rising to a mean height of 3,000 feet from a general level of 2,000 feet, with its sandstone escarpment capped by a slightly tilted roof of limestone.

Farther east than Jebel Tuweiq other stratified rocks succeed one another in a long gradual descent to the shallow Persian Gulf. Here is a land-step formation very different from that on the west side of

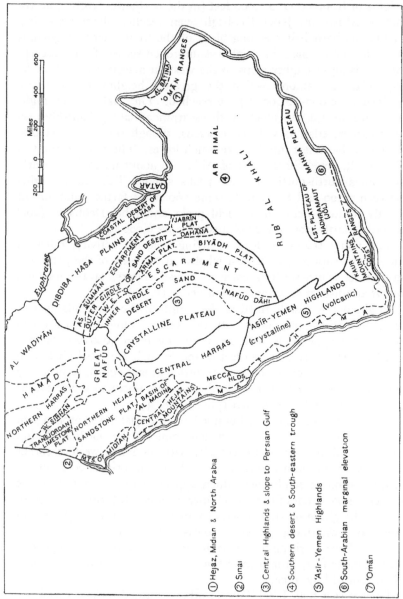

FIG. 4. *Physiographic Regions of Arabia*

① Hejaz, Midian & North Arabia

② Sinai

③ Central Highlands & slope to Persian Gulf

④ Southern desert & South-eastern trough

⑤ 'Asir-Yemen Highlands

⑥ South-Arabian marginal elevation

⑦ 'Omān

the peninsula. Nevertheless, besides the Tuweiq range, some beds stand above the general level as slighter elevations, while the long curved bow of the Dahana sand-desert again connects the northern Nafūd with the great southern desert. Thus is formed the eastern side of the girdle of sand-desert encircling the stratified rocks of the central highlands. The structure of the long gradual eastward declivity is described in more detail later (pp. 47–49).

North of the northern sand-desert (the Great Nafūd) rocky steppe reaches as far as the lowlands of Mesopotamia. It is composed of sandstones and limestones (Cretaceous and Eocene) and later Tertiary covering-layers. Down the middle of the northward projection of Sa'ūdi Arabia a broad watershed extends south to the Great Nafūd, and northward nearly to Palmyra, far outside the area under review in this book. Its almost unbroken surface, usually covered with pebbles and stone sherds, is the Hamād proper, the 'dry' or 'barren' Syrian desert. But on its eastern slope a series of shallow valleys leading north of east towards the Euphrates constitutes the region called Al Wadiyān ('the Wadis'), and on its western side others drain towards Wadi Sirhan, a long depression with no outlet, running north-west from Jauf. Between Wadi Sirhan and the Gulf of 'Aqaba the north-west corner of the peninsula is peculiar. Its features comprise other inland-drainage depressions, the fantastic landscapes of the Tubeiq hills, and scenery among the grandest in Desert Arabia.

South of the crystalline tableland and its veneer of stratified rocks sloping to the Persian Gulf the great sand-desert, the Rub' al Khali, stretches from the inner margin of the Yemen highlands to the mountain chains of 'Omān. The broad trough in which it lies reaches to the south Arabian marginal ranges, and even beyond the sand-desert, as an expanse of low-lying coastland, forming a gap 300 miles wide between the southern marginal ranges and the mountains of 'Omān.

The southern marginal ranges extend from the south-east extremity of the Yemen highlands to a point beyond the Qara mountains in Dhufār. Though cut into separate blocks and ranges, they comprise the south Arabian marginal elevation which borders the Gulf of Aden. Altitudes above 6,000 feet are found in its massifs, south of Wadi Hadhramaut.

Lastly, the high ranges of 'Omān show resemblances to the folded and thrust-faulted mountains of south Persia. The highest rises to nearly 10,000 feet.

The principal physiographic divisions are considered below in more detail (pp. 37–57). But their form in Arabia is so closely bound up with their geological history, and with the drainage systems of the peninsula, that these two subjects are best considered next.

(iii) GEOLOGY

The ancient crystalline rocks forming the common basement of north-east Africa and Arabia comprise gneiss and granites of unknown age together with strongly folded schist. After prolonged denudation had planed down this complex, which extended as a unit from the Nile to the Euphrates and from Syria to Abyssinia, the desert-formed Nubian sandstones were deposited in patches upon it during the long period between early Palaeozoic and Cretaceous times. At some points near its edge occasional beds of limestone alternate with the predominating sandstones. In Sinai, Transjordan, and Palestine such beds contain fossils which serve to date them. The lower horizons are Cambrian, and rather higher ones record advances of the sea in Carboniferous and Triassic times. The sea encroached much farther on to the shield during the Middle and Upper Jurassic[1] and probably formed one sheet of limestones as a strip from Syria, through the borders of Mesopotamia to Arabia, and through Nejd and the Hadhramaut to Somaliland, eastern and southern Abyssinia. The sea then withdrew, and desert covered the bulk of these Jurassic marine deposits; but before long the sea again moved up, so that the sandy limestones of the south and the alternation of limestone and sandstone over much of eastern Arabia mark the presence of Middle and Upper Cretaceous seas respectively. The series of rocks about this time point to slight oscillation in sea-level. A notable advance

[1] There is strong evidence for assigning the fossils from a number of points in the Jurassic limestones of the Tuweiq escarpment, in central Nejd, to the Middle Jurassic (Callovian) rather than to the Upper Jurassic as was at first supposed. Several of the species are the same as those found in Middle Jurassic beds in Somaliland, while one well-characterized species has been found in Sinai as well. These finds indicate that the same marine organisms lived in Middle Jurassic times in a sea extending, probably as a bight, from Sinai through central Nejd and the Hadhramaut to Somaliland. At Dhāla' and elsewhere north of Aden slightly younger (i.e. Upper Jurassic) fossils have been found. Turning to a more recent epoch, fossils of Upper Cretaceous age have been discovered in the limestones of the 'Arma plateau, 30 to 40 miles east of the Tuweiq escarpment; one species is an oyster also found in the beds known as Senonian in Persia, and in many localities in north Africa; other species from the 'Arma plateau are also assigned to the Senonian phase of the Upper Cretaceous. (A fuller account will be found in the Appendix on 'Stratigraphy and Palaeontology' by L. R. Cox, in Philby's *The Empty Quarter*, 1933, pp. 383–387.)

of the sea occurred again in the Middle Eocene, marked mostly by formation of limestones, but there are also local deposits of gypsum and salt. Then, after a considerable interval during which land conditions prevailed, there was a minor advance of the sea in the Miocene, when limestone was again formed locally, followed by saliferous deposits a little later, before the sea once more withdrew. Though dry land has been extensive from the Mio-pliocene onwards, oscillations are still operating, and late movements are recorded by the presence of a series of raised beaches along several parts of the Arabian coast.

Great volcanic activity occurred in early Tertiary times in south-west Arabia and Abyssinia. During Eocene eruptions an immensely thick series of lavas was discharged, accompanying faulting movements; these eruptions gave rise to the series of trap, which in central Yemen, for instance, reaches a thickness of more than 2,000 feet. This activity must be clearly distinguished from the later phase, when other floods of lava broke through in the Pliocene and continued into sub-recent, if not historical, times.

The geological history of Arabia falls into two parts. The first is concerned with a conflict between a shield moved gently up and down and an encircling sea trying to swamp it, the second with the up-arching of the shield and its break-up through the development of great splinters, which left the Red Sea, with associated gulfs and valleys, ensconced between the high and often broken edges of Arabia and Africa. The first part has already been considered; it has been shown that the sea reached its high-water mark in the Jurassic and then retreated intermittently until the Middle Eocene, when its last considerable advance was recorded. The second part starts with faulting of the Eocene sediments in the direction north-north-west to south-south-east and the depression of an ancestral Red Sea. The sea then penetrated from the north into the depression formed by the faulting, but was subsequently cut off from it again. Local shrinkings of the enclosed sea thus formed gave rise to great deposits of rock-salt, probably during the Miocene. Such are the deposits near the present Red Sea coast, at Jīzān, Luheiya, and Salīf, and the inland salt-mines extending in a series, roughly west to east, from the region of Marib and Beihān to beyond Shabwa.[1]

There is not much evidence about the timing of the principal

[1] See H. St. J. B. Philby, 'The Land of Sheba', *Geographical Journal*, xcii, p. 113 (Aug. 1938), and R. A. B. Hamilton, 'Six Weeks in Shabwa', op. cit., c, p. 109 (Sept. 1942).

episodes in the formation of the Red Sea and Gulf of Aden troughs, because most of the intersecting faults which have led to these results are hidden beneath the sea. But there is no reason to doubt that events resembled those in Palestine, where the sequence has been worked out from the fossiliferous rocks exposed by the process of faulting. The process began in the Eocene, and later episodes may have taken place in two main phases—in the late Miocene and late Pliocene. The movements in the earth's crust did not take place once for all at any point, but intermittently, though they were most active at the periods mentioned. Nor have they all been in the downward direction, for there are many ancient beaches raised to high elevations on the coasts (p. 62). The Red Sea and Gulf of Aden became connected at Bab al Mandeb in the Pliocene, and even later the Mediterranean was temporarily connected with the Red Sea. Down into historic times there have been uplifts and smaller subsidences on nearly all the coasts of Arabia. Students of medieval and earlier history of the Yemen record that for many centuries the sea has retired, that old harbours have disappeared and new ones have been created, where formerly only deep water was to be found. The same process has occurred to a less extent elsewhere in the Red Sea.

In the Red Sea and Gulf of Aden rifts three series of faults have been distinguished: the first running north-north-west to south-south-east, spoken of as the 'Eritrean' series; the second running due north and south, the 'Meridional' series; and the third running from west-south-west to east-north-east, at right angles to the Eritrean series and spoken of as the 'Aden' (or 'Somali') series. In the Red Sea the system of faulting is remarkably regular. The Eritrean and the Meridional series cut one another off obliquely into alternating zones, so that a direct north–south fault on the west coast corresponds to one farther north on the east coast. Not only the coastal faults but the deep enclosed central trough of the Red Sea is subject to this regular system of obliquely intersecting faults. Only quite near the southern end of the Red Sea is the structure complicated by faults of the third or Aden series (fig. 12).

Though the terms *rift* and *rift-valley* are used in this book, attention may be called to the difference of opinion which exists as to the manner of formation of these troughs. Some experts prefer to call them *ramp-valleys*. While a rift implies tension for a time over a part of the earth's crust, a ramp implies compression. The former term implies that the keystone of the broad arch of east Africa and Arabia dropped whilst the arch was stretched; the latter term implies that there was strong contrary pressure on two components of this block, which moved together over a third narrow strip. Their bevelled edges bore on the centre block and strove to press it down. Its reaction tilted their inward edges up and away from the depressed strip. It is significant that all the faults but one in a carefully surveyed part of the Hadhramaut indicate movement away from the Gulf of Aden, movement of a kind which might easily have happened if the ramp hypothesis be correct. On the other hand, the known faults of the Red Sea coasts, and those assumed from soundings to be present on the floor of that sea, appear to intersect regularly, with none of the curves which might be expected according to the ramp theory. Gravity measurements made along the Red Sea coasts and in the Gulf of 'Aqaba have revealed strange anomalies without clearly supporting either theory.

One result of these uplifts and subsidences has been the formation of raised beaches, occasionally three, one above the other, old dune-walls, or uplifted coral reefs, as well as old submerged reefs in places. Two phases of uplifting, followed by a slight subsidence, appear to have been the rule round most of the Red Sea coasts and in the Gulf of Aden. In the Hadhramaut a raised beach from 50 to 60 feet above sea-level is cut across by the mouths of wadis, into some of which the sea penetrates, forming narrow creeks where the salt water is cut off from the sea during the ebb-tide. At many points on the Red Sea coast the living coral reefs along the outer edge of the shallow coastal shelf are interrupted opposite the mouths of wadis, because corals cannot live in the fresh water and silt which periodically rush down from these valleys. Possibly through subsidence of the land, bights of deep water (*sherm* and *mersa*) have originated at these points, forming the best harbours in the Red Sea, such as Suākin, Port Sudan, and Yenbo' al Bahr (described in more detail in Chapter III). In east Arabia, at the northern extremity of the 'Omān mountains, on either side of the Ras Masandam promontory, steep-sided valleys, cut deep into the high mountain-land, have been drowned. While there appears to have been subsidence of at least 1,600 feet at that point, an uplift of nearly 1,000 feet is indicated farther south.

The Eocene phase of volcanic activity gave rise, as stated, to out-pourings of trap of great thickness in Abyssinia and the Yemen. It was succeeded, from the Pliocene to recent times, by a later volcanic period, the evidences of which appear in a broad band from the volcanoes of Armenia and the Taurus as far south as Tanganyika Territory. But this zone of volcanic formations does not always follow the course of the great rifts closely. In Arabia the volcanic zone reaches from the Hauran in Syria through the eastern Hejaz to 'Asīr, the Yemen, and the islands of the southern Red Sea. The volcanic belt broadens out along the eastern rampart of the Abyssinian highlands, throwing a branch north-eastward along the north coast of the Gulf of Aden. This branch consists of detached patches, of which the Aden peninsula itself is one. It extends as far as the north-eastern side of the mouth of the Wadi Maseila (Wadi Hadhramaut), marked by the extensive lava-fields in the coastal area between Shihr, north-east of Mukalla, and Seihūt, on the far side of the wadi-mouth.

Throughout Arabia these volcanoes have the same general form; groups of small cones, rarely standing more than 1,300 feet above the surrounding level, and encircled by common lava-fields composed of separate or confluent floods. Most of these volcanoes show little sign of weathering, their condition indicating eruption in very recent geological times. Each group of cones, craters, and lava-fields together constitutes that type of landscape so characteristic of west and south-west Arabia, a *harra*.

The later volcanic period was subdivided into at least two phases. Thus, on the volcanic crags of Aden traces of Pliocene raised beaches tell of uplift since the volcano came into being. But at Bir 'Ali, on the coast between 60 and 70 miles south-west of Mukalla, the volcanic formations reach the sea with no such beach-lines. There are records, traditions, or indications of eruptions having taken place in historical times in the following places: the *harra* of Kheibar; the *harra* of Al Madina, where a volcano erupted, according to the historian Abu'l Fida, about A.D. 1256–1257; the threefold Harrat al 'Uweiridh, extending from the latitude of Al 'Ulā and Madāin Sālih 150 miles north-westwards to that of Tebūk (the whole of these *harras* are believed to be identical with the Harrat an Nār—'*harra* of the fire' of Arabic writers—known to have been active in historical times); the volcano of Al Bedr in Jebel Thadra (roughly north-west of Harrat ar Rahā, a detached *harra* regarded as the northernmost part of Harrat al 'Uweiridh), reported to have once vomited fire and stones, destroying many beduin and their camels and sheep, so that the beduin no longer ascend the mountain or allow their animals to graze there;[1] Jebel Yar in 'Asīr (believed to have been active only about a century ago); the *harra* of Arhab, north of San'ā (active possibly about the third century A.D.); Jebel Tāir and

---

[1] Musil, *The Northern Hejaz*, 1926, p. 215; according to his map Jebel Thadra lies at about 27° 02′ N., 37° 02′ E.

8. *In the Harra of Arhab, north of San'ā*

9. *Jebel al Kohl, an extinct volcano 15 miles north-north-west of San'ā*

10. *An extinct volcano north-east of Aden from the air*

11. *Warm pond at Huweimi, Western Aden Protectorate, fed by hot spring*

the Zubair islands in the Red Sea. Several craters in the south are in the fumarole stage of declining activity, that is, emitting vapour from fissures: such are Jebel Haidar al Lissi[1] near Dhamār on the high plateau of the Yemen, and some craters in the Afar (Danakil) country on the African side of the Red Sea.

Hot sulphurous springs also break forth at a number of points, at various altitudes. Some have given rise to thermal establishments of local importance. Such are several springs in 'Asīr; also Hammam 'Ali, at an altitude somewhat below 6,000 feet, in the wadi of the same name, west of Ma'bar in the Yemen. Other hot springs, without any thermal establishment, occur at Huweimi (152° F.), at about 2,200 feet in the Wadi Natīd (south-west Aden Protectorate); near Sidara, in Wadi Hajr (western Hadhramaut); near Bat-ha, in Wadi Maseila (lower Wadi Hadhramaut), close to an extensive lava-field; and many, mostly sulphurous, at Tabāla, seven miles north of Shihr (south coast over 30 miles north-east of Mukalla). Much farther north, in the Hejaz, there are warm sulphurous springs at Al 'Ulā, south of Madāin Sālih) and at Kheibar. It is also remarkable that some of the springs far away on the eastern side of the peninsula, in Al Hasa, are warm and some sulphurous. For instance, a warm spring, 'Ain al Harra, exists at Mubarraz, just north of Hofūf. These warm springs of Al Hasa are remote from any visible volcanic formations, in the limestones of the gentle slope of sedimentary rocks towards the Persian Gulf. This list of hot springs is doubtless far from exhaustive; for instance, warm springs are found at many places in the sultanate of 'Omān, notably at An Nakhl (106° F.) in the Western Hajar range, south-west of Muscat.

Local earthquakes are mentioned fairly often by Arab historians, but there is nothing to suggest that they were widespread. Al Khazraji records an earthquake in the western Yemen in A.D. 1258 which 'threw down many places'; a succession of shocks in the neighbourhood of Aden in August 1387, by which some houses were demolished; and a series of shocks, up to about forty in one day, at Mauza' (Moza), some 18 miles east of Mocha, in March and April 1394. A modern historian of the Yemen, 'Abd al Wasi', mentions, among others, one in the mountain district of Al Heima, west of San'ā, in 1873–1874, and another in the district of Mocha in 1896–1897; while in 1909 an earthquake in Weilan (Wa'lān), south of

---

[1] This mountain is spelt on maps Haidaralesi, Haidar al Issi, &c.; the correct spelling, *al Lissi*, denotes kindling material.

San'ā, is recorded to have demolished many houses and cost several hundred lives, though this may be exaggerated.[1]

Alluvial deposits occur in patches in wadi-beds and on the coastal plains. Among aeolian (wind-borne) deposits must be classed the dunes, crescentic or elongated ridges, of the sand-deserts; also the dust-deposits or loess composing the plain round San'ā and other parts of the high plateaux of the Yemen. The loess is, incidentally, excellent material for brickmaking and serves to prevent evaporation of water from the underlying strata. Hence in places such as San'ā plain these deposits are perforated by many deep wells, while the bricks for the city walls and parts of its houses are made of this substance. The loess and other wind-borne deposits in the Yemen highlands are geologically very recent; for instance, north of San'ā the floor of Kaulat al Hauri, a perfectly formed extinct but recent crater, is filled with still more recent wind-borne deposits. The age of the dunes in the sand-desert is more difficult to compute, but may be regarded as Recent or Sub-recent.

(iv) DRAINAGE

The following outline concerns the drainage systems of Arabia as a whole, though particular parts of these systems have been mentioned in the preceding sections, and other references to them will be found in the sections on the chief physiographic divisions of the peninsula which follow.

Moreover, it has seemed fitting to consider not only the valleys, many of which are normally dry, but the water which flows in them either perennially or at intervals. And, since it is impossible to dissociate the water from man's agelong struggle to conserve and make the best use of it, a general survey is added of human devices, ancient and modern, to this end. This does not, however, exclude further reference to these devices in the chapters dealing with climate and with the people, their history and their administration.

Rivers (fig. 6)

At the present day the greater part of Arabia is a land of 'episodic rivers',[2] i.e. of valleys which are dry on the surface, or contain only

---

[1] For Al Khazraji, see *Pearl Strings* (translation by Sir James Redhouse, Gibb Memorial Series), vol. i, 1906, p. 154, and vol. ii, 1907, pp. 170, 238. The history written by 'Abd al Wasi' is *Tarikh al Yemen*, Cairo, 1928.

[2] 'Episodic', the term used by certain German geographers, seems the best description of these rivers; 'ephemeral' does not accurately describe them, since the flow of water, when it does occur, may be long maintained.

isolated pools, during the greater part of the year. But these almost countless dry wadis may carry torrents (*seil*), sudden and violent, after rainstorms, though some only do so at intervals of many years. The extent of these floods is discussed more fully below. The dry wadis are also important because they almost always carry underground water, to be reached by wells sunk in their beds; when it is near enough to the surface, chains of oases result. Thus many dry wadis form travel routes of the first importance.

Perennial streams and rivers, however, exist in several parts of the peninsula. But, with the single exception of the Hajr river in the south-western Hadhramaut (p. 24), they are not continuous from source to mouth throughout the year. They are encountered in the interior of the 'Asīr–Yemen highlands, in the mountains near Tāif in southern Hejaz, which catch the summer rains of the south-west monsoon, and in the mountains of 'Omān; in a large part of Wadi Maseila (the lower portion of Wadi Hadhramaut) and its tributaries, especially Wadi Hun and Wadi 'Adīm; in the central highlands of Nejd, and on the east side of the peninsula in Al Hasa. The last of these, in particular, are dependent on water percolating underground from a distance, not on the local rainfall.

In the south-western highlands some streams and rivers flow eastwards towards the arid interior, in which their waters disappear; such is the Wadi Khārid, north-east of San'ā, one of the remnants of a system which watered the ancient Minaean and Sabaean centres of culture (p. 219). But many flow westwards or southwards through the steep-sided mountain escarpments towards the sea. These rivers naturally swell during the monsoon rains, when they are liable to rush down their valleys in sudden spates. In the dry months they dwindle. Though perennial in the highlands, and sometimes as low as 1,000–2,000 feet in the foothills, their waters fade away when they reach the hot coastal plains. This is partly caused by evaporation and by seepage into the porous soil, partly by the demands of irrigation. For example, the Wadi Tiban is affected in its lower course by the irrigation of the oasis of Lahej; while some 30 miles north-east of Aden the Nazi'a 'canal' was cut about eighty years ago from the Bana river to irrigate the fertile coastal oasis of Abyan.[1] A further example may be added from the heart of the peninsula: in southern Nejd, near the oasis of Gheil in the Tuweiq mountains, a stream

---

[1] Incidentally a long-standing subject of dispute between the lower Yāfa'i tribes, in whose territory the river lies, and the Fadhli, whose fields are irrigated by the canal.

breaks from the pebbly bed of the Ashaira torrent, to flow perennially as far as is possible before the waters are exhausted by the demands of irrigation.

The Hajr, the only perennial river from source to mouth, lies in the south-western Hadhramaut, but is not part of the Wadi Hadhramaut system. A separate river, it flows directly from the highlands to the sea through an extensively cultivated valley. It owes its existence, at any rate partly, to the hot springs at Sidara about 60 miles from its mouth (photo. 15).

Floods and Torrents

The sudden spates to which the perennial rivers are subjected, and the torrents (*seil*) which at intervals pour down the dry valleys, sometimes bring calamity in their train. In central Nejd the old city of Yamāma, south-east of Riyādh, is believed to have been destroyed by a flood in Wadi Hanīfa. Farther south in the same region serious damage, with loss of life among human beings and stock, was caused in the upper part of Wadi Dawāsir and one of its tributaries in the summer of 1917; the wadi had not been known to flow within living memory, but a violent flood, descending from the mountains, caused destruction and loss of life in the Tathlīth channel; it even reached the group of villages (Dām, Mishrif, &c.) composing the Wadi Dawāsir oasis, where it obliterated a small hamlet and wrecked many wells in the wadi-bed. On the pilgrim road between Riyādh and Mecca frequent floods descend north-eastwards from the Wadi Turaba (in its lower reaches Wadi Subai'), scattering uprooted scrub on the steppe-land about the mouth of the latter, near Qunsulīya. Other instances could be given.

The Sinai peninsula, like the adjacent parts of north Arabia, is subject to violent winter storms (p. 191), sometimes causing dangerous floods in the steep-sided wadis. A particularly destructive flood occurred on 3 December 1867, in Wadi Feiran, west Sinai; after little more than an hour's rain the torrent was 8 to 10 feet deep; an Arab encampment was swept away, and nearly thirty people, with scores of camels, donkeys, sheep, and goats, perished; but only two human bodies were found, the rest being buried under debris or swept right down to the sea.[1]

Several of the principal cities of Arabia are subject to sudden floods. At Al Madina, in A.D. 773, the water of the Wadi Qanāt rose

[1] F. W. Holland in *Ordnance Survey of the Peninsula of Sinai*, Part I, 1869, pp. 226–227.

so high that a channel had to be dug to divert part of the flood, though, during the caliphate of 'Othman, a dike had been built to protect the town. References by historians to serious floods in Mecca are so numerous that few examples can be mentioned. In A.D. 700 a heavy storm in the valley of Mecca swept away the kit of pilgrims encamped there and forced them to climb the hill-sides; though only a little rain fell in Mecca itself, the flood swept through the city, submerged the courtyard in which the Ka'ba stands, and caused the collapse of several houses, after which the Caliph 'Abdul Malik employed Christian architects to build dams. In A.D. 1399 (probably November) a violent downpour lasting two days resulted in a flood which submerged the mosque to a depth of 10 feet; the threshhold of the Ka'ba was under water, its steps were carried away, many manuscripts of the Koran were lost, and about sixty people were killed by falling houses in the city; next morning the mosque could not be entered for mud and debris, and circumambulation of the Ka'ba was impossible for two days. In A.D. 1422 a flood again submerged the mosque, covering the Black Stone, while a new gate and nearly 60 feet of the city wall were destroyed.[1]

In San'ā the summer afternoon thunderstorms frequently turn the streets into swirling brooks, while the usually dry seil-bed traversing the old city is filled to overflowing. Ibn Battuta in A.D. 1330 noted how the storms washed the paved streets. Floods of exceptional magnitude in San'ā are also recorded by Arab historians. In A.D. 912 the Carmathians finally captured the city during exceedingly heavy rains; it is said that the conqueror, 'Ali ibn al Fadhl, caused the channels carrying off the water to be closed; the water entered the Great Mosque, and captured women were cast into it; the water was retained in the mosque, which it filled to the ceiling.[2] The lowland city of Zabīd and its surrounding valley have also suffered several times from destructive floods, as in A.D. 1342, when most of an outlying village was swept away and many lives were lost. Nor has Ta'izz escaped, despite its elevated situation; in A.D. 1366 many houses were carried away by a torrent and their occupants drowned.[3] Still farther south, a battle between contending Zurei'id princes of

---

[1] For floods in Al Madina and Mecca, see F. Wüstenfeld, *Geschichte der Stadt Medina*, 1860, pp. 154–155, and *Geschichte der Stadt Mekka*, 1861, pp. 119, 147, 191–192, 202, 264, 282–283.

[2] Al Janadi, translation by H. C. Kay, in *Yaman, its Early Mediaeval History*, 1892, pp. 199, 200.

[3] Redhouse's translation of Al Khazraji's history of the Rasulid dynasty, *Pearl Strings*, vol. i, 1906, pp. 255–256; vol. ii, 1907, pp. 63, 92, 118, 132–133, 173, 215.

Aden (*c.* A.D. 1135) was interrupted by a torrent descending the Wadi Tiban.

In the canyons of the Hadhramaut and elsewhere, cities and villages have been sited on the sides of the valley-bed, out of reach of floods. In Wadi Maseila, though the wadi-bed is used by travellers when dry, the volume of water at times of flood is tremendous. High-water mark can be seen 20 feet up the vertical walls of the wadi in narrow parts of its course, while debris remains caught in lofty trees. Travellers must then use paths high up the sides of the valley. Cultivation of the *seil*-bed is naturally impossible in such places, and crops are therefore planted on terraces of alluvial soil brought down by the river in former times, and through which later torrents have cut a channel. Such terraces may now be as much as 30 feet above the river-bed. Much higher up this wadi system, in the Wadi Hadhramaut proper, 10 feet of flood-water has been recorded in date-gardens near Shibām after heavy rain in November. In some places where the silt brought down by such floods spreads out on the coastal plains it may form the rich alluvial soil of oases (e.g. Lahej). But in most of the steeply inclined, deep valleys running down to the Red Sea the detritus is left high and dry, only to be quickly reduced to dust by the sun and wind.

Valley Systems

It follows from the configuration of the peninsula that a number of comparatively short, steeply inclined valleys descend from the western marginal ranges and from the south Arabian marginal elevation to the sea. The whole Red Sea coastal region, from Midian to Bab al Mandeb, is a network of such wadis. The same features occur on both coasts of the Sinai triangle, and on the African coast of the Red Sea. They extend moreover round the south coast of Arabia as far as the heights continue, to Dhufār or beyond, and reappear on the north-east coast of 'Omān, particularly in the region of the Bātina coastal plain, where many such short valleys descend from the Hajar ranges. They are, however, much less numerous in the stretch of low-lying coast between Dhufār and 'Omān, and on the gentle eastern slope to the Persian Gulf they are absent.

The general direction of these valleys is at right angles to the coast, but there are exceptions, as in the basin of Al Madina, where some of the principal wadis run from north-west and south-east roughly parallel with the coast. The whole basin here is drained by the Wadi Hamdh breaking through the coastal ranges westwards, a drainage

12. *Volcanic plug on the way up Jebel Jihāf, Amiri highlands, Western Aden Protectorate*

13. *Upper part of Wadi Tiban, Western Aden Protectorate, about 3,800 feet, in late October*

14. *Wadi Dhahr, north-west of Sanʿā*

15. *Wadi Hajr, near Sidara, Eastern Aden Protectorate*

pattern which, in some respects, forms a counterpart in west Arabia of Wadi Hadhramaut in the south; another example, on a much smaller scale, is Wadi Watir in eastern Sinai (p. 92). Many of these Red Sea coastal valleys are routes inland, some even feasible for motor traffic; e.g. Yenbo' to Al Madina by Wadi Hamra, Rābigh to Al Madina by Wadi Safrā, and Al Līth to Mecca by Wadi Yalamlan. In the western Yemen the Wadi Hammam 'Ali, upper tributary of the Wadi ar Rima, and part of the Wadi Sahām have been used as routes for the motor-road between San'ā and Hodeida. Some of the valleys of this region descend thousands of feet in less than a hundred miles.

The Wadi Hamdh appears far the longest episodic river on the western side, being over 300 miles from its source north-east of Al Madina to its mouth; but if the Wadi 'Aqīq, which rises just south of Tāif and runs to join Wadi Hamdh at Al Madina, be included, the total course of the two is well over 400 miles. The head valleys of Wadi Hamdh are in the *harra* of Kheibar. At the point where this wadi (having been joined by Wadi 'Aqīq) bends westward to break through the marginal range, in about 25° 40′ N. Lat., it is joined by Wadi al Jizil, descending from a diametrically opposite direction, that is from its head-valleys to the north about the Harrat al 'Uweiridh, and adding at least another 100 miles to the Hamdh–'Aqīq system.

In western Yemen the Wadi ar Rima, perennial in its upper course, covers over 80 miles as the crow flies, its actual course being considerably more. The Wadi Tiban, perennial almost to the sea, probably covers over 100 miles from its extreme head-waters in the southern Yemen to its outlet in the bay of Aden. This wadi forks some 30 miles inland; its western channel reaches the sea-shore, but the eastern branch fades out. These valley systems are incompletely surveyed, and at the corner of the south-western highlands the watershed between streams flowing west to the Red Sea and those flowing south to the Gulf of Aden is extremely complex, broken up by a close but irregular network of greater valleys and their tributaries.

Other normally dry valleys are: (i) Al Wadiyān, the group of wadis descending gently eastward towards the Euphrates valley from the high land of the Syrian desert; (ii) the groups of wadis draining into the depressions of Wadi Sirhan and the Juba (or Jauf), and into other inland basins in north-west Arabia; (iii) a succession of valleys descending the south-western or landward slopes of the 'Omān ranges towards the depression of the great desert; (iv) the wadis leading northward from the high country north of Wadi Hadhramaut, and those running north-eastward from the Mahra country and the Qara mountains (Dhufār), all towards the southern fringes of the great desert.

Last to be considered are the four great wadis—Wadi ar Rima, Wadi Sirra, Wadi Dawāsir, Wadi Hadhramaut—stretching, even as much as 1,000 miles, from the eastern side of the watershed formed by the western marginal ranges, right across the peninsula in a north-easterly or easterly direction. These, together with Al Wadiyān and the valleys draining to inland basins, are believed to be relics of pluvial periods, when Arabia enjoyed a moister climate than now. They deserve special notice, though the first three may be crossed in many parts of their lower and middle courses almost without the traveller being aware of their presence. While these are numbered (1) to (4) below, other important channels, draining eastwards from the marginal ranges but losing themselves in the deserts of the interior, are numbered (2a), (3a), (3b).

(1) *Wadi ar Rima*[1] ('Wadi Rumma' of older books). Its several head-valleys rise in the lava-formations east of Kheibar; it runs through the province of Al Qasīm, past 'Aneiza. North-east of Al Qasīm it disappears beneath the sand for more than 30 miles, but its course can be traced on the surface by the growth of *qordhi*.[2] From the point where it reappears the lower course of the wadi is known as Al Bātin ('the depression'), which runs north-eastwards to join the Shatt al Arab near Basra. The channel of the whole wadi falls more than 5,000 feet in 1,000 miles. In the upper part, Wadi ar Rima proper, alluvial deposits help to check rapid evaporation, but moisture from the upper reaches does not normally reach Al Bātin, which only keeps moist after plentiful rains.

(2) *Wadi Sirra, Wadi Birq, Wadi as Sahaba.* This great wadi system is the central of the three which drain the middle part of the peninsula towards the east. The several valleys which unite to form the upper course of the main channel rise in the highlands of western Nejd, near the pilgrim route from Riyādh to Mecca, north-east of Sakha. As the Wadi Sirra, the valley then runs nearly due east to Jebel Tuweiq, and, as the Wadi Birq, it cuts through the middle of this range. The bed of the Wadi Sirra is several hundred feet above that of Wadi ar Rima, to the north, and still more above that of Wadi

---

[1] Not to be confused with the valley of the same name in the western Yemen, mentioned above.

[2] According to Musil (*Northern Nejd*, 1928, p. 38), an Umbelliferous plant, *Deverra* (= *Pituranthos*) *chlorantha* (p. 198).

16. *Al Jumum village, Wadi Fātima, Hejaz*

17. *Looking west down the Wadi al Leiman from Madhiq*

18. *A shallow cavern with stalactitic forms in the Wadi Dareija, near Dhāla', Western Aden Protectorate*

19. *Wadi 'Irma, near Shabwa*

Dawāsir, to the south. On the east side of the Tuweiq mountains the valley turns almost due north, and, as the Wadi Ajeimi, runs parallel to the mountains, to join the Wadi Nisāh, which has also cut through the Tuweiq range from the west. The united valleys lead eastward to the great Wadi Hanīfa, which descends from the north-west and collects them east of the ruined site of Yamāma. The resulting single channel, Wadi as Sahaba, though traceable through the greater part of its eastward course to the Persian Gulf, which it reaches south-east of the Qatar peninsula, has long ceased to function as a river-bed. To-day it probably never carries water beyond the western edge of the Dahana sand-belt, which lies across its course. The existence of this great system of valleys, however, explains the former importance of Yamāma and its vanished empire (p. 233), and the present-day prosperity of Riyādh, Suleimīya, and other towns, villages, and oases.

(2a) *Wadi Kara, Wadi Turaba, Wadi Subai'*. This important system is the most northerly part of the drainage of the main marginal range running eastward; north of it the drainage runs northwards by the Wadi 'Aqīq into the Wadi Hamdh system, as described above. Wadi Kara rises in the main marginal range, well over 100 miles south-east of Mecca, from the same watershed as, but west of, the Wadi Ranya mentioned below. Instead of joining the Dawāsir system as does Wadi Ranya, the system at present under consideration probably joins Wadi Sirra. Wadi Kara runs north-east and unites with Wadi Turaba (which also rises in the marginal range but farther north) at the oasis of Turaba, some 110 miles east of Mecca. From Turaba, under the name Wadi Subai', the valley extends in a north-easterly and then in a more easterly direction through Khurma and past Qunsulīya to the edge of the 'Arq Subai' sands, in which it can be traced as a series of depressions, probably on its way to join Wadi Sirra, though this is not established.

(3) *Wadi Dawāsir*. This wadi system drains the mountains of 'Asīr south-eastwards. Like the Wadi Sirra, it cuts through the Jebel Tuweiq range. It then runs into the Empty Quarter where its lower course is not yet determined, though it is believed to traverse the southern part of the great desert to the Persian Gulf. Including the longest of the valleys which unite to form the Wadi Dawāsir proper, the system may well be the most extensive in all Arabia. The Wadi Tathlīth ('the Trinity') rises at about 8,500 feet at 'Aifa in 'Asīr, and leads about 200 miles northwards, receiving several important tributary valleys on its left bank. Another main constituent is Wadi Bīsha,

which rises some miles south of Bīshat ibn Salīm, south-east of Abhā. This runs north and north-east, roughly parallel with the Tathlīth but farther west, receiving tributaries, till it joins Wadi Ranya. All these eventually unite to form the Wadi Dawāsir proper, at a point some 40 miles west of the Wadi Dawāsir oasis, which consists of Dām, Mishrif, and other villages. Thence the wadi turns east, cutting through the southern part of the Tuweiq range at Suleiyil, about 50 miles east of Dām. The destructive floods which occasionally descend from the upper valleys, notably the Tathlīth, have been mentioned (p. 24). Flood-water sometimes descends as far as the Farsha channel, a few miles east of Suleiyil, at the eastern end of the cut through the Tuweiq range. Beyond this point Wadi Dawāsir has been traced as a bush-lined channel for more than 30 miles. Then nothing more is known of it till at a point about 380 miles east-south-east, in the heart of the Rub' al Khali, a line of wells near Shanna (lat. 19° N., about long. 51° 8' E.), in a valley-bottom, is continued eastwards as a series of gypsum patches (photo. 52). In this region there are also deposits of freshwater shells. This is believed to be a section of the lost channel of the great wadi across the Empty Quarter.

(3a) *Wadi Habauna* and (3b) *Wadi Nejrān*. These systems also rise in the main marginal range, and are believed originally to have joined Wadi Dawāsir. At any rate they cannot bend south to Wadi Hadhramaut, as the slope northwards from the northern edge of the Hadhramaut elevation must cause them to descend towards the Empty Quarter.

Wadi Habauna, rising in 'Asīr, south of 'Aifa and at other points almost down to the boundary between Sa'ūdi Arabia and the Yemen, becomes a single wide channel at Salwa, east of Habauna oasis, and runs past the wells of Huseinīya into the sands of the Empty Quarter. It probably joined Wadi Dawāsir at or near Shanna thus covering 500 miles even without allowing for windings.

Wadi Nejrān drains the marginal range from the southern limit of Habauna to some distance south-west of Sa'da in the northern Yemen. Its main channel, collecting five tributaries at or near Sa'da, descends as Wadi Marwan to the gorge of Madhiq, whence it enters the oasis of Nejrān and assumes that name. In its course through this large and now isolated oasis, formerly a centre of ancient pre-Christian and Christian culture, the wadi always has trickles of water in its channel. It runs out to a point in the Empty Quarter about 10 miles east of the oasis, beyond which it has not been traced. At the edge of the desert it is joined by a series of wadis draining the northern

20. *Jau as Sahaba, south of the Wadi as Sahaba, east-central Arabia*

21. *Al Farsha, Wadi Dawāsir, east of Suleiyil, central Arabia*

22. *Wadi Hun, a principal left-bank tributary of the Wadi Maseila (lower Wadi Hadhramaut), east of Tarīm*

23. *The town of Khoreiba in the Wadi Lū an, principal right-bank tributary of the Wadi Hadhramaut, above Shibām*

Yemen, e.g. Wadis Fara' and Hishwa, probably also by Wadis Hima and Khabb.

(4) *Wadi Hadhramaut* differs in many ways from any of the preceding. Though the general direction of its upper course is from west to east, it bends south-east and finally almost south, breaking through the coastal ranges and opening to the Indian Ocean instead of reaching the Persian Gulf. The remarkable system of deep canyons, with almost vertical cliffs rising from steep scree-slopes, formed by the main wadi and many of its tributaries, is an outstanding feature of south Arabia. The wadi is very wide near its head, but becomes progressively narrower, and over considerable stretches of its course it is a permanently flowing river.

The country east of the 'Asīr–Yemen highlands, especially east of their southern part, is still so little surveyed that it is impossible to be certain which of the wadis descending the eastern slopes find their way to the Hadhramaut system. The great wadis running south-eastwards from the Yemen Jauf, and many others (such as Wadi Abrad, Wadi Beihān, Wadi Markha, and Wadi Jardan) running east, north-east, or even north-west, all united formerly to form the head-waters of Wadi Hadhramaut. Some of the wadis descending the eastern slopes are perennial in their upper courses (e.g. Wadi Khārid, north-east of San'ā), but their channels may now be lost in the tongue of desert, the Ramlāt Sabatein, projecting south-west in the angle between the 'Asīr–Yemen highlands and the south Arabian marginal ranges.

Husn al 'Abr, whence Wadi Hadhramaut runs in a general eastward direction to a point east of Tarīm where it bends south-eastwards, is about 356 miles from the sea; but the total length of the system is much greater. Thus, the head of Wadi Jauf is roughly 175 miles west, and that of Wadi Beihān roughly 160 miles south-west, of al 'Abr, and these are measurements in a straight line. The channel of the Hadhramaut itself is said to be clearly recognizable to beyond Shabwa, some 60 miles south-west. The valley contracts remarkably in its descent. Though it is between 4 and 5 miles wide about 75 miles east-south-east of Husn al 'Abr, between Hauta and Henin, in its lower reaches the valley in places contracts to less than 100 yards. Its bed is more than 3,000 feet above sea-level at Husn al 'Abr, while beyond Tarīm, 130 miles lower down, it is less than 2,000 feet. In the remaining 226 miles to the sea, therefore, it descends nearly 2,000 feet. From Husn Dhoban Maseila, nearly 3 miles below Tarīm, the valley is called Wadi Maseila (the 'valley of floods'). In this lower part it holds two long stretches of perennial river. The first flows from a point almost level with Tarīm to Basaʻ, for about 60 miles, receiving as perennial tributaries the Wadi ʻAdīm on its right bank, south of Tarīm, the Wadi Hun on its left (north) bank, some way to the east, and the Wadi Sena on the right bank, still farther east. Below Basaʻ, the wadi-bed, called Al Lizʻa, is normally dry for more than 40 miles, but water wells forth again at Marakhai and flows perennially for about 50 miles to Buzūn; the volume is increased by the hot springs at Bat-ha between these two points. Below Buzūn disconnected pools continue as far as Qalʻana, but in times of flood the *seil* sweeps right down to the sea. The principal tributary of the lower stretch of river is Wadi ʻAkīd, on the right (south) bank. The cleft in the coastal range, where the wadi breaks through to the sea, is a striking feature, particularly when seen from ships, a little west of Seihūt.

In all that part of the country where the main Wadi Hadhramaut runs from west to east a most characteristic feature is the number of tributary valleys debouching into it both from the north and south. To the north the land rises to 3,500 feet between the wadi and the desert, but to the south altitudes of 6,000 feet and more are attained. These barren *jōls* are dissected into detached blocks of tableland by an extraordinarily intricate network of canyons and valleys. Two of the most important tributary dry valleys are Wadi ʻAmd, from the south-west, and the mighty chasm of Wadi Dūʻan, which comes some 60 miles from the south. These two open into Wadi Hadhramaut on its south side at Qaʻudha and Haura respectively (photos. 22, 23, 58, 59).

Lakes, Surface-waters, Springs, &c.

The foregoing account of the valley systems necessarily excludes certain other drainage features of the peninsula. It is only possible to mention some examples of these.

Salt-lakes. The principal salt-lakes lie in the depression at the base of the Qatar peninsula, in the Persian Gulf. Parts of this area, e.g. Nakhala, have been recorded as below sea-level. There the salt-marshes may become lakes after heavy falls of rain or, near the coast, after exceptionally high tides. The largest salt-lake, Sabkhet al ʻAmra, about 7 miles long and $1\frac{1}{2}$ miles wide, is an extension of a lagoon which comparatively recently separated the Qatar peninsula from the mainland. In parts it is bordered by a broad belt of rock-salt. Farther south are the *jaubs* or *jibān*, low-lying strips of salt-desert.

Freshwater Lakes. Apparently the only one is the tarn Umm al Jebel (ʻthe mother of the mountainʼ) situated at an altitude between

24. Ferns overhanging pool at Jebel Jihāf, Western Aden Protectorate, c. 6,500 feet

25. Waterfall in Wadi Dareija, near Dhāla'

26. Ancient cistern south of Dhamār, central Yemen

27. Ancient reservoir formed by damming valley near Haz, north-west of San'ā

28. *Majīl al Asʿad, an old rectangular reservoir south-east of Sanʿā*

29. *Draw-well at Bir al ʿAzab, Sanʿā. Dung drying in right foreground*

30. *Waterhole in Jabrīn oasis, Nejd. Acacia trees in foreground*

31. *Well in Riyādh*

1,500 and 2,000 feet in Aflāj, east of the Tuweiq range. Its length is three-quarters of a mile, its broad edges are reedy and grassy. The lake, which is fed by springs (like other pools near it, and in Kharj, to the north), lies near a group of reservoirs in the limestone, varying from cisterns a few yards across to a pond 500 yards long by about 60 broad. The important oasis of Saih, to the north, is irrigated from the lake and the reservoirs by a system of aqueducts.

Springs. Not all the mountain springs of Arabia are destined to become surface rivers, even intermittent ones. In Midian, for instance, water from the many mountain springs disappears into the limestone after a short distance, without being used for agriculture. The same applies to many springs in the western mountains farther south. Springs independent of local rainfall are plentiful in certain of the limestone districts, e.g. the Hajar ranges of 'Omān, the oases of Hofūf and Al Qatīf in Al Hasa, and in the island of Bahrein.[1]

Springs are not entirely wanting on the coastal lowlands. In particular those at 'Ayūn Musa in Sinai, a few miles south-east of Suez and a mile inland, deserve mention. Here palm-groves are watered by trickling streams emerging from a number of outlets on a terrace raised appreciably above the coastal plain. These springs, which may be connected with faults, are situated on an elevation, due to accumulation of vegetable debris and wind-borne material. They are unlike most Arabian springs, but resemble in their raised form those of the great oases of the Libyan desert.

Hot springs, associated with volcanic activity, have been mentioned above, p. 21.

In the 'Asīr–Yemen highlands springs often form rushing brooks. These are led along irrigation channels and descend hundreds of feet from one terraced field to the next, each field being retained by stone walls on the steep mountain-side. In some places water is led almost horizontally in earth-banked channels along the sides of steeply sloping wadis; at others through long plastered conduits to fill way-side tanks. In these districts the springs are the direct result of the high summer rainfall.

In some districts the water channels descending from springs are partly subterranean, flowing through underground conduits pierced at intervals by circular shafts in the roof. These shafts may be

---

[1] The terms *verkarstet* and *Karstquellen* have been used of parts of these limestone districts, implying a formation with many surface-pits, swallow-holes, and underground streams. This is not the case in Bahrein, and it appears that the terms as usually understood are not applicable elsewhere.

designed to admit workmen for inspection and repair of the conduits, but some have arisen, as with the Persian *karez*, through the practice of sinking shafts at intervals to find the water-level, then excavating tunnels between the shafts. Certain underground water-courses in 'Omān need to be thoroughly cleaned at least every ten years; the cost is divided among the landowners, while neglect spells failure of the supply and consequent ruin of date-gardens. Under-ground water-channels are found in Wadi Fātima, west of Mecca, and water is brought to the holy city through similar conduits from 'Ain Zobeida to the south-east; water is similarly distributed to the several quarters of Al Madina from the tepid source of 'Ain Zarqa, 2 miles south of that city. Subterranean channels are also found in parts of the Yemen (e.g. in the mountains west of San'ā), in the central highlands of Nejd, in Al Hasa, and above all in 'Omān. In the last-named territory they are called *felej*; in Nejd the term *kharaz* (Persian *qanāt* or *karez*) is used. Similar structures are found in Persia and central Asia and as far east as Shensi in China. In several parts of Arabia their construction is attributed either to Persian workmanship or at any rate to Persian influence (e.g. Al Qatīf in Hasa, and south-east of Riyādh at Firzan ridge in the Tuweiq hills—a ridge believed to commemorate the Persians in its name).

These and other devices for conservation of water are closely linked with the human history of the country, and will be referred to again in the chapters dealing with history and agriculture. Mean-while a brief survey of them may be completed here.

Cisterns, Dams (photos. 26–28, 303)

Even in the mountainous districts receiving abundant rainfall at certain seasons, the rain alone is rarely enough for cultivation. Surface-water is therefore collected from slopes and gullies (*sha'b*, *sha'ūb*) and stored in reservoirs, often very ancient. The simplest kinds are made by damming small valleys and hollows, masonry being added to natural rock where needed. A type, widespread in the south-western highlands, consists of large masonry-lined and plastered cisterns, sunk below the surface and fed only by surface drainage. On these structures, so numerous in the Yemen tablelands, the life of much of the countryside and of its ancient civilizations have depended for many centuries. The cisterns are usually quad-rangular or circular, in diameter from 20 to 130 feet, and from about 13 to 26 feet deep; the walls may have a single slope, nearly vertical, or they are stepped. Some have flights of stairs to the bottom, others have none. A few are subterranean, with only a small opening to the surface. In the highlands they are generally single, but the famous Tanks of Aden, usually assigned to the period of Persian rule (A.D. 570–628), form a wonderful descending chain along a steep narrow gully in the side of the crater. Walls of masonry are built across the valley, every feature of the adjacent crags is used to increase the capacity, and the overflow of each tank is led into the next below. Examination of remains of reservoirs in the Little Aden peninsula, and at Khor 'Umeira, on the coast 60 miles west of Aden, may indicate that the whole series were constructed a century or two earlier.

At Jidda rain-water from the mountains is led, by a complicated system of channels, into great reservoirs just east of the city. These fill to the brim when water rushes from the valleys after storms in the coastal ranges. The floors of the reservoirs are honeycombed with deep wells, which increase the storage capacity but result in brackish underground water mixing with the surface-water. Farther inland, fresher water is stored in carefully walled and roofed cisterns along the edges of the mountain watercourses. In recent years, however, the bulk of the water-supply has been provided by distillation of sea-water.

In parts of the limestone plateaux of the Hadhramaut cisterns with small mouth openings are met with, called *naqba*. Usually they are roughly hewn in the porous limestone above impervious strata. Very characteristic of the Hadhramaut also are the small wayside water reservoirs (*siqaya*) with domed or pyramidal roofs, and openings in the sides through which the vessel provided can be pushed in and withdrawn full of water. These siqayas, founded by charitable people for the benefit of wayfarers, are usually endowed by their founders, and so are periodically refilled by men paid to perform this task (photo. 33).

Even in the arid central districts of Nejd, great water-pits may occur in cavities of the rock. Such are several natural reservoirs at Qurain (west of the ruins of Yamāma), from which the surrounding land is irrigated by means of open conduits (p. 33). The most striking, 'Ain adh Dhila', measures roughly 100 by 70 yards. It is enclosed by walls of the living limestone, towering above the water 30 to 40 feet, except on one side, where there is a gradual descent to the water's edge. Its depth is seemingly unplumbed.

Again, at Khafs, about 46 miles north-north-west of Riyādh, two pools lie at the foot of the cliff forming the edge of the 'Arma plateau, where it rises nearly 500 feet in a precipice of limestone surmounted by sandstone; the larger pool, Ghadīr al Khafs, is almost permanent, some 80 yards by 50, and about 18 feet deep in the centre, though the depth varies somewhat with the rainfall; the smaller pool, about 40 by 20 yards, is very shallow; the whole area is preserved for grazing of the royal herds.

Dams on a large scale, either impounding the water in valleys or acting as the central feature in systems of controlled flooding, belong to the great works of antiquity. They are found especially on the eastward slope of the 'Asīr–Yemen highlands. Most famous was that at Marib, from which (it has been said) an area as big as Bohemia was irrigated; but Wadi Markha possessed a like system, and others existed. In Wadi Markha water seems to have been admitted, through sluices in the dam, into strips of cultivable land separated by walls radiating fanwise. In the Hadhramaut remains of an ancient dam, strongly built of masonry and cement, can be seen in Wadi Maseila at Qōz Ādubi, somewhat below the point where Wadi Sena enters the main wadi. Dams also existed in Nejd, in Wadi Hanīfa near Riyādh.

Aqueducts. Ruins of aqueducts are numbered among the pre-Islamic remains on the inner slope of the Yemen highlands, and in the angle between their southern end and the southern marginal ranges. An aqueduct of hewn stone was seen by travellers between Jauf and Marib in 1870. Ruined aqueducts exist in the district of Nisāb, south-east of Beihān. The aqueduct along which water formerly flowed from Bir Hamīd to Aden is assigned to late medieval times.

Canals. The Nazi'a 'Canal', hardly a canal in the ordinary sense, but a large irrigation channel, constructed to irrigate the oasis of Abyan (near the coast, north-east of Aden) from the waters of Wadi Bana, has already been mentioned (p. 23).

Wells. Far the most widespread form of irrigation is derived from wells, at which oxen, camels, or donkeys, descending an inclined plane, draw up a large leather bucket by a rope passing over a wooden pulley. The bucket is emptied into the irrigation channel by a man at the well-head. A more elaborate installation has several pulleys side by side, with several animals descending the inclined plane abreast; to each beast two ropes are attached, the upper passing over the pulley and hauling up the bucket, while the lower, running over a wooden roller, causes the bucket to pour its contents into a channel at the well-mouth. This dispenses with the need for a man at the well-

32. *Drawing from a well, Aden colony*

33. *Wayside fountain, or Siqaya, in the Hadhramaut*

34. *Desert scenery near Dār al Hajj, Hejaz railway*

35. *Scarped rocks of Madāin Sālih, Hejaz*

36. *Ardh as Sawwān, the Desert of Flint*

37. *The hard remnants of the Tubeiq hills*

38. Pass of Habran, Jebel Shammar

39. Steppe-desert of Jebel Shammar

head. Such are the many great wells, often 15 feet in diameter and 60 or more feet deep, in and about the city of San'ā (photos. 29, 245, 246).

This raising of water by animal power is used, in varying forms, throughout the coastal plain of 'Omān, in much of the Hadhramaut, in many parts of the Western Aden Protectorate and of the high plateaux of the Yemen, and in most of the oases of central Arabia (Nejd). At Teima, in the north-west, sixty to a hundred camels can be harnessed at the same time to the venerable well-pit, the Haddaj, vast and inexhaustible, so that 100,000 gallons can be lifted daily in 20-gallon hide buckets. In the high Yemen tablelands the use or absence of these wells is determined by local conditions. Thus, while San'ā, standing on a plain, is almost entirely dependent on water raised from deep wells in the porous loess, Ta'izz and Ibb, built on the spurs of high mountains, are supplied with mountain water through streams and aqueducts.

The life of the nomad tribes of the desert also depends on ground-water. Their wells and springs are of varying depth. In the great southern desert many water-holes are between 3 and 30 feet deep, occasionally between 60 and 70. Wells of great depth and antiquity, with masonry-lined shafts, are found in hollows in the northern Nafūd, proving, as remarked elsewhere, the stability of the sand-dunes over long periods.

While wells do not usually exceed 70 feet, there are isolated instances of greater depths. In Wadi 'Amd (in the Hadhramaut) a well of drinking-water reaches over 390 feet. Modern water-borings include the wells sunk to between 100 and 200 feet in the solid rock at Aden. Windmill pumps were introduced into Bahrein island through the indirect agency of American medical missionaries, when the Mission hospital was inaugurated there early in the present century; and one was erected by the Turks at Tāif, but it no longer operates.

Modern adaptations of the irrigation works of ancient times, great and small, may still be used to reclaim arid districts for cultivation. The land-settlement of the Ikhwān initiated in recent years in Sa'ūdi Arabia is mentioned in Chap. V, p. 285.

(v) Chief Physiographic Divisions of the Peninsula

1. *The Hejaz, Midian, and North Arabia* (figs. 7, 8, 10; photos. 34–39)

The first two of these terms may still be used in a geographical sense, to denote the northern part of the high western margin, from the northern end of the 'Asīr–Yemen block to the east shore of the

Gulf of 'Aqaba. It is also geographically convenient to preserve the old distinction between the Hejaz proper and Midian. The former extends from the northern limit of 'Asīr to a line drawn approximately from Al Wejh, on the coast, to Al 'Ulā. Midian and its hinterland, Al Hisma, fill the space between this line and the Gulf of 'Aqaba.

In these two regions the highlands are much dissected into smaller massifs. This is caused, at least partly, by faults running east-north-east in the region of Mecca, at right angles to the main or 'Eritrean' series. The crystalline ranges about Mecca mostly rise less than 1,500 feet above a network of broad valleys. The fine sandy soil of the latter is driven against the flanks of the mountains by the prevailing north-west winds.

The volcanic tracts (*harras*) also are much cut up, notably the Harrat Sfeina, north of Mecca, which is dissected into slabs of table-land towards its western edge, and, much farther north, the Tubeiq hills. These latter are described in more detail below. But several other harras occur in the long gap between Sfeina and Tubeiq: specially the great Harra of Kheibar, lying 5,000 feet or more above sea-level. The ancient oasis of Kheibar is under its western edge, at an elevation somewhat below 3,000 feet, and about 70 miles north of Al Madina. It stands in the largest of the proverbial 'seven dark valleys of Kheibar', which lie close together 'like a palm leaf, in the Harra border—gashes in the lava field'; they cut through to shallow clays beneath, and these, in turn, overlie sandstone. These valleys, with others, drain westwards into the basin of Al Madina. The oasis comprises a group of villages, the principal one built under a long detached basalt crag crowned by the ancient citadel, standing isolated in the Wadi Zeidīya. The water-supply is derived from many warm sulphurous springs, rising between the basaltic lava and the clays below. Though the soil of the valley-floors is saline, the water is not brackish. Moreover, if the salt-crusts be cleared away for several seasons, the soil becomes cultivable and of increasing fertility.

The great series of harras lying west of the Hejaz railway, and extending 150 miles or more north-west from the latitude of Al 'Ulā, is also much dissected (fig. 8). It is divided into three main sections by narrow transverse gaps; the northernmost, Harrat ar Rahā, is separated from the southern sections, the Harrat al 'Uweiridh proper, by the depression of Al Jau, containing a layer of deep clay favourable to plant growth.[1]

---

[1] Musil, *The Northern Hejaz*, 1926, p. 215.

The Tubeiq hills, about midway between Teima and Amman, owe their strange, fantastic scenery to the gradual erosion of a sandstone range capped with lava, the material eroded from which has been largely carried by winds south-eastward, contributing to the Great Nafūd. Lava-capped blackened sandstone table-mountains, or black cores of basalt watching over denuded sandstone slopes, are left as ruins. The whole landscape is one of extreme desolation, sunscorched and waterless in summer, fog-bound in winter; with an intricate maze of gullies, and with labyrinthine passages, almost too narrow for a loaded camel, between sandstone ramparts; and in the foothills, separated by broader spaces, the blown sand silts against the lower slopes as breakers surge upon rocks (photos. 7, 37).

Between the separate massifs of the western highlands low-lying country extends far inland. The deepest and most impressive passage through the highlands is the Wadi Hamdh, which drains the great basin of Al Madina (p. 27). The basin itself is an elongated depression with axis parallel to the Red Sea; the Wadi Hamdh breaks through the highlands in a direction somewhat north of west. Other basins farther north also have their long axes parallel to the Red Sea, notably that east of Al Hisma, and the great Wadi Sirhan, which is alined south-eastwards for over 200 miles from Qasr al Azraq, east of Amman, to the depression of Al Jauf, just north of the Great Nafūd (p. 41). But basins of inland drainage, such as that of Al Jafr, east of Maʻan, are only found in this part of Arabia west of the Hamād (the Syrian desert) and the Great Nafūd.

The oases in this region, excepting desert wells, are extremely few. At the north end of Wadi Sirhan, across the boundary of Transjordan, lies Qasr al Azraq, with a ruined hunting-palace, so named from its beautiful blue pools. Forty-five miles down the Wadi Sirhan to the south-east is Kāf, an oasis with several subsidiary villages at about 1,400 feet, and with the volcanic crater of Jebel Maqqal (somewhat over 2,200 ft.) immediately to the north. These are known collectively as Quraiyāt al Milh ('salt hamlets'), from the only local industry. Many salt-pans lie in the bed of this great enclosed wadi; 40 miles south-east is the wide glistening salt-marsh of Nuqrat al Hadhaudha. Thence for 120 miles or more south-eastwards down the Wadi Sirhan, though occasional wells are found, there is no permanent human settlement. A vast lava-field, covering the Cretaceous limestone, extends south from Hauran to a point near the great salt-marsh, ending near the volcanic cone of Bureik, which reaches nearly 1,600 feet. East of the south-eastern end of Wadi Sirhan Cretaceous sandstone crops out from beneath the limestone. In this sandstone plain, extending to the northern border of the Great Nafūd, the wide depression of Juba, curving more than 30 miles from south-west to north-east, holds the important oases of Al Jauf and Sakāka, comprising groups of small villages amid palm-groves. Jauf al 'Amr itself lies at the extreme south-west, Sakāka more than 25 miles east-north-east. The Juba depression lies about 200 feet below the surrounding plain, but despite its nearness to Wadi Sirhan it appears to be independent. Wadi Sirhan is bounded by lines of faulting on either side.[1] The Juba depression, on the other hand, has probably been formed by erosion, the sandstone having worn away more quickly than the neighbouring limestone, which is protected by a hard roof of flint. The two depressions, Wadi Sirhan and the Juba, altogether drain about 36,000 square miles of country.

The northern crystalline borders of Arabia form one mountain group, but they also are interrupted by gaps. Even the mountains of Midian, some of which reach great heights,[2] do not carry the main watershed, but are pierced by valleys descending from the much lower volcanic region (c. 5,500 ft.) to the north-east.

East of the Gulf of 'Aqaba two important watersheds lie roughly parallel to one another and to the gulf: (i) immediately behind the coastal lowlands the ridge of Al Farwa separates the wadis which cut westward through the coastal ridge to the gulf, from those which drain southwards to the Red Sea east of Ras Fartak; the chief of the latter wadis is Wadi al Abyadh, which in its lower reaches broadens and is called Wadi al Efāl;[3] (ii) the ridge of Al Mu'affara, dividing the valleys running south to the Red Sea from those running to the inland drainage area (known as Al Mehteteb) north of Tebūk.

---

[1] The Cretaceous rocks appear to be overlaid by Tertiary (Pliocene and Eocene) deposits on its banks (Philby, *Geographical Journal*, xii, 1923, p. 251).

[2] Two mountains about 25 miles inland, north-east of Muweilih, exceed 7,000 feet; namely Jebel Debbagh, *c.* 7,700 feet, to the south, and Jebel Harb, only just over 7,000 feet, north of it; see map accompanying Alois Musil's 'Northern Hejaz, a Topographical Itinerary' (*American Geographical Society Oriental Explorations and Studies*, No. 1, 1926). According to H. von Wissmann, 'Übersicht über Aufbau und Oberflachengestaltung Arabiens' (*Zeitschr. Gesellsch. für Erdkunde zu Berlin*, 1932) the coastal ranges of Midian reach 9,597 feet, and the figure 2,925 (metres) is shown on Map 4 of that work, not far from the promontory at the southern end of the Gulf of 'Aqaba; this high figure is almost undoubtedly an error, for neither the 1 : 1,000,000 map (Sheet North H-36) nor the Admiralty charts indicate such altitudes.

[3] Believed to be the plain inhabited by the Bythemani, of which Agatharcides of Cnidus wrote in the second century B.C.; for this paragraph see Musil, *The Northern Hejaz*, pp. 96, 103.

South-west of the northern part of Wadi Sirhan lies the Ardh as Sawwān ('land of black stones', or Desert of Flint), a smooth black expanse, 70 miles long. It is intersected by dry wadis, e.g. Wadi Bāyir, 300 yards from bank to bank at Bāyir, which has deep-cut water-channels in its bed. The Ardh as Sawwān ends to the south-east in the isolated rocky outcrops of the Hausa hills, a northern outlier of the fantastic Tubeiq already described; south-westwards it extends to the inland drainage depression of Al Jafr, nearly due east of Ma'an, in Transjordan (photo. 36).

The Tubeiq hills rise towards their western end to nearly 4,000 feet; eastward they fade into a rolling country of sandstone rocks and dunes, finally sinking to the dead level of Al Biseita plain, which lies south of the eastern end of Wadi Sirhan, between that depression and the north-western extension of the Great Nafūd known as Al Areij.

South of the Tubeiq hills lies an utterly desolate region of wasted sandstones, desiccated, scoured, and polished by the westerly winds of ages. The sandstone ruins are of every fantastic form imaginable, solitary pinnacles, pylons, and pyramids, isolated table-mountains, grim formations like ruined castles, and acres of rocks worn to the shape of giant mushrooms (photo. 103). All the wastage has been blown eastwards, like that from the Tubeiq hills. Scenery of the same type characterizes much or all of the district of Al Hisma, north-west of Tebūk; it extends south-east as far as the Umm Jalad ridge at the northern end of the Harrat ar Rahā, where it gives place to flat plateaux overlooked by dark knolls and separated by level sandy stretches; north-west it reaches to Jebel Sherā, a flat ridge with a broad layer of yellow clay, the natural boundary of sandy and rocky desert, beyond which is cultivable country.

South of this again, between Wadi Fajr and Wadi Neyyāl, two drainage channels running north-east, lies Al Hūl, a desolate tract of red rocky flagstones and a little sand. This gives place farther south to black stony ground and then to white steppe. Still farther south lies a great white saline depression containing the very ancient and important oasis of Teima. Though Teima lies over 3,000 feet above sea-level, it is in a self-contained hollow. It comprises one principal and two subsidiary settlements, with copious supplies of water and extensive cultivated lands producing varied crops.

The Great or Northern Nafūd is the largest expanse of sand-desert in Arabia after the great southern desert. At its widest it measures 200 miles each way. Its shape is irregular, the whole area amounting to 30,000 square miles of wind-blown sand, in a vast depression, piled high above the surrounding steppe. Since the general fall of this part of Arabia is towards the distant Euphrates, the Nafūd slopes from about 2,400 feet on the west to 2,200 feet on the east. Tongues of sand-desert project from the central expanse, such as that of Al Areij mentioned above; this, which runs north-west towards the Tubeiq hills, can be crossed in a day. There is always a descent to the edge of the Nafūd, though its sand-dunes tower above the surrounding country; in the extreme south-west they are heaped to at least 600 feet; in the centre to 400 feet; to the north and north-east they are shallower. Only on the extreme east has the Nafūd no definite margin. The Shammar tribesmen regard the Nafūd as ending in the east where the sand becomes too shallow for *ghadha*-bushes[1] to grow; the south-eastern part, in particular, is characterized by *khubūb*, 'stony dells walled in by parallel sand drifts' called *'urūq*; the *khubūb* (plural of *khabb*) may be over 100 miles long, varying in width from a few yards to about 2 miles, and up to 100 feet deep.[2] Everywhere else the edge is marked and a single pace will often take a man from deep sand to hard stony desert. From a distance the sands appear carmine or rose-red, especially in low morning light, or golden red at sunset; at midday they are glaring white to persons on the ground. The wonderful colouring is not, however, peculiar to the northern Nafūd. The Dahana of eastern Arabia also appears carmine from a distance, while in south Arabia the rose-red colour has been noted from aeroplanes even at midday in distant sands, though they seem ochreous from directly above.

There is no surface-water within the Nafūd. The few reliable wells occur where the bed-rock is exposed beneath the sand, where cyclonic storms have cut out curious horseshoe depressions called *falj*, at rare intervals. Such is the famous depression of Shaqīq, on the main track across the Nafūd from Jauf to Jebel Shammar. It contains several ancient wells of great depth, their shafts masonry-lined above and rock-hewn beneath, proof that the general form of the dunes and hollows changes little over long periods.

Among the dunes of the Nafūd pasturage is plentiful, tall desert-grass, tamarisk, and great spreading bushes of *ghadha* with far-flung roots. After even slight rains the dune-slopes flush green. Incidentally the south-western corner of this Nafūd is one of the places where 'singing sands' have been noted (p. 50).

---

[1] A species of *Haloxylon* (p. 198).
[2] Musil, *Northern Nejd*, 1928, pp. 11, 19, 41.

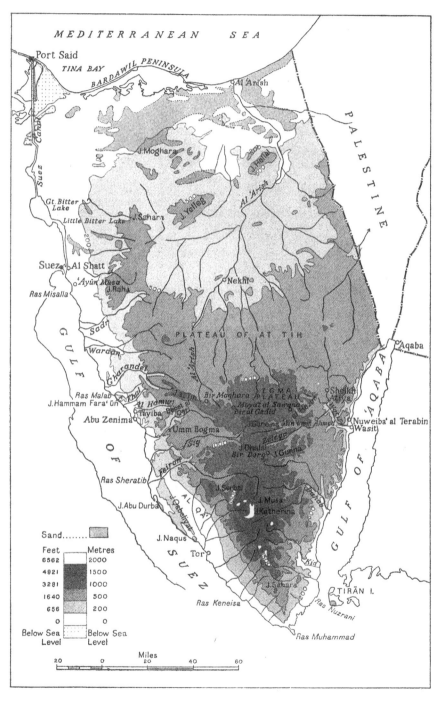

MEDITERRANEAN SEA

Port Said
TINA BAY
BARDAWIL PENINSULA
Al 'Arīsh

PALESTINE

Suez Canal

J.Moghara
J.Halāl

Gt. Bitter Lake
J.Yelleg
Al 'Arīsh
Little Bitter Lake
J.Sahara

Suez Al Shatt
'Ayūn Musa
J.Rāha
Nekhl

Ras Misalla

GULF

Sadr

PLATEAU OF AT TIH

Wardan

Gharandel

Ras Malab
J.Hammam Fara'ūn
El Homur
Tayiba
J.Tih
Bir Moghara
EGMA PLATEAU
Sheikh 'Atiya
'Aqaba
Ogeh
Moyat el Sawana
Bir al Gadid

Abu Zenima
OF
Umm Bogma
Ganeina Um Shmei
P.Nuweiba' al Terabin
Wasit

Sig
zelega
J.Dhalal
Bir Berg J.Gunna

SUEZ
Peiran

Ras Sheratib

AL QA'

J.Abu Durba
J.Serbal

Qedeiyat
J.Musa
Katherina
GULF OF 'AQABA

Sand........

J.Naqus
Tor

Feet   Metres
6562   2000
4921   1500
3281   1000
1640   500
656   200
0   0
Below Sea   Below Sea
Level   Level

Ras Keneisa
J.Sahara
TIRĀN I.
Ras Nuzrani

Ras Muhammad

Miles
20   0   20   40   60

FIG. 9. *Sinai*

2. *The Sinai Peninsula* (fig. 9; photos. 40–47)

The triangular region between the gulfs of Suez and 'Aqaba is that principally dealt with, though the term 'Sinai' has in recent years been extended to include all the country as far north as the Mediterranean, bounded on the west by the Suez canal and on the east by the frontier of Palestine.

The area denoted in this wider sense, about 23,000 square miles, is divisible into three main topographical sections. In the north lie wide open sandy plains, flanked near the coast by low-lying dune-country and relieved by isolated groups or ranges of hills, such as Moghara, Yelleg, and Hellal. Across the centre stretch elevated tablelands of sedimentary strata, Jebel at Tih and the superimposed Jebel Egma. In the south rises a labyrinth of pointed peaks and jagged ridges of crystalline rock, separated by almost countless watercourses; among these wild granite mountains the highest points of Sinai are found, in Jebel Musa and the 8,650-foot Jebel Katherina. The low coastal plain is narrow on the shore of the Gulf of 'Aqaba; on the shore of the Gulf of Suez it is wider and is prolonged to the Mediterranean by the belt of low country flanking the canal and the Bitter Lakes.

The elevated triangular block between the rifts of the gulfs of Suez and 'Aqaba, though politically part of Egypt, is, geologically speaking, mainly a fragment of Arabia, composed of granite and schists covered with a mantle of sandstones and limy sediments. It is deprived of its topmost layers in the south, and it falls away on either side towards the rifts in tilted steps, with faults mainly parallel to the coast on either side.

Sinai has three main drainage systems. Not only the part north of the peninsula proper, but also the tableland of Jebel Egma, is drained by the Wadi al 'Arish and its tributaries, debouching into the Mediterranean at Al 'Arish, 90 miles east of Port Said; this system accounts for half the total area. South of the tablelands, the divide between the drainage to the Gulf of Suez and that to the Gulf of 'Aqaba forms an almost straight line from the southernmost point of Jebel Egma to Ras Muhammad, at the southern extremity of the peninsula.

Manganese and iron ores occur at the base of carboniferous limestone, in the immediate neighbourhood of faults, on the west side of the peninsula, at Umm Bogma, 10 miles inland (p. 80). Copper was mined in the same district in ancient times, and turquoises were exploited by the Egyptians in predynastic days and later; the remains of Egyptian temples have been investigated at Serabit al Khadim, a few miles north-east of Umm Bogma, and turquoises are still found after heavy floods in Wadi Maghara.[1] Early in the present century an abortive attempt was made to drill for coal near Bir Berg, at the southern end of the lower tableland; nothing was found but thin seams of lignite and shales with plant remains; the Arabs named the wadi in which these operations took place Abu Berima ('father of screws').

South of Al Shatt, opposite Suez at the head of the gulf, the undulating coastal plain consists of recent marine sandy beds with many common Red Sea shells of species still living. Sinai as a whole is well supplied with springs and wells (some masonry-lined), but the peculiar springs of 'Ayūn Musa have been described on p. 33. Between them and Jebel Raha, the ramparts of the interior, borings in search of oil have passed through more than 2,000 feet of Tertiary deposits, mainly foraminiferal marls of the Miocene with a small thickness of underlying Eocene limestone.[2]

The great tableland of Badiet at Tih ('desert of the wanderings') reaches points from 3,900 to 5,290 feet above sea-level along its escarpment facing south-west. At the north-west end the ramparts are deeply cut into, notably by the Wadi Wardan, Wadi Gharandel, and their tributaries; springs and pools are numerous. Here also the strata have been invaded by massive dikes and sheets of basalt; the dikes occupy faults or fissures which were frequently a main factor in determining the position of valleys. South of these indentations the escarpment continues as a somewhat sinuous but unbroken line of lofty cliffs, mainly of Cretaceous limestone, capped in places by alluvial gravels, for about 30 miles south-east, till the deep indentations of Wadi Sig and Wadi Zelega are reached. Just north of the former the escarpment rises to 4,700 feet, but between these two wadis Jebel Dhalal projects south-westward into the lower country as a promontory reaching 5,290 feet, and presenting a famous exposure of sandstones of the Nubian series.

At the southern extremity of the Tih proper, north of Wadi Sig, immense cliffs overlook golden-coloured plains (Debet al Qeri), beyond which is a maze of black peaks of crystalline rock, the mountains of southern Sinai. The surface of the tableland, sloping northwards and draining to Wadi al 'Arish, is scored by many watercourses, the heads of which are on the crest of the great escarpment; many of them form, in their upper reaches, deep narrow gorges cut

[1] Joan M. C. Jullien, *Royal Central Asian Journal*, xxix, 1942, p. 226.
[2] Beadnell, *The Wilderness of Sinai*, p. 16 (1927).

40. *Wadi Sawana, Egma plateau, Sinai*

41. *Escarpment of the Tih, Jebel Dhalal*

42. *Wadi Megebila, descending to the Gulf of 'Aqaba*

43. *Alluvial deposits in the Wadi Thal, Sinai*

45. *Convent of Saint Catharine, Sinai*

44. *Wadi Watir, below 'Ain Furtaga*

46. *View from the summit of Jebel Musa*

47. *Foothills of Jebel Bodhia, Sinai*

in the Cretaceous (Turonian) limestone. Occasional but heavy rains are largely absorbed by the limestone, through the northward-dipping strata of which they filter, to reappear as springs farther north. The valleys running west from the margin of the escarpment to the Gulf of Suez catch far less of the rainfall than might be expected from the deep notches cut in the escarpment by their heads. Certain grits of the Upper Cretaceous (Senonian) are extensively quarried for the manufacture of grindstones or querns, especially west of Bir al Gedid, in the southern part of the Tih.

On the east side of the peninsula the lower tableland is much more broken up. South-east of Jebel Egma extends a lower step called Al Hezim, corresponding to the Tih, but far narrower and much indented by the heads of wadis. All the country between the eastern escarpment of Jebel Egma and the coast of the Gulf of 'Aqaba (where the very narrow coastal plain is in places interrupted by spurs of the mountains extending right into the sea) is so broken that it is impossible to describe it briefly in detail. Faults, in some cases trough-faults, are much in evidence, notably the Atiya fault, which determines the meridional direction of Wadi Watir in the upper part of its course, and the Shefalla fault, some miles to the east, a marked feature in the landscape extending for many miles meridionally, as well as a cross-fracture joining the northern end of the Shefalla fault. A little south of Sheikh Atiya, the tomb of a *weli*, the Wadi Watir diverges from the line of the fault and follows a serpentine course south-eastward to the coast of the Gulf of 'Aqaba at Wasit; throughout its length it receives many tributaries from west, east, and south, the whole network draining an area extending some 50 miles from Jebel Gunna, at the extreme south-western part of the lower tableland, to the north-east. In its lower part Wadi Watir breaks through ranges of crystalline rock by a tortuous gorge between cliffs of granite from 1,200 to 1,500 feet high. Scenery of desolate grandeur is also exhibited by its southern tributary, Wadi al 'Ain, which is wide and open in its upper reaches, but near its junction with Wadi Watir becomes a narrow twisting ravine between vertical cliffs, a death-trap at times of flood. Wadi al 'Ain is named from the springs of 'Ain umm Ahmed, which lie in its bed at the head of the gorge, marked by a group of palms, and giving rise to a brackish stream. Eastern Sinai is well provided with such springs and with wells.

Eastward of Jebel at Tih, the inner and higher tableland of Jebel Egma (about 1,500 square miles) is bounded by a magnificent escarpment of white chalk and chalky limestone,[1] increasing in height southwards; on the western side it runs 37 miles south-east in an almost straight line. At its southern extremity the cliffs are over 1,200 feet high, the summit, Jebel Ganeina, 5,338 feet, being the highest point anywhere in Sinai apart from the high mountains of the south. Since the surface of the Egma plateau, like that of the Tih, slopes down to the north, the shallow winding watercourses, flanked by gentle slopes, with which it is scored, drain northwards into Wadi al 'Arish. The escarpment presents no gullies of any size cutting back into the plateau. The cliffs in many places are almost unscalable, yet defiles do exist, such as Naqb al Zibda ('the pass of butter') in the north-west, so called from the soft, smooth marl and shale over which the track leads, or the long zigzag Naqb Gedid, leading up from Bir al Gedid, much used by beduin who pasture their flocks on the Egma but bring them down to the Tih for water, a procedure rendered necessary by the lack of permanent water-supplies on the Egma, except for a few rock-cisterns (*galut*) dependent on surface-water after rain, and the places (*themail*) where water can usually be found at shallow depths in its north-eastern corner; in ancient times rain-water was conserved in cisterns artificially cut in the limestone. From Jebel Ganeina the cliffs of the Egma trend 20 miles east-north-east to Moya't al Sawana, where Jebel Umm Afruth, a long promontory of the Egma projecting on to the lower tableland of Al Hezim, exhibits Tertiary strata (including nummu-litic limestone) more recent than those of the tableland. North of this, the eastern escarpment extends 15 miles nearly due north to Jebel Heyala, whence it fades out northwards as a number of irregular outliers.

Amid the grand mountain scenery of the south Jebel Katherina (8,651 ft.), the highest point in the peninsula[2] and in the whole kingdom of Egypt, is surmounted by a chapel dedicated to Saint Catharine (the Alexandrian maiden martyred in 307 after she had sought refuge in Sinai). North of this, and forming part of the same massif, Jebel Musa (7,496 ft.) is the principal claimant to be the veritable Mount Sinai; a chapel and a mosque stand side by side on its summit; the bold precipices of its 'brow', Ras Sufsafeh, the

[1] In the middle of the chalky limestone a softer and darker band of more shaly consistency has been determined as marking the passage from Cretaceous to Eocene.

[2] The height here given is taken from the International 1: 1,000,000 map, North H 36, 1941, where 2,637 metres (8,651 ft.) is marked. Beadnell, however (*Wilderness of Sinai*, p. 166), gives 8,681 feet.

traditional point of the promulgation of the Mosaic Law, overlook the spacious plain of Al Rahab, the only place among these mountains where a large concourse could have gathered. The plain, surrounded by a noble amphitheatre of hills, slopes down to the mountain. North of Jebel Musa, at its foot, the great fortress-convent of Saint Catharine, founded by Justinian in 530 as the Convent of the Transfiguration, partly to afford to anchorites protection from molestation by nomads, excels in picturesqueness any other convent in Egypt. A tower still more ancient, ascribed to the Empress Helena, and standing near the traditional sites of the Burning Bush and Jethro's Well, served as its nucleus. The abundant running streams in gullies of the mountain irrigate the outlying gardens of the convent, where cypresses, poplars, apples, olives, and almonds impart a Grecian aspect to the scene amid the desolate magnificence of its surroundings. There is unfortunately no continuity of tradition, especially in late Jewish and early Christian times; consequently the identification of Mount Sinai is doubtful. Jebel Serbal, more than 20 miles west-north-west, is considered to have strong claims which are not, however, supported by local tradition; though considerably lower (6,792 ft.), it is 'unsurpassed (in Sinai) in its bold and stately ruggedness'. Incidentally, a recent traveller has seen the clouds round the summit of Serbal glowing fiery red after a violent rainstorm, in a manner so spectacular as to have easily impressed a primitive people.[1]

3. *The Central Highlands of Arabia and the slope to the Persian Gulf* (figs. 7, 8, 10; photos. 6, 48, 49)

In the middle section of the Arabian peninsula the basement or shield of crystalline rocks, which forms so large a part of the western marginal ranges, is extended far to the east, where its surface slopes downwards and is hidden beneath sedimentary rocks. The outcrops of the latter occur roughly in curved bands, the oldest (probably Lower or Middle Jurassic) lying near the centre of Arabia. Thence more recent formations (Upper Jurassic, Cretaceous, Tertiary), in some cases separated by strips of sand-desert, form a series of escarpments facing west, and descend in a long and gradual slope till they pass beneath the shallow waters of the Persian Gulf. The crystalline shield, together with the innermost and most elevated outcrops of sedimentary rocks, forms the high steppes of central Arabia, desolate and semi-desert, with a few jagged teeth of volcanic rock sticking up from below. It is bounded on the east by the broken and irregular

[1] Joan M. C. Jullien, *Royal Central Asian Journal*, xxix, 1942, p. 227.

strips of sand-desert running south from the northern Nafūd, expanding southwards into the smaller Nafūd Dāhi, and eventually joining the north-western part of the Rub' al Khali. These strips have originated from the disintegration of sandstones, possibly Triassic in part, but mainly Jurassic. The desert band forms the western side of the sand-girdle encircling the highlands of Nejd.

The contrast between the western and eastern sides of the peninsula is indeed very great (fig. 3). On the west the marginal coast-ranges or the mighty abrupt seaward-facing escarpments; on the east the long gradual slope down to the Persian Gulf, broken by occasional escarpments of sedimentary rocks, gently tilted, which, being harder, have escaped erosion to the surrounding level. The innermost and highest of these escarpments forms the crescentic plateau of Jebel Tuweiq, 700 miles long, rising precipitously from about 2,000 feet above sea-level to a mean altitude of 3,000 feet, in the very heart of the peninsula, and pierced by the Wadi Sirra or Birq, south of Riyādh, and by the Wadi Dawāsir at Suleiyil, 50 miles or more from its southern end (p. 29).

The structure is clearly seen on the journey by the pilgrim road from Tāif, north-east to Riyādh, and thence to Al 'Oqeir on the coast of the gulf of Bahrein. As Jebel Tuweiq is approached from the south-west, alternate bands of limestone desert and rolling sand combine to form a dreary wilderness. The sandy strips are southward projecting arms of the great northern Nafūd, and they merge to the south in the Nafūd Dāhi, a sand-desert cut off from the Rub' al Khali by the Wadi Dawāsir. Between the desert and the western cliffs of Tuweiq the Dhruma valley forms a shallow trough.

At the east foot of Tuweiq again is a depression, in which Riyādh and its sister-settlements lie amid their palm-groves. Thence the country descends in three steps, the Suleiy downs, the Jubeil slope, and the 'Arma limestone plateau, to the Dahana. The only one of these which rises much above its surroundings is the plateau, known as 'Arma in the north and Biyādh farther south, which stands up 300 feet. The Dahana, a curving ribbon of sand-desert, seen on the horizon as a low, dull pink barrier, has a uniform width of 20 to 25 miles for a long distance. At this point its direction is nearly north and south; it curves north-west to join the northern Nafūd and south-west towards the western end of the Rub' al Khali.

Beyond the Dahana is the outermost limestone step, the As Summān (or Hajara) step, less marked than the others and sometimes absent. This broad band of steppe-desert is much honeycombed

49. *The Saqta gorge, Tuweiq range*

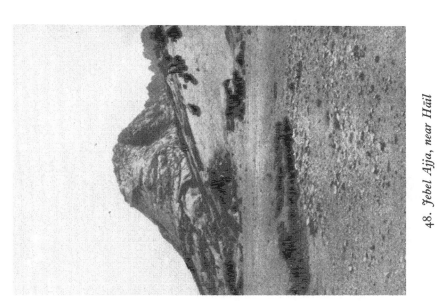

48. *Jebel Ajja, near Hāil*

50. *The sands, Wadi Mugshin, Rub' al Khali*

51. *Halt for prayer, central sands, Sanam, Rub' al Khali*

52. *Gypsum bed in the Rub' al Khali*

53. *Raven's nest in ghadha bush, between Maqainama and Bir Fadhil, Rub' al Khali*

54. *Jebel Sabir, 9,800 feet, southern Yemen*

55. *The middle part of the Wadi Siham, east of Hodeida*

with 'chimneys', caves, and underground water reservoirs (*dahal*). East of As Summān appear slight billowings of the early Tertiary strata. Shallow valleys from north to south have been formed, with minor escarpments on either side marking the strata. There is no running water, and they are irrigated from springs fed by water which has percolated long distances underground from the more elevated land-steps in the interior. Such 'artesian oases' (as they have sometimes been termed) occur at Hofūf, in Bahrein island, and at Al Qatīf on the coast. Consequent on the structure the oases of Al Hasa (Hofūf) have two broad parallel belts of palms and fertile ground, along two of the shallow valleys, with a wide strip of bare stony plain between them (p. 567).

Along the coast of the Persian Gulf, north of the Qatar peninsula, the country is largely a desert of limestone rock in various stages of disintegration, with strips and patches of sand-desert in places, especially from Jubeil southwards to the latitude of Al 'Oqeir and even farther south. Between Hofūf and the coast at Al 'Oqeir lies a rolling sea of loose sand some 50 miles broad; in many places water is found at shallow depths.[1]

4. *The Southern Desert and South-eastern Trough* (figs. 10, 11; photos. 50–53)

The north and north-west of the Arabian peninsula have been outlined in section 1. The central portion has also been sketched, in a line from south-west to north-east, in section 3.

Farther south the topography is different. The western marginal ranges are continued in the distinctive elevated block of the 'Asīr–Yemen highlands. From the inner escarpments of these, the vast south Arabian sand-desert, the Rub' al Khali ('Empty Quarter') and its north-eastern extension, Ar Rimāl ('The Sands'), stretch as a broad zone across the peninsula, almost reaching the coast of the Persian Gulf in north-eastern Trucial 'Omān. From the elevated central parts of the peninsula farther north the general surface slopes gradually south-eastwards to a broad trough (possibly a wide synclinal fold) between the central highlands and the elevated southern border of Arabia. West of the 'Omān mountain chain this trough passes almost imperceptibly into a depression, the southward continuation of the Persian Gulf and Mesopotamian lowland. It extends to the south-east coast, facing the Indian Ocean, where a low-lying coast-line 300 miles long extends from the district of Ja'lān, south of

[1] H. St. J. B. Philby, 'Across Arabia' (*Geographical Journal*, lvi, 1920, p. 448).

Ras al Hadd, to the extreme north-eastern end of the marginal ranges and *jōls* of south-west Arabia.

The south Arabian sand-desert, largest in the world after the Libyan desert, is about 780 miles long from west to east, with a maximum breadth, from its southern margin, north of Dhufār, to the base of the Qatar peninsula, of over 300 miles. The unevenness of the slope from the central highlands is shown by depressions containing deposits of salt and gypsum, especially in the east. Its sand is partly of limestone particles, in contrast to that of the *nafūds* and the *Dahana*, which is mainly of quartz grains. Its western part, the Empty Quarter proper, is utterly lifeless and uninhabitable. Ar Rimāl in the north-east has, on the other hand, wells and occasional pasture after rain. The greatest dunes are found in its southern and south-eastern parts, where huge crescentic billows of sand reach to 600 or even 700 feet. Farther north, and in parts of the west, they become gradually more gentle and flattened, till the desert merges into a hard gravelly surface.

In general, the wells in the great desert are numerous to the east, where they are shallow, full, and very brackish, so that even camels will not drink from some of them. Westwards the wells become progressively rarer, deeper, and sweeter, but less reliable.

The Empty Quarter has one feature unique in the whole of Arabia. This is the group of craters, formed by the impact of meteorites on the desert sand, which gave rise to the tradition that an ancient city, Wabar, stood there, but was destroyed by fire. The craters lie in the eastern part of the desert, at Al Hadida, about 50° 40' E. long. and 21° 29' N. lat., in the heart of Ar Rimāl. As to size, the diameter of some reaches 100 yards. They have black slaggy walls formed by the fusion of the quartz sand-grains into silica-glass. The surrounding sand is filled with beads of black glass and bombs of cellular white material covered with a thin lustrous black vitreous layer. Fragments of meteoric iron testify to the origin of the craters.

'Singing sands' have been mentioned (p. 42) as occurring in the south-western corner of the northern Nafūd. They have been heard also in the great southern desert, at Neifa, about 51° E. long. and 20° N. lat., and on the southern fringe at Yadila, about 52° 5' E. long. and 18° 7' N. lat. At Neifa a natural amphitheatre is surrounded by steep slopes of thick soft sand 200 feet high. When the sand at the top is disturbed, shutes descend with a grating sound, rising in a steady crescendo until the moving mass has gone some 50 feet down the slope, when the quality of the sound changes suddenly to a deep musical booming lasting two to three minutes, during which the sand descends a further 50 to 70 feet, when motion and sound cease abruptly; nor do the lowest 60 or 70 feet of the slope seem ever to produce sound. Apparently, when the surface grains at the top begin to roll down, they entrain those immediately beneath, which engage those beneath them, and so on, causing the grating noise; but at a certain depth a 'gliding plane' is reached, below which the grains are too tightly packed to move, and the deep booming is produced by the passage of the moving upper layers over this immobile sloping floor. At Yadila the word *huneina* ('bellowing') was applied to the sound; two tribes of the Rub' al Khali, the Rashid and the Murra, respectively call singing sands *al damam* and *al hiyal*.[1] Other singing sands are found at Abul Dufuf ('father of drums'), a lofty cone of pure white sand 15 miles south of Ranya oasis, some 200 miles east-south-east of Mecca; at Bedr Hunein, 10 miles from the Red Sea coast, up Wadi Safrā towards Al Madina; and Al 'Oqeir, on the Persian Gulf.

5. *The 'Asīr–Yemen Highlands* (figs. 10, 11; photos. 54–57)

These highlands present on their western face an almost continuous series of mountain ramparts, rising in mighty steps to the western marginal ranges. The plateaux are not merely the bent-up edge of the Arabian land-mass, broken off by the subsidence of the Red Sea rift. They are an uplifted block, falling away along lines of faulting on its eastern edge towards the desert interior, as well as on its western edge towards the coastal plain. The escarpment on the eastern side is much lower and, on the whole, less abrupt. The 'Asīr–Yemen highlands and the much larger block of the Ethiopian highlands are in fact a single uplifted block, cut in two by the Red Sea and Gulf of Aden rifts. The Ethiopian highlands also rise in steps, by a series of precipitous escarpments on the seaward side, while to the west they have another fault-margin, forming a steep descent to the Sudan lowlands.

The highest mountains (10,000–12,000 ft.) of all Arabia are found among the ranges of these highlands. The loftiest peaks probably occur in the still unsurveyed ranges of north-central Yemen, but not farther north than about lat. 16°; Jebel Hadhur Nebi Shu'aib, west-south-west of San'ā, is one of the highest. In 'Asīr altitudes decrease, though the highest point, Jebel Suda, reaches 9,250 feet, while

[1] See Philby, *The Empty Quarter*, 1933, pp. 204 sqq., and 393; and Bertram Thomas, *Arabia Felix*, 1932, p. 169.

even the detached spurs, as far north as Tāif in the southern Hejaz, attain considerable heights and a point south of Tāif reaches over 8,300 feet. Gold, lead, and iron were worked in this little-known region in the past, and some minerals may still be worked there; in central Yemen, near Dhamār, sulphur was, and possibly still is, exploited in at least one crater. Again, in the Kaur mountains, which link the south-eastern Yemen to the Hadhramaut, altitudes between 8,000 and 9,000 feet have been recorded.

The central and southern Yemen highlands form the massive corner-stone of Arabia, with one face looking west to the Red Sea, the other nearly south to the Gulf of Aden. In their interior they consist of extensive tablelands, at altitudes from under 8,000 to over 9,000 feet, sheets of volcanic trap overlying the Cretaceous sandstones exposed principally in the north and north-east, and the Jurassic rocks beyond. There are two volcanic harras, with cones some of which rise to over 9,000 feet, in the Arhab district north of San'ā, and near Dhamār in central Yemen. One of the latter group of craters emits vapour from fissures. Hot springs occur at a number of points in the marginal ranges. From the general level of these tablelands more or less isolated massifs and peaks rise to 10,000 feet and more. Near the edge of the precipitous seaward escarpment, south-west of San'ā, Jebel Hadhur Nebi Shu'aib exceeds 12,000 feet. It is probably the highest mountain in the modern State of the Yemen, and is presumably composed of volcanic rock. Near their outer escarpments the highlands are much broken up into separate domed summits and jagged ranges. Some mountains have the form of isolated blocks of tilted tableland at altitudes above 7,000 feet, while the massifs are separated by undulating plains at elevations between 3,000 and 5,000 feet. Thus, near Ta'izz in southern Yemen the general level of the rolling tableland is about 4,500 feet; but the isolated igneous massif of Jebel Sabir reaches 9,800 feet, and other mountains to the east nearly reach, or even exceed, 8,000 feet. Extensions of the coastal lowlands penetrate at some points in the form of broad valley floors into the rocky foothills and jagged outer ranges.

It is possible that, besides faults of the Eritrean and Meridional series, some of the Aden series, at right angles to the Eritrean, have assisted in breaking up the edges of the elevated 'Asīr–Yemen block, especially in the south. In contrast with the western and southern margins, the inner (eastern) edge of these highlands generally presents more nearly horizontal strata, often penetrated by volcanic 'necks',

56. *View eastwards from summit of Jebel Harir, 7,790 feet, over Yāfaʻi country, Western Aden Protectorate*

57. *Jebel Fiddi, 7,500–8,000 feet, Wadi Dhahr, north-west of Sanʻā*

58. *The Hadhramaut seen south-westwards from the air*

59. *View eastwards across the eroded plateau of the Jōl from the air*

some older, some comparatively recent. To the eye the richly coloured bands of the rock-layers compensate to some extent for the sparseness of vegetation. Reddish volcanic cones and dark grey lava-fields, geologically young, contrast strongly with the older horizontal layers of the dark brown volcanic trap or black columnar basalt, and still more sharply with the red, yellow, and light grey Cretaceous sandstones or the paler limestones, marls, and clays of the Jurassic. The gently rounded forms of the last-named are very different from the steep outlines of the sandstones.

Erosion, working backwards into the western and southern escarpments, has worn away the recent deposits of loess and pebbles in the floors of the broad highland valleys. For, owing to the abundant monsoon rains, springs break forth at various altitudes in the western ranges. Perennial rivers and streams flow in the interior through valleys with luxuriant tropical vegetation in the middle altitudes (2,000–5,000 ft.). Few, however, normally continue throughout the year across the coastal lowlands to the sea. Another series of springs emerge at the eastern foot of the ranges, on the high plateaux. Many unite into rivers, which descend the eastern slopes to fade out in the arid interior of Arabia. Yet the wadis in which they flow may extend, though usually dry, far across the peninsula (pp. 29–31).

6. *The South Arabian Marginal Elevation* (fig. 11; photos. 58–63)

This term is used to denote all the high country lying between the great southern desert and the sea, from a point a little west of the 56th meridian to the southern extremity of the Yemen highlands. This southern elevation can hardly be designated 'coastal ranges', because it consists largely of barren *jōls* or blocks of tableland. 'Marginal elevation' expresses the geological structure and comprehends the whole assemblage of plateaux, ranges, and mountains.

On the north-east it is separated from the coastal mountain-ranges of 'Omān by a 300-mile gap of low-lying barren coast and hinterland. Greater altitudes begin some distance west of the 56th meridian, north-east of Dhufār, and are found, though with breaks, from there to the extreme south-west corner of Arabia. Between Dhufār and southern Yemen the whole southern margin of these highlands is upturned, like the northern margin of Somaliland, consequent on the separation of south Arabia from east Africa. In the border ranges of Dhufār and of the extreme north-eastern part of the Aden Protectorate, the edge so formed falls steeply to the sea, and the coastal lowlands are narrow. Behind Qamr bay, north of Ras Fartak, the steep face of the limestone tableland lies farther back from the coast. From Ras Fartak a great block of highlands, lying somewhat obliquely to those farther north-east, stretches a long distance to the south-west, but is occasionally interrupted where wadis break through to the sea. South of the Wadi Hadhramaut, between that great valley and the sea, large blocks of the limestone tableland, the barren *jōls*, reach over 6,000 feet; at Kōr Seibān, north-west of Mukalla, more than 7,000 feet has been recorded. North of Wadi Hadhramaut the tableland sinks lower (3,500 ft.), till it is covered by the southern fringe of the great sand-desert. The landscape is broken into separate blocks by canyons, the central Wadi Hadhramaut itself, its northern and southern tributaries, and those valleys which drain seawards from the *jōls* (p. 32). West of Mukalla, between the limestone tableland and the sea, clefts running from east to west break up the mountain country into steep-faced table-mountains, capped by Eocene limestone, or into granite spikes and towers. The clefts form wide basins with old sea- or lake-terraces and recent volcanic rocks. Some of the limestone blocks exceed 7,000 feet in height.

This part of the south Arabian coastline thus presents an interchange of steep mountain slopes falling almost sheer to the sea and lowland plains of varying width. The narrow plains of Dhufār and north-eastern Mahra-land give place to wider plains behind Qamr bay; farther west, space can only be found for the city-port of Mukalla by stringing it out along the narrow foreshore below the steep escarpment (photos. 98, 308).

Farther south-west, a broad coastal plain lies east of Ahwar, in the region of Hauta and 'Irqa. Low-lying wadi-beds reach far inland, separating the coastal tablelands of the Hadhramaut from the mountains between Wadi Meifa'a and Wadi Ahwar, and the latter from the mountains behind Shuqra. These oblique highland blocks are formed of igneous rocks, also of limestones (Jurassic) and sandstones (Cretaceous), like the mountains of the Aden hinterland. The southern Tihama plain, broad behind Aden, is mainly a desert of silt and sand, with oases lining the river-valleys, as at Lahej. Relics of volcanic action, such as the Aden peninsula itself, may have been islands, like those in the Red Sea, since joined to the land by desert. The coasts are described in more detail in Chapter III.

In the inner angle between the Yemen highlands and the south Arabian marginal elevation, desert country, partly of sand-dunes, partly level gravel plain, extends some way south, thereby narrowing the plateaux and mountains connecting the south-eastern corner of

61. *Spring of Khiyunt, Dhufār*

60. *In the bed of the Wadi Arbot, Dhufār*

62. *Wadi Arbot from Fuzah, Dhufār*

63. *Qara mountain meadows, Dhufār*

the Yemen highlands with the high country farther east. This region is very little surveyed, but the principal connecting link consists of the granitic Kaur ranges, running roughly west-south-west to east-north-east. They have been likened to the backbone of this part of Arabia. The chief is the Kaur al 'Audhilla, the highest part of the 'Audhali country; much of it is above 6,500 feet, while points between 8,000 and 9,000 have been recorded. The eastern part of the range, called Kaur al 'Awaliq from the 'Aulaqi tribes in whose country it lies, reaches as far east as Yeshbum. Only three routes up the Kaur ranges from the coastal lowlands are possible for pack-animals: the Wadi 'Alam, the Wadi Rughub, and the Talh pass. The first (westernmost) leads on to the south-eastern part of the Yemen plateau, the other two lead on to the plain of Nisāb. Other routes from small ancient seaports farther east also lead up to this plain, which is part of the roughly triangular area between Nisāb, Beihān, and Shabwa, believed to have been the point of convergence whence the great incense-route of antiquity led northwards.

North of Nisāb the country is strewn with pre-Islamic ruins such as Qohlan, Markha, Al 'Uqla, Shabwa, comprising walled cities, irrigation works, temples, and burial-places. There are many rock-salt deposits, such as those of Shabwa, where the salt is taken from mines, and the better deposits at 'Eiyad in Wadi Jardan, over 20 miles south of Shabwa, and at 'Eiyadin in the Bal Harith country, at the end of Wadi Beihān, some 60 miles west of Shabwa. At 'Eiyadin oil is collected for use in native lamps, while oil-bearing rocks also occur farther north, between Marib and Shabwa.

7. 'Omān (fig. 10)

Parallel with the coast of the truncated toe of the Arabian boot are the ranges of 'Omān. The mountains rise from the sea at Ras Masandam, the apex of a promontory almost cut off from the mainland by steep-walled valleys drowned by subsidence. Jurassic limestone predominates, especially in the north. The chain is divided into several separate massifs by deep transverse passages, the principal components being the western and eastern Hajar ranges. Highest in the middle, Jebel Akhdar reaches over 9,000 feet, with steep-walled table-tops of Cretaceous limestone. These mountains and the western Hajar fall steeply towards the coastal plain, Al Bātina, the most fertile part of the sultanate of 'Omān, extending along the wide curve of coast between its northern frontier and its capital, Muscat.

Al Bātina (said to mean 'the interior country', enclosed between mountains and sea) is a plain about 12 to 30 miles wide, with a belt of date-gardens extending almost continuously next the shore for over 150 miles, and in places reaching a depth of several miles; it has other cultivation, and the rest of the plain bears scrubby vegetation, providing sustenance for camels and wood-fuel for the towns and villages in which dwell perhaps 100,000 persons. The Bātina has no surface water, but near the coast fresh water is only 8 to 10 feet below ground. Inland the depth increases till cultivation ceases at a point where the water is 30 feet or more below the surface. Water is raised almost entirely by oxen.

Many date-palm oases are also situated in valleys descending from Jebel Akhdar and the Western Hajar, and crossing the Bātina. Watered by springs in the arid mountains, these oases, including very small ones, number probably several hundred, with a total population estimated as double that of the Bātina. Some of the largest oases have four or five thousand people each, and thousands of palms, the cultivation of which in some cases has reached a higher level even than in the Bātina. The largest, Semāil, in the wadi of that name, between 20 and 30 miles west of Muscat, has gardens extending for many miles between the mountains. An Nakhl and Nazwa are other important oases south-west of Muscat.

Wadi Semāil runs nearly due north to the Gulf of 'Omān. On the southern side of the mountains rises the much longer Wadi Hanifein, taking a southerly course towards the Arabian Sea at the Ghubbat al Hashīsh, level with Masīra island. The pass, on opposite sides of which these two wadis rise, separates Jebel Akhdar from the Eastern Hajar, and is a principal means of communication between coast and interior. South and south-east of the Eastern Hajar lie the sandy districts of Al Ja'lān and Sharqīya.

At the northern end of 'Omān, Ras Masandam and the maze of barren mountains immediately south of it form the district of Ras al Jebel (or Ruūs al Jibāl), a small, politically detached part of the sultanate of 'Omān, separated from the main territory by a 'corridor' of Trucial 'Omān.

Divergent views have been held concerning the structure of the 'Omān mountains. The opinion has been expressed that the ranges belong structurally to those of Persia. The most recent investigations do not, however, appear to support this theory. The Persian ranges nearest to 'Omān run east-north-east,[1] while those of 'Omān

---

[1] The ranges of Persian Makran are described in B.R. 525, *Persia*, pp. 99–104.

extend from north to south in their northern part, curving round in the south till their direction is nearly west to east. Moreover, their structure does not indicate that they were formed as part of the great belt of mountains extending from the Alps to the Himalayas. Whatever be their nature, they are strangely isolated from the rest of Arabia, to which the peninsula is connected by low-lying desert.[1]

[1] See B.R. 524, *Iraq and the Persian Gulf*, pp. 129 sqq.

CHAPTER III

THE COASTS

THE Gulf of Suez and the Red Sea, between latitudes 29° 58′ N. and 12° 38′ N., together may be taken as 1,380 miles long, and the Gulf of 'Aqaba as about 100 miles. If the coasts on either side were merely parallel straight lines, this would give a total coastline of nearly 3,000 miles. But allowing for curves and indentations, the length is very much greater, and there is also to be considered about 700 miles of the south coast of Arabia, from Cape Bab al Mandeb to Ras Dhurbat 'Ali. Well over 4,000 miles of coast have, therefore, to be discussed in this chapter.

The Red Sea varies in breadth from about 16 miles at Bab al Mandeb, its narrowest point, to 230 miles at right angles to its axis near Massawa. The Gulf of Aden extends from the head of the gulf of Tajura, 85 miles south-west of Bab al Mandeb, over 600 miles east-north-east to a line drawn northwards from Cape Gardafui. Its width is about 150 miles from Aden southward to the African coast, but increases eastward.

Political Divisions

These coasts fall under eight separate States or territories. The *Kingdom of Egypt* has both coasts of the Gulf of Suez, all the west coast of the Gulf of 'Aqaba except a few miles at its head, and the west coast of the Red Sea as far south as the Sudanese frontier at Bir Shalatein, at the mouth of Wadi Hodein, almost abreast of Mirear island (*c.* lat. 23° 8′ N.).[1] The Egyptian Ports and Lights Administration is responsible for the lighthouses in the Gulf of Suez and on the islands at its mouth (Ashrafi, Jubal Seria, and Shadwān); also for those on The Brothers and Daedalus in the main Red Sea.

The *Anglo-Egyptian Sudan* extends from Bir Shalatein to Ras Kasar (*c.* lat. 18° N.): *Eritrea* from Ras Kasar to Ras Dumeira where it abuts on French Somaliland.[2]

---

[1] On the 1:1,000,000 map, sheet N.F. 36, 1934, two frontiers are shown; the 22nd parallel, and the administrative frontier, which bends north-east to the point stated.

[2] On the 1:1,000,000 map, sheet N.D. 37–38, Italian military edition, 1934, the frontier touches the coast about 18 miles farther south-east, at the village of Der Elua, opposite Perim island. But the boundary between French Somaliland and Eritrea, reaching the coast at Ras Dumeira, where there is a French frontier post,

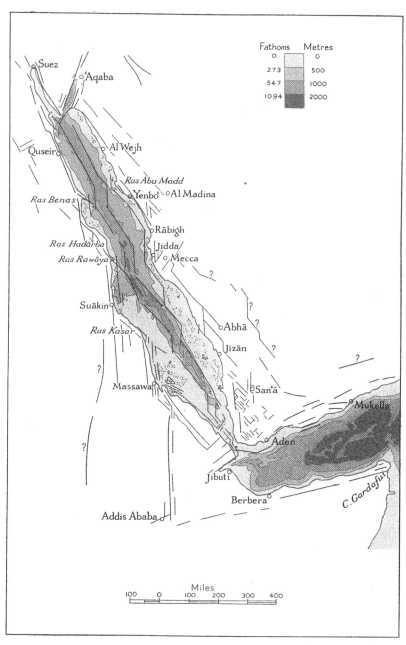

Fathoms   Metres
   0   0
  273   500
  547   1000
 1094   2000

Suez
'Aqaba
Quseir
Al Wejh
Ras Abu Madd
Yenbo Al Madina
Ras Benas
Rābigh
Ras Hadārba
Jidda
Ras Rawāya
Mecca
?
Suākin
?
Ras Kasar
Abhā
?
Jīzān
?
?
Massawa
San'ā
?
Mukalla
?
Aden
Jibuti
C. Gardafui
Berbera
Addis Ababa

Miles
100   0   100 200 300 400

FIG. 12.   *The Red Sea and Gulf of Aden. Faults and configuration of the sea-floor*

On the eastern side, *Palestine* and *Transjordan* abut on the Gulf of 'Aqaba at its head; *Sa'ūdi Arabia* has all the east coast of this gulf from a few miles south of 'Aqaba, and all the Red Sea coast as far south as the Yemen frontier, just north of Meidi (102 miles north of Hodeida); thence the *Kingdom of the Yemen* extends to Cape Bab al Mandeb, including almost the whole of that promontory. Lastly, the *British Protectorate of Aden* includes all the south Arabian coast from the frontier south of Cape Bab al Mandeb to Ras Dhurbat 'Ali; the Protectorate includes no part of the Red Sea coast, but Perim island is British and is part of the Colony of Aden proper (as distinct from the Protectorate).

The status of some of the southern Red Sea islands was left 'indeterminate' when the Turks renounced their rights by the Treaty of Lausanne, 1923. Kamarān island has since been occupied (though not annexed) by Britain, for the sanitary service of the Mecca pilgrimage, and the lights on Abu 'Ail, Centre Peak (south-west of Zubair island), and Jebel at Tāir were (until the present war) maintained chiefly by Britain, in one case partly by Italy.[1]

The Red Sea Rift or Trough-fault

As explained in Chapter II, the Gulf of 'Aqaba and the Red Sea lie in rifts which are part of a ramifying system, extending from southern Syria to Tanganyika Territory, comprising also the Gulf of Aden and possibly submerged branches on the floor of the Indian Ocean (fig. 12). The deep Gulf of 'Aqaba lies in the lower part of the Syro-Palestinian rift, while the deep Red Sea, and its shallow northern continuation the Gulf of Suez, lie in the Red Sea rift or 'Eritrean trough-fault', one of the most clearly defined members of the whole system, though its coasts were till recently among the least known parts of the world. The Red Sea trough is by some experts thought to be less well understood than the Syro-Palestinian or the East African rifts.

was fixed by the Franco-Italian Protocols of 24 January 1900 and 10 July 1901. In 1934 Laval and Mussolini drew up a pact by which France promised to cede to Italy an area of 309 sq. miles, withdrawing the frontier to Der Elua, and recognized Italian sovereignty over the island of Dumeira. This pact was never ratified by the French Senate, and although the *Statesman's Year Book* (1938–43) and the officially inspired *Guida dell' Africa Orientale Italiana* (1938) give the impression that this area was actually ceded, and maps were printed in consequence, the Italians never occupied it.

[1] Under the Anglo-Italian Agreement of April 1938 the need for British officials of the sanitary service to reside on Kamarān was recognized; also the need for personnel to maintain the lights on Abu 'Ail, Centre Peak, and Jebel at Tāir; while Italian officials for the protection of the fishing population were to be allowed to remain on Great and Little Hanīsh islands and on Jebel Zuqar (Zukur).

Coastal faults of the Eritrean series (north-north-west to south-south-east) interdigitate in the Red Sea with those of the Meridional series, while soundings indicate that there may be submerged faults in the sea-bed following a similar structure. Alternate sections of these two series, therefore, appear to truncate one another obliquely, or even to cross one another. For instance, coastal faults running due north and south on the west side correspond to similar faults lying farther north on the east side. The same statement applies to the trend of the present coastline when this follows the direction of the principal faults, as is often the case. Thus, the nearly meridional trend of the African coast south of Ras Rawāya (Ras Abu Shagara) corresponds to the general meridional trend of the Arabian coast farther north from about Rābigh southwards to Jidda. This structure has been taken to indicate dislocation and pushing obliquely to one side of sections of the trough during the long process of its formation. At any rate, these ideas correspond with four natural divisions into which the Red Sea proper falls, and which are described on pp. 95–98.

Faults of the Aden series (west-south-west to east-north-east) enter little into the picture, except in one narrow zone near the southern end, where they cross the main faults of the Eritrean series at right angles. But in the Gulf of Aden they are the dominating feature; there almost every important fault belongs to the Aden series.

Depth of the Red Sea and Configuration of its Floor

The long trough of the Red Sea narrows funnel-wise at both ends. Its outer margins on either side are formed by the seaward escarpments of the coastal ranges, escarpments often broken up (as described in Chapter II) into land-steps on a great scale. On both sides of the sea these escarpments are separated from the coasts by a gently sloping coastal plain of varying width. The coastal plain is continued below sea-level, as a shallowly submerged step, to the edge of an abrupt steep slope, falling away to greater depths. Soundings seem to indicate the existence of steps formed by faulting below the surface; for in many parts the slope from the edge of the coastal step descends to a depth of 1,600 feet, where there is a step in the sea-bottom, from the edge of which a second steep slope falls away to the narrow innermost trough. This central trough, extending almost the whole length of the Red Sea proper, reaches depths of 6,000, at some points over 7,000 feet. The greatest depths, between latitudes 26° and 20° N., range from 6,000 to 8,520 feet. The latter point, the deepest of all, is almost midway between Port Sudan (on the African coast) and Al Līth. Another great depth, 7,590 feet, lies much farther north, about latitude 25° 25' N., nearly abreast of Sheibara on the Arabian coast. Depths of over 4,800 feet reach as far south as latitude 16° N.

Tides

Variation in water-level is a matter of practical importance in the Red Sea owing to the presence of many reefs (p. 66). Tides vary from place to place; for instance there is a tidal variation of 7 feet at Suez, of 2 feet at The Brothers islets, of little more than 1 foot in the south of the Gulf of Suez, and in some places it is imperceptible. But besides tidal rise and fall, there is also a marked seasonal alteration in water-level of 2 or 3 feet. From December to March strong southerly winds raise the level in the north of the Red Sea, while from July to September it is lower than the winter level by as much as 3 feet as a result of strong northerly winds.

Formation and Age of the Red Sea

Diverse theories have been advanced to account for the whole rift-system, but whether or not the earth's crust was rent apart to form the Red Sea trough, its sides seem to have been crushed one against the other, resulting in the alternation of sections of faulting in the Eritrean and Meridional directions. If the Arabian peninsula tended to drift away eastwards from the African land-mass, and also, though perhaps not simultaneously, in a more northerly direction towards the mountain folds of Anatolia and Persia, the eastward drift may have caused the Eritrean faults and the northerly drift the Meridional faults.

The Red Sea trough was formed in successive phases from Eocene times to the present, and the possibility of further modification should not be excluded. The first movements apparently started in the south, and in their train began the great outpourings of volcanic trap previously mentioned (p. 17). Whether subsidence of the trough took place contemporaneously with these processes is not known, for indications of trough-formation as early as Eocene times exist only in the northern parts of the Red Sea. Only among Oligocene and Miocene rocks is evidence found of that stronger faulting which allowed the Mediterranean to flow south into the trough. This Miocene sea then had no outlet to the Indian Ocean, so that, when cut off from the Mediterranean by an uplift of land between Syria and the Libyan desert, the Red Sea became an inland sea, possibly continued as a chain of lakes at its southern end. In this phase evaporation caused the formation of gypsum and rock-salt deposits. Later movements, in Pliocene times, led to the formation of the deep central trough, and probably opened the outlet to the Gulf of Aden.

The formation of those parts of the coastal ranges which follow the chief marginal faults of the trough is believed to have occurred in Oligocene or Miocene times. Some of the land-steps and elevated blocks rising from the coastal plain are more recent in origin. Their comparatively recent submarine deposits, sandstones, marls, clays, and conglomerates, with gypsum and rock-salt in the Miocene layers, and associated with oil-bearing beds in places (e.g. the Farasān islands), once covered the floor of the oldest, widest, and shallowest rift, formed by the first subsidence. Since this sea-floor has again become dry land, terrestrial formations (alluvium and wind-borne deposits) have been added.

Uplifts and Subsidences of the Red Sea and Gulf of Aden Coasts

The later history of these coasts can be followed from the raised beaches and other evidences of uplift and subsidence, to be discussed here more fully than in Chapter II.

(a) *The Red Sea*. The raised beaches of these coasts may be classed in three categories: (i) those formed by abrasion, wearing down of the local rock or of terrestrial or marine deposits; (ii) those formed by the piling up of material, for instance at the coastal edge of river-deposits, large quantities of which were laid down at the foot of the ranges during ancient pluvial phases of climate; and (iii) old coral reefs. The form of the land above and below sea-level has determined which type should prevail at any point.

Studies in the northern Red Sea indicate that a raised beach at an average height of 50–65 feet is the most uniformly distributed. The southern point of the Sinai peninsula exhibits three beaches, mainly of ancient coral reefs. The uppermost, probably late Pliocene, is between 200 and 300 feet above sea-level, the second between 30 and 80 feet; the lowest is 20 feet below the present fringing reef. Therefore a twofold uplift, followed by slight subsidence, is indicated.[1] The Red Sea would at one time have extended from the

---

[1] 'Uplift' and 'subsidence' are used to denote vertical movement of the land relative to adjacent sea-level. Similar effects would occur with a changing sea-level relative to a stationary land. Neither land nor sea-level are absolutely fixed, but it is generally agreed that the greater movement occurs in the level of the land, and round the Red Sea different lands have moved relative to each other.

(a) *The Sinai coast south of Tor*

(b) *The African coast south of Ras Dhib*

(c) *Shadwān Island*

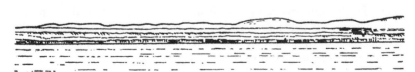

(d) *The Arabian coast north of Al Wejh*

FIG. 13. *Raised beaches of the Red Sea*

Gulf of 'Aqaba to the Dead Sea, where the water-level was 1,390 feet higher than at present.

On the Sinai coast of the Gulf of Suez, particularly south of Tor, two raised beaches are recognizable (fig. 13 a), but they do not correspond in level with those on the west coast of the gulf opposite. North of Tor the raised beaches are less easy to trace, since two isolated land-steps separate the coast from the broad coastal plain; but two old coral reefs raised respectively 35 and 750 feet above sea-level have been found on Jebel Hammam Musa.

On the south part of the African coast of the Gulf of Suez (fig. 13 b), and on Jubal and Shadwān islands (fig. 13 c), raised beaches are again visible; on the flank of the Zeit hills (p. 87) there are three, the highest nearly 500 feet above sea-level; on Jubal island, where the strata incline slightly northward, the three beaches are at about 80, 250, and 500 feet respectively; on Shadwān island, besides these three, there is a fourth at nearly 700 feet.

In the Gulf of 'Aqaba on the Arabian coast between 'Aqaba and Haqal three or four beaches are recognizable, consisting of sand and coarse pebbles, with reefs and fragments of coral. Their nature indicates formation by successive shrinkings of the sea rather than by uplifts of the land.

The position of the highest raised beach varies greatly in different parts of the Red Sea coast. On the Egyptian coast it ranges between 230 and 790 feet above sea-level. Two beaches occur on the Eritrean coast near Massawa, the upper 330 feet above sea-level. Along the Danakil coast the raised beaches slant upwards from south-east to north-west, from a point 30–60 feet above sea-level near Assab to about 590 feet at Adailo.

On the Arabian coast raised beaches have been traced only in parts. In the north a cliff between 80 and 100 feet high, appearing from far out at sea as a light grey stripe, and extending from the mouth of the Gulf of 'Aqaba to Al Wejh (fig. 13 d), seems to represent the lowest beach. Higher ones are recognizable in places. The lowest also occurs on the islands off the coast, which, like the outer part of the coastal plain, consist of uplifted coralline limestone. Near Jidda there is no obvious trace of the three beaches so plainly developed farther north, except a low cliff 12–20 feet high (the same applies to the vicinity of Port Sudan, on the opposite African shore, though here the sandstone steps of the coastal plain, and old coral reefs appear to be raised to nearly 1,000 feet). Farther south, near Hodeida, no clearly defined raised beaches are visible; there is only a sharp rise or cliff between

12 and 20 feet high, at the coast, though the surface of the coastal plain, consisting largely of wind-borne deposits, bears also beds of marine shells. These, of species still living in the Red Sea, occur as far as 12 miles inland, and nearly 200 feet above sea-level. The Farasān and Kamarān islands consist mainly of recent (Quaternary) coral reefs and other marine deposits, elevated usually only 3–15 feet, though reaching 260 feet in the highest hills of the Farasān islands (p. 134).

(b) *The Gulf of Aden and 'Omān.* At the head of the Gulf of Aden, the gulf of Tajura exhibits two raised beaches, the upper 130–165 feet above sea-level. In British Somaliland diluvial beach and reef deposits occur as far as 12 miles inland. In Socotra old coral reefs are met with 50 feet above sea-level. On parts of the south coast of Arabia (and of the Persian Gulf also) two raised beaches are found. But no such formations occur in northern 'Omān, where, on the contrary, a subsidence of at least 1,600 feet has drowned valleys and produced deep inlets. Farther south in 'Omān, however, uplift seems to have occurred, for in Wadi Hatta (30 miles north-west of Sohār) two recently formed raised beaches slant upwards from the coastal plain; as they rise they diverge, the upper reaching 1,045 feet in the wadi and reappearing on the western side of the mountain range at 1,230 feet, just above a sandy plain extending westward; this plain is believed to be an old beach, and the whole area may have been raised to over 1,200 feet at its highest point, and displaced eastward.

South of Muscat well-defined raised beaches are traceable for a long distance, elevated between 820 and 980 feet. In the north-east of the Aden Protectorate, north of Ras Fartak and near Nishtūn, a wide, sloping, ancient beach lies 165 feet above the present cliff. Near Mukalla the lower (Quaternary) beach is over 60 feet above sea-level; the upper (Pliocene) varies between 300 and nearly 500 feet. The coastal plain near Wadi Meifa'a, perhaps also the immediate hinterland of Aden, was submerged in Pliocene times. In the crater of Aden layers of fossil shells have been found well over 300 feet above sea-level, and several old beach-lines are traceable.

It is risky, in the present state of knowledge, to draw comparisons between the Red Sea coasts and the southern and eastern coasts of Arabia. Yet a general uplift since the late Pliocene seems clear enough, except in the Ras Masandam area, where subsidence has occurred. If the highest raised beaches could be proved to have been formed simultaneously, it would follow—since they slant and vary in height above sea-level—that strong bendings of the rocks have taken place, particularly on the African coast of the Red Sea and in parts of 'Omān.

Islands and Coral Reefs in the Red Sea

Almost every known form of coral reef (Arabic *shab*, plural *shuʿūb*) is represented, including fringing and barrier reefs, simple island reefs, and atolls. Reefs are most plentiful and luxuriant in the middle part of the length of the Red Sea, rather less so in the south, despite the great breadth of the shallow-water coastal step and the number of rocky islands. In the north less favourable climatic conditions partly account for their paucity in the gulfs of Suez and 'Aqaba, but this cause will not entirely explain their relative fewness in the northern part of the main Red Sea.

The reefs in the Gulf of Suez have generally 2–3 feet of water over them, and in the summer they occasionally dry in places. A slight ripple always breaks on the weather side. In the main Red Sea they are covered usually by 5 feet or less of water, but the sea seldom breaks on them. Speaking generally, they extend in long strips parallel to the coast, and divide the Red Sea into a deep central channel and two inshore channels, of which the central alone is suitable for through navigation by large vessels. The reefs are, on the whole, more numerous on the Arabian than on the African side. The inshore channel on the Arabian side is wide, formed partly by small detached reefs and sunken rocks, partly by more extensive reefs and islands; many of its anchorages are insecure. The inshore channel on the western side is similar, but much narrower. Both these channels are connected with the central channel by openings in the reefs which, especially in the northern part, are in some cases very wide. Approach to the shore is frequently difficult owing to the great extent of reefs, but good anchorages are found behind them in a number of places (p. 68). Across the entrance to the Gulf of Suez from the Red Sea there are numerous islands and reefs, but there are good passages through them. Two islands with reefs obstruct the entrance to the Gulf of 'Aqaba, and the channels here are narrower and more difficult.

At certain times in summer, when large tracts of smooth water are covered with a brown scum composed of minute algae, shallowly submerged reefs are similarly discoloured. It has, indeed, been thought that the much disputed origin of the name 'Red Sea' may be due to brown or red discolorations caused by minute algae. Otherwise, when the coral sand outside the reefs is stirred up by strong winds or tidal streams, the water has usually a milky appearance, though some reefs (e.g. those outside Jidda) appear dark green.

Just as the raised beaches provide evidence of uplifts of the land or former sea-levels higher than the present one, so the existing coral-reefs give some indication of conditions in past ages below the present sea-level. The reefs are still, however, incompletely known in many parts of the Red Sea, especially those remote from important harbours.

The barrier reefs and atolls can usually be regarded as evidence of sinking of the land. For instance, Sanganeb reef, north-east of

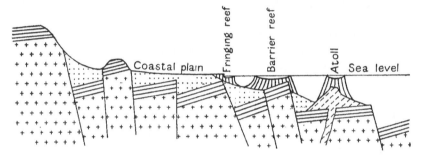

FIG. 14. *Generalized Geological section at Port Sudan*

Port Sudan, is a beautifully formed elongated atoll, the slopes of which descend steeply on every side to depths over 2,000 feet, indicating subsidence of the sea-floor and of the (probably volcanic) base on which the atoll stands. Between Sanganeb and the coast lies a barrier reef, which also slopes steeply along its outer side to a depth of more than 2,000 feet. On the inner side of the barrier reef, between it and the fringing reef along the coast, the inshore channel is in places nearly 1,000 feet deep, while farther south, between Port Sudan and Suākin, it reaches depths between 1,300 and 1,600 feet. Usually the inshore channel between barrier reef and fringing reef is not more than some 300 feet deep. So a very great subsidence would have had to take place in the neighbourhood of Port Sudan and Suākin, if this cause alone were responsible for the great depths. More probably recent subsidence on a great scale is not the sole cause, but rather the existence of far more ancient submerged mountains, which by recent slight subsidence have favoured the formation of coral reefs of considerable thickness (fig. 14).

Besides islands of coralline limestone, rocky islands also occur on the barrier reefs, indicating that the reefs stand on submerged mountains. Drowned mountain-ranges (roughly parallel to the coasts), which only here and there reach above the surface, but are near enough to the surface for the growth of coral, probably account for most of the barrier reefs. In the islands of Jubal Seria and Ashrafi (the former immediately north, the latter some way north-west, of Jubal island at the mouth of the Gulf of Suez), the coral is, respectively, about 10 feet and nearly 30 feet thick.

In short, the relief of the sea-floor near the coast may be compared with that of the coastal plain. Even below sea-level, isolated moun-tain-chains and single mountains lie parallel to the main line of faulting of the coastal range. These submerged mountains are mostly step-formations like those on the land. They form the bases of most of the coral reefs (except the simple reefs fringing the coasts), hence the steep slope of the reefs on their outer side. The submerged ranges would also appear to have a fairly uniform elevation, so that they only reach the surface in a few places.

Harbours in the Red Sea

Very characteristic of the Red Sea, and closely connected with coral formations, are certain long narrow bights of deep water, pene-trating nearly perpendicularly into the coast for some distance, then throwing out deep lateral gulfs, often at right angles, so that the whole inlet in many cases assumes a cross- or T-shape. These inlets com-prise the most important harbours of the Red Sea as well as many smaller anchorages. They are known variously as *sherm* (or *sharm*, plural *shurūm*), *mersa* (or *marsa*, plural *marāsi*), and *khor*.[1] In some cases (but not all) the mouth of a wadi opens at the back of each branch of the inlet; but under present climatic conditions such wadis only discharge rain-water into the bight at long and irregular intervals.

The two best-known 'sherms' are those of Port Sudan and Suākin (figs. 15, 16). As stated above, the inshore channel along the coast (within the barrier reef) north and south of Port Sudan reaches great depths. At Port Sudan a channel between 600 and 700 feet deep penetrates the outer edge of the coral reef fringing the coast. The gap in the reef is still over 200 feet deep at the level of the coast itself. The inlet penetrates the land obliquely north-westward, then forks

---

[1] Though there is no fixed rule, the term *mersa* is more frequently used on the African coast, 'mersas' and 'khors' being interspersed in the southern part. On the Arabian coast, *mersa* is comparatively seldom used; 'sherms' succeed one another in the north, 'khors' in the south.

into two narrow branches, a longer and a shorter, extending approximately north-west and south-west. A dry wadi opens at the head of each branch. The water is still nearly 90 feet deep at the point of bifurcation, and depths of over 30 feet continue deep into the land along either branch. The banks of the harbour form mostly a low cliff some 6 feet high; there is usually a narrow fringing reef, at the edge of which is a sudden descent to a depth of about 30 feet.

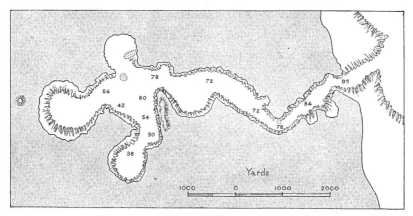

FIG. 17. *Khor Shin'āb* (*Key on fig. 15*)

At Suākin a deep narrow channel crosses the fringing reef from north-east to south-west, between 200 and 300 feet deep at the outer edge of the reef, and still nearly 100 feet some distance in. The channel penetrates south-westward into the land at right angles to the coast, being still over 60 feet deep some way within the harbour mouth. It bifurcates into a northern and southern branch, each broader than those at Port Sudan, and with an islet lying at the point of bifurcation; the southern branch again bifurcates, two deep channels with broad heads being separated by another islet, linked to the town of Suākin by a narrow causeway.

The cross-shaped form is shown best by Khor Shin'āb, on the African coast a little north of Ras Rawāya (fig. 17). Here a channel nearly 100 feet deep cuts across the fringing reef and is continued as a narrow inlet perpendicular to the coastline; the inlet, after a sharp bend, branches into three at its head. Outside the fringing reef the sea-floor falls away to a depth of nearly 800 feet.

Many variants of the typical cross-form occur. Thus Mersa Gwiyai, one of a number of inlets north of Port Sudan, has the form of an irregular L (fig. 18). Sherm Jubba, on the Arabian coast, is T-shaped, with a channel nearly 100 feet deep at its mouth, and over 40 feet deep where the arms branch out (fig. 19). At Rābigh, on

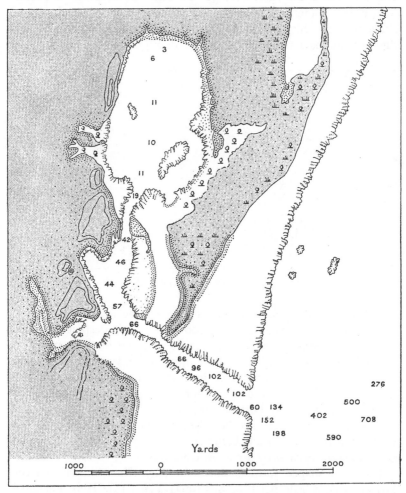

FIG. 18. *Mersa Gwiyai* (*Key on fig. 15*)

the other hand, the harbour appears at first sight a large, roughly triangular, expanse of water, connected with the sea by a narrow opening, but soundings show the typical cross-form of deep narrow channels below the surface; slight subsidence may have caused the

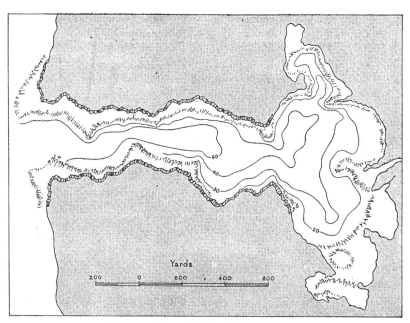

FIG. 19. *Sherm Jubba* (*Key on fig. 15*)

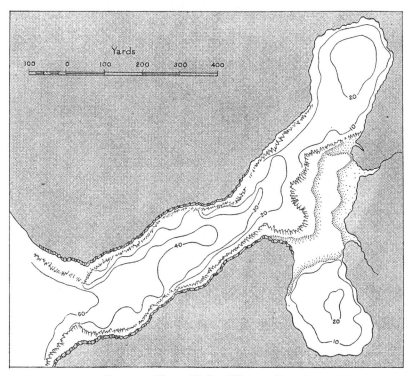

FIG. 20. *Sherm Yahar* (*Key on fig. 15*)

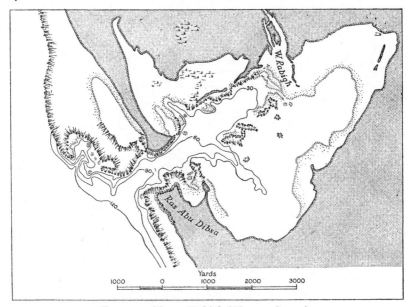

FIG. 21. *Sherm Rābigh* (*Key on fig. 15*)

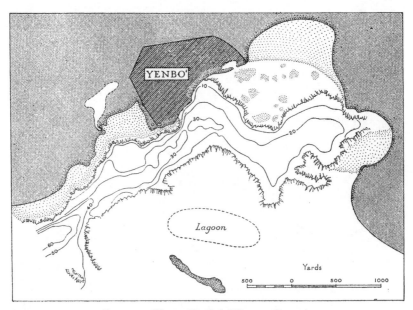

FIG. 22. *Sherm Yenbo'* (*Key on fig. 15*)

broadening of the sheet of water above (fig. 21). The two most important harbours on the north Arabian coast, Yenbo' and Al Wejh, are designated *sherm* by the Arabs. The former, though appearing as a broad open harbour, is a true sherm, of rather irregular shape, in which the south side of the narrow deep inlet is formed, not by the

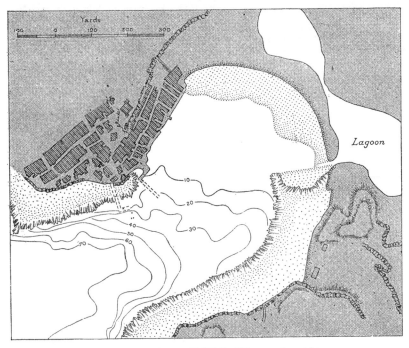

FIG. 23. *Sherm Al Wejh* (*Key on fig. 15*)

coast, but by a wide fringing reef on which an islet rests (fig. 22).[1] Al Wejh has a broader inlet, more rounded in outline, into which deep water penetrates in a broad tongue (fig. 23).

These deep inlets, of great economic importance as anchorages, occur on almost every part of the Red Sea coast except the southernmost. A list is given in Appendix A, p. 584. Several theories have been advanced to explain their origin, the cause of which is probably not the same in every case. Some may be valleys drowned by

[1] Reference is made here to the port of Yenbo' itself, not to an inlet called 'Sherm Yenbo' ', some distance from the town, along the coast to the north-west. The latter is indeed a true sherm, a deep narrow winding inlet with branches, though irregular in form.

subsidence, for instance those in which a dry wadi opens into the head
of the main inlet, or in which wadis open into the lateral gulfs, as at
Port Sudan. In a past climatic phase of greater rainfall, fresh water
discharged from these valleys would kill the coral of the fringing reef

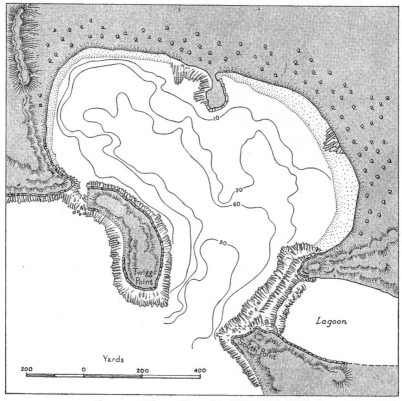

FIG. 24. *Sherm Dumeigh* (*Key on fig. 15*)

and form a gap, while the setting in of a later dry phase would check
this process and allow the growth of the small fringing reefs along
the sides of the inlets. Still later, if the inlet becomes a harbour, the
growth of these small reefs is again checked by the fouling of the
water by shipping. If submergence of valleys explains these cases,
a slight later uplift is required to explain the low cliffs along the
sides of a bight such as Port Sudan. Many of the inlets are not
sunk in coralline limestone but in the sand and pebble deposits of
the coastal plain; killing of coral cannot explain such cases as these.

Moreover, in many instances there is no dry wadi opening into any of the branches. Some cases seem better explained by movements in the earth's crust, such as the formation of cross-faults and the subsidence of narrow troughs at right angles to one another; this would account for the exceptional depth of the inshore channel along the coast between barrier reef and fringing reef near the mouth of such an inlet as Port Sudan. In the development of sherms as a whole, submergence of valleys, later uplifts of the land, and the natural laws regulating the growth of coral, all doubtless have played their part. These factors have probably entered also into the formation of certain deep oval inlets such as Ghubbet as Sughra on Great Dahlak island, and Khor as Saghir on Great Farasān island, both of which may become sherms in the future through growth of coral reefs.

Divisions of the Red Sea (fig. 25)

The Red Sea falls naturally into six major divisions. These are the gulfs of Suez and 'Aqaba, and four sections into which the Red Sea proper can be divided, depending on the configuration of the shores and the sea-bed.

In the detailed description which follows, the gulfs of Suez and 'Aqaba are considered first; then after a brief outline of the four structural divisions of the Red Sea proper, taken from north to south, there follows an account first of the African side in its political divisions of Egypt, the Sudan, and Eritrea, then of the Arabian side in its geographical divisions of Midian, Hejaz, 'Asīr, and Yemen.

THE GULF OF SUEZ AND STRAIT OF JUBAL (figs. 26, 27)

The Gulf of Suez stretches between latitudes 29° 58′ N. and 27° 49′ N.; though its coasts are formed by parallel faults continuing the north-north-west to south-south-east direction of the Red Sea, it is shallow. Soundings in the middle of its breadth range between 120 and 270 feet from north to south, while at the strait of Jubal, where the gulf opens to the Red Sea, there is a sudden descent to more than 3,000 feet.

The parallel faults bounding the gulf are cut off at the northern end in the deserts of the isthmus by the Sahara–Syrian fault system, at right angles to the Eritrean series. Isolated land-steps rise on both sides of the gulf—on the Sinai coast north of Tor, and on the African

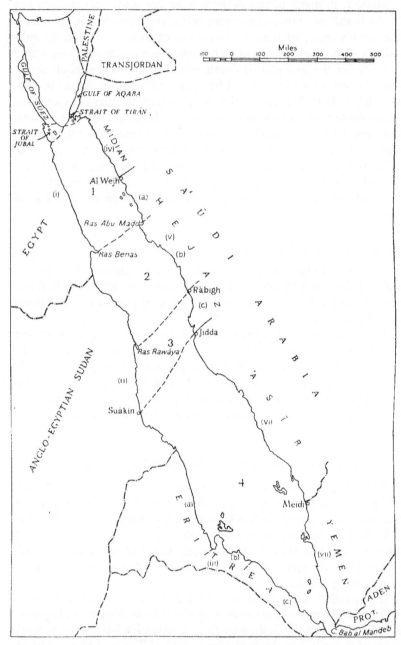

FIG. 25. *Divisions of the Red Sea and its coasts*

side farther south, where the Zeit hills extend southwards to the mouth of the gulf and continue as a group of islands to Shadwān.

East Coast of the Gulf of Suez (fig. 26)

The general trend of the west coast of Sinai, north-north-west to south-south-east (the direction of the Eritrean series of faults), is well marked. The higher elevations of the peninsula are some distance inland, and the coastal belt of country below about 650 feet is broad. Yet from Ras Malab southwards to Tor there are isolated hills and ranges near the coast exceeding 1,600 feet or reaching 2,000 feet at a few points; notably the range of Jebel Qabeliyat, north of Tor, an isolated land-step parallel to the coast and separated from the interior mountains by a long, fairly wide, low-lying strip, Al Qa'. The coral reefs along this coast extend farther out to sea and have more outliers than on the west side of the gulf.

The eastern side of Suez bay is low and sandy, and approach to the canal is made difficult by patches of coral. Kad al Marākib and Ras Misalla are two low sandy points 8 miles apart, between which is a shallow bay backed by a sandy, shell-strewn plain, gently undulating and covered in places with detritus washed down from the older rocks of the interior. About a mile inshore from the middle of the bay the oasis of 'Ayūn Musa ('The springs of Moses') lies among palm-groves and tamarisks on the brow of a slope (p. 33). For long it was a place of importance and the chief source of fresh water for shipping in the Red Sea; later it became a residential suburb and the main source of water for Suez, being abandoned for this purpose after the completion of the Sweet Water canal. Even now the groves are owned by inhabitants of Suez and Cairo and are tended by gardeners who live in huts among the trees. Beduin tradition associates it with the place where the Israelites landed after crossing the Red Sea (*Exodus* xv).

From Ras Misalla to Ras Sadr (Sudr), 16 miles, thence to Ras Metarma 10 miles beyond, and again on another 20 miles to Ras Malab, the coast is low and sandy, as are all these capes, and bordered by reefs. This part of the coastal plain, about 50 miles, is one of the longest waterless stretches in Sinai; its hard, yellow, pebble-strewn surface is bare of vegetation except in the wadis. It is, however, easy going for camels, and along it runs the caravan track from Suez through 'Ayūn Musa and on down the west side of Sinai. The three main drainage systems on this side of the tableland of At Tih, the wadis Sadr, Wardan, and Gharandel, reach the gulf near the three capes named above, Wadi Gharandel expanding among the sand-

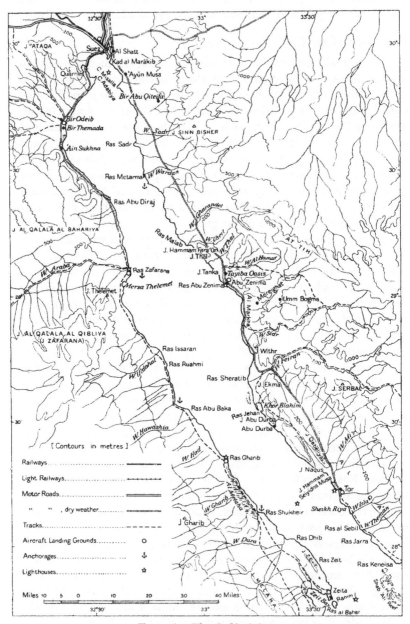

Fig. 26. *The Gulf of Suez*

hills near its mouth to form an oasis which has been identified with the Elim of Exodus. About 18 miles east of Ras Sadr an isolated, white, cliffed mountain, Jebel Sinn Bisher (Jebel Sadr), rises above 2,000 feet, in a break formed by Wadi Sadr in the tableland of At Tih, the mean elevation of which is slightly lower. About 12 miles north-west of this mountain an unsuccessful boring for oil was made in 1922 at Bir Abu Qiteifa on the coastal plain, involving the construction of a road from Suez suitable for heavy tractors, and of a pipeline to bring fresh water from Al Shatt on the canal.

From Ras Malab the coast trends south-east for 22 miles, then generally south for 24 miles to Ras Sheratib, bordered by reefs throughout. Wadi Useit reaches the sea near Ras Malab, Wadi Thal 7 miles farther on (photo. 43). Between the two a range of hills rises abruptly from the sea, breaking the coast into a series of rocky ridges separated by pebble-strewn coves and inlets. Three miles south-east of Ras Malab is Jebel Hammam Fara'ūn ('bath of Pharaoh'), 1,620 feet high, with a precipitous cliff so near the sea that it is only just possible to make a way round it at low tide. Hot salt-springs gush out near the foot of the cliff at a temperature of 160° F.; these, and the hot caverns near by, are used by the Arabs for medicinal purposes. Beduin avoid the place after dark, believing that Pharaoh was drowned here, and that his uneasy spirit howls round the desolate mountain in the sudden storms which arise on this part of the coast. A more prosaic explanation of the storms and fierce seas is perhaps to be sought in the narrowing of the gulf between Ras Malab and Ras Zafarana (p. 86), together with the winds which rush down the ravines on either shore. The highest point in this coastal range is Jebel Thal (Useit), which rears its sharp peak to 1,696 feet 3 miles farther south.

Beyond Wadi Thal a tract of low hills faces the sea in a precipitous scarp 230 feet high, forcing the coastal track inland. These hills, of dazzling white chalk, end at Jebel Tanka, 11 miles south-east of Ras Malab. Wadi Al Hamur, emerging from the hills of the interior among dark basaltic rock which contrasts strongly with the limestone, bends sharply south before reaching Jebel Tanka, passes Tayiba oasis a few miles inland, and reaches the coast as Wadi Tayiba north-west of Abu Zenima. In its southward stretch, which contains the oasis, a lovely spot with palms and feathery grasses (Tayiba means 'beautiful'), the wadi is followed by the caravan track from Suez, since the hills leave no room by the sea.

South-east of Jebel Tanka a semicircle of hills encloses the plain and bay of Abu Zenima. Ras Abu Zenima is a low and gravelly cape, just over 3 miles beyond Jebel Tanka, and close eastward, on the north shore of Abu Zenima bay, are the pier, storehouses, &c., of the British company working the mines of iron and manganese at Umm Bogma, 15 miles east-south-east and some way inland. The bay, with a sandy beach, affords good anchorage sheltered from the north and north-west, though it is unsafe during strong southerly winds, when landing is impracticable. The pier is 438 feet long, with a transporter at its head. West of it a sand and coral bank extends southwest for half a mile. North of the village and a quarter of a mile inland is an emergency landing-ground used by the R.A.F. The village is linked by telegraph with Suez and Tor, and the mining company's lorries run once or twice weekly to Suez, 65 miles away. The boats which take the ore to Suez return with mail and stores and, as there is no spring at Abu Zenima, with fresh water in 100-gallon tanks.

For 4 miles beyond the bay hills are close to the coast. They end abruptly on the edge of the plain of Al Markha, which extends 14 miles southward with an average width of 4 miles, rising gradually from the coast with a stony and gravelly surface dotted with bushes but completely lacking shade. A light railway 11 miles long from Abu Zenima runs south-east between the hills and the sea, then turns inland across the northern edge of the plain to Mereighat on the inland border, where it meets the aerial ropeway which conveys ore over 6 miles of rough country from the mines at Umm Bogma. Along the seaward edge of the plain runs the Suez–Tor caravan track.

At the southern end of the plain of Al Markha hills approach the coast again, and Jebel Withr rises to 1,470 feet 20 miles south of Abu Zenima. Between Jebel Withr and Jebel Abu Durba, 19 miles south, is a low coastal plain about 5 miles across at its widest. Wadi Feiran breaks through the hills behind to reach the gulf at Ras Sheratib, where the low sandy cape projects seawards, bordered by shoals. This wadi is the longest on the west coast of Sinai, and it provides a broad, easy route into the mountains, past Jebel Serbal, almost up to the monastery of St. Catharine.

From Ras Sheratib the coast trends south-east to the southernmost point of the peninsula. Granite hills, partly sand-covered, rise near the coast for 20 miles from about 9 miles south-east of Ras Sheratib. Jebel Jehan and Jebel Abu Durba, both over 1,400 feet, form an isolated group cut off from the rest of the range by a wadi which reaches the sea at Abu Durba, a small place with an insignificant production of oil. At the northern end of these hills Khor Blahim (8 miles south-south-east of Ras Sheratib) is the chief feature of the coast, a large lagoon less than 50 feet deep in the middle and 3 miles wide; the narrow opening to the sea at the southern end is only 70 yards wide, with 4 feet of water. The hills end in Jebel Hammam Seiyidna Musa ('baths of our lord Moses'), about 840 feet high, with hot salt-springs issuing from the base at a temperature of 77° F. Jebel Naqus is an isolated hill (1,220 ft.) 2 miles north-west, where there are musical sands (p. 50). Farther inland, parallel to the coastal hills, is the range of Jebel Ekma (c. 2,070 ft.) and Jebel Qabeli-yat, already mentioned as geologically an isolated land-step, separated by the broad low-lying plain of Al Qa' from the high mountains of the interior. The highest of the central mountains lies between 35 and 40 miles to the east, but Jebel Musa (Mount Sinai, c. 7,500 ft.) is only visible from a small part of the gulf near Jebel Hammam Fara'ūn, being hidden by the highest mountain of all, Jebel Katherina (c. 8,650 ft.), to the south-west and by other high mountains west and north-west.

Three miles south-east of Jebel Hammam Seiyidna Musa the town and small harbour of Tor are well marked by palm-groves. Apart from a few stunted palms near the beach about 4 miles north, these are the only trees visible from the sea south of 'Ayūn Musa. The harbour is a small inlet opening south-westwards between reefs, sheltered on the west by a low coral spit and on the south-west by an isolated reef. There are four jetties, the southernmost of which has water laid on. Tor village lies north of the harbour, with houses of unburnt brick, mosques, and nearer the sea a few well-built stone houses. This solitary little port and quarantine station rouses to great activity during the pilgrimage season, which lasts 2 or 3 months. The pilgrim enclosure, with barracks and hospital, is about half a mile inland. Close south-east of it is a landing-ground controlled from Cairo and used by the R.A.F. There is also a meteorological station and telegraph and telephone communications. The coastal track from Suez through Abu Zenima is reported usable by motors, but only a camel track leads to the interior. Dugong (sea-cow, *Halicore taberna-culi*) is caught off Tor and used for making native sandals in Sinai. In the dunes near by singing sands have been noted.

South of Tor a broad coastal plain, as much as 12 miles wide, slopes upwards to the base of the high mountains at about 1,000 feet. It is a southward extension of Al Qa', and continues to the southern tip of the peninsula, with the coastal track keeping to its seaward edge. A result of the existence of the detached Qabeliyat range, parallel to the coast, is that some wadis descend from its southern end in the

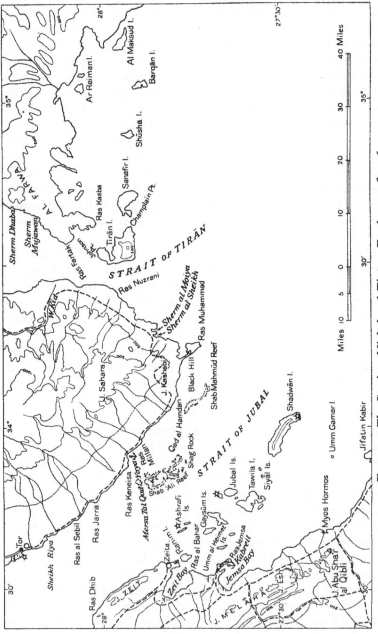

FIG. 27. *The Straits of Jubal and Tirān. For key see fig. 26*

same direction. These unite with a parallel drainage system, extending down Al Qa', which collects tributaries from the high mountains of the interior on its left bank. The united system bends south and converges with the coast north-west of Tor. Otherwise, south of Tor, almost to the end of the peninsula, a series of ten wadis descends from the high mountains and crosses the coastal plain at right angles to the shore.

Six miles south of Tor lies the harbour of Sheikh Riya, opening southwards and sheltered on the west by a low, sandy point fringed with coral reefs. Ras as Sebil (Ras Sebila) and Ras Jarra are two low capes, respectively 7 and 12 miles south-east of Sheikh Riya. Ten miles farther on is the low, sandy Ras Keneisa (Iknaisi). Fringing reefs extend a mile off shore in this stretch, and several outlying patches are present over 6 miles from the shore in the case of Poynder shoal, which lies nearly 8 miles west of Ras Keneisa.

The north-eastern side of the Strait of Jubal is a sandy plain stretching 14 miles inland to the base of the mountains. The coast is reef-bound, reefs lying in places 8 miles off shore and causing an abrupt change from deep blue to bright green water. Shab 'Ali, a large group of coral reefs $3\frac{1}{2}$ miles at its northern end from Ras Keneisa, divides the strait into a narrow inner (NE.) channel and a broader main (SW.) channel, the latter lying between it and the islands described below (p. 89). The main channel is 12 miles wide between Shag rock (a small rock standing 3 feet above the water at the south end of Shab 'Ali) and the Ashrafi lighthouse (fig. 27).

The anchorage of Mersa Tal Qad Yaya is sheltered by a reef extending east-south-east from Ras Keneisa, and 9 miles south-east of the same cape is another anchorage, Mersa Tawila, a bight in the shore reefs. Near by, from Ras al Millan the coast trends south-east for 11 miles to Qad al Hamdan, an inlet with a promontory extending west-south-west on its eastern side. Beyond this the coast trends nearly east for $6\frac{1}{2}$ miles, then south-east 5 miles to Ras Muhammad. But an important reef, Shab Mahmūd, extends 6 miles south-east from a little south of Qad al Hamdan; this reef lies parallel with the isthmus and peninsula of Ras Muhammad, 7 miles to the east.

Ras Muhammad, the extreme southern point of the Sinai peninsula, is 5 miles from the base of the narrow isthmus joining it to the mainland. The cape has an abrupt cliff 90 feet high and a flat top; a little to the north the ground descends to a low plain of gravel and dead coral. Black Hill, near the southern end of the isthmus and $2\frac{1}{2}$ miles west of the cape, is a black rounded elevation 190 feet high; a flat sand-coloured hill almost as high lies to the south-east. From the middle of the strait of Jubal these hills look like islands, while Tirān island, at the mouth of the Gulf of 'Aqaba, is visible over the cape 20 miles north-east. The mainland of Sinai north of the isthmus is hilly. Jebel Kashabi, 3½ miles north of the isthmus, reaches 1,069 feet; from it a range trends northward to Jebel Sahara, 4,785 feet high.

West Coast of the Gulf of Suez (fig. 26)

The African shore of the Gulf of Suez is in general low and sandy, and an arid coastal plain, varying from 2 to 20 miles in width, extends inland to the hills and mountains which form the eastern rim of the Egyptian desert. West of these coastal ranges the desert plateau slopes away to the Nile valley between the latitudes of Cairo and Asyūt. The watershed between the gulf and the Nile follows a winding course, generally nearer the Nile in the north, but approaching the gulf in the south, so that the southern wadis of the coastal belt are shorter and steeper than those nearer the head of the gulf. In two places broad gaps of relatively low country lead inland from the coast to the Nile valley. Elsewhere the much eroded but still rugged ranges, chiefly of granite or schist, with limestone in the north, and bare of vegetation save in the valleys, buttress the desert plateau as a barrier between the gulf and the Nile.

This stretch of coast is almost without economic activity. Communications are extremely poor, for access to the Nile valley, where the economic life of Egypt is concentrated, is barred by barren hills and behind them by desert. There are no made roads nor railways except at the head of the gulf, and only a track follows the coast all the way from Suez to the strait of Jubal. In some sections this is fit for light motors, but it is in no sense a through route, with numerous wadis crossing it and the hills in places pushing it into the sea. Approach to the coast on the seaward side is made difficult by reefs, and there are few anchorages. Only where mineral wealth is being exploited, as at the oilfield on Ras Gharib, and near the limestone quarries of Jebel 'Ataqa (p. 85), are there any facilities for shipping. On the other hand, weather conditions are excellent for aviation, with little rainfall, which makes it possible to use flat stretches of the coastal plain for landing-grounds. The only real dangers are occasional sandstorms, winter thunderstorms, and the dust-haze and mirage of summer.

Suez bay, at the head of the gulf, extends 6 miles southward to Cape Adabiya. The north-west shore is low and sandy, backed by a desert plain across which roads and railways connect Suez with Cairo and the Nile delta. In the south, where reefs and banks fringe the coast, the limestone hills of Jebel 'Ataqa rise abruptly from the sea, trending north-west and reaching a height of 2,857 feet 10 miles west of Suez. The track from Suez down the west side of the gulf keeps close to the shore of the bay, climbing the foothills of Jebel 'Ataqa to force a passage between the range and the sea. Quarries on the east flank of Jebel 'Ataqa are linked by tramway to a small pier about two-thirds of the way round the bay. Cape Adabiya is a low sandy spit which forms the eastern side of Adabiya bay, a good and almost landlocked anchorage, protected by 'Ataqa reef, in the south of Suez bay.

Suez lies on the north shore of Suez bay, on the flat, sandy desert plain, north-west of the mouth of the Suez canal. The site is historic, for the mound immediately north of the town is thought to mark the ruins of the Ptolemaic fortress of Clysma, and possibly an earlier settlement of the period of the Pharaohs. It is the site of Kolzum, a seventh-century trading-centre at the end of the canal which then joined the Red Sea to the Nile. By the thirteenth century Suez had replaced Kolzum, and after the Ottoman conquest of Egypt in the sixteenth century Suez became a naval station. It was of little importance when the French occupied it in 1798, and the battles which followed the English occupation in 1800 ruined it. Before the Suez canal was built it was a miserable Arab village, obtaining its water from 'Ayūn Musa until the Sweet Water canal from the Nile at Cairo was opened in 1863.

The town stands on mudflats on the south-west bank of Suez creek, into which the Sweet Water canal opens. The Arab seamen's quarter, Al Arba'in, is on the north-west outskirts, west of the railway. In the south-east of the town are the Government and business premises and the European quarters. To the south-west, fronting the shore of Suez bay, are two oil refineries, the property of the Anglo-Egyptian Oil Company and of the Egyptian Government. Suez is a quarantine station for pilgrims to Mecca. The harbour is an artificial construction built on land reclaimed from the sea. It consists of an island joined to the mainland by a stone causeway across the shallows at the head of Suez bay. Port Tewfik, the property of the Suez Canal Company, lies on the east and south-east of the island, and Port Ibrahim, the property of the Egyptian Government, occupies the north-west. The New Port is to the west, enclosed by breakwaters between Port Ibrahim and the mainland. A road and railway along the causeway link the port with the town, and from thence there are roads and railways north to Ismailia and west to Cairo. A light railway links the New Port with quarries on Jebel 'Ataqa, and a track follows the coast of the Gulf of Suez to Hurghada. There is a landing-ground 2 miles north-west of the town, near the junction of the Cairo and Ismailia railways.

South of Cape Adabiya the coast recedes westwards in a broad bay between Jebel 'Ataqa and the more imposing mass of Jebel al Qalala al Bahariya (North Qalala plateau). Once round the spurs of Jebel 'Ataqa the shore is low, trending south-west for 22 miles from Cape Adabiya. The country behind this northern part of the bay is comparatively low, forming one of the gaps mentioned above, and numerous wadis come down from the interior to lose their water in the hummocky plain which borders the gulf. They provide routes for several paths from the coast to the Nile valley. Bir Odeib and Bir Themada have perennial water-holes on the coastal plain, and there is a Frontier District Administration camp and an aircraft landing-ground at Bir Odeib. Farther south, 'Ain Sukhna has sulphur springs, and a stretch of salt-marsh borders the coast to the north of it. Here the hills of Jebel al Qalala al Bahariya, of limestone like Jebel 'Ataqa, approach the coast, and for 20 miles border the south-east trending shore of the bay, in places rising abruptly from the water with so little passage that camels have to wade round the spurs. Inland they form an intricate mass of ravine-furrowed highlands, reaching to within 20 miles of the Nile, and rising to 4,350 feet less than 10 miles from the coast. Ras Abu Diraj marks the end of the mountainous stretch and the southern point of the broad bay.

For about 20 miles beyond, to a point south of Cape Zafarana, the country is low and sandy, rising gradually westwards. Coral reefs border the coast. This lowland, an alluvium-filled depression sunk between faults of the Aden series which have left the upstanding masses of Jebel al Qalala al Bahariya and Jebel al Qalala al Qibliya (South Qalala plateau) flanking it to north and south, is the second gap giving access to the Nile valley. In the middle of it Wadi Araba, starting from 50 or 60 miles inland, opens to the sea near Cape Zafarana. Close to the lighthouse on the cape is a Frontier District Administration camp and a military landing-ground. The track from Suez follows the coast, crossing a number of dry wadis, and a branch goes up Wadi Araba. About 5 miles south of Cape Zafarana is Mersa Thelemet, a small bight which opens between the coast reefs. There is anchorage here and to the south of Zafarana reef.

From Mersa Thelemet the coast trends south-south-east for 57 miles to Ras Gharib. Low, undulating desert plains rise gradually from the reef-fringed coast towards the mountains, from 10 to 20 miles inland except where Jebel Thelemet (2,142 ft.) in the north of this section reaches to within 3 miles of the coast. The high table-land, called as a whole Jebel al Qalala al Qibliya or Jebel Zafarana, backing the coastal plain and rising to summits over 4,000 feet, is the northern end of the Red Sea hills, which from here continue unbroken along the west side of the gulf and on down the Egyptian coast of the Red Sea proper. Heights increase southwards, but the most conspicuous summit overlooking the gulf is the solitary precipitous peak of Jebel Gharib, which reaches 5,760 feet and dominates the scene from the sea. The only anchorages on this stretch of coast are in the small bay north of Ras Abu Baka and at Ras Gharib. At Ras Gharib is the most important oilfield in Egypt, and although operations only began in April 1938 it had quite outstripped the Hurghada field (p. 100) in 1939, when it produced 4,350,000 barrels, 80 per cent. of the total Egyptian output. Besides the buildings near the lighthouse on the cape there are three oil tanks at the base of an iron jetty 180 feet long, which extends south-south-east from the south side of the cape. An aircraft landing-ground, licensed to Anglo-Egyptian Oilfields, Ltd., and usable by all types of aircraft, lies $2\frac{3}{4}$ miles south of the lighthouse, near the track from Suez. This track is reported fit for light motors in some sections, but besides this there is only a rough path from Ras Gharib up the Wadi Had westward through the hills. Ras Gharib is connected to the telegraph line which runs close to the coast all the way from Suez to Quseir.

From Ras Gharib the coast continues 29 miles to Ras Dhib, inclining slightly more south-east. It is low and reef-bound, indented halfway by a bay, south of which Ras Shukheir rises in gravel cliffs to 250 feet, sheltering the anchorage. As far as Ras Shukheir the shore is backed by the salt-swamp of Al Melaha, which swallows the drainage of several wadis coming down from the hills and leaves little room for the coastal track on its seaward side.

Beyond Ras Dhib the scene changes as the coast bulges eastward round the granite range of Jebel Zeit, which with its fringe of Nubian sandstone forms one of the land-steps mentioned above (p. 75). The Zeit hills lie only a mile or less inland, rising to 1,503 feet at the highest point and displaying three old raised beaches (p. 64), the highest 500 feet above sea-level. These beaches form low cliffs, against which the waves, breaking on the submarine reef, dash in showers of foam and spray, wearing away the coast in steep-sided gullies and leaving at the foot of the cliff a mass of reef-boulders and coral sand which gives protection from more active denudation. The Zeit hills are an outlying range, separated by a desert plain about 13 miles wide from the parallel detached range of Jebel Melaha, which is slightly offset to the south. The coastal track, which branches into two at Ras Shukheir, keeps to this plain inland of the Zeit hills. The eastern branch skirts the base of the promontory formed by the southern end of the hills to reach Zeita, where a small bay provides anchorage near the oil-wells on the seaward flank of the Zeit hills. Except for Zafarana (p. 86) this is the best anchorage on the west side of the gulf, but the oil-wells have gone out of production.

The Mainland Coast on the South-west Side of the Strait of Jubal (fig. 27)

The coast from the Zeit promontory nearly to Hurghada, 42 miles south-south-east, may be regarded as the African side of the strait of Jubal, the entrance to the Gulf of Suez from the Red Sea. The southern end of the Zeit promontory is low, connected by reefs with the low, sandy Ranim island. Westward of the promontory Zeit bay (Ghubbet ti Zeiti) is a sheltered, land-locked inlet with a narrow entrance. Ras al Bahar, the southern entrance-point, projects north-east-wards, and the entrance to the shallow bay (30–40 ft.) is still more narrowed by reefs. The bay itself is free of reefs and has a sandy beach, with swamps at the head. It is used as an emergency seaplane anchorage. Low country, with sand and coral hillocks, surrounds it, and the track from Suez and Zeita skirts the shore to continue south along the coast. Most of the drainage from the seaward side of Jebel Melaha and from the landward side of the Zeit hills finds its way into the bay.

South of the Zeit promontory, from where Zeit bay etches into the plain behind the Zeit hills, the low coast is set back some miles to the west, so that the Melaha range is nearer the sea. The coastal plain, 8 miles wide at Zeit bay, narrows southward to only 2 miles. Behind it the Melaha range, with a core of volcanic rocks, has summits of over 1,300 feet and rises to a double peak in Jebel Esh (10 miles south of Ras Jemsa). The range ends abruptly, 11½ miles south-south-east of Jebel Esh, in Jebel Abu Sha'r al Qibli, inland from the site of Myos Hormos, a seaport famous in antiquity. Behind the Melaha range the Red Sea hills tower in granite highlands to over 5,000 feet less than 30 miles inland.

On the coast the promontory of Ras Jemsa (Gimsa), rising in yellow-white hills over 260 feet high, projects $3\frac{1}{2}$ miles south-eastwards about 5 miles south of Ras al Bahar. It is two-pronged, the narrow eastern branch (Jemsa peninsula) being the longer, and the whole promontory appearing in plan like the profile of a gnarled hand. The first oil-well in Egypt was bored on the north-east side of the peninsula, in 1908, and for a time Jemsa was a busy little port. But there is no production now, the only signs of this activity being the old oil-wells and the jetty. On the south side of the peninsula there is another jetty near disused sulphur mines. Jemsa anchorage is too exposed to the north to be satisfactory, but Kabreit anchorage on the south, protected by reefs, is good. Many reefs lie off the coast, and two small islands, Umm al Heimet and Umm al Heimet Seria, lie on the reefs between Jemsa promontory and the Gaysūm islands (*below*). Jemsa bay (Ghubbet ti Jemsa), between the Jemsa promontory and the mainland, has a broad entrance and is truncated at its head, where wadis from the Melaha range lose themselves in swamps. Its southern shore is bordered by reefs. From its southern entrance-point the coast trends south-east for 33 miles to a point opposite Jifatin Kabir island. Reefs encumber the shore, while inland the Melaha range comes to an end over half-way towards Hurghada, causing the coastal plain to broaden up to the foot of the Red Sea hills. At the end of this stretch the coastal plain is broken by the flat-topped hill of Dishat Abu Hurghada, which rises to 180 feet overlooking the sea opposite Jifatin Kabir island.

The Islands in the Strait of Jubal

Off this stretch of coast lie several groups of islands which continue the Zeit hills south-eastwards. The chief are the Ashrafi islands, Gaysūm islands, Jubal, Tawila, and Shadwān, the largest. The channels between them are intricate and filled with reefs. Three lighthouses stand at the edge of the strait, on the reef east of the Ashrafi islands, on the north-east point of Jubal Seria, and on the south-east point of Shadwān. The Ashrafi islands are low, composed of dead coral and sand from 6 to 15 feet high; the coral is about 30 feet thick (p. 68). North and South Gaysūm islands, considerably larger but also low and mainly flat, lie 3 miles to the south. South Gaysūm has white sandy cliffs on its north shore, and a conical dark brown hillock 100 feet high at its north end. On the south side is an Arab fishing-village. Jubal island, over 3 miles south-east of South Gaysūm, has a rounded summit reaching 410 feet; its east side is steep, with depths

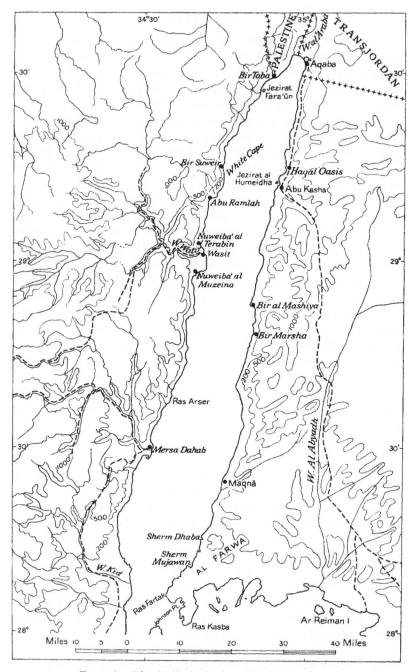

FIG. 28. *The Gulf of 'Aqaba. For key see fig. 26*

between 200 and 300 feet a mile off shore. Jubal Seria lies on the same reef, immediately north of Jubal. Tawila, south-west of Jubal, is a large, irregular coral island where oil-boring has been carried out. It is low, but rises to 50 feet on its east side. Shadwān ('seal') island is over 10 miles from north-west to south-east, a rugged brown extension of the Zeit range, with hills, scored by ravines, rising to between 700 and 990 feet. Small cays and islets in this archipelago are not all enumerated, but mention should be made of Umm Gamar (Gumārh), a small island with coral cliffs about 50 feet high on the eastern side. It lies near the south end of a steeply sloping coral reef, about 11 miles south of the north-west end of Shadwān, and a shorter distance from the north end of Jifatin (Giftūn) Kabir island (p. 99).

Southward of Dishat Abu Hurghada the coast and off-lying islands are described under section (i) of the Red Sea proper (pp. 98 ff.).

THE GULF OF 'AQABA, SOUTH-EAST COAST OF SINAI, AND STRAIT OF TIRĀN (figs. 27, 28)

The Gulf of 'Aqaba resembles that of Suez in filling the end of a rift and in being bounded by coast faults. But it differs from the shallow Gulf of Suez in being deep and almost without reefs. At its head there is a shallow step, then an abrupt descent to about 2,160 feet; 4,600 feet is reached half-way down the gulf, while the floor shallows again to 2,400 feet abreast of Ras Fartak.

Between latitudes 29° 33′ N. and 28° 05′ N. it is 110 miles long from north-north-east to south-south-west, the breadth varying between 7 and 17 miles. Mountain ridges leave only a narrow strip of coastal lowland on both sides. The ridges continue beyond the head of the gulf, enclosing Wadi al 'Araba, to the Dead Sea, 1,290 feet below the level of the Mediterranean. In many places the mountains rise like walls, and passage over them is very difficult. Even the coastal strip is difficult to traverse, and there is no continuous track for any distance on either shore. Anchorages are few, and most of these are exposed to southerly winds. Native shipping makes little use of the gulf, partly because the coast is barren and desolate, with very few inhabitants, but mainly because the northerly winds which prevail for the greater part of the year raise a considerable swell.

Politically, four States touch the shores of the gulf (p. 58), the frontiers converging at its head, a truncated bay, about 3 miles wide. The northern side, where Wadi al 'Araba opens to the gulf, is low and flat, but high mountains rise to east and west. 'Aqaba village stands on the east side.[1]

West Side of the Gulf of 'Aqaba

The extreme north-west corner of the gulf, in Palestine, is known as Umm Rashrash, but except for the huts of the police-post has no sign of habitation. On the long southward-projecting promontory of Taba, 5 miles south of the Palestine police-post, is an Egyptian post, on the frontier between Egypt and Palestine, which is marked by a cairn. Bir Taba, on the south side of the promontory, is an insignificant settlement with a well of brackish water. Five miles farther south, Jezirat Fara'ūn (Pharaoh's island), a conspicuous landmark, rises sharply out of the sea about 300 yards off shore. This small islet (also called Graia) is a rocky ridge, depressed in the middle, and covered by the ruins of a castle ascribed to the Crusaders. It is surrounded by a low wall, which, like the fortress, is built of the same reddish-brown rock of which the islet is composed. There is no water-supply, and the difficulty of sailing there in shark-infested wind-troubled waters has kept all but a few visitors away for at least eight centuries. The island provides anchorage off each end, according to wind.

From here southwards a narrow gravelly beach usually lies between mountains and sea, but in places steep spurs of the mountains cross the beach, forcing caravans to turn inland and climb steep narrow passes, or to round the ends of spurs at low tide. Between Jezirat Fara'ūn and White Cape, 17 miles farther south, three small bays provide anchorage sheltered from the north-east, and Abu Ramlah, 4 miles farther south, marks another anchorage. The narrow coastal plain widens to 3 miles round the mouth of Wadi Watir, 10 miles south of Abu Ramlah. Nuweiba' at Terabin, with its palmgroves and deserted fort, stands where the plain begins to widen. Its neglected well, in a ruined courtyard, is the only supply of drinking-water on the 36-mile stretch of coast south from Taba, that at Bir Suweir being too salty even for camels. Good quality manganese has been reported near the shore in this district, but labour difficulties prevent development. Wasit, a place of little interest with a few brackish wells and scattered palms, lies 2 miles farther south, where Wadi Watir, leaving the hills by a gorge only 150 paces across, reaches the sea through a channel in the barren shell-strewn beach. Very small vessels can anchor south of its sandy point. The wadi provides

[1] For 'Aqaba see B.R. 514, *Palestine and Transjordan*, pp. 522–524.

64. *Jezirat Fara'ūn, Gulf of 'Aqaba*

65. *Egyptian frontier post at Taba*

66. *Western shore of the Gulf of 'Aqaba near Nuweiba' at Terabin*

67. *View east-south-east to 'Aqaba. New Imperia wharf in foreground*

68. *Looking south-east to the new fishery wharf, a mile south of 'Aqaba. Granite hills of the Sa'ūdi frontier behind*

the only recognized route inland (photo. 44) on this side of the gulf, comparing in significance with Wadi Feiran (p. 80) on the west coast of Sinai. Four miles farther south, Nuweiba' al Muzeina, distinguished from its counterpart to the north by its lack of water, stands where the plain narrows suddenly and the dark ranges approach the coast again. Ras Arser, a sandy point about 32 miles south of Wasit, gives anchorage in its lee. Mersa Dahab, 7 miles farther south, is a harbour which affords good shelter on the south side of the low, sandy, reef-fringed Dahab promontory. Wadi Dahab, after collecting the drainage of several valleys from the high mountains, opens to the sea north of the promontory. The wadi and one of its tributaries offer a rough and circuitous route from the coast to the monastery of St. Catharine, about 34 miles directly inland. Southwards, about 37 miles of coast extends to Ras Nuzrani in the strait opposite Tirān island. There are no wadis of importance in this stretch until Wadi Kid is reached, where the mountains stand back from the sea. This wadi contains a perennial stream, with palm-groves near the shore. South of it the coastal plain is wider and the high mountains about 15 miles inland. The Sinai coast between Ras Nuzrani and Ras Muhammad is more indented than farther north; two small bays, Sherm ash Sheikh and Sherm al Moiya, separated by a rocky projection, provide anchorage for small vessels. A narrow reef extends the whole way from Mersa Dahab to Ras Muhammad, and approach to this coast is dangerous even for small boats except near the two sherms mentioned above.

East Side of the Gulf of 'Aqaba

The Transjordan–Sa'ūdi Arabian frontier touches the shore a few miles south of 'Aqaba village. An islet, Jezirat al Humeidha, lies in a small bay 20 miles south of the frontier, connected with the mainland by a reef at its northern end. A good anchorage, between islet and mainland, sheltered from all winds, can be entered from the south. Along this stretch of coast there is a track from 'Aqaba as far as Abu Kasha, 26 miles to the south. But mountain spurs reach down to the sea, and in places, as at Katib al Mubassi where the road has been artificially cut in soft marls, the way is dangerous. The waves cut into the soft rocks and the track crumbles away; during storms the sea sweeps over the path and completely blocks the passage. Haqal oasis stands among palm-trees on the shore of a small bay 3 miles north of Jezirat al Humeidha. It has a number of salt or brackish wells and sp..ings which cause violent fever, the only freshwater spring being south of Wadi al Mabraq, and some way inland.

Mountains, seamed with deep or shallow wadis, continue close to the coast for over 50 miles. At Abu Kasha the caravan road turns inland up a wadi, crosses the watershed ridge of Al Farwa into Wadi al Abyadh (p. 40) through a maze of peaks, ravines, and rocky ribs to the Red Sea coast. On the coast of the gulf there is little of interest. At Bir al Mashiya, 20 miles south of Abu Kasha, temporary anchorage can be found south of a sandy rock-fringed point. Between Bir Marsha, where there is a copious well, 4 miles south of Bir al Mashiya, and Maqnā, 34 miles farther south, mountains rise steeply from the sea, and the coastal strip is crossed obliquely by wadis draining south-westwards. The oasis of Maqnā, at the mouth of the wadi of the same name, is a collection of palm-leaf huts among date-groves, with a ruined fort to the south-east. The coastal range dies away north of the oasis, and limestone hills behind it form the watershed between the gulf and Wadi Abyadh. Few points south of Maqnā exceed 1,600 feet, and a white rocky plain rises gradually to the interior. The broad coastal lowland along the head of the Red Sea proper joins the narrow strip along the east side of the gulf, forming a long promontory less than 650 feet high. This ends in a double prong, with the rounded cape of Ras Fartak on the north and Ras Kasba (Ras al Fasma) on the south, at the eastern entrance to the gulf. Sherm Dhaba and Sherm Mujawan, two small coves 12 and 17 miles north of Ras Fartak, provide anchorage.

The Strait of Tirān, between Ras Nuzrani and Tirān island, is 4 miles wide at its narrowest and full of reefs. Tirān island, irregular in shape and about 7½ miles long from north to south, lies in the middle of the entrance to the Gulf of 'Aqaba, forming the east side of the strait. It is a low sandy plain with hills in places, the peak in the south rising to 1,720 feet. A long inlet, Foul bay, deeply indents the north-east coast, leaving a low peninsula of sand and dead coral to the north, connected with the rest of the island by a narrow isthmus. A reef joins this peninsula to the mainland at Ras Fartak. Much of the west coast of the island is low undercut coral cliffs, but two small sandy beaches usually afford landing. The south-west coast is steep and cliffed, with a narrow coral reef off shore. From Champlain point at the south-east extremity, for nearly 3 miles north-westward, the coast is a sloping sandy beach. There is little vegetation on the island, and the only fresh water is that left by rain in holes in the rocks. Johnson point, the north-west tip, gives anchorage on its south side; other anchorages are in a small bay on the south coast west of Champlain point and off the south-east coast.

Sanafīr (Sinafir) island is 2 miles east of Tīrān, south-south-east of Ras Kasba on the mainland. Broken limestone hills rise from the eastern part, nowhere more than about 200 feet high. A promontory juts southward from the north-west corner, forming the west side of a bay, reef-bordered on the north and east shores. The bay is used as an emergency seaplane anchorage, and a level space in the middle of the island serves as an emergency landing-ground for aircraft. The island has no water; rainfall is slight and usually restricted to December, January, and February. Mirage is frequent, and sandstorms, which occur at any time of the year, may be severe and prolonged in summer.

Natural Divisions of the Red Sea Proper (figs. 12, 25)

(1) *From the Southern end of the Sinai Peninsula to the line Ras Benas–Ras Abu Madd*

In this northern section the direction of the coast is controlled by faults of the Eritrean series (fig. 12). The escarpment of the coastal range on the African side is formed by a long line of faulting in a north-north-west to south-south-east direction, curving slightly east at its southern end along the Ras Benas peninsula to Seberget (Zeberged, St. John's) island. The abrupt descent to the 1,600-foot line is parallel to the coast range, and the shallow-water step only a few miles wide. At the entrance to the Gulf of Suez the elevated land-step of Jebel Zeit and its continuations, Jubal and Shadwān islands, extend as far south as the abrupt slope to the deepest central trough. The little islands of The Brothers and Daedalus, coralline limestone on volcanic bases, stand on the edge of this submerged escarpment. Soundings indicate that the submerged eastern escarpment of the deep central trough is parallel to that on the west.

The alinement of the Arabian coastal ranges and plain is roughly parallel to that on the African side. The coastal plain is narrow, but its submerged extension, the shallow-water step, is broad and studded with islands in the south between Al Wejh and Ras Abu Madd. The descent from the shallows to 1,600 feet is nearly parallel with the foot of the coast range. The deep central trough appears to be truncated at its northern end, possibly by a cross-fault continuing the line of the Gulf of 'Aqaba.

In the part of Arabia abutting on this section of the Red Sea, parallel faults of the Eritrean series lie far inland. The long narrow plain of Al Hisma, an inland drainage depression along which part of the Hejaz railway was laid, has the same direction. Again parallel, but much farther inland, is Wadi Sirhan. A section of the Hejaz railway farther south, from Al 'Ulā to Al Madina, lies in a broad plain the axis of which is a prolongation of Al Hisma. The volcanic harras between these two plains and the western escarpment of the high plateau are ranged in the same direction.

(2) *From the line Ras Benas–Ras Abu Madd to the line Ras Rawāya–Rābigh*

In this section faults of the Eritrean direction meet with others of the Meridional series. That 'crossings' of faults of these two series occur is at once visible from the African side. Here the escarpment of the coastal range south of Ras Benas runs due south, and about the latitude of the wide bay of Mersa Shab a long line of faulting continues due south far into the range, at an angle with its eastern escarpment, while the coastal range slants south-south-east to Ras Rawāya. The north-north-west to south-south-east line of faulting between Mersa Shab and Ras Rawāya represents the oblique truncation at the northern end of two faults of the Meridional series, for south of Ras Rawāya both coast and coastal range run due south. The chief line of faulting in this series appears here to be dislocated several times, and the parts pushed sideways, an instance of the structure already mentioned (p. 60).

On the Arabian side, in the region between Rābigh and Al Madina (a district better known than some) the course of valleys and ranges also indicates crossing of faults of the Eritrean and Meridional series.

(3) *From the line Ras Rawāya–Rābigh to the line Suākin–Jidda*

In this short section the central trough as a whole reaches its greatest depth, much of it being below 6,600 feet. Soundings indicate that the submerged steps in the sea-floor run meridionally in the northern part, but slant in the Eritrean direction in the south. In the central trough the northern (Meridional) section is shorter than the southern (Eritrean) section. This is again a part of the sea where the Meridional lines of faulting appear to have been dislocated and pushed sideways to the east. The escarpments of the shallowly submerged coastal step on either side do not always appear parallel with the edge of the deeply submerged step.

(4) *From the line Suākin–Jidda to Bab al Mandeb*

From about the latitude of Suākin southwards the character of the Red Sea changes (fig. 12). The shallow-water steps on both sides broaden so that they include about three-quarters of the total width.

The steep descent to the central trough appears uninterrupted, and in the north the greatest depth of all is reached (8,520 ft.).

On the African side the transition into this southern section is very peculiar. North of Port Sudan the shallow-water step falls abruptly to depths of more than 2,600 feet. Opposite Port Sudan and again opposite Suākin it is deeply indented so that depths of 1,900 and 1,300 feet respectively are found near these harbours. But south of them the shallow-water step projects outwards, bearing many coral reefs and islands, between which and the coast lies a deeper channel. After bending eastward at Suākin this channel ends blindly against the projecting part of the shallow-water step. Outside the shallow-water step a number of islets and reefs opposite Suākin rise steeply from great depths, indicating a submerged volcanic landscape. South of Suākin the islands and reefs of the Suākin archipelago extend far out to sea, separated from each other by very varying depths.

At Ras Kasar, the frontier between the Sudan and Eritrea, the sea-bottom descends steeply to 1,300 feet near the coast. Still farther south the Dahlak islands stand on a broad shallow platform penetrated from north to south by two deep submarine inlets. The eastern side of this platform is penetrated by several fairly deep troughs (300 feet and more), trending meridionally in the north, but in the Eritrean direction farther south.

From the Baraka mouth, south of Suākin, the African coast strikes south-south-east to Ras Kasar. The coastal range is parallel, but the direction of the valleys indicates that several Meridional faults are here cut off obliquely by a coastal fault of the Eritrean series. From Ras Kasar southwards the faults bounding the coastal range again lie meridionally. Opposite the Dahlak islands several land-steps formed by faulting appear to be pushed eastwards, especially on the Buri peninsula. Thence the western marginal fault of the Red Sea rift coincides with the actual coastline, running south-south-east even beyond Bab al Mandeb. This long coastal fault apparently joins the marginal system of faults bounding the Abyssinian highlands on the east, a system which extends southwards until it abuts on the south Abyssinian rift, where the Red Sea and Gulf of Aden rifts join the east African rift system.[1]

[1] According to one view at least, the south Abyssinian rift separates the true Abyssinian highlands on the west and north from the Somaliland highlands, which comprise part of south-east Abyssinia and Somaliland. Between the Red Sea coast south of the Buri peninsula, and the Danakil desert, the Danakil highlands are another separate block. A rift extends south from Annesley bay, forking into two; the eastern branch, forming the western limit of the Danakil highlands, runs south

The deep central trough of the Red Sea appears to slant in the Eritrean direction immediately south of the Suākin–Jidda line. Farther south, between Ras Kasar on the African coast and Wasm on the Arabian, begins a short Meridional part. It then slants south-south-east again between the broad shallow-water shelves on which stand the Dahlak and Farasān islands, continuing thus for a long distance with only a short Meridional stretch between Jebel at Tāir with the Zubair islands, and the Hanīsh islands. These three island groups are all volcanic, the two former rising from the central deeps, the Hanīsh islands from the eastern edge of the trough. Finally the trough slants south-south-east again, shallowing to about 300–650 feet through the straits of Bab al Mandeb, beyond which it reaches the much wider Gulf of Aden.

The direction of the ranges and faults on the Arabian side is insufficiently known. About Jidda the margins of the ranges strike meridionally, but north of Al Līth they appear to slant south-south-east, a direction which seems also to prevail on the inner edge of the coastal highlands here. East of Al Qunfidha and east of Jīzān, the seaward escarpment lies north–south, but slants south-south-east between the two. The foot of the Yemen coastal range extends north–south except for a few short stretches. But farther inland the mountain chains, fault valleys, and steps lie mostly north-north-west to south-south-east, obliquely cut off at their northern ends by the meridional outer margin of the coastal range, and crossed at right angles by short faults of the Aden series.

Farther north in Arabia, faults of this last series (west-south-west to east-north-east) only appear near Mecca, but on the African side they apparently cross the faults of the Eritrean series at right angles in the elevated Danakil country south-east of Assab. Near Great Hanīsh island the main trough of the Red Sea also seems to be crossed by a small transverse trough in the Aden direction. The gulf of Obok or Tajura is similarly alined, forming a narrow extension of the wide head of the Gulf of Aden.

THE AFRICAN COAST OF THE RED SEA

(i) *The Coast of Egypt* (fig. 29)

South of the strait of Jubal, Egypt, without allowing for indentations and projecting points, has a coastline of over 330 miles on the

to the deepest depression, hundreds of feet below sea-level, of the Danakil desert which divides the Danakil highlands from the Abyssinian highlands. The western branch of the rift forms the eastern limit of the true Abyssinian highlands.

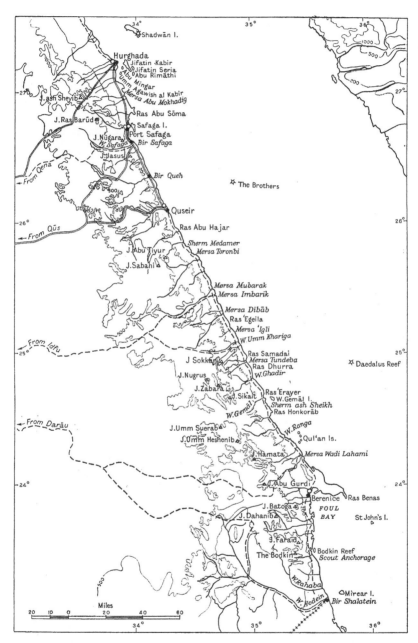

FIG. 29. *The Red Sea Coast of Egypt (Key on Fig. 26)*

Red Sea between the points 27° 20′ N., 33° 42′ E., and 23° 09′ N., 35° 35′ E. Throughout its length the Red Sea hills rise from a narrow coastal plain, carrying the watershed between the Nile and the sea at varying distances (20–50 miles) inland, much broken on the seaward side by short steep wadis, and composed mainly of granites, schists, and other crystalline rocks. The Miocene limestones and gypseous beds which border the hills on the seaward side die out at Ras Benas. The general slope of the coastal plain is considerably steeper than the slope down to the Nile valley on the other side of the hills, hence the watershed lies much nearer to the sea than to the Nile. Mineral deposits, gold, copper, iron, emeralds, and phosphates, exist in the Red Sea hills and on the coastal plain, some of them exploited in antiquity, but the only modern workings are the phosphate mines near Safaga and Quseir, the products before the war being exported chiefly to Japan as phosphate of lime, or used for the manufacture of superphosphates. Reefs border the coast everywhere except at a few favoured harbours, making it dangerous for shipping, though there are many good anchorages among outlying reefs. In places, as near Berenice, sand dunes have accumulated on the plain, but have no great development on this coast of Egypt.

Apart from Hurghada, Port Safaga, and Quseir, there are very few permanent settlements near the coast. The strip between the mountains and the sea is a desert plain with rainfall so slight as to be negligible. What there is is extremely variable both in quantity and distribution, confined to sudden showers which flood the wadis but have no lasting benefit. Winds are generally from between west and north, more westerly in winter, northerly in summer. Thunderstorms are frequent in winter and sandstorms at any time of the year. Thus it is difficult to maintain centres of population, and most of the inhabitants of this part of Egypt are semi-nomadic Arabs.

In the north the five Jifatin (Giftūn) islands lie from 14 to 20 miles south of Shadwān island and from 1 to 9 miles off the mainland at Dishat Abu Hurghada (p. 89). Jifatin Kabir, the largest, is 7 miles long, with a rugged hill extending from the northern end to reach 350 feet in the middle; the southern end is a plateau of dead coral 10 to 20 feet high. Jifatin Seria, a much smaller island east of the south end of Jifatin Kabir, also rises to over 300 feet. Abu Rimāthi, only a mile long, with a narrow point at its north end, is south of Jifatin Seria. Between these and the coast are two others: Umm Agawish al Kabir, coralline and 15 feet high, and Umm Agawish as Saghir, low and rocky. Abu Mingar is a small flat island of sand and coral on the reef west of Jifatin Kabir; it is divided into two by a narrow creek, the northern part bare, but the southern covered with low bushes. All the islands are reef-fringed, and there are outlying reefs in the vicinity, but the channel between Jifatin Kabir and Jifatin Seria provides well-sheltered anchorage.

The mainland coast from abreast the islands trends generally south-south-east for over 80 miles to Quseir. For the first 60 miles reefs are discontinuous, but abreast of Safaga island they extend over 6 miles off shore, and in the last 20 miles a narrow reef borders the coast. Though there are small harbours and anchorages, and the names *Mersa* and *Sherm* occur, it does not appear that any north of Quseir have the peculiar structure of true sherms.

At Hurghada the summits of the mountain range are about 30 miles inland, but abreast of Safaga island the range converges with the coast, remaining close to the sea thence to Quseir. The highest point in Egypt is Jebel ash Sheyib (7,165 ft.), 28 miles south-west of Hurghada, and beyond this heights decrease. Jebel Ras Barūd, 16 miles south-east of Jebel ash Sheyib, is 4,700 feet high, but south-wards the altitudes are generally less than 2,000 feet.

On the coast, Dishat Abu Mingar is a headland 278 feet high, which, prolonged by Merlin point, of steep bare coral ledges rising to 240 feet, projects eastward towards Jifatin Kabir island. In the bay between this headland and that of Abu Hurghada $3\frac{1}{2}$ miles to the north (p. 89) is the settlement of Hurghada, on a plain surrounded by bare hills of sand and coral. Hurghada owes its existence to the oilfield, worked by the Anglo-Egyptian Oil Company. Most of the oil wells lie on the landward slopes of Dishat Abu Hurghada, where production started in 1914. After reaching 288,000 tons in 1919, output declined (173,650 tons in 1935), and at the end of 1940 was only 20 per cent. of the total Egyptian output. Crude oil is shipped to the Company's refinery at Suez. The settlement is in two parts: one, on the oilfield, has the Company's offices and workshops, the European and native quarters and the Post Office; the other, $2\frac{1}{4}$ miles south-east, is near the shore, and consists of the native fishing-village and the Frontier District Administration camp, with barracks and police station. There is no local water-supply, and all water has to be shipped from Suez. The two piers are connected by light railway (2-ft. gauge) and by motor-road with the oilfield and its settlement. Water is laid on to both piers, and crude oil from the wells to the North Pier only. Communications are poor; there are tracks along the coast to Suez and Safaga, and inland to Qena on the

69. *Coastal track to Safaga*

70. *The small Egyptian Red Sea port of Quseir in 1938*

71. *Quseir from the air*

72. *Daedalus Reef and lighthouse in 1935*

Nile. The Post Office has telegraph lines to Suez and Safaga, and there is a landing-ground on the outskirts of the oilfield settlement, $2\frac{1}{2}$ miles west-north-west of the piers. Seaplanes anchor off the piers and in rough weather between Jifatin Kabir and Abu Mingar islands. The foreshore is reef-fringed except between the piers, where boats can be run up on the sandy beach.

For about 6 miles beyond Hurghada the coast trends south, reef-fringed and flat, with the hills gradually approaching the sea until Dishat adh Dhaba (315 ft.) pushes south-east for 2 miles to form the north side of a small bay, Mersa Abu Mokhadig, where there is anchorage protected by Sa'al Hashish, a low islet on a reef a mile south of Dishat adh Dhaba. Another small but well-sheltered boat-harbour lies 3 miles farther south. Over 5 miles to the south-east, Ras Abu Sōma is a gravel-topped double headland projecting $2\frac{1}{2}$ miles seaward, somewhat higher than the surrounding coast; it provides anchorage west of its south-eastern end. For 18 miles south of Ras Abu Sōma, as far as Bir Safaga, the general south-south-east trend of the coast is interrupted, and fronted by reefs and islets it forms a wide bay, broken by small capes. Safaga island, 6 miles long, lies in the middle of the bay; it is low and sandy, but with a conspicuous table-topped hill over 70 feet high on the north-east, capped by a beacon. Reefs fringe the island, and there are mangrove swamps on its west coast. The stretch of water between the island and the mainland is used as an emergency seaplane anchorage, sheltered from all quarters except the south-east.

Port Safaga, which is entered between the detached rocks off the south end of Safaga island and the north end of Spit reef, is the outlet for the phosphate mined by a British company at Umm al Huweitat, up a southern tributary of Wadi Safaga near Jebel Jasus. There is a small settlement on the mainland consisting chiefly of the company's houses and phosphate works, with the Egyptian Frontier Force camp at the south end on the shore. Of the two small piers only the southern one is now used, and it is equipped with a transporter crane at the terminus of a narrow-gauge railway. This line follows the shore south for 8 miles, then turns inland for a further 8 miles up Wadi Safaga and its tributary to the phosphate mines. Reefs border the shore south of the southern pier, but there is anchorage close inshore north of it, and seaplanes have been successfully hauled up on the beach on either side of the northern pier. On the promontory which encloses Port Safaga on the north is an emergency aircraft landing-ground used by the Egyptian Air Force. Except for

the sand-dunes which surround the landing-ground, the Safaga neighbourhood is low and flat, though mountains rising inland reach 1,230
feet within a mile of the coast, and Jebel Nugara 2½ miles south-west
of Port Safaga has a summit of 2,730 feet. The coastal track which
links Port Safaga northwards with Hurghada and the Gulf of Suez,
and southwards with Quseir, is usable by motors in dry weather
(photo. 69). Vessels of the phosphate company call regularly at the port.

Bir Safaga (Safaja Ulbur) lies near the mouth of Wadi Safaga, up
which a track branches inland to the Nile valley at Qena, and an
alternative dry-weather motor-road to the coastal route branches
inland to join the track linking Quseir with the Nile at Qūs. From
Bir Safaga the south-south-east trend of the coast is resumed for
200 miles to Ras Benas. The small Arab village of Bir Queh (Kuweh,
Quei‘), 22 miles from Bir Safaga, has a good boat-harbour, and there
is another 7 miles farther south. But there are no sheltered anchorages
for larger vessels, and the coast is reef-fringed between Bir Safaga
and Quseir (40 miles).

Quseir ('the little fortress') is a small native town, with European
quarters on the north and north-east outskirts. Though in the past
it was the terminus of an ancient caravan route from the Nile to
the Red Sea, and the place where routes from Coptos and Myos
Hormos joined before passing on to Berenice, it owes its present
importance solely to its phosphate mines. The town and phosphate
works stand on a low, blunt, sandy point, in bare desert country.
A few miles inland lie the Red Sea hills, outliers of which, Jebel
Quseir and Jebel Gehenna, reach 446 and 715 feet respectively, to
west-north-west and west-south-west of the town. The sandy point
forms the north shore of a small bight, where there is a short break
in the coast reef opposite the mouth of a wadi. The reefs prevent
landing everywhere except on the small beach south of the town or
at the two jetties. In the town streets are regular and at right angles
to each other; houses are built of stone. There are two hospitals,
a Post Office, and a Frontier District Administration Station. Water
is obtained from the Government evaporating plant near the jetty
and from the Phosphate Company's plant, there being no natural
supply. Electricity is supplied to Government buildings and to the
European quarter from the Company's plant. The phosphates are
mined entirely by an Italian Company, which besides a jetty, hospital,
and the road to the mines, also owns a school. There is no other
industry in the town apart from the mining and export of phosphates.
A light railway (2 ft. 6 in. gauge) links the jetty with the works and

the mines, and in 1938 a railway was under construction from Quseir to Qena. The tracks north to Safaga and inland to Qūs are usable by light motors, and there is a landing-ground near the coast 2½ miles west-north-west of the town.

In the 160 miles of coast between Quseir and Ras Benas there are few well-marked inlets, only Sherm Medamer, Mersa Mubarak, and Sherm ash Sheikh being listed among typical sherms with deep-water channels (p. 584), though there are a few other anchorages. Sherm Medamer is 20 miles south of Quseir and 10 miles south of Ras Abu Hajar, a cape marked by the black conical hill of Jebel 'Esel 2½ miles south-south-west. Mersa Toronbi, about 10 miles south-south-east of Sherm Medamer, is a small bight with water 50 feet deep, giving anchorage sheltered from the north-west. Mersa Mubarak, or Mubarak inlet, 12 miles farther on, must be distinguished from Mersa Imbarik (Ma Mubarak), another small bight between reefs 1½ miles south-south-east of it. The former, though insufficiently known, appears to be a two-armed sherm of typical form.[1] About 13 miles south-south-east of Mersa Mubarak is a cove, Mersa Dibāb, with the steep-sided Elphinstone reef about 7 miles off shore. Completely sheltered anchorage is afforded by Mersa 'Igli (Zebara), a narrow cove with entrance only 100 yards wide, 8 miles beyond Mersa Dibāb. Between the two is the reddish double hill of Ras 'Egeila, and 16 miles south-south-east of Mersa 'Igli the low reef-fringed point of Ras Samadai projects from the coast. Close south of this point is Mersa Tundeba, another anchorage, with the small boat-harbour of Wadi Ghadir 7 miles farther on. Ruins on low hillocks south of Wadi Ghadir are thought to be those of Ptolemy's *Nechesia*. Ras Dhurra to the north and Ras 'Erayer (Uriah) to the south of Wadi Ghadir are low capes. Between Ras 'Erayer and Ras Honkorāb (Umm al 'Abbas), 14 miles south-east, where a conspicuous sugar-loaf hill rises to more than 300 feet near the coast, is Sherm ash Sheikh (Sherm Lūli), the third of the typical deep-water sherms north of Ras Benas. This cove, up to 90 feet deep, is a good anchorage, reached through a narrow opening in the coast reef. Wadi Gemāl island, low and rocky, lies among reefs 4 miles off shore and north-east of Sherm ash Sheikh. The 50-mile stretch of coast between Ras Honkorāb and Ras Benas is fronted with reefs and islands. The Qul'an (Gulhan) group, 20 miles south-east of Ras Honkorāb, consists of four low sandy islands with anchorage off the southernmost. On the mainland opposite the islands the Miocene limestone, on which the coastal plain is developed

---

[1] Report of H.M.S. *Penzance*, 1933.

all the way from Safaga, gives place to Nubian sandstone, which in turn
is buried by more recent deposits of sand and coral before Ras Benas
is reached. Mersa Wadi Lahami, 8 miles south of the Qul'an islands,
gives good anchorage. Ras Benas is the eastern end of a hilly peninsula, the most prominent feature on the Egyptian coast, extending
nearly 20 miles south-eastward. A narrow, sinuous plateau of white
limestone forms the backbone, reaching an elevation of 616 feet. A
darker mass of granite hills 643 feet high lies near the junction of the
peninsula with the mainland, and a similar mass at the south-east end
reaches 633 feet. The north side of the peninsula is a gently sloping
sandy plain across which short grassy wadis drain the interior.
This plain is continued as a narrow sandspit, Ras Benas, nearly
5 miles long, with a sheikh's tomb at the end. On the south coast
of the peninsula the hills come down to the sea except near the
mainland where a small sandy plain intervenes and sends out south-
westwards a spit 4 miles long, which encloses the anchorage of Port
Berenice.

The mountain range, which lies so near the coast north of Quseir,
recedes south of Ras Abu Hajar, but gains in height. Thus Jebel Abu
Tiyur, 16 miles south-west of the cape, is 3,600 feet high, and farther
inland Jebel Sabahi is over 4,800 feet. From the vicinity of Mubarak
inlet a broken line of lesser heights lies near the coast until it dies out
opposite the Qul'an islands. Inland from Ras Dhurra, Jebel Nugrus
rears its granite head to 4,937 feet 22 miles from the coast near the
head of Wadi Ghadir, the centre of a cluster of mountains between
Wadi Umm Khariga and Wadi Gemāl. On the north-eastern flank
of this group the craggy granite ridge of Jebel Sokkari (Sukari) rises
to 2,066 feet, 13 miles west of Mersa Tundeba, and here the ancient
gold-mines have recently (1937) been reopened by the Egyptian
Government with a potential output of 40 tons of ore per day.
Other high mountains in this group are Jebel Zabara (4,465 ft.)
and Jebel Sikait (2,530 ft.). As a whole the highland mass is
known as 'the Emerald mountains', for there are ancient emerald
mines in several places; other minerals including gold and iron ore
are found.

South of Wadi Gemāl a still higher mountain mass backs the coast
between Ras Honkorāb and Ras Benas. It is composed chiefly of
schists, with some gneiss and granite, the latter forming the lower
summits, and contains some of the loftiest peaks in Egypt. Jebel
Hamata (6,552 ft.), 22 miles from the coast opposite the Qul'an
islands, is the highest summit, and second only to Jebel ash Sheyib in

Egypt. Jebel Umm Suerab and Jebel Umm Heshenib in the north, behind Wadi Ranga, are over 4,000 feet, and Jebel Abu Gurdi, the terminal peak of a south-easterly extension, reaches 5,124 feet.

The last 60 miles of the Egyptian coast, between Ras Benas and the frontier with the Sudan, trends south, receding to form Foul Bay. Almost the whole stretch is foul with reefs and sunken rocks, and there is anchorage for steam vessels only at Port Berenice and Scout anchorage 35 miles farther south. Though there are several curiously shaped inlets, none can be listed with certainty among the sherms in Appendix A. The coast is low and rocky, with only a narrow sandy plain about 5 miles wide before high mountains rise towards the interior. Port Berenice lies in the north-west corner of Foul Bay, in the angle between the Ras Benas peninsula and the mainland. Its inner harbour, lying to the north-west of the sandspit which projects from the peninsula is much encumbered with reefs, but is a safe operating area for seaplanes on its north-west side, with depths of 5 to 15 feet. The outer harbour, reef-bordered in the south, is indented with small coves and lagoons, separated by low coral plateaux, and the best anchorage is in North cove, entered through a gap in the fringing reef. There is an emergency aircraft landing-ground on the west shore of the inner harbour. Overlooking a lagoon on the west shore of the outer harbour, 4 miles south-south-west of the landing-ground are the ruins of ancient Berenice, founded in 275 B.C. by Ptolemy II and named after his mother; it was the terminus of the main desert routes and for about 500 years a centre of Egypt's maritime commerce with Arabia and India (p. 215). Scout anchorage is 32 miles farther south, sheltered from the north by Bodkin reef, but 3 miles off shore. Mirear island, low and sandy, lies in a maze of reefs 22 miles to the south-east, 8 miles seaward of the point on the mainland where the Sudan frontier reaches the sea.

Two groups of mountains lie near the coast in this section south of Ras Benas. Jebel Dahanib (4,160 ft.) is the highest summit in the northern group, but it is 20 miles inland, and other summits lie between it and the sea. Jebel Batoga, 8 miles inland and about the same distance south-west of the ruins of Berenice, reaches 2,628 feet. In the southern group, Jebel Faraid (4,480 ft.), only 7 miles inland, is the highest peak, but the Bodkin, a little farther inland and to the south, a sharp pinnacle of granite 4,035 feet high, almost on the Tropic of Cancer, is more conspicuous. The foothills of these two mountain groups are only 3½ miles from the coast in the north, but in the south they stand back about 8 miles, and there is a further widening of the coastal plain round the mouths of the wadis Rahaba and Hodein near the frontier.

Communications on the Red Sea coast are undeveloped. Hurghada is linked with Qena on the Nile by a road suitable for motor traffic in dry weather, and lies on a similar road along the coast from the Gulf of Suez through Port Safaga to Quseir. Quseir is linked with the Nile at Qūs by a dry-weather motor-road, a branch of which goes north to Bir Safaga as an alternative to the coastal road. A railway is reported under construction from Quseir inland to the Nile at Barāhma, between Qūs and Qena, but the only existing railway on this coast is the short mineral line already mentioned (p. 102). A track continues along the coast from Quseir to the frontier, with branches inland to the Nile valley from Mersa Imbarik, from a point south of Mersa 'Igli, from Mersa Wadi Lahami, and from the frontier at Bir Shalatein. In the north, Hurghada and Bir Safaga have tracks to Qena. Hurghada and Port Safaga are linked by telegraph lines, an extension of the line along the west coast of the Gulf of Suez.

As well as the islands already referred to near the coast, there are three other groups farther out to sea. The Brothers (p. 95) are two coral islets 38 miles out from Quseir to east-north-east. Both are fringed with narrow reefs, and North islet has a lighthouse 119 feet high, and an iron jetty 180 feet long on the south-west side. Daedalus reef, 56 miles east of Mersa Tundeba, and 114 miles south-south-east of The Brothers, is usually submerged, but may be uncovered during the low-water period (p. 61). It has a lighthouse 100 feet high and an iron jetty which extends to the edge of the reef (photo. 72). Seberget (St. John's) island is a volcanic cone 700 feet high bordered by coral reefs, 32 miles south-east of Ras Benas and 94 miles south-south-east of Daedalus reef. It is inaccessible except for a small boat-passage through the reefs on the north-east, barren and without water, but occasionally visited by fishermen in search of the turtles numerous in the vicinity and valuable for their shells.

(ii) *The Coast of the Anglo-Egyptian Sudan* (fig. 30)

The coast of the Anglo-Egyptian Sudan stretches from Bir Shalatein to Ras Kasar (23° 09′ N., 35° 35′ E. to 18° 00′ N., 38° 32′ E.), discounting all but the major irregularities a distance of over 420 miles, comprising parts of all the natural divisions of the Red Sea except the first (p. 96). For this reason it is more complex in outline than that of Egypt, and in addition it contains nearly all of the

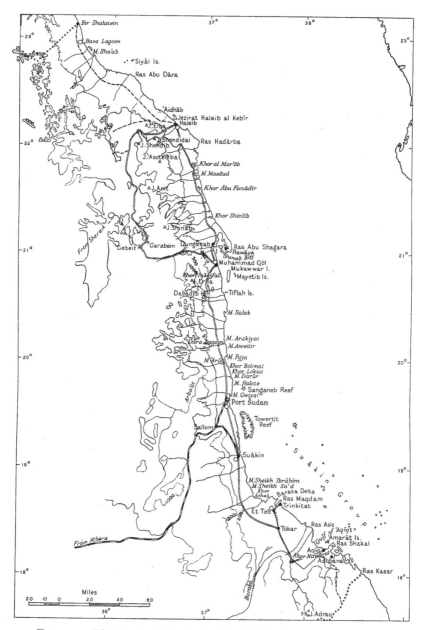

FIG. 30. *The Coast of the Anglo-Egyptian Sudan (Key on Fig. 26)*

twenty-six inlets listed as true sherms on the African side of the Red Sea. The whole coast is studded with reefs and islets, between which and the mainland is a protected channel extending southwards from Rawāya (Ras Abu Shagara), half a mile wide in the north, but considerably wider south of Suākin. Gaps in the reefs give entrance to the channel from seaward, those off Port Sudan and Suākin being important factors in the location of those ports. The coast is generally low and sandy, backed by a plain which varies from 8 to 20 miles in width and behind which lie rocky mountain ranges, the high eastern rim of the Nubian desert, where several summits exceed 7,000 feet. The coastal belt may be divided into four roughly parallel north–south strips. The seaward fringe is impregnated with salt, and contains salt pans devoid of vegetation; occasionally mangroves line the water's edge. About a mile inland is a belt of hard sand dunes, bearing fleshy-leaved bushes, and behind that a zone of coarse hard sand with fine gravel, overlaid in places with soft sand which occasionally forms dunes. The last strip is the stony belt adjoining the foothills, bare of vegetation except in the wadis. Most of the streams draining to the Red Sea rise on the eastern side of the mountains and have short courses. These, especially in the north where rainfall is slight, carry little silt, and splitting into many channels on leaving the foothills, lose themselves in the sand of the coastal plain. But in the south, with heavier rainfall, there are several longer watercourses, such as the Arba'āt and the Baraka, which rise well behind the mountains, break through the range, and reach the sea through deltas. These, especially the Baraka, bring down much silt, which is spread out over the plain when the rivers flood.

The coastal plain north of Port Sudan has few settlements and little cultivation, the climate being similar to that of the Red Sea coast of Egypt. But south of Port Sudan rainfall increases, and, still slight and variable, is mainly confined to the winter, between October and February. Winds are generally northerly, but in the south from June to September strong south winds blow and dust storms are common. Economically, the Red Sea coast of the Sudan is important for the cotton produced in the Tokar district, where millet is also grown for human consumption, and for the salt which is extracted from some of the lagoons. Mineral wealth, mainly gold, is known to exist in the mountains, but mining is not well developed. Communications are better than on the Egyptian coast; and since Port Sudan and Suākin are the only ports for the whole of this vast country, they dominate the economic activity of the coastal zone.

For 52 miles from Bir Shalatein on the frontier with Egypt the coast trends south-east and then east, continuing the broad curve of Foul Bay to Ras Abu Dāra. The coastal plain here is about 18 miles wide, sandy and undulating, with a cover of sparse scrub. Hasa lagoon is 11 miles south of the frontier, a crescentic shallow lagoon about 2 miles long. It is enclosed between sandspits on the north and south, and protected seawards by sandy islets and a bank of sand and mud. On its western shore are mangrove swamps and sand-dunes, with low hills rising 5 miles inland. The only entrance to the lagoon is by a narrow boat-channel round the end of the northern spit, and depths inside never exceed 15 feet. The lagoon provides an emergency anchorage for seaplanes, and has a military landing-ground on the west shore. Mersa Sha‘ab, a large inlet inaccessible to vessels because of reefs, is 9 miles farther south-east, and from here to the low point of Abu Dāra the coast is bordered by a reef with many outlying patches. The three Siyāl islands, low and sandy, lie 10 miles north of Ras Abu Dāra, surrounded by rocks and reefs.

From Ras Abu Dāra the coast trends south-east for 62 miles to Ras Hadārba (Cape ‘Elba), reef-fringed for 55 miles and unapproachable for steam vessels though there are several anchorages for dhows.

About 30 miles south-east of Ras Abu Dāra are the ruins of ‘Aidhāb, called Suākin al Qadim (Suākin the Ancient). The harbour served Mecca pilgrims during the Middle Ages, and ‘Aidhāb was a market for goods from central Africa as well as for those from India shipped through Aden, with caravan routes to the Nile at Aswān, Idfu, and Qūs. The population, depending entirely on imported means of subsistence (even water had to be supplied from elsewhere), was engaged chiefly in conveying goods by land and sea, supplementing this with fishing and pearl-diving. The height of prosperity was reached between 1058 and 1368, but after Indian trade reverted to the north of the Red Sea at the end of the fourteenth century, ‘Aidhāb sank into oblivion (p. 245).

About 12 miles beyond the ruins is the irregular inlet of Mersa Haleib, sheltered by Jezirat Haleib al Kebīr and coral reefs, and with two good anchorages reached through channels at each end of the long reef which lies off the village. Haleib village, a collection of reed huts and matting tents surrounding an old fort, straggles among palm-trees between a blockhouse on a small hill to the south-west and the sea. Its wells yield very hard water, strongly purgative to those unused to it, but local supplies include mutton, fish, eggs, and even grouse. There is a small coral pier off the village and an aircraft landing-ground to the south-east. The harbour is used as an emergency seaplane anchorage. Tracks, reported usable for light motors, lead north-west along the coastal plain to the frontier, south along the coast to Port Sudan, and inland through the mountains to the Nile at Shereik. Ras Hadārba, 20 miles south-east of Mersa Haleib, is a projection of quicksands where the coast suddenly changes direction almost to due south. In the section between this point and Ras Abu Dāra the coastal plain narrows to about 8 miles as granite mountains approach the sea. This impressive group, towering to great heights above the coastal plain, is very conspicuous from the sea or land, though frequently rendered almost invisible from near at hand when shrouded in mist. Jebel Asoteriba (7,270 ft.) is the highest peak, 29 miles south-west of Ras Hadārba; Jebel Shendib (6,289 ft.) and Jebel Shendidai (5,010 ft.) lie towards the middle of the group, west of Ras Hadārba; and Jebel 'Elba (4,685 ft.), 18 miles west of Haleib, is the most prominent summit in the north. Jebel Hadārba, an outlier of the main group, rises to 731 feet only 6 miles inland from the cape. These mountains are remarkable for their rich vegetation and ample water-supplies, both derived from the wet mists which cling about the slopes. Consequently there are considerable settlements of Arabs at the foot, and the track inland from Haleib crosses the region, with branches to these centres. The Egyptian coast has nothing to compare with the 'Elba district in these respects.

The next section of coast, 74 miles long between Ras Hadārba and the tip of Ras Abu Shagara, trends south-south-east, and contains eleven of the twenty-six sherms on the African shore of the Red Sea (p. 584). A narrow reef, unbroken except by the entrances to the sherms, extends the whole way, and there are many outlying reefs. All the sherms named on p. 584 provide anchorage, except Mersa Masdud, 24 miles south of Ras Hadārba, which is closed by the fringing reef. The coastal plain widens southwards until it is 20 miles across at Ras Abu Shagara, and behind it the divide between the Nile and the Red Sea is only about 30 miles inland, with numerous short wadis descending the steep eastern slopes to lose themselves in the coastal plain or to enter the sea at the heads of the sherms. The highest summits are Jebel Asoteriba (7,270 ft.), 20 miles inland from Khor al Mar'ōb, Jebel Arit (5,912 ft.) farther inland west of Khor Abu Fanādīr, and Jebel Shin'āb (4,511 ft.), 30 miles west-south-west of Khor Shin'āb. There are no centres of population on the plain, and water is to be found only at a few points, but in the foothills and among the mountains wells are numerous. The coastal track from Haleib skirts the heads of the sherms and keeps close to the sea throughout this section, but there are no routes of any importance inland.

The Abu Shagara peninsula is the most prominent feature on the Sudan coast. It projects south-eastward for 15 miles, ending in three points, the eastern and western of which are low and sandy, while the central point, Ras Abu Shagara, is bluff, reaching a height of 127 feet less than a mile inland. On the western side of the peninsula is a large salt lagoon, from which salt is extracted at the Rawāya works.

From Ras Abu Shagara the coast trends slightly east of south for 145 miles to Suākin, forming the African side of the third structural division of the Red Sea (p. 96). Dungunab bay lies between the Abu Shagara peninsula and the mainland, its entrance encumbered with reefs, shoals, and islets. It provides good anchorage, with a passage round the south end of the reef which projects from Ras Abu Shagara. The shores are low and sandy, and near a small bay on the west side lies Dungunab village with its meteorological station, the first permanent settlement on the coast south of Haleib. Muhammad Qōl is another Arab village, 14 miles farther south, with a fort, jetty, and custom-house, a small port for the export of Rawāya salt. It lies on the south shore of a small bight where there is a break in the fringing reef, and near the shore to the north-west is an emergency aircraft landing-ground. The anchorage is off the south-east end of the jetty, but except for small craft must be approached from southwards of Mukawwar island. Muhammad Qōl is on the coastal track between Haleib and Port Sudan, and another track, also usable by light motors in dry weather, leads inland through the gold-mining district of Gebeit and Garabein, 50 miles inland, then turns north behind the watershed to reach the coast again at Haleib. Eight miles south of Muhammad Qōl the inlet of Khor Inkeifal affords good anchorage for native craft. Mukawwar island, 5 miles seaward of this inlet, is a narrow rocky sandstone tableland 6 miles long and 310 feet high, steeply cliffed and reef-bordered, with mangroves and a low sandspit at its southern end. The Mayetib islands are two rocky islets on the reef east of Mukawwar, and the three Tiflah islands lie 7 miles south.

From here southwards the low, sandy coast is reef-bordered all the way to Port Sudan. There is anchorage at Dabādīb on the mainland opposite the Tiflah islands; Mersa Salak, 14 miles south of Dabādīb hill, has another anchorage in a small bay. From this point a series of outlying reefs extends 18 miles southwards, leaving a channel 3–4 miles wide between them and the shore reefs. Towards the south of this channel Mersa Arakiyai is a reef-fringed landlocked cove, with anchorage off the east side of the coral islet in the entrance; 4 miles farther south is Mersa Aweitir, an anchorage for native craft near the Dāra lagoon from which salt is extracted for export. Then comes a break in the outlying reefs, but the inner channel begins again at Mersa Fijja, 7 miles south of Dāra. Between Mersa Fijja and Port Sudan there are several inlets, of which Khor Bolonai, Khor Lokiai, and Mersa Gwiyai are thought to be true sherms. Anchorage for small vessels can be obtained in Mersa Fijja, also a true sherm, and at Mersa Darūr, where there is a dilapidated stone landing-pier on the east side of a low, flat islet connected with the mainland by a causeway. The Arba'āt river reaches the sea through Mersa Darūr, depositing the silt it brings down in the winter floods, so that the head of the harbour is silting up. The delta region is cultivated and is a centre of locust outbreaks. Mersa Halote is a small inlet closed by the fringing reef 4 miles south of Mersa Darūr, and 7 miles farther south is Mersa Gwiyai, with good, sheltered anchorage for boats. Port Sudan is 4 miles south of it.

In this section between Ras Abu Shagara and Port Sudan the sandy coastal plain widens from about 5 miles behind Muhammad Qōl to over 10 miles near Port Sudan. Except for Dāra, there are no permanent settlements south of Muhammad Qōl. Inland the mountains tower in rugged masses, with several summits over 5,500 feet; Jebel Erba (7,273 ft.) is the highest, conspicuous from the sea, 18 miles inland from Khor Inkeifal. There are no obvious or easy routes through the mountains to the interior in this section, and the track from Haleib following the coast keeps inland among the foothills for 25 miles south of Muhammad Qōl, leaving only a path along the shore until it reaches the sea again at Mersa 'Arūs.

Port Sudan lies on the coastal plain, here about 7 miles wide and covered with coarse grass and sparse scrub. The town, built of coral, is divided into three parts, north, east, and south, and occupies the three points between the forked sherm (p. 68; fig. 15) which forms the harbour, and the sea. Until 1905 the settlement was no more than the burial ground of a Moslem saint, Sheikh Barghut, whose tomb is conspicuous on the northern entrance-point of the harbour. When the railway between the Nile at Atbara and the Red Sea was built, Port Sudan was selected as a terminus because its harbour offered better facilities than that of Suākin. The railway was opened in 1906, and since then, with the rapid development of both town and port, Port Sudan has almost entirely supplanted Suākin. It was opened officially in 1909. The town is lit by electricity, and water-supply comes by pipe-line from an underground source in the Arba'āt valley, 18 miles north-west of the town. The salt-pans on the southern outskirts of the town supply the whole country, and considerable quantities are exported annually. The railway, which from the Town station has branches across the north-west arm of the harbour to East Town and round the south-west arm to South Town, links Port Sudan through Sallom junction with Suākin and Atbara, where it meets the Nile valley line. Rough roads follow the coastal plain north to Haleib and south to Suākin, and there are several tracks inland. In normal times there is regular steamer communication with Red Sea ports. The landing-ground for aircraft is 2 miles south-west of the town, alongside the road to Suākin.

Suākin stands on the open desert plain, and like Port Sudan is in three parts, grouped about the harbour (p. 69; fig. 16). It is an ancient Arab settlement and was once the chief slave port on the Red Sea. But since the foundation of Port Sudan it has lost its importance, mainly because its harbour is difficult to enter. It is still, however, the port for Sudan pilgrims to Mecca. The quarantine camp and hospital are on the north shore of the main entrance channel. The old town, almost deserted, though once the richest part, occupies Suākin island (photo. 73), where the south-west arm of the sherm forks again. The area on the mainland, Al Kaff, lies south-west of the island and is larger, enclosed within the old fortified wall. It is joined to the island by a coral causeway. Outside the wall is the suburb of Shata, which contains the railway station, whence the line continues round the southern outskirts nearly to Graham Point, the southern entrance-point of the harbour. Quarantine or Condenser island, so-called from the old installations, lies north of Suākin island, where the main channel of the sherm forks, and is joined to the mainland by a causeway. The town is lit by oil lamps, and water is supplied to Al Kaff and Suākin island by pipes from wells in Shata. The railway links through Sallom junction with Port Sudan and Atbara. Rough roads connect with Port Sudan in the north and Tokar in the south, and tracks lead inland to the railway between Sallom and Sinkāt. There is a landing-ground 1 mile south of the town, just west of the Tokar road.

In the 38-mile stretch between Port Sudan and Suākin there are several small inlets, none of them true sherms. The dangerous Towertit reefs lie about 4 miles off shore and the inlets are not used as anchorages. The coast is formed by a raised coral reef, behind which a flat desert plain rises gently to the mountains. Small shrubs and tufts of grass spring up on the plain during winter rains, when the mountains are hidden in mist, but there is no perennial water. This section of coast is important for its railways to the interior.

The last 120 miles of the Sudan coast, between Suākin and Ras Kasar, lie in the fourth structural division of the Red Sea (p. 96), characterized by the great breadth of the shallow-water step, along which the Suākin group of reefs and islets extends as far as Khor Nawarat, only 20 miles short of the Eritrean frontier at Ras Kasar. Several inlets provide anchorage for small boats in the 16-mile stretch between Suākin and Mersa Sheikh Ibrāhīm, the latter being one of the two true sherms on this part of the coast. Mersa Sheikh Sa'd, 4 miles south-east of Mersa Sheikh Ibrāhīm, is a sheltered anchorage where it is possible to land boats. From this point the coast curves east in a broad bay to Ras Maqdam, a low cape backed by sandhills, on the north-west edge of the Baraka delta. Mersa Maqdam, west of the cape, is a capacious anchorage, and east of the cape is Trinkitat harbour. The harbour is the outlet for the cotton grown in the Baraka delta and has a pier 120 yards long, with two jetties for dhows east of it. A light railway links it through Et Teb with Tokar, 16 miles to the south, the centre of the cotton district. Between Trinkitat and Ras Asis, 28 miles south-east, the coast, formed by the Baraka delta, is low, barren, and covered with salt flats. Ras Asis is a sandspit which projects 4 miles east-south-east from the eastern edge of the delta, marked by a beacon. Between it and Ras Shakal is the 13-mile-wide gulf of 'Aqīq, with the two low sandy 'Amarāt islands in the entrance and 'Aqīq village on the south shore. There is a small jetty at the village where it is possible to land. Ras Shakal is a sandy point joining these islets. Immediately east of it, Khor Nawarat is a deep, branching inlet, the second sherm in this stretch of coast, completely sheltered by a chain of coral islets across the mouth. Landing is possible on the beach east of Adobana village. The last 20 miles of coast to Ras Kasar is much broken, with several sandy or rocky islets off shore.

South of Port Sudan the mountains again approach the sea, and the coastal plain is only about 10 miles wide until Khor Ashat is reached, 30 miles south of Suākin. A well-defined line of foothills, with some of its summits over 2,300 feet, extends from Sallom junction, where the Port Sudan and Suākin railways converge, to Jebel Eshanak (2,034 ft.), just south of Khor Ashat. Behind this range an extensive highland rises to well over 5,000 feet, stretching inland for about 90 miles. Several tracks cross the mountain belt to link the coast road with the railway. South of Khor Ashat, while the ranges continue southwards the coast trends east away from them, and the Baraka delta forms a broad plain reaching as much as 40 miles inland. This plain is the first area so far encountered on the African side of the Red Sea where cultivation is of importance. The reason is to be found in the increase of winter rainfall, though the amount is very variable, and in the summer floods of the Baraka, which, rising in the Eritrean highlands, benefits from the summer monsoon. The channels by which the river reaches the sea migrate over the whole plain, at present being concentrated in the south-east. The dry north-western half of the delta, floored with clay and silt, is covered in places with sand-dunes and salt flats, and in this region *dukhn* (bulrush millet) is grown as a food-grain when heavy rain causes local floods between the dunes. In the Tokar district cotton is grown as a summer crop, irrigated by the floods of the Baraka, and in the unirrigated parts of the delta dukhn is grown as a winter crop dependent on rainfall. Sandstorms are notoriously common throughout the year in the Tokar district, rendering it almost uninhabitable in June and July, when Trinkitat harbour is practically deserted. Et Teb, on the railway between Trinkitat and Tokar, has an emergency landing-ground for aircraft, and Tokar is linked by road with Suākin and 'Aqīq, with a track up the Baraka valley to the interior. East of the Baraka, high mountains rise within 35 miles of the sea, in a group which extends over the frontier into Eritrea, sending spurs and ridges towards the coast between 'Aqīq and Ras Kasar. Jebel Adrau (8,307 ft.), close to the frontier 46 miles south-west of Ras Kasar, is the highest peak in the Red Sea hills of the Sudan. A large area of this highland block south of 'Aqīq is reserved for game.

(iii) *The Coast of Eritrea* (figs. 31, 32)

In shape Eritrea resembles a triangle with a long tail stretching from the south-east corner down the Red Sea coast. It has a coastline of over 550 miles, discounting irregularities, from latitude 18° N. to latitude 12° 43′ N., and on the landward side has common boundaries with the Anglo-Egyptian Sudan in the north and west, with Ethiopia (Abyssinia) in the south, and with French Somaliland in the extreme south-east. The triangular part is occupied largely by the Ethiopian plateau and its northern continuation, known as the Rore, on either side of the Anseba valley. This slopes westwards to the Sudan plains, and falls steeply from its high eastern rim to the coastal plain north of Massawa and in the south to the Danakil desert. East of the southern half of the plateau is the Danakil depression, a

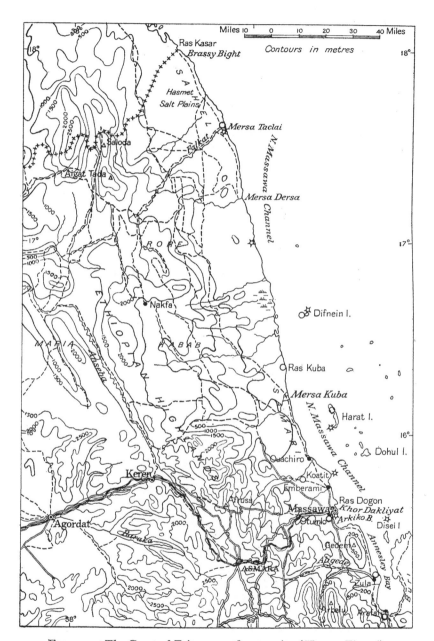

Miles 10   0   10   20   30   40 Miles

Contours in metres

Ras Kasar
Brassy Bight

18°   18°

Hasmet
Salt Plains

Saloda

Mersa Taclai

Aigat Tada

Mersa Dersa

17°   17°

Nakfa

Difnein I.

Ras Kuba

Mersa Kuba

Harat I.

16°   16°

Dohul I.

Ouachiro

Koatit

Emberami

Keren   Ras Dogon
                                                   Khor Dakliyat
Ahuss   Massawa   Arkiko B.
Agordat   Otumlo   Disei I.

Baraka   Gedem
                                           Abgede

ASMARA   Zula

                                           Arata

FIG. 31.   *The Coast of Eritrea, northern section (Key on Fig. 26)*

sunken block occupied by salt lakes and desert plains, which reaches the coast south of Massawa. East again of this the Danakil highlands trend south-east, filling, with the maritime zone of varying width, the region between the frontier and the coast.

The economic and strategic significance of Eritrea arises from its position on the Red Sea coast, where Massawa is the most important port on the Red Sea, and was the chief gateway to the whole of the former Italian East African empire. The Italians carried out a comprehensive road-building programme, designed to link Massawa through Asmara with the interior. Thus the port is connected by trunk roads with Tessenei, an important cotton-growing settlement in the west, through Adua with Gondar in the south-west, and through Dessie with Addis Ababa in the south. Another trunk road was built inland from Assab across the Danakil highlands to Addis Ababa, and Assab was developed as a second port to relieve congestion at Massawa. Eritrea was used as the base of Italian operations in east Africa which led to the creation of the empire in May 1936, comprising Eritrea, Italian Somaliland, and the Ethiopian empire.

Of economic importance in the coastal zone are the fishing and salt industries, the former carried on almost entirely by Arabs. The great diversity of species is a hindrance to marketing organization, as is also the hot climate, which makes the establishment of refrigerating plant a necessary step before the industry can expand. Another physical obstacle is the presence of coral reefs, so that drag nets cannot be used, and fixed nets, pots, and harpoons have to be employed instead. Sharks are the chief species caught, the salted flesh being exported to the east coast of Africa and to the Persian Gulf, while the tails and fins are dried and sent to the Far East, where they are regarded as delicacies as well as having pharmaceutical uses. Pearl fisheries are important along the whole coast, especially in the Dahlak islands. Salt extraction from lagoons at Massawa, Assab, and Ouachiro is the most important mineral industry in the maritime zone. Agriculture in the coastal lowlands depends on the floods caused by summer rain in the highlands, sometimes with a second crop from local winter rains. Maize and millets are grown as food crops, with cotton in a few areas where its production forms part of Italian settlement schemes. But agriculture is almost impossible on a commercial scale without irrigation, and there are several centres of locust outbreaks along the coast.

The coast of Eritrea falls naturally into three subdivisions controlled by geological structure. These are (a) between Ras Kasar and

Annesley bay (Golfo di Zula), fronting the Ethiopian or Abyssinian highlands; (b) between Annesley bay and Amfile (Hanfela) bay, where the Danakil depression reaches the sea; and (c) between Amfile bay and Ras Dumeira on the frontier with French Somaliland, fronting the Danakil highlands.

(a) *Ras Kasar–Annesley Bay.* In the first subdivision the coast trends south-south-east for 200 miles, reef-bordered and with few inlets or promontories. Between Ras Kasar and Mersa Taclai (40 miles south) the 600-foot line is from 6 to 12 miles off shore, but between it and the coast reefs there are two deeps; south of Mersa Taclai the inshore channel of the Red Sea (p. 66) is continued in the north Massawa channel. Immediately south-east of Ras Kasar, Brassy bight is a small bay where dhows anchor off the coast reef. The coast is low and sandy, with swamps and salt flats near Hasmet, for 40 miles to Mersa Taclai. The latter is a small boat-harbour with two dilapidated moles, at one of which boats can unload, and there was an Italian military landing-ground on the north-west shore. Scrub and low dunes cover the sandy plain, which here stretches 5 miles inland to the foot of hills about 440 feet high. Beyond Mersa Taclai the coast continues low and sandy to Massawa, and between the coast reef and Dahlak bank the north Massawa channel extends for 160 miles south-south-east. There is anchorage almost anywhere on the west side of the channel, though most places are exposed to south-easterly winds. The best anchorage is in the outer part of Khor Dakliyat, a small bay between Ras Dogon and the 'Abd al Qadir peninsula which overlooks Massawa harbour. Emberami, 7 miles north of Massawa, has a landing-stage for native craft. In general this coast has a barren aspect, its sandy monotony relieved only by occasional palm trees, mangrove swamps, salt flats, and dunes. Work was in progress in 1938 on the construction of salt-works near Ouachiro, an Arab village on the river of the same name 16 miles north of Massawa. A large lagoon near the coast, equipped with overhead ropeway and two power-stations, was expected to yield 120,000 tons annually. A coastal track from the Sudan frontier passes Mersa Taclai, but turns inland at Mersa Dersa, 22 miles farther south, continuing along the foothills and only reaching the coast again at Mersa Kuba (74 miles south of Mersa Dersa), whence it follows the coast to Massawa.

The coastal plain in this section, called Sahel in the north, Samar in the south, is formed by terraces of marine sedimentary rocks, with, near Massawa, intercalated volcanic beds and occasionally an outcrop

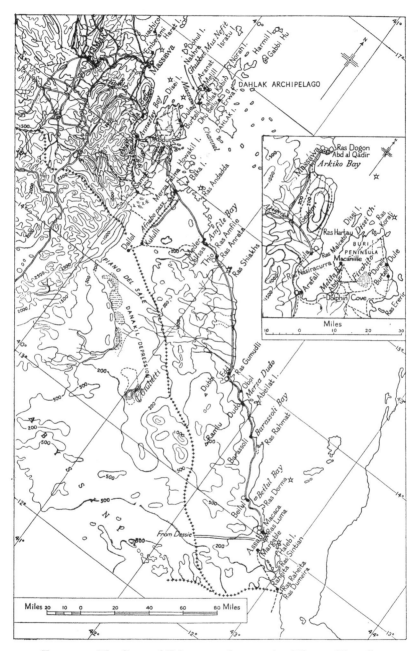

FIG. 32. *The Coast of Eritrea, southern section (Key on Fig. 26)*

of ancient crystalline rocks. Loose sand covers the surface, accumulating in dunes, and over this barren expanse the wadis descending from the plateau inland distribute their water in shifting channels to the sea or lose it before reaching the shoreline. Low hills, outliers of the scarp behind, break the surface near the coast. Rainfall is scanty, but increases towards Massawa. It is confined to the winter months, when north-east winds blow in from the sea. This is one of the hottest regions of the world, for besides direct heating from the sun there is the additional factor of the summer monsoon winds which descend from the plateau and are warmed in doing so. The only important area of cultivation is at Mersa Taclai, where 700 acres are devoted to cotton, dependent either on rainfall or on the floods of the Falkat river. The Italian Air Force had landing-grounds at Ras Kuba and Koatit.

Behind the plain the scarp of the Ethiopian highlands rises like a broken wall, about 25 miles inland in the north, 15 miles inland nearer Massawa. Steep narrow valleys have carved the crystalline rocks of the scarp face into a series of sharp ridges, making movement even along the foothill zone difficult. The summits lie about 40 miles inland in the north, but approach the coast in the south; Saloda, near the Sudan frontier, reaches 8,218 feet, Aigat Tada, 44 miles south-west of Mersa Taclai, is 8,438 feet high, and in the south, Afruss, 40 miles west of Massawa, is 8,058 feet.

Behind the scarp lies the elevated northern portion of the Ethiopian highlands, known as the Rore, which extends westward to the Baraka river whose valley follows a great fault of the Meridional series. The Anseba valley divides the highland into two blocks, the Habab on the east and the Maria on the west. In both, the erosion of the original crystalline plateau has produced a landscape of parallel ridges and valleys alined meridionally, and many of the rivers which break eastward to the coastal plain have upper basins parallel to the scarp.

Massawa lies on a flat sandy plain on the south side of the 'Abd al Qadir peninsula, at the northern entrance point of Arkiko bay. It has had a long and varied history, and for centuries was part of the Abyssinian dominions. It was captured by the Turks in 1557, remaining a Turkish possession for two hundred years. At the end of the eighteenth century it passed to Egypt from the Sharif of Mecca, and after the Turks had been reinstated in 1850 it was handed back to Egypt in 1865. In 1885 it was occupied by the Italians, and was the capital of the Italian colony until replaced by Asmara in 1900.

It was occupied by British forces on 9 April 1941, after the Italians had attempted to block the harbour by scuttling ships.

The harbour is an irregular deep-water inlet enclosed on the north by the 'Abd al Qadir peninsula and on the south by Massawa and Taulud islands, which are joined to each other and to the mainland by causeways (photos. 74–76). The outer harbour is 1,500 yards long and 350 yards wide, extending south-west. At the head of this a narrow channel continues into the western arm, Taulud bay. The northern arm of the harbour, Gherar bay, is separated from the western by the Gherar peninsula. The commercial port is in Taulud bay and the naval base on the east shore of Gherar bay. In many places the shores of the harbour are fringed by coral reefs, and there are no beaching positions. Extensive salt-pans border the north-west side of Taulud bay and stretch across the head of Gherar bay.

The town lies on Massawa and Taulud islands, the Gherar and 'Abd al Qadir peninsulas, and has a suburb at Adago Berai on the mainland about a mile north-west of Taulud island. Great improvements have been effected during Italian occupation. Much of the old town on Massawa island has been rebuilt, and it now contains the commercial and native quarters. The administrative and new residential district is on Taulud island, the military district on the Gherar peninsula, and industrial and commercial buildings are on the Gherar and 'Abd al Qadir peninsulas. Water-supply is from a well at Moncullo, 5 miles west of the town, from distilling plant on Taulud island, and from wells sunk in the Tamarisco valley at Dogali, about 12 miles west of the town. From the station on Taulud island a single-track railway (95-cm. gauge) connects Massawa through Otumlo, where there is an airport, with Asmara, then on through Keren with Agordat. A first-class road was completed in 1938 from Massawa to Asmara, and a fairly good motor-road follows the coast to Assab. Northward there is only a track along the coast.

(b) *Annesley Bay–Amfile Bay*. The second subdivision of the Eritrean coast is more complex, for here faults of the Meridional series are crossed by others of the Eritrean series, and the resulting land-steps are dislocated towards the east, producing a broken and irregular coastline. In this section of about 100 miles, discounting irregularities, there are three large bays and two long projections of the coast. Annesley bay, or the gulf of Zula, penetrates inland for 30 miles with a minimum width of 5 miles about half-way down. It lies between the Gedem massif on the west, immediately south of Arkiko bay, and the Buri peninsula on the east. The low, sandy

73. *Suākin Island and causeway to Al Kaff from the air in 1932*

74. *Taulud Island and causeway to Massawa Island, seen from the west-south-west*

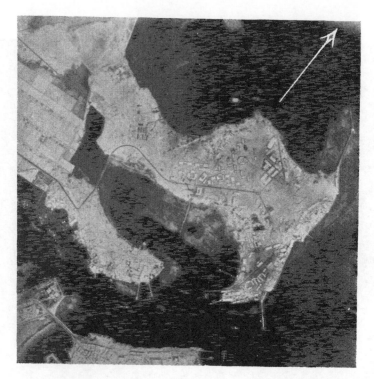

75. *Massawa from the air in 1940. 'Abd al Qadir peninsula*

76. *Massawa from the air in 1941. Massawa and Taulud Islands*

western shore rises gently to Jebel Gedem (3,034 ft.) in the north, and more steeply to Arbalu (7,887 ft.) in the south. Between the two highlands the Aligede river reaches the sea, with Zula village on its right bank a little way inland. There is a landing-stage at the village, and an aircraft landing-ground 3 miles north-north-east. The coast on either side is bordered with mangroves. Ras Malcato, a sandy point projecting south-east of the Aligede mouth, has a wireless-telegraphy station and was the base for Lord Napier's expedition in 1868. Near by, on the opposite bank of the river, are the ruins of Adulis, an ancient city and port, founded by fugitive slaves from Egypt, and under the Romans a harbour (Axume) and caravan station whence the products of Africa reached Rome. Near the head of the bay, about 13 miles beyond Ras Malcato, is Arafali village at the foot of the extinct volcano Dola (528 ft.). Tracks from Massawa along the western shore of the bay, from Samoti in the Danakil depression, from Mersa Fatma on the coast east of the Buri peninsula, and from the eastern shore of Annesley bay all converge on Arafali. The eastern shore of the bay, generally low and sandy but with hills near the sea in places, is formed by the Buri peninsula. About 12 miles round the bay from Arafali is Dolphin cove, a bight in the coast reef with a low, flat shore rising to the rocky ridge on which stands Jebel Abdur (803 ft.). Black lava ridges covered with brushwood south of the cove give place to more open sandy country farther north, and about 9 miles northward of the cove Melita bay penetrates a mile inland, protected on the west by Ras Nasiracurra, but almost filled by the coast reef and with mangrove swamps on the shore. Macanille village is at its head, and both this point and Dolphin cove, on the coastal track from Arafali, are the meeting-places for tracks which fan out over the Buri peninsula. From Ras Nasiracurra to Ras Hartau, the north-western extremity of the peninsula, the coast is offset to-wards the west, and Annesley bay narrows correspondingly. This 12-mile stretch on the east shore is backed by one of the dislocated land-steps (p. 60), which forms low granite hills. The coast is reef-bordered most of the way, and Ras Hartau at 138 feet is one of the higher points on the east shore of Annesley bay. Thence for over 10 miles north-eastward to Ras Korali the coast is deeply indented and fronted with coral reefs and islets, forming the south-east side of Disei channel, the eastern entrance to Annesley bay from the south Massawa channel. Disei island, on the eastern side of the entrance to Annesley bay about 4 miles off the Buri peninsula, is volcanic, with a number of conical peaks culminating in Mount Disei (335 ft.)

near the northern end, and a small village on its east coast. Within
Annesley bay there are anchorages at Ras Malcato, Arafali, Dolphin
cove, and Melita bay.

The north-east coast of the Buri peninsula, between Ras Korali and
Ras Ererir, is 20 miles long, sandy and reef-bordered, with few irregularities. The only anchorage is off Umm Namūs island. A track follows
the coast from end to end, passing the villages of Dule and Burteli.

The Buri peninsula, 12 miles across at its narrowest, but wider at
the northern end, projects 30 miles seaward from its base where it is
20 miles across. It is generally low and undulating, formed in the
south of black, twisted lava flows, and in the north of granite. The
highest point in the south is Jebel Abdur near the west coast (803 ft.),
and in the north Jebel Dureli (764 ft.). The middle is occupied by
the salt lagoon of Firahito, nearly 5 miles long, triangular in shape,
with its base in the south about 4 miles wide.

East of the Buri peninsula is Howakil (Ouachil) bay, the second of
the large bays in this section of coast. It is 36 miles wide at the mouth,
between Ras Ererir and Ras Andadda, a maze of reefs and islands,
and with an irregular reef-fringed shore. Howakil island, the largest
and most conspicuous, is in the middle, shaped like an inverted
comma, with the head in the south culminating in a sharp volcanic
peak 722 feet high, and the tail in the north of low coral. The Italian
Air Force had a landing-ground on the island, but water is scarce.
Baka island, almost as large, is a flat-topped plateau over 500 feet
high with abundant water, half-way between Howakil island and the
south-east shore of the bay. There are several anchorages among the
islands, but the only settlement of any importance on the mainland
is Mersa Fatma in the south-east corner opposite Baka island. Here
it is possible to land, and the Italians have had plans for developing
it as a port. It lies between Massawa and Assab, on the coastal track
which is reported motorable. A Decauville line goes inland to Kululli,
36 miles to the south, but this is now abandoned. Schemes for development included the construction of a canal from Mersa Fatma to the
northern end of the Danakil depression, here known as the Piano del
Sale (Salt plain). This canal was to serve for navigation and for the
production of electricity, and through it sea-water was to transform
the Danakil depression, much of which is below sea-level, into a great
inland lake with an area of 1,800 square miles. By this it was hoped
to improve the climate of the district. But there were various obstacles
to the scheme, chief of which was the value of the minerals already
known to exist in the Piano del Sale, and the desire to explore for

petroleum. Under the Italians the salt deposits, mainly potassium chloride, sodium, and magnesium, were exploited by the Compagnia Mineraria Coloniale, and during the War of 1914–1918 20,000 tons of potassium chloride similar to the Stassfurt deposits were supplied to the Allies. Greater production would be possible in future if the region were linked by railway to Mersa Fatma. The Decauville line never reached beyond Kululli, and since it was allowed to fall into disrepair there is only the track from Dallol (just over the frontier in Ethiopia) through Kululli and out by the Afnabo pass to Mersa Fatma, where there is also an aircraft landing-ground.

From Ras Andadda the coast trends south-east for 20 miles, with several projecting points separating small bays, but reef-bordered all the way, and backed by low volcanic hills. South-east of this stretch is Amfile (Hanfela) bay, 12 miles wide, encumbered with islands and shoals, but with several anchorages. Its shores are low, and backed at varying distances by volcanic hills. Small coral islets are in places tied to the land by sandspits, for example at Meder village about half-way round the bay, where the coastal track reaches the sea again after cutting across the base of the series of promontories which separates Howakil and Amfile bays. The track passes through Lelissa, another village on the south-east shore, then continues south-east along the Danakil coast.

The whole stretch of coast between Annesley bay and Amfile bay with its associated islands forms the south-west side of the south Massawa channel. On the north-east side lies the Dahlak archipelago, which with its reefs and banks extends for nearly 200 miles parallel to the coast (fig. 32). The islands are mainly of coral, low, reef-fringed, and sometimes wooded. Dahlak is the largest island, with an area of about 340 square miles, its nearest point 12 miles north-east of the tip of the Buri peninsula. The north and west coasts of the island are deeply indented, and contain most of the settlements. The chief village is Dahlak Kabir, on a small bay in the south-west coast, but it is little more than a collection of huts round a few good wells. North of it is a large inlet, Ghubbet Mus Nefit, where depths reach 540 feet. The island of Nakhra (Nocra), coralline, with patches of grass and a few dūm palms, lies in the entrance. The landing-stage for boats from Massawa is on the south-west side of Ghubbet Mus Nefit, opposite Nakhra island, and it serves also for loading boats with limestone used for building in Massawa. Farther round the south-west shore of the bay there is a good beach of fine sand. On the north side of the peninsula which forms the north shore of Ghubbet

Mus Nefit are the villages of Melill and Aranat, centres of the pearl fisheries. Another large inlet is on the north coast, with Erwa island almost blocking the entrance. Dhu Bellu (Dubellu), the ancient cultural centre of Dahlak island, now in ruins, has an anchorage in an opening in the coast reef on the west shore of the inlet. Dahlak depends mainly on water brought from the mainland and stored in tanks, but has some cisterns for rain-water. The rainfall is slight, occuring between October and March, when vegetation quickly springs up, supporting a few goats, asses, sheep, and deer. Coral mounds rise above the low surface, and there are palm-trees in places. There is an aircraft landing-ground and wireless-telegraphy station in the south-east. The island of Norah, 10 miles north of Dahlak, is the second largest in the archipelago. Formed of sand and coral, rising to a low summit on the south-west, it has a few date-groves and one or two fishing-villages. None of the other islands is of special significance, but some have been used by the Italians for landing-grounds, namely Difnein, Harat, Harmil, Gabbi Hu, and Norah, all lying north or north-west of Dahlak.

The relief of the interior, like the coast itself in this section, is varied and complex. Behind the western shore of Annesley bay, and continuing southwards beyond the head of the bay as the western margin of the Danakil depression, rises the steep eastern escarpment of the Ethiopian highlands, flanked by a piedmont zone of younger volcanic rocks which includes the Gedem massif (3,034 ft.) and the hills behind Arafali. The crystalline rocks of the escarpment are incised by deep, narrow, and tortuous valleys, so that they form buttresses separated by basins elongated parallel to the general line of the escarpment, here controlled by faults of the Meridional series. Thus the ascent from the coast is not so difficult as would be the case were the slope not broken by this step formation. The highlands west of the scarp are part of an old crystalline plateau, once worn smooth by erosion, then uplifted and tilted westwards, after which erosion was renewed; and the rivers have again cut deeply into the old surface, destroying its once level character except near the eastern rim, where the crest of the escarpment, broad and gently rolling, retains its old form, and is important because in spite of its height it offers the only easy route from Massawa to the interior. Thus a major trunk road climbs from Massawa to Asmara, then follows this natural 'ridgeway' through Dessie to Addis Ababa, the capital of Ethiopia, used by the Italians as the administrative centre of their East African empire.

77, 78. *Assab town and harbour from the air in October 1940*

79. *Assab, from the sea, March 1938*

80. *Jidda, from the sea*

81. *The sandy coastal Tihama, between Hodeida and Bājil*

East of the Ethiopian highlands the great Danakil depression continues the line of Annesley bay inland for nearly 200 miles, extending far beyond the Eritrean border. It is a rift valley, much of it below sea-level, containing salt lakes which are the remnants of a great arm of the sea, now cut off by volcanic outpourings. Most of its floor is a sandy desert plain, the Piano del Sale, but the relief is diversified by volcanic cones associated with the instability of the earth's crust caused by the depression of the rift. Such are the peaks of Alid (2,985 ft.), 17 miles south-east of Arafali, and several smaller ones around Samoti, 12 miles farther south-east. Thus the country south of the Buri peninsula and Howakil bay consists of volcanic hills of varying heights, some of conical form, others, developed on lava-flows, in the form of ridges, with small sandy plains between them, unfit for cultivation except where river floods can be utilized.

(c) *Amfile Bay–Ras Dumeira.* The third subdivision of the Eritrean coast, about 210 miles long without allowing for indentations, is simpler in form than the last, trending south-eastwards with a line of faulting in the Eritrean direction. From Ras Amfile, the south-eastern entrance-point of Amfile bay, the coast trends east-south-east for 24 miles to Ras Shiakhs, low and sandy and with several shallow bays. Ras Anrata, a low coral point, projects seawards about 5 miles south-east of Ras Amfile; on it stands Thio village, where there is a small landing-pier and an aircraft landing-ground. Besides the coastal track, there is another inland to Dallol, the centre of the mineral industry in the Piano del Sale (p. 120). The coastal plain in this section is covered with gypsum and sand-dunes, with a few wells of brackish water near the mouths of the wadis. From Ras Shiakhs for nearly 60 miles south-eastwards to Edd the coast is sandy and low, with no prominent features. The desert plain behind is about 15 miles wide, a desolate expanse of dunes and salt flats with a few settlements clustered round brackish wells where the coastal track crosses a wadi. Edd is a larger village, near the head of a bight, with customs offices and a picturesque mosque; a military landing-ground lies 4 miles inland to west-north-west. Enclosing the bight on the east is Ras Gumudli, a promontory formed by a lava-flow from the volcano of Dubbi (5,183 ft.) which lies 25 miles south-east and erupted as recently as 1861.

Between Ras Gumudli and Ras Rahmat, 40 miles south-east, the coast is more indented and there are several islands off shore. Near Edd volcanic hills approach the sea and come down to the shore throughout this stretch. Mersa Dudo, a small inlet 14 miles south-east of Ras Gumudli, provides anchorage and has a village with a well at its head. The eastern side of Mersa Dudo is formed by a blunt double promontory of basalt, rising to two summits of 833 feet and 584 feet, the higher to the west. Abeilat and Sadla islands, also volcanic, lie 3–4 miles off the tip of the promontory, giving anchorage off their shores. The next inlet is Barassoli (Bahar Assoli) bay, with Barassoli village at its head, 22 miles south-east of Dudo. The bay has sandy shores, but is surrounded by hills of reddish lava; in it and seawards of it there are many rocks and islets, with some anchorages. The three Quoin islets are 14 miles north of Barassoli village. Skirting the bay is the motorable coast track from Edd. South-east of Barassoli bay a mangrove-bordered lagoon penetrates 6 miles inland between the mainland and two sandspits, blocked at the entrance by Rahmat island and its fringing reefs. Ras Rahmat is the tip of the northern sandspit. The country inland of the section between Ras Gumudli and Ras Rahmat is a torrid desert of lava plains and volcanic cones, with pockets of sand and salt-bearing clay. Water is scarce, and the few wells there are brackish or salty, and occasionally, as at Obol, sulphurous.

From Ras Rahmat the coast trends south for 30 miles, then curves round to the east, forming Beilul bay, which is enclosed on the east by the promontory of Ras Dorma. The southward trending stretch is low, with a sandy, reef-bordered beach, but round the bayhead desolate, sun-baked, basalt hills come close to the shore. Beilul village lies about 2 miles inland from the south-west corner of the bay, in an oasis shaded by palms and acacias. It has a good supply of drinking-water, and the Italians constructed a military landing-ground somewhere in the vicinity. The village is on the coastal track, and several other tracks lead inland through the hills and over the boundary into Abyssinia. A large coral reef, marked on Italian maps as an island, lies in the middle of the bay.

For 20 miles south-east of Ras Dorma the coast is low and reef-bordered. It then recedes southwards to form Assab bay, which is 20 miles wide between Ras Luma and Ras Sintian, with low swampy shores backed by a dune-covered plain, out of which rise low basalt hills. A fringing reef follows the shore in most places, and the bay is encumbered with many low reef-bordered islands and sand cays which prevent swell from entering the bay but have no effect when south-easterly winds cause a rough sea. Haleb island, north-west of Ras Sintian, is the largest island. Assab, a port of growing importance, lies on the north-west shore near the entrance to the bay.

From the sandy, mangrove-fringed coast the land rises slightly behind Assab, with sand-dunes and low hills partly scrub-covered. This gives place about 5 miles inland to barren volcanic hills. Assab was the first territory acquired by Italy in Africa. It was purchased in 1870 from the Sultan of Raheita for use as a coaling station when the Suez canal was opened. In July 1882, despite opposition from Great Britain, Egypt, and Turkey, it was declared an Italian colony. Later, after the unification of Italian possessions as the colony of Eritrea, Assab functioned as the capital of the province of Danakilia Meridionale (photos. 77–79).

On 11 June 1941 Assab was occupied by British forces. The town was still largely under construction, but it stretches about 1½ miles north and south of Ras Buja, with the European quarter and Government buildings to the north and the native quarter (Arabs and Danakils) to the south. The only industrial establishment is the salt-works 3 miles south of the town on the shore of Assab bay. Most of the salt was exported unrefined to Japan, average annual production being about 100,000 tons. The water-supply for the town and the salt-works comes from wells 10 miles south of the town. A first-class road leads north-west along the coast from Assab, through Macaca, where the Italians had an aerodrome, to Beilul, whence it proceeds as a track to Massawa. The new Assab–Dessie road, 322 miles long, adds to the importance of Assab by providing the shortest route from the sea to Addis Ababa. South of Assab there is only a track to Ras Dumeira.

Margable village is the only other settlement on the bay, and from Assab south-eastwards the coastal track is no longer motorable. Beyond Assab bay a bight lies east of Ras Sintian, entirely filled by the coast reef. Ras Raheita is a bluff about 250 feet high formed of basalt, projecting seawards from 14 miles south-east of Ras Sintian. Inland of it is Raheita village near the boundary with French Somaliland. The boundary reaches the sea along Ras Dumeira, another rocky promontory, off which lies Dumeira island, conspicuous with its double peak 260 feet high (p. 58).

The whole of this third subdivision of the Eritrean coast is backed by the Danakil highlands, an uplifted block with average height not much above 3,000 feet. This block, formed partly of limestone and granite, is covered on its flanks by volcanic rocks resulting from geologically recent activity, some associated with the coastal fault and some with the fault on the interior margin bounding the Danakil depression. The volcanic regions are in general the highest. In the southern half of the highlands volcanic activity has pervaded the whole block, so that basalt lava flows and extinct cones extend beyond the frontier to the edge of the Piano del Sale. The highest summit is Ramlu (5,905 ft.) near the frontier south of Edd. Dubbi, the second highest, has already been mentioned (p. 123).

The only important line of communication in this section, apart from the coastal track, is the trunk road inland from Assab to Addis Ababa.

The Arabian Coast of the Red Sea

The coastal zone on the Arabian side differs from that on the African side in several respects. One is that the coast itself is everywhere low and flat, with no headlands or cliffs of any height. Further, the coastal plain is generally wider than on the African side, extending as a continuous strip for the entire length of the sea. Thirdly, the mountain rampart, compared with the African side, rises to higher summits latitude for latitude behind most sections of the Arabian coast and has fewer gaps leading to the interior. Water-supplies on both coasts of the Red Sea are scanty, but if anything, the Arabian coast has to depend on ship-borne supplies to an even greater extent than the African side.

The geographical divisions of the Arabian coast, Midian, Hejaz, 'Asīr, and Yemen are described below in order from north to south.

(iv) *The Coast of Midian: Ras al Fasma–Al Wejh* (fig. 8)

This section, between points 28° 03' N., 34° 40' E. and 26° 15' N., 36° 25' E., is about 200 miles long, trending east in the north for 36 miles between Ras Kasba (al Fasma) at the entrance to the Gulf of 'Aqaba and 'Ainūnā (Ayunah) bay, then south-east following the direction of the Eritrean faults. In the northern half, north of Ras Abu Massarib, the coast is low and sandy, fronted by coral reefs and islands. South of Ras Abu Massarib, steep overhanging cliffs of coral and sandstone, less than 100 feet high, rise directly from the water, fronted by a submerged ledge of rock 40 yards wide, nearly awash at its outer edge. The coastal plain, generally sandy, with salt incrustations and swampy stretches, rises gradually to the crystalline highlands, which are higher and nearer the coast in the north. Flocks of sheep and goats are supported on the pastures of the plain unless the rain fails, when the beduin retreat to the mountains. The Midian coast contains thirteen true sherms (pp. 584–585), and most of them provide anchorage.

The 36-mile stretch of coast between Ras al Fasma and 'Ainūnā bay is deeply indented, and the sandy plain is backed by the elevated tableland which farther north gives place to the mountains bordering the east shore of the Gulf of 'Aqaba. In this region faults of the Eritrean series interdigitate with others parallel to the Gulf of 'Aqaba, and to this is probably due the fact that inlets are numerous, and that deep water penetrates to the shore in some places, while in others reefs and banks on which stand several islands make approach difficult.

At 'Ainūnā bay the Eritrean faults assume the dominating role in the trend of coastline and coastal mountains, and from this point the Arabian shore of the Red Sea slants east-south-east as far as the Jidda district, which falls in the third natural subdivision (p. 96). The coastal plain as far as Ras Abu Massarib, 70 miles south-east of 'Ainūnā bay, is barely 5 miles wide, and several summits in the north exceed 6,500 feet. There is anchorage near some of the off-lying islands, also in Sherm Yahar, in Sherm Jubba, and in Sherm Qafafa. Muweilih, 30 miles south-east of 'Ainūnā bay, is a beduin market, on the coastal track, with a caravan route inland to Tebūk. It consists of a few stone buildings and palm-leaf huts, with a fort, but there is only a roadstead sheltered by coral reefs. Dhaba is a similar village 28 miles beyond; it makes use of the anchorage in Sherm Qafafa about a mile north of it, where a wooden jetty enables dhows to land cargo. There may be oilfields in the vicinity, for there is certainly a visible seepage along the coast.

From Ras Abu Massarib the coastal plain widens gradually until at Al Wejh it is 25 miles across. But access to it from the sea is difficult. Steep coral cliffs, the rocky ledge at their foot, and off-lying reefs and islets are all obstacles, though there are several good anchorages in this 80-mile stretch. These are in Sherm Na'mān, between Na'mān island and Ras Abu Massarib, Mersa Zobeida (not listed among the true sherms), Sherm Dumeigh, Sherm 'Antar, and Mersa Za'am; the latter is not a true sherm, but it is possible to land on the sandy beach at the head. The coastal track keeps to the inner margin of the plain in the section, and there are no settlements until Al Wejh is reached. This is described on p. 539.

(v) The Hejaz Coast: Al Wejh–Jidda (fig. 10)

The Hejaz coast, stretching between latitudes 26° 15' N. and 21° 30' N., is over 400 miles long, and besides part of the first and fourth natural divisions of the Red Sea, includes the whole of the Arabian sides of the second and third.

(a) *Al Wejh–Ras Abu Madd.* This section, of 120 miles, comprises the Arabian side of the southern half of the first natural division. For 13 miles beyond Al Wejh, to the northern Sherm Habban, coral and sandstone cliffs, a continuation of those in the preceding section, rise directly from the water. Sherm Habban, and Sherm Minaibara, 5 miles to the east of it, both true sherms, provide anchorage, the former completely landlocked. Between Sherm Habban and Ras Kurkumai the coast recedes to form an open bay 15 miles wide at the entrance. Into this bay Wadi Hamdh, with the greatest valley system anywhere in western Arabia (p. 27), empties its episodic waters. Opening from the hills about 20 miles from the sea in a great trough 15 miles across, it distributes its water through a score of channels in a north-westerly direction across the coastal plain, each channel, whether dry or flooded, marked by a dark line of scrub. Sheer from the plain, Jebel Raal rises to over 3,000 feet, a hogback split in the middle standing sentinel over the wadi where it leaves the highlands at Abu Zereibat. Several short wadis also empty into the bay, and the shores are low and sandy all the way round. Ras Kurkumai is a blunt promontory which rises to a summit of 400 feet 2 miles inland.

Between Ras Kurkumai and Ras Abu Madd the coast, still low and sandy, is indented with wide bays, and fronted with reefs and low coral islands, among which there are several anchorages. There are no sherms in this section, and Umm Lejj is the only village on the coast. Al Hasani island, 12 miles out from the village, differs from the rest of the islands in being high and rugged. A sandy beach opposite a gap in the reef on its eastern side offers a landing-place for boats. The coastal track from Al Wejh, the broad, well-beaten pilgrim road, keeps inland until it has crossed the Wadi Hamdh at Abu Zereibat, then approaches the coast to pass through the oasis of Semna, where there are groves of date-palms and little gardens clustered round shallow, wood-lined wells in the valley bed, 5 miles inland. The coastal plain in this section is about 15 miles wide, narrowing south-eastwards, a flat sandy expanse, covered in places with thorn trees, and here and there mud-flats or glistening expanses of salt-encrusted clay, and towards the south-east an old lava-bed (Harrat Jelib) half-buried in sand.

(b) *Ras Abu Madd–Rābigh.* This section of about 190 miles falls in the second natural division of the Red Sea (p. 96), where, at any rate in the interior, faults of the Eritrean series are crossed by others with a meridional trend, though the coastline appears to reflect only the Eritrean alinement. There are many more settlements in this division than in the preceding one, both on the coast itself and following the wadis inland among the hills. Besides the seaports of Yenbo' and Rābigh, described on pp. 540, 541, there are five other sherms of typical structure, three of which provide anchorage, and it is through this section of coast that Al Madina maintains contact with the sea.

Ras Abu Madd is the sandy tip of a broad low promontory. For 45 miles from this point the coast trends south-east to Ras Baridi, a higher promontory; another Sherm Habban and Sherm Hassey are in this section, the latter providing anchorage in its inner part. Sherm Mahar, between the two, is another good anchorage, with a valley at its head extending into the hills, bordered by overhanging walls. A high tableland, one of the massifs mentioned on p. 38, lies behind the coast, culminating in Jebel Hajina, over 5,000 feet, 23 miles north-east of Ras Baridi, and the coastal track from Umm Lejj keeps to the inner margin of the tableland, with a branch to Sherm Mahar. Spurs from the massif reach seaward, terminating in bluffs and promontories.

From Ras Baridi to Rābigh the coast recedes eastwards in a gentle curve, much indented, and reef-fringed to within 15 miles of Rābigh. Sherm al Khor, east of Ras Baridi, though reef encumbered, gives anchorage, and 17 miles south-east of it Sherm Yenbo' (p. 73) is the best harbour between Ras al Fasma and Jidda. Then for 45 miles the coast is low and swampy, bordered with mangroves and with no inlets of importance. Sherm Bureiqa, at the end of this stretch, is a typical sherm with anchorage for small craft. South of it Ras Abyadh is a low, sandy, reef-bordered point, and beyond it the coast continues low to Rābigh, with anchorage only in Ghubbet ar Raus, an inlet between the sandspit of Ras Abyadh and the mainland. The fringing reefs end at Sherm al Kharrar, 45 miles south-east of Ghubbet ar Raus.

The coastal plain, known as the Tihama, is of varying width, for several highland massifs, alined from north to south, come close to the coast between Yenbo' and Mastura, 180 miles to the south-east. Inland from Yenbo' it is about 15 miles wide, with a surface of sand and shingle in gentle swells and shallow valleys. In the distance, 38 miles away to the north-east of the town, Jebel Radhwa rises sheer from the plain to a flat-topped summit 6,000 feet high. East of the town a group of lower hills, outliers of the highland block which separates the plain of Al Madina from the coast, encloses the Yenbo' plain, coming down towards the sea in broken ridges and twisted crags of reddish lava, with rolling dunes piled against the seaward flanks. Between these hills and Jebel Radhwa, Wadi Yenbo' opens to the plain, where it forms a delta similar to that of Wadi Hamdh. Thorns and tamarisks mark the channels, while inland the wadi contains nearly a score of villages, set among palm-groves where wells tap the water of the wadi bed. Another line of villages occupies a similar position in Wadi Hamra, which reaches the coast near Ghubbet ar Raus. Between Wadi Hamra and Rābigh the steep, saw-toothed ridge of Beni Ayub, another outlier of the main scarp, trends from the north towards the coast at Mastura, about 15 miles from the sea, and the lower hills of Jebel Hasana flank Wadi Safrā barely 10 miles inland. The ruined village of Mastura, 2 miles from the shore, is the centre of the third section where the coastal plain, here of dazzling white sand, widens between Beni Ayub and the blue-black cindery lava hills behind Rābigh.

The coastal track between Yenbo' and Rābigh keeps to the seaward edge of the plain, and there are several branches inland; the chief of these are from Yenbo' up the wadi to the Hejaz railway at Muarda; from Yenbo' east to Hamra then to the Wadi Safrā and to Al Madina, a motorable route; from Rābigh to Hamra, also motorable, thence by the same route to Al Madina; and from Ghubbet ar Raus to Hamra, following Wadi Hamra.

(c) *Rābigh–Jidda*. This stretch of 100 miles is the Arabian side of the third natural division of the Red Sea, and here the coastal zone has been influenced largely by faults of the Meridional series. Dislocated land-steps are alined from north to south, as are also the lava-beds in the northern half of the region, but in general the rim of the Arabian tableland is lower here than to the north or south, and the climb up to Mecca does not much exceed 900 feet. From Rābigh the low sandy coast trends first south, then south-west, to Ras Hātiba, a distance of nearly 60 miles. Four inlets in this section are thought to be true sherms but are imperfectly known. Mersa Dhunaib and Mersa Umm al Misk are used as anchorages, but the two large inlets near Ras Hātiba are too much encumbered with reefs.

Between Ras Hātiba, a low sandy point, and Jidda, 40 miles beyond, the coast trends south-east, with the landlocked inlet of Sherm Ubhar penetrating 7 miles inland in the middle, a typical sherm used as an anchorage. Jidda and its surroundings are described on p. 542.

The low shore, off which lie a number of reefs and islets, is backed throughout this section by a sandy desert plain of varying width. Behind Mersa Dhunaib the lava hills which flank Jebel Rahab reach within 5 miles of the sea. Farther south, Jebel Dha'l Lama rises to

1,650 feet behind Ras Hātiba, with sand-dunes piled against the sea-ward slopes. Separated from it by a valley, in which lies 'Usfān, the Qirfan hills, with summits over 1,900 feet, trend south-east between Sherm Ubhar and Jidda, only 3 miles from the head of the sherm in the north but with a wide embayment north-east of Jidda. Although the plain is usually a waste of sand, there may be a fairly thick cover of vegetation, tussocks of grass and thorny scrub, when the winter rains are heavy, and occasionally near Jidda millets and water-melons are grown. The coastal track from Rābigh keeps to the seaward margin, skirting the swamp at the head of Sherm Ubhar, with motor-able branches from Jidda to Mecca and 'Usfān.

(vi) *The Coast of 'Asīr: Jidda–Meidi* (fig. 10)

This section, about 450 miles long between latitudes 21° 30' N. and 16° 27' N., forms the Arabian side of the northern half of the fourth natural division of the Red Sea (p. 96), where the margin of the tableland, here considerably higher than farther north, is formed by long faults of the Eritrean series, cut off between shorter sections of Meridional trend, with the farther complication in the north, near Mecca, of faults parallel to the Aden series. The coastline appears to be parallel to the plateau margin; thus between Jidda and Ras al Aswad it trends south, between the latter and Al Qunfidha south-east, between Al Qunfidha and the Yemen border, alternately several times in both directions. There are seven typical sherms on this coast, all in the southern half. The seaports of Al Qunfidha and Jīzān are described on pp. 544, 545.

The characteristic broadening of the shallow-water step in this section is obvious from the innumerable reefs, banks, and islands which lie off shore and extend many miles out to sea; the chief island group is that of Farasān, which corresponds in position with the Dahlak archipelago off the Eritrean coast (p. 121).

From Jidda the coast trends south for 11 miles to Ras al Aswad, a low sandy point which extends north over the coast reef. Thence for 95 miles the trend is south-east in a broad arc convex westwards; throughout this stretch the coast is low and sandy, with many small bights in the narrow fringing reef, some of which are used as anchor-ages, though usually without much shelter. A string of tiny villages follows the shore, spaced with almost regular intervals of 4–5 miles. Behind them the monotonous sand-wastes of the Tihama swallow the water brought down in wadis from the hills, here about 20 miles inland. The hills rise to the highlands south-east of Mecca and Tāif, where Jebel Daka reaches 8,346 feet. The coastal track from Jidda keeps to the middle of the plain, following a line of wells where the wadi beds fade into the sand. A branch track from Wadi Sawadiya goes north-east to Mecca, motorable in dry weather.

From Mersa Qishrān, at the end of this stretch, the coast is slightly concave westwards for 110 miles to Al Qunfidha, but much more deeply indented, and with the Farasān bank, well out to sea, obstructing the approaches. Qishrān island is a narrow sandy island 17 miles long, parallel to the coast, with Da'ama island off its eastern end half a mile off shore from Al Līth. Behind it lies a lagoon, entered through Mersa Qishrān between the western end of Qishrān island and the mainland. Al Līth (20° 9′ N., 40° 16′ E.) is a small town 2 miles inland, with anchorage in the outer road unprotected from the prevailing north-westerly winds, and an inner anchorage in Mersa Ibrāhīm, a bight opposite Da'ama island. It stands on an island in Wadi Līth, the channels on either side being dry except after rain. The inhabitants, chiefly fishermen and their families, live in low mud houses or straw huts of conical shape. Behind the town is a thick palm-grove, and the plain to the east produces maize, millets, and water-melons after rain. The coastal track from Jidda passes through the town, and a motorable branch from it goes up Wadi Mafran and on to Tāif in the highlands, forking up Wadi Yalamlan to Mecca.

Thence to Al Qunfidha, about 90 miles to the south-east, the coast is formed by several sandy points and spits separating large bights. Mangroves, mud-flats, and sand-dunes line the shore, and the plain behind undulates in low dune ridges, while off shore lies a maze of reefs, shoals, and islets. The plain is only about 10 miles wide, with the coastal track and a few small villages on the seaward edge. The escarpment behind rises to a narrow crest over 6,500 feet high 25 miles from the coast, its alinement north–south from Mecca to Al Līth, then stepped back behind the latter, trending south-east, until another north–south stretch intervenes, offset to the east, 70 miles inland from Al Qunfidha.

The last section of the 'Asīr coast, the 230 miles to Meidi, is more diversified, for an intricate system of faults breaks up the highland interior as well as the maritime fringe, and the region has also been affected by volcanic activity, the counterpart, and probably a linear extension of the volcanic zone of Eritrea (p. 123). The mountains of the interior, much higher than those farther north, receive a heavier rainfall, and as a result many wadis cross the coastal plain, expanding in deltas when they reach the sea. Cultivation is more abundant, natural vegetation thicker, and this stretch of the plain is regarded as an outbreak area of locusts. But in its human affinities there is little to distinguish this from the preceding sections of the Tihama and its highland border. There is the same line of fishing-villages along the coast, the coastal track, the episodic wadis and their dependent centres of population and cultivation. Well out to sea the Farasān bank with its associated reefs and islands serves a double function of providing anchorage for those with local knowledge and of making approach to the coast difficult for the unwary. One feature distinguishes this part of the coast from the last; it contains seven of the true sherms listed in Appendix A, these providing more sheltered anchorage than most of the inlets. Starting from Al Līth, there is an inner channel all the way between the Farasān bank and the mainland, correspond-ing to the Massawa channels on the African side (p. 116).

Between Al Qunfidha and Hali, 39 miles to the south-south-east, there are several projections from the low coast, and the plain is about 17 miles wide, crossed by several wadis between which long spurs push seawards from the high steep escarpment of the 'Asīr highlands, here 70 miles inland and trending north–south. Hali village lies a little way inland from the bight east of Ras Hali, near the mouth of Wadi Dofar.

Between Hali and Khor 'Itwad, where for 90 miles the indented coastline curves gradually round to the east in a broad arc convex westwards, volcanic hills lie near the sea, narrowing the plain to less than 3 miles in places. Khor Nahūd, 25 miles from Hali, is a typical sherm, the first of five in this section. It offers good anchorage and has a low sandy shore. Behind it the hills, here very close to the shore, rise to two summits over 3,000 feet high, outliers of a more extensive elongated volcanic range. Khor al Birq, another sheltered anchorage and typical sherm, is 2½ miles farther south-east. Then the hills recede about 12 miles inland, and in the 65 miles of coast between Khor al Birq and Wadi Rim there are two more sherms, Khor al Wasm and Khor Makra, both of which provide anchorage. Qotanbul island, 2 miles off shore, and 12 miles west-north-west of Khor Makra where Wadi Rim reaches the sea, is volcanic, with a small peak 330 feet high, precipitous on the western and southern sides and steep everywhere else. Then for 38 miles south-east of Wadi Rim the hills are again close to the coast. Shuqeiq village, 18 miles south-east of Khor Makra, stands a little way inland on the plain, which is here fertile and well watered; there is a landing-place on the beach off the village. Khor 'Itwad, 10 miles south-east of the

village, is a typical sherm, but anchorage can be found almost anywhere along this coast.

From a point 11 miles south-east of Khor 'Itwad the coast trends
south in a narrow strip of bush-covered land 15 miles long, terminating in Ras Turfā. Between this reef-bordered spit and the mainland there is anchorage in the long inlet of Khor al Ja'afira, with the
island of Ferafar in the entrance. Here the hills withdraw farther into
the interior, and the coastal plain widens to 15 miles, a width it retains
beyond Meidi and in fact throughout the Yemen. As far as Jīzān,
14 miles south-east of Ras Turfā, the coast is low and sandy, but
southward of Jīzān rocky cliffs rise from the water. A reef borders
the coast practically all the way between Ras Turfā and the Yemen
border just north of Meidi. Khor al Wahla and Mersa Bagla are two
sherms between Jīzān and Meidi, both with anchorages.

The coastal track keeps inland along the lower slopes of the hills
from Khor 'Itwad southwards, passing As Sabya, but from As Sabya
there is a branch to Jīzān, whence a parallel track continues along
the seaward edge of the plain.

Off the coast between Khor 'Itwad and Meidi lie the Farasān
islands, the largest of which is about 30 miles out from Jīzān. Like
their counterpart on the opposite side of the Red Sea, they contain
two irregularly shaped islands very much larger than the rest, Farasān
and Segīd, corresponding to Dahlak and Norah. Most of the islands
in the group are coralline, but Disan island, towards the north-west, is
volcanic and provides a link between the volcanic zone of Danakil
and that of 'Asīr. Both Farasān and Segīd are fairly high, with an
undulating surface; and both have water-supplies. There are several
fishing-villages and anchorages on the sinuous coastline. Segīd lies
in a bight on the north coast of Farasān, connected with the latter
by a sandy spit which enables camels to pass from one to the other.
Disan, another of the larger islands, west of Segīd, has no water
and is not permanently inhabited.

(vii) *The Yemen Coast: Meidi–Bab al Mandeb* (fig. 11)

The Yemen has a coastline of about 280 miles on the Red Sea,
between latitudes 16° 27′ N. and 12° 40′ N. The general trend is
slightly east of south, but there are many irregularities. Sandy, mangrove-bordered beaches slope gently up to the coastal plain, an undulating, almost waterless expanse about 15 miles wide, sparsely covered
with low bushes and dry grass tussocks. Behind this is the upper
Tihama, a much broken zone of foothills about 30 miles wide, seamed

82, 83. *Undercut coral islets and cliffs on the east coast of Kamarān Island*

84. *Kamarān village seen across the harbour from the north-east. Lazaretto pier in foreground*

85. *Kamarān harbour and village from the north-east, seen from the air. Quarantine station in foreground*

with stony valleys. And then, towering to heights of over 9,000 feet, the Yemen highlands dominate the scene, their crystalline, volcanic, and limestone rocks carved into a great variety of forms by the plentiful rains of the summer monsoon. The lower Tihama misses the summer rainfall, being too low and hot for condensation to take place, but the scanty population make use of such water as reaches the plain in the wadi beds, and grow millets and sesame for food, and some cotton and indigo. The commerce of the more productive highlands is carried on through the seaports of Meidi, Luheiya, Hodeida, and Mocha, which are described on pp. 545–549.

From the boundary a few miles north of Meidi, to Luheiya, 54 miles to the south, the coast is low and sandy, fringed by a reef with many outlying patches and islets. There are no large indentations, and the most prominent points are Ras al Khatib (the delta of Wadi 'Ain) and the delta of Wadi Mur, on the south side of which Luheiya stands. Eight miles farther south Ras Haram is a low sandy point bordered with mangroves, at the entrance to Kamaran bay, which lies between Kamaran island and the mainland. The bay is over 20 miles wide, its eastern shore reef-fringed and irregular, with one or two villages. The southern shore is formed by a hilly promontory about 6 miles wide, which terminates in two sandy points, Ras Harifi on the north and Ras Bayadh on the west. Between the two is a bight, on which stands As Salif, a pretty village with a mosque, where there are large deposits of rock salt. The village has a stone pier, used for loading salt, though it was reported to be in ruins in 1931.

Kamaran island forms the west shore of the bay (fig. 33). It is administered from Aden and is used as an advanced flying base, with a fortnightly mail service to Aden. The island, 14 miles long from north to south, 6 miles at its widest from east to west, is low and reef-bordered except for a short gap on the east side. Its name, meaning 'two moons', arises from the belief that under certain conditions a reflection of the moon may be seen in the water on both sides of the island at the same time. In the Middle Ages it was the headquarters of the Portuguese, who built the fort which was later destroyed by the Turks. Under British administration it is a quarantine station for pilgrims to Mecca. The north and east coasts are deeply indented, and about half-way down the east coast is Kamaran harbour, sheltered from all except easterly winds which here are of rare occurrence. The low cliffs of North point and Milton point overlook the entrance, but the head of the harbour is low, with a mud bank partly fringed with coral. The village lies on the south-west shore of the harbour, and

FIG. 33. *Kamarān Island*

on the northern shore is a large quarantine station and offices, with a wireless-telegraphy station between it and North point. There are two stone piers on the north shore of the harbour, the coal pier to the west equipped with a 2-ton crane, and the Lazaretto pier to the east with water laid on. The chief activity in the harbour is caused by pilgrims, and most of the local population are employed in the quarantine station, but there is also an export trade in charcoal and dried fish. A short distance inland, and north-west of the harbour on the sandy, scrub-covered plain, is the B.O.A.C. landing-ground, connected by trolley-track with the coal pier. There are three other villages on the island besides Kamarān, mostly populated by fishermen and their families. Part of the catch is exchanged for vegetables on the Yemen coast, but most of the inhabitants of the island are poor, with the single exception of the pearl merchants. The pearl-fishing village is on the north-west side, a miserable collection of huts among beautiful surroundings, fouled with the smell of oyster-shells left to rot in the sun. The divers go out in canoes and dhows to the pearling banks, live there for a few days while food and water last, fishing in the morning, then singing and playing musical instruments during the hot afternoon under the shade of sails rigged on sticks in the sand. There is no shade or plant cover of any kind on the banks, and all supplies have to be carried by the divers. Shells are brought back to the island to be opened; the pearls are then graded and weighed by the merchants, and every two or three months are sent to Bombay to be sold. Another occupation of the islanders is the netting of brilliantly plumaged singing birds, which alight to rest on the thorny bushes of salt-encrusted hollows in the waste of sea, sand, and rock. These are sold or exchanged for fish. (Photos. 82–85, 88.)

Nearly 60 miles out to sea from Luheiya, and rising from the deep central trough, is the small volcanic island of Jebel at Tāir ('Bird Island'). It slopes gradually from the shore to the foot of a range of hills about 500 feet high, the change in slope making a conspicuous notch when seen from the sea. On the range are two peaks which reach 800 feet; west of the summit is a lighthouse. There are a few huts and water tanks on the south side, and more water tanks on the beach north of the lighthouse, for the use of the keepers. Landing is possible near both these points between May and September.

About 40 miles farther south-east, also in the central part of the Red Sea, are the Zubair islands, another volcanic group of nine small islands and islets. The largest is Jebel Zubair, with three peaks over 500 feet high. Centre Peak island, the southernmost of the group, also has three peaks, rising above the rocky coast. The highest of these (566 ft.) bears a lighthouse. All the islands are bare and rugged, but are occasionally visited by Arab fishermen (photo. 86).

From Ras Isa, the southerly bulge of the promontory south of Kamarān bay, the coast forms a wide bay with Ras Ketenib at the southern entrance, 16 miles south-east of Ras Isa. There is anchorage in the bay, and the sandy shore is backed by low sandhills. Another bay lies between Ras Ketenib and Ras Katib, 7 miles to the south. The southern part of this bay is Khor Katib, divided into four basins by reefs and islets, enclosed on the west by the narrow northward-projecting peninsula, 6 miles long, which ends in the sandy point of Ras Katib. Hodeida (p. 547) lies 6 miles south-east of the base of this peninsula, backed by a low ridge. To the south the coast, still low, is indented with two small bays (photo. 90). Khor Ghuleifiqa is an inlet similar to Khor Katib but with more capacious anchorage. Its western shore is formed by a low promontory 7 miles long, with an island off the end terminating in Ras Mujāmilla. Thence, from the base of the promontory for 30 miles south-south-eastward to Ras Mutaina the coast is but little indented and almost featureless, with one or two small anchorages and boat harbours.

Still monotonously low and sandy, the coast recedes eastward between Ras Mutaina and Mocha, 50 miles away. There are more villages in this stretch, and anchorage can be found off any of them. From Mocha, where there is a slight westerly bulge in the coastline, to Cape Bab al Mandeb, for 50 miles the coast is fronted by an extensive reef. The only projecting point is near Dubab village, 30 miles south-east of Mocha, then 10 miles farther on the broad Bab al Mandeb peninsula projects south-westward 10 miles out into the strait.

From the deep central trough of the Red Sea, 19 miles out from Ras Mutaina, rises Jebel Zuqar island, the largest of the volcanic group which includes the Hanīsh islands. Jebel Zuqar is about 10 miles long from north to south, 8 miles at its widest from east to west, irregular in shape, rugged and barren, and with a lofty summit (2,047 ft.) about a third of the way in from the northern extremity. It has no permanent inhabitants, but like the Zubair islands is visited by fishermen from Kamarān and Mukalla in search of sharks' fins (pp. 531, 536), fish, and turtle.

Great Hanīsh island, 10 miles farther south, is the second largest in the group. It is elongated from north-east to south-west, 11 miles long, rugged, and with a central summit of 1,335 feet. Near the south-western end a low strip of sand crosses the island, so that the tip

86. *Zubair Islands from near 'Saddle Island'*

87. *Abu 'Ail Islands*

88. *Pearl oysters on Kamarān island*

89. *View westwards from the air across Perim Island. 'Azalea Point' in left foreground; 'Obstruction Point' in right foreground*

90. *Hodeida from the south, with lagoon in foreground*

appears as an off-lying islet. All the islands in the group are rugged and barren, and a chain of islets continues south-westwards to Beilul bay (p. 124) on the African coast.

The Bab al Mandeb peninsula is formed of volcanic rock, and rises to several summits over 500 feet high. On its western side is the entrance to Khor Ghureira which extends more than half-way across the peninsula; the entrance is almost closed by two banks. The southern coast is indented with small reef-fringed bights, and off Cape Bab al Mandeb is a small island, Sheikh Malu (Oyster Island), which is connected with the cape by a rocky shoal ledge.

Throughout the Yemen there is a coastal track at varying distances from the shore. Between Meidi and Luheiya it follows the seaward edge of the Tihama, then diverges inland to Zeidīya, 14 miles inland from Kamarān bay. From this point a track continues south along the upper Tihama, linking the larger centres of population which stand near the junction of the foothill zone and the lower Tihama. From Zeidīya a branch goes to As Salīf on the coast, and from there follows the coast to Hodeida. Thence there is no track, and few villages near the shore, until the upper Tihama track from Zabīd approaches the coast south of Ras Mutaina. But from this point onwards to Cape Bab al Mandeb there is a track within a short distance of the sea.

The Straits of Bab al Mandeb, and Perim Island (fig. 34)

The straits of Bab al Mandeb, 16 miles across at the narrowest, are divided into two by Perim island. Large Strait, 12 miles wide, lies between the latter and the African coast from Ras Dumeira (p. 125) to Ras si Ane in French Somaliland. The Somaliland shore, 20 miles long, is low, sandy, and nearly straight, bordered throughout by a reef which broadens south-eastward, entirely filling the bight between Ras si Ane and the mainland. The latter cape is the northern tip of a promontory which extends $1\frac{1}{2}$ miles northward from the mainland coast, rising at the end to a rugged volcanic hill, reddish in colour and nearly 450 feet high. Small Strait, between Perim island and Cape Bab al Mandeb, is less than 2 miles wide and dangerous to shipping.

Perim island, a British possession administered from Aden, is important as a coaling and signals station, and has a seaplane harbour, with a fortnightly mail service to Aden. It is bare and rocky, composed of volcanic rock strewn with boulders. The highest point is at the eastern end, on an elongated rounded summit surrounded on all sides by steep slopes down to the sea (photo. 89).

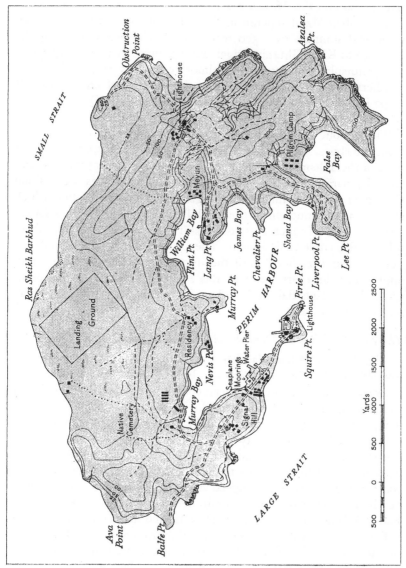

FIG. 34. *Perim Island*

The greatest east–west length is $3\frac{1}{2}$ miles, the narrowest from north to south, about 1,200 yards, towards the eastern end. The north-west part of the island is flat and sandy with a sparse covering of scrub. An aircraft landing-ground occupies the middle of this stretch. The southern coast is very irregular, with sandy bays and hilly promontories and peninsulas backed by steep slopes. Coral reefs encumber the heads of all the bays. The harbour, sheltered from all but southerly winds, is on the south side, entered between Pirie point and Lee point, less than 1,000 yards apart. Inside the entrance the harbour extends north-west in Murray bay, and north-east in William bay, both much indented. The seaplane moorings are on the southern shore of the former, and between them and Pirie point are several piers and slipways. On Pirie point are the oil tanks, from which a pipe-line with floating extension runs along the oil jetty. Water, laid on to Water Pier, is supplied by two condensers, and there is another condenser at Meyun village near the pier on the south side of William bay. Perim port was closed to shipping in November 1936, when the Perim Coal Co. withdrew from the island.

THE SOUTH COAST OF WESTERN ARABIA

This last section of coast to be described extends from Cape Bab al Mandeb (12° 40′ N., 43° 30′ E.) to Ras Dhurbat 'Ali (16° 37′ N., 53° 15′ E.), comprising the coast of the Aden Protectorate, here described for convenience in its western and eastern divisions marked off by Wadi Sanam (13° 34′ N., 47° 17′ E.).

As in the Red Sea, the topography of the coastal zone is controlled by great faults, here chiefly of the Aden series alined from west-south-west to east-north-east. Resulting from this is a marked absence of natural harbours, and, in general, harbours of practical importance are only to be found where volcanic activity has modified the monotonously regular profile of the coast. Behind an irregular strip of sandy plain, mostly barren desert relieved only where springs or the flood water of wadis coming from the interior make cultivation possible, rises the highland rampart of the south Arabian marginal elevation, decreasing in elevation and complexity of structure from west to east. Thus the coast itself is of little economic importance, and serves chiefly as the link between the sea and the more productive and populous valleys of the interior. A vivid description of this coast about A.D. 60, written by a Greek mariner, shows how little the life of this zone has changed with the centuries. A string of fishing-villages by the water's edge, a few agricultural settlements collected round springs or strung out along the wadis, sandy beaches where fish dry in the sun and native boats are built to the ancient pattern; the plodding camels bringing incense and hides down from the interior to the harbours for export, or taking foodstuffs and clothing inland, their routes marked out by water-holes and springs in the coastal strip and by the gaps cut by wadis in the hills—all these are the essential features of human activity in the coastal zone to-day. At few points are changes easily visible, and these are the result of external political influences, concerning the development of ports and in one or two places the building of motor roads.

The Coast of the Western Aden Protectorate (fig. 11)

The coast of the Western Aden Protectorate has fewer features of interest, apart from Aden itself, than that of the Hadhramaut farther east. A coastal plain of varying width, in general a sandy desert with little cultivation and few settlements, rises gradually to high ranges of igneous and volcanic mountains, flanked by tabular plateau-blocks of limestone and sandstone much dissected by watercourses. These mountains, the southern end of the Yemen highlands, are difficult of access from the south coast, where in any case harbours are lacking, and in consequence the coast of the Western Aden Protectorate has not the historical interest of that farther to the east, much less has it economic significance in modern times, apart from the colony of Aden which is described separately on pp. 549 ff.

Between Cape Bab al Mandeb and the Little Aden peninsula, a distance of 100 miles, the coast, generally low and sandy but with occasional low cliffs and rocky promontories, has several wide bays. There are neither islands nor reefs off this stretch, but a broad submerged shelf extends 16 miles seawards, sloping gradually to depths of about 240 feet at the outer edge where an abrupt step marks the descent to the deep central section of the Gulf of Aden (fig. 12).

The coastal plain, about 10 miles wide in the west, broadens to 25 miles behind Aden; though stony in the west, it is generally covered with loose sand, on which grows a scattered collection of low shrubs and tussock grasses. Gently undulating near the sea, the plain rises in high sandhills on the landward margin, and behind these the southern flanks of the Yemen highlands rise to over 2,500 feet within 30 miles of the sea.

Many wadis come down from the highlands, the larger expanding into deltas soon after leaving the hills, the smaller forming restricted

91. *Little Aden (Jebel Ihsan) from the north shore of the Bay of Aden. Wading birds on wet sand in foreground*

92. *The Crater of Aden seen westwards from the air. Holkat Bay in foreground between Ras Marshag and Sira island. Little Aden under cloud in distance beyond Bay of Aden*

93. *Aden peninsula. Lighthouse on 'Elephant's Back', south-west coast*

94. *Aden peninsula. Lighthouse on Ras Marshag, east coast*

deltas near the sea. In this section Wadi Tiban is the largest; it reaches
the sea near Aden harbour, and is perennial in parts. Cultivation depends on flood waters from the mountains, and is therefore limited
to the wadis. Along the smaller watercourses the Arabs have dammed
back the soil to form plots for cultivation where otherwise there would
be only the sandy or stony bed of the wadi. This is not necessary in
the larger wadis, for, as already noted, the delta commences close to
the landward margin of the plain. The chief crops are dates, dhura
(*sorghum* millet), dukhn (*bulrush* millet), sesame, and a little cotton.
This part of the Arabian coastal plain is suspected as a locust outbreak area, though investigations are not yet complete.

The first large bay is Ghubbet al Haika, 25 miles wide between
Cape Bab al Mandeb and the low sandy point of Ras al 'Āra. The
shores are low and sandy, and there are wells of fresh water in the
wadi beds near the edge of the sea. The bay has good anchorage,
protected from the strong winds of the north-east monsoon. Native
dhows occasionally ply to Aden from Bir Suqaiya in the north-west
corner of the bay and from Ras al 'Āra in the east. The plain behind
the bay is stony or gravelly, intersected by many wadis. A track
follows the coast round Cape Bab al Mandeb to Mocha in the west,
and to Aden in the east, linking the points where water can be obtained. From it at Bir Suqaiya another track follows the landward
border of the plain, eventually reaching Aden. At An Nabiya, 7 miles
inland at the foot of the Jebel Hajar, there is an abandoned R.A.F.
landing-ground on the east bank of Wadi Hurim. Another landing-
ground, recently extended, is at Ras al 'Āra.

East of Ras al 'Āra the coast continues for 13 miles round the delta
of Wadi Timnan, low and sandy at first, but with 20–30-foot cliffs of
hard sand, broken by gullies, east of the wadi mouth. The cliffs die
out at the entrance to Khor 'Umeira, a shallow oval inlet almost enclosed by a westward-projecting sandspit which leaves only a narrow
entrance barely 6 feet deep. The western end of the inlet is encumbered with sandbanks, but the eastern is used as an emergency seaplane anchorage. Behind it a narrow sandy plain rises to a group of
hills centred on Jebel Kharāz (2,760 ft.), 5 miles inland. From this
hill-group short wadis radiate in all directions, some southwards to
the coast, some westwards and north-westwards to Wadi Timnan,
and some north-east and east to Wadi Shahar. On the north-west
shore of Khor 'Umeira is Dar am Umm village, with an aircraft
landing-ground east of it. The coastal track here meets a track from
the Yemen interior down Wadi Timnan.

East of Khor 'Umeira is the delta of Wadi Shahar, over which the plain extends 20 miles inland behind the low sandy coast. Ras Qa'o (Jebel Marsa) is a small dark bluff 145 feet high on the eastern edge of the delta. Behind it are the two conspicuous sandhills of Jebel Sumamma (550 ft.) and Jebel am Birka (753 ft.), respectively 2 and 3 miles inland. Between Ras Qa'o and Ras 'Imrān the coast recedes to form Bandar 'Imrān, a broad bay 21 miles across at the mouth, with low sandy shores. Ras 'Imrān, the eastern entrance-point, is a rocky promontory 738 feet high; off it lies the rocky crescent of Jebel 'Aziz island, 350 feet high. There is anchorage at the eastern end of Bandar 'Imrān, sheltered by the cape, and the bay is reported suitable for seaplane operations throughout the north-east monsoon and often during the south-west monsoon. Near the village at the base of Ras 'Imrān is an aircraft landing-ground. Another, no longer used, is at Bir am Makhnūq, about half-way round the bay. The coastal plain stretches inland for 20 miles, flat and sandy near the sea, but covered with high dunes farther inland. Behind it the mountains rise towards the Yemen border, where Jebel am Khurf reaches 4,390 feet and Jebel Khulaqa 4,383 feet. No wadis cross the sandy waste of the plain, but the water of those coming down from the mountains is collected by Wadi Dar on the west and by Wadi ar Riya' on the east, chiefly by the former, which ends in a swamp behind Ras Qa'o. The coastal track from Khor 'Umeira passes through Bir am Makhnūq on its way to Aden, and there is also a beach track passable at low water.

Bandar Fuqum is another bay between Ras 'Imrān and Ras Fuqum, the western extremity of the Little Aden peninsula. It is just over 6 miles wide at the entrance, shallow, with low swampy shores backed by a scrub-covered plain in which Wadi ar Riya' and several parallel watercourses lose themselves before reaching the sea. The Little Aden peninsula on the east side of the bay is a rugged granite mass, originally an island but now joined to the land by the sands of the extended deltas (photo. 91). It is described with Aden on p. 549.

East of Aden the coast curves round towards the north-east in the wide bay of Ghubbet Seilān, between the deltas of Wadi Tiban and Wadi Bana. The flat, sandy coast, swampy in the west, is backed by a low, featureless plain, which, covered with sand hummocks bearing stunted bushes, extends nearly 30 miles inland towards the north-west. Cultivated fields border Wadi Bana on both banks, reaching to the foot of the hills. Ras Seilān, the eastern entrance-point of the bay, is a rounded sandy point immediately east of the mouth of Wadi Bana, with Sheikh Abdulla village about 1½ miles to the north. Thence for 30 miles the coast trends north-east, with a sandy beach, to Shuqra. Wadi Hasan reaches the sea 6 miles north-east of Wadi Bana, its lower course, which forms the western limit of the Fadhli country, parallel to the Wadi Bana and joined to it by an irrigation canal. Between Wadi Hasan and Shuqra a range of hills, reaching 2,330 feet in Jebel Amzūq, lies nearly parallel to the coast, leaving a coastal plain which narrows from 10 miles in the south-west to 3 miles in the north-east. Behind the range Wadi Hasan runs south-west until within $1\frac{1}{2}$ miles from Wadi Bana it makes an abrupt right-angled bend round the western flank of the hills to take an independent course to the sea. The divide between Wadi Hasan and the short wadis which cross the coastal plain lies along the high ridge at the back of the range, barely 2 miles seaward of Wadi Hasan, but 10 miles from the coast. Shuqra, the capital and chief port of the Fadhli district, is a small town divided by a strip of scrub-covered sand into two parts; the Sheikh's house and principal buildings are grouped to the east, the commercial and fishing quarters to the west. The culti-vated area extends north of the town between Wadi Udeba and Wadi Mathwan; maize and dates are grown, and there are salt-works on the east bank of Wadi Mathwan. A break in the coast reef forms a boat harbour, and there is good anchorage half a mile outside the reef.

Beyond Shuqra the coast trends only slightly north of east for 50 miles to Maqātīn Kabir, lacking prominent features and backed by a narrow plain up to the foot of the Fadhli mountains, here only 4 miles inland. The mountains are a lofty lava-covered range of broken peaks, the highest of which is Jebel al 'Urūs (5,702 ft.), 19 miles north-east of Shuqra. Many short watercourses furrow the seaward flanks and die out on the coastal plain, steep-sided and clothed with thick vegetation in their upper reaches. Behind the range is an elevated basin with considerable areas of cultivation. From the western fringe of this basin Wadi Hasan collects many tributaries; in the central part of the basin there are many wells, around which small villages have grown up. The northern edge rises to the high plateaux, over 6,000 feet, of the south Arabian marginal elevation. On the coastal plain most of the villages are near the shore, linked by the track from Aden. The only track inland goes from Shuqra, passes to the west of Jebel al 'Urūs, then through some of the villages in the upper Hasan basin, to Laudar, a local route-centre on the northern border, where the R.A.F. have a landing-ground. Maqātīn on the coast is no longer a permanent settlement, and fishermen who use it

from time to time erect rough shelters. The anchorage is west of a
rocky point and of four off-lying islets, white with guano. Behind
the ruins of Maqātīn a wide stretch of mud-flats reaches 5–7 miles
inland to the lava-flows on the edge of the hills.

From Maqātīn a hundred miles of slightly sinuous coast extends
to Ras al Ghusain (Cape Quseir). Wadi Ahwar, one of the largest on
the south coast of Arabia, reaches the sea 17 miles east of Maqātīn,
forming a wide re-entrant in the hills, up which goes the most direct
track from the coast to Shabwa. The coast of the Ahwar delta is low,
with small rocky points. The plain behind is sandy, undulating, and
scrub-covered, but a large area of cultivation lies mainly on the east
bank of the wadi. Ahwar town, the chief residence of the 'Aulaqi
Sheikh, is on an eastern distributary 5 miles inland. About a mile
north-east of the town is an R.A.F. landing-ground. The 'Aulaqi
district extends along the coast from Maqātīn to Wadi Sanam, 40
miles east of Wadi Ahwar. From the bare sandy coast a dreary plain
stretches 10 miles inland, and then a barren, rugged mountain range
rises like a wall, reaching north-eastwards as far as Wadi Meifa'a.
Wadi Sanam marks the boundary between the Western and Eastern
Aden Protectorates at the coast, although the territory of the Dhuyaib
tribe, east of the wadi, is not included politically in the Hadhramaut.

The Coast of the Eastern Aden Protectorate (fig. 11)

This includes, besides the section between Wadi Sanam and Ras al
Kalb, the coast of the Hadhramaut, from the latter point to Ras
Dhurbat 'Ali. Physically it is more varied in feature than the coast of
the Western Aden Protectorate, largely as a result of more intricate
rock structure and peculiar volcanic topography. At the western end
of the Hadhramaut rugged mountain blocks rise to between 7,000
and 8,000 feet, succeeded eastward by lower table-topped, scarp-
bounded uplands whose height decreases to 2,000 feet behind Ras
Fartak. The region between these highlands and the sea is drained
by short, steep, intermittent streams, with a few larger wadis breaking
through from the landward side of the mountain rim. Widely scattered in the coastal zone are hot, usually sulphurous, springs which
commonly deposit gypsum in quantity. Some are used to irrigate
groves of palm-trees and fields of millet, and the tobacco cultivation
at Gheil Ba Wazīr is based on springs in an extensive gypsum flat.
When moisture-laden winds blow in from the Gulf of Aden a cloud
bank covers the coastal plain, but only the seaward fringe of the
coastal highlands towards the east has enough rainfall for a thin

growth of vegetation, largely incense trees. Fishing is the chief activity of the coast to-day; the inhabitants of shore settlements wade out with hand-nets or cast from small canoes, and the fish are dried on the beaches, then packed in bundles for transport to the interior, where they are used for camel fodder or for manure. The beduin eat the fish either raw or cooked, and by allowing the fish to decompose in pits obtain fish oil. Sardines abound in the winter months; sting-rays, porpoises, and sharks are also caught, but lobsters are rejected as their use is not known. The only harbours of any note are Mukalla (described on p. 554) and Shihr. Small dhow harbours are at Bandar Ruweini near Mukalla, Hāmi, Sharma bay, Qarn, and Cape Quseir.

Historically this part of the south coast of Arabia is of great interest. From Bir 'Ali, west of the Hadhramaut border, to Ras Fartak, it was once part of the incense country, whose western part has now dwindled owing largely to decrease in demand for the product, for it still grows in quantity in the wild valleys of the interior. On this trade were based the great empires of southern Arabia (pp. 218 ff.), and from the sandy coastal strip camels transported bales of the precious gum through the hills northward, skirting the eastern Yemen highlands, then on to Damascus, Babylon, or Tyre. On the coast, Cana and Syagrus (Ras Fartak) were collecting centres with storehouses, whence routes converged on Wadi Hadhramaut, believed to be part of the great incense road which played such a significant part in the political growth of empires in early times (fig. 35). Now Cana lies buried in sand near Bir 'Ali, and most of the incense comes from the Dhufār coast, outside the region here described, though Damqūt and Qishn still perpetuate the ancient trade in the Hadhramaut, exporting annually about 100 and 200 tons respectively.

From a point a few miles east of Wadi Sanam the coastline trends north-eastward, broken by a few projecting points, to Ras al Ghusain (Cape Quseir), a rounded sandy point in the delta of Wadi Meifa'a, 45 miles beyond Wadi Sanam. In this section 'Irqa and Haura are two small fishing-villages on the coastal track.

Between Ras al Ghusain and Ras Asīda is the broad bay of Ghubbet 'Ain, 22 miles wide at the mouth, with anchorage at Bālhāf in the eastern corner. The headland of Ras Asīda, projecting from deep water, rises inland to a dark conical hill 160 feet high, sheltering the anchorage from easterly winds. The coastal plain behind the bay contains several villages where maize and date-palms are cultivated, watered from springs. The R.A.F. has a landing-ground at Bālhāf.

East of Ras Asīda an elliptical group of lava-covered hills lies between the wadis draining to Ghubbet 'Ain on the west and Wadi
Hajr on the east. The volcanic coast in this 35-mile stretch is indented with small bays and projecting points, and there are several
off-lying islets. On either side of the promontory of Ras ar Ratl (Rotl
or Kaidi), an extinct crater with a hollow cone sunk in the middle, its
steep outer rim fringed with coral at water-level, there is shelter for
boats. Farther east the small bay of Husn al Ghorab (Ghūrāb) is set
in an amphitheatre of dead volcanoes, with a solitary flattened crater
making a conspicuous landmark against the shining white sand of the
shore (photo. 129). The crater-lake is a prominent feature in air
travel. There is anchorage in the bay, and Bir 'Ali village, walled and
with a single palm-tree, lies in the north-east corner. In the flat
ground between the crater and the village are the buried ruins of an
ancient town, believed to be the port of Cana (p. 223) described so
vividly in the first century A.D. by the Greek author of the *Periplus
of the Erythraean Sea*. Cana, possibly the Canneh of Ezekiel (xxvii.
23), was the chief port of the incense country until replaced by Shihr
in the Middle Ages, and much interest centres round its location.
Other sites have been suggested, notably Bālhāf and Ras ar Ratl
within 15 miles and to the west of Bir 'Ali, and Ras Majdaha, 6 miles
to the east, but none agrees so closely with the description in the
Periplus. Nor are these alternatives so obviously the meeting-points
of caravan routes from the interior.

The black snout of Ras Majdaha, 20 miles east of Ras Asīda, is a
high point, the end of a line of lava hills which reaches 10 miles inland. It shelters a good anchorage in a small bay on its western
side. Majdaha, on the shore of the bay, has an emergency landing-
ground near by. Ras al Kalb, 17 miles east of Majdaha, is the rounded
sandy extremity of the Hajr delta and is regarded as the western
limit on the coast of the political division of the Hadhramaut. Behind
the delta a broad extension of the coastal plain north-westwards up
the wadi forms a well-marked re-entrant in the hills, but apart from
one or two villages near the coast it is a desolate region without even
a coastal track, for this ends on the shores of Ghubbet 'Ain.

For 45 miles from Ras al Kalb the coast trends north-eastward to
Mukalla. Hills come down close to the sea, particularly in the middle
of this stretch, which, with promontories rising several hundreds of
feet from deep water, is more rugged than any so far described on the
south coast of Arabia. Ras Rahmat (Rajaima), the first prominent
point after the low shore of the Hajr delta, 8 miles north-east of Ras

95. *Bālhāf village*

96. *Bandar Burūm*

97. *The shore west of Mukalla*

98. *Mukalla from the air*

al Kalb, is a limestone headland 300 feet high, piled high on its south-west flanks with sand blown by the monsoon from the delta plain. Its name 'lull of the wind' is derived from Arab experience during the south-west monsoon, for once the dhow is round the point on the eastward journey the violence of the wind decreases. Ras Asasa (al Hamra) is another rocky point 8 miles farther north-east. Between it and Ras al Himār is a small bay with a village on the shore. Ghubbet Kulun (Gullun) is another bay, with indifferent anchorage, between Ras al Himār and Ras Burūm, the latter cape being the end of a craggy limestone promontory 1,100 feet high. On the north-east side of Ras Burūm is Bandar Burūm, a safe anchorage during the south-west monsoon. Surrounded by date-palms, the fishing-village of Burūm stands on the shore at the foot of the hills, which here send a long spur to the sea. A considerable part of Mukalla's trade is diverted here during the south-west monsoon. Beyond Radham Bluff, the northern entrance-point of Bandar Burūm, the hills withdraw inland and the coast is low and sandy for 16 miles to Mukalla. Wadi Khirba reaches the sea in this section, with Fūwa village and its landing-ground a little way inland on the north side of the mouth.

East of Mukalla the coast is regular in outline, an unbroken stretch of low sand for 50 miles nearly to Sharma bay. A coastal plain about 10 miles wide, crossed by a few wadis, rises gradually to a high range of mountains, an unbroken mass between Wadi 'Adīm, a southern affluent of Wadi Hadhramaut on the west, and Wadi Maseila, the lower course of the latter, on the east, the seaward face of the range being cut off by a great fault of the Aden series. Several villages with good water-supply stand on the plain, those on the seaward edge supplementing their cultivation of maize and dates with fishing, the fish being dried and sold for human consumption, fodder, or manure. The R.A.F. has a landing-ground 17 miles from Mukalla, on the way to Shihr.

Shihr, 35 miles east-north-east of Mukalla, is a small port with an open roadstead trading chiefly in dried fish. The town is at least 700 years old and has seen many different occupations. The first recorded visit by Europeans was in 1532, when Manuel da Vasconcello from Goa captured a native vessel with a rich cargo. Other Portuguese visits followed, and from accounts of this period it appears that 'Xaer' was an entrepot with considerable trade with India and Aden. Fishing was important as long ago as the time of Marco Polo, and he too speaks of the trade with India and of the export of horses and incense. It was also a slave-trading station until well into the

nineteenth century. To-day Shihr has nothing of its former importance. The town, walled on the three landward sides, has wide streets,
though many of the houses are ruined. Huts of sticks and mats have
replaced them by the north wall. The water-supply comes through
a covered aqueduct from a large open tank fed by open channels from
a spring at Tabāla, 6½ miles to the north, where there are many springs.
Of the hot springs at Tabāla some are heavily impregnated with sulphur. From Shihr a good motor-road goes inland, then westward
through Hibs and Gheil Ba Wazīr, where it again bends seawards to
Shuheir, continuing along the coast to Mukalla. A branch-road
leading north-west from Shihr is completed to Tarīm, but is in very
bad condition, though cars can get through.

At the eastern end of this stretch of coast, Hāmi village stands in a
ravine, with its patch of cultivation at the base of a dark double-peaked
hill. Cliffs on either side of the mouth of the ravine break the low
outline of the shore, and there are hot springs in the neighbourhood.
There is anchorage off the village, but Sharma bay, which opens just
east of it, provides better anchorage. Sharma bay is about 8 miles
wide, with several villages near the shore and bluff hills coming down
almost to the sea. Qarn, on the north-east shore, has a small dhow
harbour. Dīs and Thaubān (Thubba), some way inland, both have
hot springs.

Then for 9 miles between Sharma bay and Ras Baghashwa limestone cliffs rise almost vertically to 300 or 400 feet. Beyond this the
coast for 70 miles is low, sandy, uncultivated, and of desolate appearance to the mouth of Wadi Maseila. The mountains continue unbroken until Wadi Maseila breaks through in the east. Quseir, a
walled town of stone houses, whose population is engaged chiefly in
shark fishing, is a little way inland from a low rocky cape, 14 miles
from Ras Baghashwa. Reida (Reidat al Abdul Wadud), a further
13 miles north-eastwards in a district noted for its hot springs, is a
small trading town exporting incense, aloes, ambergris, and sharks'
fins, with anchorage off the beach and an aircraft landing-ground.
Near Reida appear the relics of volcanic activity. The first tract
contains several low cones, about 100 feet high, surrounded by sheets
of black basalt in striking contrast to the glaring sands of the sun-
baked plain. Similar cones and lava-fields, called *Hariq* (burnt places)
by the Arabs, extend to Wadi Maseila; the Palinurus shoal, a patch of
rock and coral 10 miles off shore from Museina'a, and the deep hole,
probably a submerged crater, off Reida beach, are also connected with
these features. Lava, welling out from the cones, has found its way

99. *The beach at Shihr*

100. *Qarn seen westwards from the air*

101. *Queseir (Hadhramaut) in 1937*

102. *Qishn in 1937*

into the watercourses, and appears at the coast as black rock filling gashes in the white limestone. Around Museina'a, the site of a large ruined town 13 miles east-north-east of Reida, there are swamps, with mangroves along the coast.

The great Wadi Maseila opens to the sea near Seihūt, with a ruined fort on each side of the entrance. The coast of the delta is straight and low, until Ras 'Iqab rises in a rocky headland east of the wadi mouth. Seihūt has only an open roadstead, but is of some importance as a port because of its connexions with the interior through Wadi Maseila. Its chief trade is in dried fish and fish oil; some of its inhabitants are also engaged in shark fishing. The town is well built, but dirty.

From Ras 'Iqab to Ras Shurwein, a distance of 24 miles, the coast-line is irregular, and there are several small bays with sandy beaches between rocky promontories. The bays afford shelter for small boats during the north-east monsoon, but a sea-breeze causes surf on the beaches and makes landing difficult. The hills come down almost to the sea, with blown sand piled high against their western flanks; they rise to well over 3,000 feet less than 25 miles inland. A few fishing-villages stand on the seaward edge of the narrow plain, but there is no coastal track.

Ras Shurwein is a high vertical cliff at the eastern end of a promontory which rises to a conical peak of 1,905 feet about 2 miles from the cape, bearing two sugar-loaf hills of 1,840 feet on its western shoulder. A wedge of ravine-furrowed highland joins the promontory to the coastal range. North-east of the promontory is Qishn bay, 15 miles wide, with the steep cliffs of the cave-riddled limestone promontory of Ras Darja at the north-east entrance-point. The shores of the bay are low and sandy, separated from the high ranges inland by a barren stretch of sandhills. There is anchorage in Bandar Lask, the western corner of the bay, and a sheltered cove on the other side, close westward of Ras Darja, is used for landing small boats when surf makes landing impossible elsewhere in the bay. Qishn village is about 9 miles from Ras Shurwein, near the shore of the bay. It exports incense, salt, and dried fish to Zanzibar and the Persian Gulf; imports are chiefly foodstuffs and cotton goods. The village, surrounded by palm-groves, is in two sections, with an emergency landing-ground between them.

Beyond the cliffs of Ras Darja a 28-mile stretch of low sandy coast is backed by a narrow plain covered with sandhills, gradually rising to the hills inland, with an expanse of salt marsh at the western end.

Most of the villages are engaged in fishing and have small areas of cultivation. Khaisāt, formerly an important centre of the slave trade, is a little port close to Ras Fartak, exporting salt, salt fish, and sharks' fins, and importing rice, cotton goods, tobacco, dates, and timber for the interior.

At Ras Fartak, the ancient Syagrus, a long spur from the Fartak mountains ends in high limestone cliffs, the highest and most prominent headland on the Hadhramaut coast. Here the coastline makes a great northward bend into Qamr bay, and for 8 miles north of the cape precipitous cliffs nearly 2,000 feet high rise sheer from the water in a great escarpment. Farther round the bay the cliffs decrease in height, becoming more irregular in profile, until they fade into the sandy beach off Tābūt village, 22 miles north of Ras Fartak. From Tābūt the coast curves gradually round to the east, and a wide plain stretches inland, gently rising to the plateau behind the Fartak range. Al Gheidha, 40 miles north of Ras Fartak, is the largest town on Qamr bay, and with an open roadstead it serves as a small port, exporting dried fish, tobacco, and ghi, importing rice, grain, dates, sugar, and clothing. About 28 miles north-east of Al Gheidha the Falik (Fatk) mountains approach the sea, leaving but a narrow strip of sand between them and the water's edge. North-east of these mountains the broad valley of Wadi Shagawat enlarges the coastal plain, and beyond this again another mountain spur comes down to the coast. Immediately east-north-east of this spur Damqūt (Damghūt) lies where a short valley opens at the western end of the Qamr mountains, surrounded on the landward side by almost inaccessible slopes, and with cliffs on the seaward side. Landing is possible on the reef off the town, and shark fishing is carried on. Ghi, hides, and incense are exported.

Beyond Damqūt the cliffs continue for about 8 miles, then give place to a sandy beach-fringed plain bordering the hills. Ras Dhurbat 'Ali, a rocky promontory 200 feet high, projecting from the marginal plateau, marks the eastern limit of the Hadhramaut, where the Aden Protectorate lies adjacent to 'Omān.

Socotra island off the eastern horn of Africa, at the entrance to the Gulf of Aden, and the Kuria Muria islands are described separately in Appendixes F and G.

CHAPTER IV

CLIMATE AND VEGETATION

CLIMATE

THE popular conception of Arabia as a hot land is justified by the facts that the peninsula is nearly bisected by the tropic of Cancer and that the general average temperature is about 80° F., ranging from about 70° in the north to well over 80° in the south. But the altitude of the entire western half greatly lowers its temperature, so that here the winter weather can on occasion be quite cold, with sharp night frosts and even heavy snowfall. Indeed no greater climatic contrast within a limited area can be imagined than that between the healthy, dry, bracing highlands with their sudden changes of temperature and the monotonous, damp, enervating heat of the shores of the Red Sea and the Persian Gulf, where during the hot season the mean day and night air temperature is near blood-heat, and the wet-bulb temperature up in the eighties or even nineties. Every part of Arabia at low or moderate altitudes is liable to experience maximum day temperatures of over 100° during a large part of the year, and extensive areas over 110°, generally when dusty *khamsīn* winds from the south prevail. The lower deserts of the Rub' al Khali and the shores of the Persian Gulf record over 120°, whilst the surface of the desert sand can, even in winter, be heated up to much higher temperatures under the powerful Arabian sun.

Arabia is only part of a far larger desert tract in Asia and Africa, the aridity of which is broadly caused by its position in the path of the north-east trade winds. But the peninsula is not nearly so rainless as is commonly supposed; the beduin in fact possess quite an extensive folk-lore connected with rainfall. It can probably be said that no part of Arabia escapes occasional showers, or rare but sudden and heavy storms which fill the wadis. The northern half of Arabia receives winter rains from Mediterranean depressions moving eastwards across Palestine to the Persian Gulf, sometimes accompanied by violent thunderstorms, especially in the mountains of Sinai. The mountains of 'Omān extract fairly abundant winter rain from the north-east monsoon, and the mountains of the Yemen get still heavier summer rains from the south-west monsoon. Thunderstorms occur locally at times in the 'Omān and Yemen mountains. They bring most of the summer rain which falls on the San'ā tableland in the lee of the rainier outer rampart of mountains, which catch the moist south-west monsoon. Wandering tropical cyclones occasionally visit the south coast and may greatly increase the trifling rainfall of Aden.

The shores of Arabia exhibit that curious and interesting anomaly, not uncommon in the tropics, of high atmospheric humidity associated with rainlessness. The moisture is there, but the prevailing air-circulation prevents its precipitation as rain. It condenses, however, in many places into copious night dews and mists, and the wet mists which cling to the slopes of the Yemen highlands at all seasons of the year are apparently a more critical factor in the successful cultivation of coffee than the actual rainfall.

Sources of Information

Detailed knowledge of the climate of Arabia is very fragmentary. There are several meteorological stations, with records of varying length, on the coasts of the Red Sea, Gulf of Aden, and Persian Gulf. The statistical records kept in these places, taken in conjunction with the reports of travellers in the interior, and with records kept for periods of some length in San'ā, enable a tolerably good picture of the general climatic conditions of the whole peninsula to be formed. But a long time must elapse before charts of Arabia, showing the distribution of the elements in the manner familiar in well-known countries, can be produced.

Meteorological Units

Throughout the following account temperature is quoted in degrees Fahrenheit; the Fahrenheit degree being little more than half the Centigrade degree, fractions of a degree may more easily be disregarded. Temperatures are always those of the air (unless soil or water is specified), as taken by thermometers screened from direct sun-rays.

Pressure is given either in millibars or inches of mercury, or both, according to the context (30·0 in. = 1,018·9 mb.; 1 in. = 34 mb.).

Rainfall is given in inches (1 in. = 25·4 mm.).

Owing to the arbitrary nature of the northern boundaries of Arabia as here considered, observations from Palestine and 'Iraq are frequently quoted to suggest the trend of climatic conditions over the Syrian desert. Observations from ports on the African shore of the Red Sea are included for comparison with those on the Arabian shore, whereas in the Persian Gulf reference is almost exclusively to the Arabian shore.

GENERAL FACTORS OF CLIMATE

The climate of any locality or region on the earth's surface in so far as it depends on purely geographical factors is determined by its latitude, its altitude, its position with respect to land and water, and the direction and constancy of its prevailing winds and associated pressure systems, such as depressions and anticyclones. To these must be added the nature and relief of the land, and the temperature of the ocean currents, since the climatic effects of prevailing winds depend largely upon the regions over which they have blown.

Arabia's latitude would make it essentially a hot country, but this character is strongly modified and complicated by the large extent of elevated land in the western part of the peninsula and by the vast expanses of desert surface, which produce violent extremes of temperature between summer and winter, day and night, and one day and another. Thermal vicissitudes in association with general aridity thus mark the climate as pronouncedly of the continental type. The coastal districts are anomalous in suffering from a humid atmosphere with liability to drenching dews and morning mists without adequate rainfall.

Theoretically the region belongs to the planetary wind and pressure belt of the north-east trade winds, and in effect the desert of Arabia, like those of northern Africa, is a trade-wind desert. The simple trade-wind system is, however, profoundly modified in the Arabian region both in winter and summer by the great neighbouring land-masses of Asia and Africa, which disturb the uniformity of the sub-tropical high-pressure belt, causing it to split up into a number of anticyclonic centres, with the result that nowhere do the trade winds blow unmodified by regional conditions. Over the Arabian area this regional modification is very striking when the average wind and pressure charts for January and July are examined. In January there is a region of high barometric pressure (1,040 mb.) over central Asia which guides a general flow of air from the north-east over Arabia, causing an intensification of the theoretical trade-wind circulation; but in July the establishment of a low-pressure area over central Asia with a well-marked centre over north-west India (990 mb.), taken in conjunction with a marked expansion over the Mediterranean of the Atlantic high pressure, leads to the complete suppression of the NE. trade wind by the south-west monsoon over the Arabian Sea and to a general northerly or north-westerly current over Arabia and the Red Sea, which is a disguised arm of the NE. trade wind proper to these latitudes. Hence the broad features of the atmospheric circulation over Arabia are determined by the position of the peninsula with respect to Asia, Africa, and Europe; but the detailed pattern of the winds depends on more local geographical factors, such as the deep trench of the Red Sea, the high plateaux of western Arabia, and the depression of the Persian Gulf. To the effects of these topographical factors on the wind-system of the region must be added that of the land-mass of Arabia itself on the barometric pressure; for in winter a weak system of high pressure and in summer of low pressure forms over the peninsula, being superposed on the major features of the pressure distribution, and these have an influence on the direction and strength of the winds of the Gulf of Aden and Red Sea, as will appear below.

WINDS

Since, therefore, in winter the general air current across the Arabian region is from the north-east, in summer from the north or north-west over the northern part of the area, and from the west or south-west over the southern part, the regional characteristics of the prevailing winds can be described as follows:

Winds of the Red Sea and Gulf of Aden

The prevailing winds over these areas blow more or less parallel with the shores. Three regions may be distinguished.

1. In the Red Sea north of 20° N. latitude the wind is mainly from the north-north-west all through the year, though between October and May it occasionally blows from the south through the influence of Mediterranean coastal depressions. The northerly winds occasionally reach gale force (force 8 or more) in the Gulf of Suez and northern part of the Red Sea, most frequently in the summer. In the Gulf of 'Aqaba the strongest winds blow down the gulf, that is from north-north-east.

2. South of 20° N. latitude the winds of the Red Sea go through a well-marked annual variation. From October till April the prevailing direction is from the south-south-east, gale force being attained on one or two days a month. Occasionally during this period the wind blows lightly or moderately from the north, but in May the general direction becomes north-north-west and remains so till late in September. Gale force in summer is not reached.

103. Giant mushroom rock eroded by the wind

104. Mabraq an Naqa', the 'place where the camel knelt', near Madāin Sālih. Sandstone monoliths eroded by wind-blown sand

105. *Wind-eroded rocks of Jebel Ethlib, near Madāin Sālih*

106. *Desert between Madāin Sālih and Al 'Ulā*

3. In the Gulf of Aden the prevailing winter wind, still following the coast, is easterly or south-easterly in the straits of Bab al Mandeb where it sometimes blows a gale. In May the winds are variable, but from June to September they blow steadily from the west into the main current of the SW. monsoon in the Arabian Sea.

At all seasons of the year there is, in consequence of the configuration of the continents, a break over the Red Sea area in the continuity of the theoretical NE. trade winds, though it is not very conspicuous in the transitional months of April and October. In July, when the low-pressure centre in north-west India maintains a gradient for NW. winds throughout the length of the Red Sea (as mentioned above, p. 155) this break is most prominent, but in January it is more localized and complicated than in the summer. In winter a development of relatively high pressure, both over the Sahara and Arabia, together with an extension of the Sudanese lower pressure over the middle portion of the Red Sea, leads to NW. winds in the north of the Red Sea and SE. winds in the south, though the precise direction of these currents is largely determined by the trend of the coastline. These oppositely directed winds converge upon an area of relatively low pressure with light variable winds or calms, the average position of which in the Red Sea is between 20° and 18° N.

Investigations carried out some years ago at Kamarān island in connexion with Imperial Airways on the upper air currents of the Red Sea showed that the NE. trade usually extends upwards to a height of about 20,000 feet. This in itself agrees with the interpretation here given of the NW. and SE. winds of the Red Sea as surface deflections of the general current. The prevailing winds of the Red Sea are liable to interruption at times by barometric depressions which, however, are not frequent, as well as by land and sea breezes which are strong in the later summer months, particularly in the southern part of the Red Sea. In winter, when a depression passes eastwards over the Mediterranean, the winds become variable in the Gulf of Suez but do not acquire gale force. Should, however, a depression pass eastwards over Egypt, strong northerly winds spring up in its rear in the south of the Gulf of Suez, in the north of the Red Sea, and in the Gulf of 'Aqaba. These winds strike very cold since, besides blowing from a cold quarter, they are chilled by the snow-clad mountains of the Sinai peninsula. Shallow depressions in autumn, winter, and spring frequently develop over the Anglo-Egyptian Sudan, causing the wind to draw from the south on their eastern side. The hot southerly winds called *khamsīns* carry fine dust and are liable to bring sudden sandstorms reducing visibility to very narrow limits. The name *khamsīn*, however, which in Egypt signifies this dry southerly wind, is applied also to a dry northerly wind which occasionally blows in the Gulf of Aden during the SW. monsoon. The latter fails and the N. wind suddenly rises with great violence at Aden, raising clouds of dust with much lightning without thunder and a quick rise of the barometer of about 4 millibars. This northerly wind is known in Aden as the *kawi* (in the sense of a hot iron) and in the interior of the Eastern Aden Protectorate as the *kharīf*, or autumn wind, said to ripen the date-crop. Another less violent type of northerly squall occurs at Aden towards the end of the SW. monsoon. It differs from the *khamsīn* in carrying no sand, in bringing dark clouds instead of reddish, and in not producing any rise of the barometer.

Tropical cyclones seldom visit the Gulf of Aden and Arabian Sea, and those which do are generally felt most on the west coast of India. The seasonal incidence differs somewhat from that which obtains in most areas subject to tropical revolving storms. Ordinarily tropical cyclones, which require abundant supplies of moisture, are most frequent in the later summer and early autumn months in those oceanic areas where the NE. trade wind is likely to encounter the SE. trade wind, which at this season crosses the equator, thereby becoming deflected to a SW. current; or conversely where the SE. trade wind encounters the deflected NE. trade wind as a NW. current. But, as has already been noted, in the Arabian Sea the NE. trade is cut off in summer by the Asiatic monsoon system, and here it is rather just before and after the season of the SW. monsoon that the air currents are sufficiently irregular and conflicting to engender revolving storms. Up to the end of 1925, the total number of cyclones reported was 42, of which the number between January and March was 0, in April 4, May 7, June 11, between July and September 0, in October 6, November 12, and December 2. By far the most severe visitation in comparatively recent times in this region was that between 30 May and 3 June 1885. The storm, in the centre of which the barometer fell as low as 966 millibars, moved westward through the Gulf of Aden and caused many vessels to founder near Aden. The hurricane brought heavy rain and was preceded by much lightning to eastward, a lunar halo, threatening sky, northerly squalls, a swell from the east, and marked uneasiness among the sea-birds near Perim and Aden.

Winds of the Persian Gulf and Gulf of 'Omān

The winds in the Persian Gulf are mainly north-westerly through the greater part of the year, but in the Gulf of 'Omān they change direction from northerly in winter to southerly in summer in association with the setting in of the SW. monsoon in the northern part of the Arabian Sea.

During the winter months of December, January, and February the general NE. or N. winds from the interior of Asia are deflected along the Persian Gulf into a NW. current, partly in consequence of the configuration of the land and partly in consequence of local irregularities in the distribution of pressure. In the southern section of the Persian Gulf and along the Arabian shore of the Gulf of 'Omān the prevailing wind-direction in this season is more westerly. The normal winter winds are, however, frequently disturbed by the passage of depressions from the Mediterranean, so that an alternation between SE. and NW. winds is characteristic of this season. During March, April, and May the Mediterranean or 'western' depressions decrease in frequency, and during the monsoon period between June and September the NW. winds become strong and steady in the Persian Gulf, with the establishment of the great low-pressure system extending westward from north-west India through Persia to Arabia. In the Gulf of 'Omān the monsoon winds are more variable and blow mainly from the south-east, being locally deflected from the main SW. current of the Arabian Sea. From the middle of September to November there is a gradual change to the winter regime. Tropical cyclones rarely influence the Persian Gulf, but not uncommonly affect the Gulf of 'Omān just before and after the SW. monsoon or during temporary intermissions of it.

Although long-continued gales are uncommon even in winter, the Persian Gulf is liable to sudden squalls which are a menace to navigation at all seasons. Thus in winter line-squalls are associated with the arrival of the cold front of a Mediterranean depression, and in summer with dust-storms. In the spring northerly or westerly squalls sometimes occur in the evening in association with thunderstorms, and these are particularly heavy near the head of the gulf in May. In the autumn very violent squalls locally known to the Arabs as *uhaimir* may be experienced. They appear to come from any direction, and the air is said to be very clear before their arrival. Electrical activity is noticeable during these disturbances, and St. Elmo's fire has been observed on board ship at this season.

Land and sea breezes are strongly developed during quiet, settled weather, but their direction depends on the trend of the coast. The effect of the breezes may be to deviate the wind due to the general pressure gradient, to reinforce it, or even to reverse it. The land breeze which sets in about midnight and dies away at sunrise rarely extends more than 10 miles seaward and is naturally most pronounced during the colder months from October to March. The sea breeze is most vigorous in spring and autumn, since during the heat of summer it tends to be obliterated by the vigorous NW. winds.

On the steep mountainous shores of the Persian and 'Omān gulfs as well as on the Makran coast katabatic winds, like the *bora* of the Mediterranean only less violent, may occur.

Of various Arabic or Persian names given to local winds of the Persian and 'Omān gulfs, *shamāl* ('north') is the best known. It is here used for any form of strong NW. wind, though in 'Iraq it is more strictly confined to the steady northerly winds of summer.

Winds of the Interior of Arabia

In default of systematic observations from vast tracts of desert, little precise information can be given about the interior winds of the peninsula. But a good deal can be inferred from our knowledge of the coastal winds and of the winds of the northern border lands, as also from the mean wind and pressure charts of the surrounding regions. It is always vitally important to interpret charts of average wind and pressure dynamically and not statically, because such charts merely summarize a perpetual succession of changes, many of which deviate very widely from what is depicted on the mean chart. The mean monthly wind and pressure charts of the British Isles, for example, showing for the most part a barometric gradient for SW. winds, become meaningless unless thought of as compounded of all kinds of temporary distortions from day to day or year to year, including fairly frequent reversals to persistent spells of NE. wind. In Arabia the daily changes may not be so profound as in Europe but they are nevertheless important, more especially in the north in winter and the south in summer.

Thus in January and neighbouring months the Syrian desert or Hamād shares to a considerable extent in the alternations between mild rainy westerly winds from the Mediterranean and cold dry easterly winds from Asia, which are characteristic of Palestine, Transjordan, and 'Iraq. Farther south NE. winds blow more regularly across the peninsula and help to account for the remarkably rigorous character of the high eastward-sloping plateaux of the Nafūd and Nejd.

In June, July and August dry N. winds embrace the entire peninsula except Yemen, the Hadhramaut and Dhufār, which come under the influence of the SW. monsoon system of winds; but even here the reign of the SW. monsoon is not so complete as in India, and all over the southern half of the peninsula there are frequent oscillations in summer between damp and enervating S. winds and dry, more bracing N. winds, in accordance with the temporary changes in the position of the main currents; the northerly *kharīf* winds in the interior of the Eastern Aden Protectorate have been mentioned (p. 158).

The mountainous character of much of Arabia, together with the intense heating and cooling to which the irregular surfaces are subjected in the dry air, would lead to the inference that sudden local and rather violent winds must be common in the country. The expectation appears to be borne out by travellers' accounts of sand-storms and dust-storms, eddy winds, and the like. On this as on the African side of the Red Sea there exist some of the most impressive sand-dunes in the world.

TEMPERATURE

The Red Sea and Arabian peninsula are roughly bisected by the Tropic of Cancer, and the general regional isotherms reduced to sea-level show a mean annual temperature of 80° practically coincident with the tropic line in this region—clearly one of the hottest on earth. In January, the coldest month, the migration southward of all the isotherms brings that of 65° practically into line with the tropic, so that even then the air is on the broad average decidedly warmer than it is in England in the warmest month, July. But in this month all correspondence in Arabia between the isothermal lines and the parallels of latitude vanishes. Just after the high solstice such a vast expanse of land surface has been heated by the sun on either side of the tropic that the isotherm of 90° makes two large closed loops, one over North Africa and the other over western and central Asia including nearly the whole of Arabia. Since this is a sea-level isotherm, such heat is actually experienced only on the low eastern side of the Arabian peninsula; but there are places on the shores of the Red Sea and Persian Gulf where the average day and night temperature between June and August is upwards of 95°. Hence human beings there have to endure for many weeks an external temperature near that of the blood, associated with high humidity and a truly terrific force of direct sun-heat unmitigated by the clouds of the rainy tropics. Such conditions make the fierce summer heat of Spain and Italy, often so formidable to visitors from northern Europe, appear quite mild.

Red Sea and Gulf of Aden Temperature Distribution

The mean annual temperature of the air varies from about 70° in the Gulf of Suez to about 85° in the southern part of the Red Sea, whence it declines a little in the Gulf of Aden, except on the African side. The figures for both Massawa and Berbera, namely 86°, are among the highest known on the surface of the globe, and the same figure is given for Kamarān island, though based on a much shorter record. Over the Red Sea itself the mean air temperature exceeds 80° south of 20° N. lat.

During the hotter months of the year maximum temperatures exceeding 100° occur everywhere along the shores of the Red Sea and Gulf of Aden, but they rarely exceed this level over the open sea itself. The fact, however, that the temperature of the sea surface in the southern part of the Red Sea rises in August to 89° helps to raise the vapour pressure and render the heat very oppressive. At Port Sudan, Massawa, and Berbera the average daily maximum is over 100° (as high as 107° at Berbera) between June and August, and on the whole the heat appears to be more severe on the African than on the Arabian shores, perhaps owing to a smaller frequency of cooling on-shore winds. During the occurrence of the *khamsīn* very high temperatures exceeding 110° have been recorded on the African side of the Red Sea and Gulf of Aden and less frequently on the Arabian. Thus an extreme maximum of 118° has been recorded at Quseir, of 117° at Port Sudan, 117° at Berbera, 115° at Jidda, 113° at Tor (as early as April), and 112° at Massawa. There are more climatological stations, with more complete records, on the African shores of the Red Sea than on the Asiatic shores, so that the suggestion as to the more intense heat on the former needs to be received with caution pending fuller investigation. In particular data are needed from the port of Hodeida, for comparison with the nearly opposite port of Massawa, in the same way that the existing record at Jidda can be compared with that at Port Sudan, or the record at Aden with that at Berbera.

Whereas in the hot season the mean day and night temperature varies from a little above 80° in the north of the Red Sea to over 90° in the south and the Gulf of Aden, in the cool season the corresponding figures are 60° and 80° approximately. In the south of the Red Sea and the west part of the Gulf of Aden the air temperature in winter never falls below 60° and the sea temperature keeps as high as 78°. North of 20° N. lat. the night minima sometimes fall below 50° on the Red Sea and its shores, but they appear never to drop to freezing-point even on the banks of the Suez canal. Along the central axis of the Red Sea the average temperature is a little higher in winter than along its shores, just as it is a little lower in summer.

The high night temperatures at all seasons render the climate in the southern part of the Red Sea very oppressive, affording little relief from the heat of the day. A short distance inland on both sides, however, the climate is much more extreme, so that care should be taken to guard against night chills and exposure to the sun.

In the extra-tropical portion of the Red Sea the coldest month is definitely January on the average, but the hottest is August rather than July; and a characteristic feature here, as in the entire Mediterranean region, is the maintenance of high temperatures right through September. In the tropical part of the Red Sea the effect of the double passage of the overhead sun is to reduce the annual range of temperature and to lengthen the hot season, so that the hottest month tends to be rather indefinite between June, July, and August, and to be determined more by local factors. Even May and September can be almost as hot.

The following table for Tor on the coast of the Sinai peninsula, Jidda in the middle of the Arabian shore of the Red Sea, and Aden has been prepared to indicate representative thermal characteristics of the region. The difference between the mean temperature of the coldest and warmest months indicates the annual range and that between the average maximum and minimum in these months the diurnal range.

	Mean annual tempera- ture	Hottest month				Coldest month			
		Month	Mean temp.	Mean max.	Mean min.	Month	Mean temp.	Mean max.	Mean min.
Tor (1905–1930)	72	August	84	94	76	January	57	69	48
Jidda (1881–1891)	81	August	88	93	83	February	71	77	67
Aden (50 years)	83	June	90	95	84	January	76	80	73

It will be noticed that the range of temperature both seasonal and diurnal is greater at Tor than at the two tropical stations. This place, too, shows an extreme range of temperature between 111° in April and 35° in February, the latter figure suggesting that actual frost may occur now and then a few miles inland, as in fact it does in Sinai. At Jidda the absolute extremes are 115° in June and 55° in January, and at Aden 109° in June and July and 61° in February.

The characteristics of Tor generally resemble those of Suez. Jidda is cooler in summer than Port Sudan on the opposite coast, where the range of temperature is considerably greater and there has been an extreme minimum of 50° in January.

Tables, nearly complete, have recently become available, showing the highest and lowest temperatures periodically recorded at Mukalla, on the south coast, over nearly 7½ years (April 1938–July 1945), and at Seiyūn, in the Wadi Hadhramaut at about 2,340 feet above sea-level, over more than 3½ years (Dec. 1939–June 1943). At Mukalla temperatures of 100° or more were recorded in June, July, and August in 1938, 1939, and 1940 (in 1938 also in May); in 1941 and 1942 no temperature of 100° or over was recorded, though points little under 100° were reached in the hot months; in 1943 and 1944, 100° or more in June, July, August, and September (in 1944 also in May and in the later months of the year). The lowest minima were temperatures a little above or below 70°, the thermometer falling to 67° in December 1938 and to the same figure in November and December 1943. In the interior, at the comparatively high altitude of Seiyūn, much wider divergences between maximum and minimum are recorded; 110° was reached in June in 1940, 1941, and 1942 (in 1942 the same figure was recorded in July and August); while temperature fell to 30° in January 1942 and to points under 50° in November, December, March, and April of the several years.

Aden has a particularly complicated monthly distribution of mean temperature, June being the hottest month with 90°, followed by July and September with 88°, May 87°, and August 86°. This place is notably cooler than Berbera in British Somaliland, but the range of temperature is rather less.

Temperature Distribution on the Persian Gulf and the Gulf of 'Omān

The Persian Gulf and Gulf of 'Omān are situated, respectively, in a higher latitude than the Red Sea and Gulf of Aden, Muscat lying almost exactly on the northern tropic. This results in a cooler winter on the Persian Gulf as compared with the Red Sea, though the summer heat is about the same. At the head of the gulf, near the mouth of the Shatt al Arab, the annual range of temperature is great, the heat in summer surpassing anything known on the coasts of the

Red Sea but the cold in winter reaching frost levels. The following comparison between Shuaiba near Basra, 70 miles from the mouth of the Shatt al Arab, and Muscat, on the Arabian shore of the Gulf of 'Omān, will suffice to indicate the thermal regime.

	Hottest month			Coldest month		
	Month	Mean max.	Mean min.	Month	Mean max.	Mean min.
Muscat (38 years, 1902–40)	June	98	88	January	75	66
Shuaiba (16 years, 1922–38)	August	112	80	January	62	42

Muscat, though thermometrically cooler than Massawa, is described as one of the hottest harbours in the world in June, when the sun is overhead at noon and heat is reflected from its surrounding barren rocky hills. The recorded absolute extremes of temperature are 116° and 49°. At Shuaiba, which endures an average August daily maximum of 112°, the thermometer has been known to soar to 125° in the screen, but there has been a winter night minimum of 19°, or 13 degrees of frost—cold which would be accounted moderately severe in England. At Kuweit a minimum of 27° F. has been observed. The sea-surface temperature of the Persian Gulf is excessively high in August, when it is rarely below 90°, and may exceed 98° in that month and in September, making conditions on board ship very trying.[1] In February the sea-temperature is as high as 70° at the entrance to the strait of Hormuz and 64° on the western side of the Persian Gulf, but even the latter figure is several degrees higher than the temperature of the sea-water around the Scottish coasts in August. In the Gulf of 'Omān the SW. monsoon arrests the continual rise of the sea-temperature through the summer, so that the maximum of 87° occurs in July. Out in the Arabian Sea the maximum of only 84° occurs in June.

Temperature in the Interior of Arabia

Less than half of the surface of Arabia is at, or near, sea-level; for apart from the higher mountains of 'Omān, Yemen, and 'Asīr (8,000–c. 12,000 ft.) much of the vast extent of irregular tableland in the west of the peninsula reaches approximately 5,000 feet. This is the primary factor in the distribution of temperature over the peninsula in comparison with the Red Sea and Persian Gulf

[1] Temperatures exceeding blood-heat, 98·4°, were recorded from just below the sea surface in September 1917.

depressions on each side of it. Some of the familiar school atlases, which show Arabia crossed by the mean annual isotherm of 80° reduced to sea-level, also represent by colours the distribution of the actual temperature as lowered by altitude. These values are not, of course, derived from actual temperature records in the little known Arabian interior, but are deduced from the law that on the average the temperature falls at the rate of 3·3 degrees Fahrenheit for each 1,000 feet of ascent above sea-level. The vertical rate of cooling of the air, or 'lapse-rate', cannot much exceed this value without setting up unstable atmospheric conditions, though it may locally and temporarily be less or even reversed—as in the case of cold weather 'inversions', when it may be warmer on the top of a mountain than around its base. The rate of cooling with height is more variable and irregular on mountain slopes than in the free air because of differences of exposure to sunshine and wind, and because broad plateau surfaces heat up and cool down more rapidly than narrow ridges or isolated peaks; but in the long run such local factors cancel out, so that if the normal temperature at sea-level is known it is possible to calculate approximately how much lower the average temperature must be on a mountain top of known height in the vicinity.

Hann applied this rule to the highlands of Yemen, calculating what the normal temperature should be in every month of the year at San'ā, for comparison with the temperature actually observed there by Glaser during nine complete months in 1883. For this purpose Hann took the mean of each of the twelve normal monthly temperatures at three places on the Arabian coast, Aden, Perim island, and Jidda; the mean of the geographical positions of these three, 15° 36' N. lat., 42° 31' E. long., is not far from that of San'ā, namely 15° 22' N. lat., 44° 12' E. long. Taking the altitude of San'ā from analysis of the barometric data to be 2,371 metres = 7,706 feet above sea-level,[1] and applying the rule for reduction of normal temperature with height, he found that in none of the nine months did the calculated temperature differ by as much as one degree Centigrade or two degrees Fahrenheit from the mean temperature of the respective months as deduced from Glaser's record. Hann's device for obtaining base temperatures was ingenious, and the agreement between the calculated and observed temperature was notable; but he omitted to add that the very possibility of such a close correspondence seems to depend on a fair measure of uniformity of temperature over the area represented by Aden, Perim, and Jidda,

[1] Actually the altitude of San'ā may be slightly greater.

and (considering that Glaser's record was only from January to mid-October, in a single year) on the probability that the temperature at San'ā does not vary very much from one year to another. While the calculated normal yearly temperature at San'ā works out at 17·5° C. (63·5° F.), as compared with 27·9° C. (82·2° F.) for the hypothetical position of the city at sea-level, the probable mean temperature for the whole of 1883 as deduced by sine-curve analysis from Glaser's incomplete observations agrees exactly with this figure, so that 1883 would seem to have been a highly typical year on the high tableland of south Arabia.

Thus, on the high Yemen tableland the average temperature over the year is no higher than that of southern England at the height of summer. A peculiarity of the seasonal course of temperature at San'ā is the small range between the mean of the coldest month and that of June, the warmest, the two means being about 59° and 68° respectively, a difference of only nine degrees Fahrenheit. Glaser's record (1883), as stated, extended from January to mid-October, but did not include November and December. The much more recent observations of Dr. P. W. R. Petrie indicate that in San'ā, in some winters at least (e.g. 1937–8), the coldest weather, with several degrees of frost, occurs in December or even November; though at Aden and elsewhere on the coast January is on an average about one degree Fahrenheit colder than December. Petrie's lowest night-minimum was 17° F., while in January 1938 the lowest night-minimum recorded (12–13 Jan.) was just over 33°. If the greater cold of December in the Yemen highlands is constant over long series of years, it may be the effect of the lowest solar altitude in the rarified air at nearly 8,000 feet above sea-level.

The maximum for the whole year in San'ā is about 82°, and the fact that June is the warmest month is partly due to the cloud and rain of July and August keeping down the day temperature in the latter months. The anomaly of the small range between the means of the coldest and hottest months is attributed by Hann, no doubt correctly, to the fact that winter is the clear season and summer the cloudy season; the strong tropical sunshine has full play in the cool season, often raising the daily maxima to nearly as high a level as the more checkered sunshine in the hot season. The effect of this would be to reduce the annual range of temperature very considerably, whereas in the northern parts of Arabia the mean annual range amounts to more than 30 degrees.

But all over the interior of the peninsula there is a wide daily range of temperature. At San'ā it may be 36 degrees or even more in the dry season, while in north Arabia 40 degrees is quoted by Philby and Euting as a typical difference between day and night.

On occasion the range of temperature is much greater than this, and many travellers in the interior of Arabia have instanced the sudden violent vicissitudes of the thermometer between day and night or accompanying changes of wind. Thus, Euting recorded in August 1883 a fall of temperature in the Nafūd from 113° at mid-day to 57° just before sunset—equal to a range of 56 degrees. More remarkable are the fluctuations alleged by Baron Nolde to have taken place near Hāil on 2 February 1893. In the middle of the day the temperature under the influence of a cold wind was no higher than 41°; it subsequently rose slowly to 44° and then about an hour before sunset suddenly leaped up to 77°, only to sink rapidly several degrees below freezing-point soon after sunset—to a minimum before dawn of 12°, or 20 degrees of frost. Since these extraordinary excursions of the thermometer took place in a spell of very cold weather previous to a widespread heavy fall of snow, and the reading of 77° was noted only a little before sunset, it is impossible to avoid the suspicion that the instrument had been accidentally exposed to the sun's rays; but as on this point there is nothing reassuring in Nolde's narrative the case must at this late date unfortunately remain undecided. Nevertheless great and rapid variations of temperature are only to be expected in the deserts of Arabia, where the sands, with their low specific heat and poor thermal conductivity, heat up and cool down very quickly by solar and terrestrial radiation respectively in the clear dry air.

Concerning the extremes of heat and cold liable to be encountered in different parts of the interior, only very guarded statements can be made. There is no reason to suppose that the summer heat of Arabia is not as great as that of the Sahara. Since daily maxima above 110° occur very generally on the coasts of the peninsula, and since maxima of 125° and 123° respectively have been observed at Basra and Baghdad in Mesopotamia, it seems safe to infer that all the eastern lowlands abutting on the Persian Gulf must be subject to summer temperatures over 120°. Max von Oppenheim, travelling through the Syrian desert in the summer of 1893, experienced for a whole week an average maximum of 117° with an absolute maximum of 129°. Even Mecca, at more than 2,000 feet above sea-level, had a maximum of 117° in June 1883 according to Semelhack.

For comparison it may be noted that there are not many authentic records of air temperature much above 130° in any part of the world, among the more notable instances being 133° at In Sala in the Sahara, 134° in Death Valley, California, and 136° at Azizia in Tripolitania. Philby, in the course of his summer journey in 1932, repeatedly noted day temperatures in excess of 110° in the neighbourhood of Riyādh and night temperatures which did not fall below 90° or 80°. The desert sands, exposed to the summer sun, doubtless sometimes reach temperatures from 170° to 180°, as in the Sahara, and even in winter the direct sun-heat is so strong that the sands can hardly be trodden without sandals. Raunkiaer in north Arabia found sand temperatures in winter as high as 118° and Glaser in south Arabia as high as 129°.

At the other extreme there does not appear to be any part of the Arabian interior which is exempt from winter night frost, though this is completely absent on the coasts except at the head of the Persian Gulf and in the Sinai peninsula. In the lower Rub' al Khali, within the tropics, it is probable that freezing temperatures are confined for the most part to the surface of the sand, that is, night frosts are mainly ground frosts and not air frosts, but with increasing latitude and altitude in Arabia frost becomes very definite in the cold season. Philby, in the winter of 1917, noted a minimum of 27° near Riyādh, and Euting, in the early spring of 1884, following a very wet winter, recorded ice every night for a fortnight in Nejd and a minimum of 23°. Nolde's minimum of 12° near Hāil in February 1893 has already been mentioned, and there is no reason to suppose that an even greater degree of cold may not occasionally occur there. The general indications are that when the weather on the lofty tablelands of Arabia is cold with night frost, the day-time temperature usually rises to 50° or higher in consequence of the strong tropical sunshine. Brief spells of continuous frost, night and day, probably occur now and then in the Syrian desert, but farther south they must be limited to the highest altitudes, viz. the mountains of the Hejaz, 'Asīr, the Yemen, and possibly 'Omān.

In relation to the latitude and in comparison with the lands on the other side of the Red Sea, winter in the high interior of Arabia is rigorous, a fact which is not entirely due to altitude and the free play of nocturnal radiation from a desert surface, since these factors also operate in parts of Egypt, the Sahara, and the Sudan. The critical factors in Arabia are the NE. winds, which frequently bring bitter cold straight from central Asia, and the full exposure of the sloping plateau surface to these winds. If the slope of the peninsula were reversed, with the high edge on the Persian Gulf and the low ground on the Red Sea, the Arabian winter would be milder, partly because of shelter from the prevailing wind and partly because the wind itself, blowing down-slope, would tend to become dynamically warmed in accordance with a well-known meteorological principle.

HUMIDITY

Humidity is an important climatic element. In the technical sense used by meteorologists it has nothing to do with aqueous condensation but refers simply to the condition of the air, either in the amount of water vapour it holds or in the ratio of this to the amount which the air would hold if saturated at the given temperature. The former quantity, called the absolute humidity, is conveniently indicated in terms of vapour pressure, the latter, known as the relative humidity, is expressed as a percentage of saturation. Both are significant in the physical processes of the weather as well as in the physiological reactions to weather and climate, and consequently the practice in some books of merely regarding the relative humidity is most misleading. Relative humidity figures have little significance unless the level of temperature to which they refer are kept in mind, and variations in the relative humidity are only a simple index of the amount of moisture in the air at constant temperatures. Mr. W. G. Kendrew in *The Climates of the Continents* has pointed out that the relative humidity in the intense dry cold of a Siberian winter is on the average as high as it is in the milder and damper English winter, namely 80 per cent., but because the air can hold so little vapour at very low temperatures the winter climate of Siberia is physiologically intensely dry. Again, in the tropics a relative humidity no higher than 70 per cent. may make the heat feel damp and oppressive, because the high vapour-pressure hinders evaporation from the lungs and skin; but on the other hand unsaturated tropical air has greater drying power over wet surfaces than cold air, because it has greater capacity for holding moisture. A very useful indication of atmospheric humidity, in that it prevents the temperature of the air from being left out of account, is the wet-bulb temperature, which is of special importance in hot countries. A wet-bulb reading over 70° generally implies uncomfortable conditions, and one over 80° conditions which are becoming dangerous to health, so that in India warnings against heat-stroke are issued by the

Meteorological Service when the wet-bulb temperature is expected to exceed 84°.

Humidity in the Red Sea and Gulf of Aden

The data available for the Red Sea and its shores concern relative humidity and wet-bulb temperature, and these should be studied in the light of the reputation of the region, based on long experience, for oppressive, damp, enervating heat. Over the open sea there is little seasonal variation in the relative humidity, and it is high throughout the year, as the following percentage figures indicate:

Gulf of Suez	. 71%
Red Sea, lat. 21° N.	. 77%
Red Sea, lat. 13° N.	. 80%
Gulf of Aden, long. 48° E.	. 80%

From these average values the relative humidity varies greatly from day to day according to the direction of the wind. The high average values are due to the prevalent air motion along the Red Sea (as described on p. 156), but when the wind is off shore the humidity may fall as low as 30 per cent.

The average wet-bulb temperatures over the open sea are shown in the following table.

	Red Sea			
	27° N. lat.	21° N. lat.	15° N. lat.	Gulf of Aden
January . .	. 61° F.	67° F.	74° F.	72° F.
April . . .	69	75	78	79
July . . .	77	81	84	81
October . .	74	80	80	78

These figures suggest danger in the southern part of the Red Sea between April and October, and death from heat apoplexy in these months is not uncommon. The great heat is often intensified on vessels proceeding southward by a light wind too weak to pass through them. At Kamarān island a wet-bulb temperature of 100° has been recorded with a relative humidity of 98 per cent., but such extreme conditions have only occurred twice in eight years. An average humidity of 80 per cent. at Red Sea temperatures inevitably means a very high vapour pressure, which fully accounts for the distressing quality of the heat encountered by voyagers.

The humidity values along the shores of the Red Sea are definitely lower than those on the open sea. In the northern part percentage values of 41 at Quseir and 59 at Tor compare very favourably with 74 at the Daedalus coral reef in mid-sea, but even in the south there are none as high as 80, though Jidda shows 69, and Perim, Zeila, and Aden 73, 75, and 75 respectively. At Kamarān island, close to the Arabian shore, where the wet-bulb temperature has reached 100°, and at Massawa on the opposite shore, known for its steamy heat, the relative humidity only averages 65 per cent. with a range between 73 in winter and 56 in summer. On the other hand at Jidda, with an average of 69, the seasonal variation is small, the maximum occurring in September with 75. The length of the Red Sea and Gulf of Suez together being nearly 1,380 miles, local differences are to be expected, but the figures may be affected to some extent by inequalities in the number of years upon which the averages are based, some of the records covering only a few years. Data are not at hand on the diurnal variation in the relative humidity, but it should be noted that it is characteristic of hot sunny climates and weather for the humidity to go up in the early morning after the air has been chilled by nocturnal radiation, and to go down in the hot hours of the afternoon when convection carries a good deal of moist air upwards. Though the humidity is greater on the open Red Sea than it is on the coasts, there is compensation in the fact that the temperature rarely rises much above 100°.

Humidity in the Persian Gulf and Gulf of 'Omān

These two seas are also notorious for their 'damp' heat, and for this side of Arabia also there are sufficient instrumental data to throw light on this reputation.

In the Persian Gulf the wet-bulb temperature at nearly all ports exceeds 78° from June to September both morning and afternoon. At Bahrein on August afternoons it averages as high as 87°, and when the dry bulb (air) temperature is between 95° and 100°, the wet bulb may read only two degrees lower—most trying conditions, especially if the wind drops to a calm. Out over the open sea wet-bulb readings from 85° to 88° were recorded on ten successive days in August 1930. The oppressive character of the summer climate in the Gulf is also brought out by the relative humidity, which averages about 70 per cent. with little diurnal variation. Inland from the coast, however, the air is much drier and the intense heat more tolerable. Thus near Basra the average relative humidity between June and September is from 20 to 25 per cent., and on some occasions the air may be almost completely dry.

During the winter months the wet-bulb temperature is below 78°, though the relative humidity is slightly higher than during the intense summer heat, exceeding 80 per cent. at the morning hour of observation at nearly all ports.

At Muscat the relative humidity is as high as 80 per cent. in the early morning, and during the whole of the period from June to September the average wet-bulb temperature is above 78°.

In relation to the intense heat the summer relative humidity on the Persian Gulf is undoubtedly high, though the actual figures fall a good deal short of those (from 85 to 95%) at places such as Bombay and Calcutta during the wet season. There, though the steamy heat, near saturation in the sunny intervals, may be distressing, the actual temperature is at any rate lower than on the Gulf, while the sight and sound of mighty downpours of rain bring refreshment to mind and body.

Humidity in the Interior of Arabia

Practically no records exist of this element in the interior of Arabia. According to Glaser's observations for the year 1883 at San'ā, not quite typical of the interior, the relative humidity averaged 48 per cent., fluctuating between 69 per cent. in the morning and 29 per cent. in the afternoon.[1] He stated that in the dry thin air of the Yemen highlands water evaporates so quickly that ice forms on winter nights, even with air temperature several degrees above the freezing-point. For comparison there are records of average relative humidity for both Baghdad (January 73%, July 37%) and Jerusalem (January 73%, July 56%).

The desiccating effect of the desert winds of Arabia on the landscape and flora and fauna are described in other parts of this book. Meanwhile it should be noted that though the air in the tropical deserts is normally dry, its capacity for moisture is so great on account of the high temperature that very large fluctuations in the humidity are liable to occur. In Arabia a southerly wind of long fetch from the heated Arabian Sea may cause the humidity to reach quite high values far into the interior; but so long as the air is coming from a dry quarter or descending in anticyclonic circulation from high levels, humidity, in the absence of large evaporating surfaces, must remain very low in the deserts, sometimes becoming almost nil. In the main Wadi Hadhramaut, during the SW. monsoon, the

[1] Recently Dr. P. W. R. Petrie has recorded in San'ā a daily variation in January of 40%, from 60% early in the morning to 20% at 2 p.m.; in March the daily variation is about 50%, the morning and afternoon figures being, respectively, 80% and 30%; while from June to October the daily variation is usually about 35%, with morning and afternoon figures, respectively, 55% and 20%.

excessive dryness of the atmosphere is very trying, though many who have experienced it find the high temperatures, e.g. 110° in Seiyūn, more tolerable on account of the dryness.

For comparison, L. J. Sutton, writing of the intensely hot semi-desert climate of Khartoum, shows that though the relative humidity is lower than in London, the average amount of water vapour in the air is rather greater, in accordance with the following figures for vapour pressure expressed in millimetres: Khartoum 8·4, Cairo 8·8, London (Kew) 7·3. Similarly Francis Rodd, travelling in the Aïr region of the Sahara in 1922 and 1927, found the relative humidity to vary between 81 and 2 per cent. with the vapour pressure on one occasion as high as 22 millibars (=16·5 mm.).

SOLAR RADIATION, SUNSHINE, AND CLOUD

Solar radiation, insolation, or more conventionally 'sunshine' is, apart from its physical effects in making weather, a very important element of climate in relation to living organisms, including man himself. Properly speaking, sunshine as a climatic element involves the intensity and quality of the direct heat and light received from the sun as well as its duration; but unfortunately scientific measurement of solar radiation is still in a primitive state, with the result that as a rule only the duration of sunshine is given in climatological descriptions.

Arabia's position in latitude about the northern tropic, together with the prevailing clear sky and relatively dry atmosphere, renders the sunshine, in the peninsula and adjacent seas alike, constant and powerful even in winter. In summer the sun beats down with over-powering force, the sensible effect of which on human beings is greatly enhanced by the extremely high accompanying temperature of the air. In addition to this there are fierce blasts of hot air from the sun-scorched rocks and sands, whilst the intense glare of the sunlight reflecting from water, buildings, and all bright surfaces has also to be contended with. In these respects the climate of the Arabian region is indeed exacting, whatever may be the compensating advantages attendant upon abundance of sunlight. In the extreme south of Arabia the seasonal variation in the length of the day practically vanishes and even in the extreme north it fails to assume the impressive contrast of European latitudes. Everywhere night falls rapidly with no lingering twilight, and then there comes all the splendour of the desert starlight and moonlight, the influence of

107. *Rainstorm at over 7,000 feet on Jebel Jihāf on a September afternoon*

108. *Afternoon clouds piling up over the southern Yemen mountains in September*

109. *Snow on the Gunna tableland, Sinai*

110. *Cloudy evening, late December, at Ibb in the Yemen*

which is so vividly reflected in Arab religion, folk-lore, and time-reckoning.

On the Red Sea coasts it is said that 8 hours of continuous sun-shine may be expected almost daily. Actual measurements of the duration of sunshine from this part of the world, however, are wanting, though what amounts to an inverted measure thereof is supplied by records of the amount of cloud on the scale 0 = completely clear to 10 = completely overcast.

At none of the Red Sea and Arabian ports is the average amount of cloud during the year as high as 5, and only at one or two places is this figure exceeded in the cloudiest month of the year. At the northern end of the Red Sea the yearly value is from 1 to 2, and the summer figure is less than 0·5. Farther south the annual proportion rises somewhat to between 2 and 3, and at Aden it reaches 4·2, the highest in the entire region, and here the winter figure exceeds 5. Along the Persian Gulf the annual figure is mostly about 2, but the highland Persian side of the Gulf of 'Omān has a rather high proportion of cloud, 5 to 7, during the SW. monsoon. At Baghdad the amount of cloud in July is as low as 0·1, but increases to 3·2 in January, the corresponding amounts for Jerusalem being 0·8 and 5·2.

According to Glaser's observations in the Yemen in 1883 the amount of cloud at San'ā, 2·6, is considerably smaller than at Aden, but the seasonal variation is reversed, summer being the cloudiest period. Recently Rathjens and Wissmann have published a table showing that the amount of cloud in San'ā may be as much as 4 during the height of the summer rains, but only 0·5 in late autumn and mid-winter; they consider the average of 2·6 perhaps too low.

The amount of true cloud is probably still smaller in the interior of the peninsula than on the coasts; but it is likely that the glare of the sun is more often tempered by blown dust and sand, which no doubt helps to engender the gorgeous sunrise and sunset colours over the desert.

From the journeys of Glaser in 1883, of Rathjens and Wissmann in 1928, and of Hugh Scott in 1937 it is clear that very imposing thundery cumulo-nimbus clouds habitually develop over the highlands of the Yemen during the summer months. In the Sinai peninsula fine cloud scenery of the fleecy alto-cumulus type, as well as other forms, are described by Paul Range as accompanying the hot and stormy scirocco or *khamsīn* winds which frequently arise in spring. The Ruwalla beduin speak of plenty of cloud during the rainless summers of northern Arabia and of haloes and mock-suns preceding rain in the winter months.

VISIBILITY

Though visibility conditions must be fairly good in a climate characterized by brilliant sunlight, they are probably inferior to those which obtain in fine weather in many cool rainy climates removed from sources of industrial pollution—such as, for instance, the Atlantic seaboard of the British Isles. For, though there is little true mist or fog in most parts of Arabia, there is, owing to the general aridity, frequent dust-haze which destroys the blueness of the sky and diminishes the range of vision, as well as drifting sand-storms which can reduce visibility to that in a very dense fog. Visibility is also interrupted and complicated by mirage, as travellers in the sun-baked deserts so often find to their embarrassment. In the south-western highlands, on the other hand, the atmosphere is often wonderfully clear and the landscape sharply defined for many miles, for instance during fine parts of the day in the summer rains and during rainless periods in the winter.

On the Red Sea fog is rather rare, occurring chiefly in winter in the northern half of the area and in summer in the southern half. In the Tihama coastal plain night fogs a few miles inland, where terrestrial radiation has freer play, are more common than off the coast on Kamarān island. On this island the chief cause of poor visibility is sand-haze, which occasionally contracts the range of vision to 550 yards on the visibility scale now in official use. Severe sandstorms, which generally occur between May and August in the afternoon, are described as advancing towards Kamarān island from the east like a huge brown sea-wave accompanied by high wind with thunder. They have been known to limit visibility to a few feet, as in an exceptionally bad nineteenth-century London fog. Dust-devils with light winds occur at all seasons.

During the SW. monsoon visibility on the coast of the Eastern Aden Protectorate becomes extremely poor, so that it has been known to be a danger to aircraft. A political officer, stationed in Mukalla during July and August, never realized the existence of a range of hills stretching to the sea between 20 and 30 miles west of the town; these are clearly visible during the remainder of the year.

More precise data on visibility are available for the Persian Gulf, where conditions appear to be similar to those of the Red Sea. On the Gulf poor visibility may be due either to early morning mist or fog, dust-haze, or salt-haze. From October to March morning mist with visibility less than one mile occurs a few times a month in calm anticyclonic weather, most commonly in December and January. Dust, however, is the most common cause of bad visibility, as on the Red Sea. During a dust-storm visibility may be only a quarter of a mile or less, and it remains poor long after the actual storm. Ordinary dust-haze reduces the visibility to between 2 and 6 miles; the following table indicates the monthly frequency.

Average Number of Days with Dust-haze in the Persian Gulf

J.	F.	M.	A.	M.	J.	J.	A.	S.	O.	N.	D.	Year
1	1	2	2	2	9	12	7	2	2	1	1	42

Dust-storms as well as dust-haze are most frequent in June and July, the fact being related to the strong NW. winds (*shamāl*) of mid-summer. At Basra the number is 7 in June and 10 in July, but on the shores of the Gulf the frequency is less. In winter dust-storms are infrequent but may occur either in association with thunderstorms or the passage of Mediterranean depressions. Another type of obscurity in the Persian Gulf is due to salt-haze. It is common in summer and may last for hours, reducing visibility to between 4 and 6 miles. Evidently haze of one kind or another is so prevalent on the Gulf during the terrible damp heat of summer that the sky, so far from being deep blue, must often look like brass.

RAINFALL

The fundamental reason why Arabia is a dry land is its domination by the trade-wind system, in which not only is the air moving southwards into warmer latitudes and so tending to dissipate cloud, but also more significantly because it is on the whole descending from higher atmospheric levels and so becoming compressed and dynamically warmed with like dissipation of cloud. Rain in appreciable quantity can only be produced by the ascent of air to higher levels where, on account of reduced barometric pressure, it undergoes adiabatic expansion and consequent cooling, with condensation of its moisture into cloud and rain. Rising air currents are associated with the circulation in cyclones, depressions, and fronts, with local instability resulting in sudden showers or storms, and with mountain barriers which obstruct the passage of the wind so that the air is forced

A 4836   N mechanically upwards. Rainfall, which is intensified by mountainous relief, known as orographic precipitation, plays a very important part in many countries, including the wetter parts of the British Isles. In Arabia itself the relatively heavy rains of both the Yemen in the south-west and 'Omān in the south-east are largely of this character.

Despite the general aridity there is probably no spot in Arabia which does not now and then receive a light shower or at long intervals a heavy storm. When these occur the steppes and deserts, except in limited areas where the white quartz sand may be chemically sterile, respond at once, especially in spring, with a luscious growth of herbage affording valuable pasture for camels, horses, and sheep. In almost any part of Arabia a sudden storm may convert a dry wadi-bed into a raging torrent, as in the arid parts of north Africa. More permanent results of the rainfall are seen in the network of rich green oases in Nejd, the fertile mountain-valleys of 'Omān, and above all in the valleys and tablelands of the Yemen. The importance of rain in the economy of the nomadic tribes is instanced in north Arabia by the fact that the beduin subdivide the winter rains according to the successive prevalence in the night sky of the stars Canopus, the Pleiades, Gemini, Sirius, and Arcturus (Appendix E, p. 603).

Around the coastline of Arabia the average annual quantity of rain, falling on from 10 to 30 days only, nowhere exceeds 5 inches, though it amounts to 7 inches at Massawa on the Eritrean shore. At the northern end of the Red Sea the amount sinks to barely 1 inch, as at Cairo, Suez, and Tor. In the interior of the peninsula there must be many areas at the lower levels where the mean annual rainfall is likewise insignificant, but it exceeds 5 inches over practically the whole of the high land in the south and west, also in the Syrian desert, which lies immediately in the track of many of the Mediterranean depressions, yielding a seasonal total of 25 inches to Jerusalem and 7 inches to Baghdad.

In the wettest parts of the south-western highlands the annual rainfall may be over 30 inches; north and north-east of Ta'izz, for instance, the south-western corner of the plateau, confronting the south-west monsoon, is estimated to receive 28–32 inches. San'ā, considerably farther north and some way east of the marginal ranges, on a plain rather below 8,000 feet, receives 15–16 inches annually; the period of variable 'little rains' extends from the end of February to the end of April, with a maximum in April; the much heavier 'great rains' approximately from the beginning of July to the end of September, with a maximum probably usually in August (though in 1883 Glaser recorded 6 inches in July against 4 in August); the rainstorms generally begin between 3 and 4 p.m. and continue till sunset. This relatively heavy rainfall, about equal to that of the driest parts of England, coupled with drenching mountain mists and dews, suffices to endow the highlands of south-west Arabia with great fertility; but in a latitude where evaporation is intense and where the demands of vegetation and irrigation on all available water are excessive, it does not suffice to send perennial streams down to the sea. (Photos. 107, 108.)

No part of the Hadhramaut appears to receive much over 8 inches annually. Its plateau is lower than the Yemen plateau and in the rain-shadow of the latter. The limestone formation increases the effective aridity; nevertheless the fall in temperature at night causes heavy dews, beneficial to the vegetation in the wadis. The Wadi Hadhramaut and its tributaries markedly affect the direction of the wind, so that, though the moisture may be derived from the south-west monsoon, much of the rainfall, in late summer at any rate, occurs when east winds form a cold front with the warm air-current (just as, in England, heavy rain often falls when dry surface-winds blow from the east, though the moisture is provided by south-west winds at a higher level). Sandstorms (*habūb*), of a different colour from those of the high Yemen plateau, often occur on summer afternoons in Wadi Hadhramaut.

The rainfall varies greatly in different parts of 'Omān. At Muscat, on the coast, the average deduced from a long record is about 4 inches, nearly all concentrated into the winter NE. monsoon season. In lowland districts of the interior the rainfall is probably even less, but in the high mountains there is a good rainfall and perhaps occasional snowfall; much of these mountains must receive at least from 5 to 10 inches, while some spots may (as stated above) receive even more than 20 inches. Yet in the Masandam peninsula the rain is never enough to support large villages; behind Daba, on the east coast, the Shihuh people can keep few animals besides goats on the hill-tops rising to over 5,000 feet; horses are unknown, donkeys few, and only few camels obtain sustenance from the acacia jungle in catchment folds of the hills. Again, in the Sifala district, SE. of Muscat, an almost total drought lasting ten years from 1920 caused the springs to dry up, with consequent death of date-palms in the oases, to such an extent that the wealthy owners of date-gardens emigrated. On the other hand, in Dhufār, within the arc of the Qara mountains, the SW.

monsoon brings rain sufficient in quantity and regularity to support fairly dense tropical forest and grassland (photos. 63, 124).

The essential difference between the high interior of the Yemen and the mountains of the 'Omān peninsula is that the former gets most of its rain in summer with the SW. monsoon, while the latter, being much farther north, have most of their rain in winter with the NE. monsoon. Torrential rains are thus liable to occur in mid-winter in the 'Omān ranges, and the snowfall may be considerable; but the effect of the summer SW. monsoon in 'Omān is weak, though thunderstorms may occur. In the high Yemen the total rainfall is more copious but the proportion of snow much smaller.

As a rough estimate, therefore, it would not be far wrong to put the mean annual rainfall of the whole of Arabia at about 7 or 8 inches. The rainfall, however, is in most parts exceedingly variable and erratic. Thus at Aden the annual totals have ranged from nil to 8 inches round an average of 2, and nearly the whole of this 2 inches may easily fall in a single storm. Similarly at Jidda the average quantity of rain is only 3 inches a year, but 4 inches fell in a single storm lasting 2½ hours in November 1931.

Taking the region as a whole, and especially the coasts, rain is more plentiful in winter than in summer. The Mediterranean depressions occasion fairly widespread winter rains in the northern half of the peninsula, and passing on to the Persian Gulf (where they are known as 'western depressions') bring considerable rainfall and snowfall to the mountains of 'Omān. The NE. monsoon (trade) augments the rainfall of 'Omān through orographic uplift and also produces slight rain of similar origin along the southern Arabian coast, as well as heavier precipitation in Socotra Island. The SE. or S. winds of the southern Red Sea bring a certain amount of orographic winter rain to the highlands of Eritrea.

The summer rains of Arabia, if less widespread than those of winter, are more concentrated. They affect most of the southern interior of the peninsula northward to about the latitude of Mecca, and are associated with the SW. monsoon system of winds, or occasionally with depressions spreading northward from the Arabian Sea, known as 'eastern depressions', which now and then develop into tropical cyclones. These summer rains, most pronounced in the Yemen, are usually ascribed to the SW. monsoon, but this is only partially correct. The wind charts for the month of July indicate a predominance of SW. wind in the Gulf of Aden,

W. wind in the straits of Bab al Mandeb, and NW. wind in the southern Red Sea, so that on the average the air currents converge upon the Yemen. The full current of the SW. monsoon certainly does not flow directly or persistently on to the Yemen mountains as it does on to the Western Ghats of India. If it did, the rainfall would be much heavier than occurs in the Yemen, and more like that in the neighbouring mountains of Ethiopia—which possibly prevent a certain amount of moisture from reaching south-west Arabia. Much of the moisture supplying the Yemen rains must come from the Red Sea rather than the Indian Ocean. But the moisture-laden winds, whether from off the Red Sea or the Gulf of Aden, on striking the outer mountain ramparts of the Yemen provoke copious condensation of mist and rain, whilst the residue of the moisture, passing to leeward, supplies the afternoon thunderstorms which account for practically all the rain falling on the elevated plateau upon which San'ā is situated. Thus the summer rains of south-west Arabia might be described as being as closely related to the currents which feed the SW. monsoon as to the SW. monsoon itself. They must be regarded as partly due to the very high relief of the land and partly to thunderstorm instability, the storms themselves being favoured by the small depressions which move in from the Red Sea. The fact that, as mentioned above, the air currents on the average converge on the Yemen is itself favourable to rainfall. By a curious anomaly the SW. monsoon occasions less of the scanty annual rainfall of the Aden coast than the NE. monsoon; so that the seasonal variation, if it counts for anything at all in a place where an erratic long-period average of 2 inches a year may be made up anyhow and anywhere, is opposite to that in the high Yemen. At infrequent intervals of years a wandering tropical cyclone may visit Aden during the summer with a few inches of rain, but nothing like the quantities—perhaps 20 to 30 inches in a couple of days—yielded by hurricanes in the West Indies, China Sea, and elsewhere.

A considerable proportion of Arabia's rainfall is contributed by thunderstorms. In summer 'Omān and especially the Yemen are foci of thunder and hailstorms of considerable intensity, which form almost daily among the mountains and of which a few may drift into the lowlands. In northern Arabia thunder is rare during the rainless summer months, but it often accompanies the winter rains, especially the cold fronts of Mediterranean depressions. In Palestine and Sinai severe and protracted hailstorms have occurred at this season in recent times—an interesting fact in the light of biblical testimony.

The hailstones are said to be large enough sometimes to kill young camels.

Snow falls fairly often in the interior of northern Arabia, at no great altitude. Thus in the Syrian desert it is said to fall every winter in large flakes if only in small quantity. In Sinai it often falls thickly on the mountains (photo. 109). In Palestine, with heavy winter rainfall, severe snowstorms occur every few years on the high plateau of Judaea, where snow 2 feet deep may lie in Jerusalem. In the northern Nafūd there is often only hoar-frost when snow is present in the Hamād, but much depends on the altitude of the country. At the beginning of February 1893 Nolde came in for a real fall of snow in the heart of Arabia near Hāil; a widespread covering of snow several inches deep gave to the Arabian landscape a truly wintry character, which the beduin maintained was exceptional and unseen for more than fifty years. But unless Arab weather memories are longer and more reliable than those of ordinary countrymen in England, their statements should not be taken too literally. No doubt the snowfall in question was unusually heavy, but it should be noted that even at Tāif, within the tropics and only some 3,000 feet above sea-level, snow is said to fall every four years, and every year on the neighbouring mountains. Farther south, in ʻAsīr, mountains from 6,000 to 8,000 feet high are said to hold snow more regularly than those of 12,000 feet on the other side of the Red Sea—in keeping with the more rigorous character of the Arabian winter previously described. On the Yemen mountains snowfall is limited by the fact that winter is the dry season, but it may cap the highest summits on the rare occasions when winter rain falls at Sanʻā. In the mountains of ʻOmān snowfall is heavier, partly because they lie farther north, but chiefly because winter is there the wet season.

Dew in Arabia is often copious enough to take the place of rain in the economy of vegetation. In the damp air along the Red Sea and Persian Gulf shores the dew on summer nights may be so drenching as to give in the mornings the appearance of rain having fallen. In the interior deserts the air is drier, but more vigorous nocturnal radiation cools the air to the dew-point, so that even there dewy nights are known, and in the more northern parts damp night fogs in late autumn are said to precede the winter rain. In the western ranges bordering the Yemen Tihama fog-drip is a most valuable source of atmospheric moisture, as it is available at all seasons at altitudes suitable for coffee cultivation.

SEA, SWELL, AND CURRENTS

The circulation of the sea and the motion of its surface in direction and speed are the product of tide, wind, density difference connected with temperature and salinity, and the configuration of the coastlines. As the subject belongs more to oceanography than to climatology it is referred to but briefly in this chapter, in connexion with the meteorological factors concerned, more particularly in the Red Sea.

There the tidal oscillation is relatively small and self-contained with little disturbance from the Indian Ocean, so that the currents flowing through the straits of Bab al Mandeb are in the main drift currents produced by the NE. and SW. monsoons in the Arabian Sea; but theoretically there must be a net inflow of water through the straits to make good the great loss of water by evaporation from the surface of the Red Sea, into which no rivers drain and upon which little rain falls. From October to March, the period of the NE. monsoon, the SE. winds in the Gulf of Aden and southern Red Sea sometimes drive the water northward at the rate of 20 to 30 miles a day, but often there is no current. During the period of the SW. monsoon, June to September, the water may be driven southward by the NW. winds in the Red Sea at a similar or greater speed, but sometimes in the northern part the set of the current is northward at a somewhat slower rate. Southward of the strait of Jubal there are many local and irregular currents caused by, and setting with, the prevailing winds. Strong currents, too, occasionally set right across the Red Sea and may be reversed within a few miles. All these irregularities, with further complications due to the numerous fringing coral reefs, render navigation difficult and dangerous to sailing-vessels but are of little concern to steamers. Violent land winds during the night and sea breezes by day may also cause local heavy swells and high waves.

In the Arabian Sea the currents are governed mainly by the monsoons. The monsoon currents, however, are not very steady, and though sets in directions corresponding to the prevailing monsoon are most frequent, they may be experienced in any direction. The currents are stronger and less variable during the SW. than during the NE. monsoon. Owing to the conformation of the coasts the effect of the SW. monsoon is to produce a clockwise circulation in a wide belt of water adjacent to the coasts, that of the NE. monsoon an anti-clockwise movement. The swell of the SW. monsoon rolls round Ras al Hadd and is felt off Muscat or even nearer the entrance to the Persian Gulf; at the strait of Hormuz a heavy swell without any wind preceding or following it usually portends a gale. In the Persian Gulf the sea is said to get up quickly, being 'short and hollow'. At the entrance, when the tidal stream is opposed by a heavy *shamāl*, the sea breaks very heavily, being out of all proportion to the force of the wind, but it quickly subsides.

  In the vicinity of tropical revolving storms, such as occasionally beset the Arabian Sea, abnormally strong currents may be encountered, which cannot be explained by the strength of the wind experienced on board. It is then particularly important not to forget the law according to which, in the northern hemisphere, currents set at 45° to the right of the wind direction. When a tropical cyclone approaches or crosses the coast there is liable to be a dangerous piling up of water against the shore.

REGIONAL CLIMATOLOGY

As will already have been gathered in the account of the separate meteorological elements, the hot, damp, enervating, and often malarious coastal lowlands of the Arabian peninsula are strongly differentiated from the cool, dry, and bracing highlands of the western interior. Here exhilarating tropical sunlight, invigorating winds, sharp changes of temperature, and now and then the tonic sight of frost and snow in mid-winter, if perhaps a little too drastic for weakly persons, would appear to have a splendid effect on the health of naturally robust constitutions. It has been claimed that the highlands of Nejd have a climate as healthy as any in the world.

The several parts of Arabia, both coastal and inland, vary greatly in climate, though records are not to hand in sufficient detail for them to be described, either according to the physical or political divisions of the area, without monotonous repetition of what has already been said. Therefore separate accounts of the climate of the various topographical divisions are not attempted, except in the case of the south-western highlands and that of the Sinai peninsula. For these two interesting regions, supplementary information is fortunately available.

The South-western Highlands

The kingdom of the Yemen enjoys a climate strongly differentiated from that prevailing in most parts of Arabia because it is everywhere, except on the coast, dominated by high mountains. These ramify

into the 'Asīr territory of the Sa'ūdi kingdom to the north, and into
the Aden Protectorate to the south, where they send a long high
spur eastwards towards the Hadhramaut, greatly to the alleviation
of heat and drought. The inner marginal range of the Yemen,
culminating in Jebel Hadhur Nebi Shu'aib, over 12,000 feet, is a
definite climatic divide between moist conditions on the steep western
slopes and a drier climate on the broad tableland sloping gently
eastward. But the intervention between the marginal range and the
Tihama of the coastal ranges and tumbled foothills, containing deep
luxuriant valleys and penetrated by ribbons of the Tihama, gives
the country a much more complicated orography, and the whole
kingdom falls into a number of distinctive climatic provinces which
may be briefly described.

Inwards from the coast, with its climate typical of the southern
Red Sea, the Tihama desert extends up to about 30 miles. Here falls
of rain are rare, but mist, drizzle, and clouds are less rare; while
with increasing distance from the sea the amount of dew increases
owing to stronger nocturnal cooling. During the fiery midday heat
turbulent wind eddies raising sand-spouts and dust-devils shroud the
whole Tihama in dust. As the mountains are approached rain
becomes more abundant so that the country begins to show cultivation. Agriculture does not, however, depend on sparse showers,
which may fall at any season, but on the summer rains in the mountains, which cause sudden spates in the dry valleys, providing water
for irrigation. The millet crop of the Tihama depends on this
flood water.

The 'mountain-Tihama', that is to say the region where inlets of
the coast plain wind into the coast ranges, is liable to short but heavy
afternoon thunder-showers. These may fall at long intervals, at any
season, but more frequently in March and April and again between
July and September, the seasons of the 'Little Rains' and 'Great
Rains' in high Abyssinia. The storms cause flooding in the wadis,
but only the largest rivers such as the Wadi Surdad and Wadi Siham
retain running water all the year (photo. 55). Irrigation is necessary in
the dry strips of the mountain-Tihama, but in some places the rains
alone suffice to bring the fields to harvest, and the wadis are bordered
by a strip of naturally fertile land.

The valleys of the coastal ranges and the western slopes of the
marginal range between 4,000 and 7,000 feet comprise the most
fertile country in all Arabia, with a flora and fauna characteristic of
the moist tropics and every kind of tropical produce. In the deep

valleys there form at night dense wet mists which, during the day, rise and cling to the mountains in tatters of cloud (photo. 111); moisture accruing from these hot steamy mists all through the year constitutes the principal condition for the successful cultivation of coffee. In addition there is a moderate rainfall from thunderstorms, which never fail between June and September. The lightning issuing from the storms hovering round the western ranges of the Yemen affords a fine spectacle from Kamarān island almost every summer evening. The higher parts of the marginal range, above 8,000 feet, are stormy, raw, and damp, being usually in the wet season shrouded in driving mist and rain. In summer thunderstorms are said to leave the summits white with hail for hours, whilst in winter every precipitation gives a canopy of true snow to the highest summits and of soft hail lower down, the latter phenomenon not requiring such cold conditions. According to Glaser inhabitants at the high levels in the winter of 1884–85 were marooned in their houses for eight days by snow a metre deep.

Thus the mountains of the Yemen succeed by various meteorological processes in extracting a good deal of the moisture contained in the vapour-laden atmosphere of the Red Sea shores, but it must be repeated (p. 181) that there is no really heavy monsoon rainfall from 50 to 100 inches and upwards, such as would inevitably fall if there existed between July and September a barometric gradient for strong and steady SW. winds.

The bulk of the orographic rain and cloud which shrouds the western declivities of the Yemen fails to surmount the crest, so that the plateau to the east has a much drier climate, reflected in a flora, fauna, and agriculture more akin to those of the temperate zone. Apart from the tropical sunshine the climate of the tableland, as represented by San'ā, may be called warm temperate, since the mean temperature varies between 59° in the coldest and 68° in the warmest month. Owing to the development of clouds and storms in summer the maximum temperatures appear rarely to exceed 90°, whereas 80° is quite common on sunny winter days. On the other hand, the winter nights can be very cold, and frosty spells occur every year. The temperature on the heights surrounding San'ā frequently falls well below the freezing-point, and even in the city a night minimum of 17° was recorded by Dr. Petrie in December 1937. Presumably the incidence of frosty nights is the determining factor in inducing apricots, figs, walnuts, and other trees to shed their leaves in winter, though drought may also be a contributory cause. Certainly the day-time warmth in winter is more than ample for the active growth of vegetation whose lower limit is generally placed at 42° F. Possibly the deciduous habit in these fruit-trees, which may have been imported from colder regions, will ultimately disappear after more complete acclimatization has taken place (photo. 261).

Ice is observed at San'ā on winter mornings more frequently than the occurrence of frost would appear to warrant, an anomaly due to the low pressure at nearly 8,000 feet, combined with the low humidity, which results in such rapid evaporation of water that its temperature can drop to the freezing-point when that of the air is several degrees above it. Similarly on the high tableland persons may shiver in a brisk wind with the thermometer at 90°, in consequence of the excessive evaporation of sweat, whereas down on the coast they would remain bathed in perspiration. At the altitude of San'ā the lowered temperature of the air greatly reduces the oppressiveness of the heat in the direct rays of the sun, as compared with places on the coast such as Hodeida, Aden, or Mukalla. But it should be noted that high up on the tableland the intrinsic intensity of the sunlight is, in consequence of the rarefied air, actually greater than at sea-level; therefore in any evaluation of the physiological and medical aspects of the climate of San'ā the effect of the strong actinic rays and other constituents of the sunshine, as well as of the low barometric pressure, would need to be considered.

On the plateau the rainfall is less than on the western crests of the Yemen, averaging about 15–20 inches a year, with considerable fluctuations. Though an occasional wet day may occur at any time of year, the bulk of the rainfall is in the form of showers and thunderstorms, occurring first towards the end of the period of the NE. monsoon in March and April, and again with much greater intensity during the period of the SW. monsoon between July and September. The correspondence with the 'Little' and 'Great Rains' of the Ethiopian highlands is fairly close, though the rain in the highlands of south-west Arabia is less in total amount and probably less regular. At San'ā the storms do not break every day, and when they do it is almost always in the afternoons after clear sunny mornings. They are brief but rather heavy, though the greatest amount of rain recorded by Glaser in any one storm during the summer of 1883 was only 2 inches—not very remarkable by the standard of European thunderstorms. The downpours often cause the wadi traversing the city of San'ā to overflow, and thick hail has been known to linger in shady spots all day.

It is of historic interest to note Ibn Battuta's account of the daily afternoon rainstorms at San'ā in A.D. 1330, when the rain drove people indoors and washed the paved streets. The accounts of damage by flood, frost, and earthquake given by the modern Arab historian 'Abd al Wasi' are probably exaggerated. Thus in A.D. 856 a flood from the high Bilad Senhan country, south-east of San'ā, is said to have destroyed 20,000 people, 400 houses, and 8 mosques.

During the heat of the day in the dry winter season local dusty whirlwinds drift about the San'ā plain, and in the rainy summer season large-scale sandstorms from the deserts of the interior, favoured by the conditions conducive to thunderstorms, sometimes shroud the country in a thick veil. In certain valleys of the highlands opening northward, hot dry winds from the south, of the *föhn* type, are known.

Dull skies and damp winds are naturally uncommon, though not unknown, on the dry sunny tableland of the Yemen. Splendid formations of thundery cumulus and cumulo-nimbus cloud are an almost daily phenomenon of the rainy season, whether the storms actually break or not. The rifted storm clouds, playing with all their intensity of light and shadow on black volcanic crags and tawny mountains much enhance the grandeur of the scenery.

Sinai Peninsula

Mainly an austere arid mountainous wilderness, very unlike the Yemen in many respects, Sinai yet resembles the south-west corner of the Arabian peninsula, in that its mountains, rising to 8,000 feet, differentiate the climatic conditions from those in the neighbouring parts of Egypt, Transjordan, and Midian, as well as from the coastal lowlands of Sinai itself. Apart from the meteorological record at Tor, systematic information about the weather and climate of Sinai is very meagre. Nevertheless that which is available from the interior of the peninsula derives special interest from the association of the region, actual or traditional, with the Exodus, and more generally from the fact that it forms part of that wider geographical arena whose landscape features are depicted in the Bible with so much vividness and poetical power.

During the rainless period between June and September, when steady northerly winds prevail, the higher plateaux, sun-baked though they be, are naturally more temperate, at any rate at night; but the heat in the lower basins and enclosed wadis is insupportable, and even in winter there are days of uncomfortably high temperature, with overpowering sunshine. The winter weather in the peninsula is variable and rigorous at the higher levels. While there are many days with northerly wind and brilliant sunshine (as in the Nile Valley), on other days the Mediterranean depressions, bringing rain on the coast, cause the wind to back temporarily westward with clouded sky. On these occasions the effect of the Sinai mountains is to cause an extension southwards of the coastal rainfall. Fierce bitter winds then often sweep across the tableland, with driving rain, and during the colder spells with E. winds the Sinai mountains share in the snowfalls of the highlands of Palestine. According to the monks at the convent of St. Catharine (5,000 ft.) in southern Sinai, snow was lying 3 feet deep on one day in February 1937, a scene reminiscent of February in the Scottish highlands. Much of the winter rainfall of Sinai comes in the form of sudden storms with thunder, lightning, and hail, often during the passage of the cold front of a depression, causing the wadis to fill and swell with such rapidity that it is notoriously dangerous for travellers to encamp in these channels. An important contributing factor in the generation of the sudden winter storms is the warming of the surface air by the powerful sunshine while the upper air remains very cold, giving rise to thermal instability with consequent convection. In summer, on the contrary, storms, as all over the Mediterranean area, are much less frequent, because the stable anticyclonic circulation with downward settling of the air currents, dispels any tendency to storm generation despite the tremendous heat. Frost of some intensity is common in winter in the higher mountains and is not entirely absent even near the sea. In general the eastern coastal plain on the Gulf of 'Aqaba is colder in winter than the western plain on the Red Sea, on account of exposure to the seasonal NE. monsoon. In autumn, and also especially in spring and early summer, occasional depressions form over lower Egypt, causing the wind over northern Arabia to draw into the south or south-east with intense heat. In Sinai these hot dusty *khamsin* winds are particularly dreaded, because their already high temperature is still further raised by the effects of descending the lee sides of the various mountain scarps. Hence when a *khamsin* spell occurs in May or June, the time of greatest frequency, the temperature soars far above 100° F. and numerous cases of heat prostration and some even of death ensue. As the barometer commences to fall on the approach of a *khamsin* the visibility is at first very clear, distances seem near and foreshortened, and the mountain ridges appear sharply outlined. Later the sky becomes mottled with clouds through which the sun shines with a lurid light, and at night haloes or coronae encircle the moon. The contours of the mountains then become blurred by the dust and sand raised by the wind, which blows in fiery puffs. The traveller is tormented by swarms of flies and by intense thirst in a temperature which may rise as high as 120° F., but only should he miss the water-holes is his plight necessarily perilous.

Meteorological observations for a whole year, September 1915 to 1916, were taken by Paul Range (who was attached to a German military post) at Hemme in the northern part of the peninsula (30° 18' N., 33° 33' E.), situated on the south-eastern slopes of the Jebel Moghara range at about 630 feet, some 75 miles south of the Mediterranean coast. During this period, which appears by comparison with longer periods in neighbouring regions to have been rather warmer as well as drier than usual, the mean temperature of the air was 65°, ranging from 50° in January to 82° in June, which was abnormally hot, being not only a little hotter than July but much hotter than August. The absolute extremes of temperature were 34° on nights in January and February (actual frost occurring at other places in the vicinity) and 115° on *khamsīn* days in May and June. Even higher temperatures are said to have occurred at Jericho and in the Dead Sea basin during a severe three-day *khamsīn* in the middle of May. The rainfall of the period was 87 millimetres (3·4 in.), none occurring between May and August. The wettest day, with over an inch of rain, was in late January, when snow fell on the mountains without, however, lying below 1,000 feet. The normal seasonal winter rainfall is estimated at 100 millimetres (4 in.), enough according to the beduin to ensure a modest harvest of common grain crops. Most of this scanty rainfall is in the form of showers with squally westerly winds, and the winter weather is often chilly, cloudy, and changeable. Dew was a common phenomenon at Hemme, and fog or mist often formed in hollows on calm clear nights in autumn and winter, indicating that the air in tropical or subtropical deserts holds plenty of vapour, while the aridity of the country is simply due to inadequate rainfall far in defect of evaporation. During the year in question at Hemme, the rainfall (3·4 in.) may be compared with an evaporation of 40 inches, more than ten times as great. September and October were pleasant months, while even during the heat of summer a sea-wind, except during a *khamsīn*, would spring up about midday, preventing the afternoon becoming hotter than the forenoon as it normally should.

The above is apparently the only instrumental weather record from the interior of Sinai, but there are a number of descriptive sketches from other parts of the peninsula. Thus Beadnell encountered a flood on the eastern margin of the Egma plateau in late November, illustrating the risk to which desert encampments are exposed in winter: 'a terrific thunderstorm raged from 5 p.m. until after midnight . . . it was touch and go for six hours, as although we had piled heavy cases and rocks on the tent-ropes, the ground speedily became so soft and waterlogged that the pegs would scarcely hold' (*The Wilderness of Sinai*, 1927, p. 113). 'Fortunately', he adds, 'storms in the desert are generally short-lived. When the sun comes out temporary discomforts are forgotten in appreciation of the abundant pools of the best water ever available, while the Arabs are filled with satisfaction at the contemplation of the fresh herbage which will spring up in a very short time.' The same writer, ascending Jebel Katherina on 11 March 1924, found little snow left, but passed many frozen rain-pools, and the early morning was keen and chilly.

Numerous references to weather and climate in association with the lavish if somewhat austere beauty of this wild and desolate region are given in Mrs. J. M. C. Jullien's book, *Once in Sinai*. One day early in 1937 the clouds which were still enveloping the summit of Jebel Serbal (6,792 ft.) after a violent rainstorm glowed fiery red like an immense furnace till the sun sank. In such a climate the red granite of the mountains in southern Sinai must often endow the landscape with intense, not to say, fierce colours.

'The lofty isolated position of Jebel Serbal makes its neighbourhood peculiarly liable to thunderstorms and unseasonable rainstorms, and to this fact as much as to the rivulet is due the outstanding fertility of the oasis lying in its shadow. The appearance of the mountain may even be embodied in its name, for according to Palmer the words Jebel Serbal mean the *mountain of the coat of mail*, and he adds that they are derived by a beautiful metaphor from the appearance of the smooth granite on its summit when clothed by rain with a sheet of glittering water.'

Another climatic picture from her book supplies just that touch of local colour which mere statistics can never give:

'There are no rivers, the mountains are bare rock; nature has carved only with frost and flood the watercourses which serve the Beduin as highways, and there are practically no others. The climate is wonderful: the air is dry and pure, and so invigorating that it fills the traveller with energy and takes the edge off every hardship. The winter, though short, is severe in the high country, while soon after April the heat becomes insupportable for the average European. A rare good fortune had landed me in Sinai in time for the brief and magical spring, when grass and flowers are conjured from every rock, when days are pleasantly warm and the nights not too cold, when winter floods are over and the wilderness wears such a serene and gracious aspect that to wander there for forty years were a not unwelcome condemnation.'

The changes of Arabian climate in past geological periods cannot be discussed in detail. There is little doubt that the peninsula was affected by pluvial periods accompanying glaciation in adjacent countries, particularly Abyssinia and east Africa. The great valley-systems of Arabia can hardly have been formed except under moister conditions than those prevailing at present, possibly during pluvial periods corresponding with those in east Africa. But desiccation within historical times has probably been only very gradual, for there is no evidence in history of a complete reversal from moist to arid conditions. Sinai is of peculiar interest in this connexion. The late Professor J. W. Gregory, in an article published in the *Geographical Journal* (1930), maintained that there are no grounds for the contention that the climate of Palestine in Biblical times was essentially different from that of the Holy Land to-day. It would be of considerable scientific interest to know, bearing in mind that the storms of Mount Sinai normally occur in winter, at what time of year the Law was given—when amid the thunder and lightning of the smoking mountain 'Moses drew near unto the thick darkness where God was'. (*Exodus* xx. 21.)

VEGETATION

THE flora of Arabia is not rich and, excepting the neighbourhood of Aden, has been the subject of comparatively few writings.

The geographical range of plants in Arabia is affected more by rainfall than by temperature. The rainfall is in its turn determined by the presence or absence of rain-bearing winds from the sea and the condensing effect of mountains and forests. The framework so established is then superimposed on a geographical pattern, which owes its origin to the geological history of the different parts of the peninsula.

The vegetation of Arabia and Socotra is considered under nine main headings: i. The coastal areas; ii. The dry central plateau; iii. Sinai; iv. The western escarpment; v. The Qara mountains;

111. *Mist rising at Menzil Sumara, north of Ibb, 8,000 feet,*
early morning in December

112. *Morning cloud clearing from the western face of Jebel Jihāf, over 7,000 feet,*
in September

113. *Dūm-palms (Hyphaene) and Suaeda on sandhills near the road between Sheikh 'Othman and Fuqum, Aden Colony*

114. *Grove of 'ilb (nebq) trees at 4,800 feet near Dhāla'*

vi. The mountains of 'Omān; vii. Socotra; viii. Flowerless land-plants; ix. Marine vegetation.

THE COASTAL AREAS

The Red Sea Coast is bordered by a narrow strip of low country between the sea and the western escarpment. This consists of an outer desert zone and an inner steppe zone. Some botanical collections have been made near 'Aqaba, Jidda, Al Qunfidha, Luheiya, and Hodeida by Forskål, Ehrenberg, Schimper, Hart, and Schweinfurth. The vegetation is similar to that of the opposite African coast. Hart states that at 'Aqaba *Cressa cretica*,[1] a herb with ash-grey hairy leaves and small white flowers, is a characteristic species along the shore or saline flats. In some places there is a close growth of the thistle-like *rattaf (Nitraria retusa)*, supposed by some to have been the lotus of the ancients, two oraches,[2] and a rush.[3] A wild rue[4] with a sickening and persistent smell is found in the wadis. The *dūm*-palm[5] reaches its northern limit here, also the *nebq* tree or *'ilb*; [6] henna,[7] date-palms, and tamarinds are cultivated. The characteristic trees in the wadis are *seyāl*[8] and a tamarisk called *tarfā*.[9] A kind of mistletoe,[10] dependent on the sunbird for the pollination of its crimson flowers, is parasitic on the *nebq*.

At a single locality on the coast of the northern Hejaz, an early botanical traveller, Bové, found three species of the indigo genus,[11] a spider-wort,[12] and a species of the jute genus.[13] Southwards the coast is lined with tamarisk. The town of Yenbo' is surrounded by a sandy plain where grows the arenaria-like *Robbairea prostrata*. Farther south, at Rābigh, occurs the white mangrove,[14] called *shūra* by the Arabs. This, about the size of an olive-tree, forms small woods in salt-marshes and on islands on the coast of the Red Sea from about the neighbourhood of Jidda southwards, including the Hanīsh and other islands. The trunks are sometimes partially submerged at high water; the short finger-like lateral roots grow straight up into the air; these specialized roots (pneumatophores) supply the subterranean parts of the trees with oxygen. The man-

---

[1] Convolvulaceae.
[2] *Atriplex leucocladum* and *A. Halimus*.
[3] *Juncus maritimus*.
[4] *Ruta tuberculata*.
[5] *Hyphaene thebaica*.
[6] *Zizyphus Spina-Christi*.
[7] *Lawsonia inermis*.
[8] *Acacia fasciculata*.
[9] *Tamarix gallica*.
[10] *Loranthus acaciae*.
[11] *Indigofera articulata* and *I. oblongifolia*.
[12] *Cleome brachycarpa*.
[13] *Corchorus Antichorus*
[14] *Avicennia marina*.

grove formation is well developed on parts of the coast of 'Asīr, and particularly about Luheiya (Yemen), where there is a belt of *shūra* 400 to 500 yards broad along the water's edge. At Hodeida itself mangroves are lacking, but on adjacent parts of the coast the white mangrove is joined by the red mangrove,[1] the only recorded locality for this species in Arabia; the seeds of the red mangrove germinate precociously while still attached to the parent plant, a fact which Forskål, when told by the Arabs, did not believe.

At some places on this coast, from the region of Jidda south to Aden, an almost leafless caper-shrub[2] resembling a miniature barbed-wire entanglement grows in the desert. The same caper is found with the *nebq* tree in the desert about Jidda. A small island opposite Al Qunfidha is entirely covered with *Suaeda*,[3] *dalūq* to the Arabs. The trunk of this plant is as thick as a man's arm and is used for firewood.

The coast near Hodeida is flat, with lagoons surrounded by swampy tussocks of *Aeluropus mucronatus* grass (photo. 90). Two kinds of dwarf palm are found on the shore. To the north of the town there is a sandy beach 200–300 yards wide, succeeded by small dunes with the grasses *Aeluropus* and *bokār*.[4] A little farther inland comes the *asal* zone where *Suaeda monoica* and *S. fruticosa* are dominant, the dark green succulent *Salsola foetida* and *S. Forskåli* very common, while the grasses are represented by species with sharp-pointed leaves.[5] On the landward side of this zone the *Salsola* disappears and the reddish-yellow sand is covered with silver-grey hummocks of *bokār* grass.

About Migaiet at Tānnem, some 14 miles north-east of Hodeida and 10 miles inland, the character of the desert changes. The leaf-less green-barked shrub, *markh*,[6] appears like bundles of rods; it becomes dominant farther inland. The spiny grasses[5] disappear and the *bokār* is interspersed with the other grasses.[7] *Ewāl*[8] and a blue-flowered acanthus with thistle-like leaves, called *shauk al ajūs*,[9] are characteristic. Elsewhere in the inner zone of the Tihama occur thickets or woods, composed of trees of the caper family,[10] with date-palms and screw-pine.[11]

---

[1] *Rhizophora mucronata.*   [2] *Capparis decidua.*
[3] *S. fruticosa.*   [4] *Panicum turgidum.*
[5] *Aeluropus mucronatus* and *Sporobolus pungens.*
[6] *Leptadenia pyrotechnica.*
[7] *Aristida coerulescens, Pennisetum dichotomum, Rottboellia hirsuta.*
[8] *Jatropha villosa.*   [9] *Blepharis edulis.*
[10] *Cadaba formosa* and *C. glandulosa.*   [11] *Pandanus tectorius.*

The wadis are marked by groups of flat-topped umbrella-like acacias, yellow-flowered[1] and white-flowered.[2]

The Southern Coast. The vegetation here is determined largely by the topography, coastal plains alternating with mountains falling sheer to the sea. The coconut palm occurs in a narrow area near the coast, from a point a little west of Aden to about the mouth of Wadi Maseila, and again along the whole coast of Dhufār (p. 205), where luxuriant groves are found; these are its limits in Arabia.

There is a particularly luxuriant growth of *dūm*-palms and *Suaeda* on the dunes near Hiswa, on the north shore of the bay of Aden, and *Suaeda* is also plentiful about Khormaksar, on the narrow sandy isthmus connecting Aden with the mainland.

Aden has been more thoroughly investigated botanically than any other part of the peninsula. Though it is remarkable for its lack of vegetation, 250 species have been recorded. The commonest plant is a large kind of mignonette[3] called *amhir* by the Arabs, and the most conspicuous a bushy green caper, *lasaf*;[4] next come a large herbaceous spider-wort[5] with golden-yellow flowers, and rusty-looking acacia bushes.[6]

A strange-looking euphorbia,[7] the *rummīd* of the Arabs, forms leafless intricately branched shrubs with pale green fleshy branches. The almost globular fleshy trunks, naked branches, and fragrant rosy flowers of the *ʿadan* bush[8] make it a conspicuous object on the crags about Aden and the ravines of Jebel Shamsan. This plant, which occurs also up to over 3,000 feet in the mountains of the Western Protectorate and the southern Yemen (photo. 116), is favoured by local gardeners. From the standpoint of plant-geography one of the most interesting plants of Aden is a species of the genus *Kissenia*, the only Old-World representative of the South American family Loasaceae; the species found in south-west Arabia occurs also in Somaliland, while a second species occurs in south-west Africa.

The long-thorned acacia, *samr*,[9] is the commonest tree in most of the Hadhramaut wadis, and in the drier wadis *nebq*[10] replaces the date-palm. Frankincense[11] grows in some of the smaller wadis; it was originally described from specimens from Rakhyūt, at the western end of the Dhufār coast, about 12 miles west of Ras Sājir.

---

[1] *A. Ehrenbergiana* and *A. orfota.*
[2] *A. arabica.*
[3] *Reseda amblycarpa.*
[4] *Capparis galeata.*
[5] *Cleome brachycarpa.*
[6] *Acacia Edgeworthii.*
[7] *Euphorbia Schimperi.*
[8] *Adenium arabicum.*
[9] *Acacia spirocarpa.*
[10] *Zizyphus Spina-Christi.*
[11] *Boswellia Carteri.*

In the Wadi Maseila, Wadi Hajr, and elsewhere grows a tree which is normally a constituent of mangrove formations on the coast, the *ariata*,[1] 50–70 feet high. *Ithil* (tamarisk)[2] and *rakh* are also found in the Wadi Maseila and elsewhere, especially in sandy places. The Wadi Hajr is remarkable as a perennial stream where there are high jungles of grass and slender palms of an unidentified species. Mangrove swamps have been reported by Bent from parts of the low coast near Dhufār, and by Miles as forming a dense mass, 30–40 feet high, on Mahut island, in the deep inlet of Ghubbat al Hashīsh ('the gulf of grass'), west of Masīra island, as well as in the estuary of the Kalbu river, draining into the head of that gulf; but the species has not been identified.

The barren elevated *jōls* of the Eastern Aden Protectorate, separated by deep wadis like cracks in the bottom of a sun-dried pond, and lying both north and south of the Wadi Hadhramaut, though hardly a 'coastal area', may be mentioned here. Little is recorded of such vegetation as the *jōls* support. Freya Stark has listed[3] *sabr* (a species of *Aloe* related to *A. rubroviolacea*) and other plants, *kardah*, *qurith*, *deni*, &c., not identified. Dragon's-blood trees (*Dracaena*), so characteristic of Socotra (p. 208), occur also on the mainland; one found at 1,200 feet in the hills near Dobeiba, Wadi Hadhramaut, is believed to be a different species[4] from that found in Socotra. Van der Meulen reported that a single dragon's-blood tree on the Eocene limestone at Kōr Seibān, north-west of Mukalla, was called *arab*; about Kōr Seibān *qaradh*[5] is the commonest tree.

The Eastern Coast. On the eastern side of the peninsula the central plateau slopes gradually down to the Persian Gulf and there is no considerable distinctive coastal area except the Bātina coastal plain, between the Hajar ranges and the east coast of 'Omān; this plain is 150 miles long and 12 to 30 miles wide. Besides a continuous line of date-gardens and other cultivation, acacias are frequent. The rocky basalt slopes near Muscat have a peculiar flora of the caper family,[6] also an ephedra-like leguminous plant,[7] and some annuals.[8] The turnsole (*tourne-sol*), a plant of the euphorbia family,[9] similar

---

[1] *Conocarpus erectus.*   [2] *Salvadora persica.*

[3] Freya Stark, *The Southern Gates of Arabia*, pp. 91, 92 (1936).

[4] *Dracaena serrulata.*   [5] *Acacia senegal.*

[6] Capparidaceae, including *Capparis elliptica* and *C. galeata*, also *Cleome brachycarpa*, *C. papillosa*, *C. droserifolia*.

[7] *Taverniera glabra.*

[8] A cruciferous plant, *Morettia parviflora*, and a plant, *Herniaria maskatensis*, related to the British rupture-wort.   [9] *Chrozophora oblongifolia.*

115. *Avenue of Terminalia trees on road north of Lahej in November. Altitude 600 feet*

116. *A small Adenium arabicum bush in flower close to the Tiban river, altitude 3,800 feet, October. Western Aden Protectorate*

117. *Camels grazing near Madāin Sālih*

118. *A halt in the Dahana*

to the kind formerly much used in England for colouring jellies and confectionery, is found on the driest hills.

To the north of 'Omān the coast is low, flat, and sandy, with scanty vegetation. A representative of the lily family,[1] with yellow star-like flowers and leaves like bundles of wire, is common near Kuweit, as is a campion[2] with white flowers. Mangroves were recorded by Theophrastus to have been seen in 324–323 B.C. by the soldiers of Alexander the Great on Bahrein island, where they are not found now.

The pebbly plots called *hazm* (plural *huzum*) have a peculiar flora, including a cruciferous plant, *kulkulān*[3] and a small poppy with purple-black flowers.[4]

In swamps *haram*,[5] an almost leafless plant, is the commonest species; *artā*[6] is also found. These belong respectively to the families Chenopodiaceae (goosefoots) and Polygonaceae (knot-grass, &c.).

THE CENTRAL PLATEAU

The central plateau of Arabia slopes from the western escarpment towards the east. It may be subdivided into four regions: 1. The stony desert of the Hamād; 2. The red desert of Nafūd; 3. The rocky area of Central Nejd; 4. The sandy Rub' al Khali.

1. The *Hamād* is usually absolutely level and almost bare of vegetation, a flat black expanse of gravelly soil with small round pebbles. Here and there are depressions with fine deposits of salt in which water accumulates after rain. These are surrounded by zones of vegetation.[7] In depressions *shih*,[8] *rūte*,[9] and *sha'rān*[10] are characteristic; sometimes *jirjīr*,[11] woad,[12] *m'harūt*,[13] are also present. The roots of *m'harūt* grow 16 to 24 inches long and 9 inches in diameter; they are edible and may be baked like beans.

The stony plains have an annual vegetation which springs up after

---

[1] *Gagea* sp. [2] *Silene tenuis.* [3] *Savignya aegyptiaca.*
[4] Probably a variety of *Papaver hybridum.*
[5] *Haloxylon recurvum.* [6] *Calligonum comosum.*
[7] These zones of vegetation may contain a cranesbill, *dhama* (*Erodium laciniatum*), a rockrose, *rukrūk* (*Helianthemum* sp.); *ummu rueis* (*Scabiosa palaestina*); *wubēra* (*Scabiosa Olivieri*); *zneima* (*Ifloga spicata*); *sa'ēd* (*Iris Sisyrinchium*); *sneisle* (*Bupleurum semicompositum*); *shiqāra* (*Erucaria aegiceras*); *sam'* (*Stipa tortilis*); *qaf'a* (various species of *Astragalus*); *krēta* (species of *Plantago*); *kamsha* (*Paracaryum arabicum*); *nefel* (various species of *Trigonella*); *niqd* (*Asteriscus graveolens*).
[8] *Artemisia herba-alba.* [9] *Salsola lancifolia.*
[10] *Suaeda.* [11] *Senecio coronopifolius.*
[12] *Isatis microcarpa.* [13] *Scorodosma arabica.*

rain and quickly withers. *Samh*,[1] a fleshy annual from whose seeds a substitute for flour is made, is seasonally abundant.

The Wadi Sirhan (p. 39) is a broad depression which has some water at all seasons and marshy spots with thickets of tamarisk (*tarfā*). Poplars (*gharab, rurab*) grow beside the main channel and thistle-like *msa*,[2] with its red edible fruits.

2. *The Nafūd* (pp. 41–42) is a sandy desert with many dunes which stand up from 300 to 500 feet above the level of the desert. The most frequent characteristic of the larger species is a member of the goose-foot family,[3] the *ghadha*,[4] specially abundant on the southern slopes of the Nafūd; it is a large shrub, or sometimes a small tree up to 25 feet, with clean white bark and green needle-like jointed twigs.

A curious parasite with a long red juicy spike of flowers[5] grows on the roots of the *ghadha*. Known to the Arabs as *tarthūth* or by the indecent name *zubb al ardh*, it is the favoured food of the oryx.

After the spring rains the pasture of the Nafūd is richer than that of other parts of the desert. A tall grass called *nasī*[6] grows in some quantity, and there are stretches of bare sand. *Qordhi* (*korzi*),[7] a shrubby umbelliferous plant with finely divided leaves, thrives only on sandy tracts supplied with ground water (p. 28).

3. *Central Nejd* consists of eroded rocky country intersected with wadis. The characteristic trees of the latter are tamarisks, both *ithil* (more than one species) and *tarfā*,[8] also in some places *talh* (*Acacia Seyal*), *salīm* (*Acacia flava* and possibly other species), *sarh* or *sarha*,[9] and *bēn*.[10] This tree, from which ben-oil is made in other parts of the East, also has the Arabic name *yesar* in parts of eastern Arabia, while the pod is called *zubb al bēn* and the seed *habb al bēn*. *Rakh*[11] appears in the more sandy places. After the level plain of the Kuweit coast low flat-topped sandstone hills begin in the Summān district. A scabious,[12] a glasswort,[13] and a composite[14] have been found here. The common brushwood is *'Arfaj*,[15] a low woody plant with daisy-like flowers, the club-shaped root of which is easily dragged from the ground. *'Arfaj* is not found in the Tuweiq hills south of Wadi Dawāsir.

---

[1] *Mesembryanthemum Forskahlei.*
[2] *Nitraria retusa*, called *rattaf* and *gharqad* in some districts.
[3] *Chenopodiaceae.*   [4] *Haloxylon persicum.*   [5] *Cynomorium coccineum.*
[6] *Aristida Forskahlei.*   [7] *Deverra chlorantha.*
[8] *Tamarix mannifera.*   [9] *Cotoneaster nummularia.*
[10] *Moringa peregrina.*   [11] *Salvadora persica.*
[12] *Scabiosa palaestina.*   [13] *Salicornia fruticosa.*
[14] *Anvillea Garcini.*
[15] *Rhanterium epapposum*, but *'arfaj* is also the name of another plant.

In the Dahana vegetation is like that of the Nafūd. *Artā*, the representative of the knot-grass family already mentioned (*Calligonum comosum*, family Polygonaceae), is abundant. About Riyādh tamarisk[1] is abundant and a labiate[2] is plentiful in hollows, where a small iris[3] also occurs.

Oases, such as that of Hofūf, produce a sedge,[4] reeds,[5] grass,[6] rushes,[7] even the maidenhair fern,[8] and water ferns.[9]

Samh[10] covers the stony plains of northern Nejd and is a valuable food plant; a second species, called *da‘a*,[11] is used in the same way. The characteristic tree is *talh*.[12] Copses of dwarf willow (*ghāf*) occur in places, as in the upper Wadi Hanīfa north-west of Riyādh.[13]

4. *The Rub‘ al Khali*, covering an area ten times that of England and Wales, is entirely devoid of trees, and the vegetation consists of extensive areas dotted with the polygonaceous shrub,[14] known as *abal* in this part of Arabia (but *artā* elsewhere), and sharply defined belts of the chenopodiaceous shrub known locally as *hādh*.[15] There are stretches of bare sand called *hamra* and minor zones of the sedge *birkan*[16] and a grass called *qasla*. After rain the sedge *andab*[17] is the first green thing to appear, then *abal*[18] and later *alqa*,[19] the *birkan* mentioned above, and the *zahr*,[20] a pretty yellow-flowered plant of the genus called 'caltrops' from the resemblance of the sharp-spined seed-vessels to the military instruments formerly used to impede cavalry.

From south to north there are belts of *abal*, with *birkan*, and *zahr*, *hādh*, and *ghadha*.[21] But *ghadha* areas are not as common as in the Nafūd; the plant is, however, found to the south of the Qatar peninsula, accompanied by *tarthūth*[22] (photo. 53).

On the eastern fringe euphorbias, several species of acacia, tamarisk, and dwarf palms[23] are present. In the north, in the district of the 'jaubs' (plural *al Jibān*, the estuaries), there are areas of *haram*[24] and *shinān*,[25] which are even more salt-loving than *hādh*.

[1] *Tamarix articulata.* [2] *Teucrium Oliverianum.*
[3] *Iris Sisyrhynchium.* [4] *Fimbristylis*, a species near *F. ferruginea.*
[5] *Phragmites communis.* [6] *Dactyloctenium aegyptiacum.*
[7] *Juncus acutus.* [8] *Adiantum Capillus-Veneris.*
[9] *Ceratopteris thalictroides.* [10] *Mesembryanthemum Forskahlei.*
[11] *Mesembryanthemum nodiflorum.* [12] *Acacia Seyal.*
[13] Philby, *Arabia of the Wahhabis*, 1928, p. 69; both dwarf willows and dwarf poplars are said to be called *ghāf*. [14] *Calligonum comosum.*
[15] *Cornulacea monacantha.* [16] *Fagonia glutinosa.*
[17] *Cyperus conglomeratus.* [18] *Calligonum.* [19] *Dipterygium glaucum.*
[20] *Tribulus macropterus*, Zygophyllaceae. [21] *Haloxylon persicum.*
[22] *Cynomorium coccineum.* [23] Probably a species of *Nannorhops.*
[24] *Haloxylon recurvum.* [25] *Arthrocnemum glaucum.*

SINAI

The flora of the Sinai peninsula has been carefully investigated and thirty-six species, out of a total of nearly a thousand, are known only from this area. These include a delphinium,[1] a St. John's wort,[2] and a mullein.[3]

The desert merges with the sand-dunes on the north coast and presents the usual type of desert flora found from Sind to the Sahara. Some 300 species have been found in the desert area, and this number includes only five trees, the date-palm, a wild fig,[4] and three different tamarisks.[5]

The broom-like *retam*,[6] a shrub with white flowers having a purple calyx and smelling like the flowers of the English bean, is characteristic of the Tih desert; it is the *rothem* of the Hebrew Bible, mistranslated 'juniper' in the English Authorized Version (*1 Kings* xix. 4, 5; *Psalm* cxx. 4; *Job* xxx. 4), though the Revised Version gives 'broom' as a marginal alternative for the first two and uses that word in the text for the third. In the wadis of the Tih grows *rattaf*,[7] a prickly shrub with scarlet fruits and fleshy leaves, also called *gharqad*. A Mediterranean element in the vegetation of the low hills of the Tih is represented by a small bulbous plant with yellow squill-like flowers,[8] a convolvulus,[9] a globularia,[10] and other species.

The south coast is rather wetter and there is a southern element in the flora, represented by two acacias,[11] the *bēn*,[12] *nebq*,[13] and spiny trees of *zukkum*.[14] The *dūm*-palm[15] and a tree related to (though outwardly unlike) the European lime,[16] as well as large clumps of *rakh*,[17] are found on the shores of the Gulf of 'Aqaba.

The upper slopes of Mount Sinai are characterized by plants of north temperate aspect, resembling for example the flora of northern Persia. Most of the species which are only known from Sinai are restricted to these higher altitudes. They include a pink,[18] a primula,[19] and other species.[20]

[1] *Delphinium deserti.*　　[2] *Hypericum sinaicum.*　　[3] *Verbascum Schimperianum.*
[4] *Ficus pseudosycomorus.*　　[5] *Tamarix macrocarpa, T. aphylla, T. mannifera.*
[6] *Retama roetam.*　　[7] *Nitraria retusa.*　　[8] *Gagea fibrosa.*
[9] *Convolvulus oleifolius.*　　[10] *Globularia arabica.*　　[11] *Acacia tortilis* and *A. Seyal.*
[12] *Moringa peregrina.*　　[13] *Zizyphus Spina-Christi.*　　[14] *Balanites aegyptiaca.*
[15] *Hyphaene thebaica.*　　[16] *Grewia tenax.*　　[17] *Salvadora persica.*
[18] *Dianthus sinaicus.*　　　　　　　[19] *Primula Boveana.*
[20] *Buffonia multiceps*; the campions *Silene leucophylla* and *S. Schimperiana*; the vetch-like plants *Astragalus Fresenii* and *A. Kneuckeri*; the umbelliferous plant, *Ferula sinaica*; *Thymus decussatus*; the labiates *Nepeta septemcrenata* and *Ballota Kaiseri;* the scrophulariaceous plant *Anarrhinum pubescens*; the plantain *Plantago arabica*; and *Pyrethrum santaloides.*

Of the vegetation associated with the wanderings of the Israelites, the *rattaf* has been suggested as the plant used by Moses to sweeten the bitter Waters of Marah[1] (identified with 'Ain al Hawara, near the west coast about 40 miles south of 'Ayūn Musa). The traditional identification of the bush which 'burned with fire . . . and was not consumed',[2] made probably by anchorites living in Sinai about the third century, is with a bramble,[3] which is not inconsistent with the etymology of the Hebrew word used;[4] there is no evidence to support suggested identifications with either a hawthorn (*Crataegus*) or an acacia, while, although the species of *Dictamnus* (dittany or candle-plant) secrete a volatile and inflammable ethereal oil, so that the air round the plant is sometimes ignited on hot calm days, these do not occur in Sinai. The origin of the Israelitish *manna* has long been disputed, but the name is now applied by the Arabs to the gummy exudation of a tamarisk[5] caused by the punctures made by a scale-insect or coccid. Two coccids[6] are said to be concerned.

THE WESTERN ESCARPMENT

The flora of the western escarpment, and particularly of the high south-western mountains, is the richest in Arabia. Just as roughly half the human population is crowded into the south-western corner of the peninsula, so the south-western highlands, with their perennial streams and several distinct types of climate, have a number and diversity of species of plants disproportionate to that of the peninsula as a whole.

Where the steep slopes catch the monsoon rains, narrow bands of fringing-forest follow the mountain rivers in their steep descent, forming a zone of tropical vegetation akin to the forests on the African side of the Red Sea. In places, e.g. in the hot valleys of the Yemen such as that about Madinat al Abīd, *c.* 4,000 feet, very large wild figs[7] and leguminous trees form patches of forest. A tree[8] of the same family as mahogany is characteristic. In some wadis at from 2,000 to 3,000 feet tamarisks reach the size of tall forest trees, though reckless felling often allows few to survive. Beside streams, at 2,000–5,000 feet, occur dense clumps of a dwarf date-palm,[9] and low scrub of grey-foliaged bushes of wild indigo (*Indigofera*) (photos. 119, 120).

[1] *Exodus* xv. 25. [2] *Exodus* iii. 2.
[3] *Rubus sanctus.* [4] Löw, *Flora der Juden*, iii, p. 183.
[5] *Tamarix mannifera.* [6] *Trabutina mannipara* and *Naiococcus serpentinus* var. *minor.* [7] *Ficus salicifolia* and *F. populifolia.*
[8] *Trichilia emetica.* [9] *Phoenix reclinata* according to Rathjens and Wissman, possibly identical with *P. abyssinica.*

On the higher slopes are found purple, lily-like amaryllids,[1] and many flowering bushes and herbs; among these, members of the acanthus family are conspicuous, notably low, sometimes prickly, *Barleria*-bushes, with blue, lilac, or peach-yellow trumpet-shaped blossoms, brick-red and yellow *Justicias*, violet-blue *Ruellias*, rose-coloured *Crossandras*, and purple-lipped *Anisotes*, not to mention prickly-leaved branching bushes of acanthus itself[2] (photo. 121).

In the south-western highlands, above 7,000 feet, the flora becomes less numerous in species, but extremely interesting. In 'Asīr, for example, near Suda north of Abhā, a dense forest of junipers and other trees extends down the steeper mountain-slopes from above 9,000 to 7,500 feet; small bush-junipers grow at nearly 10,000 feet on Jebel Jalal, south of San'ā, and scattered trees on Jebel Sabir, above Ta'izz. The high mountains of the Yemen have plants recalling those of Europe, such as a buttercup,[3] while a primula[4] with tiers of golden-yellow flowers brightens the edges of springs and small waterfalls.

In the broken rocky mountain-spurs some real 'alpines' occur, including a rock-pink,[5] a creeping plant of the gentian family with purple-tinged white flowers,[6] and a blue-flowered creeping campanula[7] with succulent edible roots (related to the rampion, cultivated for the same purpose in Europe). A white iris[8] grows in patches up to 8,000 feet; the Arab custom of planting it on graves may account for its wide distribution from Spain and Barbary along the Mediterranean and down to the south-west Arabian highlands.

Some plants found in the Yemen, from considerably below to above 7,000 feet, are also characteristic of the Abyssinian highlands, e.g. a trailing clematis with small white flowers[9] and a white wild rose.[10] A widespread African buddleia[11] with orange spikes of scented blossoms is lopped into the form of small trees. White jasmine,[12] trailing over rocks and the stone terraces of fields, is found up to nearly 10,000 feet. Low woody bushes with white daisy-like flower-heads[13] grow on rocky ground at the same high elevation. A low-growing scarlet hibiscus[14] ranges in altitude over several thousand feet up to 7,000. Clumps of vernonia, with knapweed-like heads of

---

[1] *Haemanthus.*
[2] *Acanthus racemosus.*
[3] *Ranunculus multifidus.*
[4] *Primula verticillata.*
[5] *Dianthus uniflorus.*
[6] *Swertia polynectaria.*
[7] *Campanula edulis.*
[8] *Iris florentina*, also called *I. albicans.*
[9] *Clematis simensis.*
[10] *Rosa abyssinica.*
[11] *Buddleia polystachya.*
[12] *Jasminum officinale.*
[13] *Antithrixia abyssinica* and species of *Phagnalon.*
[14] *Hibiscus meidiensis.*

vivid magenta, colour steep rocky slopes. In moist clefts of the south-western mountains are nearly a dozen species of ferns (photo. 24) including two maidenhairs, also a horsetail[1] and a selaginella;[2] most of these are widespread in Africa and the east, some are restricted to Abyssinia and south-west Arabia. The Red Sea, however, is to some extent a barrier, for some plants found in India and the Yemen, such as the genera *Iris* and *Dianthus* and the dodder-like *Cassytha filiformis*, do not occur in Africa, while the giant lobelias of the African mountains, though extending north to Eritrea, are not found in the Yemen.

Among the richly represented euphorbia family, the prickly suc-culent cactus-like forms are specially characteristic of south Arabia and distinct from those of Africa. Every type of climate has its particular endemic species. Miles of stony rolling plateau in the middle altitudes are covered with a dense growth of several species, mostly 3–4 feet high, some taller. The candelabra-like tree-euphorbia or *'amaq*,[3] 10–12 feet high and growing at altitudes up to 7,000 feet, is planted round enclosures (photo. 122). On stony steppes at 9,000 feet or more a low compact pincushion-like species,[4] exuding when torn a latex dangerously caustic to the skin, may be found beside a plant of the asclepiad family (a species of *Stapelia*) with stems like grotesque fleshy fingers a few inches high.

Towards the east of the escarpment, as the rainfall lessens, plants characteristic of the dry Mediterranean lands appear: for example the resurrection plant or *kaf maryam*,[5] a cruciferous plant in which, in the dry season, the leaves fall, the branches fold inwards, the roots are loosened from the ground, and the plant is blown like a wicker ball before the wind, with pods closed until a wet spot is reached; also a blue-flowered, almost stalkless, wild chicory,[6] which forms dense tufts in short turf. Acacias,[7] tamarisks, and willows appear as the rocky steppes of central Arabia are approached.

The coffee- and *qāt*-trees, restricted to the south-western highlands, are discussed in the chapter on Agriculture (pp. 490–493).

Frankincense, Myrrh. Since the principal source of frankincense in Arabia is Dhufār, this product is discussed under the Qara moun-tains (p. 205).

The areas yielding myrrh are mainly parts of 'Asīr, the Yemen,

[1] *Equisetum ramosissimum.*
[2] *Selaginella yemensis.*
[3] *Euphorbia Ammak.*
[4] *Euphorbia officinalis.*
[5] *Anastatica hierochuntica.*
[6] *Cichorium Bottae.*
[7] *Acacia abyssinica.*

and the Western Aden Protectorate. Myrrh (see also Chapter IX, p. 532) is one of a group of 'oleo-gum-resins', of which the constituents are a volatile oil, a gum (soluble in water), and a resin (not soluble in water). It is produced by stunted trees or shrubs of the genus *Commiphora*, belonging (like *Boswellia*, the source of frankincense) to the family Burseraceae. Much confusion exists, and the various forms of the product have still not been exactly correlated with the trees which yield them; the names 'myrrh' and 'bdellium' are often used without precision.

The resins exploited commercially are now mainly brought from Somaliland, but over fifty years ago 'myrrh' was collected in Fadhli territory, north-east of Aden, particularly in Jebel al 'Urūs and Jebel an Nakhai; the abundant trees, identified as *Commiphora simplicifolia*, were called locally *qafal*, a name used for more than one species and best known in connexion with the *qafal* wood exported to Egypt and sold in the Cairo bazaars. Apparently myrrh is no longer collected in Fadhli country. Records of nearly sixty years ago, and others a little over ten years old, point to parts of 'Asīr and the northern Yemen, all at high elevations, as the most important centres of resin-collection. Deflers mentioned Suda, over 50 miles north-north-west of San'ā, as an important centre, adding that small cups (*finjān*) were placed below incisions in the trees; Rathjens and Wissman mention Hajja, some 25 miles south-west of Suda.

Commiphora-trees of various species are an important element in the vegetation in several parts of the south-western highlands at intermediate altitudes; in the Haraz district, for instance, between Hajeila and Manākha, they form a scrub, bare in winter. A species of *Commiphora*, known to the Arabs as *qataf*, yields a resin said by Forskål to have been used by Yemeni women for cleansing the hair, while the same writer also mentioned *qafal* resin as a purgative.

The balsam-tree (*Commiphora opobalsamum*)[1] is the source of an oleo-resin called 'balsam of Mecca' or 'balm of Gilead', and apparently also of the resin called 'Hadhramaut myrrh' or *meetiya* (p. 533). Living trees of various species of *Commiphora* were among the plants brought to Egypt by the expedition of Queen Hatshepsut (*c.* 1600 B.C.). The balsam-tree was also cultivated in Egypt and Palestine, whence it was described by medieval pilgrims,[2] from whom the fourteenth-

---

[1] Arabic *bisām* (root of Greek *balsamon*), or *abu shamm* ('father of perfume').
[2] e.g. Burchard of Mount Sion (1283) and Ludolph von Suchem (1336–1341), *Palestine Pilgrims*, xii, pp. 62, 68 (1897).

119. *A giant tamarisk in the Wadi Jaira, c. 3,000 feet, March 1938*

120. *Dwarf wild date-palms (Phoenix reclinata) in the Wadi Ghailama, c. 2,200 feet, March 1938*

121. *A prickly Barleria bush in flower on Jebel Jihāf, c. 7,000 feet, September*

122. *Tree-Euphorbias (E. Ammak) growing on a rocky hill between Ibb and Makhadar, c. 5,000 feet, January*

123. *Euphorbia officinalis growing at c. 9,000 feet north of Ṣanʻā*

124. *Vegetation in the Wadi Nihaz, Qara mountains*

century account in the travels under the name 'Sir John Mandeville' was derived.

One species of *Commiphora* is restricted to the Qara mountains (Dhufār), and another member of this large genus grows in Socotra.

THE QARA MOUNTAINS (DHUFĀR)

The mountains, about 8 miles wide, are a belt of Upper Cretaceous and Eocene limestone rising to 3,000 feet. On their seaward face thick forests of deciduous trees, comparable in size with those of an English wood, wild figs, giant creepers, and others, adorn the valley slopes. Above are rolling yellow meadows of long grass, grazed by herds of cattle. The 'Indian' south-west monsoon reaches this area and drizzling rain falls in these mountains during the summer months. The groves of coconut-palms on the coast have been mentioned (p. 195). (Photos. 63, 124.)

At about 500 feet a libaniferous (resin-bearing) tree, *mulukh*, is found in the wadis; its resin is said to exude naturally from the branches and to be 'edible', possibly in the sense of a chewing-gum. On the lower slopes of the mountains from 600 to 1,000 feet grow the following: *mushta, thamar, la'ilāub, al khaimur, mughalīf, hurāum, mitān* (a heavy wood, said not to float), *subāra*, and *klafaut*.

The vegetation of the montane zone, from 2,750 to 3,000 feet, includes *tishgaut*, a low bushy gum-bearing tree growing on the watershed, the gum of which is flattened into cakes and sometimes exported; also trees called *tikidauhaut, laifīt, zurfit, ra'i zintiraut, gushar, qarhahaur*, and *dhubdhubaut*.

Frankincense. All the frankincense in the world is produced in south Arabia and Somaliland. The Qara mountains, the largest district in Arabia yielding this resin, produce the best quality. A smaller area exists in the province of Hajr (p. 224), in the Eastern Aden Protectorate; here the trees still flourish in little dry secluded valleys opening off the Wadi Hajr, and the right of collecting the resin is rented to Somalis, who cross from Africa for this purpose.

From a botanical standpoint the subject is less complicated than that of myrrh (p. 203) because, though the south Arabians distinguish several kinds of frankincense, all collected in Arabia is derived from the same species, *Boswellia Carteri*, a member of the same order, Burseraceae, as the myrrh-producing plants. It is a stunted tree or, as the trunk is divided, strictly a large shrub, with leaves like those of the ash, but stiff and hairy, and small green flowers. In tapping, which is done between March and August, an incision is made and a narrow strip of bark removed below the cut; from 3 to 7 days are allowed, according to the weather, for the milky juice to dry, and, if the sun is not hot enough, the resin has to finish drying on the ground. Dhufār is said to be the only region where two yields of resin are still collected each year, as when in Pliny's time the white 'summer' resin and the red 'spring' resin were differentiated.

The resin is exported from the small ports of the Mahra and Dhufār coast—from west to east, Qishn, Al Gheidha, Jadhib, Rakhyūt, Rīsūt, 'Auqad, Salāla, Hāfa, Tāqa, Marbāt, Sudh, and Hadhbaram—to Aden, where it is sorted and graded by women working in sheds. The best quality is exported from Marbāt and Hadhbaram; that from Qishn is considered inferior. Arab traders call the best Hoja'i; inferior qualities, usually from near the coast, are Shihri, Samhali, and Rasmi.

The inhabitants of the Qara mountains, using different names, recognize three kinds of resin produced by the *mughur* (frankincense tree). In descending quality they are (i) *negedi (nedji) mughur*, from trees on the wadi slopes of the landward side of the mountains, between 2,000 and 2,500 feet; (ii) *shazari mughur*, from the mountain-region of that name, at the junction of the western end of the Qara mountains with Jebel Qamr, and (iii) *sha'abi mughur*, a poor quality from the coastal plain about Rīsūt. The Qarāwi herdsmen who own the mountain-groves rent the collecting of the resin to Kathīri and other tribesmen.

In Somaliland the same tree, called *mohor*, produces resin like false amber with a pinkish tinge, while other species of *Boswellia* yield similar resins, e.g. the *yehar* tree (*B. Frereana*) yielding *loban maidi*, a pale topaz-yellow substance.

Colour and size determine the value of frankincense, which may vary from £80 to £10 a ton. As examples of quantity, in the five years 1929–34 amounts totalling 1,547 tons (value 430,907 rupees or £32,318) were imported into Aden from ports on the coast of the Eastern Aden Protectorate and Dhufār; the amounts varied from 130 tons (value 26,125 rupees or £1,959) in 1932–3 to 525 tons (value 150,435 rupees or £11,283) in 1930–1.[1] Besides these exports from the south Arabian coast, British and (former) Italian Somaliland contribute somewhat smaller totals. Much of the 'incense' now used, however, contains no frankincense; its composition varies, but the chief ingredients are usually gum-benzoin and sandal-wood.[2]

---

[1] W. H. Ingrams, *Report on the Hadhramaut*, pp. 72, 73 (1937).
[2] C. J. S. Thompson, *The Mystery and Lure of Perfume*, p. 58 (1927).

The long history of frankincense, like that of myrrh, cannot be fully discussed here.[1] Probably some of the supposed allusions to it by ancient writers refer really to mastic, the gum of the lentisc (*Pistacia lentiscus*). The first European recorded to have seen the Arabian frankincense tree was Androsthenes, who was sent (324–323 B.C.) on one of the expeditions ordered by Alexander the Great to sail round Arabia; his account was used by his contemporary, Theophrastus (*History of Plants*, book ix, chaps. 3, 4). In the second century A.D. Arrian gave a precise account, referring to Dhufār as the centre of the trade. The Chinese writer Chao Ju-Kua, about A.D. 1250, mentioned place-names which have been identified with Marbāt and Dhufār as centres of the 'milk-perfume' (*ju-hiang*) trade.[2]

THE MOUNTAINS OF 'OMĀN

The several massifs of the Western and Eastern Hajar ranges, separated by deep transverse passages, and culminating about the middle in Jebel Akhdar (the 'green mountain'), over 9,000 feet, with limestone table-tops (p. 55), have received only a single brief visit from one botanist, Aucher-Eloy. The higher parts of the range produced some plants of a northern type, a primula,[3] a violet,[4] a juniper,[5] and a honeysuckle.[6] Lower down, on almost inaccessible rocks, grows the *bēn* tree;[7] and on the slopes Compositae of the genus *Pulicaria*,[8] related to fleabane; and *Gallionia Aucheri*, a plant of the family Rubiaceae also found in western India.

SOCOTRA

The flora of Socotra, on account of its great scientific interest, has been more thoroughly investigated than that of the mainland. Some six hundred species of flowering plants and ferns have been recorded from the island, and among the cryptogams 130 species of lichens and 16 mosses have been reported. The flora resembles that of the Somali coast and south Arabia, but some 200 species are only known from the island.

---

[1] See the full account by G. Birdwood, 'On the genus Boswellia', *Trans. Linnean Soc.* xxvii, pp. 111-148 (1870); Freya Stark, *The Southern Gates of Arabia*, chap. i, pp. 9-11, and Appendix (1936).

[2] *Chu-fan-chi (A Description of Barbarous Peoples*, translated 1911).

[3] *Primula Aucheri.*

[4] *Viola cinerea.*

[5] *Juniperus macrocarpa.*

[6] *Lonicera Aucheri.*

[7] *Moringa peregrina* (p. 198).

[8] *Pulicaria crispa* and *P. orientalis.*

The trees are remarkable for their swollen, gouty trunks, resembling those of the African baobab. The bulbous trunks of cucumber trees[1] and isfed[2] are a conspicuous feature.

In the valleys there are woods of a local red-flowered frankincense-tree called ameiro[3] and above 1,000 feet forests of the dragon's-blood tree (damm al 'ahwein);[4] this is 20–30 feet high with the habit of an umbrella pine. A varnish can be prepared from the ruby-coloured resin, the 'cinnabar' of Pliny (called qatir in Arabic, edah or idihab in Socoteri). But none of the local resins or gums appear to be exploited commercially now; the trade in dragon's-blood resin shifted to Sumatra, where the palm Calamus draco yields a similar product.

The red rocks of the mountain peaks are blackened with lichens. A wild pomegranate[5] with small yellow fruit, and wild oranges are also reported. A fern with edible roots recorded by Wellsted remains unidentified.

Aloes, the drug obtained by evaporation of the juice of these plants, was formerly exported in large quantities from Socotra. Apparently a very small amount is still exported from the island, and from the mainland of the Eastern Aden Protectorate, but the trade, one of the oldest known, has greatly declined. Socotran or hepatic aloes is obtained from Aloe Perryi (Socoteri tāyif, Arabic sabr). A hole dug in the ground is lined with a skin, and the leaves are piled round it, points outwards, till the pressure makes the juice exude; the juice is at first called tāyif diho or tāyif rhiho, both diho and rhiho being used for water; when nearly firm it is tāyif geshisha, and when hard and dry tāyif kasahal. So-called 'Mocha aloes', the produce of one of the mainland species, perhaps A. rubroviolaceum (sabr), is inferior to that of Socotra.

'Abd al Kuri, the much smaller island to the west, lacks most of the conspicuous Socotran plants, such as the cucumber-tree, the dragon's-blood, and the isfed; but peculiar to this island are a succulent euphorbia,[6] a mignonette,[7] and a pretty morning glory.[8] For 'vegetable blubber', an article of diet, see p. 210.

FLOWERLESS LAND-PLANTS

Very little has been written about the lower plants, or cryptogamic flora, of Arabia. Excepting in the mountains of Sinai, south-west

[1] Dendrosicyos socotrana.
[2] Adenium socotranum.
[3] Boswellia ameero.
[4] Dracaena cinnabari.
[5] Punica protopunica.
[6] Euphorbia abdelkuri.
[7] Reseda viridis.
[8] Convolvulus Grantii.

125. *Dragon's-blood tree, Dracaena cinnabari, alt. c. 1,300 feet*

126. *View from summit of Jebel Dryet (alt. c. 4,940 feet) of the Socotran mountains and forest of dragon's-blood trees*

127. *Euphorbia arbuscula, near Ras Ahmar, eastern Socotra*

128. *Socotran Frankincense tree, Boswellia ameero, northern slopes of Jebel Hauweri (1,220 feet) near Ras Haulaf*

Arabia, and Socotra, lichens and mosses are on the whole doubtless very scarce, but at least eight kinds of lichens, as well as several mosses, were collected in the high south-western mountains in 1937–38 (British Museum Expedition). Burton found a freshwater alga called *ishnik* (*Chara foetida*) in Midian.

Several travellers mention fungi. Doughty states that certain tall white agarics (toadstools) 'being boiled with alum in the urine of camels that have fed of the bush el-humth (*al hamdh*) yield the gay scarlet dye of the beduin wool-wives'. Truffles are called *jibāt* or *fuq'a*; Huber recorded two kinds near Hāil, one being a small red kind which is white within, lying deep beneath the ground and appearing about a month after the autumnal rains. There are also one or more white kinds called *zebeidi* or *belūh*. Burckhardt (vol. i, pp. 60, 225) calls them *kemma* or *kemmaia*, and states that a black kind (*jibāt*) is found besides the white and red (*khalasi*), while they are sometimes so numerous that families live entirely on them in the season (*Terfezia Claveryi* and *T. Boudieri* var. *arabica*; the black species is possibly *T. Metaxasi*). In Kuweit truffles called *fuq'a* are generally found in company with a plant (*rukruk*) of the cistus family,[1] on which they are almost certainly parasitic. An edible fungus, *faqa'a* (a species of *Phellorium*), like a stalked puff-ball, is sold in the Kuweit bazaar. Edible agarics, *haubar* of the Ruwalla beduin, are also known. A fungus, *faswat al 'ajūz*, identical with the British stinkhorn[2] is recorded by Burton from Midian.

Three species of the curious genus *Podaxon*[3] have been found in south-west Arabia; the Arabic name of one has been given as *chourl al ga'r*. This genus is characteristic of dry semi-desert areas and certain species have been recorded as always found on or near the nests of termites (so-called 'white ants'). It has been suggested that *Podaxon* may be one of the fungi cultivated by the termites in their fungus-gardens, but the balance of evidence is against this theory. The usual fungi found in termite hills are an agaric,[4] the stag's-horn fungus,[5] and a small yellow cup-fungus.[6]

A fungus called *taktak*, which grows under the sand, is used as a remedy for colds. The dried fungus is also smoked in a pipe by persons suffering from rheumatism, but is not edible.

[1] *Helianthemum Lippii.*
[2] *Ithyphallus impudicus.*
[3] *Podaxon arabicum, P. Schweinfurthi, P. Deflersii.*
[4] *Collybia albuminosa.*
[5] *Xylaria nigripes.*
[6] *Peziza citrina.*

Marine Vegetation

Several species of marine flowering plants or sea-grasses, *surām* (certain species of *Cymodocea*,[1] and species of *Enhalus*, *Halophila*, and *Thalassia*[2]), are common in the deeper water along the Red Sea coast, and as far as Aden, but have not been recorded elsewhere.

Marine algae (seaweeds) are almost absent from the rocks at Aden, but 166 species have been recorded from the Red Sea, of which only 20 are also found in the Mediterranean. This total includes 30 species of *Sargassum* (which have been described as sometimes floating like that in the Sargasso sea), and a microscopic red-purple alga[3] which is sometimes present in such quantities as to colour the sea in places, a fact suggesting a possible origin of the name 'Red Sea'.

Only a poor algal vegetation can be expected in the inner part of the Persian Gulf, owing to the shallowness and the high temperature of the water, which may be nearly 97° F. near Bahrein. The salt content is 4·1 per cent. near Bushire and the bottom sandy and muddy. A brown sponge-like alga[4] forms an extensive belt along the beach at Bushire and is found at Bahrein.

The algae are not entirely useless; Captain Owen records[5] that, at the time of his visit to 'Abd al Kuri island, the chief vegetable food of the inhabitants consisted of a kind of 'vegetable blubber like a puff toadstool but full of water', varying in size from that of a goose's egg to a 4-lb. shot. The outer pellicle was transparent but the inner of a bright lead colour.

Additional information regarding plants of economic importance will be found in Appendix D, pp. 590–602.

---

[1] Potamogetonaceae.
[2] Hydrocharitaceae.
[3] *Trichodesmium erythraeum.*
[4] *Colpomenia sinuosa.*
[5] W. F. W. Owen, *Narrative of Voyages to explore the Shores of Africa, Arabia and Madagascar*, vol. i, p. 351 (1833).

CHAPTER V

HISTORY

INTRODUCTION

IN no country has geography determined history more than in Arabia. Except for the south-west, most of it is so unproductive that foreign invasion has been very rare. As in Persia, the position of the deserts has hindered the unification of those regions in which the strongest states have arisen, the Yemen, the Hejaz, the oases of central Nejd and 'Omān. The aridity of many districts has forced nomadic life and tribal organization on their inhabitants. Warfare has been almost incessant throughout their history; their political allegiance has usually meant little and changed readily without affecting their way of life and the nature of their society. Similar geographical conditions extend north of the peninsula in the Syrian desert, and the Arabs, skilled in desert travel, have been able to move freely across it to plunder, trade, or settle in the valleys of the Euphrates and the Jordan.

The coasts have always been better known than the interior. The monsoons helped the development of commerce in the Indian Ocean, and the long inlets that separate Arabia from Africa and Persia are natural trade-routes. For centuries Eastern products have been brought up the Red Sea to Egypt for distribution in north Africa and Europe, or taken overland from the Persian Gulf to the Syrian ports. For a time the sea route from India by the Cape of Good Hope was used in preference, but since the opening of the Suez canal in 1869 most of the trade between Europe and Asia has passed through the Red Sea. The latter is nowhere much more than 250 miles wide and can be crossed by small craft trading between Africa and Arabia. On both sides of the deep central channel are shallows and coral reefs through which coastal vessels thread their way to the entrepots situated at the few good harbours; foreign merchants and governments have been interested mainly in them and in the possible watering-places and coaling-stations along its torrid, mostly barren, shores.

In this chapter an account will be given of the history of the Hejaz, 'Asīr, the Yemen, and the territory now comprising the Aden Protectorate and the Colony of Aden, a summary of events in Nejd being included when desirable. Whenever possible the history of the Red Sea as a whole will be considered. Otherwise, the history of the African coast will be only briefly indicated.

There are four principal periods of Arabian history, and the historian has to rely on evidence of a different kind for each.

I. *From the earliest times to Muhammad*: Knowledge of this period comes primarily from inscriptions and coins found in Arabia, supplemented by references in Egyptian, Babylonian, Assyrian, Greek, Roman, and Byzantine sources. The medieval Arab writers who deal with it must be used with great caution. Western Arabia in this period was divided among several independent States. Its commercial importance was great; its political history is rather obscure.

II. *From Muhammad to about* A.D. *1500*: For this period reliance must be placed almost entirely on Arab historians. Arabia was now the Holy Land of a great religion and, for a short time, the centre of a vast empire, later becoming one of the least important provinces and sinking into disunion and isolation.

III and IV. *From about* A.D. *1500 to the present day*: Arabic histories can now be compared with European official documents and travel books. The struggle for the control of trade that followed Vasco da Gama's voyage caused European and then Turkish intervention, and some part of Arabia has been under foreign control ever since. In this period Europeans have explored most of the interior, but some areas are still little known. For convenience this period is divided into two sections: III, from 1500 to 1900, and IV, the twentieth century.

I. FROM THE EARLIEST TIMES TO MUHAMMAD

Before the Rise of the South Arabian Kingdoms

Derivation of the name Arabia

The derivation of the names Arabia and Arab is uncertain. Some Arabs say that they are so called because they lived in the 'Araba part of the Tihama south of Mecca. It is, however, generally agreed that the term Arab means nomad or desert-dweller.

From earliest times Arabia was divided, partly by the southern desert stretching nearly across the peninsula and making contact between north and south difficult, but also by the existence of two peoples, racially akin but differing widely in their habits and ways of life. The northern Arabs of the Hejaz and Nejd were nomads based on the few existing oases, while the southern Arabs were a settled people with a highly developed civilization. This has led Moslem genealogists to assert that the Arabs descended by two different lines from a common ancestor, Shem the son of Noah (Sa'm ibn Nūh), deriving the northern Arabs from Adnan, a descendant of Ishmael (Isma'il), and the southern from Qahtān, identified with the Biblical Joktan (Yoqtan) of *Genesis* x. 25. Really the Arabs know nothing of their early history, and have adopted Hebrew genealogies wherever possible. Little reliance can be placed on the legends with which Moslem writers have tried to conceal their ignorance of the *Jāhalīya*, or Age of Ignorance, and previous periods (p. 230).

Prehistoric Man in Arabia

Though no systematic survey of the whole country has been made, Arabia is known to have been inhabited since the Palaeolithic (Old Stone) Age. The earliest implements found are Chellian, one of the earliest known Stone Age cultures. Flints of the Neolithic (New Stone) and Bronze Ages have been found in the Empty Quarter and in the Hadhramaut. In Sinai Chalcolithic hoes and Bronze Age flint tools like those of southern Palestine have been found in the north coastal sandy belt near Sheikh Zuweid. So far no skeletons of prehistoric man have been discovered, either in Sinai or in the Arabian peninsula proper.[1]

The search for remains has hitherto lain largely in the south, especially in the Hadhramaut, where excavation has revealed stone implements assigned to the Levalloisian phase of Palaeolithic culture, but usually crude in comparison with examples of the same type from north Arabia, Palestine, and Africa. This may be due partly to lack of contact with more progressive peoples, such as would result from the separation, early in the Pleistocene, of Arabia from east Africa, a probable centre of cultural diffusion in Palaeolithic times. The apparent absence from south-west Arabia of examples of the important Palaeolithic culture-group known as 'hand-axe industries', widely distributed in east Africa, supports the theory of early separation of the two continents. Objects made of volcanic glass (obsidian) in geometric forms, triangles, crescents, trapezoids, &c., of the culture-group called 'blade-industries', are also believed to owe their appearance in the Hadhramaut to east African influence; the evidence

[1] The few skulls found in burial sites in Wadi 'Amd, Hadhramaut, by the Lord Wakefield Expedition, are believed to be of a date several centuries B.C., but within historical times.

indicates that these objects, which existed in Europe and the Mediterranean before the third millennium B.C., survived in south Arabia
into the first millennium B.C., since they were contemporaneous with
pre-Islamic temples well within that period.

At the northern end of the area under review, prehistoric rock-
drawings of ibexes, dromedaries, and other animals have been found
at Kilwa (Transjordan), a site rich in Palaeolithic, Mesolithic, and
later remains; the representations of dromedaries are perhaps the
earliest known. In the south rock-drawings also occur; for instance,
representations of ibexes, suns, and crescent moons are found on the
incense-road south of Shabwa, between Wadi Yeb'eth and Wadi
'Irma, where the beduin are said still to scratch ibexes to this day.

Early Egyptian Contacts with Sinai

Though the name Sinai, mentioned in several Old Testament
books (e.g. *Exodus* xix. 1; *Numbers* xxxiii. 15), can probably be traced
to the moon-god Sīn (p. 225), a Babylonian deity of whose cult it was
an early site, yet the Egyptians mined copper and turquoises in Wadi
Maghara. Probably they never held the greater part of Sinai, as
many battles with the nomads are recorded on stelae; the earliest
inscription shows Semerkhet of the First Dynasty smiting a kneeling
beduin. There are traces of the use of turquoises in Egypt as early
as the First Dynasty; but the first sculptured relief directly connected
with the mines relates to Sa-Nekht III of the Third Dynasty (2815–
2690 B.C.). Remains exist of the working-galleries, slag-heaps, and
huts of Egyptian mining communities of the Fourth and Sixth
Dynasties. Hathor, primarily a sky-goddess, but portrayed in Sinai
supporting the full moon between horns, may there have been
worshipped as a moon-goddess. Her temple at Serabit has many
non-Egyptian features, such as standing stones and an inner cave-
sanctuary, due to contact with Semitic religious forms. Since Sinai
was the corridor of Egypt to her empire in Syria and Palestine, a
chain of forts guarding the route was set up in the Eighteenth
Dynasty (*c.* 1700–1400 B.C.).

Egyptian Exploration of the Arabian Coasts

The early Egyptians tried hard to control the spice-route (p. 219),
a branch of which led from Ma'an or Petra via Aelana ('Aqaba) to
Egypt. Whether Punt ('God's Land' of the Egyptian inscriptions)
was in Ethiopia, or on the Somali coast, or in south-west Arabia, is
undecided; its products, as shown in inscriptions, could have come

from the Somali or Arabian coasts of the Gulf of Aden, and the Egyptians may have traded with both.[1] Their voyages are recorded as early as the Fifth Dynasty, but intercourse probably took place much earlier, since myrrh and spices for embalming were needed even by the First Dynasty Pharaohs. The best-known expedition to the southern ports was sent by Queen Hatshepsut of the Eighteenth Dynasty, c. 1600 B.C., to bring back myrrh-trees (p. 204). The Red Sea coasts, however, were mainly explored under Ptolemy II towards the end of the third century B.C. The Seleucid rulers of Syria vied with the Ptolemies in their demand for incense, though they obtained it partly from the Gerrhaeans in the Persian Gulf. The Ptolemies, however, anxious to cut the incense-route south of the point whence a branch led north-east to Syria, established a port on the Red Sea coast at Ampelonē, north of the latitude of Yathrib (Al Madina). They hoped thus to strike simultaneously at Seleucids and Nabataeans, but were eventually defeated by the latter, who captured Ampelonē, probably renaming it Leucē Cōmē (p. 231). The Egyptians knew the south coast between Bab al Mandeb and Mahra-land, but little beyond.[2] The *Periplus of the Erythraean Sea*, written by an Alexandrian Greek of unknown name about the first century A.D., deals with the African and Asiatic shores of the Indian Ocean, including parts of the south Arabian coast, especially about Shihr.

Mesopotamian Contacts with Arabia

It is believed that the Akkadians and Sumerians had intercourse with Arabia, possibly bringing copper from 'Omān. Narām-Sin, descendant of Sargon, the Semitic founder of Agade (Akkad), is recorded in an inscription of the third millennium B.C. to have conquered Magan. Wood and stone were brought for temple-construction about the same period from Magan and Melukhkha, names identified with parts of Arabia; the former may possibly have been 'Omān.

Records of Assyrian penetration are quite definite. Shalmaneser III, c. 854 B.C., conquered an Arab chief named Gindibu (Jundub) at his 'royal city' Karkar, north of Hama (Syria), taking 1,000 camels

[1] W. H. Schoff, translator and annotator of *The Periplus of the Erythraean Sea* (1912) is convinced (pp. 218–19) that the reliefs in the Egyptian temple of Deir el Bahri represent Dhufār, that the non-Arab people depicted were inhabitants of that country, and that the trees shown were its frankincense-trees; but there is not agreement on this point.

[2] W. W. Tarn, 'Ptolemy II and Arabia', *Journ. Egyptian Archaeology*, vol. xv, pp. 9–25, 1929; Arrian, *Anabasis Alexandrou*, vii. 22.

—one of the first allusions in history to the camel, and the first Assyrian mention of an Arab. Assyria vied with Egypt in trying to control the trade-route from the south to Petra and was specially concerned with its northern branch thence to Damascus. Though never penetrating far into the peninsula for long, the Assyrians had many dealings with the northern tribes and some relations with south Arabia. Tiglath-Pileser IV (745–727 B.C.), Sargon II (722–705 B.C.), Sennacherib (705–681 B.C.), and Esarhaddon (681–669 B.C.) all warred against the Aribi, believed to have been mainly northern beduin, who harassed the trade-routes, aided by Egypt and Babylonia, both hostile to Assyria. Esarhaddon tried to control the Aribi by setting over them an Assyrian nominee as their queen. Finally their king, Uaite', driven out by his own people, sought refuge with Natnu of Nabaite, possibly the Biblical Nebaioth, 'firstborn of Ishmael'. Sargon defeated the Tamud, the Ibadidi, and the Marsimani; the Tamud (Thamūd of the Koran) remained a recognized tribal organization till the rise of Islam, but nothing more is heard of the others. The first mention of a south Arabian, doubtless one of the Yith'i-amaras who were Mukarribs of Saba (p. 220), is that Sargon received gold, horses, camels, herbs, and other products from 'It'amara the Sabaean'. Adumu, a fortified city, believed to be the Dumah of *Genesis* (xxv. 14) and of *Isaiah* (xxi. 11) and the Dūmat al Jandal of Islamic conquests, identical with the modern (northern) Jauf, was raided by either Sennacherib or Esarhaddon and its gods carried into captivity. According to Xenophon (*Cyropaedeia*, i. 5. 2), Nebuchadnezzar subdued the 'king of Arabia' during his campaign against Egypt in 567 B.C.

The Neo-Babylonian king Nabonidus (Nabuna'id), resided at Tema (Teima) during several years of his reign (555–538 B.C.). He probably introduced the worship of the moon-god Sīn, for the deity shown on the Tema Stone bears the horns of a bull, the moon-god's symbol in Arabia; moreover, an Aramaic inscription on the stone, of the fifth century B.C., describes the introduction of a new god. The contact of Arabia with Neo-Babylonia ended with the fall of Babylon to the Persians in 538 B.C. Little is known of Achaemenid or Parthian contacts with Arabia in the following centuries, but Nearchus, commander of Alexander's fleet, touched at Ras Masandam in the strait of Hormuz on his voyage from the Indus to the Tigris in 324 B.C., and before his death in the following year Alexander sent out three naval expeditions to explore the Arabian coasts, one being commanded by Androsthenes (p. 207).

Palestinian Contacts

The Arabians and Hebrews were near neighbours and closely akin in speech. Yet, apart from the wanderings of the Israelites in Sinai, ending either in 1450 or 1200 B.C., contact between the two peoples cannot be proved before the time of Solomon, who with his ally Hiram, King of Tyre, sent trading fleets from the Gulf of 'Aqaba to south Arabia early in the tenth century B.C. '. . . king Solomon made a navy of ships in Ezion-Geber . . . on the shore of the Red Sea, in the land of Edom . . . and the navy also of Hiram . . . brought gold from Ophir (and) great plenty of almug trees and precious stones' (*1 Kings* ix. 26; x. 11). Nevertheless any references in the Old Testament to frankincense must be taken as indicating contact with either south Arabia or Somaliland, or both. Thus in *Exodus* xxx. 34, 35, 'pure frankincense' is included in a list of components of the incense to be used in the Tabernacle; in *Leviticus* ii. 1–3, it is directed that frankincense be put upon 'meal offerings'; in *1 Chronicles* ix. 26–30, certain Levites had charge of special rooms in the Temple where frankincense, spices, wine, oil, and many other things were stored; while later, as recorded in *Nehemiah* xiii. 4–9, it was considered sacrilege that one of these chambers had been occupied as a dwelling.

Of references to the incense traffic in the days of Israel's prosperity only the following can be cited: *Isaiah* lx. 6, 'the multitude of camels shall cover thee, the dromedaries of Midian and Ephah; they all shall come from Sheba; they shall bring gold and frankincense . . .', a passage plainly indicating the overland route. On the other hand, *Ezekiel*, inveighing in his chapter xxvii against the Kingdom of Tyre, reviews the countries to which the people of Tyre made long trading-voyages by sea, including (verse 23) '. . . Canneh and Eden, the traffickers of Sheba . . .'. It seems agreed that this Eden is Aden, while Canneh is Pliny's Cana, now Husn al Ghorab near Bir 'Ali (p. 148). The 'abundance of spices' (*1 Kings* x. 10) given by the Queen of Sheba to Solomon may well have included frankincense.[1]

The *Book of Job* may, from its vocabulary, be derived from an Arabic source. Local tradition affirms the southern Yemen to have been the 'land of Uz', the setting of the book, a tradition borne out by the allusion in chapter i. 15 to 'the Sebaeans' having fallen on Job's sons and taken them away. But Job's likening of his brethren (chapter vi. 15–17) to a deceitful brook, 'black by reason of the ice,

[1] All Biblical quotations above are from the Revised Version. For these and other references see W. H. Schoff, *The Periplus of the Erythraean Sea*, pp. 120 sqq. (1912).

and wherein the snow hideth itself', yet shrinking and vanishing 'when it is hot', would seem to indicate the north-west Arabian mountains, where brooks swell in the winter rains—whereas in the south-western highlands they swell in summer and shrink in winter. The allusion in the following verse to 'caravans of Tema' and 'companies of Sheba' applies equally to north-west and south-west Arabia.

'Arabia', 'Arabians', and Arabian names are found in the Old Testament several times. South Arabia is mentioned in *Psalm* lxxii: 'the kings of Sheba and Saba'. But the Hebrews, like the Assyrians, had most intercourse with the north Arabians of the Syrian desert, and 'all the kings of Arabia' (*Jeremiah* xxv. 24) doubtless means their sheikhs. Ezekiel (xxvii. 21) mentions Tyre as being supplied with sheep and goats by 'Arabia and all the princes of Kedar', the latter being probably the Kidri of Assyrian records, settled near Petra. By the time of Herodotus (5th century B.C.) 'Arab' and 'Arabia' designated the peoples and country between the Mediterranean and the Euphrates to the north, and as far south as the Indian Ocean.

The South Arabian Kingdoms

Classical authors and south Arabian inscriptions are the chief sources of information concerning the four principal and certain minor states in the area now known as the Yemen and the Hadhramaut, while the most reliable of numerous Arabic authors is Al Hamdāni, who wrote in the tenth century A.D. The classical authors divided the country into Arabia Petraea, i.e. Sinai and the adjacent part of north-west Arabia; Arabia Deserta, consisting of the Syrian desert, the northern Hejaz, and northern Nafūd; and Arabia Felix (Arabia Eudaemon of the Greeks), comprising not only the southern Hejaz, the Yemen, and the Hadhramaut, but Dhufār and indeed the whole country south of Arabia Deserta.

Apparently the first European traveller to notice south Arabian inscriptions was C. Niebuhr, who was shown copies, though he did not see the originals, in the Yemen in 1763. J. R. Wellsted published part of an inscription from Naqab al Hajar (in Wadi Meifa'a, Eastern Aden Protectorate) in 1838. Louis Arnaud examined the ruins at Marib and copied many inscriptions in 1843; Joseph Halévy brought back copies of nearly 700 from the north-eastern Yemen in 1869–1870, while Eduard Glaser, during twelve years from 1882, obtained copies of some 2,000. The language was deciphered by Emil Rödiger and by Gesenius. Not all the inscriptions so far discovered have been deciphered; they are mainly votary, or stelae recording irrigation works and repairs, and texts recording notable happenings, an invaluable contemporary record of events in south Arabia, which will prove still more useful after some of the events are satisfactorily dated by scientific exploration.[1]

The State of Ma'īn (Ma'an)

The earliest of these states was the Minaean, centred at Ma'īn, in the district of Jauf, in the north-eastern Yemen. It appears to have been not strictly monarchical, but ruled by a Grand Council, which is considered still to survive in the 'Grand Council of Ma'an', consisting of the three rulers of the 'Aulaqi confederation of tribes in the Aden Protectorate, far south-east of the original centre. Rising to power at least as early as 1000 B.C. and continuing till about 650 B.C., Ma'īn at its zenith included much of south Arabia. During its later stages the neighbouring kingdom of Saba increased in importance, till Ma'īn was finally overthrown by one of the Sabaean Mukarribs.

The Minaeans were great traders, with colonies in the land of Midian at Dedan (Al 'Ulā) and Al Hijr (Madāin Sālih), also at Ma'an (now in Transjordan), a form of the name also used for Ma'īn in south Arabia. Several of these stations were on the 'incense-road', to control which was, as mentioned above, the object of Egypt, Assyria, and the Seleucids over long periods. The incense-road (p. 147) led north-north-west through Saba and Ma'īn to Mecca; thence through Yathrib (Al Madina), Dedan, Al Hijr, and Teima to Ma'an and Petra; from one of which a branch extended north to Damascus, another via Aelana ('Aqaba) to Egypt. The Minaeans carried the worship of their god Wadd (p. 225) as far north as Delos in the Aegean. Wadd is mentioned in inscriptions found near Madāin Sālih;[2] in others the protection of the gods of Ma'īn is invoked for travellers by land and sea.

The Kingdom of Saba

The best known of the south Arabian kingdoms, the name of which, Saba, Sheba, or Sab'u, has often been used incorrectly to designate the whole of Arabia Felix, lasted from about 950 B.C. to

[1] See Corpus Inscriptionum Semiticarum (Paris, 1889–1908) and volumes v–vii entitled Répertoire de l'Épigraphie Sémitique, translated by G. Ryckmans (Paris, 1929), covering the south Arabian inscriptions.

[2] Pères Jaussen et Savignac, Mission Archéologique en Arabie, Paris, 1909, vol. i, p. 250.

115 B.C. Its early *Mukarribs* were priest-kings, but about 650 B.C., at the end of the 'first Sabaean period', these were replaced by *Mulūk Saba* ('kings of Saba'). Their capital was at first Sirwah, later Mariaba, the modern Marib, with its famous dam built by Yith'i-Amara Bayin, probably the ruler who conquered the kingdom of Ma'īn, though Arab tradition ascribes its building to the mythical Luqum ibn 'Ad (the descendants of 'Ad being a race of giants, believed to have inhabited south Arabia in ancient times and to have constructed the buildings of huge masonry, ruins of which still stand).

As yet no evidence has been found in south Arabian inscriptions of the existence of a 'Queen of Sheba'. There is nothing intrinsically improbable in the idea, since female rulers have occurred in Arabian history both before and after Muhammad (pp. 216, 248). But the rulers of Saba do not figure in inscriptions till considerably later than the time of Solomon. If the queen mentioned in *1 Kings* x, and *2 Chronicles* ix, and later named Bilqīs in the Koran and Mākedā by Ethiopian writers, is an historical personage, it is uncertain whether she resided in Ethiopia (as the Abyssinians claim) or in south-west Arabia, or even at one of the Sabaean trading-posts farther north on the incense-route.

Inscriptions indicate that the grouping of the south Arabian kingdoms altered considerably in the period under review. Towns such as Nask, on the frontier between Ma'īn and Saba, constantly changed hands. The Greeks considered the Sabaeans a peaceful people, possessed of great wealth from the incense trade; but evidently south Arabia was a scene of constant strife, at least in the early part of the first millennium B.C. The Sirwah inscriptions record a Sabaean expedition, in alliance with the Hadhramis, against Ausan (p. 222), in which there were over a thousand dead and four thousand prisoners.

The earliest mention of Saba in Greek literature is by Theophrastus, 288 B.C. (*History of Plants*, XI. iv. 2): 'now frankincense, myrrh, cassia and cinnamon are to be found in the Arabian Peninsula, about Saba, Hadramyta, Kitibaina and Mamali' (Mahra). In the time of Pliny (c. A.D. 77) the land of the Sabaeans reached the western and southern coasts of Arabia. Strabo, who lived between 64 B.C. and A.D. 21, wrote (XVI. iv. 19) 'bordering upon these people is the very fertile country of the Sabaeans, a very large tribe in whose country myrrh and frankincense and cinnamon are produced. . . . On account of the abundance of fruits the inhabitants are easy-going in their mode of life. . . . Those who live close to one another receive in continuous succession the loads of aromatics and deliver them to their next neighbours as far as Syria and Mesopotamia.' The wealth of Saba was based on the incense trade, as recorded by the Greek travellers. Strabo remarks: 'from their trafficking both the Sabaeans and the Gerrhaeans have become richest of all; and they have a vast equipment of both gold and silver articles such as couches, tripods and bowls, together with drinking vessels and very costly houses'. Pliny notes, besides the spice trade, their gold mines, their irrigated agricultural land, and the production of honey and baskets.

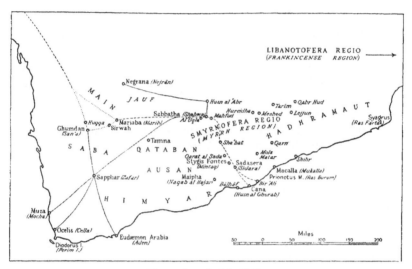

FIG. 36. *Arabia Felix*

Traditionally the Sabaean kingdom declined through the bursting of the great dam at Marib early in the Christian era, but the major causes were probably the diversion, under the Seleucids and Parthians, of the spice trade from the incense-route near the coast to the central overland route via the Persian Gulf, and the increase of commercial navigation in the Red Sea by the Romans about the third century A.D. When the classical authors were describing Saba it had already been replaced as the primary southern kingdom by that of the Himyarites.

The Kingdom of Qataban

This state appears, from south Arabian inscriptions and the classical authors (among whom Theophrastus, 288 B.C., first mentioned it), to have arisen some centuries B.C. and to have been finally absorbed in the Himyarite kingdom early in the Christian era. Its rulers, like those of Saba, were termed Mukarribs. Their capital, Tamna, is identified with the modern Timna' in Wadi Harīb, roughly 100 miles east-south-east of San'ā. According to Strabo (XVI. ii. 2), Qataban controlled the territory from the Sabaean border to the coast, thus embracing the modern Beihān and An Nuqūb to the east of Harīb, and the south-western Yemen mountains. Qataban was probably not independent for long at a time, but either allied with, or subject to, Saba or Himyar.

Ausan

Believed to have originated from Qataban more than six centuries B.C., and to have been eventually absorbed into Qataban again, Ausan was stated by the author of the *Periplus Maris Erythraei*, about A.D. 60, to have been for a time first among the south-west Arabian states, and to have possessed the African coast about Zanzibar. Hence this was still called in the first century A.D. the Ausanitic coast, and governed by the Mapharitic chief, a name perpetuated to-day in the Ma'afir tribe of the Yemen lowlands.

The Himyarite Kingdom

The Himyarites (Homeritae of the *Periplus*) rose to power in the second century B.C. and continued, despite a brief Abyssinian invasion in the fourth century A.D., till their overthrow by the Axumites (northern Abyssinians) in A.D. 525. Traditionally Himyar was descended from Qahtān, identified with Joktan of *Genesis* (chap. x), descendant of Shem. The present ruling house of the Yemen claim descent from the last Himyarite princes, and almost every trace of pre-Islamic culture in the Yemen is to-day ascribed to the Himyarites. The latter apparently absorbed Qataban and later Saba, and for a time early in the Christian era they claimed lordship over the Hadhramaut. The Sabaean capital at Marib was superseded by Zafar (or Sapphar), about 10 miles south-west of Yarīm near a mountain called Jebel Zafar to this day (Zafar of the Himyarites is not to be confused with Zafar, the ancient name of Dhufār, on the south-east coast). The Himyarite princes took the title 'king of Saba and Dhu Reidan', the latter according to Arab historians being the royal stronghold in Zafar, though there are also ancient ruins on Jebel Reidhan above Al Qasab in Wadi Beihān, nearly 100 miles to the north-east. The Himyarites minted a silver and gold coinage of Hellenistic type. The wars of their later monarchs (*tubbas*) with the Abyssinians and Persians, and other events, are mentioned below (pp. 228–230).

129. *Husn al Ghorab, 'Raven Castle', the starting-point of the old incense road*

130. *Ruins at Balid, 'Ophir', Dhufār*

131. *Himyaritic inscription on rock at Husn al Ghorab*

132. *Himyaritic inscriptions on old fort at 'Uqla, south face*

At one period the Himyarite state extended north-eastward along the coast, including Pliny's port of Cana (probably the Canneh of *Ezekiel* xxvii. 23), the ruins of which cover the promontory of Husn al Ghorab ('raven castle') near Bir 'Ali; Ptolemy's Maipha Metropolis (mod. Naqab al Hajar, in Wadi Meifa'a) may have been their inland capital. It is evident from the *Periplus* that all incense collected in the 'frankincense country' *par excellence*, the modern Dhufār, was first stored at a harbour on 'a great promontory facing the east' called Syagrus (mod. Ras Fartak), whence it was shipped to Cana, and there again stored, till it was taken northwards by the main incense road to Sabbatha (Shabwa). A section of the Wahidis, in whose country the ruins of Cana and Maipha lie, is called Beni Himyar to-day. The boundary between the Himyarites and Sabaeans in this region appears to have been an impressive masonry wall 200 yards long, which the ancient incense road pierces by a narrow passage, in Wadi Bana[1] north of Bir 'Ali (photo. 136).

In Himyaritic times the Romans, helped by the Nabataeans, made their one attempt to open the riches of south-west Arabia to Roman commerce and to incorporate it, like Nabataea, in their empire. In 24 B.C. Aelius Gallus, prefect of Egypt under Augustus, landed with an army at Leucē Cōmē, on the Red Sea coast north of the present Yenbo'. The expedition marched south-eastward along routes some distance inland, probably skirting the inner edge of the marginal highlands, for roughly 900 miles. At first the Romans met no one, but suffered great losses from sickness during the desert journey. Farther south they encountered the inhabitants and took the town of Negrana, believed to be Nejrān, and still farther south inflicted a crushing defeat on their enemies. Apparently they never reached Mariaba (Marib) itself, but took places called Athlula and Nasca, probably south of it; after penetrating even farther and laying siege to a town they were forced to retire from lack of water.[2] Though the Romans passed the former Sabaean capital on the east, their southernmost point may have had nearly the same name, Mariba, now a hill-ruin south of Nisāb. Recently the sheikh of this district asked technical assistance from the Aden Government in finding the spring sources and repairing the ancient system of aqueducts, because (he said) an occupying British army from the north had in ancient times blocked the springs and broken the aqueducts before withdrawing; when told that no British army had ever invaded his

[1] Distinct from Wadi Bana in Abyan, some 150 miles to the west.
[2] Strabo (xvi. 4. 22); Dio Cassius (book 53, xxix. 3).

country, the sheikh persisted that in any case it was a northern army of *Ahl Fareng*, 'Frankish people'. He may have been repeating a half-forgotten tradition of the Roman incursion.[1] The Marsyaba, the farthest people reached by Aelius Gallus, may be represented by the Mas'abi tribes, now some distance west of this point.

The Kingdom of the Hadhramaut

The fortunes of this kingdom cannot yet be told chronologically, but they were much intertwined with those of the states on the west, and with the Habashat, ancestors of the present Mahras, to the north-east. Legends apart, an independent Hadhramaut kingdom did exist for considerable periods. Very early, an inscription in Ma'in records the building of some towers by a Hadhrami king closely related to the Minaean ruler. Later the Hadhramis were allied with the Sabaeans against Ausan (p. 220). At one period the Hadhramaut conquered Qataban; an inscription considered not later than the second century B.C. records a peace between the kings of Saba, Qataban, and Hadhramaut. Probably in the first century B.C. the Hadhramis overthrew the Habashat (who had earlier been supreme in the incense country), many of whom then migrated to Tigré in northern Abyssinia. In the *Periplus* (1st century A.D.) the King of the Hadhramaut is described as ruling the frankincense country and also the islands of Kuria Muria, Masira, and Socotra, formerly belonging to the Habashat. Later in the Christian era the Hadhramis were subject to the Himyarites (p. 222).

The Hadhrami capital was at first 'Irma (or 'Arma), in the wadi of that name south-east of Shabwa (photo. 19). The identity of the king who transferred the capital to Shabwa is established. Shabwa was called in ancient times Sabbatha, the Sabota of Pliny, who records that the section of Sabaeans inhabiting it were the Atramitae (Hadhramis). The kings were crowned at a rocky place less than ten miles to the west, called Al 'Uqla. Shabwa was reputed to contain more than 60 temples, but its ruins indicate that these could not all have been within the walls, but must include sites in the surrounding district. The temple-ruins within the city are believed to have been those of a temple of 'Athtar (Venus). It is again clear from the *Periplus* that, while all incense from Dhufār was brought by sea to Cana and thence by road to Shabwa, that collected from the much smaller area in the Hadhramaut itself—probably near the Wadi Hajr, where some incense is still collected—was brought direct to Shabwa by camel. The whole

[1] R. A. B. Hamilton, *Geographical Journal*, vol. ci, p. 115, March 1943.

incense-traffic therefore passed northwards through Shabwa, where large dues were exacted in kind. Taxes had also to be paid to the Minaeans and other communities farther north, and eventually to the Nabataeans at Petra. The Hadhramaut and other southern kingdoms thus depended on the traffic, and when the incense ceased to be carried overland the south Arabian states, with their buildings and agriculture, declined.

'Sessania Adrumetorum' was possibly 'Azzān of the Hadhramis. There, according to ecclesiastical legend, the bones of the Three Magi were found early in the fourth century by the envoys of the Empress Helena, and were taken thence to Constantinople; whence in the twelfth century, in the time of the Emperor Manuel Comnenus, they were translated to Milan and later (1164) to Cologne. Some foundation for the legend may exist in the flight of a number of Magians from persecution in Persia to eastern, and possibly southern, Arabia.[1]

Pre-Islamic Religion of South Arabia

In the ancient astral worship the principal deity, Sīn, the moon-god (pp. 214, 216), was conceived of as masculine. Known to the Minaeans as Wadd, and by other names in the other states, he took precedence over his consort Shams, the sun-goddess, possibly identical with Al Lāt of the Hejaz and north Arabia. The son of Sīn and Shams was 'Athtar, a male form of the Babylonian goddess Ishtar or the Phoenician Astarte. Despite the ideas of marriage and birth, there is no evidence of anthropomorphism in the worship of this triad, from which spring many heavenly bodies regarded as lesser deities, some of which were only phases of the same body, e.g. the waxing and waning moon. Classical authors equated these deities with their own; 'Athtar and Shams changed their sex, becoming respectively Venus and Apollo (Arrian, *Indica*, chap. xxxvii). As stated (p. 219), Minaean merchants carried the worship of Wadd to north Arabia and even to the Aegean; a pillar representing him is said to have stood at Dūmat al Jandal (the northern Jauf, p. 40), and an altar in his name was found at Delos. Melik (Maqrieh) was a deity associated with the priest-kings of Saba; and Nasr, the vulture-god (also worshipped in the Hejaz), with the Himyarites. Wadd, Nasr, and other deities are mentioned in the Koran (*Sura* lxxi) as gods of the unbelievers; while in *Sura* xli Moslems are expressly

[1] *The Book of Ser Marco Polo*, transl. by Sir H. Yule, 3rd ed. revised by H. Cordier, vol. i, 1903, p. 82; Gibbon, *Decline and Fall of the Roman Empire*, chap. 50.

forbidden to adore the sun and moon. Yāfa', still the name of a powerful tribal confederation in the Western Aden Protectorate, may have been a deity worshipped on the 'Audhali plateau at Am 'Adia, where an ancient building among ruined terraces is inscribed 'Yafā' is great' in relief-characters of Phoenician type. The south Arabians offered incense and live bulls as sacrifices; sculptured bulls' heads occurred in their temples as emblems of the moon-god, because of the resemblance of the horns to a crescent moon. Veneration of springs and possibly of a rain-god are mentioned below. There were centres of local pilgrimage as in the pre-Islamic religions of north Arabia (p. 234).

Religious and other Buildings

The temples erected to the worship of these gods were usually square or rectangular, containing a sanctuary opening off a court surrounded by a portico with octagonal or square pillars. Some were elaborately decorated, with coloured wall plaster and carving, and had their eave-spouts adorned with bulls' heads. Two temples have been excavated. That at Huqqa, north of San'ā, was dedicated to the sun-goddess, Dhāt Ba'dān, probably a local name, and has been assigned by its excavators, Rathjens and Wissmann, to the third century B.C. The other, at Hureidha (Hadhramaut), was dedicated to the moon-god, Sīn; near-by tombs, containing Neo-Babylonian seals, were probably of the period between the sixth and fourth centuries B.C. The rectangular ground-plan and colonnades of these and other temples, such as at Ma'īn, Sirwah, Riyan, and Madinat Haram, are comparable with those of the earliest Islamic mosques, for example the Great Mosque at San'ā; it is evident whence the plan of the mosques is derived. On the other hand, the temple, oval in ground-plan, at Haram Bilqīs near Marib, has been compared with the ruins at Zimbabwe, Southern Rhodesia.

A primitive cult of trees and pillars may have existed. Many springs were, and still are, venerated; notably in the south-western mountains, tombs of Moslem saints stand close to springs which have doubtless been sacred from pre-Islamic times. At Qabr Hūd (tomb of the Prophet Hūd), the most holy spot in the Hadhramaut, the present buildings surround a great boulder, now held to have been the hump of the prophet's camel, but this site and many others were probably sanctuaries of the older religion. The existence of a shrine of Mola Matar (literally 'lord rain'), particularly venerated by the beduin, in the mountains north-west of Mukalla, perhaps

133. *Tomb at 'Alam Abyadh, about 30 miles north-east of Marib*

134. *Ancient palace-wall in Hajar, Shabwa*

135. *Nabataean rock-cut tombs at Madāin Sālih*

136. *Pre-Islamic boundary-wall at Bana, north of Bir ʿAli*

indicates that a rain-god also was worshipped, though the tomb, 15 feet long, is now said to be that of a prophet descended from 'Ad.[1] Compare the ancient north Arabian religion (p. 235). Among several forms of ancient tombs are circular, blockhouse-like buildings forming vast necropolises in the desert east of the Yemen Jauf, and sepulchres hewn in cliffs, in many cases accessible only with ropes from above, in the Yemen.

On the incense-road in Wadi Hajr (believed to be Ptolemy's river Prion) are monuments called *marqas*, consisting of an upright stone with a sculptured representation of a bearded face and a dagger, while other stones are set in front and at the sides, so that the whole structure, perhaps a wayside place of prayer, resembles a chair. In the Sei'ar country, north-east of Shabwa, and again in Mahra country, there are structures called *'urum*, consisting of piles of stones in a line, a dozen or more, with upright stones and a circular enclosure either in the middle or at the end. These 'urums are usually by the roadside or on the crests of neighbouring hills, but whether intended for defence or as 'hides' for huntsmen is unknown. In them are found carved representations of pairs of feet, such as are associated with crosses in Socotra.

Ruins of pre-Islamic buildings are mainly of limestone, basalt, or granite, not commonly of brick; the joints are fine, sometimes with leaden tie-bolts or, as in the Marib dam, copper nails. Structures for water-storage in general have been discussed in Chapter II (pp. 34 ff.). Pillars, cylindrical, quadrangular, or polygonal monoliths up to 10 feet high or more, were a frequent architectural feature, occasionally bearing inscriptions round the edge of the capital. Remains of castles or palaces exist, especially in the south-west, as at Shabwa or Haz (north-west of San'ā). Others, destroyed in the Abyssinian and Persian wars, are described by Arab writers, particularly by the tenth-century savant Al Hamdāni, in whose time the ruins of the famous stronghold of Ghumdan (precursor of San'ā) still stood. It was said to be twenty stories high, with the upper part of polished marble, and four bronze lions, through which the wind roared, on the roof. Sculptured friezes have been found, also statues and bronzes, mainly copies of Hellenistic models of late date; but small stone statues, representing seated human figures, crudely wrought and probably much older, may have been figures of ancestors formerly placed in the rock-sepulchres of the Yemen. A bronze statuette from an ancient fort at the entrance to Wadi Jardan, the

[1] H. Ingrams, *Arabia and the Isles*, pp. 166–167, 213–216.

Gorda of Ptolemy, west of Shabwa, is considered imported Greek work of the fifth century B.C.

Christianity in Arabia and the Abyssinian and Persian Conquests

Northern Ethiopia was colonized, probably in the second or first millennium B.C., by immigrants from south Arabia; the Habashat (p. 224) gave the name 'Abyssinia' to the country, and the Ag'azi the name *Ge'ez* to the language. The Arab settlers gradually conquered the indigenous 'Hamites', the dominant peoples in Abyssinia having arisen from the resulting fusion. Later these northern Ethiopians formed in the present province of Tigré the kingdom of Axum, mentioned by the writer of the *Periplus* in the first century A.D. The early settlement from south Arabia naturally fostered close commercial relations between the two countries, and the Axumites also traded, from their port at Adulis, on the western shore of Annesley bay, with Ptolemaic and with Roman Egypt. The early centuries of the Christian era saw a revival of Red Sea trade with Egypt and an increase of traffic with India.

Christianity began to penetrate south-west Arabia at an uncertain but very early date. Tradition, especially in the eastern churches, has it that missionaries started work in Arabia Felix in apostolic times. Both Eusebius and St. Jerome mention a probable visit of St. Bartholomew. In the fourth century missionaries went to both sides of the Red Sea, and it has been claimed that Frumentius, apostle of Ethiopia, also visited south-west Arabia. More definite evidence exists that, in the reign of Constantius II, Theophilus Indus, 'invested with the double character of ambassador and bishop', took charge of the newly formed churches in Abyssinia, south-west Arabia, and Socotra. Though he is said to have been an Arian, Christianity in those lands assumed mainly a Monophysite type. Theophilus founded a church in Aden and got permission from the ruler of the Himyarites to build others in the city of Ẓafar and elsewhere. Nejrān appears not to have become Christian till about A.D. 500, under the influence of Phemion, a Syrian Monophysite. In Socotra ruins of Christian churches exist to this day, while the place-name Kallansiya (or 'Kalenzia'), in the north-west of the island, is believed to be derived from *ecclesia*. Traditions of Christian kings and towns exist in the Hadhramaut, and in what is now Nejd some of the chiefs of Kinda (p. 232) are said to have been Christian.

Judaism also penetrated early, possibly soon after the destruction of Jerusalem in A.D. 70. The names recorded indicate that most

Jews who settled in south Arabia were Aramaean or Arabian converts. Possibly several of the Himyarite rulers embraced Judaism; at any rate the last *tubba*, Dhu Nuwās, was a Jew who, perhaps associating Christianity with the commencing domination of the Abyssinians, almost stamped it out by a massacre at Nejrān and elsewhere about A.D. 523. This led to an invasion by an Abyssinian army under Aryat, sent by the Negus Kaleb Ela Asbeha, to avenge the murdered Christians. This attempt by the Abyssinians to help their co-religionists may have been partly prompted by the desire of the Emperor Justinian for an alliance with Abyssinia against the growing power of Persia, and his anxiety to divert the silk trade with China from the overland route through Persia to the sea-route. Whatever the cause, the Abyssinians were, according to the contemporary historian Procopius, victorious, and Dhu Nuwās was slain. A Christian Himyaritic ruler was set up, but soon overthrown by a revolt in the Abyssinian army of occupation, led by Abraha (Abramus), previously a Christian slave of a Roman merchant in Adulis. Abraha defeated Aryat, but was not recognized as viceroy of the Yemen till the Negus had sent several unsuccessful expeditions against him. Afterwards Abraha, wishing San'ā to rival Mecca as a centre of pilgrimage, built there a magnificent church, *al Kalis* (*ecclesia*), remnants of which may still be incorporated in the Great Mosque. Local tradition holds that, after this church was defiled by pagan Arabs associated with the cult of the Ka'ba at Mecca, Abraha led an army against Mecca, accompanied by elephants, about A.D. 570, but that the Abyssinians were destroyed by small-pox within sight of the Holy City.

Their defeat, from whatever cause, in the 'Year of the Elephant' weakened Abyssinian power in Arabia, which was not, however, finally overthrown till the invasion of the Persians in the reign of Nushirwan (Chosroes I). The Sassanian ruler sent to Aden a force under Wahriz, who defeated the Abyssinians under Maruk (Masrud), last viceroy of the dynasty of Abraha, about A.D. 575, and placed on the throne an exiled Himyarite prince, Seif Ibn Dhu Yazan. The latter, celebrated in Arab story as a national hero struggling against the Abyssinian yoke, appears to have begged Nushirwan for help, which was gladly given in order indirectly to weaken the influence of Byzantium. The second Abyssinian occupation had lasted about half a century, an earlier and shorter one having occurred in the fourth century A.D.

Seif Ibn Dhu Yazan at first resided at the stronghold of Ghumdan

(San'ā) as co-viceroy with Wahriz. But the Yemen soon became a Persian satrapy and so continued till Badhan, the last Persian satrap, embraced Islam in A.D. 628, the sixth year after the Hijra. Persia then ceased to have a determining influence in Arabia.

The final bursting of the famous dam at Marib occurred in the Abyssinian period, probably between A.D. 542 and 570. That this has been assigned to various dates, ranging from the second to the sixth century, can be explained by the occurrence several times of leaks, which were repaired. According to Glaser two inscriptions record large breaches, respectively in A.D. 450 and 543, the second being inscribed in the name of 'Abraha, envoy of the Ge'ezetic (Ethiopian) king'. The final burst has been variously ascribed to a great flood (which might also be an effect of the catastrophe), to earthquake, volcanic eruption, and the digging of rodents. Reference is made to the event in the Koran (*Sura* xxxiv. 15). Some Arab chroniclers state that a rat moved a stone which fifty men could not have shifted, thereby bringing about the disaster, on which later Arab imagination has seized to explain the whole agelong decline of south Arabian trade and prosperity; but the real causes lay in the diversion of trade from the overland incense-route to the sea-route, in internal divisions resulting from the introduction of Christianity and Judaism, and in subsequent submission to foreign rule. The local effect was, however, considerable; Al Hamdāni, writing in the tenth century, describes how the gardens of the Yemen became waste land;[1] and either an earlier breach of the dam, or the final one, appears to have caused certain powerful tribes to move north. The Beni Ghassān, who migrated to Transjordania, east of the Roman frontier, started a new chronology dating from a burst of the dam, believed to have occurred late in the third century A.D.; the Beni Lakhm migrated to the desert west of the Euphrates (p. 232), where Hira, not far from the later Najaf, became their border town.

THE HEJAZ BEFORE ISLAM

'The Age of Ignorance' (Al Jāhalīya)

This name, meaning the age before Arabia had any revelation or inspired book, really denotes in the Hejaz, and, indeed, in the whole of the peninsula north of the Rub' al Khali, a period of little over a century, just before the coming of Islam.

[1] Al Hamdāni, *Al Iklil* (translation by N. A. Faris), book viii, p. 34.

The grouping of several families into an encampment (*hayy*) of several encampments into a clan (*qaum*), and the federation of kindred clans into a tribe (*qabīla*), with its own pasture and water-supplies, beyond which the tribe could not move without risk of hostile encounter, led then, as later, to tribal wars, many of which are recorded in Moslem tradition as well as in pre-Islamic poems and proverbs. These large-scale raids usually occurred over such things as water-rights, pastures, or camels. Thus the *Harb al Basūs* (war of Basūs), between the Beni Taghlib and Beni Bakr tribes of north-east Arabia, was fought, towards the end of the fifth century A.D., over a she-camel and ended with a battle called the Day of Shearing. Soon after, a similar war broke out between the related 'Abs and Dhubyān tribes of central Arabia, over the unfair conduct of the latter tribe in a horse-race. Both these feuds lasted several decades, the latter extending into Islamic times.

Northern Arabic spread in this period, finding its finest expression in poems (odes, *qasīda*), and superseding the south Arabian dialects as the classical language. Poets played an important part in pre-Islamic history. The famous seven *Mu'allaqāt* ('suspended') odes, still honoured as masterpieces throughout the Arabic-speaking world, are said to have been awarded the annual prize at the fair of 'Ukaz ('Akaz) near Mecca, a sort of 'eisteddfod' whither hero-poets yearly resorted to celebrate their exploits. The prize-winning odes were inscribed in golden letters and hung on the walls of the Ka'ba. Many English translations exist, giving an excellent account of beduin life and manners in pre-Islamic times.[1]

The influence of three important border-states must be briefly mentioned: the Nabataeans and, later, the Ghassānids of Transjordan and the Lakhmids of Hira.

The Nabataeans (Nabathu or al Anbāt) were an Arabian tribe, best known as traders and merchants with their capital at Petra, the Sela of the Old Testament, whence they controlled the trade-routes between south Arabia and the Mediterranean (p. 219), setting up ports on the Gulf of 'Aqaba and on the Red Sea coast at Leucē Cōmē (p. 215). Their inscriptions also are found at Al Hijr (Madāin Sālih). The Nabataeans successfully held the balance of power between the Ptolemies and Seleucids, but were finally annexed by Trajan as a Roman border-state in A.D. 105. The modern Huweitāt beduin are regarded as their descendants.

[1] R. A. Nicholson, *Literary History of the Arabs*, 2nd ed., pp. 71–140, 1930; Sir Charles Lyall, *Ancient Arabian Poetry*, 1885.

The Ghassānids, Monophysite Christians of the Syrian school later called Jacobite, and within the Byzantine sphere of influence, originated in the south-west, claiming descent from 'Amr Muzeiqīya ibn 'Āmir Mā' al Samā ('water of heaven'), who moved north from Marib after one of the breaches of the dam (p. 230).

The Lakhmids, claiming a similar origin, were almost continuously at war with the Ghassānids. Being clients of the Persians, they less readily adopted Christianity. No Lakhmid sovereign was converted till the last, Al Nu'mān III, in the sixth century. Nevertheless there were bishops of Hira, one of whom, a Nestorian, lived as early as A.D. 410.

Certain Christian doctrines, later incorporated by Muhammad in the Koran, probably reached the Arabian peninsula from these sources. Sinai also was a Christian sphere, inhabited by hermits fleeing from Roman persecution. They first lived in rude huts or caves, but later both churches and monasteries were built; the most famous, the monastery of St. Catharine, having been founded by the Emperor Justinian *c.* A.D. 530 as the Convent of the Transfiguration, about the nucleus of a more ancient tower ascribed to the Empress Helena (p. 47). Two names of the fourth century, St. Onophrius and St. Julian Sabbas, are also worthy of mention. The latter, an ascetic hermit of Edessa (now Urfa in southern Turkey), went with his followers to Sinai and built a church. St. Onophrius, a monk of Thebes, lived alone in extreme asceticism in a cave, where he was discovered after many years by the Egyptian monk Paphnutius, who wrote his life; hence many convents where solitude is rigorously enforced are dedicated to him. Excavations at S'baita (Auja Hafir), just within the frontier of Palestine, have revealed remains of several churches.

The Kingdom of Kinda. The powerful tribes of Royal Kinda (*Kinda al Malik*), first mentioned in the fourth century A.D., probably originated in the south-west as vassals of the Himyarite *tubbas*. During the fifth century their kingdom, founded by Hujr, dominated central and north Arabia; excepting the ancient kingdoms of the south-west, their rulers alone within the peninsula were entitled king (*malik*). Hārith ibn 'Amr, grandson of Hujr, rivalled the power of Hira and Ghassān, invading 'Iraq between A.D. 505 and 509, and deposing Mundhir of Hira. The poems of 'Amr (or 'Imru) al Qeis, son of Hārith, in the Mu'allaqāt, tell of the feud between Kinda and Hira. The kingdom of Kinda also made one of the first recorded attempts to form a central Arabian confederacy, an experiment which later served as precedent to the Hejaz and Muhammad. The struggle for supremacy between the sons of Hārith led in A.D. 612 to the battle of Kulab, 'the day of the barred gates', when many tribes fought on a site still unidentified. 'Amr al Qeis spent the rest of his life unsuccessfully trying to regain his patrimony.

Yamāma. This ancient city, in Wadi Hanīfa south-east of Riyādh, was capital of a kingdom at the time of the rise of Muhammad, and had been possibly the capital of the whole empire of Kinda. The Hanīfa valley is said to have been closely set with prosperous oases for 80 miles or more. Most of these have disappeared, and Yamāma itself now consists of four small hamlets, with a total population of about 2,000, in the angle formed by the junction of Wadi Nisāh and Wadi Hanīfa. According to tradition the inhabitants opposed Muhammad and were doubly afflicted by locusts and plague. But, since ruins of clay buildings appear from beneath sands on the side nearer the Hanīfa channel, a catastrophic flood in the latter was probably the main cause of the downfall of Yamāma; only settlements such as Riyādh, above flood-level, survived. The catastrophe may not have occurred till some time after Muhammad, as Yamāma figures in early Islamic history.

The Lihyānites and several other north Arabian peoples possessed cultures of which little is known. The Lihyānites (*Lechieni* of Pliny) had their capital at Deidān (Dedan of the Old Testament, modern Al 'Ulā), formerly a Minaean outpost on the incense-route, the ruins of which include tombs with sculptures in high relief, dating from *c.* 500 B.C. to 300 B.C. As late as Ptolemaic times the Lihyānites struggled with the Nabataeans for control of the trade-routes; and after the fall of the Nabataean power they seem also to have held Al Hijr. At the time of Muhammad their descendants were under the control of the Qureish. Relations between Lihyānites and Thamūd (p. 216) are not clear; the former may have been a section of the latter. The Thamūd, who in early times held Al Hijr (Madāin Sālih), are mainly known for the story of their destruction, the prophet Sālih and his she-camel being sent to them in vain (Koran, *Sura* vii. 71; ix. 71). In Lihyānite and Thamūdic inscriptions the epigraphy is related to that of south Arabia, though the language itself is northern Arabic.

The Beni Teiy (Tayi), a powerful north Arabian confederation claiming south Arabian origin, were at one period Christian. Jebel Shammar was frequently called in pre-Islamic literature 'the two mountains of Teiy', and in later times the Shammar, probably of northern origin, displaced (or perhaps absorbed) the ancient Teiy nation. The latter figure later, in Islamic times (p. 244). Their most famous member, Hātim at Tei'i, proverbial in Moslem records for his beduin generosity, is believed to have died *c.* A.D. 605.

Among many names of tribes and confederacies in pre-Islamic times, met with again in Islamic history, are the Ma'addites, near Mecca; the Beni Kalb, about the Nafūd; the Asad, between the Teiy and Kinda; and the Hawāzin, who fought against the Qureish and the Kināna on the Ayyām al Fijar, 'days of transgression', so called because they fell within the holy months when fighting was prohibited under the ancient religion.

The Rise of the Qureish (Koreish)

Muhammad's own tribe, of northern (Nizāri) stock, became guardians of the Ka'ba and the holy well, Zemzem, at Mecca, about a century before the Prophet's birth. Traditionally they are said to have acquired the art of writing and their idolatrous beliefs from Hira. They rose to power under Zeid ibn Kilab ibn Murra, sur-named Qussei, who defeated their rivals, the Beni Khuza'a. The latter had wrested from the true descendants of Ishmael the guardian-ship of the Ka'ba, believed to have been built by Adam after a celestial prototype, and rebuilt after the Flood by Abraham and Ishmael, with whom the Archangel Gabriel deposited the Black Stone set in the south-east corner of the structure. With the coming of the Qureish the Ishmaelite line was resumed. Qussei earned the name Al Mujamini (the congregator) by collecting the Qureish into the Meccan valley. He allotted quarters in the city to each family, and built the Dar al Nadwa, where the notables assembled to discuss tribal matters and the administration of the pilgrimage. The ordi-nances of Qussei were perpetuated after his death.

Muhammad was born in A.D. 570 or 571, the Year of the Elephant, i.e. of Abraha's expedition against Mecca (p. 229). The failure of Abraha, soon followed by the defeat of a Persian army near Kufa by the Beni Bakr, marked the end of Arab subjection to foreign sway and opened the way to a new era in Arabian history.

Pre-Islamic Religions in North Arabia

Though the beduin were not naturally religious, each tribe or clan had its own deities, the outward forms of which are mentioned below. Besides the main god or gods there was primitive nature-worship.

Certain springs were sacred, the most famous being the well of Zemzem in the court of the Ka'ba at Mecca, believed to have been that which supplied water to Hagar and Ishmael. *Ba'l* represented the spirit of springs and underground water generally. Special trees and caves were held sacred; thus the goddess Al 'Uzza was believed to reside in a tree at Nakhla. Sacred areas, usually mountains or caves, were places of pilgrimage. Astral beliefs centred (as in south Arabia) on the moon, in whose light the beduin grazed their flocks. To this day the Ruwalla imagine that the moon beneficently regulates their life, distilling dew and causing vegetation to grow, while the sun would malevolently wish to destroy life.

The principal deities, the goddesses Al 'Uzza (equivalent of Venus), Al Lāt ('the goddess'), and Manah (all mentioned in the Koran, *Sura* liii. 19, 20), had their sanctuaries in the Hejaz; but were known far and wide, e.g. Al Mundhir III of Hira offered a captured son of his rival, the Ghassānid King Al Hārith, as a sacrifice to Al 'Uzza, *c.* A.D. 544. Allah (*al ilāh*, the god), the principal, but not the only, god of Mecca, is mentioned in the Safa inscriptions in Syria centuries before Islam. Several passages in the Koran attest the esteem in which Allah was held even in pre-Islamic times; the name 'Abdullah (servant of Allah) was used, being incidentally that of Muhammad's father. Of other gods Hubal, though possibly of Syrian origin, had a place in Mecca; Jalsad was a god of the Kinda; Dhu al Khalasa and Yaghuth were worshipped in the Yemen, the former (like Hubal at Mecca) being said to give oracular answers through arrows by means of which lots were drawn.

Buildings and Idols (compare p. 226). Mecca was a holy city long before the coming of Islam. The traditional origin of the Ka'ba has been mentioned (p. 234). In fact the pagan Ka'ba was cube-like (whence the name) and of primitive simplicity, originally roofless, but housing the venerated meteorite, the Black Stone, and other idols (*frontispiece*). It was rebuilt before the age of Islam, wreckage of some Greek ships from the Red Sea shore being used. The Black Stone is set in the south-east corner of the present structure. Nejrān also had a Ka'ba, probably consisting of a great basaltic rock, still standing at Taslal though long disused. San'ā had a third Ka'ba, still represented by a small domed building in the Great Mosque (photo. 182). At Petra was a kind of Ka'ba where Dhu al Shara (Dūshara, later associated with the vine) was worshipped under the form of a black quadrangular stone, about 4 feet high. A square stone at Tāif represented the goddess Al Lāt (compare the erection of a sacred stone by Jacob, *Genesis* xxviii. 18, 19). Weapons, garments, and rags were hung as gifts in a sacred palm-tree in Nejrān, and offerings were made to the tree (probably a *sidr*-tree, *Zizyphus*) of Al 'Uzza at Nakhla. After the conquest of Mecca by Muhammad many idols were destroyed.

The tribesmen also believed (and still believe) in spirits, mainly hostile (whereas the gods were, on the whole, friendly), out of which Moslem theologians later built up an elaborate demonology. The four principal types are *sheitan*, *jinn* (plural *jānn*), *'afrit*, and *marid*, the last being very powerful. The greatest demon, *Iblīs*, created of smokeless fire, rebelled against God in refusing to worship Adam, made of earth. Among simple people the *jānn* are largely personifications of the terrors of desert and mountains, or of wild animals. A jinn may assume human form, sometimes of huge size and very hideous; or various beasts and reptiles are sometimes said to be 'jinn'. A madman, *majnūn*, is one possessed by the *jānn*. 'Afrits may be spirits of wicked men, haunting their place of burial. At the coming of Islam many of the inferior pagan gods were deprived of most of their power and degraded to the position of *jānn*, whose number was thereby greatly increased.

II. FROM MUHAMMAD TO ABOUT A.D. 1500

The Moslem State and the Arab Caliphates

Muhammad and the Moslem State

MUHAMMAD was born at Mecca about the year 570 in one of the poorer Qureish families. When about 40 years of age he received the first of what he believed to be revelations from God delivered by the Archangel Gabriel. He began to preach religious and social reform, teaching the doctrine of rewards and punishments after death, denouncing idolatry, and insisting above all on absolute monotheism and his own prophetic status. He strongly condemned the blood feud; the brotherhood of the faith was to supersede all other ties. He respected the sanctity of the Ka'ba, but his attacks on polytheism and its ethics gave offence and there was some persecution. Some of his supporters fled to Abyssinia, but in 622 he and as many of his followers as were able migrated to Yathrib, thereafter called 'the city of the Prophet', *madīnat an nabī*, or simply 'the city', *Al Madīna*; hence the European name 'Medina'. This event is known as the Hijra (flight), and the year in which it occurred became the first of the Moslem era.

Muhammad was now free to harry the valuable Syrian trade of Mecca and to organize his community as he wished; the regulations he made became the Law of Islam. He showed himself an able administrator, negotiator, and general, was undeterred by defeat and moderate in victory, and his troops owed much to the fervour and discipline which he instilled. The Meccans were beaten at Badr (624) and failed to follow up a success at Uhud (625); an attack by them on Al Madina was repulsed (627). There the Prophet became an absolute ruler, expelling the Jews (624–627), and making tributary to him their rich settlement at Kheibar (628) as well as other villages and tribes. Even when Mecca was taken in 630, Al Madina remained his capital; in the same year a beduin coalition was defeated at Hunein. Tāif surrendered soon after and Muhammad gained converts, allies, or sympathizers in most parts of Arabia. He did not, however, set up a regular administration, and his representatives were agents, collectors of tribute, and missionaries, rather than governors. There was probably still much hostility or indifference to Islam in the peninsula when he died at Al Madina in 632.

There is no doubt about the chief events of Muhammad's life, but much that is told of him is legend, and the evidence is not easy to interpret. In Europe he has been regarded as a Christian heretic, an impostor, an epileptic, a social reformer, an ambitious politician, or a religious enthusiast. The opinions of Moslem sects differ almost as much. While many pray for his intercession and some have mystical views about him, orthodox theology sees in him the last and greatest of the prophets, whose memory is to be revered, but still only a man, no more to be worshipped than other men.[1]

Muhammad died without appointing a successor and left no son. As the 'seal of the prophets' no one could succeed him, but someone was needed to take his place as temporal head of the community. So his friend Abu Bekr, an austere and simple man, the father of his wife Ayesha, was informally chosen 'Successor (*Khalifa*, Caliph) of the Prophet of God'. In spite of their respect for lineage and their interest in genealogy, the Arabs have never accepted the principle of primogeniture, and, at least in theory, the Caliphs were always elected. Their government was at first patriarchal and was conducted with the help of the surviving Companions of the Prophet.

[1] Some account of the beliefs and practices of Islam will be found in Chapter VII, pp. 378 ff.

They had no spiritual power of any kind; in a sense, indeed, no Moslem ruler can even legislate; he can only administer the Canon Law (*shar'*) revealed by God, which all the faithful are bound to observe. This is the traditional orthodox theory and is still maintained by the 'ulema of Nejd; its practical importance has varied; its validity is denied by some Egyptian modernists. The *shar'* is interpreted not by the State but by learned men (*'ulema*, plural of *'alim*) who devote their lives to its study. It is found primarily in the Koran, the collection of Muhammad's revelations made after his death, which orthodox theology holds to have existed uncreated from eternity. This is supplemented from the 'Tradition' (*hadīth*), that is, his recorded sayings and actions, many of which have been invented either to give support to particular opinions, or as legal fictions to supply deficiencies in the existing code. From very early times there was also a party which regarded as rulers and religious teachers by divine right certain members of his family, usually called Imams,[1] of whom the first was his cousin and son-in-law, 'Ali ibn Abi Tālib. These heretics, or *Shī'a* (sect), separated into many sects according to which of his descendants they recognized and to their theory of the Imamate.

The Arab Empire

The Arabs were accustomed to almost incessant war among themselves. Now, uneasily united under a government and a religion which tried to impose peace among them, they attacked the neighbouring countries which they had visited as raiders, mercenaries, and merchants, and whose weakness they knew. Within the next hundred years they acquired one of the largest empires in history, extending from China to the Atlantic and from Provence to the Punjab. Fanaticism had little to do with this expansion. Their new subjects were mostly Christians, Jews, or Zoroastrians, who were free either to become Moslems or to pay tribute (*jizya*), not as a penalty for not accepting Islam, but as a tax instead of military service, for which, as a rule, only Moslems were liable. For financial reasons the new subjects were sometimes encouraged to pay the tribute; others, such as the famous generals, Khālid ibn al Walīd and 'Amr ibn al 'Ās, were late converts and far from bigoted. The pious deplored the luxury that resulted from these early conquests, in which many of Muhammad's closest associates took no part. An attempt in recent times to explain them as the last of a series of migrations of Semitic

[1] See Chapter VII, pp. 385 ff.

peoples driven from Arabia by desiccation has been seriously challenged.[1]

Byzantium and Persia were exhausted by a struggle that had lasted a quarter of a century, in which neither had gained anything. Agriculture had been ruined by war and taxation; the loyalty of the nobility and the administration had been undermined; the Byzantine emperor was a usurper; Persia had had twelve rulers since the murder of Chosroes II in 628. Both empires had subject populations: Arabs, already settled in Syria and 'Iraq, and Copts, Armenians, and Aramaeans, speaking their own languages, mostly belonging to heretical Christian sects and therefore often persecuted, as was orthodoxy itself when the ruler was a heretic. Islam offered toleration to all. Its own spiritual appeal is shown by several strong Christian movements which in some ways resembled it; Leo III, the Iconoclast, was accused of 'arabizing'. There had been centuries of controversy and civil strife to decide the interpretation of the doctrines of the Trinity and the Incarnation, and many turned with relief to a faith which denied them both. Its dogmas and precepts were easy to understand and it was free from the less attractive features of oriental Christianity—morbid asceticism, hair-splitting theology, and, above all, a corrupt and ambitious clergy—for it had no priesthood.

The Byzantines had studied fortification and tactics; their army, recently reorganized, was well trained and equipped, but small. Attacks by Slavs and Avars kept part of it in Europe, and they could no longer afford to subsidize the nomad border chiefs or hire them as mercenaries. The Arabs were eager for booty, accustomed to warfare and hardship, and they suffered less from the heat than the heavily armed Greeks of more temperate regions. A frontier raid on Muta east of the Dead Sea was repelled during Muhammad's lifetime. Immediately after his death the Moslems were occupied in consolidating their power in the peninsula, which the Arab historians represent as having apostatized, though it is likely that some parts were now subdued for the first time. Their most dangerous enemy, the rival prophet Museilima of Yamāma (p. 233), was defeated and killed by Khālid at the battle of the Garden of Death (633). Strong forces were then sent against the Byzantines by Abu Bekr and the next Caliph, 'Omar (634–644). Safe from pursuit in the desert they attacked the long frontier where they pleased. Reinforced by Khālid

---

[1] Caetani has stated the case for this view in *Studi di storia orientale*, vol. i, 1911. His historical and geographical evidence has been criticized by Alois Musil, *Northern Nejd*, 1928, Appendix X.

after a brilliant march from Hira by way of Jauf, they were victorious at Ajnādein (634) and on the Yarmuk (636), and with the fall of Caesarea (640) the whole of Palestine and Syria was conquered. The emperor retreated to Asia Minor, where his successors organized a system of local defence. The passes over the Taurus were easy to hold and the climate inhospitable; the hardy and loyal population provided the imperial army with some of its best troops, and the navy, refitted after long neglect, threatened the coast behind the invaders. The Arabs raided far across the Anatolian plateau, but never retained a foothold.

'Iraq was as hard for the Persians to defend as was Syria for the Byzantines, and its loss was likely to be fatal, for it was the metropolitan province, the richest of the Sassanian Empire, in which the central authority was already weak. Al Muthanna, a beduin who had been fighting for Islam in Al Hasa, successfully carried the war into the delta. A Persian revolt saved the Arabs from the consequences of defeat at the battle of the Bridge (634) and after the great victory of Qadisiya (637?) they occupied the Sassanian capital, Ctesiphon. The last royal army was destroyed at Nihavend in Persia (642?) and many of the satraps, now independent, readily made terms. The fugitive king, Yezdigird III, the last of the Sassanian dynasty, was murdered in 652.

Meanwhile Egypt had been conquered by 'Amr ibn al 'Ās in 640. The loyalty of its inhabitants had been estranged by ruinous taxation and the violent persecution by the Byzantine Orthodox of the Monophysite Church, to which most of them belonged. The Byzantine army in Egypt, in the main recruited locally, was only sufficient for internal security; its discipline was bad and there was no supreme commander. The Arabs pressed on in the west to Tripoli, and in the south to the First Cataract, the boundary of the Christian kingdom of Nubia, which, however, kept its independence in spite of raids.

The Caliph 'Omar was more anxious to consolidate these conquests than to extend them. Arabic gradually became the language of nearly all the natives of Syria, Palestine, 'Iraq, and Egypt, and Islam the religion of most. But 'Omar, a strong ruler, and a simple and frugal man of great piety, was assassinated in 644, and the third Caliph, 'Othman (644–656), accused of nepotism and misgovernment, was murdered after a troubled reign. These Caliphs had lived at Al Madina, though there were many larger, richer, and more suitable cities, and the centres of military and political activity were already

Damascus in Syria and Kufa in 'Iraq. The fourth Caliph, 'Ali ibn Abi Tālib, the Prophet's son-in-law, therefore removed to Kufa after his election. Mu'āwiya, the powerful governor of Syria, refused to recognize him and civil war broke out. 'Ali, brave and eloquent, but lacking in political astuteness, was assassinated and his son Hasan abdicated. Mu'āwiya succeeded to the Caliphate and so founded the Omeiyad dynasty (661–750)—so named from one of his forefathers, 'Omeiyah—under which the Arab Empire reached its greatest extent. Three attempts were made to take Constantinople, the most determined being in 716–717, but the strength of its position and fortifications, the energy of Leo III, the use of 'Greek Fire', Byzantine sea-power, the rigours of winter, and difficulties of supply were too much for the Moslems.

Systematic conquest of the Byzantine province of Africa, which comprised Tunisia and parts of Algeria and Morocco, began about 670. As always, the Arabs were delayed by fortified towns, such as Carthage, which was not finally taken till 698. The Berbers resisted vigorously, but the straits of Gibraltar were crossed in 711. Roderic, King of the Visigoths, was defeated, most of Spain and Portugal overrun, Narbonne, Arles, and Marseilles taken, Bordeaux sacked, and Burgundy raided. This was the limit of expansion in Europe. An advance on Tours was checked at Poitiers (732) by Charles Martel, who soon after, in alliance with the Lombards, recovered Arles.

During the same period there was much activity in the Mediterranean and expansion eastwards. The Moslem fleet, first organized under 'Othman at Alexandria and Acre, took part in the sieges of Constantinople; Pantellaria was seized and descents were made on Cyprus, Rhodes, Crete, Sardinia, Corsica, and probably Malta. In the East conquest was directed by Al Hajjāj, the stern and able viceroy of 'Iraq. Afghanistan and Baluchistan were subdued; Muhammad ibn al Qasim invaded India, conquered Sind, and took Multan. The Turkish principalities beyond the Oxus submitted to Quteiba ibn Muslim, and the Arabs reached Kashgar. These vast areas were more lightly held than the nearer conquests of 'Omar's reign. In them, the Arabs were a small minority, and native families kept much of their authority. But in spite of serious rebellions by Berbers and Turks, Islam gradually became the faith of most of the conquered peoples both in the West and in the East, and, except in Europe, has remained so.

The Omeiyads have been more favourably regarded by European

R

than by Arab historians, who blame them for secularizing the Moslem State. They largely maintained the Byzantine administrative system and many of the same officials. In effect, each Caliph now appointed his successor. As patrons of letters and the arts, they kept a brilliant and luxurious court in or near Damascus. Some, such as Mu'āwiya I, had great political ability; others were merely dissolute; none but 'Omar ibn 'Abd al 'Aziz was intolerant in religion. Their relations with the Syrian Christians were good; St. John Damascene and Yazīd I were companions in youth. The Arabs, however, had not enough national consciousness to preserve a purely political unity. Bitter tribal feuds were carried all over the empire and involved the dynasty itself. The several sects of the Khawārij, or 'seceders', demanded an elected Caliph and complete equality among Moslems, and were in constant revolt. Husein, son of 'Ali and Muhammad's daughter, Fatima, rebelled against Yazīd I in 680. Killed at Karbala, he has ever since been revered as a martyr by the Shi'as.

The descendants of Muhammad's uncle, Al 'Abbās, skilfully exploited these dissensions. They won support among Persian converts by playing on their legitimist sympathies and on their resentment at being treated as a subject race. Civil war began in 747; the Caliph Marwān II was defeated and killed in 750, and the Caliphate passed to the Abbasids, whose rule lasted for 500 years. The surviving Omeiyad, 'Abdurrahman, escaped to Spain, where he remained independent.

The Abbasids inherited the Omeiyad Empire and ruled it from 'Iraq. Baghdad, founded in 762, became their capital. In many ways their rule was of the traditional Persian kind, and they relied primarily on Persians from the province of Khorasan, especially after the victory of Al Mamūn in the civil war between the sons of Harun ar Rashid. The religious basis of their power was stressed and sayings were ascribed to Muhammad which enjoined unquestioning obedience to the Caliph. On accession they assumed names with religious significance, were very devout in public, and sometimes bigoted. Gradually they lost power, and during the ninth century they became mere puppets of their Turkish bodyguard. Certain Shi'a dynasties arose, such as the Idrisids of Morocco, which ceased to recognize them, and many of their nominal subjects in the provinces made their own offices hereditary and became virtually independent. In such cases the only signs of the Caliph's authority were diplomas of investiture which he was powerless to refuse, public prayers for him on Fridays, and sometimes the appearance of his name on the coinage. Such were his relations with the dynasties of western Arabia.

The Hejaz during the Arab Caliphates

For the Hejaz, one of the most unproductive and disloyal provinces of the empire, this was a period of diminished political and commercial importance, increasing isolation and considerable disorder. Mecca enjoyed great sanctity, but its prosperity depended chiefly on the annual pilgrimage and endowments, and its food-supply on Egypt. Al Madina, where Muhammad was buried, was only less sacred and there was much rivalry between them. Its situation, nearer to the great administrative cities of Islam, Damascus, Baghdad, and Cairo, made it a more suitable residence for the Caliph's governors than Mecca, but rendered it dependent on Egypt when they ceased to be appointed. Tāif under the Caliphs was ruled by a deputy of the Governor of Mecca; the principal local family was the Beni Thaqīf. The numerous descendants of 'Ali, who had much property and influence in Mecca, Al Madina, and Yenbo', were disaffected to any rule but their own, and unable to agree among themselves. Those who dominated Mecca were descended from the Caliph Hasan, those at Al Madina from his brother Husein who had been killed at Karbala. These families were generally favoured by the beduin, and as the Caliphate declined they achieved more independence, playing off Egypt and 'Iraq against each other and conciliating the Yemen. The support which they had in the Hejaz was purely dynastic and not, as in most Moslem countries, associated with mystical and rationalist heresies.

The wars of conquest brought vast wealth to the Holy Cities but took away the most energetic leaders; Al Madina, when no longer the capital, and Mecca became centres of learning, poetry, and music, and retreats for the pious and the discontented. But the Omeiyads became so unpopular because of their secular government and their feud with the family of 'Ali, that on the death of Mu'āwiya I, 'Abdullah ibn az Zubeir was proclaimed Caliph at Mecca and for a short time was acknowledged in south Arabia, 'Iraq, and parts of Syria. He was killed when Mecca was besieged by Al Hajjāj (692). As long as the Caliphs were powerful there were only occasional revolts, but the work of the scholars, jurists, and theologians of Al Madina showed a hostility which has influenced Moslem historiography and political theory. The religious policy of the Abbasids enhanced the prestige of the two cities, and from this time dates the exclusion of all but Moslems from them. Muhammad was supposed to have said that no unbelievers were to be allowed to live in Arabia, and 'Omar I expelled some Christians and Jews, but there were Christians in Arabia long after his time, and the Omeiyads employed Christian workmen on the mosque at Mecca. Socotra was still Christian at the beginning of the sixteenth century, and there are to this day Jewish communities of ancient stock in the Yemen and the Aden Protectorate (p. 369).

The Abbasid Caliphs often sent a separate governor to Mecca and lavished money on it, but revolts became commoner and more dangerous. Late in the ninth century the Beni Ukheidir, a Hasanid family, won control of Yamāma and so of the communications between 'Iraq and the Hejaz. About the same time the sect of the Carmathians first appeared in 'Iraq, Syria, and Arabia, and in 899 their leader Abu Sa'id founded a state in Al Hasa which became, and may have been from the first, a republican oligarchy. Their origin and tenets are obscure, but they were connected with the Isma'īli branch of the Shi'a, since their 'Iraqi founder, Hamdān Qarmat, was a pupil of 'Abdullah ibn Meimūn, second founder of the Isma'īlis. The Carmathians were a secret society of communistic tendencies. They discarded prayer, fasting, and pilgrimage and were detested by the orthodox. Under Abu Tahir they raided Yamāma, 'Omān, and southern 'Iraq. The Caliphs purchased freedom from attack, but pilgrims could not cross Nejd without paying toll. In 930 the Carmathians plundered Mecca and carried away the Black Stone, but they returned it in 950. They were not always successful against Turkish troops in Abbasid employ, and their gradual decline was helped by internal discord. They were finally overthrown in 1077–1078 by 'Abdullah ibn 'Ali, chief of the Ibrahim ibn Muhammad clan of the 'Abd al Qeis, a tribe of Al Hasa.

The Sharifate of Mecca. The Sharifate—the more or less independent rule of Hasanid families at Mecca—began about 950 with Ja'far, the first of the Musāwi dynasty. In 1011 the Sharif Abul Futuh proclaimed himself Caliph and joined the Beni Teiy, then in revolt in Syria against the Fatimids, the heretical Isma'īli Caliphs of Egypt, who, however, forced him to submit by supporting a rival at Mecca. The Musāwis died out in 1061. During the anarchy which followed, the Beni Sheiba, hereditary keepers of the Ka'ba, seized its treasures for their own use, thus provoking the intervention of the Yemeni ruler, 'Ali as Suleihi, who installed Abu Hāshim Muhammad as Sharif. The descendants of this man struggled for power with each

other and with the Beni Suleiman, selling to the Abbasids or the
Fatimids indifferently the honour of being mentioned as Caliph in
the Friday prayers, plundering the pilgrims, and levying a poll tax
on those whose rulers could not protect them, while the tribe of
Hudheil took part in their quarrels and looted the city. The Seljuk
Turks sent troops there several times. In 1171 Salah ad Dīn (Saladin)
deposed the Fatimids and restored orthodoxy in Egypt; in 1174 and
1176 his brother Tūrān Shah passed through Mecca on his way to
and from the conquest of the Yemen (p. 248). The Abbasids alone
were now recognized, the Zeidi (Shi'a) rite was replaced by the
Shafe'i, and abuses were checked. Saladin's successors at Ta'izz had
some control in the Hejaz.

The Crusaders. Saladin's war with the Crusaders, established in
Syria and Palestine since 1099, led to two attacks on the Hejaz by
Renaud de Châtillon, the reckless lord of Kerak, east of the Dead
Sea, who harried the trade and pilgrim routes. It was suggested that
he wanted to reach Al Madina and dig up Muhammad's body, bury
it again in his own territory, and levy a tax on Moslem visitors to
the tomb. In 1181 he raided Teima, but was forced to retire when
the Governor of Damascus invaded Transjordan in his rear. Next
year he bribed the beduin to carry ships, including five galleys, by
camel to the Gulf of 'Aqaba where they were launched, Renaud himself remaining behind. Two galleys besieged the fort on the island
of Qarya (L'île de Graye) off 'Aqaba (Ailat), which had been taken
by the Christians in 1116 and recovered by Saladin in 1170. The
others cruised in the Red Sea, taking merchantmen and pilgrim
vessels and burning sixteen ships at 'Aidhāb, which they sacked;
'Aidhāb, on the Sudan coast nearly opposite Jidda,[1] was at the
height of its prosperity from the mid-eleventh to mid-fourteenth
century, as a harbour for Mecca pilgrims and an import market
for goods from central Africa and India, which were shipped via
Aden. In 1183 an Egyptian fleet put to sea, raised the siege of
Qarya, and overtook the second squadron on the coast of the
Hejaz. The Crusaders, some 300 in number, landed and marched
inland, pursued by the Moslem sailors, and were all killed or captured and executed, a few of them in the valley of Mina at the
Feast of the Sacrifice.

About the year 1200 Qatāda, ancestor of all the later Sharifs of

---

[1] Authorities do not agree about its position. On the 1:1,000,000 map, North
F.37, 'Aidhāb is shown about 22° 20′ N., over 30 miles north-west of Ras
Hadārba.

Mecca, seized power. His vigorous policy aimed at making the whole Hejaz an independent state. He raised an army, built and garrisoned a fort at Yenbo', subdued Tāif, made war on Al Madina, and extended his rule as far south as Hali. His successors became more dependent on Egypt after the capture of Baghdad by the Mongols in 1258, and the subsequent transfer of the Abbasid Caliphate to Cairo under the protection of the Mamluk Sultans (p. 267) who, in the fifteenth century, took charge of the customs at Jidda and maintained a body of cavalry at Mecca.

South-west Arabia

The history of south-west Arabia during this period is obscure and very confused. The inhabitants disliked the authority of the Caliphs but were disunited when it was removed. Desire for independence was natural in a distant country conscious of a glorious past, difficult of access, able to feed itself, and with commercial connexions outside the Arab Empire in southern India and elsewhere. The population included numerous Abyssinian mercenaries and slaves. In the mountains were many strongholds whose chiefs maintained virtual independence for generations, providing refuges for heretics and rebels. Christianity and, still more, Judaism had been strong. Acceptance of Islam was often nominal, and local cults were important. Orthodox Sunnis of the Shafe'i rite prevailed in the Tihama, and the Zeidis, a moderate branch of the Shi'a, in the highlands. There were also Carmathians, Isma'ilis, and Ibādhis, a Khāriji sect dominant in 'Omān. Several unstable dynasties arose, but the extent of their territory and the names and dates of the rulers are not always known. In one respect they compare favourably with the Sharifs of the Hejaz; most of them were patrons of letters and keen builders; many, particularly among the Zeidi Imams, were themselves distinguished scholars, poets, or theologians.

There were many revolts against the Caliphs, some in favour of descendants of 'Ali or of pre-Islamic rulers. Under the last Omeiyad Caliph, Marwān II, Yahya ibn 'Abdullah of Kinda established an Ibādhi State in the Hadhramaut which lasted twelve years (c. 745–757). In Abbasid times the Alids became stronger and, as in the Hejaz, were often supported by the tribes. Tradition attributes the conversion of the Yemen to 'Ali; in the mosque of 'Ali at San'ā is said to be a Koran written by him and stained with the blood of the children of the governor appointed by him; they were reading it when they were killed by an Omeiyad general. The Abbasid Caliph

Al Mamūn sent against the Tihama rebels Muhammad ibn Ziyād, whose descent from a famous viceroy and supposed relative of Muʻāwiya I made him unlikely to compromise with the Shiʻa. He made his capital at Zabīd and founded the dynasty of the Ziyadids (819), whose territory is said to have extended from Hali to Shihr, including the Yemen, Nejrān, and Hadhramaut. Their exact status is not clear; they were orthodox, always acknowledged, and at first paid tribute to the Caliphs, who for a time continued to appoint governors at Sanʻā. But in the middle of the ninth century they began to use the umbrella which is the emblem of sovereignty, and made no more payments. Their authority was greatest in the Tihama; much of the plateau was ruled under their suzerainty by Jaʻfar al Manākhi, who founded a dynasty at Mudheikhira; its power was broken by the Carmathians about 904, but it was of local importance long after.

About 840 Yaʻfur ibn ʻAbdur Rahmān, who claimed descent from the Himyarite kings, rebelled against the governor at Sanʻā, whom he expelled. The Yaʻfurids were recognized as governors by the Caliph in 872 and at first acknowledged his supremacy and that of the Ziyadids. Towards the end of the century, however, they had to fight three new-comers, the Zeidi Imam Yahya ibn Husein, the Carmathian ʻAli ibn al Fadhl, and the Ismaʻīli Mansūr al Yemen, of whom the last was the least formidable.

Yahya, like all the Imams in the Yemen, assumed a pious official name and was known as Al Hādī ilal Haqq, 'the guide to the Truth'. In 893 he founded the Rassid dynasty, so named from his grandfather Al Qasim ar Rassi, a direct descendant of Muhammad through Hasan, son of Fatima and ʻAli; his dynasty is still reigning in the Yemen to-day, though not all the Imams have been his descendants. In this early period their power, based on the northern city of Saʻda, was limited, though remarkably persistent. After a bad defeat by the Rasulids (successors of Saladin's Eiyubid governors) of Taʻizz in the thirteenth century, the history of these Zeidi Imams, always obscure, becomes almost hopelessly so until after the Turkish conquest in the sixteenth century.

The other serious opponent of the Yaʻfurids, ʻAli ibn al Fadhl, was an Ismaʻīli who won over the Yāfaʻis, made Mudheikhira his capital, took Sanʻā, and sacked Zabīd. He renounced his allegiance to the Fatimids who were the Ismaʻīli Imams, became a Carmathian, called himself 'Prophet of God', allowed wine-drinking, and tried to divert the Meccan pilgrimage to Harf. His connexion, if any, with

the Carmathians of Al Hasa is not known. After his death in 915
the Ziyadids and Ya'furids partially recovered, though they again
declined in the second half of the tenth century.

The Ya'furids often lost San'ā to the Zeidis, or to the tribal chiefs
of Hamdan and Khaulan, respectively north-west and south-east of
the capital. At one time they recognized the Fatimids. They had
little power after about 1000, but still held Kaukaban about 1280.
Several subordinate rulers, such as Suleiman ibn Tarf of 'Aththar
in the northern Tihama, the chiefs of the Beni Kurandi in Janadīya
and of the Beni Ma'an in Lahej, Aden and Hadhramaut became
virtually independent of the Ziyadids; after 981 the authority of
the latter was exercised by ministers, mostly African slaves, one
of whom, Husein ibn Salāma, built mosques and wells along the
pilgrim road from the Hadhramaut. Another of these ministers
murdered his master in 1018, only to be put to death by an Abyssinian rival, Najāh, who founded a new dynasty in 1021, which also
recognized the Abbasid Caliphs. But the Najāhid power was not
great except in the Tihama. In 1037 the Isma'īli 'Ali as Suleihi
revolted and by 1063 he had expelled the Najāhids and conquered
the whole Yemen, which he ruled from San'ā. An ornament to the
new Suleihid dynasty was Saiyida binta Ahmed, a highly cultivated
and energetic lady, who took over the government from her indolent
husband, and conferred many benefits on the country; she removed
from San'ā to Jibla, south of Ibb. But by 1100 this dynasty also
had only local influence.

Several families from Hamdan now held San'ā in turn. At
Aden the Zurei'ids, vassals of 'Ali as Suleihi who had driven out the
Beni Ma'an, made themselves independent, ruling the principality
from 1083 till the Eiyubid conquest in 1174–1176. The Najāhids
had already recovered Zabīd, but they became less powerful than
their own wazirs, and their dynasty came to an end in 1159 when
Zabīd was taken by 'Ali ibn al Mahdi, a Khāriji whose strict regime
relied on a puritan army.

In 1174 Saladin, seeking a safe retreat from the displeasure of his
suzerain, Nūr ad Dīn, sent his elder brother, Tūrān Shah, to conquer
the Yemen; the Hamdanids, Zurei'ids, and Mahdids, were over-
whelmed and a branch of the Eiyubids, as Saladin's family is called,
reigned from Ta'izz, which Tūrān Shah thought a healthier place
than Zabīd. They used Turkish and Kurdish rather than Abyssinian
troops and tried to introduce feudalism; under them and the next
two dynasties the Yemen was governed by a military aristocracy like

the Mamluks of Egypt. About 1230 Nūr ad Dīn 'Omar, deputy of the reigning Eiyubid, made himself independent and founded the Rasulids, the most brilliant dynasty of medieval Arabia; they were probably Turks, but claimed descent from the Himyaritic Tubbas through the Ghassānids (p. 232). They ruled the Hadhramaut and Mecca for a time and were patrons of letters and architecture. There was much dissension among them, and in the middle of the fifteenth century they were dispossessed by the Tahirids. Civil wars were frequent, but the reign of 'Abd al Wahhāb ibn Tahir (1478–1488) was prosperous; he built many colleges, cisterns, and other public works in San'ā, Zabīd, and Ta'izz. The Tahirid dynasty was still in power when the Mamluk Sultan of Egypt, and later the Ottoman Sultan Selim of Turkey, decided to conquer the Yemen early in the sixteenth century (p. 260).

The African Coast of the Red Sea

At the time of the Arab conquests the southern part of this coast was held by the Negus of Ethiopia and the northern by the Beja tribes, to whom the Byzantines had probably abandoned the eastern desert of Egypt south of Klysma before the middle of the sixth century. Abyssinian pirates were numerous and in 702 they burnt Jidda, which the Caliph 'Othman had developed as the port of Mecca. The Moslems retaliated, occupied the Dahlak islands, and probably destroyed Adulis. The history of the Abyssinians is obscure in this period; though the head of their Church was still appointed by the Coptic Patriarch, the end of Christian rule in Egypt and its decline in Nubia increased their isolation and the focus of the empire moved southwards. The Beja, except for the Moslem Hadarib—said to have come from the Hadhramaut in the early days of Islam—were mostly pagan. These tribes spread south and occupied the Massawa region in the eighth century, but in 831 the area between Aswan, Dahlak, and Rih became tributary to Moslem Egypt. The revolt of 'Ali Baba in 854 was suppressed by a joint military and naval expedition and he became vassal ruler of 'Aidhāb (p. 108). In the ninth century the Juheina and Beni Rabi'a tribes of Arabs penetrated the territory of the Beja, intermarried with them, and gained much influence in their matriarchal society. The Beja and the Arabs prevented Nubia from getting control of the coast, but the attacks of the Christian Nubian king, David I, about 1270 resulted in Egyptian occupation at Suākin, which was still Christian. Some fifty years later the Nubian kingdom disintegrated; it was invaded by Arab tribes, and its last known

Christian king was dethroned, though Christianity was not extinct there in the sixteenth century.

In the early tenth century Abyssinia regained the African coast at the south end of the Red Sea, but was soon weakened by pagan invasions. In the eleventh the Dahlak islands were subject to the Najāhids (p. 248), and in the twelfth they came under the Shaddādid dynasty, whose territory probably included Massawa. A hundred years later their ruler was an Abyssinian Moslem. Meanwhile Moslem settlements had been made at intervals along the coasts of the Red Sea, the Gulf of Aden, Somaliland, and far to the south in east Africa. Zeila, largely Christian in the tenth century, was a centre of Moslem propaganda in the fourteenth; it was the port of Ifat, one of a number of Moslem states that arose in eastern Abyssinia, of which the amirate of Harar survived till the nineteenth century. The best known of these states was 'Adal on the African side of the straits of Bab al Mandeb; it comprised the tribes now called Danakil, and its name persists in the 'Adali tribe of northern French Somaliland. Their history is confused, and different states or districts were often given the same name by Arab writers. After a long struggle they became more or less tributary to the Negus, whose northern maritime province extended to Suākin by the sixteenth century.

Commerce

Without some knowledge of the Red Sea trade during the Arab Caliphates the political history of the sixteenth century is unintelligible. The extent of the empire, annual pilgrimages to the Holy Cities, and the wide diffusion of the Arabic language stimulated commerce under the early Caliphs; Arabic coins have been found as far away as Mecklenburg and Iceland. The trade of Mecca, however, declined rapidly. The city had become economically less important after the centre of the Caliphate ceased to be situated in the Hejaz, its leaders had left, and the old fairs were discontinued. The alternative trade route from the Persian Gulf to Syria benefited by the cessation of the wars between Persia and Byzantium, the better administration of 'Iraq, the extension of its canals and roads, and by the foundation of Baghdad and the development of Basra. As, however, the Abbasid Caliphate declined and security diminished, trade was diverted to Aden, which became a great entrepot, goods being brought across the Indian Ocean and transferred there to small vessels which took them to the Red Sea ports. Still later, because of exactions at Aden, ocean-going ships often sailed on to Jidda, bringing renewed prosperity to that port and to Mecca. When the Crusaders held 'Aqaba, they cut the caravan road from the Hejaz to Egypt; but they were far from consistently hostile to Moslem trade, from which they also derived both revenue and supplies, while the fashions and tastes which they adopted among themselves and popularized in Europe increased the already considerable demand for oriental products.

The commodities sent to western markets by the Red Sea route were mostly natural products either of Arabia itself, or of India, Ceylon, or south-eastern Asia—spices, aromatics, drugs, dyes, and precious stones—but there were some manufactures such as textiles and, later, porcelain. Spices were much used in medieval European cookery both as preservatives and to flavour the great quantity of salt meat then eaten in winter in northern countries, where a large number of animals were killed in autumn, owing to the lack of winter feeding-stuffs before turnips were introduced. Spices were thus a very important item of trade, and almost the whole available supply reached Europe through the Levant. Pepper, ginger, canel, cinnamon, cardamoms, cloves, mace, nutmegs, and cassia were sent from Calicut, the great emporium in southern India, either up the Persian Gulf to Basra and thence to Aleppo and Beirut, or else to Aden, or later to Jidda, there to be transhipped to *gelbas*, the small boats which carried them to Tor, whence they were taken by Damascus to Beirut or by Cairo to Alexandria. From Beirut and Alexandria they were distributed to European and north African ports mostly by the merchant galleys built specially by the Venetian State to carry light, valuable cargoes. By the close of the fifteenth century the cargo of spices brought by these galleys from the Levant is estimated at 3,500,000 lb. annually, of which 2,500,000 lb. came from Alexandria, nearly half being pepper.[1]

Shoals and uncertain winds, however, made navigation difficult in the Red Sea. The *gelbas* sailed inshore and slowly, anchoring every night, and many were wrecked, so the Basra route was often used for the rarer spices, such as nutmegs and cloves, which deteriorated on a long voyage. Some spices were also imported for home consumption by the Arabs, who use ginger and cloves to flavour coffee. Commercially by far the most important and usually the cheapest of the spices was pepper; next came ginger, much used in Europe to make spiced wine. Among other items in this trade were aloes—those of

---

[1] 'Venetian Shipping during the Commercial Revolution', *American Historical Review*, vol. xxxviii, No. 2, Jan. 1933.

Socotra being famous—alum, ambergris, sandal wood, Brazil wood, camphor, cotton, lac, mastic, myrobalans, rhubarb, sugar, sapphires, emeralds, and pearls. There was a big demand for aromatics, often used as disinfectants. The extensive silk trade mostly followed more northern routes. The chief Arabian products concerned were frankincense, myrrh, precious stones, balm, and aloes. A little canel and ginger grew in south Arabia. The use of coffee, introduced from Abyssinia, was established in Arabia by 1500 in spite of theological opposition;[1] it was not yet exported to Europe.

Most of the vast profits of this trade were divided between the Arab merchants, the Sultan of Egypt, and the Venetians. The dues exacted at Jidda, Tor, and Cairo varied, and the accounts still extant do not agree in detail. At each of these places, 5 or 10 per cent. *ad valorem*, or even more, was paid. A third of any cargo brought to Jidda had to be pepper; this was sold at the Calicut price of pepper, which was low, to the Sultan, who paid for it in copper at the Calicut price of copper, which was high; the Venetians buying pepper in Egypt had to buy a fixed proportion from the Sultan at a high price and then pay him 5 per cent. for a safe conduct for their ships. The Venetians then made a considerable profit in their turn. Naturally prices in Europe were high; for instance, in England from 1260 to 1400 the average price of pepper per lb. was roughly the same as the price of a sheep, varying from 7d. to 2s. 6d., while in the fifteenth century it was about 1s. 5d.

Europe sent in return gold, silver, slaves from eastern Europe, copper, quicksilver, tin, brass, amber, verdigris, saffron, sables, woollens, and cloth goods, much of which passed through the Red Sea and Aden. Arabia imported cotton goods, rice, and sugar from the East. The Arabs also took cloaks from Aden, Indian cotton goods, beads, copper, and spices to Africa and Madagascar in exchange for gold, slaves, and ivory; negro slaves were prized for their physique and Abyssinians for their fighting qualities; the ivory was mostly resold in India, which could not meet its own needs. Berbera and Zeila also sent meat, fruit, grain, and butter to Aden. Horses were the chief Arabian export to India, some also going to Abyssinia. The trade was lucrative, as the demand was great and they died rapidly in India. Marco Polo writes that the Indians did not know how to treat horses, fed them on cooked food, and had no farriers. The King of Coro-

---

[1] It was held by some to be included in the prohibition of wine. *Qahwa*, the Arabic word for coffee, from which (through Turkish) its European names are derived, formerly meant wine.

mandel alone wanted more than two thousand horses a year, and the price of one was over 80 gold ounces. Madder from south Arabia was also sent eastwards, and there was a transit trade in emeralds from the mines of upper Egypt.

The colonies of Arab merchants in south China moved to Malaya about 900, but there was direct communication by sea between Arabia and China until the fifteenth century. Later the junks ceased to come even as far as Malabar. Arab settlements in Africa, India, and Malaya controlled most of the trade of the Indian Ocean. Those in Africa became independent states; elsewhere, though they did much to spread Islam, especially in Malaya, they usually accepted native rule and in Malabar were subject to the Hindu Rajahs. Numerous pirates frequented Socotra and sold their loot there; Guillaume Adam (p. 256) records that the pirates had 40 or 50 vessels capable of carrying 600 or 800 men apiece.[1]

Jews from France, trading to the East, used a route across the isthmus of Suez from Farama to Qulzum. 'Amr ibn al 'Ās, after his conquest of Egypt in 640, and Harun ar Rashid (786–809) considered cutting a canal across the isthmus to assist trade, but it was feared that it would be used by the Byzantine navy. 'Amr reopened the Pharaonic canal from Bilbeis to the Bitter Lakes and thence to the Gulf of Suez, in order to facilitate the dispatch of grain direct from the Nile to the Hejaz without transhipment; but this canal finally silted up in the following century.

When the Egyptians had taken Acre in 1291 and the failure of the Crusades was complete, some Europeans who understood the dependence of Moslem power on this trade made suggestions for its destruction. The last Grand Master of the Templars advised the Pope to prohibit it to all Christians.[2] Ramon Lull thought that Egypt could be ruined in six years if this were done and if spices were bought through Baghdad, then in Mongol hands.[3] Marino Sanuto in his *Liber secretorum fidelium crucis* (written 1306–1321) proposed an alliance with Tartary and Nubia and the maintenance of a fleet in the Indian Ocean to conquer its islands and coasts. Guillaume Adam considered that three or four galleys should be built at Hormuz which could blockade the Red Sea from Socotra, where the Christians and pirates would

[1] 'De modo Sarracenos extirpandi' in *Recueil des historiens des Croisades, Documents arméniens*, vol. ii, 1906, p. 555.
[2] See his memorandum to Clement V in Baluzius, *Vitae Paparum Avenionensium*, vol. iii, 1921, p. 149.
[3] See the extract from 'De fine' in A. Gottron, *Ramon Lulls Kreuzzugsideen*, 1912, pp. 86–87.

readily help them. He wrote that the Genoese had suggested to
Argun Khan, the Mongol ruler of Persia (1284–1291), the building of
two galleys at Baghdad to harry trade in the Indian Ocean; but this
scheme was prevented by the quarrels of its promoters.[1] In 1324 a
missionary wrote from India of the damage that two galleys sent by
the Pope could do.[2] At this time Genoese were organizing the Portuguese navy.

III. THE SIXTEENTH TO THE NINETEENTH CENTURIES

ARABIA AND THE RED SEA, 1500–1750

THE discovery of the sea route to India by Vasco da Gama in 1498
had immense significance for the Moslem countries, which lost much
strategic and commercial importance when European ships could
visit any seaport in Asia. To the European of the Middle Ages the
southward extent of Africa was unknown. During the fifteenth century the Portuguese had made many attempts to find a route round
Africa in the hope of spreading Christianity, of joining the Eastern
Christians in an attack on Islam, and of securing for themselves the
profits of the Eastern trade.[3] After their first successes, it is not known
exactly when King Manoel assumed the title 'Lord of the Conquest, Navigation and Commerce of Ethiopia, Arabia, Persia and
India'.

Internal Affairs 1500–1740

There is little of importance in the internal history of the Hejaz
from the time of the Portuguese discoveries until the Wahhabi revival. After the Ottoman conquest of Egypt in 1517 the Sharifs
readily accepted the Sultan's suzerainty, and his military prestige
helped to keep peace in the sixteenth century. The authority of the
Sharifs (p. 244) was recognized in Al Madina, Yenbo', Kheibar, and
Hali, but the Turkish Pasha at San'ā prevented them from annexing
Jīzān. The Sultan repaid their resistance to the Portuguese with half

[1] G. Adam, op. cit., pp. 549–555.
[2] L. Wadding, *Annales Minorum*, vol. vi, 1733, p. 36.
[3] It used to be thought that these voyages were caused by closure, or fear or
closure, of trade routes by the Turks. For a criticism of this view see A. H. Lybyer,
English Historical Review, 1915; for a defence see A. Hyma, *The Dutch in the Far
East*, 1942, pp. 224–225.

the customs dues at Jidda and, when these decreased in value, with a grant from his own property. Though the Turks gave many pious foundations to the Hejaz, they were disliked for their venality and their strong preference for the Hanafi rite (p. 384). For several centuries the chief Qadhi at Mecca had been chosen for life from a certain Meccan family; now he was an official sent annually from Constantinople. When the Sultan tried to exclude all heretics, including Shi'a pilgrims from Persia and the Yemen, the Sharif deplored the loss of revenue and tried to protect them. Throughout the seventeenth and eighteenth centuries branches of the Hasanid family fought and intrigued for power, only uniting against the Turks, whose power was everywhere declining.

In the distant Yemen the Turks were even less successful. The Pasha at San'ā was appointed either by the Sultan or by the Pasha of Egypt. Reinforcement was difficult; the Tihama was unhealthy, and there were frequent rebellions in the mountains. The religious attitude of the Turks was even more unpopular among the Zeidis than at Mecca. A war of independence began with the accession of the Imam Al Mansūr billah Al Qasim, styled 'The Great', in 1597. The Turks had artillery, better small arms, strong forts, cavalry, and an energetic general, Sinan Pasha. The Arabs were disunited, for the Imam was not the only rebel leader, being opposed by the Isma'īlis; he was for a time a fugitive in Nejrān. Both Turks and Arabs needed money, and there were long truces. When the Imam Al Mansūr died in 1620, Al Mueiyad billah Muhammad, being elected Imam, overran most of the plateau and the northern Tihama, whence the Turks withdrew to Kamarān island. His attack on Mocha was repelled by gunfire from the roofs and from ships in the harbour; but a Turkish relief force sent from Egypt deserted and San'ā surrendered to the Imam. In 1630 the Tihama was recovered by a joint Turkish military and naval expedition under Ahmed Qansuh, but when the Imam invaded it in 1635 the Turks evacuated it on terms, Zabīd, Mocha, and Kamarān being surrendered to the Imam (1636).

After this the rule of the Imams was not seriously challenged during the seventeenth and eighteenth centuries. Their history is rather obscure, but the Imam Al Mansūr billah Al Qasim (mentioned above), though a descendant of the earlier Rassid Imams of Sa'da, is regarded as the first of the present line of Imams of San'ā. His successor Al Mueiyad was followed by the Imam Isma'īl ibn Qasim. The latter, taking the time-honoured designation *Al Mutawakkil 'alā Allah* ('the relier on God'), is said to have reigned some thirty years, dying about 1676; he lived in extreme simplicity, universally respected for his piety and administrative talents. He resided mainly at Dhoran, south-west of Ma'bar, and was buried on the lofty Jebel Dhoran.

The picture drawn by Niebuhr in the mid-eighteenth century shows the country divided into provinces, each governed by a *daula* ('dola') or military governor, directly under the Imam. The daula, who commanded the troops and collected the taxes, was aided by a secretary and a *qadhi*. The daulas were changed every few years. In the seaports the daula had under him an *amir al bahr*, or port officer, an *amir as suq*, or market officer, and generally a *sheikh al bilad* set over municipal affairs.

During this period the Imams lost such control as they had over the 'Aulaqi and Yāfa'i country, while in 1728 the 'Abdali Sheikh of Lahej became independent, taking the title of Sultan, and seizing Aden soon afterwards. In the later eighteenth century a family of sharifs at Abu 'Arīsh acquired most of 'Asīr and the northern Tihama. Mocha, of which Zeila had at some time become a dependency, remained in the hands of the Imam.

The Struggle for the Red Sea Trade, 1500–1750

The wish for an eastern ally, the existence of Christians in Asia, and the toleration of the Buddhist Mongols influenced the story of Prester John, the Christian priest supposed to rule a great empire in the East, afterwards identified with Abyssinia, where Guillaume Adam and other Dominicans arrived in the early fourteenth century. Usually no reference is made in histories of Ethiopia to this little-known episode, or to any intercourse between the Monophysite Ethiopian and the Latin Churches during the period from the conversion of Ethiopia to Christianity in the fourth century till the fifteenth-century contacts mentioned below. Guillaume Adam, a Dominican and probably French, and five other Dominicans were consecrated bishops in 1318 by one of the early Popes of the 'captivity' at Avignon. They were sent to assist Franco di Perugia, just raised to the archbishopric of Sultanieh in Persia. Guillaume Adam states that 'it was meet for him to traverse thoroughly the lands round the Indian Ocean and some islands, because the arrangement of the journey which he had to make, for the purpose of preaching in Ethiopia, required this'.[1]

[1] G. Adam, op. cit., p. 551; an attempt to trace Adam's later history is made by C. Kohler in the introduction to the work cited.

In the fifteenth century the Negus—always called 'Preste João' by early Portuguese writers—sent envoys to Europe and was represented at the Council of the Church at Florence (1438–1439), while the epic of the Portuguese in Ethiopia began with the arrival of Pedro da Covilham in 1490—to last till the final expulsion of the Jesuits in 1633.[1] The Portuguese tried to reach Abyssinia at first from Guinea and then from the ports of east Africa and the Red Sea, of which latter only Massawa was satisfactory, because much of the coast was held by Moslems. It was, therefore, for many reasons important for the Portuguese to command the Red Sea.

It is worth recalling, as bearing on the hazards undergone to obtain spices, that Pedro da Covilham is regarded as the first medieval European to have visited Arabia. He was sent in May 1487 by King John II of Portugal on a voyage of exploration in the Levant, Asia, and Africa, to learn where 'cinnamon and other spices could be found', and to discover by overland routes the land of Preste João. During his travels from Cairo to India and back, with an excursion down the east African coast, and a second journey from Cairo to the Persian Gulf, he touched several times at Aden, visited Hormuz and Jidda, and claimed to have reached Mecca and Al Madina. If his claim be true, his visit to the holy cities was more than a decade earlier than that of the Bolognese traveller Ludovico di Varthema, in 1503. Covilham subsequently reached the Court of the Negus in 1490. He was honourably received but was detained in Ethiopia, where the Portuguese mission (1520–1526) under Rodrigo da Lima found him. John Cabot also claimed to have visited Mecca as a centre of the spice trade; he told Raimondo di Soncino, envoy of the Duke of Milan in England, that he (Cabot) had formerly been to Mecca, as reported by di Soncino to the Duke in a letter dated 18 December 1497.[2]

In the struggle now beginning the Portuguese were hampered by lack of numbers, resources, and capital, by business inexperience and distance from home. They could not undertake to govern a large area and had to man their fleets partly with convicts. They were hindered by orders made at home in ignorance of changing local conditions. The terms of office of the governors were too short, usually three years, but sometimes renewed, as in the case of Albuquerque (1509–

[1] C. F. Rey, *The Romance of the Portuguese in Abyssinia*, 1929.

[2] H. Harrisse, *Jean et Sebastien Cabot* (Paris, 1882, pp. 43, 324–326), doubts whether Cabot penetrated the sacred precincts of Mecca; but see also James A. Williamson, *The Voyages of the Cabots* (1929).

1515). Discipline was bad, and subordinates often complained direct to the king. Their caravels, however, designed for long and stormy voyages, were more seaworthy than lateen-rigged dhows built only to sail with the monsoon and to repel no enemy but pirates; the Egyptian and Turkish galleys were better suited to the Mediterranean. The Portuguese had armour far superior to the oriental, and their casualties were very few. Their guns were better than the Indian, though no better than those of Egyptians or Turks, but their morale was higher than that of the Sultan's renegades and slaves. Their captains and merchants had great racial pride, a fanatical zeal against Islam, and, if expedient, their policy was ruthless.

The Arab merchants opposed the Portuguese from the first, while the Venetians were as hostile as their European policy allowed. The Portuguese, envying the commercial experience and unequalled knowledge of spices possessed by the Venetians, urged them to transfer their business from Egypt to Lisbon. But the Venetian Council of Ten considered that such a diversion of trade would be disastrous and asked the Sultan both to incite the Indian Moslems and to reduce the dues paid in Egypt, thus enabling the Venetians to undercut the Portuguese. The Sultan did neither, but sent a monk to Rome to threaten that he would destroy the Holy Places in Jerusalem if the voyages continued; but he unwisely included a protest against the treatment of the Moors in Spain, thereby incurring the hostility of the strongest European State and her allies. The Pope referred the matter to King Manoel, who replied that he would soon defeat the Egyptians and capture Mecca. Venice again tried to advise the Sultan. In 1504 the Council of Ten considered suggesting to him the digging of a canal from the Mediterranean to the Red Sea, but later omitted this part of their envoy's instructions. Nevertheless, a traveller in 1529 found 20,000 men working at Farama on a canal; it was never finished, though the project was again considered by the Turks in 1586. When at last the Sultan decided on war with Portugal, Venice, as a Christian State, declined to give him active help.[1]

Da Gama's voyage lasted from 1497 to 1499, a third of his men died, he met much hostility, and his goods were not wanted. For a time some of the Portuguese opposed the whole project of Eastern expansion, but the next voyage was a success and it was then decided to try to stop the Red Sea trade. In 1502 Da Gama sailed again, burnt

[1] The relevant documents have been published in *Archivio Veneto*, vol. ii, 1871, and *Corpo Diplomatico Portuguez*, vol. i; see also *Viaggi fatti da Vinetia*, 1543, fol. 109, recto.

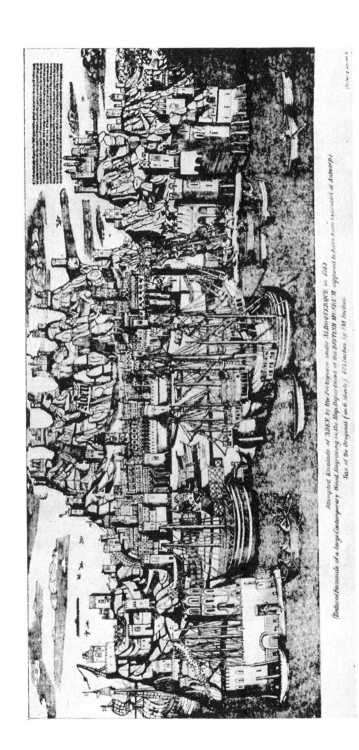

Attempted Escalade of ADEN by the Portuguese under ALBUQUERQUE in 1513

(Reduced facsimile of a large Contemporary Wood Engraving in the Map Department of the BRITISH MUSEUM supposed to have been executed at Antwerp)

Size of the Original (in 6 Sheets) 14½ inches by 19½ inches

137. *Attempted Escalade of Aden by the Portuguese under Albuquerque in 1513*

138. *Aden about 1572, showing the artificial cut through the isthmus (from G. Braun & F. Hogenberg: Civitates orbis terrarum, 1577)*

139. *Attack on Jidda by Lopo Soares de Albergaria in 1516 (? 1517) (from Gaspar Correa: Lendas da Ásia, 1860)*

a pilgrim ship, tried to expel the Moslem traders from Calicut, and left behind a squadron under Sodre which did some damage to shipping. In 1506, to help the blockade of the Gulf of Aden, Tristão da Cunha and Albuquerque were sent to take Socotra, which had been ruled from Arabia for some fifty years. They captured the island in 1507 and conciliated its Christian population. Though a useful watering place, it had no safe winter anchorage, was unhealthy and short of supplies, and was therefore abandoned in 1511. Meanwhile an Egyptian fleet was built and left Suez in 1507 under Husein, governor of Jidda. It defeated the Portuguese in the harbour of Chaul, south of Bombay (1508), but was badly beaten off Diu, west of the gulf of Cambay (1509). The first Portuguese viceroy, Almeida, who relied on sea-power and was averse from holding forts on land, was superseded (1509).

Albuquerque now became governor[1] of the Portuguese settlements and factories in western India. But those between Gujerat and the Cape, together with the conduct of the blockade, were entrusted to another officer, who, without adequate bases, could do little and was recalled in 1510. Albuquerque, in sole command, planned to occupy strategic points for the control of trade and saw that Aden was the key to the Red Sea. Aden was well fortified and, as a refuge from the Portuguese warships, it had become prosperous. Albuquerque attacked it without success in March 1513; he then entered the Red Sea, burning Arab ships and mutilating their crews, but failed to reach Jidda and put in at Kamarān, where he had very heavy losses from disease, heat, and bad food. Having explored Perim, which, being waterless, was unsuitable for a fortress, and finding Aden still strongly defended, he returned to India in August and never went back to Aden. Like others of his time, he overrated the power of Abyssinia, desiring her to join in attacks on Mecca and Suez, in which Portugal would provide the shipping and Abyssinia most of the men. Albuquerque thought he could ruin Egypt in two years by diverting the Nile to the Indian Ocean,[2] a scheme believed to have been considered long before by the Negus Lalībalā (c. 1200).

The Portuguese were more successful in the Persian Gulf where, to secure their monopoly, they needed a fortress to control the trade, just as Aden, could they have held it, would have controlled trade in the Red Sea. With this object Albuquerque captured Hormuz in 1507—the date of the first establishment of the Portuguese there,

[1] Albuquerque and most of his successors were only governors, not viceroys.
[2] *Cartas de Affonso de Albuquerque*, vol. i, 1884, pp. 278–283 and 395–402.

though it underwent a later siege. Situated on a small island near the Persian mainland in the strait due north of Ras Masandam, Hormuz effectively closed the Persian Gulf to shipping other than Portuguese, and it remained for over a century one of the most important and lucrative possessions of Portugal in Asia. The Portuguese were eventually expelled in 1622 by the English and Persians.

Albuquerque, the greatest of the Portuguese governors, was removed in 1515; the king wrote to him to assume the naval command and use the resources of India for another Red Sea campaign, but he died before the letter arrived. His successor, Lopo Soares de Albergaria, set out with a stronger force in February 1517. Meanwhile the Mamluks had decided to conquer the Yemen, either as a base to use against the Portuguese or as a refuge for themselves if the Ottoman Turks invaded Egypt. An army entered the Tihama, and a fleet sailed from Suez in 1515. Rais Suleiman, who was in command, worked for eight months on a fort at Kamarān, but failed to take Aden and returned to Jidda. Two years later Selim I, Ottoman Sultan of Turkey, conquered Egypt and was recognized by the army, which continued the occupation of the Yemen, where a Turkish Pasha was installed. When the Portuguese reached Aden in the same year (1517) the governor submitted, but instead of landing, Soares sailed to Jidda, where he did nothing, and then to Kamarān, where in three disastrous months 800 Europeans and nearly all his slaves died. In July he burnt Zeila, but he now found Aden strong enough to resist him and he therefore withdrew.

Later Portuguese expeditions were sent primarily to investigate or interrupt Turkish naval preparations to regain sea-power. Diogo Lopes de Sequeira ventured into the Red Sea in 1520, but did not meet the Turks. At Massawa he landed an envoy to the Negus, who wanted the Portuguese to build forts there and at Zeila and Suākin. In 1524 the local sheikh at Aden told Eitor da Silveira that he would pay tribute if helped against the Turks; a ship was left there to exact toll in the straits, but the sheikh imprisoned the crew. In 1529 a Turkish fleet left Suez, but was defeated by the local population at Aden and by the Portuguese in the Indian Ocean. The ports were closed to prevent leakage of information, and a larger fleet sailed in 1538 under Suleiman Pasha, a Greek eunuch. Suleiman was strong enough to be received at Aden, where he hanged the governor and burnt the town, but he was defeated at sea by the Portuguese. In 1541 Estevão da Gama, Vasco's son, sailed from Goa for Suez. Leaving his big ships at Massawa he went on to Suākin, Quseir, and Tor, but the sight of the defences and the Turkish fleet at Suez caused him to retreat. At Massawa, where food was scarce and disease rife, he landed 400 soldiers under his brother, Cristovão, to help the Negus against Muhammad Gran, a Moslem who, having obtained match-lockmen from the Pasha of the Yemen in return for tribute, had over-run Abyssinia.

In 1547 'Ali ibn Suleiman, an Arab chief, drove the Turks from Aden and asked the Portuguese for help. Payo de Noronha was sent to hold the town, but fled by night when 'Ali was defeated. The Vice-roy in India, the famous João de Castro, then sent his son, but the Turks had entered Aden before he arrived, and the Portuguese retired after storming a fort at Shihr. In 1580, 1584, and 1589 a Turkish officer, 'Ali Bey, left Mocha to make successful attacks on Muscat and on the Portuguese colonies in East Africa, but he was eventually captured. Portugal was now declining; her union with Spain in 1580 brought trouble and war with the new naval Powers, England and Holland, who infringed her commercial monopoly. After her expulsion from Hormuz in 1622 by the English and Persians she was of no importance in Arabian affairs, though she shared in the trade of Mocha till the middle of the eighteenth century. Communication with Abyssinia became very difficult, and Portu-guese influence on that side of the Red Sea ended with the failure of the Jesuit attempt to enforce Roman Catholicism (1632). The Negus and the Turks agreed together to exclude Europeans.

It will not be possible to estimate the full effect of Portuguese policy on eastern trade until the archives of Ragusa and other unpub-lished records have been examined. Spices were still dear, because bullion from the Americas kept prices high, and the Portuguese aimed not at underselling their rivals but at a monopoly. At first less spices reached Venice and Lisbon together than had formerly reached Venice alone. In 1502 the Venetians on one occasion found only four bales of pepper at Beirut. Because of a dispute between Venice and Egypt during the years 1505–1514, there was little trade between them. This dispute benefited Ragusa, which thus became a serious competitor. She had trading rights in Turkey and obtained rights in Egypt from the Mamluks in 1510 which were renewed by the Sultan Selim after he had conquered Egypt in 1517. Dues in Egypt were reduced, and by the middle of the century Egyptian trade re-covered for a while; in 1560 the Portuguese envoy to the Vatican, to whom a spy in Cairo reported, said that 4,480,000 lb. of spices, mostly pepper, reached Alexandria yearly by the Red Sea, and he therefore

suggested that Portugal should obtain her supply from the Levant.[1]
This figure may be exaggerated, since trade between India and the
Red Sea was already difficult, but it was suggested that the Viceroy
at Goa must be in revolt against Portuguese interests. In the next
century the Dutch and English diverted most of what was left of this
trade to the Cape route.[2]

The English first brought spices from the Levant in English ships
in 1511, but they also bought them in Lisbon and tried to obtain
them from Persia across Russia; they did not enter the Indian Ocean
till Drake's voyage of circumnavigation (1577–1580). The union of
Spain and Portugal (1580), the closing of the Lisbon markets, and the
rout of the Spanish Armada (1588) were additional incentives to the
venturesome English merchants to compete for trade in eastern
waters. The East India Company was chartered in 1600, and, in the
attempt to force a way into the Indian trade against Portuguese and
Dutch resistance, expeditions were sent to Aden and the Red Sea. In
1608 the company's fleet under William Keeling gave up at Socotra
an attempt to reach Aden, where Keeling had orders to try to open
a factory.

Next year (1609) Alexander Sharpie, also sent by the East India
Company, called at Aden in the *Ascension* with a cargo of iron, tin,
lead, and cloth. He was welcomed ashore by the governor, a Greek
renegade who, however, kept him under restraint, refusing to let him
return to his ship or to trade till permission had been received from
the Turkish Pasha at San'ā. Even after Sharpie had been set free,
disputes with the governor over customs dues resulted in John Jourdain, a Dorsetshire man and Sharpie's chief 'factor', being sent overland to San'ā to negotiate with the Pasha. Jourdain travelled via
Zbida (north of Lahej) and Janad, leaving Ta'izz a few miles to the
west, thence by Ibb, Yarīm, and Dhamār to San'ā. Thus the Yemen
was traversed for the first time by an Englishman, the story of whose
journey has been published.[3] On his return journey Jourdain turned
west a few miles north of Janad and visited Ta'izz, continuing to
Mocha, where he rejoined Sharpie, who had sailed from Aden, but

[1] *Corpo Diplomatico Portuguez*, vol. ix, 1886, pp. 108–112.

[2] F. C. Lane, 'Venetian Shipping during the Commercial Revolution', *American
Historical Review*, Jan. 1933, and 'The Mediterranean Spice Trade', ibid., Apr.
1940; A. H. Lybyer, 'The Ottoman Turks and the Routes of Oriental Trade',
English Historical Review, Oct. 1915; N. Mirkovich, 'Ragusa and the Portuguese
Spice Trade', *Slavonic and East European Review*, Mar. 1943.

[3] *The Journal of John Jourdain, 1608–17*, ed. Sir William Foster, Hakluyt Society,
2nd Series, No. 16, 1905.

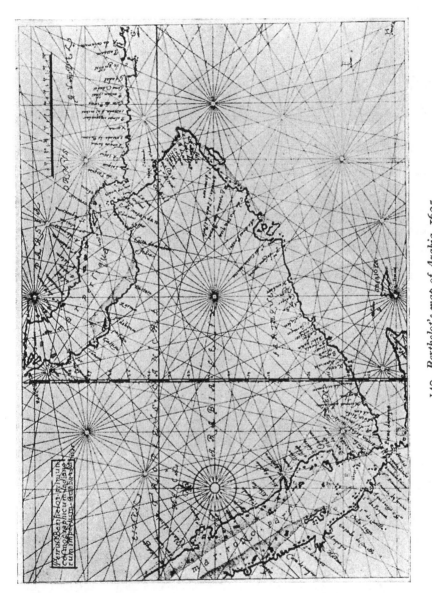

140. *Berthelot's map of Arabia, 1635*

141. *Ruined medieval hill-top fortress at Ridaʻ, Yemen*

142. *Mocha, the coffee-port, in decay*

where he did little business and could establish no factory, being without an Ottoman Imperial permit. Sharpie had first sent two of his officers, William Revett and Philip Glascock, from Aden to Mocha in an Arab vessel; these were the first Englishmen to pass through the strait of Bab al Mandeb.

Aden, then much decayed, was visited yearly by only a few small ships from India and the Persian Gulf, bringing turban cloths and cotton goods, and returning with gum arabic, frankincense, myrrh, and madder. But Aden's strong stone walls, and an outpost fort on Sira island, were guarded by the Turkish garrison, while the Arab inhabitants were kept disarmed.

Mocha, on the other hand, though an unwalled town within the Red Sea, with houses mainly of sticks and thatch, was increasingly important, being frequented by merchants from many parts of the Middle East and from India. The Indian merchants, bringing iron among other things, sailed thither with the first of the easterly winds, remaining through the winter and during most of the south-west monsoon, and leaving for India towards the end of the latter, in late August; during their stay they traded with the merchants who sailed from Suez to Mocha with the north-westerly winds, and returned to Suez with the first easterly winds of autumn (p. 156). Jourdain and Revett, mentioned above, both thought that Mocha offered scope for sale of English commodities.

In 1610 Sir Henry Middleton, another East India Company commander, sailed to Mocha, where he was imprisoned. Middleton escaped and extorted compensation by a blockade. Later he came back, traded by force, and seized Gujerati ships. He was joined in this by John Saris, who had brought a Turkish permit and had come for peaceful trade. Sir Thomas Roe, first English ambassador to the Great Mogul (1615–1619), wanted one ship from the East Indian fleet sent to the Red Sea every year. He thought £100,000 worth of goods could be sold and 100 per cent. profit made. In 1618 Andrew Shilling came to Mocha in the *Lion* and was well received; charts were made by his mate, the Arctic explorer, Baffin, while Joseph Salbank, termed a 'chief merchant' of the East India Company, visited the Pasha at San'ā. In spite of dislike of Roe's plan among the factors at Surat and by the Mogul Government, a somewhat irregular trade was maintained, though it was for a time disorganized by the Yemeni war of independence against the Turks (p. 255). Coffee, not mentioned in the Company's sale lists until 1660, had already become by far the most important export of Mocha.

The first Dutch voyage to the East was made in 1595–1597 and the Dutch East India Company was chartered in 1602. Most of its efforts were concentrated in the East Indies, Sumatra, Java, and the Moluccas. In 1614 Pieter Van den Broecke tried unsuccessfully to open a factory at Aden; he had better fortune at Shihr, where the Arabs allowed him to open one; he was also welcomed at Qishn, but left because the local Mahri Sultan was friendly to the Portuguese. In 1616 Van den Broecke visited Mocha, which had grown from a fishing village to a prosperous town in half a century; a caravan of some 1,000 camels arrived while he was there. He travelled to San'ā, where the Pasha received him courteously, but would allow no settlement without reference to the Sultan of Turkey, while he also objected to Christians being so near Mecca. On his way back Van den Broecke traded profitably at Mocha, but closed the factory at Shihr. In 1618 their ambassador secured permission for the Dutch to stay in Yemeni ports,[1] but advised them to avoid the northern Red Sea and to treat Moslem merchants well. Fearing restrictions on the rich Levantine trade, the diplomats did little to help the factors in Arabia. In 1620 Van den Broecke came too late and had to leave his goods at Aden, whence they were taken to Mocha by dhow. Dutch ships which came in 1621 attacked craft from Portuguese India; the Turks took the officials and stock of the factory at Mocha as a reprisal. Futile negotiations ensued; the factor, Willem de Milde, died a prisoner; it became unsafe for the Dutch to land, and they traded from their ships, sometimes going to Assab for supplies. In 1628 Job Grijp bought 40 bales of coffee, but the Arab revolt against the Turks made it almost impossible for him to sell the goods he had brought. Spasmodic trade continued, till in 1663 the first important cargo of coffee was sent to Holland. In 1708, at the request of the Imam (now independent of the Turks), a factory was again opened at Mocha and given the right to export 600 bales of coffee annually free of duty. Coffee was now being grown in Java, and in 1738 the Dutch East India Company decided to close the Mocha factory, although ships still made occasional calls.

A private French voyage to the East was made in 1529, and in 1619–1620 Beaulieu sailed along the south coast of Arabia. Later Colbert, the great finance minister of Louis XIV, hoped, with the help of Turkey, to revive the Red Sea trade and wanted to have consuls in the ports.[2] The traveller La Boullaye le Gouz suggested an

---

[1] *Corpus Diplomaticum Neerlando-Indicum*, vol. i, 1907, No. 58.
[2] *Lettres, Instructions et Mémoires de Colbert*, vol. ii, 1883, pp. 847–848.

alliance with Abyssinia. Nothing came of these schemes. In 1708–1709 French ships called at Aden and Mocha, a commercial treaty was made, and a factory opened. In 1711 other ships called and procured coffee bushes to plant in Réunion. The Imam refused a Turkish request that he should stop trading with Europe, but the French were offended when their goods were paid for only indirectly by remitting future customs dues; therefore in 1737 they bombarded Mocha. Though coffee sold in France for about twice its cost in Arabia, yet the trade ceased to be profitable and was gradually abandoned.

Some of the smaller European nations also took part in the Arabian trade. In 1620 a Danish fleet passed Socotra. One ship anchored there and Erik Grubbe made a trading agreement. There was a Danish factory at Mocha for a time later in the century, and about 1720 several ships sailed to Mocha from Ostend. About 1755 C. H. Braad, an agent of the Swedish East India Company, visited Mocha and reported on the commercial prospects.

The First Wahhabi State, 1740–1818

Nejd had lost all political importance after the defeat of Museilima in 633 (p. 239). With the decline of the Caliphate it became anarchic and isolated except for the pilgrim caravans that passed through. Pagan practices survived among the people. There were sacred trees, rocks, and springs (p. 235), and, as in many remote parts of the Moslem world, offerings were made at the graves of holy men. In the eighteenth century a reformation began which made Nejd a powerful state and the most puritanical country of Islam. This is the movement generally called Wahhabism, the doctrines and practices of which are described in Chapter VII, p. 384.

The founder, Muhammad ibn 'Abd al Wahhab, was born at 'Ayeina in 1703 and studied theology in Al Hasa, the Hejaz, 'Iraq, and Syria. A biographer says that he practised mysticism in Persia and gained some military knowledge. He adopted the system of Ahmed ibn Hanbal (p. 312) and was deeply influenced by the writings and example of the reformer Ibn Teimiya (1263–1328). Ibn 'Abd al Wahhab returned home and about 1740 began to denounce religious laxity. Forced by Ibn 'Arei'ar of the Beni Khālid to leave 'Ayeina, he took refuge with Muhammad ibn Sa'ūd, the head of an 'Aneiza family which had settled at Dar'īya not long before. Ibn Sa'ūd became the head of the new community and performed the duties of a Caliph. Though neither he nor his successors used this title, they always rejected the claims of any who did. Strictly they were called *Imams*, less formally *Amirs* or *Sheikhs*. Ibn 'Abd al Wahhab became leader of the *'ulema* and spent the rest of his life in teaching and controversy, and as adviser to Ibn Sa'ūd, who married his daughter; a few of his works have been printed, and others exist in manuscript in the British Museum. He died in 1791. His descendants intermarried with the royal house and are still influential.

About 1746 a long war began; in this Muhammad ibn Sa'ūd and his son 'Abdul 'Aziz, who succeeded him in 1765, slowly extended Wahhabi rule. Their most persistent enemy, Dahham ibn Dauwas of Riyādh, was finally defeated in 1773. They repulsed several attacks of the Beni Khālid, who brought artillery against Dar'īya in 1764. Raids on Al Qasīm began about 1770. By 1786 Nejd, from the Nafūd to Wadi Dawāsir, was subdued. Participation in a quarrel in the house of 'Arei'ar led to war with Thuweini, Sheikh of the Muntafiq of lower 'Iraq. At Mecca the Wahhabis were regarded as heretics. Conferences were unavailing and the pilgrim traffic from Persia and 'Iraq, though profitable to both sides, was suspended. In 1790–1791 the Sharif Ghālib invaded Nejd but had to retreat, and during the next three years the northern oasis of Jauf submitted to the Wahhabis and Al Hasa was conquered. In 1796 the Mamluk Pashas of Baghdad helped Thuweini to attack again, but the latter was murdered in the following year and his army dispersed. An expedition under 'Ali Pasha in 1798 was induced to withdraw by resistance and bribes. The Sharif Ghālib now made peace and pilgrim traffic was resumed. But the pilgrim caravan from Persia and 'Iraq was attacked by tribesmen of 'Iraq, and the Wahhabis, who had agreed to protect it, professed themselves in honour bound to avenge the attack; they therefore sacked Karbala in 1801, massacring the inhabitants and desecrating the tomb of Husein, to the horror of Islam. They raided the Euphrates valley, threatened the independence of 'Omān, and made tributary the oases along the pilgrim road from Aleppo.

In 1803 the Wahhabis broke through to the Red Sea at Hali, summoning the Sharif Ghālib to abdicate. Tāif and Mecca were taken, shrines were destroyed, and the Ka'ba was stripped of adornments. Ghālib fled to Jidda, which was held by a Turkish garrison, while the Nejdis, unused to the climate, died of plague. Then for a time the tide turned. Mecca in revolt drove out the Wahhabis. In November

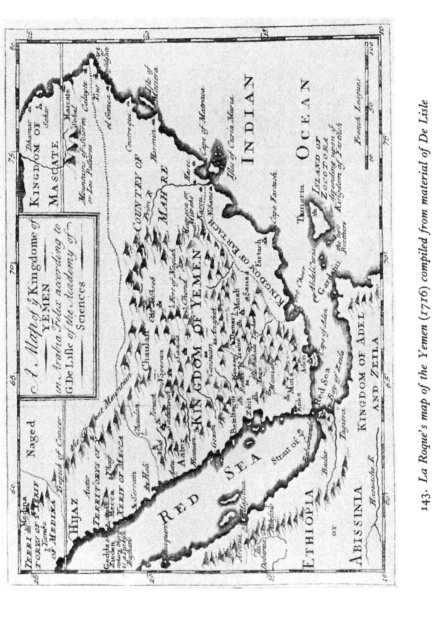

143. *La Roque's map of the Yemen (1716) compiled from material of De Lisle*

'Abdul 'Aziz was murdered by a survivor of the sack of Karbala, and was succeeded by his son and general, Sa'ūd. The following year the Harb tribesmen were won over to the Wahhabi cause and Yenbo' was seized. Al Madina capitulated; Mecca was recaptured and sacked by the Wahhabis in 1806; Jidda was surrendered by Ghālib, who now became governor of the Hejaz under Sa'ūd.

At this time the Ottoman Sultans of Turkey claimed the Caliphate and the custody of the Holy Cities. After the capture of Baghdad by the Mongols in 1258 one of the Abbasids had fled to Cairo (p. 246), where he was protected by the Mamluk Sultan, Beibars; a dynasty of Abbasid Caliphs, nominally recognized as suzerains by the Mamluks but really quite powerless, continued there until the Turkish conquest. In the eighteenth century it was said that the last of these Caliphs had resigned his rights to Selim I in the sixteenth century. The story was untrue and in any case the act would have been invalid, but the Sultan's prestige was impaired by Wahhabi rule at Mecca and a conflict was inevitable. At first the Pasha of Syria had been too slow to intervene, but now the Turks were aware of the danger. Assaults by the Wahhabis on Najaf in 'Iraq and on Damascus were repelled, and the Wahhabis were defeated by the Muntafiq of the lower Euphrates.

In 1805 Muhammad 'Ali, an Albanian soldier, the founder of the present royal house, made himself, in all but name, independent in Egypt. In later life he planned to form an Arab empire by the invasion of Arabia. With the encouragement of the Sultan, who foresaw advantages to himself whatever the result, Muhammad 'Ali collected an army under the command of his son Tusun at Suez in 1811, and attacked Arabia by land and sea. Yenbo' was captured at once, Al Madina in 1812; Tusun was joined at Jidda by the Sharif Ghālib, and the Wahhabis abandoned Mecca. Sa'ūd, who was taken by surprise by these events while advancing against Baghdad, hastened back to the west, recovered Qunfidha, and besieged Al Madina. Meanwhile Muhammad 'Ali, who had arrived in person, deposed Ghālib from the Sharifate. In 1814 Sa'ūd died and was succeeded by his son 'Abdullah. Tusun then invaded Al Qasīm, but his communications were cut by the Wahhabis, and having run short of supplies he made peace and withdrew unmolested. 'Abdullah agreed to recognize the suzerainty of the Sultan and promised to visit him; but when Muhammad 'Ali denounced this arrangement, 'Abdullah refused to go to Turkey. This gave Muhammad 'Ali an excuse to renew the invasion of Nejd in 1816. His adopted son, Ibrahim Pasha, who was in command, was joined by many of the Shammar, Harb, and Muteir tribesmen and advanced through Al Qasīm, besieged Dar'īya (north-west of Riyādh), and made a triumphal entry on 9 September 1818. 'Abdullah, who fought until only the citadel mosque was left to him, was captured and beheaded at Constantinople. Ibrahim's success was due to his artillery, to systematic bribery, and to his remarkable tenacity and organizing ability.

These events were the cause of an Englishman crossing Arabia for the first time. In 1819 the Bombay Government, deeply interested in the success of Ibrahim Pasha's campaign, since the east coast tribes were ruining the Persian Gulf trade by piracy, sent Captain G. F. Sadlier, 47th Regiment, as special envoy to congratulate Ibrahim on the capture of Dar'īya and to concert measures for the complete reduction of the Wahhabis. Landing at Qatīf in late June, Sadlier learnt that Ibrahim was already evacuating central Arabia. With no wish to explore, but bent on carrying out his instructions, Sadlier travelled to Hofūf, where he joined a force of Egyptians, and marched with them by way of Yamāma and Manfuha to the devastated oasis of Dar'īya. Thence travelling north-west to 'Aneiza, he overtook the main Egyptian army at Ar Rass, south-west of that city, only to find that Ibrahim had left for Al Madina. Sadlier had perforce to follow, and, though forbidden to enter Al Madina, he met Ibrahim in its neighbourhood early in September. The meeting had little result, and Sadlier reached the Red Sea on 20 September, having traversed the entire peninsula from east to west in less than three months. He took boat for Jidda, there to be held up another four months. His full narrative[1] was not published till 1866.

The rest of Islam hated the Wahhabis as fanatical and sacrilegious heretics. Europeans, being ill-informed, were on the whole hostile to them because of the massacre perpetrated at Karbala in 1801, and many attacks on shipping in the Persian Gulf.

THE NINETEENTH CENTURY

During the first half of the nineteenth century Muhammad 'Ali and Ibrahim Pasha dominated affairs in the Hejaz, and to a less extent farther south. They intervened less successfully in Nejd where the first enthusiasm for Wahhabi doctrines was temporarily on the wane and where rivalry began to grow between the two great families of Ibn Rashid and Ibn Sa'ūd. When in 1840 Muhammad

[1] *Diary of a Journey across Arabia* (Bombay Government Records, 1866).

'Ali was forced to give up his imperial ambitions, intervention in Arabian affairs came more directly from Constantinople.

The opening of the Suez Canal in 1869 brought the Red Sea and Arabia back into world affairs. It enabled the Sultan to take a more active part in Hejaz politics, because he could more easily reinforce his garrisons and support his nominees along the Arabian coast. Turkish intervention was also brought about from the Mesopotamian side by dynastic rivalries in Nejd. The opening of the Suez Canal was the chief cause of the revival of interest in the Red Sea among European Powers; but while France and Italy mostly confined their attention to the African shores, Great Britain, who had already obtained a foothold at Aden in 1839, intervened more directly in south Arabia.

Nejd

After Ibrahim Pasha had returned to Egypt in 1819, leaving Turkish garrisons in the chief towns, an able scion of the old ruling house of 'Ayeina, Muhammad ibn Mu'ammar, chosen by Ibrahim, was installed at Dar'īya. He had to fight the Beni Khālid and Sa'ūdi claimants and was deposed and executed in 1821 by Turki, a nephew of 'Abdul 'Aziz, who had seized Riyādh, now to be the Sa'ūdi capital. In the dunes of Harīq the Turkish troops on whom Muhammad ibn Mu'ammar relied, but whose conduct made them hated, were almost annihilated by Turki; the survivors retired to Al Qasīm, where they were reinforced from Al Madina and supported by the Muteir. Meanwhile Turki conquered the Beni Khālid, but was murdered by a rival Sa'ūdi, who was himself killed by Turki's son Feisal in 1834. The Egyptians expelled Feisal and set up Khālid ibn Sa'ūd in 1838, but on their withdrawal from Nejd Khālid was overthrown (1840).

Feisal ibn Sa'ūd recovered Riyādh and cautiously consolidated his power in southern Nejd; he reconquered Al Hasa, but ruled only nominally in Al Qasīm, and the same may be said of Hāil, where he had replaced the Ibn 'Ali family by his friend 'Abdullah ibn Rashid. 'Abdullah and his son Talāl, who succeeded him in 1847, ruled ably; they subdued the northern Jauf, Kheibar, and Teima, and Talāl promoted trade and agriculture. Feisal was succeeded in 1865 by his son 'Abdullah, who was replaced in 1870 by another son, Sa'ūd, favoured by the tribes. 'Abdullah's appeal for help gave Midhat Pasha, the Ottoman Vali of Baghdad, an excuse to occupy Al Hasa and constitute the 'Sanjaq of Nejd'; but Midhat Pasha was recalled in 1872, and the Ottoman conquest went no farther. On Sa'ūd's death

'Abdullah returned (1874), but he could neither retake Al Hasa nor obtain the governorship from the Turks, while Sa'ūd's sons were practically independent in Kharj.

Meanwhile Talāl ibn Rashid had died at Hāil, probably by suicide (1868), and was succeeded the following year, after a series of revolutions and murders, by his brother Muhammad, afterwards the greatest Arabian ruler of his generation. Muhammad ibn Rashid increased his realm as much by diplomacy as by arms, diverted the caravan trade of southern Nejd to Hāil, made the whole of Wadi Sirhan and even Palmyra tributary, and prevented the Turks from establishing themselves at Jauf, though he formally accepted their sovereignty. He had not the religious prestige of the older Sa'ūdi house, but was far more powerful than 'Abdullah ibn Sa'ūd, who had to renounce Al Qasīm (1879) and was deposed by his nephews (1887).

The events and chronology of the next few years are confused. Muhammad ibn Rashid intervened at Riyādh, but he was never recognized in Harīq and Hauta, and for a while he seems to have maintained Sa'ūdi rule in name. 'Abdurrahmān, the brother of 'Abdullah ibn Sa'ūd, together with Zamil āl Suleim of 'Aneiza, revolted in 1890. Zamil was defeated and slain at Muleida the same year. 'Abdurrahmān ibn Sa'ūd fled, accompanied by his son 'Abdul 'Aziz, destined to be the greatest prince of his line, and finally settled at Kuweit. Muhammad ibn Rashid died in 1897, leaving no son, and was succeeded by his nephew, also named 'Abdul 'Aziz. It was the families of these two men, 'Abdul 'Aziz ibn 'Abdurrahmān ibn Sa'ūd and 'Abdul 'Aziz ibn Muhammad ibn Rashid, which held the stage in northern Arabia during the first two decades of the twentieth century (pp. 281 ff., and pedigrees facing p. 286).

The Hejaz

After the deposition of Ghālib in 1813 the Sharifs of Mecca became mere nominees of Muhammad 'Ali, while real power lay with the Egyptian governors or 'Guardians of Mecca'. In 1840 the European Powers forced Muhammad 'Ali to give up his imperial schemes, which threatened the existence of Turkey; the Hejaz then reverted to the Sultan, who was represented by the 'Vali of Jidda', but Midian remained Egyptian territory till 1891. The Sharif Muhammad ibn 'Aun was now able to follow an independent policy. In 1846 Feisal ibn Turki ibn Sa'ūd bought off an attack by the Sharif by consenting to pay an annual tribute and to recognize the Sharif's supremacy over the Harb and Muteir. The Sharif intrigued at Hāil and in Al Qasīm,

144. *Luheiya and Beit al Faqih in 1763*

145. *Military exercises in the Yemen about 1763*

146. *An Arab raid (ghazu) in the Wadi Sirhan, January 1879*

and his prestige among the tribes was great. He was removed by the Turks in 1851, but his successor, 'Abdul Muttalib ibn Ghālib, could not control the rising caused by the prohibition of the slave trade, which the Great Powers had forced the Sultan to forbid. Muhammad ibn 'Aun was restored in 1856, but died two years later, being succeeded by his son 'Abdullah. British and French consuls had been stationed in Jidda since about 1825, but after a riot in which these officials were killed Jidda was bombarded in 1858. The Turks paid an indemnity and sent a commission to reorganize the government of the Hejaz. Mecca was garrisoned by Turks and Jidda connected with the Red Sea cable. After the opening of the Suez Canal in 1869 the Turks could send troops quickly by sea, consequently direct Turkish ad-ministration was established in Mecca, Al Madina, Tāif, and Jidda. The subservience of 'Abdullah and his brother and successor, Husein, to the Turks was unpopular, and Husein was murdered in 1880. The restoration of 'Abdul Mùttalib was not a success; while 'Aun ar Rafiq, who was installed as Sharif in 1882 and reigned till his death in 1905, deliberately caused anarchy by intriguing with the beduin, hoping thereby to make the Turkish position untenable.

The Yemen

Though Wahhabi doctrines made no impression on the Zeidis of the Yemen plateau, they were adopted and forcibly propagated by Sheikh Makrami in Nejrān and by Abu Nuqta of the Beni 'Asīr. The Sharif of Abu 'Arīsh had to conform temporarily, but later, with the help of the Imam, he defeated and killed Abu Nuqta in 1809. After the capture of Dar'īya in 1818 (p. 268) an Egyptian army, diverted to the Tihama, crushed the Wahhabis there and, in return for tribute, restored nominal authority to the Imam. In 1832 an officer from the Hejaz known as Turkche Bilmez ('one who speaks no Turkish'), whom the Sultan encouraged to resist Muhammad 'Ali, occupied Hodeida, Zabīd, and Mocha, but next year he was expelled by the Egyptians who, however, withdrew in 1840.

Though Ibrahim Pasha had wished to hand the Tihama over to Muhammad ibn 'Aun, Sharif of Mecca, one of the Sharifs of Abu 'Arīsh, by name Husein ibn 'Ali, with an army of 'Asīri tribesmen, disputed its possession; this Sharif's brother, with a force several thousand strong, occupied Hodeida on the very day (22 April 1840) when Ibrahim Pasha evacuated the port. Sharif Husein ibn 'Ali then assumed control of Mocha, which he ruined by his misgovernment, driving many of its inhabitants to Aden. He was hostile to the British

vice-consul at Mocha and to British subjects, insulted the commanding officer of an East India Company's steam-frigate sent thither to
protect them, and demanded directly from the Bombay Government
in insulting terms the surrender of Aden. British protests were lodged
at Constantinople but, as shown below, the Turks did not eventually
expel Sharif Husein and occupy the Tihama till 1849.

The Imam at San'ā could at first play no part in these affairs, being
distracted by the rising in October 1840 of a fanatic, Al Faqīh Sa'īd,
who proclaimed a divine mission to purify Islam and drive unbelievers from Aden. This fanatic seized Ta'izz and other places,
assumed royal state—even minting coins on which he described himself as 'Sultan of land and sea'—and was not defeated and killed till
December. The Imam then turned his attention to recovering the
Tihama from Sharif Husein ibn 'Ali, sending two missions to Aden
in 1841 to seek British aid, and even offering to cede Zeila in return.
The Political Agent at Aden had, however, been instructed to remain
strictly neutral. The Imam took no military action, though he sent a
mission to Aden a third time in 1843. Both he and the British had
referred the matter to the Porte, which sent a commissioner, Ashraf
Bey, to Zabīd in September 1842. Ashraf Bey avoided meeting the
British representative (C. J. Cruttenden, Assistant Political Agent) and
may have been bribed by Sharif Husein, who was made Pasha of the
Tihama in July 1843 in consideration of an annual tribute to Turkey.

On the death in 1844 of the Imam Al Hādī Muhammad, his successor, Imam 'Ali Mansūr, tried vigorously to recover the Tihama;
he was deposed after a few months and succeeded by his cousin
Muhammad Yahya, who continued the struggle against the Sharif.
The latter was routed and made prisoner at Bājil early in 1848,
and the Imam took possession of Hodeida, Zabīd, and Beit al Faqīh;
but no sooner had he conquered Mocha than a part of Sharif Husein's
army recaptured Zabīd. The Imam fled to San'ā, and the Tihama fell
once more into Sharif Husein's hands.

The Turks, thinking the moment opportune, sent an expedition
to the Tihama early in 1849. Tewfieh Pasha expelled Sharif Husein
from Hodeida, where also he compelled the Imam to visit him and
sign a treaty, under which the Imam was to govern the Zeidi highlands as a vassal of the Porte, with a private subsidy, but the revenues
were to be divided and a small Turkish garrison was to be stationed
at San'ā. The infuriated Zeidis almost annihilated the Turks on
the day of their arrival in San'ā, Tewfieh Pasha escaping but later
dying of his wounds; while the Imam Muhammad Yahya, who had

signed the treaty, was deposed and afterwards murdered by 'Ali Mansūr, who had been restored to the Imamate—which, however, was wrested from him a few months later, after a sanguinary conflict, by Muhammad Yahya's son, Ghālib.

Though the Turks were thus driven from San'ā, they kept their footing on the coast. Anarchy overtook the high plateau; the splendour of the Imamate temporarily waned; nine Imams tried to rule within six years.

In 1855 the 'Asīri tribesmen, taking advantage of the distractions of the Turks in the Hejaz, attacked them in the Tihama. In January 1856 60,000 'Asīris, led by a tribal chief, 'Āidh ibn Mar'ī, besieged Hodeida, but were deterred by the presence of two East India Company's vessels, sent to protect British subjects. Cholera broke out among the 'Asīris, who retreated hastily, losing a quarter of their number from this pestilence. Some years later (1871), when Hodeida was again besieged by Muhammad ibn 'Āidh, who had succeeded his father, the Turks sent Radif Pasha to subdue 'Asīr.

After a revolt of the Isma'īlis of the Yemen highlands against the Zeidis, the leading citizens of San'ā rose against the Isma'īlis. The Turks intervened in the highlands once more; Ahmed Mukhtar Pasha defeated the San'ānis, entered the city, took over the administration, and pensioned the Imam.

From this time, 1872, is dated the second full occupation of the Yemen by the Turks, which lasted till 1918. A Turkish vali was appointed to govern the Yemen, with a mutasarrif under him in 'Asīr. Superior arms and organization enabled them to control the chief towns, but the tribes were never quiet for long and the Yemenis were hostile. Some valis had military and administrative capacity, but there was much bribery, especially among the ill-paid minor officials. The religious laxity of the Turks, and the substitution of the Ottoman civil code for the *shar'*, offended both the Zeidis and the Shafe'is. Isma'īl Haqqi Pasha (1878–1882) was popular; he put down corruption and raised and carefully trained an Arab force known officially as the Hamidīya, unofficially as *Aulād Isma'īl*, 'Isma'īl's children'. This force was successful against the rebels, but was dissolved when the Pasha was recalled. The seizure of grain during a drought caused much discontent and the regime became more oppressive. It is said that the officials kept back the tax money, accused the Arabs of not having paid it, and then confiscated their property.

The election of Muhammad ibn Yahya Hamīd ad Din, styled Al Mansūr, as Imam in 1891 was followed by a general rising against

Turkish control, the garrisons were isolated, and San'ā was surrounded by some 70,000 tribesmen. The citizens suffered severely, being suspect to both parties and maltreated by the besiegers if they tried to escape. The Imam was unable to restrain his supporters. In 1892 Ahmed Feidhi Pasha (p. 288) arrived at Hodeida as vali, fought his way across the mountains via Manākha to San'ā, and burnt some 300 recalcitrant villages. He negotiated in vain with the Imam, who would not accept the civil code. The vali imprisoned many of the *'ulema* and fortified the hills round San'ā. Husein Hilmi Pasha (1897–1900) was conciliatory, gave alms to the many starving people, encouraged learning, and remedied one of the chief grievances, the compulsory use of the fez by government employees; but the army commander, 'Abdullah Pasha, secured his removal and took his place as vali. Subsequent developments are narrated on pp. 287 ff.

British Contacts with the Aden Hinterland[1]

Napoleon's conquest of Egypt had little direct or immediate effect on the Hejaz or Nejd, but since it was a serious threat to British communications with India, Perim was occupied for a few months in 1799 by troops from Bombay under Lt.-Col. Murray, who became 'Political Commissioner for the Red Sea'. Unfortunately Perim was quite waterless and guns placed on it could not command the straits; the troops therefore withdrew to Aden, where they were hospitably received by the 'Abdali Sultan of Lahej. A commercial treaty was made with this ruler, as overlord of Aden, in 1802 by Commodore Sir Home Popham, who had been sent from Calcutta as 'Ambassador to the States of Arabia', but who had previously failed to conclude a similar treaty with the Imam, although several members of his embassy visited San'ā, and Sir Home Popham himself travelled some distance into the Yemen from Mocha, being subjected to many indignities by local chiefs.

With the introduction of steam navigation some years later it became necessary to survey the Red Sea and the Gulf of Aden for a coaling-station; Sira island (immediately east of the Aden peninsula, opposite the old town) and Mukalla were found unsuitable; and negotiations were in progress for the purchase of Socotra following an agreement made in 1834 with the Sultan of Qishn and Socotra, when Aden was captured.

---

[1] The text of the treaties mentioned in this section will be found in Sir C. U. Aitchison, *A Collection of Treaties, Engagements and Sanads relating to India and Neighbouring Countries*, vol. xiii, 1933.

Aden had again attracted the attention of the Indian Government in 1837, when an attack was made on the crew and passengers of a British ship wrecked near by. Captain Haines, arriving in the war-sloop *Coote* in December, claimed compensation from the 'Abdali Sultan. Suspecting treachery, Haines withdrew but returned in October 1838, with orders to enforce the cession of Aden in consideration of an annual payment to the Sultan. As the latter sought to evade the treaty drawn up for this purpose, Haines blockaded the port, till in January 1839 two more ships, H.M.S. *Volage* and H.M.S. *Cruizer*, appeared. A demand for surrender being unanswered, the town was bombarded and finally captured by a party landing near Sira island, the Sultan and his family escaping to Lahej. Aden was the first addition to British possessions in Queen Victoria's reign.

Peace was made in February 1839; in June the Sultan signed a treaty and was granted a stipend of 6,000 dollars a year, though this was shortly suspended because of three attempts by him to retake Aden in 1839 and 1840. Further agreements were made in 1843 and 1844. But in 1846 a fanatic, Seiyid Isma'il, preached a holy war, and the Sultan of Lahej—joined as on previous occasions by the Fadhli tribes—tried unsuccessfully for the fourth time to recapture Aden. This was followed by a more comprehensive treaty and further incidents. The Sultan resumed hostilities in 1857, but after an Arab defeat the following year at Sheikh 'Othman, where the fort was blown up, negotiations were reopened. Under Sultan Fadhl ibn Muhsin (1863–1874) relations became more satisfactory, and they have not been seriously disturbed since. The 'Abdali Sultan is now the leading Arab ruler in the Western Aden Protectorate. The political and cultural influence of the present Sultan and his predecessors has been beneficial.

The Turks, after their second occupation of San'ā in 1872 (p. 273), revived the pretensions of the Imams of the Yemen to the overlord-ship of Lahej and other territories south of the Yemen highlands. Aided by disaffected tribes or tribal sections they encroached, often with temporary success, on the 'Abdali, Haushabi, and Amiri confederations. In 1873 they occupied Dhāla', the Amiri capital, and continued there more or less until 1903. In 1873 the Turks also occupied the fortified house of the 'Abdali Sultan in Lahej; the Sultan appealed for help, a British force was dispatched from Aden, and after negotiations the Turks withdrew. Following an incident in 1900 between the Humar tribe, in Turkish territory, and the Haushabi, the Porte proposed a demarcation of the frontier, offers of which it had previously rejected. British and Turkish commissioners met at Dhāla‘ in January 1902, but the Turks were obstructive and persisted in occupying Al Jalīla, in Amiri territory a few miles north of Dhāla‘. After the dispatch of a British column to Dhāla‘ the Turks withdrew to Qa‘taba; the task of delimitation then proceeded and was continued till May 1904, since when friendly relations between British and Turks were maintained until the War of 1914–1918. A fanatic styled *Al Majnūn* (the madman), who preached in the Amiri villages in 1905 against the presence of Christians, appears to have displeased the hill-tribesmen by his importunities.

Meanwhile constant difficulties had arisen with the other tribes. After the capture of Aden agreements were made with the Subeihi, Fadhli, ‘Aqrabi, Lower Yāfa‘i, and Haushabi chiefs. A convention for the suppression of the slave trade was made with the Lower ‘Aulaqi Sheikhs in 1855 and an agreement with the Amir of Dhāla‘ in 1880. In 1888 a Protectorate was established over the Fadhlis, ‘Aqrabis, Lower ‘Aulaqis, Wahidis, and Lower Haura, extended later to the Subeihis (1889), and the Lower Yāfa‘is, Haushabis, and ‘Alawis (1895). An agreement was concluded with the Sheikh of ‘Irqa in 1888. In 1876 the Mahri Sultan of Qishn and Socotra agreed not to alienate any part of his possessions except to the British Government and in 1886 accepted a Protectorate Treaty. As a result of these treaties, such disorders as occurred were generally due only to internal disputes; little more was required of the Aden authorities than constant watchfulness, arbitration, and occasional financial sanctions. The Aden authorities received but rejected several offers of alliance from chiefs who wanted their military help, including (as described above, p. 272) the Imam of the Yemen.

Aden itself, which was ruled from India by a Political Agent, later became part of the Bombay Presidency, administered by a Political Resident. It developed rapidly from a derelict condition to a prosperous town populated, in addition to the Arab inhabitants, by communities of Hindus, Parsis, and Somalis, with Persians and representatives of many other nationalities. It replaced Mocha as the principal port of south-west Arabia. Perim was reoccupied in 1857. In 1869 the peninsula of Little Aden (Jebel Ihsan) was added to British territory by purchase from the ‘Aqrabi Sultan. In 1882 the Sultan of Lahej sold to the British by treaty the town of Sheikh ‘Othman and 35 square miles of his territory, his subsidy being raised to 1,641 dollars a month. Thus the ‘Aden Settlement’ attained an area of some 80 square miles, of which Perim island accounts for 5. This territory has since become the Colony of Aden. Socotra was also brought under the supervision of the Aden authorities. The Kuria Muria islands, ceded by the Sultan of Muscat to the British Crown in 1854, are also technically under the Aden Government, though, owing to their remoteness and difficulty of access, they have long been left to the care of the British Resident in the Persian Gulf.

The Hadhramaut and Adjacent Territories

To trace the beginnings of what is now the Eastern Aden Protectorate it is necessary to follow the rise of several ruling houses, notably the Kathīris, Qu'aitis, and Kasādis, with one or other of whom the British have had official relations from 1842 onwards.

The Kathīris, who claim to have been previously sultans in Dhufār, were prominent in the Hadhramaut from the end of the fifteenth century, when 'Abdullah ibn Ja'far al Kathīr became governor of Shihr. His more famous son, Bedr Bu Tuweirak, who reigned for sixty years, brought in Zeidis from the Yemen and also Yāfa'is, and even sought Turkish protection to control the tribes. After his death (1565) his descendants divided his territory, one section, the Āl 'Isa Kathīris, establishing themselves in Shibām. Another section, the Āl 'Abdullah Kathīris, came under Zeidi domination, but early in the eighteenth century an army of Yāfa'is, brought in by one of the Āl 'Abdullah, expelled the Zeidis and themselves occupied Seiyūn and Tarīm. The Kathīris as a whole were much weakened, though the Āl 'Isa section still kept Shibām.

In the nineteenth century certain Hadhramis began to go to the East Indies to make their fortunes, while some took service in the Arab guard of the Nizam of Hyderabad. These emigrants remained intensely proud of their race, faith, and language, and often returned to the Hadhramaut to buy an estate and settle down as local chiefs, sending abroad other members of the family to take their places. It was the Kathīri Ghālib ibn Muhsin, of the Āl 'Abdullah section, who sent money home from Hyderabad to his family. They, by buying certain strongholds and then bringing several thousand 'Aulaqi soldiers from the south-west, expelled the Yāfa'i ruler of Tarīm and eventually took possession of that city (1847) and of Seiyūn (1848). Seiyūn has since become capital of the Kathīri sultanate.

While the Kathīri Ghālib was becoming wealthy in Hyderabad, another Hadhrami in the Nizam's army was 'Omar ibn 'Awadh al Qu'aiti, whose family, living at Qatn west of Shibām, had bought half the latter city from the Āl 'Isa Kathīris, so that both Kathīris and

Qu'aitis were ruling in Shibām about 1830. Many surrounding villages were still inhabited by Yāfa'is, a massacre of whom by the Kathīri ruler of half Shibām caused the beginning of trouble between Kathīris and Qu'aitis. The former were more powerful, but the Yāfa'is appealed to the Qu'aiti 'Omar ibn 'Awadh in India, who sent his three sons and soldiers to help. These besieged Shibām for sixteen years, till certain Seiyids were asked to arbitrate, and the city was again divided between Kathīris and Qu'aitis. After further incidents the Qu'aitis got sole control of Shibām in 1858, killing many of the Āl 'Isa Kathīris, though the Āl 'Abdullah section remained in possession of Tarīm and Seiyūn.

Meanwhile the first official contact of the British was with a third house, the Kasādis, who originated from one of the tribes of Lower Yāfa'. After the death in 1842 of the Kasādi Naqib of Mukalla, quarrels in his family led to the flight of two of his sons to Aden, but the Government of India, though assisting the fugitives financially, declined to intervene further.

Mukalla and Shihr belonged respectively to the Kasādi and Bureiki families. In 1850 the Turks sent a small force to annex these towns, and in 1867 a Turkish warship made a second attempt. The Turks had recently been foiled in their attempt to re-establish themselves in San'ā (p. 272), so they were seeking to extend their conquests in south Arabia in a different direction, east of Aden. But Turkish pretensions were evaded by the chiefs. The latter desired British protection, and the Kasādis on both occasions offered Mukalla to the British, who refused it, though steps were taken to dissuade the Turks from further interference. Also two treaties for the abolition of the slave trade, in 1863 and 1873, were concluded between the British and the Kasādis.

In 1866 the Kathīris captured Shihr, the Bureiki ruler fleeing to Aden. The Bureikis appealed to 'Awadh, son of 'Omar al Qu'aiti, who came from India with armed followers and drove the Kathīris out of Shihr but kept it for himself. Later he forced the Kasādi Naqib to sell him half Mukalla, a transaction which the Kasādis afterwards repudiated. In the ensuing fighting the Qu'aitis proved the strongest of the three factions. Hostilities continued by land and sea, and, in 1876, the Government of India intervened between Qu'aitis and Kasādis; but both sides were obstinate and the Government declared it would only mediate when fighting had stopped. At the end of 1876 the Resident at Aden succeeded in arranging a two years' truce. The Kasādi Naqib continued to press for British protection, failing which he would give Mukalla to anyone (except the Qu'aitis) who would take it, Turkey, France, Italy, and Zanzibar being mentioned. The Government warned him against disposing of his territory without their consent, and at length decided to support the Qu'aitis and to impose a settlement. The Kasādi Naqib retired on a pension to Zanzibar with a number of his followers, and in 1881 'Awadh al Qu'aiti took full possession of Mukalla.

In 1882 the Qu'aitis undertook not to alienate any part of their lands except to the British Government, by whose advice they were to be guided in their dealings with their neighbours and with foreign Powers. In 1884 the British announced that they would support 'Awadh al Qu'aiti if the Kathīris attacked his ports. In 1888 'Awadh signed a Protectorate Treaty; in 1902 his old title 'Jemadar', gained under the Nizam in India, was abolished and he was recognized as Sultan. He died in 1909.

Egyptian, French, and Italian Interests in the Red Sea

Since the sixteenth century the southern part of the African Red Sea coast had been under the control of petty Moslem chiefs. Suākin, though perhaps not under its direct rule, had been the port of Sennar till that kingdom disintegrated in the eighteenth century. The coast to the north had been ruled by the Turkish Pashas of Egypt. Muhammad 'Ali commenced the conquest of the Sudan, and under the Khedive Isma'īl (1863–1879) the Egyptian armies reached Berbera. The British felt concern for the fate of Socotra, but the vast empire which Egypt was attempting to form was insecurely held and maladministered. The expectation of its collapse and the opening of the Suez Canal in 1869 caused the Red Sea to be regarded as a promising field of colonial expansion, of great commercial and strategic importance. It was of particular interest to Italy, since her metropolitan territory has no port outside the Mediterranean, a handicap which she has constantly tried to overcome, either by acquiring some measure of control at the outlets of the Mediterranean and the Red Sea, or by securing a strip of land extending from the north coast of Africa to some point on the Indian Ocean.

The Italian States were too weak financially to take much part in the construction of the Suez Canal, which was begun in 1859. After the Union in 1861, the kingdom was only strong enough for limited commercial expansion. In 1865 Giuseppe Sapeto, a former missionary who knew the Red Sea well, stated in his *L'Italia e il canale di Suez* that the opening of the canal would benefit Italy more than the nations of northern and western Europe, as it would greatly shorten her communications with the East. He claimed that there were great possibilities for coastal trade and for fishing in the Red Sea, and urged the Italian Government to conclude commercial treaties and establish a naval station there. In 1869 France, which had acquired but not occupied Obok in 1862, secured a concession at Sheikh Sa'īd which, however, remained in abeyance. In the same year the Rubattino Company acquired a lease of the Bay of Assab, an act viewed by the Government of India with what Lord Cromer afterwards called 'a great deal of unnecessary ill-humour'. The project was much opposed in Italy, where it was regarded as dangerous and wasteful. In 1879 Sapeto suggested that Assab might replace Jidda as the centre of entrepot trade in the Red Sea, being much nearer to Mocha and Hodeida (*Assab e i suoi critici*). Like many other Italian writers until recent years, he was careful to show that the policy he advocated would not involve rivalry with Britain, whose aims were strategic whereas Italy's were commercial. After the French declaration of a protectorate in Tunisia (1881), Italy was even more chary of becoming a colonial competitor of Great Britain, hoping that the latter would be a check on French ambitions, which were more likely to conflict with her own.

When the Mahdi's rebellion in the Sudan began in 1882, the British, having in that year assumed almost a protectorate over Egypt, induced the Egyptian Government to evacuate the Sudan. The British took over Berbera and Zeila in 1884, though, since Zeila was still regarded as a dependency of Mocha and therefore of the Turks, payments in respect of it were for a time made to Turkey. The French occupied Obok and Tajura in the same year, and Jibuti in 1888. Cecchi, the Italian Consul-General at Aden, saw in this a threat to Zeila, where it was to Italy's interest that the British should remain. Italy had herself taken advantage of the Egyptian collapse to convert Assab into a colony (1882) and to occupy Massawa (1885). Britain's attitude to this last act has been much discussed. The contemporary opposition in Italy accused the Government of being the tool of British policy, while more recently some Fascist writers have maintained that Britain instigated the occupation in order to forestall the French. Lord Cromer held that no such suggestion was ever made, but that it had been made clear to Italy that Britain would not object to the move, a policy which in his opinion was mistaken. Relations between Britain and Italy during this period remained friendly; in 1889 the Prime Minister Depretis stated in the Italian Chamber that he favoured the acquisition of colonies for commercial but not for strategic reasons. Mancini, who was Foreign Minister from 1881 to 1885 and had read Sapeto's book, saw the possibilities of trade with Arabia, but he also envisaged the acquisition of a belt of territory reaching through the Sudan and Libya to the Mediterranean. British sympathy, necessary for this latter project, was withheld. For the next few years Italy neglected Arabia for Abyssinia, where Crispi hoped to annex a strip of territory to join Eritrea to Italian Somaliland. But neither his project nor his ministry survived the disaster of Adowa (1896). It was nearly decided to abandon Eritrea, and colonial policy was for a time discredited.

IV. THE TWENTIETH CENTURY

THE twentieth century has witnessed great changes in the Arab world. The decline of the Ottoman Empire which had been in progress for two centuries gained momentum in the twentieth, and by joining the Central European Powers in the War of 1914–1918 the Empire signed its death-warrant and the Arab world was freed from external domination. The false hopes raised by the 'Young Turk' movement and the Turkish revolution of 1908 reacted to bring about the birth of Arab nationalism in Syria, 'Iraq, and the Hejaz, though at first there was little co-ordination of effort and much rivalry between the Arab Amirs. The Sharif of Mecca, a nominee of the Young Turks, though working for an independent Arabia, helped the Turks to subdue both Nejd and 'Asīr; the Rashidi and Sa'ūdi families struggled for mastery in central Arabia; the harsh measures of Turkish valis alienated both the Yemen and 'Asīr, and necessitated strong Turkish garrisons to maintain even the semblance of Turkish sovereignty.

At the end of the war the prestige of the Sharif of Mecca, self-styled 'King of the Arab Lands', and of his sons, 'Abdullah and Feisal, stood high in Egypt and the West, since they alone of the Arab rulers had actively supported the victorious allies; but those who expected King Husein to be acceptable to the whole of Arabia failed to take into account the growing strength of Ibn Sa'ūd and the Wahhabi revival. Ibn Sa'ūd, who during the war was a passive supporter of the Allies, and in close touch with the political officers working with the British in 'Iraq, gradually consolidated his position in Nejd. Then, after the war, having first given the Hejaz troops a lesson at Turaba, he overran northern Arabia as far as the borders of Transjordan and 'Iraq, and

PEDIGREE OF KING HUSEIN AND HIS DESCENDANTS

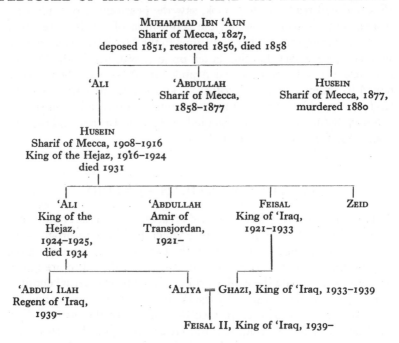

MUHAMMAD IBN 'AUN
Sharif of Mecca, 1827,
deposed 1851, restored 1856, died 1858

'ALI   'ABDULLAH   HUSEIN
              Sharif of Mecca,   Sharif of Mecca, 1877,
              1858–1877   murdered 1880

HUSEIN
Sharif of Mecca, 1908–1916
King of the Hejaz, 1916–1924
died 1931

'ALI   'ABDULLAH   FEISAL   ZEID
King of the   Amir of   King of 'Iraq,
Hejaz,   Transjordan,   1921–1933
1924–1925,   1921–
died 1934

'ABDUL ILAH   'ALIYA ⟚ GHAZI, King of 'Iraq, 1933–1939
Regent of 'Iraq,
1939–

FEISAL II, King of 'Iraq, 1939–

NOTE: The rulers of Mecca, called in European phrase 'Grand Sharif', but formerly often locally styled 'Amir', assumed the title 'Sharif' in the latter part of the tenth century, when the descendants of 'Ali were increasing their influence in western Arabia after the sack of the city in 930 by the Carmathians and the subsequent disorders (p. 244). Though the Sharifate was neither hereditary nor restricted to any one family or clan, yet certain 'dynasties' arose in succession. The first were the Musāwis, who lasted from about 950 to 1061. After a period of disorder, the ruler of the Yemen, As Suleihi, intervened among the warring descendants of Hasan and, at their own request, appointed Abu Hāshim Muhammad, first of the Hawāshim, as ruler, about 1063. A revolution occurred about 1200, when Qatāda, a descendant of the same Musa who was common ancestor of Musāwis and Hawāshim, seized the city. Descendants of this ruler, though not all in the same line, held the sharifate till the abdication of King 'Ali in 1925. The later Sharifs owed their nomination to the foreign occupying Power. The 'Abādilah House was raised to power in 1827 by Muhammad 'Ali of Egypt during his occupation of the Hejaz. The intervals between the periods of office of the Amirs in the pedigree were due to members of other branches of the 'Abādilah, or of another clan, having been appointed by the Ottoman authorities. Thus 'Abdul Muttalib, of the rival Dhawi Zeid clan, held office from 1851 to 1856 and again from 1880 to 1882. 'Aun ar Rafiq, of the 'Abādilah, a cousin of King Husein, held the position from 1882 to 1905. Another cousin, 'Ali, was King Husein's immediate predecessor, but was banished with his family to Egypt.

conquered both the Hejaz and 'Asīr. It was not, however, until 1934 that he was forced to intervene in the Yemen.

British policy throughout this period has been governed by two principles: the carrying out of pledges made during the war of 1914–1918, and the maintenance of a strong and friendly Arabia. The first was fulfilled when in 1921 'Abdullah became the ruler of Transjordan, and Feisal was elected King of 'Iraq, both events being primarily due to British initiative and support. It was not part of British policy nor was Britain under any obligation to take sides in the struggle between King Husein and Ibn Sa'ūd, since both had treaty relations with Britain.

The second principle is necessitated by the fact that the Red Sea and the Persian Gulf are vital sea and air links in the communications of the British Empire. Policy here has been directed to strengthening the ties of friendship with King Ibn Sa'ūd, with the Imam of the Yemen, and with the States which form the Eastern and Western Aden Protectorates. That British policy has so far been beneficial to Arabia is largely due to the much greater knowledge of Arabian geography and Arabian affairs, gained by such travellers and officials as Philby, Bertram Thomas, and the Ingrams, and its success is shown by the ordered progress that has taken place during this period. Even during the most critical days of the War of 1939–1945 the rulers of Arabia remained friendly to the Allied cause and were little affected by 'Axis' propaganda. The war has however brought about a strengthening of ties throughout the Arab world, and the various States met in Cairo to discuss and formulate a policy on matters of common interest. The result has been the founding of the Arab League.

EVENTS OF THE FIRST FOURTEEN YEARS

Nejd

The first ten years of the twentieth century were occupied in Nejd by the struggle for power between the Rashidi and Sa'ūdi families. But though in 1900 'Abdul 'Aziz ibn Rashid (p. 270) was the strongest ruler in Arabia, he was dependent for arms and munitions on ports under Turkish control, and he therefore coveted Kuweit, an 'Ateiba principality at the head of the Persian Gulf, which had been founded in the eighteenth century. This was nominally subject to the Vali of Basra, though actually in independent treaty relationship with Great Britain. During the nineteenth century Great Britain had imposed treaties on the rulers of 'Omān, Trucial 'Omān, and Bahrein, requiring them to suppress piracy, gun-running, and the slave trade, and to prevent the alienation of their territories. Sheikh Mubārak of Kuweit (1896–1915), in fear of vengeance for the murders by which he had gained the throne, realized that Great Britain, unlike the Turks, would not infringe his independence and might even support him against any who did. He had therefore secured a similar treaty with Britain in 1899, at the time when Germany was intriguing to obtain a railway concession through Turkey to the Persian Gulf. As a result the Turks, not daring now to attack Kuweit openly, encouraged Ibn Rashid to do so. Sheikh Mubārak, who had found the Sa'ūdi refugees, 'Abdurrahmān ibn Feisal and his son 'Abdul 'Aziz (Ibn Sa'ūd) (p. 270), useful allies, was defeated at Sarīf in 1901 by Ibn Rashid, who now repressed the Sa'ūdi faction in Nejd.

In January 1902 Ibn Sa'ūd with a few followers secretly entered Riyādh, and, having hidden in the fort opposite the house in which Ibn Rashid's governor was sleeping, killed him as he emerged at dawn, and made himself master of Riyādh. Here he was joined by his father, 'Abdurrahmān, who spent the rest of his life in comparative retirement and religious exercises. 'Abdurrahmān never acted as head of the State though he was known as Imam; he always took religious precedence of his son, whose close confidant he was, and he sometimes took administrative charge in his son's absence; he died in 1928.

At first Ibn Rashid underestimated the danger, thereby giving his rival time to consolidate his position. By the end of 1902 Ibn Sa'ūd, by better diplomacy and the lavish distribution of bribes, was in control of southern Nejd. Meanwhile Ibn Rashid divided his attacks between Riyādh, which had now been refortified and which he failed to storm, and Kuweit, where the Turks would not help him. His conduct after the battle of Sarīf had also made him unpopular, and he lost Al Washm and Sudeir. Troops sent by the Turks to recover Al Qasīm in 1904 suffered from cholera and the heat; moreover, supply and reinforcement were difficult and men were needed in the Yemen.

Meanwhile violent internal strife had destroyed the commercial prosperity of Hāil and weakened the Rashidi power from within. In 1906 'Abdul 'Aziz ibn Rashid was killed in battle against Ibn Sa'ūd and the Muteir tribesmen; his energetic son Mit'ab was soon after murdered by the head of another branch of the family, Sultān ibn Hamūd, who also killed all the other sons of 'Abdul 'Aziz with one exception, a child who was taken to Al Madina by a slave. Then Al Qasīm and Kheibar revolted against Sultān ibn Hamūd, who in turn was slain in January 1908 by his brothers Sa'ūd and Feisal, the former succeeding him as Amir at Hāil, the latter becoming governor of the northern Jauf. In September Sa'ūd ibn Hamūd and most of his family were murdered, but Feisal escaped to Riyādh.

Sa'ūd (ibn Rashid), the surviving child of 'Abdul 'Aziz ibn Rashid, now returned from Al Madina and was installed at Hāil as Amir under the regency of Hamūd ibn Subhān, who was poisoned in 1909 and succeeded by his able brother Zāmil. The latter recovered Teima, which had received a Turkish garrison, and sacked Madāin Sālih; but he lost Jauf to Nūri ibn Sha'lān of the Ruwalla tribe, and in 1910 made peace with Ibn Sa'ūd. Zāmil was murdered early in 1914 by a relative, Sa'ūd ibn Sālih, who took his place.

These events removed from 'Abdul 'Aziz ibn Sa'ūd all danger from the Rashidi family and from the Turks, with whom friendship had long been the policy of Ibn Rashid, and who could not risk international complications which direct intervention would have caused. Ibn Sa'ūd had, however, some internal difficulties to settle. The so-called 'Arāif, grandsons of Ibn Sa'ūd's uncle Sa'ūd ibn Feisal, had escaped in 1904 from their position as hostages of the Rashidi Amir at Hāil. Claiming the throne for the elder branch of their family, they rebelled unsuccessfully against Ibn Sa'ūd in 1910. Their leader, Sa'ūd ibn 'Abdul 'Aziz ibn Sa'ūd, was pardoned and remained loyal, but most of them fled to the Sharif of Mecca, now the hope of the Turks, who also intrigued with Feisal ad Duwish of the Muteir tribe and with 'Ajaimi ibn Sa'dun of the Muntafiq. In 1913 Ibn Sa'ūd suddenly occupied Al Hasa. The Turkish garrisons offered only feeble resistance and were offered generous terms. The Turks, to whom the province was of little use, did not try to regain it, and in 1914, though continuing to support Ibn Rashid against him, they recognized Ibn Sa'ūd as 'Vali of Nejd'.

The uncertain loyalty of the beduin, who had nothing at stake and might always hope to gain by a change of ruler, had hitherto been one of the chief weaknesses of any Nejdi State in a crisis. In order to revive their religious zeal and to give them common interests with the settled population, Ibn Sa'ūd now established a confraternity, in some ways like the Senusiya (Senussi) of Africa, but rigidly Wahhabi in doctrine. His policy was to induce these beduin to abandon pastoral life, sell their camels, and live in agricultural communities or colonies, recognizing no ties and no laws but those of Islam, studying the Koran, the life of Muhammad, and the Traditions, and strictly complying with the shar'. They were given money and land where there was a supply of water. They regard themselves as converts from paganism and are known as *Ikhwān* or 'Brethren'. Each colony or *hijra* has a quota of arms and ammunition according to its size. The oldest and largest is Artawiya, founded in 1912, composed of men of the Muteir and Harb tribes; its population is now about 10,000. Next came Ghatghat ('Ateiba), Dakhna (mostly Harb), and Ajfar (mostly Shammar). There are now well over a hundred colonies, and the total number of Ikhwān probably exceeds 100,000. They have added to the wealth and military strength of Nejd, have been centres of religious propaganda, and have strengthened the government against the beduin; but their violent fanaticism has been dangerous. Believing in a *jihad* or holy war against unbelievers, and tending to think of none but themselves as Moslems at all, they have embarrassed Ibn Sa'ūd's relations with foreigners, especially Europeans, and with his other subjects. The Ikhwān have also bitterly resented the use of such western inventions as motor-cars and telephones.

The Hejaz

During the nineteenth century new factors began to affect relations between Turks and Arabs. In general the Turk regarded the Arab as undisciplined, untrustworthy, fanatical, foolishly proud of an absurd genealogy, and lacking in administrative capacity. The Arab regarded the Turk as stupid, brutal, corrupt, and irreligious, but respected the Sultan's prestige—and his artillery. The Turkish reformers, wanting an efficient, centralized, rather Napoleonic state, sanctioned increasing interference by half-westernized officials in the Arab provinces. The result was a growth of national feeling on both sides. There were pan-Turanian and pan-Arab movements, while many Turks felt that all Moslems should unite to prevent their further subjection to Christian Europe. The Ottoman Sultan 'Abdul Hamid II (1876–1909) cleverly exploited this feeling and took advantage at home and abroad of his claim to be Caliph. He spent freely on pious endowments in the Hejaz, and gave many court offices to Arabs. He decreed the building of a railway from Damascus to Al Madina and Mecca (p. 521). The line reached Ma'an in 1904, and Al Madina in 1908, in spite of the open opposition of the beduin and the more discreet dislike of the Sharif, who saw that it would tighten Turkish hold on Arabia.

In 1908 the 'Young Turks' forced the Sultan to restore the Constitution, suspended since 1876. A parliament met in December 1908, in which the Arabs were represented, though inadequately. At first some of their leaders supported the new party, but soon its militant Turkish nationalism estranged them and they began to work for provincial autonomy in the Arab districts, or for a dual monarchy or complete independence. The proclamation of a Qureish Arab as Caliph had already been advocated by Kawakibi (1849–1903), a pan-Arabist who travelled in the Yemen and lived for a time at Mecca. Against the wish of 'Abdul Hamid the Young Turks had in 1908 made Husein ibn 'Ali ibn Muhammad ibn 'Aun Sharif of Mecca. He was then 53 years old, had lived among the Hejazi beduin, and later for many years at Constantinople. Deeply religious, honest, frugal, shrewd, cautious, and cultivated, yet ambitious and vain, with an imposing presence and a knowledge of Turkish politics, he was respected for the sanctity of his life. Sharif Husein assisted the Turks in 'Asīr, and in 1912 forced Ibn Sa'ūd to pay him tribute for Al Qasīm. By 1914 he had entrenched himself too well for the Turks, who now realized their mistake, to dare to remove him.

The Sharif's second son, 'Abdullah—the present Amir of Transjordan—who represented Mecca in the Chamber of Deputies at Constantinople, worked steadily in his father's interests, refusing the offers of the Turks to make him a Cabinet Minister or Vali of the Yemen. He belonged to a nationalist secret society, between which and Husein he was a useful link. Early in 1914 he sounded Lord Kitchener, then British Agent in Egypt, on Great Britain's attitude in the event of an Arab revolt; he was discouraged and reminded of the traditional friendship between Britain and Turkey. Lord Kitchener, however, privately deplored the great growth of German influence that had taken place in Turkey, which he hoped might be counterbalanced by Anglo-Arab friendship.

The Yemen

The twentieth century in the Yemen opened under the oppressive rule of the Turkish vali 'Abdullah Pasha (p. 274), and it was not long before the Zarānīq tribe of the Tihama revolted and cut the telegraph line from Hodeida to San'ā. It was also during this vali's term of office that the Turks encroached on the Amirate of Dhāla' and other territories to the south, an action which resulted in the Anglo-Turkish Boundary Commission of 1902–1904 (p. 276).

In 1904 the Imam Muhammad Al Mansūr died and was succeeded by his son, the present Imam Yahya, styled *Al Mutawakkil 'alā Allah* ('the relier on God'). The new Imam instantly revolted against the Turks and besieged San'ā. There was great scarcity in the city, where cats and dogs were eaten, while the price of a horse was 400 dollars. A Turkish supply column sent to its relief was captured by the Imam, to whom the city surrendered in 1905. Later the Turks recovered it, lost it again, and finally took it with troops under Ahmed Feidhi Pasha, who had suppressed the rebellion in 1892 (p. 274). More than half the population is said to have perished during the siege and subsequent fighting. Moreover, the whole country had suffered badly, agriculture had been neglected, and private stores of grain had been seized. The Sultan of Turkey made several attempts to come to terms with the Imam; the latter was willing to leave foreign affairs to the Turks, but insisted that the *shar'* and the traditional system of taxation should be restored and the Zeidi Qadhis reinstated; he also wished that corrupt officials should be punished and others adequately paid in order to reduce bribery, that pious endowments should be used for religious and not secular purposes, and that posts of authority in the Yemen should be given to none but Moslems. Though his terms were rejected, many of them were unofficially conceded during the governorship of Hasan Tahsin Pasha (1908–1910), and relations improved for the time being.

The next vali, Muhammad 'Ali Pasha, reverted to harsh measures, and in 1911 the Imam, issuing from his northern stronghold of Shahāra at the head of some 150,000 tribesmen, with artillery, again besieged San'ā for three months early in the year. The city was, however, well stocked with provisions, and though the Turkish Parliament would not sanction a large expeditionary force—60,000 men had been suggested by the Turkish War Minister—to subdue the country, a Turkish army, led by Ahmed 'Izzet Pasha, fought its way once more over the mountains via Manākha to San'ā. 'Izzet Pasha, who remarked that all Europe could be conquered by such men as he had had to subdue, opened negotiations with the Imam, and made an agreement which conceded in substance the Imam's demands. This agreement was to last for ten years. By it the country was divided into two administrative regions, the Imam appointing the *hukkam* or provincial governors in the Zeidi districts, and the Turkish vali appointing them in the Shafe'i and Hanafi districts. Though the Turkish Parliament rejected the treaty, it was ratified by an Imperial edict in 1913. 'Izzet Pasha left in 1912, his departure being much regretted, but under the new vali, Muhammad Nadim Bey, the agreement was loyally observed on both sides.

Meanwhile trouble had occurred in 'Asīr, where a rebellion had broken out under Seiyid Muhammad ibn 'Ali al Idrisi, a man of considerable energy and administrative ability. A grandson of Seiyid Ahmed al Idrisi—a native of Fez who had founded in north Africa the religious confraternity to which the founder of the Senusiya at one time belonged—he had studied at Al Azhar University at Cairo and in the Sudan, and had spent some time with the Senusiya. He quickly gained control of most of 'Asīr, but the Turks, with the help of the Sharif of Mecca, regained Abhā in 1911. The Italians, who at this time were at war with Turkey in Libya, exaggerated the Idrisi's importance, on account of his connexion with north Africa, gave him arms, ammunition, and money, and with their navy blockaded the ports on the Arabian coast which were in Turkish hands. Hodeida and Sheikh Sa'īd were shelled, but with little effect other than to arouse the Imam's suspicions of Italy, and to make the Idrisi unpopular throughout western Arabia. At Aden he was nicknamed *Al Iblīsi* 'the friend of the Devil'. After his death at Sabya his descendants, enriched by the offerings of pilgrims to his tomb, gradually succeeded to the local leadership formerly exercised by the Sharifs of Abu 'Arīsh (p. 256).

THE WAR OF 1914–1918

When war between Great Britain and Turkey broke out on 5 November 1914 military operations began almost at once in three regions affecting Arabia. The Turks unsuccessfully attacked the Suez Canal early in February and were slowly pushed back to Palestine, though it was not until 1917 that the British were able to launch a serious offensive on Palestine, with the co-operation of the Hejaz Arabs on their right flank. The political aspects of this campaign were controlled from Egypt. In November 1914 British troops from India occupied Basra to protect the Persian oil supply at Abadan, an aim which later developed into the conquest of 'Iraq. The political side of this campaign was managed from India. With the exception of the 'Aneiza no confederation or large body of Arabs in the country actively supported the British here, until victory was assured. The third region was the Aden hinterland where the Turks were in some strength at the outbreak of war, but the position was soon stabilized, and Aden remained throughout an important base of operations and a vital link in the sea-communications of the British Empire.

Nejd

Thanks to the pre-war travels of Captains W. H. I. Shakespear and G. E. Leachman, the Government of India was aware of the situation in Nejd and the desert south of the Euphrates. Ibn Sa'ūd's attempt to concert a uniform policy among the Arab rulers failed at once, for though Sheikh Mubārak of Kuweit renounced his allegiance to the Turks, Ibn Rashid joined the Turkish side. An inconclusive battle between him and Ibn Sa'ūd was fought at Jarrab, in which Shakespear was killed (1915), after which Ibn Sa'ūd took no further active part in the war; he was probably not strong enough to persuade the Ikhwān and the 'ulema to accept active alliance with a Christian state.

In December 1915 Ibn Sa'ūd met Sir Percy Cox, the Chief Political Officer of the Mesopotamian Expeditionary Force, at 'Oqeir and signed a treaty by which the British obtained a large measure of control of his foreign policy but acknowledged the independence and territorial integrity of Nejd and granted him a monthly subsidy of £5,000. The British imposed a blockade of Turkish territory but, despite some help from the 'Aneiza, were never able to prevent supplies from being smuggled across the desert through Hāil. Mubārak of Kuweit died in 1915 and his son Jābir in February 1917. The latter's brother, Salim (1916–1921), pro-Turkish and hostile to Ibn Sa'ūd, connived at the contraband trade.

South-west Arabia

The Imam of the Yemen remained loyal to the Turks, partly from fear of Seiyid Muhammad al Idrisi in 'Asīr, who, having failed to secure from the Turks a status higher than that of Qaimmaqam of Sabya and Abu 'Arīsh, declared against them, signing a treaty with the British Resident at Aden in May 1915. The Idrisi, with some 12,000 men, tried to take Luheiya without success, though he overran much of the northern Tihama. In June 1915 Luheiya was bombarded by the British to assist the Idrisi, who, however, resented the damage caused to the town.

In October 1914 the Turks had about 14,000 troops in the Yemen apparently ready to attack the Aden Protectorate from the Sheikh Sa'īd peninsula. Indian troops therefore landed here on the outbreak of war, demolished Turba fort at the south-east corner of the peninsula and drove the Turks inland. The garrison of Aden was also strengthened. Later the Turks reoccupied Sheikh Sa'īd, and on the night of 14–15 June 1915 they made an unsuccessful attempt to land on Perim island.

Towards the end of the same month the Turks advanced from Māwiya, near the frontier east of Ta'izz, and from Hujarīya, and, being joined by the Sultan of Museimīr with his Haushabi tribesmen, captured Lahej on 5 July. Troops from Aden had moved out to

Lahej, and the 'Abdali Sultan resisted near Tanān and Nobat Dukeim, about 17 miles north of the town, but were overcome by the Turkish guns. The Sultan himself, Sir 'Ali ibn Ahmed, a cousin of the present ruler, remained in Lahej as long as possible, and was accidentally wounded at night by the Aden troops; he died in Aden some days later. The Turks pressed on to Sheikh 'Othman, but were expelled by a surprise attack on 21 July. In August and September, attacks on Turkish posts at Fiyūsh, 8 miles north of Sheikh 'Othman, and at Waht on the Wadi Kabir, about 6 miles to the west, forced the Turks back to Lahej.

Thereafter, notwithstanding minor engagements, the Turks remained in Lahej till the collapse of Turkey in 1918, held by the Aden forces facing them, while caravans passed freely in and out of Aden through the British and Turkish lines. This strange 'peace in war' badly affected the protected tribes; besides the Haushabis, who had gone over bodily, some Subeihis, Fadhlis, and Yāfa'is joined the Turks, to whom also the Amir of Dhāla' was forced to submit. An attempt in 1916 to reinforce the Turks with 3,500 men was foiled by the Arab revolt in the Hejaz. This body was accompanied by a German mission under Baron von Stotzingen, who was to have organized propaganda in Somaliland, Eritrea, and the Sudan.

The Blockade

The blockade in the Red Sea presented great difficulties. Since Britain was at war with the Turks but not with the Arabs, the main object was to prevent munitions from reaching the former, while craft laden with *bona-fide* foodstuffs for the Arab population were to be allowed to pass. This involved the constant searching of Arab vessels. Since the Turks in the earlier part of the war freely used Arab levies, particularly in the Hejaz, boats dispatched by naval vessels to reconnoitre close inshore were often fired on by Arabs, who also tried, once successfully, to lure British landing-parties on to well-manned concealed positions. On the coast of 'Asīr matters were still more complicated, because the Idrisi (p. 288) was nominally at war with the Turks and therefore entitled to receive munitions by sea. The ports and anchorages to be watched were numerous; the Southern Patrol alone had about fifteen under its surveillance on the Arabian coast from Bab al Mandeb northwards. The Navy was also hampered in the earlier part of the war by the ships employed being too large; later, trawlers were more used. Moreover, great care had to be taken only to bombard Turkish forts and military positions, without injuring

Arabs or damaging their often closely adjacent mosques and houses. Thus, at Umm Lejj, nearly 80 miles north-west of Yenbo', the Turkish fort was put out of action early in 1916 by the guns of H.M.S. *Fox*, Senior Patrol Vessel, firing precisely up the street leading from the beach.

The Hejaz and Syria

On the declaration of war the Sultan of Turkey had, as Caliph, pro-claimed a *jihad* and tried to gain the public support of the Sharif of Mecca. An attempt was also made to introduce conscription in the Hejaz, but compulsory military service in remote parts of the Turkish Empire was already one of the chief grievances of the Arabs in Syria, some of whom had been sent to the Yemen in the hope that the rebels there would be unwilling to fight their fellow Arabs. The proposal was, therefore, unpopular in the Hejaz, where it was circumvented by the Sharif Husein. The latter adroitly avoided endorsing the call to a *jihad*; instead, he sent Muhammad's banner from Al Madina to Damascus, where it was received with much ceremony. Possibly the cautious Sharif did not fully realize the strength of the Nationalist movement in Syria, while his third son, Feisal, distrusted European ambitions in the Middle East. Even before Turkey had entered the war Mr. Ronald Storrs, the Oriental Secretary to the High Commis-sioner in Egypt, had received from the Sharif's second son 'Abdullah a non-committal but not discouraging answer to inquiries about the Arab attitude. In November 1914 Great Britain offered, in return for the Sharif's support against Turkey, to guarantee his continuance in his office and its rights, and to give general help to the Arab move-ment; while it was hinted that the Sharif might be recognized as Caliph. The Sharif then initiated a correspondence with Sir Henry McMahon, the High Commissioner, to decide the conditions on which he would join the Allies. The eight letters, known as the 'McMahon Correspondence',[1] have been the subject of much con-troversy, particularly in relation to the Palestine Mandate. So far as peninsular Arabia is concerned the mutual undertakings are clear and not very important. Sharif Husein recognized the status of Aden and the validity of existing British treaties with other Arab chiefs. Sir Henry McMahon pledged British support for Arab independence in

---

[1] The originals were in Arabic. English translations will be found in *Correspon-dence between Sir Henry McMahon, His Majesty's High Commissioner at Cairo, and the Sherif Hussein of Mecca, July 1915–March 1916*, Cmd. 5957, Accounts and Papers, Session 1938–9, pp. 573–592; and in G. Antonius, *The Arab Awakening*, 1938.

147. *The Ruwalla on the warpath, with the 'Ark of Ishmael' surrounded by its guard of honour*

148. *Feisal's army coming into Wejh, January 1917*

a wide area, including the rest of the peninsula, guaranteed the Holy Cities against external aggression, and promised to look with favour on the proclamation of one of Muhammad's descendants as Caliph. The British probably over-estimated the importance of the last question, even to Husein personally, because of the interest taken in it by Indian Moslems. In Arabia any claimant was sure to meet opposition, while elsewhere the Caliphate had become a far less moving issue than national independence.

Savage Turkish repression in Syria precipitated the Arab revolt and so 'dispensed with the necessity for a strict formulation of the limits of British concession'.[1] On 5 June 1916 Sharif Husein's eldest and third sons, 'Ali and Feisal, proclaimed Arab independence at the tomb of Hamza outside Al Madina to 1,500 recruits who had been enlisted ostensibly to help the Turks. Husein himself and his second son 'Abdullah were at Mecca, where the revolt began at dawn on 10 June; the city may be said to have fallen in a few days, though the Turkish garrison of some 1,400 men had not all surrendered till the following month.

Jidda fell principally to the British Navy, which on the night of 9 June began a bombardment of carefully located Turkish positions, intended to synchronize with an Arab attack. The latter, however, did not materialize till next morning, and then somewhat feebly, since munitions delivered on the beach south of the port to the Sharif's agents were apparently diverted to Mecca. Nevertheless the naval bombardment continued on the night of 11 June and on succeeding days, culminating on 15 June with heavy bombing of the Turkish trenches by a seaplane. The Turks ran up the white flag, negotiations resulted in unconditional surrender on 17 June, after which food and munitions for the Arabs were poured into the port.

Qunfidha and Tāif fell to 'Abdullah in September; Rābigh and Yenbo' had already capitulated; Al Madina alone was too strong to be stormed. Some 14,000 Turks were there, another 5,000 were at Tebūk, and the garrison of Ma'an was increased to over 7,000.

The adventures of two small parties of Germans in the Hejaz may be mentioned. Early in 1915 about fifty men of a demolition party which had been left on Cocos island by the *Emden*, led by an officer named Von Mucke, succeeded by means of coastal craft in reaching Al Līth on the Red Sea. Securing camels by the favour of Sharif Husein, who was still under the Turks, they reached Jidda, despite a

---

[1] G. M. Gathorne-Hardy, *A Short History of International Affairs, 1920–1938*, 1938, p. 126.

desperate encounter with Harb tribesmen lasting three days. Eventually they rejoined their compatriots in the north. The second party, consisting of Lieut.-Commander von Moeller, from a gunboat interned in China, and five reservists who had joined him in Java, met with a tragic fate. Landing on the south Arabian coast in March 1916, they reached San'ā overland, travelled thence to the coast and, screened from patrol craft by the Farasān bank, continued by dhow to Qunfidha. Thence they reached Jidda by camel early in May. Continuing northwards, against the advice of their Turkish allies, they were barbarously murdered, and their bodies mutilated, by tribesmen south of Rābigh.

Late in 1916 the Arab army of the Hejaz numbered from 30,000 to 40,000 men, but with only about 10,000 rifles. Its organization was entrusted to an Egyptian officer who had been in the Turkish army, 'Aziz 'Ali al Masri (afterwards Chief of Staff of the Egyptian Army), and later to an 'Iraqi, Ja'far al 'Askari (subsequently several times Prime Minister of 'Iraq). Its discipline and training were at first very bad and the Turks made a successful sally from Al Madina. Rābigh was threatened and it was suggested that an Allied brigade might be landed there. In January 1917 the Royal Navy, with the help of Feisal, captured Wejh. The Turkish garrison of Al Madina was henceforth on the defensive, watched by a force under the Amir 'Ali, the Sharif's eldest son. By now about 70,000 tribesmen were in revolt.

Sir Reginald Wingate, Governor-General of the Sudan, who had been made responsible for Allied military advice and supplies to the Arabs, succeeded Sir Henry McMahon as High Commissioner in Egypt early in 1917. British and French missions and a number of British advisers and instructors were sent to the Hejaz, while French-trained Moslem officers from Morocco and Algeria were also lent to Sharif Husein. T. E. Lawrence arrived in October 1916 and attached himself to the Amir Feisal. An archaeologist who had worked in Syria and elsewhere, he had not previously travelled in peninsular Arabia, but was gifted with unusual ability in dealing with Arabs and a remarkable talent for guerrilla warfare. Lawrence saw the possibility of immobilizing the large body of Turkish troops at Al Madina, where they were not so hard pressed as to be tempted to withdraw, but were to weak to launch an offensive. Their long supply lines, of which the most important was the Hejaz railway, were very vulnerable and the Turks thus lost heavily, especially from the dynamiting of trains.

The Amir 'Abdullah captured a Turkish mission on its way to the Yemen, while his youngest brother Zeid captured a convoy on its way to Ibn Rashid, the replacement of which caused a quarrel between Ibn Rashid and the Turks. Feisal, who was acquiring considerable personal prestige by his exploits, now organized the revolt from Wejh, distributing money supplied by the British, reconciling tribal feuds and disseminating nationalist ideas. He was joined by 'Auda Abu Tayi, chief of the Tayi clan of the eastern Huweitāt north of 'Aqaba, a man of great courage and energy, but with a possibly exaggerated reputation for great cruelty. 'Auda, who had his own quarrel with the Turks, having killed two gendarmes in 1908, took the lead in the operations which resulted in the capture of 'Aqaba in July 1917.

Communications between the Egyptian Expeditionary Force, now commanded by Sir Edmund Allenby, and Feisal were thenceforth conducted through 'Aqaba, where wireless stations and an airfield were built, and supplies landed. Apart from the siege of Al Madina there was no further fighting in the Hejaz. Feisal moved to the north through Transjordan, co-operating with the British armies invading Palestine. The Armistice with Turkey was signed at Mudros in October 1918, and Al Madina was surrendered on orders from Constantinople the following January.

Relations between King Husein and Ibn Sa'ūd

In October 1916 an assembly of notables at Mecca had proclaimed Sharif Husein as *Malik al bilād al 'arabīya*, 'King of the Arab countries'. His actions, provocative both to the Allies and to the other Arabian rulers, showed that he regarded himself as King of all the Arab lands whose independence had been promised by Sir Henry McMahon. The Allies, aware of rival claims and under treaty obligations to other Arab rulers, accorded him recognition only as King of the Hejaz, and tried to compose his differences with Ibn Sa'ūd.

Sir Percy Cox, who had won Ibn Sa'ūd's personal regard, tried to gain his benevolent neutrality to the Arab revolt. The Arab Bureau sent Storrs to 'Iraq, whence he set out for Riyādh, but had to return owing to sunstroke. It was then decided to send a joint mission. Cox's representatives, Colonel R. E. A. Hamilton (now Lord Belhaven) and Mr. H. St. J. B. Philby, arrived at Riyādh, but King Husein would not allow the delegates from Egypt to leave the Hejaz. Philby therefore proceeded thither, to see King Husein.

Philby left 'Oqeir on 18 November 1917, and travelling via Hofūf, reached Riyādh on 1 December. Leaving the Sa'ūdi capital on 9 December he followed the pilgrim route through Qunsulīya and

Khurma to Tāif, where he arrived seventeen days later. At King Husein's invitation he left Tāif on 28 December and, being forbidden as a (then) non-Moslem to enter Mecca, travelled north to Wadi Fātima, passing down this valley via Madhiq and Bahra; then, turning north-west through the mountains, he reached Jidda on 31 December, where he met the king. Thus for the second time Arabia was crossed from sea to sea by an Englishman, almost a century after Sadlier's journey in 1819 (p. 268). A political mission was the prime cause of the journey in both cases.

Despite Philby's efforts, however, King Husein was obdurate. In the summer of 1918 hostilities began at Khurma, a village which had been converted to the tenets of the Wahhabis and which Husein was trying to recover. His three attacks were repelled, and the British undertook to restrain him and to arbitrate after the war. Ibn Sa'ūd then marched against Ibn Rashid, whom he defeated 'in a battle of typical beduin character' at Yatab, though he was not strong enough to follow this up by an assault on Hāil. With the surrender of Turkey soon after, five Arabian states became fully independent: the Hejaz, 'Asīr, the Yemen, Sa'ūdi Arabia, and Hāil.

THE EXPANSION OF SA'ŪDI ARABIA

The Battle of Turaba

In 1919, the British Government having adjudged Khurma to the Hejaz, Husein sent 'Abdullah with 4,000 men and beduin auxiliaries to occupy the village. Ibn Sa'ūd ignored the British threat to stop his subsidy and the Amir 'Abdullah's camp at Turaba was attacked by Khālid ibn Luwei, chief of Khurma. The camp, entrenched on modern lines, was thought to be secure against attack. But on a night in the middle of May, the Wahhabis surprised it and were among the Sharifian forces before they awoke. 'Abdullah's men were killed at their guns or butchered as they arose from their beds. A handful of survivors little more than a hundred strong, including 'Abdullah and his staff, escaped to Tāif, and thence, joined by the panic-stricken inhabitants, to Mecca, where the alarm was so great that foreign pilgrims left the city and fled to Jidda.

Operations against Ibn Rashid

To the relief of all, however, Ibn Sa'ūd turned his attention once more to Ibn Rashid. Sa'ūd ibn Sālih had been followed as chief adviser to the latter by the able 'Aqab ibn 'Ajil, who had secured the retrocession of Jauf by the Ruwalla. In 1920 Sa'ūd ibn Rashid was murdered and succeeded by his nephew 'Abdullah ibn Mit'ab. A Sa'ūdi party now began to form at Hāil; and in 1921 Ibn Sa'ūd, apprehensive at Feisal's establishment in 'Iraq and his relations with the Shammar, took the field, while the Ikhwān under Feisal ad Duwish (p. 285) supported him from the east. Meanwhile the paramount sheikh of the Ruwalla, Ibn Sha'lān, recaptured Jauf. Soon after this 'Abdullah ibn Mit'ab (ibn Rashid) was deposed by Muhammad ibn Talāl (ibn Rashid) and fled to Riyādh. Muhammad ibn Talāl was defeated by the Ikhwān; Hāil, being besieged, opened its gates to avoid bombardment. Finally, in November 1921, Muhammad ibn Talāl surrendered, Ibn Sa'ūd annexed his territories and thus realized one of his greatest ambitions. In July 1922 he annexed Jauf, besides occupying Teima, Kheibar, and other border oases of the Hejaz.

Relations with Transjordan and 'Iraq

These events brought Ibn Sa'ūd to the borders of the British mandated territories of Transjordan and 'Iraq. At the invitation of the British Government in 1921, Feisal, King Husein's third son, who had already been proclaimed King of Syria and then expelled by the French, was elected King of 'Iraq, while 'Abdullah, his brother, became Amir of Transjordan. Husein remained only King of the Hejaz, though he tried to assert a paternal overlordship of his sons' dominions.

The first clash occurred in August 1922 when some three or four thousand Wahhabi Ikhwān raided to within 12 miles of Amman, the Transjordan capital, but were almost annihilated at Umm al Amad by the armoured cars and air force of 'Abdullah's British allies. Meanwhile Sir Percy Cox, who had already settled the disputed boundary of Nejd and Kuweit, arranged the Treaty of Mohammerah (1922), which assigned the Muntafiq, Dhafir, and Amarat tribes to 'Iraq, and the southern Shammar to Nejd, and also forbade tribal aggression. Ibn Sa'ūd met Cox at 'Oqeir in the winter of 1922–23, when a protocol defined the boundary separating the traditional wells and lands of the tribes concerned, and formed a neutral zone. Ibn Sa'ūd undertook to restrain his adherents, and himself to refrain from aggression against 'Iraq, Kuweit, and the Hejaz; to co-operate in maintaining the safety of the pilgrim routes through his territory; and to consent to be guided generally in his foreign policy by the wishes of Great Britain, as well as to co-operate with her in furthering peaceful conditions in Arab countries and their economic interests.

King Feisal of 'Iraq, now realizing something of the danger to his family, offered to meet Ibn Sa'ūd in conference. But the Amir 'Abdullah of Transjordan refused to attend without his father's permission, and King Husein was still obstinate. Delegates from Nejd, 'Iraq, and Transjordan, however, met at Kuweit in 1923 under the presidency of the British Resident in the Persian Gulf, Col. Knox, but nothing was accomplished, because Ibn Sa'ūd would not surrender Khurma, Turaba, Kheibar, and Teima to King Husein, nor would he restore Hāil to Ibn Rashid. Husein thereupon refused to send representatives and the conference broke up in April 1924. The end of his subsidy from Great Britain at this time gave Ibn Sa'ūd freedom of action, and war became inevitable.

The Conquest of the Hejaz

Since the Hejaz contains the holy cities of Islam, the whole Muhammadan world was interested in its fate. At the end of the war in 1918 Turkey was still the leading orthodox Moslem Power, and both Indian and Egyptian opinion was agitated by the events in Arabia. But the puritanical Wahhabis scarcely regarded Husein as a true Moslem, and he was the hereditary enemy of Ibn Sa'ūd. Husein was in a difficult position. His pretensions with the nationalists of Syria, Palestine, and 'Iraq depended on his ability to extract concessions from the mandatory power, but at the same time he could ill afford to lose British support, in fear of attack by Ibn Sa'ūd. In the event he failed through a series of political errors which lost him the support of his former friends. On the other hand, Ibn Sa'ūd showed a more reasonable desire to negotiate a settlement, and the visit of his son the Amir Feisal to London was an undoubted success.

After the disaster at Turaba in 1919, the British sent an envoy to the Hejaz to negotiate a settlement between King Husein and Ibn Sa'ūd; but the latter had already withdrawn and Husein would not permit the envoy to land. Later, as a protest against the Syrian and Palestinian mandates, Husein refused to ratify the Treaty of Versailles. In 1921 Lawrence brought an offer of an Anglo-Hejazi treaty, by which the Hejaz was to receive a subsidy and to be guaranteed against aggression, and in return Husein was to recognize Britain's special position in 'Iraq and Palestine. This proposal was curtly rejected by Husein, and later attempts in 1923 to come to terms were equally unsuccessful. At the same time Husein offended Egypt by his attitude towards the Mecca pilgrimage. His refusal to send representatives to the conference at Kuweit has been already mentioned.

On 3 March 1923 the Turkish National Assembly finally abolished the Caliphate, which had survived the abolition of the Ottoman Sultanate on 1 November 1922, though it was deprived of temporal power. Husein was in Transjordan at the time, and on 6 March he reluctantly allowed it to be announced that he had assumed the office of Caliph. This act caused a storm of indignation in Nejd and among the Ikhwān. In August another Wahhabi attack, again disastrous to themselves and at once disowned by Ibn Sa'ūd, was made on Transjordan, while a column under Sultān ibn Bijad raided the Hejaz. In September a Sa'ūdi detachment appeared before Tāif, which surrendered, and the Amir 'Ali, who was there, fell back to cover Mecca. The Wahhabis massacred some 300 persons at Tāif, a tragedy which spread alarm throughout the Hejaz. The Amir 'Ali, defeated at Hadda in the Tāif mountains, fled to Jidda, where the leading citizens persuaded Husein to abdicate and forced 'Ali to accept the throne.

Though the European Powers declared their neutrality, Great Britain protested at the massacre at Tāif; Ibn Sa'ūd therefore ordered that no further advance should be made until he could take charge in person. Meanwhile Mecca had been abandoned by King 'Ali, and had been occupied by Sultān ibn Bijad in October, though Ibn Sa'ūd only arrived there on 5 December, by which time Jidda had been fortified. With the exception of Al Madina, Yenbo', and Jidda, the Hejaz was now quickly overrun by the Wahhabis. Siege was laid to these three cities but had to be relaxed during the following summer. In December 1925 King 'Ali abdicated and retired to 'Iraq, where he died in 1934. His father Husein, who took up his residence at 'Aqaba, afterwards lived at Cyprus and died at Amman in Transjordan in 1931.

THE KINGDOM OF SA'ŪDI ARABIA

Ibn Sa'ūd was proclaimed King of the Hejaz in the Great Mosque at Mecca on 8 January 1926. There was some dissatisfaction at his taking this step without consulting Islam as a whole; already in 1925 a deputation from the Indian Caliphate Committee had arrived in Arabia, with the suggestion that the Hejaz should be given a republican constitution and placed under the control of a committee representing all sections of Islam. Ibn Sa'ūd now issued invitations to all Moslem communities to send representatives to a congress at Mecca, in order to discuss the future administration of the Hejaz, in the interests of the pilgrims. There were many abstentions, and the congress achieved nothing beyond bringing the Wahhabi leaders into contact with the rest of Islam. Their destruction of tombs and shrines in the Hejaz caused resentment, especially in Persia, which did not recognize the new regime till 1929. Relations with Egypt were also unsatisfactory, as the Sa'ūdi Government refused to allow the *Mahmal*, the finely decorated camel-litter sent annually from Egypt, to be accompanied by an armed escort as had been customary (photo. 179); consequently the Egyptians declined to send it at all.

For dynastic and doctrinal reasons Arab Nationalists did not usually envisage Ibn Sa'ūd as a member of the Arab federation which they wished to create, though many of them admired him as an example of the national virtues. He has great influence with Shukri al Quwatli, now President of the Syrian Republic. His status as an independent sovereign in friendly relations with Great Britain has been useful both to the Arabs and to the British in Palestine, in the problems of which Ibn Sa'ūd has taken a great interest.

Sa'ūdi rule in the Hejaz was readily recognized by the European Powers, beginning with the U.S.S.R., but even before the fall of Jidda Sir Gilbert Clayton was sent (October 1925) by the British Government to visit Ibn Sa'ūd in the Hejaz; he negotiated the Treaty of Bahra, which aimed at preventing raids on the frontier of 'Iraq, and that of Hadda, which determined the boundary of Nejd and Transjordan. Earlier in 1925 Ibn Sa'ūd had protested against the incorporation in Transjordan of the province of Ma'an and the port of 'Aqaba, asserting that they had been part of Husein's kingdom. A decision on their status was postponed, but Wadi Sirhan was assigned to Nejd. These agreements proving inadequate, Sir Gilbert Clayton in May 1927 negotiated the Treaty of Jidda, which has since governed relations between Great Britain and Sa'ūdi Arabia. The 'complete and absolute independence' of Ibn Sa'ūd's territories was recognized and the Treaty of 'Oqeir (p. 290) was declared void; Ibn Sa'ūd agreed to the continuance of the *status quo* under which Ma'an and 'Aqaba were administered by Transjordan, and formal agreement concerning them has never been sealed, not even by the Treaty of 1933 between Ibn Sa'ūd and the Amir of Transjordan.[1] In 1927 Ibn Sa'ūd also agreed to facilitate the pilgrimage for Moslem subjects of Great Britain, to respect British treaties with Arab chiefs of the Persian Gulf, and to co-operate in the suppression of the slave trade. The duration of the treaty was to be seven years; but it was renewed in 1934 and, by an exchange of notes in 1943, it was agreed that it

[1] *Palestine and Transjordan*, B.R. 524, p. 463.

should be automatically renewed for periods of seven years at a time unless six months' notice of denunciation were given.

Internal and External Affairs

The administration set up by Ibn Sa'ūd in Nejd and the Hejaz is described in Chapter VI. Here it will be sufficient to say that, having been proclaimed Sultan of Nejd and its dependencies in 1921 and King of the Hejaz in 1926, he became King of the Hejaz and of Nejd and its dependencies in 1927, and in 1932 King of Sa'ūdi Arabia. His greatest internal difficulty has been the fanaticism of some of his supporters. In 1926 Feisal ad Duwish (p. 285) demanded a *jihad* against all non-Wahhabis. Ibn Sa'ūd referred the matter to the 'ulema, who decided that it was within his competence as sovereign to refuse. But Feisal ad Duwish renewed his demand, beginning in 1927 and 1928 to attack 'Iraq and Kuweit. British aircraft and armoured cars intervened, but negotiations with Ibn Sa'ūd were complicated by a disagreement over the interpretation of the engagements relating to the frontier of 'Iraq. In November 1928 Feisal ad Duwish went into open rebellion. After being defeated at Sibila in 1929, he was pardoned but revolted again. He finally capitulated in 1930, an event which led to the first personal meeting of King Ibn Sa'ūd and King Feisal of 'Iraq.

Ibn Sa'ūd's relations with Transjordan were for a time unsatisfactory. In 1933 he crushed the rebellion of Ibn Ridafa, an exile who had been living in Transjordan. The complicity of the Amir 'Abdullah of Transjordan was suspected; nevertheless a treaty of friendship was signed in the same year, since when no serious difficulty has arisen between the two states. A trade agreement between Sa'ūdi Arabia and Bahrein was made in 1936: in the same year treaties were signed with 'Iraq and Egypt. In 1937 the Imam took advantage of an invitation issued by Ibn Sa'ūd to other Arab rulers, to adhere to a treaty similar in terms to that between Sa'ūdi Arabia and 'Iraq.

The Sa'ūdi-Yemen War, 1934

In 'Asīr, the mountain districts of which Ibn Sa'ūd had reduced to submission in 1920, Seiyid Muhammad al Idrisi (p. 290) died in 1922. His son 'Ali succeeded him, but was deposed by his uncle Husein. A civil war ensued in which 'Ali was supported by the Imam of the Yemen, while Husein tried to renew the traditional alliance between 'Asīr and the Wahhabis. In 1925 Husein al Idrisi accepted an arrangement almost amounting to a protectorate from Ibn Sa'ūd, who guaranteed his dominions against further encroachment and was to annex them when Husein died. Relations between Ibn Sa'ūd and the Imam were now delicate, but Ibn Sa'ūd repeatedly declared that he had no desire to recover territory lost by the Idrisi prior to the arrangement between the latter and himself. In 1932 Husein fomented a tribal revolt against Sa'ūdi domination, but the rising was suppressed by February 1933, when the Sa'ūdi forces occupied Sabya. The Idrisi fled to the Imam, whose acts, viewed by the Sa'ūdis as territorial aggressions, provoked a war with Ibn Sa'ūd in February 1934. The Wahhabis invaded the Tihama and occupied Hodeida, the governor of which, the Imam's son Seif al Islam 'Abdullah, fled to San'ā. After two months the Imam asked for peace, which was concluded by the Treaty of Tāif in May. With remarkable moderation Ibn Sa'ūd imposed only the settlement he had offered before the outbreak of war; that is, a strip of disputed territory in the south of 'Asīr was definitely incorporated in the Sa'ūdi kingdom, an arrangement which shifted the northern frontier of the Yemen some distance to the south of that shown on most maps. The frontier now touches the coast only just north of the Yemeni port of Meidi, whence it runs steeply north-eastward to the watershed, then bends south-east and finally takes a general easterly direction nearly to the edge of the Great Desert (fig. 11).

THE YEMEN

Since events in the years immediately following 1918 concerned principally Britain and the Yemen, these are outlined below (pp. 304 ff.). In general, the Armistice was followed by a chaotic period. Under the Treaty of Lausanne (1923) Turkey renounced all her possessions in Arabia, but for some time neither the status nor the frontiers of the Yemen were precisely determined. Since, however, the northern frontier with Sa'ūdi Arabia was delimited after the Sa'ūdi-Yemeni war of 1934, while modifications of the southern frontier with the Aden Protectorate have followed the Anglo-Yemeni Treaty of San'ā in the same year (p. 305), it is mainly the eastern frontiers of the Yemen which remain still undemarcated. The Imam tried in 1932 to enforce certain claims which he believed himself to have on Nejrān.

The status of certain islands in the Red Sea was left 'indeterminate' by the Treaty of Lausanne. The part played by Britain and Italy in regard to these is mentioned below (pp. 308, 340).

With the Turks the Imam's relations remained friendly. The last

Turkish vali, Muhammad Nadim Bey, who did not leave the Yemen until 1925, is said to have contributed towards the development of friendship between Italy and the Yemen. Some former Turkish officers and officials still remain in the Imam's service, including the Foreign Minister, Qadhi Muhammad Raghib, a former member of the Ottoman Diplomatic Service. In 1923 and 1924 reports were circulated of a proposal to send Yemeni delegates to the Turkish National Assembly, but in Europe this was regarded as mere propaganda.

Internal Affairs

Since the country achieved independence rebellions have occurred among the Zarānīq in the lowlands and among certain tribes north of Sanʿā. But the rule of the Zeidi Imam has on the whole been accepted peaceably by the population of the Tihama. His relations with the Ismaʿīlis in the mountains west of Manākha and elsewhere have been less satisfactory.

The old Turkish administrative divisions were at first retained, though many Turkish officials and military officers who remained in the Imam's service were gradually replaced by Yemenis, or sometimes by Syrians and Egyptians. Some designations were altered, e.g. the title ʿamil was substituted for mutasarrif. In quite recent years the Imam has made drastic changes in the administrative system and provinces (pp. 331, 357).

The Imam has tried to obliterate ancient tribal divisions in order to consolidate the country (p. 333). He also apparently wishes to improve the status of the settled cultivators. He has not shrunk from stern measures to enforce order, and has continued the ancient practice of keeping members of powerful families in the capital as hostages; usually they live under conditions of comfort, with some freedom of movement, but, when revolt threatens in their families or tribes, their captivity may involve imprisonment and chaining (p. 338).

The Imam's desire to provide his people with modern medical facilities is evinced by his having built, some years ago, a hospital in which certain European doctors worked, more up-to-date than the accommodation formerly provided under the Turkish regime; quite recently (1943), very shortly before the British Medical Mission was withdrawn, he built a new hospital as an improvement on his former establishment. The foreign medical missions mentioned below have been encouraged, and the Imam appointed one of his sons, Seif al Islam Qasim, Minister of Health.

Other ministries have been instituted (p. 330), several of them under sons of the Imam. Seif al Islam 'Abdullah in particular, as Minister of Education, has made efforts to educate the sons of farmers and tribesmen and has established a new orphanage at Raudha, north of San'ā; a school for the education of orphan boys for military service had been maintained in San'ā for some years. Progress is apparently not fast enough for some young Yemenis, since the projected foundation of a Yemeni Youth Association among young men who have migrated to Aden is reported. Besides the conferences on Arab Union recently held in Cairo, at which the Imam had a delegate, a conference on the same subject is reported to have been held in Ta'izz in 1944.

Unfortunately, besides the typhus epidemic mentioned (p. 305) and smallpox, the Yemen has suffered severely from the same famine which has affected the Aden Protectorate. The principal cause has been deficiency of rain for several seasons, but conditions have been aggravated by the attempts of interested parties to corner and hoard corn. Happily rains so heavy that the broad dry *seil*-bed running through the capital was filled with water were reported from San'ā towards the end of April 1944. An almost immediate fall in the price of grain followed.

The scarcity led to a wave of anti-Semitic feeling, which resulted in many of the Yemeni Jews leaving their ancient home in an attempt to reach Palestine. About eight hundred are reported to have arrived there at the beginning of 1944, assisted by the Middle East Refugees Relief Association. But it seems that the Imam has tried to get the emigrating Jews sent back, and many had to be segregated in camps provided by the Aden authorities on account of disease (p. 450).

Relations between Great Britain and the Yemen

After the Armistice of Mudros in 1918 the Turks evacuated the Aden Protectorate and the British occupied Hodeida. While the frontiers and status of the Yemen were still undetermined (p. 302), Lieutenant-Colonel Harold F. Jacob, First Assistant Resident at Aden, led a mission which set out from Hodeida in August 1919 for San'ā to negotiate with the Imam, but which finally had to return after nearly four months' detention by the Quhra tribe at Bājil, in the Tihama.[1] The British quitted the Yemen in 1921, handing over Hodeida to the Idrisi (p. 290). This act was deeply resented by the Imam, who took advantage of the Idrisi's weakness to seize Hodeida,

---

[1] H. F. Jacob, *Kings of Arabia*, 1923, chap. xi.

Luheiya, and Meidi, all on the coast, in 1925. Moreover, as the Imam refused to accept the decisions of the pre-war Anglo-Turkish Boundary Commission (p. 276), Yemeni forces held the Amiri country and some other parts of the Western Aden Protectorate until compelled by the Royal Air Force to evacuate them in 1928.

In 1934 Sir Bernard Reilly, then Chief Commissioner (p. 339) of Aden, headed a mission and concluded with the Imam the Treaty of San'ā. Under this arrangement, which still determines relations between Britain and the Yemen, the Imam was recognized as an entirely independent king. Modifications in the frontier between the Yemen and the Aden Protectorate, and delimitation of parts previously undefined, have followed. In 1937 Seif al Islam Husein, a son of the Imam, headed a Yemeni delegation to the Coronation of King George VI.

All dealings between the British Government and the Imam are conducted through the Colonial Office and the Governor of Aden. The Imam has an agent in Aden, while an officer of the Aden Government, visiting San'ā when questions needing discussion arise, is received with the courtesies due to the representative of a foreign Power. The only British official allowed to reside permanently was a 'Political Clerk', stationed at Hodeida. The Imam has no representative of his own in London, but since 1943 the Minister of Sa'ūdi Arabia has also acted as Chargé d'Affaires for the Yemen.

The Aden Government arranged with the Church of Scotland Medical Mission at Sheikh 'Othman (the Keith-Falconer Mission, an historic name commemorating the brilliant orientalist and missionary who died in his thirty-first year at Sheikh 'Othman in 1887) to send to San'ā, early in 1937, a British Medical Mission which, with some changes of personnel, remained there till late in 1943. Its members went to the Yemen as medical missionaries with no political motive. Their admirable work, notably under the leadership of Dr. P. W. R. Petrie, was highly appreciated by the people; though their number was small compared with the Italian medical establishment (*below*), they had the immense advantage of being able to reach Arab women of all classes, since the mission included a medical woman and a nursing sister. The mission had at length to be withdrawn, at least temporarily, to the great regret of many Yemenis, after serious epidemics of typhus, from which its own members also suffered severely.

Italian Relations with the Yemen

The acquisition of the Tihama ports by the Imam in 1925 was followed by much Italian interest in the Yemen. When the Idrisi ceased to be an independent ruler (pp. 301, 304), Italy lost an ally of some years' standing, but this was compensated for by the removal of a source of friction with the Imam. The ports were more likely to prosper now that they were under the same political authority as their economic hinterland. The War of 1914–1918 had affected the financial position of Eritrea, which was never good; partly in the hope of restoring this, the governor, Gasparini, visited the Imam at San'ā in 1926. A treaty of friendship and economic collaboration between Italy and the Yemen, valid for ten years, was signed. It was renewed in 1936 for one year, and when it expired another Italian mission headed by Gasparini visited San'ā in the autumn of 1937. This visit, accompanied by lavish distribution of 'largesse', resulted in a new treaty between Italy and the Yemen, valid for twenty-five years. One of the Imam's sons, Seif al Islam Muhammad, together with the Foreign Secretary, Qadhi Muhammad Raghib, and several prominent Yemenis, had meanwhile visited Italy in 1927, where they were received by the king and by Mussolini, and were shown much to impress them with the military strength of Italy. Another son, Seif al Islam Husein, visited Italy on a later occasion.

Pre-Fascist Italian Governments took far more interest in south-west Arabia than Fascist writers admit. Even before the Union of Italy in 1861 there was some contact with Arabia. For example, early in the nineteenth century four Italians entered Arabia as doctors with the army sent by Muhammad 'Ali against the Wahhabis (p. 271)— a forecast of the later penetration of the Yemen by Italian medical men (p. 307). Renzo Manzoni, who made several journeys in the Yemen between 1877 and 1880, wrote a book[1] which, if not adding much to geographical knowledge, was highly informative. In 1883 the brothers Luigi and Giuseppe Caprotti, merchants representing the firm of Mazzucchelli e Perera, settled in San'ā; Luigi died in 1889, but Giuseppe stayed till 1918, despite the efforts of the Turkish valis to eject him. Incidentally he and the English traveller, Wavell, were the only western Europeans in the city during its siege by the present Imam early in 1911 (p. 288).[2] Other representatives of Italian commercial firms were living in Hodeida about that time. A prominent Italian traveller, the Marchese Gaetano Benzoni (son-in-law of Ferdinando Martini, p. 307), sent to Mocha to recruit for the Italian army in Somaliland, joined the Jewish traveller Hermann Burchardt in a journey to San'ā which proved to be Burchardt's last, for the two

---

[1] *El Yemen: tre anni nell' Arabia Felice*, 1884.
[2] A. J. B. Wavell, *A Modern Pilgrim in Mecca and a Siege in Sanaa*, 1912.

were murdered near Ibb in December 1909. During part, at least, of the Turkish occupation the Italians appear to have had a far stronger consular representation than Britain in the Yemen.

After the evacuation of the Yemen by the Turks and the rise of Fascism in Italy, and because the Imam would allow no permanent foreign diplomatic or consular representatives, the Italians established a small colony of strongly Fascist medical men, and a few engineers and other technicians. Cesare Ansaldi, sent to San'ā in 1929, super-vised the hospital, was personal physician to the Imam, and practised medicine among all classes of the people, besides using many oppor-tunities of travel.[1] A number of doctors lived together in one large establishment; later the senior member was Dr. Emilio Dubbiosi, who retired to Italy in 1938 after twelve years' service in the Yemen, having also been the Imam's personal physician; he was succeeded by Dr. Passera. Single medical men were also stationed in Hodeida and Ta'izz. Much good work was done by these doctors, despite their political bias; they are credited with (inter alia) the introduction of vaccination against smallpox. It has been reported that Italy also subsidized the Imam annually with money and arms. But early in 1943 news was received that he had interned some Italians, though not all the doctors, and closed two pro-Axis radio-stations which had been broadcasting propaganda.

On the whole, however, Italy has gained little from her treaties with the Yemen. Though the Italians living there have been well situated to collect information for their Government, Italy has never succeeded in seriously influencing the Imam's policy. Probably her lack of success in the Yemen, combined with firm British opposition to Italian interference in the Hadhramaut states, caused Italian visions of the Arabian half of a colonial empire to fade, thus leading the Fascist Government to throw its whole energies into the invasion of Ethiopia (1935–1936).

Some Italians had, however, hoped much from the treaties. As early as the time of Ferdinando Martini, Civil Commissioner in Eritrea from 1897 to 1900, the Eritrean authorities had realized the possible usefulness of the Yemen to Eritrea. Martini began the prac-tice of enlisting Yemenis for labour or military service in Eritrea. These Arab soldiers, in the opinion of Colonel Harold F. Jacob (p. 304), did much to spread Italian prestige in south-west Arabia. Italy was promised colonial gains as the price of her entry into the War of 1914–1918, Jibuti, Sheikh Sa'īd, Kamarān, and Socotra being

[1] Ansaldi, Il Yemen nella storia e nella leggenda, 1933.

among those suggested. At the Peace Conference Jibuti was asked for by Italy and, though this demand was firmly refused by the French, the claim was not dropped by Italian publicists. Some distrust of Great Britain was felt, as it was thought that she had supported the French attitude. When Italy adopted an anti-British foreign policy an attempt was made to stir up anti-British feeling in south Arabia; in the Anglo-Italian Agreement of April 1938 Italy secured a clause which implied a certain recognition of her interests in Arabia, both she and Great Britain undertaking not to seek special advantages for themselves in Sa'ūdi Arabia or the Yemen.

To strengthen her position in the southern Red Sea Italy gained from France, by the Agreement of 1934, a small strip of French Somaliland and the island of Dumeira, immediately off Ras Dumeira (though she did not occupy them, p. 58); and the Jezirat Sawabih, a group of small islands off the French Somaliland coast farther south, only about 11 miles from Perim. Between the two world wars Italy supervised the fisherfolk on the Hanīsh islands and Jebel Zuqar, which were among those islands the status of which was left indeterminate by the Treaty of Lausanne; the need for this supervision was recognized under the Anglo-Italian Agreement of April 1938.

The Imam also made treaties with the U.S.S.R. (1928), Holland (1933), and France (1937). The U.S.S.R. had a mission in the Yemen for a time, a medical (woman) member of which remained in San'ā till 1938, working in collaboration with the Italian and British doctors. None of these countries, however, has any diplomatic representative. The Yemen remains closed, entry being only possible to foreigners by special permission of the Imam Yahya, who has repeatedly shown that he will not purchase economic prosperity or territorial expansion at the price of his entire independence and full sovereignty.

ADEN AND THE ADEN PROTECTORATE

The twentieth century has on the whole been a period of increasing British influence and growing prosperity. In what is now called the 'Western Aden Protectorate' the system of treaties was extended to include the Sharifs of Beihān (1903), the chiefs of Upper Yāfa' (1903), the Sheikhs and Sultans of the Upper 'Aulaqi (1904), and the chiefs of the 'Audhali confederation (1914). The boundary of the Protectorate was delimited by a convention signed in London in 1914.

To the east, in what has since become the 'Eastern Aden Protectorate', the Qu'aiti chief, 'Awadh, purchased Meifa' (some 40 miles south-west of Mukalla) from the 'Abdul Wahid in 1900; incidentally, plans have recently been made to rehabilitate and develop the Meifa' district, delta of the Hajr river (p. 24), which is potentially rich agriculturally, but malarious. In 1904 'Awadh, now Sultan (p. 279), tried to purchase Bālhāf, but was restrained by the Aden Government. He was succeeded by his son Ghālib (1909–1922), who was followed by his brother 'Omar (1922–1936), succeeded in turn by the present Sultan Sālih ibn Ghālib. The sway of these rulers has been beneficial; agriculture has been one of their special interests.

In 1918 the Government imposed an agreement (p. 342) between the Qu'aiti and Kathīri Sultans by which the former were recognized as rulers of the Hadhramaut, though they undertook to respect the special rights of the Kathīris in particular localities (pp. 310, 351).

Besides treaties existing between the Aden Government and about thirty ruling chiefs, some tribal confederations have remarkable treaties, based on the 'urf or customary law, with their own rulers (p. 347); an example is that between the 'Audhali tribes and their Sultan, the substance of which is given in Appendix C.

Aden itself, the importance of which has grown with the pacification of the hinterland and the restoration of peace with the Yemen, had been administered by a succession of senior military officers, usually Generals, styled Resident (or Political Resident), under the Government of Bombay. But on 1 April 1932 it became a Chief Commissionership under the Government of India; and on 1 April 1937 the Aden Settlement was transferred to the Colonial Office as a Crown Colony. On the same date formal recognition was given by an Order in Council to the Aden Protectorate, also under the Colonial Office, which had in practice supervised Protectorate affairs for some years previously. Sir Bernard Reilly, who served in Aden from 1912 till 1940, was the last Resident, the only Chief Commissioner, and the first Governor. The centenary of Aden as British territory was celebrated locally in January 1939.

Since 1937 the Protectorate has been formally divided into a Western division, now supervised by a British Agent at Aden; and an Eastern division, the Agent for which is stationed at Mukalla, retaining the title (held by him for several years previously) of Resident Adviser to the Qu'aiti and Kathīri Sultans, with political charge of the 'Abdul Wahid Sultanates of Bir 'Ali and Bālhāf, the sheikhdoms of 'Irqa and Haura on the 'Abdul Wahid coast, and the Mahri Sultanate of Qishn and Socotra. The Qu'aiti is often spoken of as Sultan of Shihr and Mukalla, and the Kathīri as Sultan of Seiyūn.

As there is no direct British administration in the Protectorate, the work of these Agents consists largely in attempts to induce the tribes to administer themselves and to live in peace one with another. To impose peace the Aden Government has only used military force with extreme reluctance and after due warning to the recalcitrant parties; in such cases the use of force has generally been hailed with relief by the inhabitants, in some cases even by the offenders, who could not otherwise adopt a peaceful way of life without 'losing face'. In the Eastern Protectorate a notable event was the signing, early in 1937, of a truce (among themselves) for three years by nearly 1,400 signatories, from chiefs of large tribal territories down to heads of small independent villages; some notoriously lawless tribes then consented to a mass surrender of arms. Most of the signatories agreed to renew the truce for a further ten years. Though there have been breaches of the truce, conditions are much improved. Previously, though the inhabitants of the larger towns had attained a high culture and adopted many modern inventions, intertribal wars raged almost ceaselessly, villages were divided against themselves, and even single houses at war one with another, to the ruin of agriculture and prosperity.[1]

In recent years the older system of giving presents to ruling chiefs, and of granting them the right to issue recommendatory letters to tribesmen, who then received money and arms from the Government, has been discontinued. Though tribal quarrels still occupy much time, the Aden Government has been able to attend more to education, agriculture, and public health. By the opening in 1936 of the Aden Protectorate College for the sons of chiefs, a long-standing scheme was realized. The appointment of an Agricultural Officer, with assistants, has meant encouragement of better methods among the cultivators. A medical survey of the Western Protectorate was initiated in 1939–1940; unfortunately in 1943 and 1944 all efforts had to be concentrated on checking the spread of typhus fever.

The organization of the present Arab 'Government Guards' and 'Tribal Guards' is described elsewhere (p. 352). But British-trained military forces were raised during the War of 1914–1918 from among the Arabs of the Aden Protectorate and the Yemen (which had not yet taken shape as an independent state). Lieut.-Col. M. C. Lake (who served in Aden and the Protectorate in several capacities from 1913 to 1940, being latterly Political Secretary and more than once Acting Governor) raised, first a Labour Corps, which he commanded

[1] H. Ingrams, *Arabia and the Isles*, 1942.

in 1917–1918, then a regiment called 'First Yemen Infantry', which he commanded till it was disbanded in 1925. In 1928 he raised and commanded the Aden Protectorate Levies, a force which, since much expanded, remains a model for local forces in the Protectorate.

The outbreak of war in Europe in September 1939 had little immediate effect upon Aden and the Protectorates. It was not until Italy became a belligerent in June 1940 that the area came within the sphere of hostilities. Thereafter Aden was subjected to repeated attacks by Italian aircraft. It was to Aden that the civil authorities of British Somaliland withdrew in August 1940 when the Italian advance into the country could no longer be resisted. The Colony remained in the war zone until the collapse of Axis power in Africa and the Mediterranean in 1943. The damage sustained from enemy attack was not on the whole very serious, and the general attitude of the Protectorate Chiefs and of the people of the Colony remained loyal throughout. No portion of the Protectorates was occupied by the enemy, as had occurred in the war of 1914–1918.

In the provision of man-power for the armed forces of the Crown, Aden played no prominent part. Before the war the Aden Protectorate Levies were the only force raised locally. These were placed under the Local Air Command and were mostly used for guarding airfields in the Colony. Others performed garrison duties in such places as Socotra and Masīra island. Two companies saw active service in March 1945 when they assisted the Hyderabad Lancers to reduce a rebel stronghold in the Hadhramaut. The Levies in May 1945 numbered just under 1,800. An Aden Labour Corps and Hadhramaut Pioneer Corps were also raised.

CHAPTER VI

ADMINISTRATION

INTRODUCTION

THE origin of law, and hence of administration, is the *'urf* or tribal law, which has existed in Arabia from time immemorial. This law is of a pattern, in spite of local differences. It is the law of pastoral tribes living under patriarchal conditions. Its institutions include polygamy and slavery. An outstanding feature is the blood feud, by which a murder is avenged unless *diya* or blood-money has been accepted in compensation. A tribe is responsible for the act of a member and can get rid of its responsibility only by expelling him.

Muhammad, as an Arab, inherited tribal law, in which Islamic law is rooted. Islamic law is, in fact, a reformed version (modified by Jewish and Christian codes) of the tribal law of Muhammad's time; polygamy is restricted, slavery regulated, infanticide prohibited; the acceptance of blood-money in place of retaliation is encouraged. There is, besides, a mass of rules reproducing, or modifying, or adding to the customary law. This Islamic law is called the *Shar'* (or *Shari'a*), sometimes spoken of as the canonical law of Islam, by analogy with the canon law of Christendom. The Shar' is potentially, and was originally intended to be, a complete corpus of ecclesiastical, constitutional, criminal, civil, personal, and commercial law. Its fundamental structure is embodied in the Koran alone, and that alone is absolutely binding. This structure was, however, from the earliest times reinforced by a body of law based on what was believed to be the practice (*Sunna*) of the Prophet, as illustrated by a vast mass of tradition (*Hadīth*) preserved by the Prophet's Companions and contemporaries, and by no means all of equal value. Hence arose the four great schools of Sunni theology, Hanafi, Māliki, Shafe'i, and Hanbali, of which the last, founded by Ahmed ibn Hanbal, afterwards revived by Ibn Teimiya, and finally restored to vigour in the eighteenth century by Muhammad ibn 'Abd al Wahhab, is exclusively followed in Sa'ūdi Arabia. This system, like the others, is fundamentally based on the Koran, but, unlike the others, it rejects all traditions about the Sunna which are open to challenge on the score of authenticity. The Wahhabis owe their reputation for fanaticism to their insistence on their own more circumscribed interpretation of

God's will as proclaimed in the Koran and interpreted by the Prophet.

The Shar' lays down as a punishment for picking and stealing the loss of a hand, and prohibits wine-drinking, gambling, and the charging of interest. From it has developed the extensive system of *Waqf*, or entail, whereby property is settled in perpetuity for some religious purpose, or in favour of some beneficiary and his heirs as administrator of such purpose.

Of the two main bodies of Moslems, Sunnis and Shi'as, the Sunnis (the orthodox body) are found throughout western Arabia, except for the Zeidis in the Yemen and the Isma'ilis of the Yemen and of Nejrān (pp. 386–389). The Wahhabis of Sa'ūdi Arabia are a puritan Sunni sect. The Shi'as recognize, as true successors of the Prophet, only 'Ali, Muhammad's son-in-law, and 'Ali's descendants, up to the seventh or twelfth Imam (according to sect), after which they believe there has been an interregnum to be ended by the appearance of the Mahdi. The Zeidi sect, an offshoot of the Shi'a, and of all the Shi'a bodies most akin to the Sunnis, is the ruling sect in the Yemen. The religious split has also legal consequences, as the Shi'as do not recognize the Sunni schools of law, but have their own schools.

The third system of law to influence western Arabia was the *Qānūn*, or former Turkish code. Though the Turks were Moslems, the development of their civilization and their contacts with Europeans led them to supersede the Shar' by a more modern system of Moslem law which throve in the Hejaz, where pilgrims thronged and trade flourished. One of the features of this system was the introduction of courts composed of several judges. Primitive Moslem law knew only the single judge. A legal consequence of the period of Turkish rule was that, after King Ibn Sa'ūd had conquered the Hejaz, he saw fit to introduce a Commercial Code, and set up a Commercial Court, in this advanced part of his dominions.

The latest legal system to operate in western Arabia is the law of England, introduced into Aden Colony and embracing the common law, the doctrines of equity, and the statutes of general application in force in England. English criminal law has been introduced through the medium of the Indian penal code.

Besides these four systems of law the Jewish communities have their rabbinical law, which regulates matters of marriage, divorce, guardianship, and inheritance, and the British courts in Aden also apply the personal laws of Hindus and Parsis, as well as of Moslems.

These different legal systems correspond to the different forms of administration, of which western Arabia presents a variety. The tribesmen, who cling to the customary law, may be nomad or sedentary, the nomads being usually described as beduin. Each tribe has its sheikh and elders, who lead rather than govern its members. The great Islamic states—Sa'ūdi Arabia and the Yemen, and the sultanates split off from the Yemen—are absolute monarchies. Under the Turks the divisions of western Arabia were the *vilayet* or government (each under a *vali*), *liwa* or province (under a *mutasarrif*), *qadha* or district (under a *qaimmaqam*), and *nāhiya* or sub-district (under a *mudir*). There were two vilayets, the Hejaz and the Yemen. Nejd was nominally a liwa of the Basra vilayet. In some places the inhabitants enjoyed local self-government; in others, councils participated in the work of administration. This system has vanished with the expulsion of the Turks, and the part of Arabia dealt with in this volume consists of the Kingdom of Sa'ūdi Arabia, the Imamate of the Yemen, and the British Colony and Protectorate of Aden. Traces of the Turkish administration, however, survive, especially in the Hejaz, in certain local names and titles. Aden is a British Crown Colony, administered by a Governor responsible to the Secretary of State for the Colonies and to Parliament. The Aden Protectorate, for the most part, is not directly administered by Great Britain but consists of a number of native states and tribal districts in protective treaty relations with the British Government; the rulers of the two 'Hadhramaut States' and other territories in the Eastern Aden Protectorate now act on the advice of a British Resident Adviser.

Certain titles are in use throughout western Arabia. King (*malik*) is the supreme secular title, and is that assumed by the monarch of Sa'ūdi Arabia. The ruler of the Yemen also has the title of King, recognized by several Great Powers, but is generally known by his ancient title of *Imam*, or religious leader of the Zeidis. *Amir* means a commander or governor or prince (the word 'admiral' originating from *Amir al Bahr*, commander of the sea). *Sheikh* is a very general title, meaning a patriarch, and hence the patriarch of a tribe, but it is applied also to other dignitaries, civil and religious, e.g. *Sheikh-al-Islam*, or Grand Mufti (the head of the canon-lawyers), *Sheikh-al-Bilad*, the mayor of a town; and it is frequently applied so widely that it is almost equivalent to the English 'esquire'. There are also in the Yemen and in Aden Protectorate certain communities of sheikhs who claim to be the descendants of Moslem saints. The titles 'Sharif' and 'Seiyid' indicate descent from the Prophet. In the Yemen and the Protectorate, communities of Seiyids are held in great respect and act as arbitrators. The usual title of a Moslem Shar' judge is *qadhi*, except in the Yemen, where this word has a quite different sense (p. 330). *Hākim* is also a common word for a judge or magistrate (p. 334).

The main duties of government, from the Arab point of view, are to administer a country generally and to give protection and judge disputes. To enable it to do so it has a right to tax. 'He who protects the land collects the taxes.'

Throughout western Arabia, from the kingdoms down to the sub-tribes, the principle runs that the office of ruler is elective within limits. The successor is usually chosen from a certain family of a special tribe, but the choice does not necessarily fall on the eldest son. Monarchs, however, try to secure the recognition as heir of the eldest or favourite son by obtaining the consent of 'the people of the tying and the loosing', i.e. the elders, and of the general public.

SA'ŪDI ARABIA[1]

The Realm

The component parts of Sa'ūdi Arabia are many, namely: (a) Nejd, (b) its dependencies or Mulhaqat (Hasa, Qatīf, &c.), (c) 'Asīr al Sirat, (d) Jebel Shammar, (e) Juba (Jauf, &c.), (f) Wadi Sirhan, (g) Hejaz, (h) 'Asīr al Tihama, and (i) Nejrān.

The lettering gives the chronological sequence of the development of the realm of Ibn Sa'ūd who, besides being the titular Imam of his people throughout the period of his rule, as he still is, has successively borne the following secular titles, namely: (1) *Amir* or *Amir Nejd*, (2) *Hākim* or *Hākim Nejd wa Mulhaqathu* from 1916, (3) *Sultan* or *Sultan Nejd wa Mulhaqathu* from 1921, (4) King and Sultan as *Malik al Hejaz wa Sultan Nejd wa Mulhaqathu* from 1926, (5) King as *Malik al Hejaz wa Nejd wa Mulhaqathu* from 1927, and finally (6) King of Sa'ūdi Arabia or *Malik Mamlakat al 'Arabiya al Sa'ūdiya*.

By his people in general the king is referred to simply as *Al Shuyūkh* (the plural *par excellence* of sheikh in its secular sense) or, latterly, as Malik. He is commonly addressed as *Tawīl al 'Umr* ('long

---

[1] The forms *Sa'ūd*, *Sa'ūdi* are used in this book as being well established in English writings. In the country itself a literary purist would write *Su'ūd*, *Su'ūdi*, the correct classical Arabic form, and the one used in official documents. But the name is ordinarily written without indication of the vowel, while in different parts of the country it is sounded over the whole phonetic range from *Su'ūd* to *Sa'ūd*.

of life' in the sense of 'May God give you long life!'), sometimes by his beduin contemporaries simply by his name ('Abdul 'Aziz) or by his traditional cognomina of *Abu Turki* (father of Turki, his eldest son, who died in 1919) or *Akhu Nura* (brother of Nura, his eldest sister). In the more sophisticated circles of town and administrative life he is the King or His Majesty the King (*Jalalat al Malik*), while the title of Imam is generally used in ecclesiastical circles or by those concerned to stress their own religious orthodoxy.

The succession to the throne, though not regulated by any constitutional instrument or decree, is theoretically determined by the people within certain limits. This is in accordance with the practice of the Prophet and ancient Arabian custom which, between them, insist on the suitability of a candidate for the responsibilities of the throne and give a natural preference to the established dynasty, though not necessarily to the eldest son of the ruling monarch. The relevant precedent was set by Muhammad himself, who had no son of his own and who, passing over the presumptive claim of his daughter's husband, nominated his principal 'Companion' and father-in-law for the ultimate leadership of Islam, subject to the ratification of his choice by the congregation of the faithful. This was accorded after the Prophet's death, and might be claimed as a precedent justifying the election by the people of any suitable candidate for the throne regardless of dynastic claims. This precedent has in fact often been used in Islamic history to justify usurpation or to regularize revolution—the only practical methods of changing the dynasty. The essential factor is therefore popular election, which is signified first by the acclamation of the congregation and forthwith ratified by the *bai'at*, or swearing of allegiance to the accepted candidate. There is no ballot or individual voting, but it is important to realize that such elections are the acts of the congregation which theoretically comprises the whole electorate. For this reason the time of the Friday prayer is generally the occasion for such demonstrations of the popular will, as every member of the electorate is supposed to and at least may attend the congregational prayer. In practice monarchy has become the established status of Islamic communities; and the precedent set by the early Caliphs of putting forward the candidate of their choice for election as successor to the throne during their own lifetime has prevailed in the house of Sa'ūd from the eighteenth century onwards. Accordingly in 1933, the present king readily assented to the proposal of his principal advisers that his eldest surviving son, Sa'ūd, should be nominated for acceptance by the people as their king-elect. Sa'ūd was accordingly acclaimed as *Walī al 'Ahad* by the congregation after the Friday prayers in the Great Mosque of Mecca; and his brother, the Amir Feisal, received on his behalf the traditional oath of allegiance. The question of succession to the present king was thus settled and Sa'ūd will succeed his father automatically. The succession to him will presumably be decided in the same way in due course.

The frontiers of Sa'ūdi Arabia have been crystallized in part by a series of international treaties, namely: the Protocol of 'Oqeir in 1923, the Treaties of Bahra and Hadda in 1925, and the Treaty of Tāif in 1934. By these instruments the kingdom's frontiers with 'Iraq and the principality of Kuweit have been fully settled subject to the final disposal of the two neutral zones which intervene between Sa'ūdi Arabia and these two neighbours. The Transjordan frontier has been similarly disposed of except for a small section south of 'Aqaba;[1] and the Yemen frontier from the sea to the western edge of the Rub' al Khali has also been demarcated. No final settlement of the Sa'ūdi Arabian frontier with the Aden Protectorate, the Sultanate of 'Omān, the States of the Trucial Coast, and the Qatar district has yet been arrived at, though negotiation of the matter has been proceeding for several years between the British Government and Sa'ūdi Arabia before the outbreak of war in 1939. Pending a final settlement the British Government has prescribed a *de facto* line of jurisdiction, but the old Anglo-Turkish line of 1914 from the Aden–Yemen frontier to the Persian Gulf, an extension of the agreement of 1904, is now a dead letter (p. 276; figs. 10, 11).

Constitution

Within the *de jure* and *de facto* frontiers of Sa'ūdi Arabia the supreme sovereignty resides constitutionally in the Shar' or Divine Law; and the responsibility for upholding it is vested in the king as Imam or religious head of his people—not as Caliph (successor of the Prophet) or Amir al Mu'minin (Commander of the faithful), because both these titles, once held by the Caliph-Sultans of Turkey and still used by a number of local sovereigns, imply a much wider sphere of domination and responsibility than Ibn Sa'ūd has ever claimed.

The 'constitutional' law of 1926 specifically enthroned the Shar' as supreme sovereign to be obeyed by all, including the king himself. It also made a number of other constitutional provisions on a partial or tentative basis for ultimate inclusion after any necessary revision

---

[1] For the status of the district of Ma'an see p. 300.

in a comprehensive constitutional law, which has in fact never materialized. The constitutional status of Sa'ūdi Arabia has thus to a large extent not yet received statutory form and is perhaps not likely to do so during the present reign, when so much depends on the king's own personality. It has, however, developed during the past twenty years as decree followed decree under the royal sign manual. Apart therefore from the fundamental position of the Shar' and the king recognized by the original statute, Sa'ūdi Arabia may best be regarded as an absolute monarchy limited only by the Law of God but without any written constitution in so far as the rights of the subject and the form of the administration are concerned. In other words, the constitutional position is fluid and continuously developing by a process of trial and error. There is no law or institution except the Shar' and the monarchy, which is not subject to modification.

The Shar' itself is, of course, the constitutional law of the land, fixed and immutable. It does not, however, cover the whole range of human activities even in Arabia, though, like constitutional laws elsewhere, it has an important negative effect in that no act of contumacy against it by an individual or a community can be legally condoned, and no special, commercial, tribal, or other *ad hoc* law or regulation inconsistent with its provisions can have any legal validity. It is important to realize this point and equally important to bear in mind that the interpretation of the Shar' does not rest with the executive but with the supreme ecclesiastical court or authority. No question involving interpretation of the Shar' can be disposed of without reference to such authority, whether it be the single *Qadhi* of a province or district (who in Sa'ūdi Arabia also *de facto* exercises the functions of *Mufti*), or the full bench of *'Ulema* or *Masheikh* (plural of Sheikh in the religious sense) at Mecca or Riyādh. The king, as Imam, is theoretically *ex officio* head of that bench, but he never presides at its meetings and has been known on occasion to exercise considerable diplomatic tact to get from the court of the 'Ulema a pronouncement in favour of this or that relaxation of prohibitions believed (however wrongly) to be inherent in the Shar'. The classic case of this kind is provided by a Fatwa of the 'Ulema in 1927 in favour of the use of the then new-fangled telephone, which was popularly believed to be the work of the devil but was thus authoritatively cleared of this imputation. Tobacco, motor-cars, and the wireless have all provided opportunities of examining the basic sense of the Shar', while on a recent occasion (1940) the king, at the instance of the 'Ulema of Riyādh, cancelled a projected visit of the

Amir Feisal to the capital of Nejd by aeroplane—a project which was regarded as being too literal an attempt to fly in the face of Providence.

Central Government

Under the Shar' the executive administration of the country is the sole responsibility of the king. His decision is final in all matters, great and small; and it is astonishing how wide is the range of his administrative activity—from quite petty concerns, such as the allocation of a camel or a motor-car to a pilgrim, to the highest affairs of state such as the signing of a treaty with a foreign Power. Nevertheless, even before the administration of his growing realm became as complex as it now is, the king always respected and acted on the Koranic precept: 'Take counsel among yourselves'. That precept has from immemorial antiquity been a characteristic of the beduin society of Arabia, and still operates powerfully among the great nomad tribes, whose leaders are always in council with their fellow-tribesmen to select a new grazing-ground or (as in the old days, and indeed still in some territories outside Sa'ūdi limits) to arrange the details of a raid on a neighbouring tribe. Throughout his career Ibn Sa'ūd has been faithful to this ingrained habit, which forms the fundamental basis of Arabian democracy. In the early days he seldom acted without consulting his father (who died in 1928), and the principal 'Ulema and leading tribal sheikhs such as Feisal ad Duwish, Feisal ibn Hashr, Sultān ibn Bijad, and many others. He was of course free to choose his advisers; but under the prevailing conditions of public audience it was equally open to anyone and everyone to tender advice unasked; and these audiences provided an open forum for the discussion of all matters of moment—not always on lines pleasing to the king but calculated to keep him informed of the tendencies of public opinion in his realm.

When that realm developed to the proportions of a kingdom recognized by the Great Powers it began to be felt in the king's entourage that some concession to world opinion was called for in the shape of democratic institutions of an elective or parliamentary type. The king, acutely aware of the impracticability of such a tendency, nevertheless allowed himself to be persuaded by progressive opinion; and the early attempts at constitution-making envisaged the creation of partially elective consultative bodies in order to associate the people more directly in the task of government. Such bodies were in fact created; but, apart from the municipal committees with limited local functions, it was soon found that the projected central administrative committee could not function as a democratic adjunct to the Government without seriously impeding the work of administration, which in the last resort always depended on the king's fiat. Such a committee in such circumstances could have no real responsibility or authority, and its function and shape were soon modified to suit the facts of the situation, while another committee of the same kind took shape at Riyādh. The experiment had not been a complete failure, for these committees, surviving to the present day in their more practical form, constitute an important part of the machinery of government. Their membership is determined by the king and their functions are purely advisory; but they have in fact proved so useful to the king and his Government that they have developed into extremely important branches of the civil service, responsible for much of the spade-work of the administration. In the absence of a titular Minister of the Interior—the Amir Feisal held that post for the Hejaz for a short period until it was suppressed as unnecessary—the Mecca and Riyādh committees constitute in effect the twin Home Offices for the Hejaz and Nejd respectively. Technically they only advise the king (or his deputies in his absence), but in fact they dispose of a great deal of business without reference to higher authority.

Local Government

There is no parliamentary supervision of the general administration, but municipal committees are responsible for the administration of local affairs in the principal towns and for the collection of all local taxes. In the general administration, in all its branches, the king is the supreme executive. Under him the whole country is divided into two administrative viceroyalties, Nejd and the Hejaz, which are administered respectively by the Crown Prince as *Amir Nejd* and the Viceroy-General of the Hejaz as *Naib al Malik* or *Naib al 'Amm*. Both refer important matters arising in their spheres of responsibility to the king at all times, but they retain their specific administrative functions even when the king is present in their area of jurisdiction, though it is only natural that in the presence of the king the viceroy concerned tends to refer more matters to him than when he is absent.

These two viceregal spheres are divided into provinces, each under an Amir or governor and subdivided into districts or subdistricts. The governors are directly subordinate to the viceroys, but have direct access to the king, to whom they report all important develop-

149. *Royal Palace at Mecca*

150. *Royal Palace at Riyādh*

ments in their provinces. It may here be mentioned that the great extension of wireless facilities throughout the country during the past decade has contributed much to the centralization of the administration; and practically all correspondence with headquarters is conducted over the wireless. At headquarters (Riyādh and Mecca) the Crown Prince and the Viceroy-General respectively have their own secretarial staffs, in addition to which the advisory committees already referred to are at their disposal for any work delegated to them. In practice they study and sift all reports from the provinces and make recommendations for the orders of the Crown Prince or Viceroy-General, who may in turn refer such recommendations to the king. A list of the administrative divisions of Sa'ūdi Arabia is given on pp. 355–356.

Government Departments

Parallel with this double system of internal administration under the two senior sons of the king, there are other important departments of state administered by officers of ministerial rank under the direct control of the king. The most important of these are the Foreign Office and the Ministry of Finance. The former is under the charge of the Amir Feisal who, in addition to being Viceroy-General of the Hejaz, is also the Foreign Minister and directly represents the king in all diplomatic contacts with the representatives of foreign Powers at Jidda, though he does not shape or control the foreign policy of the State. The king deals with all problems of this kind himself with the help of the Chief Secretary of the Royal Diwan, while the Foreign Office at Mecca, in which the titular Foreign Minister has the services of a competent staff (including formerly a Deputy Foreign Minister who was in practice responsible for the greater part of the work), carries on the day-to-day administration of external affairs in contact with the diplomatic corps.

The other department, the Ministry of Finance, has for more than fifteen years been under the virtually independent control of Sheikh 'Abdullah Suleiman, a Nejdi of outstanding ability, who is also Minister of Defence and who in respect of both departments is directly responsible to the king alone. He also exercises a wide measure of control over such other departments of state—e.g. Medical, Education, Public Works, Posts, Telegraphs and Wireless, Mines, &c.—as are administered not by Ministers but by Directors-General. The Minister of Finance, by reason of these multifarious activities, is by far the most important officer of state and maintains at all provincial and district centres a staff of officials responsible to himself and independent of the local governors. He alone enjoys the privilege of a bodyguard and maintains a semi-regal state comparable with that of the king and the royal princes. And he alone, by reason of his close understanding with the king, enjoys a measure of administrative independence to which even the viceroys do not aspire. His regime is in every way comparable with that of the Barmacid Ministers of the time of Harun ar Rashid; and the explanation of his power and independence is probably to be sought in the fact that he is entrusted with the administration of a department with whose intricacies and ramifications the king is not familiar.

Yet a third department, that of Justice, has already been disposed of by implication in discussing the status of the Shar'. There is no Minister of Justice as such, but the functions normally performed by such an officer in connexion with the administration of the courts fall to the ecclesiastical hierarchy already referred to. In Mecca the head of this body is Sheikh 'Abdullah al Hasan, while at Riyādh the equivalent post was, at least until recently, occupied by a member of the family of the founder of Wahhabism. The 'Ulema, as the active repositories and interpreters of the Shar', are themselves completely independent; but in practice the king exercises such control of their activities as may be needed, and of course all ecclesiastical appointments are either made or ratified by him. As Imam he has the right and duty of supervising this august body.

Finally two other administrative departments of a minor character call for mention, both being what might be classed as Civil List or Privy Purse departments under the respective control of the third and fourth sons of the king. The former is in charge of all the transport arrangements connected with the palace—no sinecure under existing conditions—while the latter is responsible for the administration of the royal household, involving a population of about 1,000 persons, including the royal ladies and children with all their servants and attendants.

'Privy Council'

One element connected with the governance of Sa'ūdi Arabia remains to be mentioned. It is a somewhat indeterminate body corresponding roughly to a Privy Council, which actually meets every evening under the informal presidency of the king to discuss affairs in general or to deal with any specific business introduced by the king.

For instance, this body finally recommended the grant to an American company of the concession for the exploitation of oil in eastern Arabia in 1933, after a full discussion of the terms proposed by the Finance Minister (p. 515). Membership of this council is not fixed, though it automatically includes the Crown Prince, the Viceroy-General, and other princes of the royal blood in residence at the place of meeting. It also includes the principal officers of state when in attendance on the king, and the king's personal staff, as well as a number of private individuals enjoying a privilege corresponding to private entrée and the members of the two advisory councils when present at the place of meeting. Nobody sits on this council as of right, but in practice individuals belonging to the categories mentioned above are honoured with a general invitation to attend, and do so when they can, unless they are notified that a meeting will not take place owing to the king's preoccupation with other work. Such meetings perhaps provide the nearest approach the country knows to absolutely free discussion of important topics. The king indeed often goes out of his way on such occasions to broach controversial topics in order to start an argument.

To sum up, the work of the realm at the highest level is conducted as follows:

(a) by the king alone, for he keeps some matters entirely to himself for discussion with perhaps a single individual concerned, e.g. the Crown Prince, or the Viceroy-General, or the Minister of Finance, or the Chief Justice, or even a private individual;

(b) by the king in council with his principal ministers and officers of state only, e.g. to discuss matters of the highest importance such as negotiations with a foreign Power or a declaration of war, &c.;

(c) by the king in council with his ministers and the members of the advisory council, e.g. important matters connected with the ordinary administration;

(d) by the king in 'Privy Council' as above described.

Subject to these various stages of control or intervention by the supreme executive the departmental administration of Sa'ūdi Arabia is conducted very much on the same lines as in other countries.

Judicature

In the chief towns of Nejd and at the seat of every amir, whether of a locality or of a tribe, there is stationed a *qadhi* or judge who, at the important places at least, is appointed or dismissed by the king himself, without any fixed rules. The qadhi judges the cases, civil or criminal, which are transferred to him by the king or by the amir. When the amir transfers a case he sends an officer with the parties to the qadhi who hears the case and communicates his decision orally to the amir's representative, who in his turn reports orally to the amir. The amir enforces the judgement. In the mornings the qadhi gives instruction on dogma and religious law, either in his house or in the mosque, and at the afternoon prayer he preaches a short sermon.

Hejazi institutions are in advance of those of Nejd, and include courts presided over by several judges, sitting together. There are three grades of courts: (a) summary courts; (b) higher courts; and (c) 'The Commission of Judicial Vigilance'. A summary court is presided over by a qadhi who has jurisdiction in petty civil cases and offences not punishable with death or loss of limb. Higher courts at Mecca, Al Madina, and Jidda have jurisdiction in civil and criminal cases which are beyond the competence of the qadhi; they are each composed of a qadhi, as president, and two of his substitutes, and beyond certain limits, e.g. in cases involving capital punishment or loss of limb, the decision is pronounced by the full court. The third court, whose name literally translated is 'the Commission of Judicial Vigilance', has a president and four 'ulema, and sits only at Mecca. It acts as a Court of Criminal Appeal or Court of Cassation. An appeal lies to this court within 20 days of notification of sentence. If the appeal is dismissed, the judgement becomes final; if it is allowed, the case is remitted to the court below for further consideration. The president of the commission is the head of the Hejazi judiciary. He has the supervision of all the courts and qadhis in the Hejaz and serves as an intermediary between the executive and the judiciary. He is assisted by an Inspector of Courts, first appointed in 1932.

As to judicial procedure, the plaintiff or complainant files two written copies of his claim, a hearing date is fixed, and the defendant is notified. A judicial confession is conclusive. Failing this, the judge, after passing sentence interrogates the defendant, inquiring whether he accepts the findings of the court. An admission by the defendant makes the sentence final. If he disputes the justice of the conviction he is entitled to a copy of the conviction and sentence and of the record of proceedings, to enable him to appeal. Notice of his appeal is transmitted to the Court of Appeal. A contumacious person can be sentenced in his absence, but the sentence is revised by the Court of Appeal. The plaintiff or complainant must appear personally, except in the case of a woman or a sick man, who can be represented. There are no barristers, in the ordinary sense, in Moslem courts, but the Hejazi Government admits certain men learned in the law to appear in courts. A class of Moslem notaries is also recognized, whose business it is to register donations, testaments, and contracts of every sort except those which relate to *waqf* land. Notaries are confined to Mecca, Jidda, and Al Madina: elsewhere, the qadhi or his officer acts as notary.

The defects of the Shar' in its relation to modern developments have to be made good by special legislation, generally in the form of decrees signed by the king but sometimes little more than departmental regulations issued by the responsible ministers. As in India, for instance, where Hindu and Moslem personal law, tribal and customary law, and so forth, continue to be recognized as necessary complements of the general (British) law of the land, so in Sa'ūdi Arabia tribal law continues to operate within the limits of its compatibility with the Shar'—and only so far—while special laws have been devised to regulate the relations of the State and its subjects with the non-Moslem outside world, particularly in commercial matters. Such laws often take the form of agreements binding on both parties and theoretically enforcible by the courts, though in practice a special commercial court, outside the orbit of the Shar', has been set up to deal with such cases which, for instance, must often involve questions relating to interest and insurance, which the Shar' condemns. A Shar' court could on no account award interest on a due debt, but the special court interprets agreements on their merits and surmounts the awkward hurdle of interest by a legal fiction. The matter is quite complicated and highly controversial, but for all practical purposes what we call interest is regarded as commission on the use of goods not fully paid for at the time of delivery, while insurance charges are treated as part of the freight charges on goods from abroad. On the whole the legal system provides a very satisfactory practical combination of the Shar' and common sense, and friction with the foreign commercial community, concentrated like the diplomatic corps at Jidda, is very rare. European criticism is perhaps more often directed, or misdirected, against what are regarded as defects or asperities of the Shar' itself in its impact on the nationals of the country and on pilgrims from abroad.

Finance

The administrative expenses of Sa'ūdi Arabia normally outrun its income, and the unfavourable balance is carried forward as a deficit from one year's budget to the next in the hope that it will be liquidated in due course. There is, strictly speaking, no national debt, but the great economic slump of 1931 and its consequences to the exchequer compelled the Government in that year to declare a moratorium on its current debts. The amount outstanding at that time was about £300,000, which was funded for repayment in annual instalments together with an extra percentage as commission or compensation (not interest). In effect this sum constituted a sort of national debt, secured only on the Government's undertaking to pay in the manner above indicated. The total debt now outstanding is not more than about half the original sum. Meanwhile the un-willingness of the Government to pledge its various sources of revenue as security against advances by banks, &c., has automatically limited the Government's credit and compelled it to live roughly within its income. Great economies have accordingly been effected in the field of expenditure, while strenuous efforts have been made to increase the revenue.

Armed Forces and Police

The army has been mentioned above as an item of expenditure on personnel and equipment. At the time of the Disarmament Conference of 1932 the Government officially returned an army strength of 734 officers and 43,437 men; and five years later it was estimated that these numbers had been doubled. This would give a standing army about 100,000 strong, but it is hard to believe that there are as many as 50,000, let alone 100,000, uniformed, paid, *Nidham* (regular) troops in the whole country to-day. The discrepancy is explained by the general impression among foreigners that there is no conscription for military service in Sa'ūdi Arabia, which is an entire misconception. *Jihad* is a universal obligation imposed by the Shar' and accepted as a matter of course. It involves the rendering of military service to the community in time of need, while in Arabia, outside the towns, every able-bodied man is a soldier by upbringing. The obligation of Jihad is discharged in two ways: (*a*) by actual service at the call of the State; and (*b*) by the purchase of exemption through payment of tax called Jihad. The latter method applies in practice only to town-dwellers, while the former applies to the bulk of the population—villagers, tribesmen,

&c. There is a further distinction between nomad and sedentary folk: all the able-bodied men of a tribe are at the disposal of the tribal sheikh, who receives a subsidy from the king on the basis of the number of men he can put into the field at need. In the towns and villages of Nejd a Jihad register is kept, showing the extent of the community's obligation (generally stated in terms of camels rather than men, who are taken for granted) in the event of a *Jihad ʿAmm* (general muster) or of a *Jihad Khas* (special muster). Thus, apart from the exempted class of taxpayers, all able-bodied males are liable to military service in the event of a general muster, which, however, is only proclaimed in the event of grave national peril. The special muster may draw on a percentage of this total strength throughout the country, or on the whole or part of the available strength in a given area, where or near which operations are in progress or contemplated. The Yemen war of 1934 provides a suitable illustration of the actual operation of this method. The regular Nidham army having proceeded to the front with its guns, motor-transport, and other impedimenta, a general muster of all the tribes and villages in the frontier districts was proclaimed. Meanwhile, in order to provide reinforcements in case of need, a special muster of certain areas farther from the scene, but not of the whole country, was instituted, and the king's third son was placed in charge of the organization of the resulting recruits for dispatch to the front as needed. The actual force mobilized for this war was reckoned at 100,000 including the Nidham nucleus, but nothing like that number crossed the frontier or saw any fighting.

The present strength of the Nidham army is not known, nor its financial allotment in the budget. This force is under the direct control and administration of the Minister of Finance in his capacity as Minister of Defence, while the Jihad forces (or militia, as they might be called) are separately administered by the Crown Prince and the Viceroy-General in their respective spheres and do not come within the purview of the Ministry of Defence, though the latter provides ammunition and rations for them when on service. Incidentally the Jihad forces provide their own rifles and camel-transport. While the king exercises an overall control over the whole military administration, the Crown Prince was formally appointed some years ago to the titular post of Commander-in-Chief of all the armed forces and would assume supreme command in the field in the event of any big military venture.

The *Shurta* or police force, in addition to its normal functions in the towns, acts as a gendarmerie in the districts. It is administered by a Director-General with his headquarters at Mecca, under the supervision of the Minister of Finance for organizational purposes and under the direction of the Crown Prince or Viceroy-General, as the case may be, for operational purposes. Like the Nidham army, the police wear uniforms of European pattern with Arab head-dresses, and are armed with rifles. They are recruited from all parts of Sa'ūdi Arabia; and the policy is to spread them all over the country in small bodies for all the work that falls to their lot, including the prevention of smuggling and the patrolling of frontier areas, the escorting of tax-collectors on their rounds, and of course the prevention and detection of crime. There is also a well-equipped Criminal Investigation Department at headquarters, and the Director-General can point with pride to the excellent record of his force both in bringing criminals to justice and in the discouragement of crime. He would, however, be the first to admit that the moral influence of the king has always been the principal factor in the success achieved. It is not so much the severity of the Shar' towards crime but its proper application in practice that accounts for the exceptional standard of law and order in Sa'ūdi Arabia. After all, other Moslem States have or have had the benefits of the Shar' without achieving comparable results.

Finally, the Marine or Coast-guard service is a small semi-military organization. This body, organized like the police, is also under the supreme control of the Minister of Finance and is administered by officials bearing the title of *Amir al Bahr* (admiral) stationed at Jidda and other important coastal towns. The prevention of smuggling, which is encouraged by the very high scale of customs duties on all imported goods, and the regulation of shipping and coastal fisheries constitute their principal functions. The checking of passports and the granting of nationalization certificates are duties of the police, but the checking of unauthorized entry into the country falls largely on the Coast-guard service, particularly in connexion with the pilgrimage.

THE YEMEN

Area and Frontiers

The modern state of the Yemen has a coastline extending roughly 250 miles from a point north of Meidi, on the Red Sea coast, to Ras Turba, on the south coast of the Sheikh Sa'īd peninsula. Inland, its frontiers adjoin Sa'ūdi Arabia and the Aden Protectorate, as shown on fig. 11. Its area has been estimated at roughly 74,000 square miles and its heterogeneous population at figures ranging from less than 2 to over 4 millions.

Central Government

The Government is centred in the Imam of San'ā, head of the Zeidi sect of Islam (p. 386), who is at once the theocratic and temporal head of the State, claiming descent from 'Ali, son-in-law of Muhammad.

In the Yemen the descendants of the Prophet are called Seiyids, and they hold a position of very special honour, respect, and reverence. From among them the Imam is chosen. He is at once the king of the country and spiritual head of the Zeidis; he is Khalifa (successor to the Prophet) and Amir al Mu'minin (Commander of the Faithful).

The Imamate follows no rule of primogeniture and any Seiyid who is otherwise suitable may in theory be a candidate for the post. In fact he may be selected from any one of half a dozen families whose ancestors at one time or another were Imams. The choice from among several eligible Seiyids is supposed to be in the hands of the 'Ulema, the men of learning. There is no reason to doubt the general opinion in San'ā that the 'Ulema will elect either him of whom they are most afraid or him who will pay them most.

There are thousands of Seiyids in the Yemen and the State is administered in their interests and especially in the interests of the reigning family. Some of the Seiyids are employed in administrative posts, but many have no regular occupation, living luxuriously on their privileges.

When the country was not under Turkish rule (i.e., excluding the periods c. 1538–1630 and 1872–1918), the Imam has wielded temporal power in varying degree, especially over the Zeidi districts, but only since 1918 has the Yemen been consolidated into a centrally controlled state. The present Imam, having made himself an absolute ruler, normally attends personally to even the smallest matters. No minister or provincial governor, not even if he be the Imam's son, dares to take any decision of importance without reference to the Imam. As, however, the latter is old and sometimes out of health, one of his sons, especially Prince 'Abdullah, may at times perform most executive functions, while the eldest son, Prince Ahmed, has been given the principality of Ta'izz, where he is allowed a high degree of independence, probably in order to train him for his future responsibilities. Though the eldest son is designated *Wali al 'Ahad* (heir to the throne, sometimes referred to by Europeans as 'Crown Prince'), all the sons of the Imam (of whom thirteen are said to be living) have the title *Seif al Islam* ('sword of Islam'). Some of the *Suyūf* or 'Seifs' have been appointed either ministers or amirs, that is, provincial governors, as explained below.

The Imam's several ministers of state are for the most part chosen from the Seiyids, and several of them are his own sons. When a 'commoner' is deemed worthy of such a dignity he is not only called *wazir* ('minister') but is given a special title, almost as if he were being raised to the peerage. The title is *Qadhi*, but it must not be confused with the ordinary Moslem usage of the word to denote a judge of Koranic law.

Of the two principal ministers, one for internal and one for external affairs, the former takes precedence and is called *al Wazir al Awwal*, literally, 'prime minister'; the present holder of the office, Qadhi 'Abdullah al 'Amri, is an example of a commoner who has been given the special title of Qadhi. Other departments are the ministries of war, justice, education, public health, and public works. In recent years ministries of commerce, agriculture, communications, posts and telegraph, irrigation and animal-care have been created by the Imamic decrees. Some of these are held by sons of the Imam.

The Imam has a council, akin to a Privy Council, called *al Majlis*; it is an innovation dating from the Turkish departure from the country, and is composed of the Imam's ministers, with some additional members who are mostly Seiyids; but, again, in cases where a 'commoner' becomes a regular member of council, he receives the title of Qadhi. The members of council have no powers but act merely in an advisory capacity.

Some Turks from the old regime—notably the second minister of state, the Minister for External Affairs, Qadhi Muhammad Raghib— stayed in the Yemen in the Imam's service, but these have necessarily tended, with the lapse of time, to be replaced by persons of other nationalities. In the employ of various ministries (health, agriculture, industry, education, and war) there are usually a number of foreign technical advisers. Of recent years these have been Egyptian, Syrian, 'Iraqi, Italian, British, and German. The Imam, when he so desires, consults any of these experts directly, but more usually through the relevant minister.

Local Government

When the Yemen emerged as an independent state after the with-drawal of the Turks in 1918, much of the Turkish system of adminis-tration was kept. The country was still divided into *liwas*; each liwa into *qadhas*; the qadhas into *nāhiyas* or groups of about twenty to forty villages; while the unit of Yemeni organization in the settled areas, and for the most part in the semi-nomad areas, remained the *qarya*, or village.

The title *amir*, substituted for the Turkish *mutasarrif*, had (like *qadhi*) a special significance in the Yemen, being used, not as in other Moslem countries to denote a prince of the royal blood, but as the designation of a provincial governor. Each governor of a liwa held the title 'amir' by virtue of being *amir al jeish* or commander-in-chief of the troops in his province; he was, however, ordinarily called simply 'the amir'. The full title *Amir al Jeish* is used for the Minister of State for War, for the commander-in-chief of the whole army, and for the officer actually commanding the troops in a province. The much more humble post of harbour-master at Hodeida carries the title *Amir al Bahr* ('ruler of the sea', cf. p. 314).

Much of the above administrative system still remains, as shown by the list of divisions at the end of this chapter (p. 357). But since 1939 the tendency of the Imam has been to abolish the historic amirates and to substitute principalities, governed by his own sons, thereby concentrating ever more power into the hands of the reigning family. Thus, he removed Seiyid 'Ali al Wazir, formerly Amir of Ta'izz, and Seiyid 'Abdullah al Wazir, formerly Amir of Hodeida, members of the princely Al Wazir family, replacing them by members of his own family. When Seiyid Abdulqadūs al Wazir, Amir of Dhamār, died of typhus in 1944, his amirate was abolished, and the main divisions of the whole country were recast and changed to principalities.

Before the abolition of the amirates the Yemen was divided into the following five liwas: (i) San'ā; (ii) North (capital, Sa'da); (iii) Tihama (capital, Hodeida); (iv) Central (capital, Dhamār); (v) South (capital, Ta'izz).

The principalities which have been substituted for the old amirates have no geographical homogeneity or continuity. San'ā takes under its wing any district appearing to need special supervision. More-over, political conditions in the Yemen are so fluid that what is written may very soon be out of date. But at the end of 1944 the arrangement was as follows:

(*a*) The principality ruled by Seif al Islam Ahmed, the Wali al 'Ahad ('Crown Prince') comprises half of the old 'North' Amirate, and the old 'South' Amirate. Prince Ahmed lives in Ta'izz and rules the southern area directly and with little reference to San'ā. His brother, Seif al Islam Motahir, deputizes for him in the north, usually residing at Qafla, which has thus become the capital of his half of the old northern amirate.

(*b*) The principality ruled by Seif al Islam 'Abdullah, comprises the other half of the old 'North' Amirate, together with the old San'ā and Tihama Amirates. This amounts in practice to two principalities, for Prince 'Abdullah lives in San'ā with his father, the Imam, over whom he is thought to be steadily gaining ascendancy, while Sa'da, and the other parts of the old northern amirate which are not in Prince Ahmed's principality, are now directly under San'ā. In the Tihama, on the other hand, Qadhi 'Ali al 'Amri (brother of the Prime Minister) acts for Prince 'Abdullah, but is in almost continuous communication with San'ā by telegraph.

(*c*) The principality ruled by Seif al Islam Hasan, whose capital is Ibb, consists of the remnants of the old 'Central' Amirate of Dhamār, many parts of which have been transferred to the San'ā Principality.

Principalities (*liwa*) are each divided into a number of districts, called *qadha* (plur. *qadhat*) and administered by '*amils*, who are usually Seiyids, but—as in the higher ranks—if a commoner is appointed he receives the title *qadhi*; originally the *qadha* meant simply the area of the qadhi's influence. Thus, persons with the title qadhi, but acting as 'amils, are met with (for instance, Qadhi Husein al Halali, 'Amil of Hujarīya, and Qadhi Muhammad ash Shami, 'Amil of Rida', were recently appointed jointly to make contact with the Government of Aden). Many of the 'amils are Zeidis, particularly in the Zeidi districts of the north and north-east. In the Shafe'i districts of the south many 'amils are Shafe'is, but there is no rigid demarcation in this respect.

Qadhas are divided into smaller districts (*nāhiya*, plur. *nawāhi*) each administered by an '*amil* (plur. '*ummal*), who is either a Seiyid or a commoner entitled qadhi. These lesser amilates, the nahiyas, are subdivided into groups of villages, each called an *azal*, under a head man generally entitled *sheikh*. Each separate village or qarya has its head man ('*aqil*).

Under the old Turkish regime the people elected their own sheikhs and 'aqils, but after the formation of the independent state these officials were nominated by the amirs of liwas; and, now that the amirates have disappeared, they are nominated by the Prince, or even directly by the central government at San'ā. This change has arisen from the Imam's policy of weakening the cohesion of the tribes so that they cannot unite against the central government.

Taxation and Finance

The various forms of almsgiving prescribed by the Koran have been organized by the Imam into taxes, paid into the *Beit al Māl* ('treasure house'), a fund which is theoretically 'common wealth'. These taxes are nominally three: (i) the *'ashur* or tithe on crops; (ii) the *zakat*, 1/40th of any capital which has been in hand for a year or more; and (iii) the *fitra* ('breaking of the fast'), a head-tax amounting to 6*d.* per head collected at the end of Ramadhan. In addition the tax money must cover the cost of collection, which has many regular and irregular ramifications. There is the 'rake off' for the soldier who collects it, then something for the 'aqil, the sheikh, the 'amil, the grand 'amil, and, of course, the Prince, so that one frequently hears that the taxes in individual cases exceed 50 per cent. The affairs of the Beit al Māl are administered in each area by the *Mamūr al Māl* (superintendent of the Beit al Māl) and his two underlings, the *Mamūr al Ambar* (superintendent of the grain store) and the *Amin as Sanduq* (treasurer or cashier).

The princes under the new regime have shown great anxiety to get more and more direct control over the Beit al Māl, therefore this system may at any time be altered in some details.

Similarly each 'amil is assisted in his district by a paymaster-general, a treasurer, and a grain-controller. The 'amil transmits the accounts for his district to the Prince, who pays to the Imam the quota for which the liwa is liable, and distributes to the people according to their need.

Forced Labour. Besides paying taxes directly in money the peasant is required either to give his own services to repair the roads, or to commute the obligation for a money payment. His beasts are also pressed into service, and he has to follow them (even when he is not required) to see that they are returned. The animals are used to convey government ammunition, corn, taxes, and soldiers sent out on missions. This practice, probably very ancient, is sometimes also exacted even by certain native rulers in the Aden Protectorate (though naturally not encouraged by the Aden Government), and it was a feature of administration in Egypt in former days.

Recruitment for Government Service. For the executive branches
the ruler of the liwa recruits clerks or secretaries (*katib*, plural *kuttab*),
many of whom have passed through the universities and are therefore
of the *'ulema* (wise men, educated class). They may rise on the executive side to the rank of 'amil, or on the judicial side to the rank of
hākim (see below), either of which posts may carry with it the title
'qadhi'. If a katib rises to one or other of these posts, he is paid
50–60 riyals a month, a salary the inadequacy of which may be a
cause of corruption.

The Judicial Systems

There are two main legal systems: the civil law as administered
by the 'amil, from whom appeal can be made to the Prince as ruler
of the liwa, and if need be to the Imam himself; and the canonical or
Koranic law (the *shari'a*) administered by the *hākim*, from whom
there is right of appeal, with permission of the local 'amil, to another
hākim. Any further appeal must go to the *Ra'is al Istinaf* (judge of
the court of appeal, in San'ā, at present Seiyid Zeid ad Dailami),
and from him, though rarely, to the Imam.

It should be noted that, in the Yemen, *shari'a* is a commoner form
of the name for the Koranic law than *shar'*. Further, the title 'qadhi'
does not denote a judge, as in other Moslem lands, but is used in
the manner already explained; and the office of *mufti*, who in other
Moslem lands aids the qadhi by interpreting the law, does not exist.
Lastly, *hākim*, a common word for a judge in Arab countries, is
distinct from *hakīm*, a physician, though both are from the same
root, the general sense comprising *hukm*, 'command', and *hikma*,
'wisdom'.

In practice there is probably not much difference between the
law as administered by Zeidis and by Shafe'is. The application of
the Koranic law may be somewhat coloured by Zeidi interpretation,
yet it must be remembered that the Zeidis of the Yemen, though
an offshoot of the Shi'a body, claim to be *al Midhab al Khamis*, the
fifth orthodox rite in Islam (p. 388). The presence of Jewish
communities is covered by the provision which has always been
made in the shari'a for administration of the law to 'protected'
minorities.

When the hākim tries the case, as in probably the majority of
instances, the complainant obtains a summons from the 'amil.
Should the defendant fail to appear, he is arrested. Witnesses are
sworn either before the hākim or in a mosque; if the complainant has

no witnesses, he takes the hand of the hākim and is sworn. The parties share the payment of fees for the hearing, which depend on the length of the case. Hākims, however, are often venal.

Besides the shari‘a and the civil law, a third system, though discouraged by the central government, is administered in many country districts. This is the ancient, pre-Islamic tribal law or ‘urf (sometimes also called hukm al qabyala or hukm bedu, 'tribesman's law' or 'beduin law'). Thus an ‘aqil may, within a tribe, settle cases of debt, personal quarrels, and disputes about land and water rights, and he may be paid for so doing. Tribal law was intended to keep the balance by application of sanctions to those who have, either intentionally or accidentally, caused damage to others; whereas Islamic law, being later and more advanced, attempts to deal also with morals, which are outside the sphere of tribal law.

In theory the Imam himself in San‘ā, and the Prince in the capital of each liwa, is accessible to anyone without intermediary, and can dispense patriarchal justice. But in practice door-keepers and other subordinates make this method of approach both expensive and precarious. The Imam has, however, exclusive jurisdiction in murder cases. If he finds the accused guilty, the family of the victim may accept blood-money (diya). Failing this, the Imam passes sentence of death by decapitation, appointing someone, often one of his own slaves, to act as executioner. Since a slave is not regarded as menial and his rank depends on that of his master, he performs this act as his master's 'hand'. This is one of the ways in which the central government has cut across tribal custom. On the principle of 'a life for a life', the death penalty may be exacted for the murder of a Jew or of other persons lacking in sharaf (nobility), such as barbers, shoemakers, blacksmiths, and bath-attendants, to whom a tribesman would not marry his daughter; but in practice a life-sentence would probably be more usual in such cases.

While for wilful murder, uncompounded, the penalty is death, the Imam tries to settle cases of manslaughter (whether accidental or due to neglect) by enforcing payment to the relatives of blood-money, assessed according to the defendant's wealth; but even he finds it difficult to refuse, if the victim's relatives, backed by their tribe, demand 'a life for a life'. Contrary to practice in the Aden Protectorate, the full diya is exacted for manslaughter of a Jew, or a non-tribesman, or any of the classes termed in the Yemen nāqas, 'imperfect'. For homicide of a woman or a slave only half the compensation is paid.

In the Zeidi legal code very severe punishments are laid down for a number of offences, but in practice are rarely—in some cases never—carried out. Such, briefly, are:

Perjury: punishable by flogging and imprisonment; in practice no punishment is inflicted, though numerous obvious cases come before the judges.

Adultery is punishable by stoning, and immorality between young unmarried people by forty stripes. But, since conviction depends on the precisely unanimous testimony of four eyewitnesses of the very act, and since the witnesses themselves are liable to be flogged as mischief-makers if their testimony disagrees, no cases of these punishments being inflicted within living memory appear to be on record.

Theft: the hand of a burglar who commits robbery with violence may still be cut off, the execution being a public ceremony. The ordinances of Islamic law are thereby fulfilled. But most Zeidis maintain that theft of Beit al Māl property cannot thus be punished, as it is 'common wealth'—a theory which can work out conveniently for government officials.

Wine-drinking by Moslems is punishable by flogging or by *ta'zir* (see below). In practice it is frowned upon officially, but indulged in privately by certain Seiyids and others, who normally escape punishment, though certain sons of the Imam have been imprisoned ostensibly for drinking (probably really for suspected treason). The Jews are allowed to distil alcohol and make wine, but only for use in their own quarters; occasionally Jews known to sell wine illicitly to Moslems are very harshly punished, their houses are razed, their stills and wine-stores are destroyed, and a heavy fine is imposed. *Ta'zir*, a rather 'bookish' punishment, is still occasionally used: a small drum is tied to the culprit's back, and this is beaten while he is led round the town amid the jeers of the people; or his face is tarred, or he is mounted facing backwards on a donkey, or in other ways shamed.

Chaining, the commonest form of punishment, may be inflicted for such small offences as quarrelling among servants or 'rowdiness' among boys. A hoop may be placed on one ankle, and two heavy links left to drag along the ground; or the two legs may be chained together—in cases of serious misdemeanour with double chains of such weight that the victim can scarcely move about.

Jews are subject to special laws regulating their dress and may not carry arms or ride horses, but they may ride donkeys or camels.

151. *Cortège of the Imam of the Yemen entering the Bab as Sabah at San'ā*

152. *Imam's palace at San'ā seen from the Arab city*

153. *Mounted escort of the former Amir of Ibb*

154. *Yemeni infantrymen*

They must not build houses more than two stories high without special permission, which is seldom granted, though recently certain Jews, who could afford to buy the favour of the Imam's advisers, obtained permission to build three stories. Jews are taxed, according to *jiziya* (tribute), one dollar, three dollars, or five dollars *per* head *per* year, according as their households are classed poor, average, or rich.

The Armed Forces

The army is divided into the *Jeish ad Difa'i*, or militia, and the *Jeish an Nidhami*, or regular army.

The *Difa'i* aims at training every man in the country to be a soldier. In theory 25 per cent. of the adult males of a given liwa are called up for training in one period of six months. After this is over they return home and 25 per cent. are brought in from another liwa, and so on, till the whole country has sent in its first 25 per cent. The process is then repeated until every man has been trained. The training takes place at San'ā, and a special military expert from outside (often from Syria) is employed to do the training. He is called the Pasha and is said to have from 15,000 to 20,000 men in training at a time. Registers of the trained men are kept as a reserve list for the regular army. Any man called up for the Difa'i may hire a substitute if he does not want to serve.

The regular *Nidhami* army is also called *Jeish al Mudhaffar*, 'the victorious army'. The members are mostly volunteers. The service is for life, and an old man who wants to retire must pay someone to take his place or send a son. In some cases, if a district, especially one of the southern (Shafe'i) areas, fails to provide a reasonable number of voluntary members to the Nidhami, some will be conscripted. Also, from the zealous northern Zeidi tribes some *barani* or free soldiers serve without pay and may leave when they like. The Nidhami is said to be over 18,000 strong.

The branches of the army are: the *'askari* or infantryman; the *'okfi* or guardsman (a local word from *'akfa*, 'to be devoted to', used for a personal bodyguard of the Imam or of the princes); the *sowari* or cavalryman; the *hijan* or camel-trooper; and the *tabshi* or artilleryman. Some soldiers are detailed for police duties under the 'amil; such a soldier is a *qanūn* and his officer is *amir al markiz* ('commander of headquarters'). The ranks correspond roughly to those in European armies as follows: a private is called *'askari, sowari*, &c., according to his section, or a private in any section, whether infantry, cavalry, &c., may also be called *nafar*; *sha'ūsh* corresponds roughly to corporal, and *beit sha'ūsh* (local Arabic form of the more correct Turkish *bash sha'ūsh*) to a sergeant; *naqib*, 2nd lieutenant; *mulazim awwal*, 1st lieutenant; *amir mifraza* (also called *uz ashab*),[1] captain; *amir tabur*, major; *amir alāy*,[2] colonel, who, if the senior officer at the capital of a liwa, also receives the courtesy title *amir al jeish* (above, p. 331). A naqib has about 20–25 men under him. The number of soldiers in each district under an 'amil may vary from less than a hundred to several hundreds.

Private soldiers draw 5–6 riyals a month and rations, but make over 20 riyals when they are sent out on tax-collection. The town gates have military guards, and incomers deposit their weapons and withdraw them on departure, just as they do at Aden, a custom which is probably very old. In the morning the drums beat and the soldiers sing a chant, and at 9 p.m. the drums beat again and there is a ceremonial parade, called the march of the Imam, which lasts for about a quarter of an hour. This occurs in the camps and barracks throughout the Yemen. There is also a ceremonial parade to the mosque every Friday in each district-capital or town of higher status, at which the local head of the civil administration takes the salute in the name of the Imam. In San'ā the Imam himself takes the salute at a great parade of the garrison on the Īd al Kabir ('great festival') and other state occasions.

Cadets are trained at a military college, and the Imam has a cartridge factory which produces 4 cases of 1,000 rounds a day. The lead is imported and the saltpetre is obtained locally. The army was estimated in 1938 at 25,000 men. Many of the rifles and much of the artillery are old. The uniform and weapons of an ordinary soldier, and of a sha'ūsh or beit sha'ūsh, consist generally of white or indigo-dyed turban, indigo shirt, white knee-length kilt, curved *jambiya* (dagger) worn in the girdle, and rifle. Officers usually wear black *kalpaks* on the head, and tunics and trousers of khaki, or sometimes other colours.

The Hostage System

By levying hostages from every tribal area in the country the Imam maintains rigid control over all. The number of hostages required from an area depends upon its loyalty. It is said that the

---

[1] A corruption of the old Turkish rank *yuzbashi*, literally 'head of a hundred'.
[2] Also a Turkish designation, formerly more often written *mīralāy*, 'commander of a regiment'.

Jauf and Barat areas are required to send a third of their male members to the hostage prisons.

The hostages are often little boys between 5 and 11. They are kept in prison—at the citadel in San'ā, at the Imam's palaces up and down the country, and at each administrative centre. The treatment they receive depends on the current behaviour of their tribes. Sometimes large numbers of them are in chains. A school is provided in the prison where the boys learn to recite the Koran. Otherwise they are neglected, having to provide and prepare their own food, and they become very dirty and verminous.

Education

San'ā has several schools for the sons of noble and wealthy families—others for the less wealthy, a school for girls, an orphanage school, a secondary school, and a university. In San'ā itself literacy is high for an Arab country; many even of the women can read and write. The orphanage school has four hundred pupils, many of whom are boarders, but those who have relatives in the city may live out. The uniform of this school is bright yellow. These boys are educated for various branches of government service. Some go to the military college and others to minor clerkships. The abler pupils go to the secondary school and thence to the university, emerging as 'ulema and entering the ranks of the *kuttab* (p. 334).

Hodeida and San'ā have girls' schools and secondary schools. Since the Crown Prince went to Ta'izz secondary education has been started there too, and a large government school is being built. The university is at Ibb. Koranic schools exist throughout the country, but teaching beyond recitation of the sacred book is only to be had at the administrative centres.

THE COLONY OF ADEN

The port of Aden, captured by Britain in 1839 from the 'Abdali Sultan, became a Residency under the Government of Bombay and its area was extended by purchase (p. 276). On 1 April 1932 control was transferred to the Governor-General of India in Council, and Aden became a Chief Commissionership. On 1 April 1937 it was constituted a Crown Colony (p. 309).

Administration

The Colony is administered by a Governor, aided by an Executive Council. There is at present no Legislative Council. The Civil

Secretary deals with Colonial, as distinct from Protectorate, affairs. The Chief Secretary, under the Governor, deals with both. British forces are under the command of the Air Officer Commanding (under whom are also all Imperial troops in the Protectorate; see p. 352). The Aden Settlement was created a corporate body in 1900.

A constitutional development of some importance occurred in 1944 when an Order in Council was passed providing for the establishment of a Legislative Council in the Colony of Aden, and for the creation of municipalities at Aden and Sheikh 'Othman. The latter were set up in April 1945. The inauguration of the Legislative Council had not taken place by the end of the war, but was expected to follow in a short time.

Perim was administered by an Assistant to the British Resident till 1929, then by the Manager of the Perim Coal Company as Government Agent. In 1936 this company closed down and the Commissioner of Police, Aden, became Administrator: he makes regular visits, usually by air (p. 139).

The Kuria Muria islands, ceded to the British Crown by the Sultan of Muscat in 1854, are technically part of the Aden Colony, not of the Aden Protectorate. They are adjacent to the coast of 'Omān, and so remote and difficult of access from Aden that the Government of Aden has no dealings with them, and they have for all practical purposes been put under the charge of the British Resident in the Persian Gulf (Appendix G, p. 616).

The status of the island of Kamarān, in the Red Sea, about 200 miles north of Perim, taken by Britain from the Turks in 1915, was left 'indeterminate' by the Treaty of Lausanne (1923). It was afterwards occupied (not annexed) by the British, and is under the administrative control of the Governor of Aden, on behalf of the Government of India. A quarantine station for pilgrims travelling to Mecca from the East is maintained on the island (pp. 135, 469).

Law

The Civil Courts in the Colony exercise their jurisdiction in conformity with usage, and in the absence of usage in conformity with the substance of the common law, the doctrines of equity, the British and Indian statute law in force when it became a colony, and the ordinances passed since. The personal law of Moslems, Hindus, Jews, and Parsis is applied in matters of marriage, divorce, guardianship, and succession. The Indian Penal Code is in force. The Civil Courts consist of:

(1) The Supreme Court, presided over by the Chief Justice, with unlimited jurisdiction.

(2) The Court of the Registrar (of the Supreme Court). His jurisdiction includes claims up to the value of Rs.1,000.

(3) The Court of Small Causes, i.e. cases not over Rs.500 in value, also presided over by the Registrar.

Criminal Courts are:

(1) The Supreme Court, in which all trials are by jury.

(2) The Chief Magistrate's Court and Divisional Magistrates' Courts, with powers limited to a sentence of two years' imprisonment or fine of Rs.1,000.

Civil and criminal appeals lie to the Supreme Court from the courts below, from the Supreme Court to the High Court of Judicature at Bombay, and from the High Court to the Privy Council. Forty-three civil appeals and 58 criminal appeals were lodged in 1938.

There is a considerable amount of petty civil litigation. During 1938, 37 suits were disposed of by the Supreme Court, 265 by the Court of the Registrar, and 1,376 by the Court of Small Causes.

During 1938, 5 persons were convicted in the Supreme Court and 1,658 in the Magistrates' Courts. Motoring offences, offences against the person, and cases of insult and of affray were numerous.

The Commissioner of Police had in 1938 about 300 men of the land and harbour police, and 200 men of the armed police, under his command. The superintendence of the small prison was entrusted to one of the Medical Officers.

Education

The Government provides schools, a Director of Education, and a standing committee. There are also private schools, some of which are aided by the Government. In 1938, 1,425 pupils attended government and state-aided schools, where they were taught as far as possible in their vernacular, generally Arabic, except in Indian schools, and in those of the local Jews. During the same year, secondary schools (including unaided schools) had an average number of 656 on the rolls. Some pupils came up to the primary schools from primitive Moslem schools which teach the Koran, or from Jewish schools which teach the Talmud.

Public Health

The Government medical staff consisted in 1938 of a dozen doctors, as well as a Medical Officer of Health. The Senior Medical Officer is also Port Health Officer.

ADEN PROTECTORATE

Treaties and Agreements

It has been shown (pp. 274 ff., 308 ff.)that the Protectorate developed gradually after the British occupation of Aden in 1839, from the negotiation of treaties at various dates between the Government of Aden and a number of ruling chiefs. Despite the difference in history of the western and eastern parts of the Protectorate, and the formal definition (since 1937) of a 'Western Aden Protectorate' and an 'Eastern Aden Protectorate', the treaties previously made with the principal ruling chiefs in the two divisions were identical in form.

These treaties[1] were treaties of protection, in which the chiefs on their part agreed not to cede their territories to any foreign Power. To-day over fifty chiefs throughout the whole Protectorate are in more or less direct correspondence with the Government of Aden; some thirty are in direct treaty relations, while seven of these, accorded salutes when they visit Aden, are known as 'gun chiefs'. Two only, in the whole Protectorate, are accorded the title 'His Highness', namely the 'Abdali Sultan of Lahej in the Western and the Qu'aiti Sultan of Shihr and Mukalla in the Eastern Protectorate. A list of these 'treaty chiefs' and others of almost equivalent status, with remarks, is set out on pp. 361–363.

Much of what is now the Eastern Aden Protectorate was previously divided by a feud between the Qu'aiti and Kathīri families and their followers (pp. 277–279). In 1882 the Qu'aiti rulers bound themselves to abide by British advice in their dealings, not only with foreign Powers, but also with neighbouring tribes. The Treaty of 1882 was strengthened in 1888 by the conclusion of a Protectorate in the common form of the treaties with the Protectorate chiefs. In 1918 the Kathīri made a treaty with the Qu'aiti Sultan and agreed that the Hadhramaut in its wider sense—i.e. the Wadi Hadhramaut and adjacent Qu'aiti and Kathīri territories—should become one entity, and further that, by virtue of their treaty with the Qu'aiti, the Kathīri Sultans would come into the sphere of the British Protec-

---

[1] Texts and dates of Aden Protectorate Treaties are given in Aitchison, *Collection of Treaties, Engagements and Sanads*, vol. xi, 1930.

torate. In 1937 the Qu'aiti and Kathīrī Sultans asked for a British Resident Adviser, who was at the same time given political charge of the three other sultanates of the Eastern Aden Protectorate, namely the Wahidi Sultanates of Bālhāf and Bir 'Ali and the Mahri Sultanate of Qishn and Socotra, and subsequently (1938) of the two small sheikhdoms of 'Irqa and Haura in the south-western corner. In addition to the usual Protectorate treaties there are 'Advisory Treaties', dated respectively 1937 and 1939, with the Qu'aiti and Kathīrī Sultans, as well as 'Advisory Agreements' with the Wahidi Sultans.

In 1937 as a corollary to the Order creating the Colony of Aden in that year, an Order in Council was made giving formal recognition to the Aden Protectorate; while in 1939 the Qu'aiti–Kathīrī agreement was revised as a tripartite agreement, and, by arrangement between the Colony of Aden and the Qu'aiti and Kathīrī States, the Aden Postal Union was established on the lines of the Malayan Postal Union; under the terms of this agreement the three contracting parties have their own postage stamps.

Area and Divisions (fig. 37)

The whole Protectorate extends about 700 miles, measured in a straight line, from Ras Turba, on the south coast of the Sheikh Sa'īd peninsula, to Ras Dhurbat 'Ali, the boundary between the Mahra tribes in the Protectorate and the Qara and other tribes of Dhufār in the Sultanate of 'Omān. In depth the Protectorate varies from about 100 miles near Aden to a greater but undefined distance farther east. It embraces an area of more than 112,000 square miles, of which the larger Eastern Protectorate accounts for between 60,000 and 70,000. The inhabitants of the whole Protectorate are estimated at approximately 600,000, probably nearly equally divided between the Eastern and Western divisions. Near the coast the boundary between the Eastern and Western Protectorates is Wadi Sanam (about 6 miles south-west of 'Irqa), separating the Lower 'Aulaqi tribes on the west from the 'Abdul Wahidi sultanates on the east; between 50 and 60 miles north the boundary passes between Yeshbum in the Western, and Habbān in the Eastern Protectorate; beyond this it lies in a general northerly direction, skirting the territories of the Upper 'Aulaqi and Beihāni tribes, which are in the Western Protectorate, while the Bal 'Ubeid are in the Eastern; the boundary reaches the frontier of the Protectorate in the desert. 'Eiyad ('Ayad) and Shabwa are in the Eastern Protectorate.

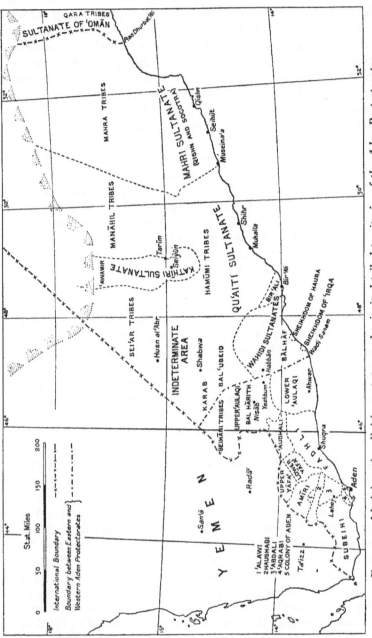

FIG. 37. *Administrative divisions, states, and principal tribal territories of the Aden Protectorate*

Besides the afore-mentioned 'treaty' states and districts, here and there are self-governing villages, more or less dependent on the ruler of the district. There are also tribes which are not subjects but allied to the district chief. The extent of the alliance varies. It may involve an undertaking by the tribe to respond to the district chief's call at any time, or it may be simply an engagement of friendship and an undertaking to co-operate in matters of mutual interest. These villages and tribes are within the Protectorate by virtue of their semi-dependence upon tribes which have entered into treaty relations with Britain. The various tribal territories and districts differ immensely in extent and importance. The 'Abdali Sultanate of Lahej and the Qu'aiti Sultanate of Mukalla are sufficiently organized to be described as States, while other territories, such as the Sheikh-dom of 'Irqa, consist of a single town. The 'Hadhramaut States', the Qu'aiti and Kathīri Sultanates, are separately mentioned below (p. 349). The Mahri Sultanate comprises much of the north-eastern end of the Protectorate, east of Wadi Maseila, with the town of Qishn, on the coast nearly 40 miles north-east of Seihūt; it includes the island of Socotra (p. 609), where the Sultan resides, while a younger branch of his family represents him at Qishn on the mainland; social organization in this sultanate is almost entirely tribal, and the tribesmen on the mainland scarcely recognize the Sultan's rule.

British Administration

Although the Protectorate may be said to have commenced when the first treaty of protection was signed, it was not and is not administered by the British Government. There was no British penetration of the hinterland, and the relations with the friendly tribes were rather those of good neighbourliness than anything else. Gradually, as has been seen, the Protectorate developed until it was formally defined by Order in Council in 1937. This Order in Council provided merely for the exercise of jurisdiction which had previously been provided for under the Indian (Foreign Jurisdiction) Order in Council. The position of the Governor of Aden in relation to the Protectorate is analogous to that of the Governor of Burma in relation to the Shan States. The Political Secretaryship, dealing with Protectorate affairs, was abolished some years ago. The Western Protectorate is under the charge of a British agent, stationed at Aden, with a number of political officers under him. The Resident. at Mukalla has become the Agent of the Eastern Protectorate but retains his function of Resident Adviser to the Qu'aiti and Kathīri Sultans; his staff now includes a political, a military, and other assistants.

Education. The Aden Protectorate College for the Sons of Chiefs, though situated in the Colony of Aden, is intended for chiefs' sons from all parts of the Protectorate; its opening in 1936, with only seven pupils, meant the realization of a scheme mooted long before; the College has flourished, and the waiting list at present (1945) numbers over fifty.[1] Otherwise, education is in varying phases of development in different tribal territories.

The important subject of *child welfare* is receiving attention, and a child-welfare worker has joined the Residency staff at Mukalla.

Agriculture in the Protectorate is mainly under the charge of a British Agricultural Adviser with assistants; but the Qu'aiti State has its own Agricultural Department.

Tribal Administration

The general system is one of communities ruled over by chiefs, split into smaller tribes, each ruled by its headman, and again split into villages under village headmen. Most chiefs are elected, either by their family or by their tribe. The main difference is that some belong to the tribe while others do not. The Sultan of Lahej, for instance, as well as the Amir of Dhāla' and the Sultan of Mukalla, are of descent foreign to the tribes over which they rule. The Sultan of Mukalla belongs to the Qu'aiti sub-tribe of the Yāfa' tribe, whose territory lies west of the Hadhramaut. In both the Qu'aiti and the Kathīri States, the sultans have by treaty the right to nominate their successors subject to the approval of His Majesty's Government. Elsewhere new chiefs elected by the family only and not by the tribesmen do not, as a rule, favour elected headmen in their villages but prefer to appoint outsiders as headmen whom they pay as retainers.

The Sharif of Beihān was originally the chief of a community of Sharifs settled in a district inhabited by two tribes. He negotiated a treaty of protection and friendship with Great Britain, concluded a truce with a rival community of Seiyids, consolidated his relationships with the tribesmen, and was accepted as chief by both tribes. He is a kind of limited monarch. He does not claim taxes from the land or trade except in his own settlements.

The chief who is a member of the confederation of tribes which he

---

[1] In 1943 plans were announced for the creation, after the war, of a new College, under the auspices of the British Council, to serve the needs of Protectorate pupils as a whole.

governs is elected from a certain family of the central tribe by his fellow tribesmen and the 'aqils or heads of the tribal sections. The chief's eldest son has no customary right to succeed, although sometimes he is accepted by the tribesmen as the heir to the throne during the chief's lifetime. As a rule, when the chief dies, a nephew will succeed. The titles of chiefs vary: many are sheikhs, but there are a number of sultans, an amir, and a sharif. High-sounding titles do not always mean that the holders are of more consequence.

The more advanced administration of the Hadhramaut States is outlined below (p. 349).

Municipal Administration

The townsmen of the Hadhramaut are divided into four classes: merchants, artificers, labourers, and servants. The leading merchants to some extent govern the affairs of their towns and have developed the beginnings of municipal organization. The municipal affairs of Tarīm are run by wealthy Seiyids who frame a budget and expend large sums on dispensaries, schools, and other public and charitable services, as well as on settling tribal feuds. An undertaking has been given by the Government of the Qu'aiti State to set up a municipal council in Mukalla.

Law

The British Government does not interfere with domestic affairs. It is not concerned when a tribesman kills a fellow tribesman, and not much more concerned when a member of one tribe kills a member of another. But, if travellers are molested on the trade routes, the responsible chief has to arrest the culprit and make full restitution for any robbery committed. There are agreements with some tribes to maintain a force of road guards for the protection of trade routes.

As in the Yemen (pp. 334–335), the two chief systems are the Moslem canonical law (*shar'*) and the primitive tribal law (*'urf*). In the Aden Protectorate much older systems of administration than in the Yemen still obtain, although they bear a certain relation to the tribal law as still administered in the Yemen. Appendix C (p. 587) contains a free translation of an agreement between the various tribes the 'Audhali confederation and their Sultan, made in 1929, an agreement which no doubt very closely resembles those of feudal Europe in its earlier stages, i.e. between the serf (as he ultimately became) and the overlord. It represents a stage beyond intertribal anarchy; the tribes have placed themselves under a family with royal powers, the representative of which, however, is by no means an absolute monarch. This agreement lays down the rights of the Sultan and of the tribes on certain specific points, while certain general legal points are also defined. Similar agreements in writing or by word of mouth no doubt exist among all the confederations in the Aden Protectorate. The law in this document is customary law which has been put into writing, though generally customary law is handed down only by word of mouth. It is of quite a different nature from Islamic law. In the Yemen the tribal law is no doubt somewhat similar to that exemplified in this document, with the substitution of 'Sheikh' for Sultan.

In 1936 the Resident Adviser induced the tribes of the Eastern Protectorate, to the number of 1,400 signatories, to make a truce for three years. A Board of Arbitration was set up, with an Arab Secretary; and a Legal Adviser was appointed, in order that the Shar' should not be overlooked in coming to decisions. Difficult cases were referred to sub-committees, but all cases, whether referred to sub-committees or not, had to be considered by the board. Over 600 cases were entered in a short time and a large number of them disposed of satisfactorily. When the truce expired there were difficulties in obtaining the unanimous consent of all the signatories to an extension, but the sultans proclaimed an extension for ten years and this has been accepted by the vast majority of the tribes and people. In consequence of this truce the number of murders in the Hadhramaut is much reduced.

In the ill-defined part of the Protectorate called Mushreq, east of the Yemen, there exists a class of judges called *manqads*, whose name is derived from a root meaning to 'pick up' or 'investigate', and who are possibly remnants of the legal system of one of the pre-Islamic kingdoms. The chief of these is the hereditary judge, elected from a particular family influential in local affairs. Once elected, he has the title *Manqad al Manaqid* ('Judge of Judges') and, without consulting anyone, he appoints four or five other manqads from outside his own family, his choice not being limited by social status or tribe. The manqads then jointly perform the duties of a final court of appeal, pronouncing judgements according to a very broad code which they describe as 'The holy law, tribal custom, and the right' (*ash sharia, al 'ada, wa'l haqq*), of which they seem to prefer tribal custom (cf. pp. 312, 335). No tribesman, having put his case to a manqad, would either withdraw it or refuse to abide by the decision. Manqads dress as poor men, carrying no arms and behaving humbly, but they are treated by both tribesmen and chiefs with great respect; indeed in some cases their actions carry more weight than those of the chief. When a chief manqad dies and a new one is elected, all the other manqads are suspended till their appointments are confirmed by the new chief manqad.

The Hadhramaut States

The Qu'aiti State is so considerably organized as to be worthy of separate notice. His Highness the Qu'aiti Sultan, principal chief of the Eastern Protectorate, is an absolute monarch as far as internal affairs are concerned, though he has devolved many of his powers to the State Council. His principal palace is at Mukalla, where the old palace of the Kasādis (p. 278) has been turned into government offices.

The State Council, which has been set up on the lines of the Malayan State Councils, is presided over by the Sultan, and the *ex officio* members are the Resident Adviser, the Heir Apparent, the Assistant to the Resident Adviser, the State Secretary, the Legal Adviser, and the State Treasurer. There are also six nominated members, of whom two must, and three may, be unofficial. This council is the Sultan's cabinet.

At the head of the administration is the State Secretary, who supervises all departments of government and is Governor (*Naib*) of the Mukalla province. The Government departments number twenty-one, of which the most important are the Secretariat, the Treasury, and the Military, Education, Medical, and Agricultural departments. The Customs have a large staff, distributed amongst all the ports, and this department also superintends the work of the ports. The Senior Medical Officer is also Port Health Officer.

The State is divided into five liwas (provinces), each administered by a naib (governor, literally 'representative'; formerly the title was *muqaddam*). The provinces are as follows, their capitals having the same name except in the two cases mentioned: Shihr (the oldest province); Mukalla; Dū'an (capital, 'Aura); Hajr (capital, Jōl Ba Hawa); and Shibām. Each naib has a paid staff, while *qaims* (district officers) are stationed in important Qu'aiti towns, that is, towns which are not autonomous.

There are many autonomous towns, governed by particular tribes or families, in the internal affairs of which the Mukalla government does not interfere. Relations with the tribes over the country are maintained chiefly by the Beduin Affairs department of the central government, and by the naibs and qaims on whose towns they economically depend. The Sultan has written agreements of two types with the tribes: (a) engagements containing an undertaking to respond to the Sultan's call in any matter and at any time; and (b) engagements of friendship and co-operation in matters of mutual interest.[1] In cases of doubtful loyalty hostages, who may be changed every month, are given by the tribe and kept in Mukalla town prison and elsewhere (not in the new central criminal prison outside the town). Some tribes receive presents and subsidies, and tribal 'aqils visiting provincial headquarters may be given presents and entertained.

The basic *law* consists of Moslem law within the towns and tribal custom outside, augmented by decrees of the Sultan passed by the State Council, and by his Edicts. Many disputes are adjusted by *mansabs*, some of whom ride about their districts on peace-making missions (photo. 158); *mansab* is derived from *nasab*, to 'set up', and mansabs are usually elected by their respective families. The Qu'aiti administration does not greatly interfere with tribal usage in the country, but, within the towns and certain demarcated areas surrounding them, murder and loot are regarded as offences against the Government. Murderers are liable to death in these areas, while thieves, besides restoring their loot, are liable to imprisonment or deportation—amputation of the hand being no longer enforced by Government. Payment of a debt may be exacted from any available fellow tribesman of an absconding debtor, a method similar to that employed in some other parts of the Protectorate. Routes between Qu'aiti towns are also sacrosanct.

Cases to which Moslem canonical law applies are heard by local qadhis at the bigger towns of the interior, but an appeal lies to the Sharia division of the Supreme Court at Mukalla, which consists of three qadhis and has both an original and an appellate jurisdiction. Within each liwa the provincial court of the naib can, generally speaking, settle all cases, but there is right of appeal to the Judge's division of the Supreme Court at Mukalla and eventually to the Sultan in Council. Commercial and bankruptcy cases are heard by the Commercial Court in Mukalla. District officers (qaims) hold district courts, with right of appeal to the provincial courts. In Mukalla and some other towns there are police magistrate's courts (*Hukm as Suq*), with powers of imprisonment up to twelve days.

[1] For lists of tribes under these agreements, see W. H. Ingrams, *Report on the Hadhramaut*, Colonial No. 123, p. 92, 1937.

There is also a system of Tribal Courts, divided into Chiefs'
Courts for autonomous towns and Beduin Courts for nomads.
Right of appeal lies from these to the Provincial Beduin Courts of
Appeal, and to the Judge of the Supreme Court acting with tribal
assessors.

Education is making great strides. Some 1,700 boys and about 200
girls are attending government elementary schools on the coast.
The Government is extending primary education to the interior;
there is a boys' intermediate boarding-school at Gheil Ba Wazīr
(north-west of Shihr). Special schools exist for weaving and spinning,
and a 'children's village' boarding-school for 300 poor children at
Mukalla. The educational activities of the Hadhrami Beduin Legion
are mentioned below, p. 353.

Child Welfare work and Agriculture in the Qu'aiti State have been
mentioned on p. 346.

The Kathīri Sultanate forms enclaves within the Qu'aiti Sultanate.
It consists of the directly ruled towns and villages of Seiyūn, Tarīm,
Taris, Al Ghurfa, Mariama and Al Gheil, and the Shenafir Confederation of tribes, the Āl Kathīr, the 'Awāmir, the Āl Jabir, and the Bajri.
This sultanate has a State Secretary but not so many organized
official institutions as the Qu'aiti Sultanate. For example, the Tarīm
town council, dispensary, roads, and schools are almost entirely
supported by the wealthy Seiyids. The preservation of their ancient
jurisdictions by autonomous communities is well exemplified at
Tarīm, within the walls of which is an enclosure containing a few
houses inhabited by the Seiyids of Al Haddad; these are entirely
under the jurisdiction of their own mansab, and are not tried by the
Kathīri Sultan, even if they commit offences in the city of Tarīm.

The military forces and police of the Hadhramaut States are discussed with those of the Aden Protectorate as a whole (p. 353).

Slavery

The slave trade is dead, but the descendants of slaves still serve
their original masters. Slavery exists only in some parts of the
Protectorate, being uncommon except in Lahej, and the two Hadhramaut States; even in the latter, the Qu'aiti State now has a law
regulating slavery and manumission, all government slaves have been
freed, and any other slave who wishes to do so can claim his freedom.
The status of by far the larger number of slaves is purely technical;
they are in fact free to do anything they please, and often have shown
themselves uncontrollable. A chief's responsibility for his slaves is

a very real one, and, should he sell or part with a slave, he will be considered to have acted shamefully. Some of the slaves of the beduin, however, have not been well treated. Many other chiefs besides the Qu'aiti Sultan have signed agreements declaring that the slave trade is illegal and agreeing to free slaves who wish to be liberated.

Army and Police

The Imperial military forces are under the immediate command of the Air Officer Commanding at Aden (p. 340). Joint Headquarters at Aden consist of Air Headquarters with its various departments, and Headquarters, Royal Artillery. The garrison includes a Royal Air Force Squadron, a Heavy Battery, a company of Royal Engineers, a section of armoured cars, and the Aden Protectorate Levies. The Levies, drawn from various tribes in the Protectorate, are commanded by a British Lieutenant-Colonel with a number of British officers; their headquarters are at Sheikh 'Othman; they have been greatly increased since they were first raised by a British officer in 1928 (p. 311). There is a naval office at Aden under a naval Officer-in-Charge. Other Imperial military units, temporarily in being since 1939, are the Aden Labour Corps and the Hadhramaut Pioneer Corps.

Besides these imperial forces several forces have been raised under the colonial administration in recent years for local security purposes. They are maintained either directly by His Majesty's Government, or jointly by the Government and Arab rulers, or wholly by the latter. Troops maintained jointly by His Majesty's Government and a local chief are known in the Western Protectorate as 'Tribal Guards'. These, started some years before the War of 1939, are maintained by their respective chiefs as far as possible, the Government helping when the chief cannot bear the whole cost. In return, they are supervised by a British officer appointed by the Government and, while adding to the authority of their own chief, they must be used in a manner approved by the Government. Later, a force of 'Government Guards' under direct government control was raised. Tribal and Government Guards are jointly known as 'Protectorate Guards'. In the Eastern Protectorate counterparts exist under somewhat different names.

As to troops maintained wholly by Arab rulers, the Lahej army is divided into the Lahej Trained Forces, a smartly equipped body of a few hundred men, a few retainers, and the irregulars. The irregular

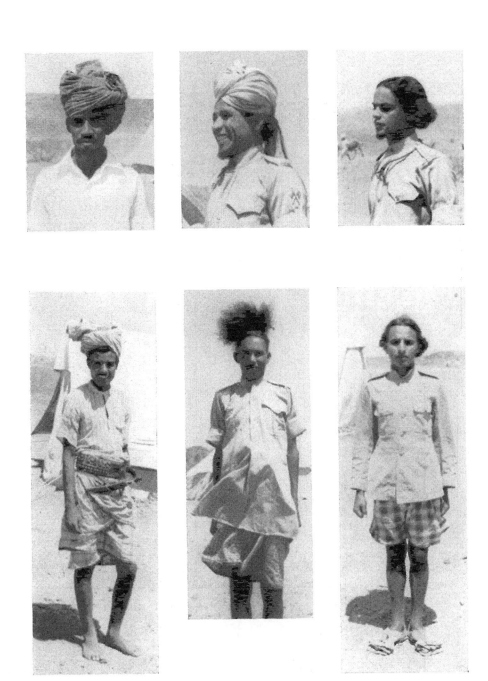

155. *Native types in the Aden Protectorate R.A.F. Levies*

156, 157. Parade of the Amir's troops at Dhāla', 1937

158. A mansab on his rounds in the Hadhramaut

tribesmen are rarely called up, and the Sultan keeps their arms locked in his armoury.

In the Eastern Protectorate the Sultan of Mukalla has a small regular army of several hundred men, consisting mostly of beduin, partly of Yāfaʻis and Africans; they are organized into a battery of mountain artillery, a small camel bodyguard, three companies of infantry, a machine-gun company, and a band. The Sultan also has 450 irregulars, all Yāfaʻis; the Quʻaiti irregular forces originally numbered over a thousand, but some have been gradually transformed into a gendarmerie of about 300 to police the towns of the interior, while the coast towns are policed by a civil police force of about 100. The state forces, regular, irregular, and gendarmerie, are controlled by the Military department under a Military Secretary with a small General Staff. The reorganization of the troops has taken place mainly under Indian officers, under the guidance of the Resident Adviser's military Assistants, who are now Indian or Arab.

Early in 1937 the Kathīri armed constabulary was formed, mainly from the Sultan's slaves.

Under British auspices a camel patrol was recruited to police the Al Kaf road (from Shihr to the Wadi Hadhramaut), its duties being to see that the tolls were paid and that the beduin did not barricade the highway. This patrol has since become part of the Hadhrami Beduin Legion, formed in 1940 to give security among the nomad tribes of the Hadhramaut, on the lines of the Desert Patrol of the Arab Legion in Transjordan. The Hadhrami Beduin Legion numbers about 370, with 100 recruits; it has specialist branches for education and agriculture among the beduin, boarding-schools for beduin boys and girls, district schools for nomads, and a small hospital.

These several forces are summarized below, the source of maintenance being given in brackets in each case:

Western Aden Protectorate

Government Guards (maintained entirely by H.M. Government).

Tribal Guards (partly H.M. Government, partly the Amir of Dhālaʻ and the Fadhli and Haushabi Sultans, respectively).

Lahej Trained Forces (the Sultan of Lahej).

Eastern Aden Protectorate

Hadhrami Beduin Legion (maintained by H.M. Government, with a contribution from the Mukalla Government).

Kathīri Armed Constabulary (mainly H.M. Government, partly the Kathīri State).

Wahidi Tribal Guards (partly H.M. Government, partly the Governments of Bir 'Ali and Bālhāf).

Mukalla Regular Army (the Mukalla Government—but H.M. Government pays the African Company, which guards a Royal Air Force aerodrome).

Qu'aiti Gendarmerie (the Mukalla Government).

Mukalla Civil Police (the Mukalla Government).

Prisons

The extensive use of corporal punishment among the Arabs limits the number of prisons required and some of the chiefs, in medieval fashion, confine their prisoners within their own premises. The Amir of Dhāla', till recently at any rate, kept prisoners in chains in his mountain-keep on Jebel Jihāf. The Haushabi Sultan's prisoners sleep on the ground floor of the palace and in the day-time shuffle about outside in their chains, pretty much as they please. Where British influence is effective this state of affairs is being altered and the larger States now have their separate prisons. Mukalla, for instance, has an up-to-date prison for criminals as well as 'lock-ups' at the police stations.

ADMINISTRATIVE DIVISIONS OF SAʿŪDI ARABIA

Areas administered by the Crown Prince as Amir Nejd

Province	Unattached districts	Sub-districts of provinces
1. Wadi Dawāsir	..	Suleiyil
2. Aflāj	1. Hauta	..
	2. Harīq	..
3. Kharj	..	Dilam (headquarters)
		Qurein or Suleimīya
4. ʿĀridh	..	Riyādh (headquarters)
		Mahmal
5. Sudeir	..	Majmaʿa
		Ghāt
		Zilfi
		Artawiya
6. Washm	..	Shaqra (headquarters)
		Marrāt
	3. Duwadami	..
	4. Sirr	..
	5. Mudhnib	..
7. Qasīm	..	Boreida (headquarters)
		ʿAneiza
		Rass
8. Jebel Shammar	..	Hāil (headquarters)
		Teima
9. Hasa (or Ahsa)	..	Hasa (headquarters at Hofūf)
		Salwa
		ʿOqeir
		Dammam
		Qatīf
		Jubeil
		Qariya
10. Juba (or Jauf)	..	Hafar al Bātin
		Sakāka (headquarters)
		Jauf
		Quraiyāt al Milh

Areas administered by the Viceroy-General of the Hejaz

1. Jīzān	..	Sabya
		Abu ʿArīsh
		ʿArdha
		Khauba
		Samta
		Muassam
		Haqu
		Feifa

Areas administered by the Viceroy-General of the Hejaz—continued

Province	Unattached districts	Sub-districts of provinces
Jīzān (*contd.*)		Beni Malik (Qahba)
		Madhāya
		Shuqeiq
		Qahma
	1. Birk	..
2. Al Qunfidha	..	Hali
		Rijal al Ma
		Sha'bein
		Maheil
	2. Al Līth	..
	3. Jidda	..
	4. Mecca	..
	5. Tāif	..
	6. Beni Malik	..
	7. Rābigh	..
	8. Yenbo' (Yanbu')	..
	9. Amlaj	..
	10. Wejh	..
	11. Dhuba'	..
	12. Muweilih	..
3. Al Madina	..	Al 'Ulā
		Hanākīya
		Kheibar
	13. Khurma	..
	14. Turaba	..
	15. Ranya	..
	16. Dhafir	..
	17. Bīsha	..
4. 'Asīr al Sirat	..	Abhā
		Khamīs Musheit
		Kheibar
5. Nejrān	..	Nejrān (headquarters)
		Habauna
		Badr
	18. Haraja	..
	19. Dhahran	..

THE ADMINISTRATIVE DIVISIONS OF THE YEMEN

THE following list, though not entirely complete, is as full and up to date as at present available. As noted in the text (pp. 331-2), the geographical and traditional divisions of the Yemen into five liwas of Sa'da (North), Ta'izz (South), Hodeida (Tihama), San'ā (North-east), and Dhamār (Central) have been replaced by four princedoms. The old Sa'da province with its four governorships or qadhas has been split into two: (i) two qadhas under Prince Ahmed of Ta'izz and managed for him by his brother Prince Motahir with capital at Qafla; (ii) two qadhas directly under San'ā and nominally under the King, but also under the influence of Prince 'Abdullah who lives in San'ā and acts for his father.

The Yemen is therefore now divided into principalities as follows:

(i) San'ā with half of Sa'da: directly under the King, for whom Prince 'Abdullah frequently acts.

(ii) Ta'izz with the other half of Sa'da under the Crown Prince with Prince Motahir acting for him in the north.

(iii) Hodeida: under Prince 'Abdullah, for whom Qadhi 'Ali al 'Amri acts, because Prince 'Abdullah lives with his father at the capital.

(iv) Ibb: under Prince Hasan.

These principalities are divided into qadhas (plur. *qadhat*) and nāhiyas (plur. *nawāhi*) as follows:

I. SAN'Ā

Seven qadhas: (i) San'ā, (ii) Anis, (iii) Reima, (iv) Dhamār, (v) Mahweit, (vi) Rida', and (vii) Haraz.

The following long list of places ranking as nāhiyas now come under:

(i) *Qadha San'ā:*

Wosab al 'Āli, cap. Ad Dan	Al Hada, cap. Zoreija
Wosab as Sāfil, cap. Al 'Ahad	Beni Bahlul, cap. San'ā
Otuma, cap. Rabu'a	Bilad ar Rus, cap. San'ā
Kohlan, cap. Jehama	Beni Hasheish, cap. Sir
Sifyan, cap. Al Harf	An Nihm, cap. Sir
Marib, cap. Marib	Ayal Siraih, cap. San'ā
Al Juba, cap. Al Juba	Muheim, cap. San'ā
Al Beidha, cap. Al Beidha	Hamdan, cap. San'ā
Bilad al Bustan, cap. Metna	Arhab, cap. San'ā
Al Jauf, cap. Al Gheil	Beni al Harith, cap. Raudha
Harib, cap. Harib	Barat, cap. Al Inan

(ii) *Qadha Anis:*

Nāhiya Anis, cap. Dhoran
   ,,   Jahran, cap. Ma'bar

(iii) *Qadha Reima:*
Nāhiya Reima, cap. Reima

(iv) *Qadha Dhamār:*
Nāhiya Dhamār, cap. Dhamār
    ,,   Maghrab 'Ans, cap. Dhoba

(v) *Qadha Mahweit:*
Nāhiya Heima ad Dakhili, cap. Mafhaq
    ,,   Heima al Khariji, cap. Al 'Er
    ,,   Mahweit, cap. Mahweit

(vi) *Qadha Rida':*
Nāhiya Rida', cap. Rida'
    ,,   Juban, cap. Juban
    ,,   Suwadi, cap. Suwadi

(vii) *Qadha Haraz:*
Nāhiya Haraz, cap. Manākha

The qadhas taken over from Sa'da are (i) Qadha Sa'da and (ii) Qadha Tawila.

(i) *Qadha Sa'da*, with eight nāhiyas (names of capitals not available): Nāhiya Razih, Jum'a, Saqin, 'Amrān, Khamir, Al Jurf, As Sunera, and Reida.

(ii) *Qadha Tawila*, with five nāhiyas (their capitals mostly of same name): Nāhiya Kaukaban, Al Ahjir, Shibām, Thula, and Beni 'Abbās.

II. TA'IZZ

Four qadhas: (i) Ta'izz, (ii) Qama'ira, (iii) Mocha, and (iv) Hujariya.

(i) *Qadha Ta'izz*, with four nāhiyas:
Nāhiya Ta'izz, cap. Ta'izz
    ,,   Al Mowadim, cap. Dar an Nasr
    ,,   Al Misrakh, cap. Misrakh
    ,,   Shera'ab, cap. Runa

(ii) *Qadha Qama'ira*, with three nāhiyas:
Nāhiya Māwiya, cap. Māwiya (also capital of the whole Qadha)
    ,,   Khadir, cap. Dimna
    ,,   Al Hisha

(iii) *Qadha Mocha*, with two nāhiyas:
Nāhiya Mocha, cap. Mocha
    ,,   Maqbara, cap. ?

(iv) *Qadha Hujariya*, with four nāhiyas:
Nāhiya Moqatara, cap. Turba (also capital of the whole Qadha)
    ,,   Qobeita, cap. Haifan
    ,,   Jebel Habeishi, cap. Yefris
    ,,   al Waza'īya, cap. Al Waza'īya

The qadhas taken over from Sa'da are (i) Qadha Huth and (ii) Qadha Hajja.

(i) *Qadha Huth,* with five nāhiyas:

Nāhiya Shahara
  ,, Wafla (capital of all this part of the old Sa'da Amirate)
  ,, Al Ahnum
  ,, As Suda
  ,, As Sirahah

(ii) *Qadha Hajja* with eight nāhiyas:

Nāhiya Ash Sharifein
  ,, Ash Shighadira
  ,, Beni 'Awam
  ,, Maswar
  ,, Kohlan
  ,, Meidi
  ,, Haradh
  ,, Hajur ash Sham.

III. HODEIDA

Five qadhas: (i) Qadha Zabīd, (ii) Qadha Beit al Faqīh, (iii) Qadha Bājil, (iv) Qadha Zeidīya, and (v) Qadha Hodeida.

(i) *Qadha Zabīd,* with three nāhiyas:

Nāhiya Zabīd
  ,, Hais
  ,, Khokha

(ii) *Qadha Beit al Faqīh,* with four nāhiyas:

Nāhiya Lijan
  ,, Al Hūseinīya
  ,, Beni Sa'īd
  ,, Beit al Faqīh

(iii) *Qadha Bājil,* with four nāhiyas:

Nāhiya Luheiya
  ,, Zohara
  ,, Al Wa'idhat, cap. Zohira
  ,, Bājil

(iv) *Qadha Zeidīya,* with four nāhiyas:

Nāhiya Ibn 'Abbās
  ,, Dhohi
  ,, Al Qanawis
  ,, Zeidīya

(v) *Qadha Hodeida,* with five nāhiyas:

Nāhiya Hodeida, cap. Hodeida
  ,, Duraihimi
  ,, Al Marawia
  ,, Mansūriya
  ,, Bura', cap. Bura'

IV. Ibb

Five qadhas: (i) Ibb, (ii) ʿUdein, (iii) Dhi Sifal, (iv) Qaʿtaba, and (v) Yarīm.

(i) *Qadha Ibb*, with four nāhiyas:

Nāhiya Ibb
,,　　Makhadar
,,　　Hubeish
,,　　Jibla

(ii) *Qadha ʿUdein*, with two nāhiyas:

Nāhiya ʿUdein
,,　　Modhaikhara

(iii) *Qadha Dhi Sifal*, with two nāhiyas:

Nāhiya Dhi Sifal
,,　　Sabira

(iv) *Qadha Qaʿtaba*, with three nāhiyas:

Nāhiya Qaʿtaba
,,　　Nadira
,,　　Damt

(v) *Qadha Yarīm*, with two nāhiyas:

Nāhiya Yarīm
..　　Khoban

STATES AND PRINCIPAL TRIBAL DISTRICTS OF THE ADEN PROTECTORATE

NOTE: (i) The Western and Eastern Aden Protectorates are so different in social organization that the two lists have to be differently arranged; (ii) in the whole list, only 'treaty chiefs' and some others of almost equivalent standing are enumerated, i.e. those who are in direct treaty relations with the Government, or at any rate in direct correspondence and/or in receipt of stipends; many minor chiefs, without special privileges, are not shown; (iii) the number of guns which the most important chiefs are accorded as a salute on their periodic visits to Aden are indicated in the fourth column; (iv) the first nine tribal areas in the Western Protectorate, shown in capitals in the first column, are the original 'Nine Cantons'; their number has been increased to eleven by the addition of the 'Audhali and Beihāni.

I. WESTERN ADEN PROTECTORATE

Tribal area	Treaty chief	Capital	Remarks
'ABDALI	His Highness the Sultan of Lahej	Lahej	Premier chief of the Western Aden Protectorate; suzerain of the Subeihis and to a less extent of the Haushabis, also recognized to some degree as overlord by the Amir of Dhāla'. 11-gun salute. (The 'Abdali State is the only area in the Western Protectorate with an organized government.)
AMIRI	The Amir of Dhāla'	Dhāla'	9-gun salute.
Quteibi	The Quteibi Sheikh	Ath Thumeir	Government has a 'road agreement' with this sheikh, who is treated as a treaty chief; he is to some degree under the influence of the Amir of Dhāla'.
FADHLI	The Fadhli Sultan	Shuqra	9-gun salute.
YĀFA'I	*Lower Yāfa'*		
	The Lower Yāfa'i Sultan	Al Qāra	9-gun salute. (The heads of the Lower Yāfa'i sections have no special privileges, and are not listed.)
	Upper Yāfa'		
	The Upper Yāfa'i Sultan	Mahjaba	..
	The Naqibs of Mausata	Al Qudma	These naqibs are co-chiefs.
	The Dhubi Sheikh	Dhī Sūra	..
	The Maflahi Sheikh	Al Jurba	..
	The Hadhrami Sheikh	Ash Shibr	..

Tribal area	Treaty chief	Capital	Remarks
YĀFA'I—*contd.*			
	The Bo'si Sheikh The Daudi Sheikh		These two sheikhs, though without treaty, are tribally of the same status as the foregoing and are treated much as treaty chiefs.
Sha'ibi	The Saqladi Sheikh	Bakhāl	The Sha'ibi, till recently treated as part of Upper Yāfa', tend to be regarded more and more as separate.
HAUSHABI	The Haushabi Sultan	Museimir	To some extent under the influence of the Sultan of Lahej.
'AULAQI	*Lower 'Aulaqi* The Lower 'Aulaqi Sultan *Upper 'Aulaqi* The Upper 'Aulaqi Sultan The Upper 'Aulaqi Sheikh	Ahwar Nisāb Yeshbum	.. .. ..
'ALAWI	The 'Alawi Sheikh	Al Qasha'a	..
'AQRABI	The 'Aqrabi Sheikh	Bir Ahmed	..
SUBEIHI	The Barhimi Sheikh The 'Ātifi Sheikhs		The Subeihis acknowledge the overlordship of the Sultan of Lahej.
	The Rija'i Sheikh The Dubeini Sheikh The Mansūri Sheikh The Makhdūmi Sheikh The Khalīfi Sheikh The Atawi Sheikh		These six sheikhs have only 'road agreements' with the Government, but are otherwise of much the same status as the two preceding sections of Subeihis
AUDHALI Dathina	The 'Audhali Sultan The Dathina Sheikhs	Laudar	The practically independent Dathina Sheikhs are mostly under 'Audhali, but in some cases under Fadhli or 'Aulaqi influence.
BEIHĀNI	The Sharif of Beihān	An Nuqūb	
Mas'abi	The Mas'abi Sheikh		Recently regarded as semi-independent and given a minor agreement for protection of a landing-ground.

II. EASTERN ADEN PROTECTORATE

This corresponds to the provinces of Hadhramaut and Shihr of the Arabian geographers. The name Shihr is now restricted to the town and province of Shihr in the Qu'aiti State, but the words *Shahr* and *Mahr* have a common origin and Shihr originally meant the Mahri country.

Province	State, &c.	Treaty chief	Executive authority	Capital	Remarks
THE HADHRAMAUT	*The Hadhramaut States:* (i) The Qu'aiti State of Shihr and Mukalla	His Highness the Qu'aiti Sultan of Shihr and Mukalla	The Mukalla Government	Mukalla	Premier chief of the Eastern Aden Protectorate; both the Sultan and the British Resident Adviser have 11-gun salutes. Government fully organized in 21 departments; state council of official and unofficial members. State divided into five provinces under Governors.
	(ii) The Kathiri State of Seiyun	The Kathiri Sultan of Seiyun	The Seiyun Government	Seiyun	9-gun salute.
	The Wahidi Sultanates: (i) The Sultanate of Balhaf	The Sultan of Balhaf	The Balhaf Government	'Azzan, Balhaf	The Sultan resides at 'Azzan; seat of government at Balhaf.
	(ii) The Sultanate of Bir 'Ali	The Sultan of Bir 'Ali	The Bir 'Ali Government	Bir 'Ali	...
	The Sheikhdom of 'Irqa	The Sheikh of 'Irqa	..	'Irqa	
	The Sheikhdom of Haura	The Sheikh of Haura	..	Haura	
	The indeterminate area	*Remarks:* This includes the tribes between the Qu'aiti State on the east, the Rub' al Khali on the north, the Wahidi Sultanates on the south, and the 'Aulaqis and Beihanis on the west; they inhabit wadis such as Rakhya, Duhr, Yeb'eth, and Jardan, including also the Bal 'Ubeid confederation and the desert of Ramlat Sabatein. Formerly acknowledging the Wahidi Sultans as their *Dola*, these tribes are now practically independent, though tending to acknowledge the Qu'aiti Sultan. Territory partly policed by Hadhrami Beduin Legion.			
THE MAHRI SULTANATE OF QISHN AND SOCOTRA	..	The Sultan of Qishn and Socotra	..	Hadibu in Socotra (Tamrida on European maps) and Qishn on the Mahri coast.	The Sultan is accorded a 9-gun salute. The ruling Mahri clan, Bin Afrar, is divided into two families. The Sultan, belonging to the senior branch, governs Socotra. The younger branch represents him on the mainland at Qishn, and a cadet of this branch usually lives at Seihut. The Mahri tribesmen of the mainland do not recognize the Sultan as ruler.

CHAPTER VII

THE PEOPLE

NUMBERS AND DISTRIBUTION

DESPITE its vast area, Arabia is estimated to support no more than 6,000,000 people. No census appears to have been made in any part, and estimates have varied between 2 and over 10 millions.[1] Taking 6 millions as one of the most recent and best-founded estimates, at least half live in the fertile south-western corner; thus the Aden Protectorate is believed to contain 600,000 and the Kingdom of the Yemen at least between 2 and 3 millions. Other populous centres are the cities of the Hejaz, the oases of the north-west and of Al Hasa in the east, the settled districts of central Nejd, and of the Sultanate of 'Omān, the last territory having perhaps 500,000. A sparse nomadic population roams over the arid parts of the peninsula, while the great southern desert is to a large extent uninhabited.

The total sedentary population is much greater than the nomadic; the former has been calculated as nearly three times the latter. Thus Arabia agrees with all the lands of the 'dry belt' stretching across north Africa and central Asia except Mongolia.

It has been calculated that nearly two-thirds of the total population are husbandmen, a little over one-quarter beduin, while about one-twelfth live in towns of over ten thousand people, of which there may be between twenty and thirty. The husbandmen are largely accounted for by some two or three million settled cultivators in the south-western highlands and roughly 200,000 in 'Omān. The huge area covered by the rest of the land supports a further body of cultivators dwelling in oases and a larger number of beduin, while yet another fraction are town-dwellers. In the northern part of the peninsula the *Solubba* (or *Sleyb*), possessing donkeys but neither camels nor horses, wander in small family groups from camp to camp

[1] Six millions is the figure given by Carleton Coon, *The Races of Europe*, 1939, p. 401. The old official *Handbook* gave 4½ millions. H. von Wissmann, in the section 'Arabien' in Fritz Klute's *Handbuch der geographischen Wissenschaft* (about 1936, p. 192), made a detailed estimate of the separate parts; in particular he reckoned the population of 'Asīr and the Yemen much higher than formerly, and that of other parts either higher or lower, so that the total for all Arabia was 8,800,000; he stated that Carl Rathjens then reckoned the total over 12 millions. These estimates seem unduly high.

of the beduin, to whom they act as tinkers and leather-workers. It is impossible to give precise numbers. A fishing-population is scattered along the coasts and on the islands.

Many transitional stages exist between nomads and settled agriculturalists. Many beduin of the Hejaz, Hadhramaut, and elsewhere cultivate the land to some extent in places where they make long stays. In 'Asīr and the eastern Yemen there are tribes or confederations including separate clans of settled cultivators and of beduin. Elsewhere a ruling stratum may dwell in oases, while others remain nomadic. In Nejd there are comparatively new settlements of Wahhabis termed *Ikhwān* ('brethren', p. 286). The periodic wanderings of nomads are dealt with below (p. 400).

RACIAL AND ETHNIC ELEMENTS

The greater part of Arabia is peopled by a branch of the Mediterranean race. Its northern ethnic frontier is not the present political boundary but a line skirting the southern edge of the 'Fertile Crescent'. In Arabia north of the Rub' al Khali, Nejd, with a mixed population of pastoral nomads and much less numerous settled cultivators, forms a natural unit with the tribesmen of Transjordan and the Syrian desert; such tribes as the Ruwalla and the Shammar are also included in northern Arabia. In the Hejaz the population is largely sedentary, living partly by agriculture and partly by trade, and drawing much wealth from the annual multitudes of pilgrims. The highlands of 'Asīr and the Yemen are populated by settled cultivators and townsfolk, though the high plateaux taper off gradually into pastoral country on the north and east. The Hadhramaut has a varied population with at least four ethnic elements: (*a*) beduin, living in the side valleys, of partly non-Mediterranean Veddoid stock (*below*), with only borderline affiliation to the 'white' races; (*b*) tribesmen of the Wadi Hadhramaut proper, tracing their ancestry to the Yemen and other parts of Arabia; (*c*) an artisan class of varied ancestry; (*d*) the aristocracy of Seiyids, direct descendants of the Prophet. In the north-eastern corner of the Aden Protectorate, beyond Wadi Hadhramaut, lies Mahra-land; here, and in Dhufār and other adjacent parts of the Sultanate of 'Omān, as well as in Socotra island, dwell the Mahra, Qara, Shahara, and other non-Arab tribes, speaking pre-Arabic Semitic languages. The origin of the non-Mediterranean peoples in south Arabia is obscure; culturally the Veddoid peoples have primitive traits relating them, on the one hand, to the aboriginal Australians and Veddas, on the other hand to the cattle-breeding Todas in India and Bantu in east Africa.

South-west Arabia has also an ancient community of Jews, estimated at 100,000, the distribution of whom is mentioned below (p. 391).

There are more or less isolated ancient communities of African origin probably dating from the period of Abyssinian domination, such as *Hajūr* ('Hujeris') of the southern Yemen and the *Subiān* of the western Hadhramaut. Somalis and Indians live in several of the larger ports, e.g. about 10,000 Somalis and a community of Parsis in Aden. The population of the ports and holy cities of the Hejaz is also very mixed. Some Turks have remained, either in commerce or as officers of the kings of Sa'ūdi Arabia and of the Yemen. The racial affinities of the south-west have been further complicated by the introduction of many slaves from Africa, especially to the Hadhramaut, in recent times, and of a Malay element due to wealthy Hadhramis marrying Malay and Javanese women in the East Indies and bringing their sons to the homeland.

On the shores of the Persian Gulf are settled Jews from 'Iraq, arabized Persians, and Persian traders. 'Omān has also many Persians and Baluchis from the Makran coast; the latter have immigrated in great numbers and, by their greater industry, are ousting the Arabs of 'Omān from ownership of date-gardens.

In Sinai the population (estimated in 1917 at a little over 5,000) includes peculiar elements. Though several important beduin Arab tribes are now represented, at the Muhammadan conquest (c. A.D. 640) the interior was inhabited exclusively by Arabs of one tribe (the Aulād Suleiman) and by Christian monks and hermits. The 'Gebelia' (*Jebeliya*) or mountain folk of southern Sinai are descendants of slaves sent by the Emperor Justinian from Egypt and the Black Sea shores in the sixth century as menials to the priests. When the beduin later deprived the convent of St. Catharine of its outlying possessions, these slaves became Moslems and adopted the habits of Arabs, from whom they are now indistinguishable; the last Arab to die a Christian was buried in the convent garden in 1750. In the early nineteenth century the Gebelia still did not intermarry with the beduin Arabs, and to this day they provide the servants needed in the monastery. Some, such as the date-gardeners in Wadi Feiran, have become settlers, stigmatized by the Arab nomads as 'fellahin'.

The few Europeans and Americans in Arabia comprise the staffs of legations and business people in Jidda; medical men in the cities of the Yemen; the British colony in Aden and a few government officers in the Aden Protectorate; the British representatives, American doctors, and a few Portuguese in Muscat; oil-experts in east and south-east Arabia generally.

Physical Characteristics

The purest living representatives of the Mediterranean race of 'white' men, without admixture of the Alpine and other elements present in northern Europe, form a zone extending from Spain through north Africa to Arabia, parts of 'Iraq and the Persian highlands, across Afghanistan into India, and throwing a branch south along both sides of the Red Sea to southern Arabia, the Ethiopian highlands, and the horn of east Africa. In this zone of comparative racial simplicity the brunet Mediterranean race exists in several regional sub-races, believed to be of unsullied *Homo sapiens* stock, complicated only in the mountains of north-west Africa by survivals derived possibly from an older species. The most characteristic and highly evolved sub-race is the central, moderate-sized, Mediterranean type, best exemplified skeletally by the predynastic Egyptians, and found living to-day in greatest purity in Arabia.

The *'Mediterraneans'*, the Arabs proper, have hitherto been most thoroughly examined in south-west Arabia. Out of 1,500 adult males, some 400 inhabitants of the high plateaux of the Yemen showed an average stature of 164 cm. (5 ft. 4½ in.). Yemeni highlanders are usually slightly built, with skin from sallow to dark brown and high-bridged noses, convex to straight in profile; nearly beardless, with hair thick and wavy, sometimes hanging in long open curls. The head is intermediate in form between those of extremely long-headed and short-headed peoples, a condition termed 'mesocephalic'; it protrudes at the back and in general shape resembles the heads of Nordic races, though the average measurements are considerably smaller.

Head-hair is nearly always black, but beard (when present at all, and then with bare patches between moustache and chin) was of various brown or red shades in a considerable proportion of the men examined. Eyes are usually dark brown, green-brown is frequently found, but black or light brown are in a minority. Lips are moderately thick, the chin is moderately prominent. Eyebrows are medium to very thick, but brow-ridges slight. Many of these characteristics, especially the moderate degree of development of various features, are considered marks of the pure Mediterranean race. Southern

'Iraqis, for instance, among whom there is a strong Irano-Afghan, as well as an Atlanto-Mediterranean element, are on the average taller, with larger faces, straighter hair, heavier beards, more prominent and thicker-tipped noses, and heavier brow-ridges than the Arabs of the Arabian peninsula; while the men of Kuweit seem, in several of these respects, more closely related to the 'Iraqis.

The gipsy-like *Solubba* (p. 408) are the purest Mediterranean group in north Arabia, conforming in several physical characteristics to the standard of the Yemen highlanders (photo. 162).

Representatives of the Atlanto-Mediterranean type, very long-headed, long-faced and bearded, are found in the Yemen as tribal and village sheikhs, army officers, &c.; the purest centre of this race is probably in northern Arabia, but its members have yet to be studied (photos. 161, 164). The *seiyids*, acknowledged descendants of the Prophet, are lighter complexioned than their neighbours; a Nordic strain may have become blended with some of these noble families.

Members of certain old families in the Hejaz, medium to tall, broad-shouldered and tending to heavy weight, with large heads, short, or mesocephalic, constitute an Alpine-looking type of uncertain origin, but not purely Mediterranean. The population of the Hejaz cities may be less than half Arab, though the extremely mixed extraneous elements have so far blended little with the indigenous people.

The physical character of the nomadic peoples of central and north Arabia has been comparatively little investigated. Measurements of 270 Ruwalla tribesmen gave an average stature of 162 cm. (a little under 5 ft. 3 in.), showing them to be shorter than Yemenis; but other beduin, such as the Shammar, are taller. The heads of the Ruwalla average slightly longer than among the Yemenis, and their faces are very narrow, though there is a coarser type with broader face and straight, rather broad, nose, as well as the less numerous narrower-faced, hawk-profiled type of Arabian aristocrat (photo. 160). Incipient blondism found in 25 per cent. of the Yemeni highlanders examined occurs also in northern tribes in varying proportions, less in the Ruwalla. On the whole several of these tribes present Mediterranean characteristics.

Non-Mediterranean *Veddoids* live as a minority in parts of the southern Yemen and the Western Aden Protectorate; in the Hadhramaut they become numerically important, while still farther east they are the chief factor in the tribes of Mahra-land, at the extreme end of the Aden Protectorate, and the Shahara, Qara, and other tribes in the Sultanate of 'Omān (photos. 174–177). All these latter

159. *High-class woman of the Ruwalla*

160. *Amīr Nūri ibn Sha'lān, chief of the Ruwalla*

161. *A sheikh of the Bishr-'Aneiza*

162. *Ralib ibn Tulihan, chief of the Solubba gipsies*

163. *Boys of the Yemen highlands*

164. *Long-headed type of Yemen highland official*

165. *Jewish boy at San'ā*

tribes speak pre-Arabic Semitic languages. Veddoids decline in numbers in the 'Omān peninsula, but reappear in the Persian Makran and southern Baluchistan. The Veddoid race, including apparently both long- and short-headed varieties, and believed to be a major division of mankind, has many extensions south-eastward, existing as substrata among the peoples of the East Indian islands. It is uncertain whether the Veddoid element in Arabia is older than the Mediterranean, and whether its arrival in the country in prehistoric times is associated with the introduction of the little humped cattle from south-eastern Asia. The Qara mountaineers of Dhufār have a distinct tradition, borne out by present customs, that they came from overseas. As the tribes of Dhufār and adjacent districts can scarcely be dissociated from the non-Arabic tongues which they speak, further particulars of individual tribes are given under 'Language' (pp. 374 ff.).

Excluding blendings with Arabs of Mediterranean stock, the south Arabian Veddoids comprise a finer type, lean-bodied and hook-nosed, and a coarser type, thicker set and broader-nosed. The finer type is more numerous from Aden eastward to the confines of Mahra-land; in the latter country, and eastward among the speakers of non-Arabic tongues, the Mahra and Qara are mostly of the fine Veddoid type, the Shahara mostly of the coarse; all cultural data indicate the Shahara as a primitive local people. The coarse type seems clearly related to the Vedda of Ceylon, from which the race takes its name, and to elements in the Dravidian-speaking peoples of southern India.

Veddoids are slightly shorter than Mediterraneans, with relatively longer arms and legs, and smaller heads in which short-headedness reaches its highest degree. The skin, ranging from light to chocolate brown, is definitely darker than that of 'white' men, even in its unexposed parts. Hair is curly or wavy, not negroid; beard sparse in the fine type, heavier in the coarse; hair and beard black, except in the fine type, where perhaps one brown or red beard appears in ten, together with a few brown heads. Eyes are usually black or dark brown, with a few grey or green, which are more numerous in the fine type.

Jews were numerous in central and southern Arabia in the centuries before Islam, though their origin is uncertain. Expelled from the Hejaz during Muhammad's lifetime, they are now found in Nejrān and Jauf; in many cities and villages of the highlands and middle altitudes in the Yemen; in the Western Aden Protectorate they form a small community at Dhāla' and in the neighbouring villages; and in the district of Habbān, in the western part of the Eastern Aden Protectorate; but not usually near the coast. They form isolated enclaves, living apart from the Arabs, either in walled ghettoes, as at San'ā, or in separate clusters of houses adjacent to the smaller towns and villages. City Jews are short, slender, of light complexion, with black hair and dark brown eyes (photo. 165); wealthier families include people of particularly slender build, with small hands and feet, and very narrow heads in which, in profile, the forehead has a sweeping curve, the face is long and narrow, the nose very long, and the lips thin. Country Jews are darker and usually more heavily built, with short straight noses and thick convergent eyebrows, while some men have bushy beards. As a whole they approximate in many ways to the Palestinian Jews. While the aristocratic city group look more typically Jewish to an outside observer, both city and country groups are distinct from the Arabs. Yet such blood-tests as are available indicate that south-west Arabian Jews and Arabs belong to the same blood-group, distinct from other groups in western Asia.

Negroids and Negroes. There are several ancient groups of negroids in south-west Arabia: (i) the *Hajūr* (plural of *Hajri*, sometimes written 'Hujeris'), denoting people who either came originally from Wadi Hajr, or who resemble its inhabitants; these are believed to be descendants of slaves imported during the Abyssinian domination of the Yemen in the sixth century and are numerous in the Yemen Tihama and the middle altitudes of the southern Yemen, but do not extend on to the high plateau; (ii) the *Subiān* (plural of *sabi*, a boy), for whom a like origin is claimed; their centre is actually Wadi Hajr, but they also live in settlements outside coastal towns such as Mukalla and Shihr; they are the lowest social class, either agricultural labourers or, in the towns, wood-cutters, water-drawers, and sweepers; (iii) the *Akhdām* (plural of *khadim*), who form the sweeper class in Aden itself, and are also found in parts of the Western Aden Protectorate and the Yemen.

Negro slaves have been imported in much more recent times, especially since the rise of the sea-power of 'Omān in the Middle Ages down to the present day. Many Arabs of central Arabia and 'Omān derive negro blood from their mothers. In the Hadhramaut the Governments of the Qu'aiti and Kathīri Sultanates are large slave-holders. At Qishn (Mahra-land) negroes are said to be nearly half as numerous as Arabs. They are also numerous in the Hejaz and in Nejd; in the latter some oases are said to be peopled almost entirely by them, every important family has its negro or negroid slaves, and negroids constitute an important part of a subservient class of blacksmiths (photo. 222).

166. *Amiri boy*

167. *Dark-skinned Amiri
servant-boy*

168. *Negroid girl from Lahej*

169. *'Aulaqi man*

170. *Kathūri*

171. *Yāfaʻi*

172. *Hadhrami from Mukalla*

173. *Armenoid type from ʻOmān*

The Malay element. In modern times many Arab traders from the Hadhramaut have married wives in Malaya and the Dutch East Indies; returning to the Hadhramaut, these Arabs take with them the sons of their Malay wives, though the wives and daughters usually stay in Malaya or the East Indies. This accounts for a partly Malay element in the Eastern Aden Protectorate. There also exists in the towns and villages of the Yemen Tihama a much older element composed of people short in stature, short-headed, with broad, short faces, broad noses and dark skin, traditionally supposed to be partly of Malay origin.

Miscellaneous. The *Somalis* have arrived so recently that they show little tendency to assimilation with the older inhabitants, but live usually in their own villages, keeping their own language and customs. The *'Armenoids'* of 'Omān, with lofty foreheads, long faces and aquiline noses, and the back of the head much flattened, probably owe their presence to a very ancient trade-migration from Armenia and Mesopotamia along the Persian Gulf. It is not attempted to describe the physical traits of these, nor of the modern *Baluchi* immigrants into 'Omān; nor of the *Persian* elements on the east coast; nor of the various *Indian* communities, in ports such as Aden, Mukalla, and Hodeida; nor, finally, of the foreign communities in some inland cities such as Riyādh, the population of which was estimated in 1935 to include Indians, Somalis, Sudanese, and Javanese, numbering about 200 out of some 9,000.

LANGUAGE

Semitic Origins

Though the term 'Semite' is not ethnologically precise, and the Arabs are mainly of Mediterranean race (p. 365), yet they, in common with the Babylonians, Assyrians, Hebrews, Aramaeans, and Abyssinians, are traditionally regarded as Semites on account of their supposed descent from Shem. The term has come into general technical use to describe people of closely related speech.

The original home of the Semites is still uncertain, but the most accepted theory is that they came from the Arabian peninsula, whence waves of Semitic peoples have been migrating ever since, thrust outwards by the natural poverty of the soil rather than by any progressive desiccation of the country; the theory of desiccation within historic times being scarcely tenable in face of ancient records, all of which allude to Arabia as an arid country. But another theory, based on evidence of similarity between certain of the north-east African Hamitic dialects, suggests an African origin. All that is certain is that there have always been movements of peoples in this area, due to the infiltration of the desert tribes into the settled lands during periods of drought, or during times when the surrounding territories were not held by a dominant Power such as Rome or Persia. Unfortunately lack of early skeletal material has made it impossible to determine the racial type of the first inhabitants.

The Semitic language has two main divisions, northern and southern, of which the former is subdivided into an eastern and a western group. The eastern is represented by Babylonian, Assyrian, and the later Syriac; the western by Phoenician, Aramaic, Hebrew, and Moabite. Southern Semitic consists of the dialects of south Arabia (Minaean, Sabaean, Himyaritic, &c.), Arabic, and Ge'ez (Ethiopic). Their scripts developed separately. The eastern group took over cuneiform writing from the pre-Semitic peoples of Mesopotamia, extending its use throughout the area from the Euphrates to the Mediterranean, from the eighteenth to the fourteenth centuries B.C. The alphabet of the western script was also based on cuneiform. The Phoenicians used a script considered to be the forerunner of the Greek and all other European alphabets. Herodotus (484–425 B.C.) regarded it as the precursor of Greek, while a comparison of the letter forms (e.g. Greek *alpha*, Phoenician *aleph*, an ox) suggests a common source. Whether the script of the Serabit texts, discovered at Serabit al Khadim in central Sinai near the turquoise mines, is a precursor of Phoenician is not decided, as it has not been satisfactorily translated; it is dated at earliest to the Twelfth Egyptian Dynasty (1990–1777 B.C.), earlier than the first known Phoenician inscription, found in 1923 on the sarcophagus of King Abram at Byblos and believed to be contemporaneous with Pharaoh Ramses II (1292–1223 B.C.).

The south Arabian peoples, Minaeans, Sabaeans, and Himyarites, wrote a fully matured script which, though still obscure in origin, may have developed separately from western Semitic. But the view is also held that the south Arabians were the inventors of the alphabet as a rival to the cuneiform and pictographic scripts of Babylonia and Egypt, which it eventually displaced; and that the Phoenicians, coming from the south, brought their southern alphabet with them, developed it on cursive lines, and passed it on to the Greeks. South Arabian had twenty-eight letters, the increase of five over Hebrew being due to a wish for increased precision in expressing the dentals and sibilants. It was written from right to left, although some of the oldest inscriptions were written *boustrophedon*, i.e. alternately from right to left and from left to right. The earliest inscriptions, believed to date back earlier than 1100 B.C., are often huge, carved in relief as well as incised. (Photos. 131, 132.)

The classical language of Ethiopia, Ge'ez, may have derived its name from the Ag'azi, a south Arabian tribe which crossed the Red Sea into Abyssinia. Ethiopian early literature and inscriptions, of which none have been found earlier than the first century B.C., are written in Ge'ez, which marked a return to the syllabic form, as the vowels were indicated by diacritical points.

The Arabs use a script of twenty-eight letters, developed from western Syriac. Its earliest written form appears in a trilingual inscription found at Zabad, south-east of Aleppo, and dated A.D. 512, and in the bilingual Greek and Arabic of the Harran, A.D. 568. There is, however, a third-century inscription in classical Arabic, but written in Nabataean characters. The earliest extant Arabic literature consists of pre-Islamic poems composed between A.D. 500 and 622; at first preserved by oral tradition, they were not written until Abbasid times, A.D. 750–900. The material of the oldest Arabic book, the Koran, was not collected and written until after the battle of Yamāma in A.D. 633. Arabic retained its case-endings, while Hebrew had already dropped its endings when these early Arabic works were first written.

Classical Arabic

Classical Arabic probably developed from a single dialect, which may have originated in east-central Arabia, and was later raised to the position of a common language, with rules defined somewhat artificially by grammarians. Attempts to elevate vernacular dialects into new literary languages have failed, and the grammatical framework of Arabic, as written (for example) in good modern newspapers, is identical with that of the old poetic language, a result to which veneration for the Koran has largely contributed. Though the Koran was written in the dialect of the Qureish, it was later assimilated, so far as vowels and orthographic signs go, to the classical language of the poets; but they did not venture to change the consonants originally committed to writing, even if these corresponded ill with classical pronunciation. The consonantal orthography of the Koran therefore remains the norm, which has largely given classical Arabic its predominance and wide diffusion.

The attempt to read and interpret the Koran correctly has caused a great development of phonetics and grammar, the former exactly defining the old Arabic consonants, while the latter has restricted the ambiguity inherent in Semitic tongues. These compare unfavourably in this respect with Aryan languages; for though many fine distinctions exist for nouns, enabling very abstract concepts to be expressed, development of the verb has been one-sided, and shades of meaning rendered in Aryan languages by simple auxiliary verbs are often left unexpressed. Arabic has, however, greater power of expression than other Semitic languages, for many subordinating conjunctions exist where the others have only simple co-ordination.

Other forms besides classical Arabic have existed from the outset, and the migrations and mixing of Arab tribes have doubtless caused changes in the spoken tongue. Modern Arabic forms cannot always be derived immediately from classical Arabic. To-day the language is spoken (partly side by side with other languages) in Arabia, 'Iraq, Syria, and Palestine; in all north Africa as far south as the western head-waters of the Nile and the confines of the Sahara, as well as some districts south of the Niger; in Zanzibar and parts of the East African mainland; and in Arab colonies as far east as the East Indies. It is also spoken in Malta (though Roman characters are used) and was formerly in Spain, the Balearic islands, and Sicily. Dialectically several separate regions have been recognized, but only certain differences in pronunciation of particular letters can be mentioned here. Thus the letter *jīm*, usually transliterated J, is sounded as G in Lower Egypt and parts of central and south Arabia where the familiar *jebel* becomes *gebel*; as GY in other districts of central and south Arabia; and as J (or Z as in *azure*) in Nejd, at Mecca, and elsewhere. Vowels may be heard sounded throughout 'the whole phonetic gamut', so that they have partly lost their usefulness in distinguishing between different forms. Diphthongs are differently sounded in different districts; e.g. AU (sounded in the north as in HOW) becomes a long O in parts of south-west Arabia, so that the place-name *Jauf* is usually sounded *Jōf* when applied to the oasis in north-eastern Yemen.

Non-Arabic Languages of South Arabia

These tongues, collectively known as the 'Hadara group',[1] and spoken by the Mahra, Qara, and other tribes forming part of the

[1] Bertram Thomas, 'Four Strange Tongues from Central South Arabia', *Proc. British Academy*, xxiii, pp. 231–331 (1937).

174. *Bureiki*

175. *Mahri*

176. *Qarāwi*

177. *Shahari*

178. *Pilgrims in the Great Mosque at Mecca*

179. *Procession of the Mahmal in Mecca*

Veddoid racial element (p. 368), are held to be a subdivision of the south Arabian division of southern Semitic. They are a still living branch of the tree to which the languages of the south Arabian inscriptions belong; in fact the twelfth-century geographer Al Idrisi stated that the Mahri tongue was a survival of the language of the Himyarites. These languages, possessing an interest out of proportion to the small number of people who speak them, are used in a belt of territory reaching over 200 miles, between 51° 10′ and 56° 20′ E. longitude, and embracing the Qara mountains and their extensions to east and west, as well as the bordering steppe north of the mountains. This area is cut off from intercourse with tribes to the north by the Rub‘ al Khali, and its inhabitants, with peculiar physiognomy and culture, speak four tongues different enough from modern Arabic to be unintelligible to an Arab visitor. The difference from Arabic is particularly marked in personal names and names of animals. A visitor accustomed to Arabic is struck by the frequency of lisped sibilants, lateralized consonants (resembling the Welsh *ll* in names such as Llanelly), and nasalized vowels (as in French *nom, matin*). The tribesmen are frequently bilingual to some extent, understanding Arabic as well. Their special languages are not written to-day, but analogies with other Semitic languages are apparent when spoken words are recorded in writing and looked at. A clue to their antiquity may be furnished by rude characters recalling southern Semitic characters, inscribed on archaic trilithon monuments in the area.

The four languages fall into two sections: (*a*) Shahari, (*b*) Mahri, Harsusi, and Botahari. The speakers of the two groups do not usually understand one another, whereas those who use any of the three component languages of section (*b*) generally understand a good deal of the other two languages of that section; this applies less, however, to Botahari than to Mahri and Harsusi.

The nine tribes using these languages are collectively known by the Arab tribesmen of ‘Omān as the *Ahl al Hadara*, a name the identity of which with Hadoram of *Genesis* (chap. x, ver. 27) has been suggested. Hadoram is there given as a son of Joktan (Qahtān) and therefore a brother of Hazarmaveth (Hadhramaut); these tribes and the Hadhramaut are in fact geographically next one another. In the following summary their names according to Arab usage are followed by those in the Shahari tongue in brackets; in the latter a sign like the Portuguese *til* (as in ĩ) represents a nasalized vowel, and a circumflex over a sibilant indicates a heavy lisped sound. The centre of all these tribes, *Dhufār* in colloquial Arabic, is *Ẑafūr* in Mahri, *Ẑafōl* in Shahari.

(1, 2) The *Qara* (*Ĭnharō*) and *Shahara* (*Ŝarō*) are settled tribes, both speaking Shahari. They live mainly in the Qara and Qamr mountains, are troglodytes, and possess the frankincense groves and large herds of cattle. To-day the Shahara are little better than slaves of the more numerous and prosperous Qara. If it be true, as tradition both among themselves and the Arabs affirms, that the Shahara formerly possessed all Dhufār but were invaded by the Qara, the latter presumably absorbed both the language and culture of the Shahara. To-day the Qara are the richest of all these tribes.

(3) The *Barahama* (*Bit Barām*) are a small settled tribe, also speaking Shahari.

(4, 5) The *Beit ash Sheikh* (*Inŝakht*), nomads in the steppe country, occupying Wadi Ingudan and the water-hole of Hanun (north of the mountains and north-east of Salāla), also speak Shahari, and may be of collateral descent with the Shahara. They do not raid, but suffer from raiders. The *Afār* (same in Shahari) are also a nomad tribe of the steppes.

(6) The *Botahara* (*Bit Bohōr* or *Bit Butuhōr*) are now settled along the shores of Kuria Muria bay, many being fishermen so poor that they cannot afford boats, but use inflated goatskins on which to swim to their nets. According to tradition they formerly possessed the steppes north of the mountains, but were driven east by the conquering Mahra. A probably dwindling tribe, they speak their own tongue, Botahari.

(7) The *Harasis* (*Bit Harsōs*), a small and dwindling tribe with menfolk numbering perhaps only about 200, are pastoral nomads indistinguishable in dress and culture from their beduin Arab neighbours, but bilingual, speaking both Arabic and Harsusi. The latter, perhaps a variant of Mahri, is a tongue restricted to themselves. The Harasis wander far inland, a long way north of the mountains at the eastern end of Dhufār.

(8) The *Mahra* (*Māhrō*), later invaders who (like the Qara) have driven the Botahara eastwards, are the most numerous, numbering many thousands. They extend from Jebel Zalaul and Ras Nus (west and south-west of Kuria Muria bay) westwards through the border-land of steppe on the north side of the mountains, reaching down to the coast at Jadhib and beyond. Though all speaking Mahri, their east and west wings are believed to have sprung from different ancestors. They have no paramount sheikh with undisputed title, though there is a certain head-man with unique prestige, exacting tribute from all but nomadic elements. The eastern Mahra are mostly

beduin, gathering frankincense in season; the western Mahra are mostly settled, many of those on the coast being fishermen, while a few are merchants or sailors.

(9) The *Bil Haf* (same in Shahari) speak Mahri, but own allegiance to no one. Like the Mahra, they extend far west of Dhufār. They neither raid nor are raided (like the Solubba of north Arabia). In their belts they carry a knife, not a dagger. They are servants of the shrine of Jauhari at Umm al Tabakh, where the Mahra make pilgrimages and offer sacrifices.

Religion

The religion of Arabia, the land where Islam arose, is to this day almost exclusively Muhammadan. The ancient Jewish communities of south-west Arabia, estimated at possibly 100,000 persons, constitute the largest non-Moslem body in a population of 6 millions or more. Hindus, Parsis, and Christians together number only some thousands, with very few exceptions confined to Aden, the Red Sea and Persian Gulf ports, and Muscat.[1]

The two main bodies of Moslems, Sunnis and Shi'as, are present, each being represented by several distinct schools and sects. Wahhabis are Sunni, despite their divergences from the main Sunni body. Zeidis and Isma'ilis are in origin Shi'a, notwithstanding their differences from the main Shi'a body and the close approach of Zeidi to Sunni ideas in many respects; while Ibādhis can hardly be regarded as either Sunni or Shi'a. The tenets of these several bodies are outlined below. In Arabia, however, Sunnis greatly outnumber all the non-Sunni bodies put together.

Certain of the smaller bodies, such as the Zeidis, a large minority, and the Isma'ilis, a very small community, have an interest out of

[1] About 1936 H. von Wissmann made a conjectural estimate of the various religious bodies in Arabia, as shown below. Since, however, this was based on a total estimated population of the whole peninsula of 8,800,000 instead of approximately 6,000,000, the estimate adopted in this book, von Wissmann's figures can only indicate the probable proportions of the religious bodies. His list is as follows:

Sunni Moslems	
Shafe'i, Māliki	3,750,000
Wahhabi	2,300,000
Ibādhi Moslems	350,000
Shi'a Moslems	
Zeidis (with some Shi'as of other sects) . .	2,100,000
Isma'ilis	150,000
Jews	100,000
Hindus, Parsis, Christians	17,000

proportion to their numbers; while many nomads, especially south Arabian beduin, and the primitive tribes of the south, display much ignorance of the Muhammadan religion in any form.

Islam

Islam (resignation) inculcates entire submission to the will and precepts of God, as revealed by Muhammad, last and greatest of the prophets, and as preached, according to his own teaching, by all the prophets since Adam. The dogmatical and theoretical side of Islam is termed *Imān* (faith), the practical side *Dīn* (religion).

The fundamental principles of *Imān* are expressed in the two clauses of the creed, 'There is no god but God; and Muhammad is the Apostle of God.' The doctrine of God's nature and attributes coincides with Christian doctrine, in so far as God is by both declared to be the creator, ruler, and preserver of all things, eternal, all-powerful and all-knowing, always and everywhere present, all-merciful. Orthodox Islam has, however, no doctrine of an Incarnation; Muhammad himself claimed to be no more than a man; Christ, regarded by him as the greatest prophet next to himself, is nowhere called more than a prophet and apostle, though His birth is believed to have been of a miraculous nature. As Muhammad superseded Christ, so the Koran superseded the Gospel. Yet Christ, according to Moslem eschatology, will come again to establish Islam everywhere, and as the forerunner of the Day of Judgement.

It should be recalled that, shortly before Muhammad's time, several men in the Hejaz were preaching the outwornness of the ancient pagan religion and the need for a return to 'the unity of God', with its implications. Judaism and Christianity had both penetrated Arabia (pp. 228–229). Such were the circumstances under which Muhammad was moved to teach his new faith, abolishing pagan idolatry on the one hand, avoiding the narrowness of Judaism and the corruptions of local Christianity on the other. His great veneration for the Hebrew patriarchs and prophets is traceable to the influence of a convert to Judaism, a relative of his wife Khadījah. He was far less influenced by Christianity and, despite his reverence for Christ, his knowledge of the New Testament is held to have been very slight.

Belief in angels is a prominent part of the Faith, the Muhammadan conception of angels, and of other aspects of the unseen world, being largely borrowed from the Jews, and through them from the Persians.

Besides angels, good and evil *jānn* (genii) are believed in (p. 236), the chief of the evil *jānn* being Iblīs ('Despair'), rejected by God for refusing to pay homage to Adam.

Belief is also held in God-given Scriptures, revealed successively to the prophets. The sacred books are held to have numbered originally more than a hundred, though only four survive, namely the Pentateuch, the Psalms, the Gospel, and the Koran, the first three in mutilated form. The Koran (*al quran*, 'the reading') existed from eternity in Heaven; traditionally a copy is believed to have been brought down by the angel Gabriel to the lowest heaven, in the 'night of power and destiny', in the month of Ramadhan. Portions of the book were, during a space of twenty-three years, revealed to Muhammad, at Mecca and at Al Madina, by Gabriel in human shape, or as inspirations direct from God. Opinions vary as to the length of the portions revealed at one time, from single letters to entire *suras* ('courses' or chapters). Muhammad dictated many of his inspirations to a scribe as finished suras or fragments, or they were learnt by heart by his followers from his lips. A year after his death the fragments, written on materials of many kinds, were, at the instance of the Caliph Abu Bekr, collected and faithfully copied, but with no attempt to arrange the subject-matter in sequence. A second edition was instituted by the Caliph 'Othman in the thirtieth year of the Hijra (p. 237), to decide which readings should be used in passages of which several versions existed, and to fix the text in the tribal idiom of the Qureish. Still no effort was made to attain continuity in subject-matter; the longest sura was placed after the introductory exordium, the *fatah*, and thenceforth the rest of the 114 chapters in decreasing length. The suras were not numbered in the manuscripts, but acquired distinctive and strange names such as 'The Cow', 'The Star', 'The Poets', taken from particular objects or persons mentioned therein. In some modern translations their traditional order is altered to attain a chronological sequence. Every sura is divided into verses (*āyāt*), which total somewhat over 6,000, and the book is also divided into devotional readings for use in the mosque and privately. The prose is of a well-known literary form in which the links of each sentence rhyme with one another, and the same rhyme is generally kept throughout a whole sura.

The principal doctrines laid down in the Koran are that there is one God, one true religion, and a Day of Judgement. Rewards and punishments in the future life, fully depicted, are exemplified mainly by stories from the Bible and the Midrash or Hebrew exposition of the Old Testament. Special laws and admonitions, particularly to *islam* (i.e. complete resignation to God's will), make up most of the book; these are almost all borrowed from the Jewish scriptures but, since the latter were known to Muhammad only by word of mouth, confusions in some of the Jewish stories have arisen. It is held that the Prophet's desire to unite in one the three chief religions in his country, Christianity, Judaism, and the primitive astral religion, can be traced in his original precepts.

Of the many thousand prophets sent at various times, more than 300 were apostles; six of these, namely Adam, Noah, Abraham, Moses, Jesus, and Muhammad, were commissioned to proclaim new dispensations, abrogating any which had preceded them, Muhammad's being the final dispensation. His teaching concerning the resurrection and last judgement, the state of the soul between death and resurrection, the various degrees of heaven and hell, and the predestination of good and evil, cannot be discussed here.

Dīn, the practical part of Islam, including the moral and ritual laws, places prayer, almsgiving, fasting, and pilgrimage as the four chief duties.

The five daily prayer-times are dawn, noon, mid-afternoon, sunset, and evening, though these may be modified owing to special circumstances, two sets of prayers being sometimes said together. Prayer must be immediately preceded by ceremonial ablution of the hands, face, ears, and feet, the use of dry dust or sand being allowed in the absence of water, while the use of special prayer-carpets, though not essential, is recommended, to ensure the prayers being said on a clean place. Prayer is accompanied by certain inclinations and prostrations of the body, a series of which is called a *rēka*, while the worshipper's face should be turned in the direction of Mecca, i.e. towards the *Qibla*, usually marked by the *mihrāb*, an alcove or niche in the wall of a mosque. The prayers themselves consist partly of extracts from the Koran, and, among the Sunnis, partly of *Sunna*, based on traditional teachings of the Prophet not claimed to be divinely ordained (p. 312).

Public prayers also are recited in the mosques on Fridays and are announced, like the daily prayers, by the *mu'edhdhins* (muezzins) from the minarets. Since Islam is not a sacramental religion, there is no priesthood in the strict sense. Public prayers are usually led by an *imam* (a designation with a more special meaning among the Zeidis and Shi'as generally, as explained on p. 385). The senior imam of a large mosque may be a *mufti*, or interpreter of the religious law, while the senior theologians collectively are *'ulema*. These, with the *mujtahids* of the Shi'a body,[1] collectively known as *ataba*, may be regarded as 'clergy'.

Almsgiving comprises both fixed legal alms, now abrogated in many places, and voluntary charitable gifts in money or kind, including distribution of provisions to the poor at the end of Ramadhan. As an example of modern almsgiving, many thousands of rupees were raised by private charity for soup kitchens, infirmaries, and assistance to refugees, as well as the granting of large sums for relief by at least one Arab state, during the recent famine in the Eastern Aden Protectorate.

Fasting from all food and drink, together with abstinence from smoking, the use of perfumes, and other worldly pleasures, is incumbent on the faithful between sunrise and sunset during the whole month of Ramadhan, a duty the more exacting when Ramadhan falls in the summer; the only persons excepted are nursing and expectant mothers, the sick and infirm, and soldiers on service; while the two last categories should fast an equal number of days at some other time. There are other fasts, but the fasting and mourning commemorative of the sufferings of Hasan and Husein in the first month of the Moslem year, Moharram, are less in evidence in Arabia than in 'Iraq and Persia, where the adherents of the main Shi'a body are far more numerous.

After Ramadhan, at the beginning of the month Shawāl, is the *Id al Fitr*, the festival of breaking the fast, lasting three days; sometimes called the 'little Id', the lesser of the two principal feasts of the year. The greater feast, *Id al Kabir* or *Id al Qurbān* (festival of sacrifice), begins on 10th Dhu'l Hijja and lasts three or four days, culminating in sacrifices of animals synchronizing with those performed by the pilgrims at Mecca.

Pilgrimage includes not only the great pilgrimage or *Hajj* to the holy cities, a paramount duty to be performed by orthodox Moslems at least once in a lifetime, and giving the pilgrim the right to the title *Hajji*; many lesser pilgrimages are made voluntarily to local holy places such as graves of saints (*weli*, pl. *auliya*) and prophets.

The Pilgrimage at Mecca. The pilgrimage proper, or *Hajj*, takes place only on the 9th and 10th of Dhu'l Hijja, the last month of the Moslem year, but the accessory rites constituting the *'Umra* can be performed at any time. Pilgrims usually perform the *'Umra* as well

[1] *Iraq and the Persian Gulf*, B.R. 524, p. 327.

though it is supererogatory for them; but its performance is obligatory for all others, even natives of Mecca, whenever they enter the
precisely defined sacred territory extending in all directions some
15 to 20 miles from Mecca and known as the *Haram*, a term which
in a more restricted sense means only the mosque enclosing the Ka'ba.
At specified points outside the limits the traveller, whether performing the Hajj or the 'Umra, must assume the pilgrim dress or *ihrām*
consisting of two seamless garments, one, the *izār*, hanging from the
waist to the ankles, the other, the *rida*, being thrown over the
shoulders. The head may be protected only by a sunshade or with
the hands. The instep must also be bare and sandals are generally
worn. The ihrām may be of any material except silk, the use of which
is strictly unlawful in Islam, and of any colour, though preferably
white; it must be worn until the Hajj or 'Umra is completed. The
muhrim, or wearer of the ihrām, must not use scent, cut his hair or
nails, shave, cut down any plant, or kill or drive away any harmless
animal; the penalties prescribed range from giving a handful of wheat
to the poor to sacrificing a sheep. Unless a pilgrim abstain from
sexual intercourse his pilgrimage is invalidated. The assumption of
the ihrām, like most of the pilgrim's acts, is accompanied by specified
prayers, one of which, called *talbiya*, repeated very frequently, may
be translated thus: 'Here am I, O God, here am I. Thou hast no
partner. Here am I. Thine are praise and grace and dominion.
Thou hast no partner. Here am I.'

The pilgrim is directed in the ritual, and generally boarded and
lodged, by a guide or *mutauwif*, literally one who makes another
perform *tawāf*, or circumambulation of the Ka'ba. The clients of
each mutauwif are recommended to him by their sheikhs, so that his
followers usually come from the same country. Tawāf, representing
the adoration of the angels round the throne of God, and performed
as soon as possible after arrival, consists in the pilgrim moving round
the Ka'ba seven times, keeping it on his left, and if possible kissing
the Black Stone. The pilgrim then drinks from the well Zemzem
in the court of the mosque. 'Umra is completed by the sevenfold
traversing of the distance between two raised points called As Safā
and Al Marwa, along the street known as Al Mas'ā, 'the place
of running' (figs. 41, 42). This act, called *sa'y*, represents the
distracted search for water made by Hagar, mother of Ishmael,
before her miraculous discovery of the well Zemzem. Afterwards
the pilgrim has his hair cut by one of the many barbers in Al
Mas'ā.

On the 9th Dhu'l Hijja the pilgrims attend a sermon on Mount 'Arafa, also called Jebel ar Rahma ('Mount of Mercy'), some 30 miles east of Mecca. The preaching ends at sundown and the night is spent at Muzdalfa, between 'Arafa and the valley of Mina. The following day is the *'Id al Kabir*, when the pilgrims throw seven stones at each of three pillars marking the places where the devil was driven away by the stones flung by Abraham, Hagar, and Ishmael. Then each pilgrim sacrifices an animal, usually a sheep or goat. He must remain at Mina at night until the 12th and, after returning to Mecca, circumambulate the Ka'ba for the last time, thus completing the pilgrimage (photos. 178, 179).

Many of the pilgrim rites are far older than Islam, but were adopted and given new significance by Muhammad. Since his time they have changed very little, and the *'ulema* have determined in minute detail how much variation is lawful. Under the puritan Wahhabis some practices, commonly followed by pilgrims but not strictly part of the pilgrimage, such as praying at certain venerated tombs, have been discouraged as superstitious; many commemorative domes and tombs have been demolished, but some have been preserved through the influence of the king.

The visits customarily paid by pilgrims to the birthplace of Muhammad at Mecca, his tomb at Al Madina and similar sites, are not strictly part of the pilgrimage and are discouraged by the Wahhabi 'ulema.

Other Rites and Taboos. The rite of circumcision is performed usually between the sixth and eighth year of age. Abstinence from all alcoholic drinks is enjoined and, though, largely under modern influences, many Moslems openly or secretly drink wine and spirits, very many strictly observe the prohibition, while some even taboo drinking coffee and smoking. Chewing *qāt* (p. 462) was not forbidden, for the plant was probably not brought to Arabia till centuries later than the Prophet's time. The flesh of swine, dogs, and animals that have died of disease is forbidden for human consumption; neither the flesh nor the milk of the ass are lawful, but horseflesh is not specifically forbidden. Animals must be slaughtered according to prescribed rules. Gambling and usury are forbidden. To prevent relapse into idolatry, stringent rules were made against the reproduction in sculpture or pictures of any living thing, a prohibition which has profoundly affected Moslem art; it is still observed by the majority, though not by the great body of Shi'as, particularly in Persia, nor by some Yemenis.

Sunnis

The Sunnis, so named from their acceptance of the *Sunna*, or traditional sayings of the Prophet as well as the Koran, are reckoned the orthodox body of Islam, acknowledging the first three successors of the Prophet, Abu Bekr, 'Omar, and 'Othman, as well as the fourth, Muhammad's son-in-law 'Ali (pp. 238–241); according to Sunni practice the Caliphs were elected, irrespective of descent from the Prophet. Orthodox Sunnis comprise four main subdivisions (*midhab*), not strictly sects but better described as rites or schools of religious law, according to their acceptance of the theological interpretations of one of the four great teachers, Abu Hanīfa, Mālik ibn Anas, Shafe'i, and Ibn Hanbal; the Wahhabis sprang from the last. In Arabia Māliki and Shafe'i Sunnis are computed to be the most numerous of these four schools of thought; in the south-west, Sunni Islam seems solidly Shafe'i, and certain places, such as Zabīd in the Yemen lowlands, are or were important Shafe'i theological centres. There is, however, much mingling of Moslem religious bodies, especially in ports; for instance, at Abu Baqara, a small port in the north of the 'Omān peninsula, may be found Māliki and Hanbali Sunnis, occasional Ibādhis (p. 389) from 'Omān proper, while the merchants of Persian origin may be either Shi'as or Shafe'i Sunnis.

Wahhabis. The origin of this puritanical Sunni body and of the first Wahhabi state is outlined on pp. 265–268. The name Wahhabis was given to the community by his opponents during the lifetime of the founder, Muhammad ibn 'Abd al Wahhab (1703–1791). In Arabia the members prefer to call themselves *Muwahhidūn* (unitarians) and refer to their system as simply 'Muhammadan'. They regard themselves as Sunnis of the Hanbali school, as interpreted by Ibn Teimiya (1263–1328), who in many of his written polemics attacked the cult of saints.

The general aim of Ibn 'Abd al Wahhab was to do away with all 'innovations' (*bida'*) later than the third century of Islam, though some practices which he desired to abolish, such as reverence shown to sacred trees, were not innovations but survivals from pre-Islamic times. Thus the claim of the Wahhabis to be Sunnis is clearly justified, for they acknowledge the authority of the four Sunni schools of law and the six books of tradition. Their founder's polemic writings were almost entirely against the cult of saints, as exhibited in the building of mausoleums, and their use as mosques and as centres of pilgrimage.

Strict Wahhabi precepts comprehend the following: all objects of worship other than God are false, and all who worship them deserve death. It savours of polytheism (*shirk*) to mention in prayer the name of prophet, saint, or angel, or to seek their intercession, or to make vows to any other being but God. It involves unbelief (*kufr*) to profess knowledge not based on the Koran, the Sunna, or necessary inferences of reason. But the system is said to have departed from that of Ibn Hanbal in the following points: attendance at public prayers is obligatory; smoking tobacco is absolutely forbidden and punishable with stripes; a proportion of alms must be paid not only on visible produce but on unseen profits, such as those derived from business transactions; merely uttering the creed does not make a man a believer, but further inquiry into his character is needed; the use of the rosary is forbidden and the names of God are counted on the knuckles instead. Wahhabi mosques are very simple, with little ornament; Wahhabi tenets have, in fact, greatly affected historic buildings in Arabia, and have resulted in the destruction of some monuments such as venerated tombstones.

Shi'as

Shi'as in general do not acknowledge the first three Caliphs, but only the fourth, 'Ali ibn Abi Tālib, husband of Muhammad's daughter Fatima, and a series of Imams descended from him. To the two clauses of the creed 'There is no god but God, and Muhammad is the Apostle of God' common to Sunnis and Shi'as, the latter add a third clause, 'and 'Ali is the Saint of God'. The designation Imam is used in a special sense, and an Imam is far more than a local religious leader (p. 380). The devotion of Shi'as to these Imams is based on a belief that the latter inherited the prophetic powers of Muhammad to interpret the will of God. But Shi'as are much subdivided into sects, not all recognizing the same descendants of 'Ali as Imams, and holding differing theories of the Imamate; some indeed hold conceptions almost, if not quite, amounting to incarnationism and infallibility.

The main body of Shi'as, the *ithna 'ashariya*, often called Dodekites or 'Twelvers', recognize a succession of twelve Imams, of whom 'Ali himself is the first, his sons Hasan and Husein respectively the second and third, while the fourth to the twelfth Imams form a lineal succession from Husein; the twelfth, Muhammad al Mahdi al Muntazar, is alleged to have disappeared into a cave at Samarra in 'Iraq (about A.D. 878), since when the mouthpieces of the main Shi'a body have been the superior clergy or *mujtahids*. The Dodekites are, however, far less numerous in Arabia than in 'Iraq or Persia, and for an account of their practices reference may be made to the handbook of 'Iraq (pp. 327–328).

Two bodies in Arabia of Shi'a origin, which, though relatively few or very few in numbers, are of great interest, are the *Zeidis* of the Yemen highlands and the *Isma'ilis* focused about Nejrān and at some points in the Yemen. A third body, the *Ibādhis* of 'Omān and Dhufār, can scarcely be classed as either Shi'a or Sunni.

The *Zeidis* are named from Zeid, a grandson of Husein, the third Imam. Zeid was slain about A.D. 740 at Kufa, after rebelling against the 'Omeiyad Caliph. After his death he became revered as a religious and political martyr, though his followers at first showed no cohesion. Later, two definite bodies of Zeidis, widely separated geographically, came into being. The first, near the southern shores of the Caspian, continued under a series of Persian Imams, not in lineal succession, till the twelfth century, when they ceased to exist as a separate body. The second body of Zeidis was established in the northern Yemen about the beginning of the tenth century, and has continued in the Yemen highlands to this day.

The Zeidis recognize the same first four Imams as do other Shi'as, namely 'Ali, Hasan, Husein, and 'Ali Zein al 'Ābidīn, the son of Husein. But whereas the bulk of Shi'as acknowledge Muhammad al Baqir, son of 'Ali Zein, as the fifth Imam, and his lineal descendants up to the twelfth Imam, the Zeidis recognize Muhammad al Baqir's brother Zeid and Zeid's son Yahya, and after these a series of Imams who are not Zeid's lineal descendants but belong to collateral lines. So far as ancestry goes, indeed, the Zeidi Imams need only belong to the 'Ahl al Beit'; they may be descended from either Hasan or Husein—the present Imam of the Yemen and nearly all his predecessors, the Rassid house, are in fact Hasanids. The Zeidis differ from the majority of Shi'as not only in recognizing Zeid but in their conception as to why 'Ali himself secured the office of Caliph, which according to them was due to his peculiar merits. Hence to this day the Zeidi Imamate is at any rate in theory selective. A candidate, besides belonging to one or other line of descent from 'Ali, must be an able soldier, brave, learned, pious, generous, and free from physical blemish; he should also stand forth publicly and claim recognition. The first of the Imams of Sa'da, predecessors of the Imams of San'ā, was Al Hādī ilal Haqq Yahya ('the guide to the truth, John'), grandson of Al Qasim ar Rassi, a descendant in the sixth generation from Fatima and 'Ali. The imamate is not invalidated by the succession

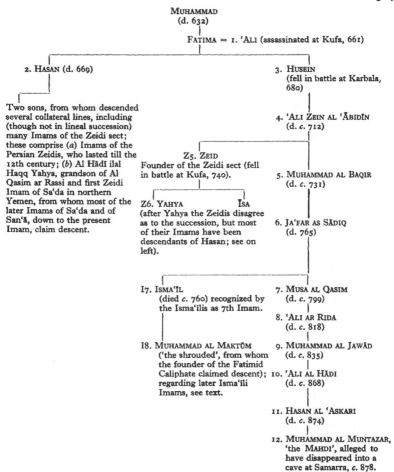

MUHAMMAD
(d. 632)

FATIMA = 1. 'ALI (assassinated at Kufa, 661)

2. HASAN (d. 669)

3. HUSEIN
(fell in battle at Karbala, 680)

Two sons, from whom descended several collateral lines, including (though not in lineal succession) many Imams of the Zeidi sect; these comprise (a) Imams of the Persian Zeidis, who lasted till the 12th century; (b) Al Hādī ilal Haqq Yahya, grandson of Al Qasim ar Rassi and first Zeidi Imam of Sa'da in northern Yemen, from whom most of the later Imams of Sa'da and of San'ā, down to the present Imam, claim descent.

4. 'ALI ZEIN AL 'ĀBIDĪN
(d. c. 712)

Z5. ZEID
Founder of the Zeidi sect (fell in battle at Kufa, 740).

5. MUHAMMAD AL BAQIR
(d. c. 731)

Z6. YAHYA   ISA
(after Yahya the Zeidis disagree as to the succession, but most of their Imams have been descendants of Hasan; see on left).

6. JA'FAR AS SĀDIQ
(d. 765)

I7. ISMA'ĪL
(died c. 760) recognized by the Isma'ilis as 7th Imam.

7. MUSA AL QASIM
(d. c. 799)

8. 'ALI AR RIDA
(d. c. 818)

I8. MUHAMMAD AL MAKTŪM
('the shrouded', from whom the founder of the Fatimid Caliphate claimed descent); regarding later Isma'ili Imams, see text.

9. MUHAMMAD AL JAWĀD
(d. c. 835)

10. 'ALI AL HĀDI
(d. c. 868)

11. HASAN AL 'ASKARI
(d. c. 874)

12. MUHAMMAD AL MUNTAZAR,
'the MAHDI', alleged to have disappeared into a cave at Samarra, c. 878.

Pedigree[1] showing relationship of the several series of Shi'a Imams. The Dodekites ('twelvers') recognize Nos. 1 to 12. The early Isma'ili Imams are numbered 1–6, I7, I8, the first six being identical with those of the Dodekites. The Zeidis also recognize Nos. 1 to 4, after whom they recognize Zeid and his son Yahya; it is said that some Zeidis also recognized Yahya's brother Isa, but there is not complete agreement as to the succession of the later Imams, who form a long series, all selected from different branches of the House of 'Ali, but not all in lineal succession. Dates are in terms of the Christian era.

[1] Full pedigree in H. C. Kay, *Yaman, its Early Mediaeval History*, p. 302 (1892).

having in early days passed away temporarily from the Rassid house, or by the occurrence of interregnums, usurpations, and the rising of pretenders, or by the deposition of an Imam and his subsequent

restoration. By the recent combination in one person of the offices of
Zeidi Imam and King of the Yemen, the imamate may tend to become
directly hereditary.

Despite the Shi'a origin of the Zeidis and their refusal to recognize
any spiritual leader not descended from 'Ali and Muhammad, they
are in philosophy and general outlook closer to Sunni Islam than to
the other Shi'a sects, so that they are often called, even by the Sunnis,
al Midhab al Khamis, the fifth orthodox rite. In worship and some
religious ordinances they display features in common with other
Shi'as. Though their tenets are puritanical, yet in architecture they
have developed peculiar forms, very beautiful and often highly
ornate.

The *Isma'ilis* seceded from the main body of Shi'as after the death
of the sixth Imam, Ja'far as Sādiq. Ja'far passed over his elder son
Isma'il on the ground of the latter's intemperance, and nominated to
succeed him his younger son Musa al Qasim, who was accepted by
the majority as seventh Imam. Though Isma'il died in A.D. 760 or
761, several years before his father, and despite his father's precautions to have the death confirmed, Isma'il's partisans claimed that he
was still alive some years after his father's death. Isma'il's sons,
involved in political persecutions, were scattered, and the later history
of the family cannot be discussed here. At present there are many
thousands of Isma'ilis, scattered in Syria, Persia and central Asia,
Afghanistan and India (possibly over 150,000); also in Zanzibar and
Tanganyika Territory. In Arabia there are many in the cities of
'Omān, with headquarters at Muttreh; a large focus at Nejrān; and
smaller groups in the north and central Yemen.

Owing to a disputed succession among the Fatimid Caliphs of
north Africa, whom they recognize, the Isma'ilis are subdivided into
two branches, usually called 'Eastern' and 'Western', the latter
termed *Bohoras* in India. The Assassins of Persia, 'Iraq, and Syria
belong to the Eastern branch, the Isma'ilis of the Yemen to the
Western. Isma'ili theology was greatly developed in Egypt under the
Fatimids, but late in the twelfth century, when it became apparent
that Egypt must submit to the orthodox Saladin, the centre of Isma'ili
propaganda was moved to the Yemen, where numerous copies of their
theological works were made. These Western Isma'ilis recognize
a line of twenty-one Imams, followed by further Imams who have
lived concealed. The number of the latter is secret, but there must
always be an Imam, since without him, according to their strange
theology, the world could not exist. Since the concealment of the

180. *Village mosque on Jebel Jihāf*

181. *The principal mosque at Dhāla'*

182. *The Great Mosque at San'ā, with local Ka'ba*

183. *Mosque and tomb of learned imam at Janadīya near Ta'izz*

Imams in the twelfth century, the head of the sect has been the Dāʿī ('he who calls', originally the director of missionary work). Though agreed as to the first twenty-six Dāʿīs, the Western Ismaʿīlis are again subdivided into Dāūdis, who recognize Dāūd ibn Qutb Shah (1591–1612) as the twenty-seventh, and Suleimanis, recognizing Suleiman ibn Hasan instead. The vast majority of Western Ismaʿīlis are Dāūdis, their Dāʿī living in Bombay or Surat, and adding to his name the title *Seif ad Dīn* ('sword of religion'). But in the Yemen alone Suleimanis predominate; their Dāʿī, known by his personal name alone, lives at Teiba in Wadi Dhahr, north-west of Sanʿā. There is a small minority of Suleimanis in India, whence pilgrims travel to the tomb of a Suleimani saint in the Yemen.

In the Yemen the Zeidis often call the Ismaʿīlis *Makārim* or *Qaramta*, 'Carmathians', probably a term of abuse, though their association with the Carmathians may have partly resulted from the domination of the Carmathian movement by the Ismaʿīli dynasty at times during the period from the ninth century to the twelfth (p. 257). The Ismaʿīlis have suffered persecution from the Zeidis in recent years. Many of their sacred writings, in some of which the names of Imams and other sacred personages are written in a secret cipher, were captured by the Zeidi Imam some forty years ago.

Superficially Ismaʿīli doctrine is very unlike orthodox Islam, and has absorbed elements derived from the metaphysics of Neoplatonism. God, who is without attributes, did not create the universe directly, but made manifest Universal Reason which created the Universal Soul, whose essential attribute is life. The Universal Soul produced primal Matter, and the combined action of five entities, Reason, Soul, Matter, Space, and Time, causes the movements of the spheres. When man, whose appearance is explained by the need of the Universal Soul to attain perfect knowledge, has attained thereto, all movement will cease. Orders in the human hierarchy correspond to these entities. Incarnate Reason (*nātik*, 'speaking') is Muhammad; incarnate Soul (*asās*, 'foundation') is ʿAli, while the ranks of Imam, Hujja, and Dāʿī correspond to Matter, Space, and Time. Despite their philosophy the Ismaʿīlis have no striking peculiarities in outward worship, and visit the ordinary mosques.[1]

The *Ibāḍhis*, in north Africa more often called *Abāḍhis*, were originally a branch of the Khawārij (Separatists) who separated from

---

[1] See W. Ivanow, *A Guide to Ismaʿīli Literature* (1933); E. Griffini, 'Die jüngste ambrosianische Sammlung arabischer Handschriften', *Zeitschr. deutsch. morgen-länd. Ges.*, vol. lxix (1915); 'Ismaʿīlīya' in *Encyclopaedia of Islam*.

'Ali when he accepted arbitration with Mu'āwiya (p. 241). They are named from 'Abdullah ibn Ibādh al Murri al Tamīmi, a learned doctor at the end of the seventh century A.D., about whom little is known, though their chronicles record that he lived in retirement, taking no part in the rebellions and excesses of the Separatists. Historically the greatest achievement of the Ibādhis was the founding of a dynasty in north Africa, where Ibādhism was introduced early in the eighth century, spread rapidly, and became the national religion of the Berbers and the pretext for a rebellion which nearly lost Africa to the orthodox Caliphate. The Ibādhi dynasty ruled for over 130 years, till overthrown by the Fatimids. Ibādhis still live in north-west Africa in compact communities, maintaining much ardour and fairly frequent communication with those of 'Omān and Zanzibar.

In doctrine Ibādhis admit the legitimacy of the first four Caliphs, but insist that Abu Bekr and 'Omar were the only impeccable examples after Muhammad; 'Othman is held to have fallen away, while they disapprove of 'Ali's actions for the reason stated above. They resemble Shi'as in being theocratic, but hold that the Imamate is not restricted to the Prophet's or any other family, but is purely elective, and may be suspended in the absence of suitable candidates. They emphasize that every Moslem must as far as possible enjoin good and reprove evil. An individual disobeying the religious law loses all claim on his co-religionists unless he perform an act of repentance, a system amounting to a kind of excommunication which may have grave civil and religious consequences. A slave may not divorce his slave wife, this prerogative being vested in the master. Only half as much blood-money is exacted from a murderer for an Ibādhi victim as for a Sunni, and only one-third as much as for a Shi'a. Usually Ibādhis keep their tenets very jealously, not mixing with orthodox Arabs except for commerce and rarely intermarrying with them. Strict Ibādhis are puritanical; in 'Omān, where Ibādhism is the State form of Islam, music is forbidden except for war and festivals.[1] They are very punctilious about ablutions, without which their prayers would be held void. Ibādhis in 'Omān will not drink out of a cup which a Christian has used, though a Shi'a tribesman in 'Iraq will often do so. They only smoke tobacco illicitly, if at all. The literate *mutawwa* (religious leader) has great power over the illiterate tribesmen. Ibādhi mosques generally have no minarets nor ornament, yet the

[1] Referring to tribes in 'Omān who use drums and pipes, an Ibādhi said: 'they are Sunnis; we Ibādhis forbid these instruments of the devil' (Bertram Thomas, *Arabia Felix*, p. 29).

184. *Turkish type of mosque (Al Bakiliya) at San'ā*

185. *Mosque at Ta'izz*

186. *Mosque at Qatn, Hadhramaut*

187. *Mosque at Seiyūn, Hadhramaut*

resemblance to Wahhabism in this is only superficial, for the bricks and stones of which they are constructed are of great sanctity; it would be sacrilegious to suggest removing doors or other fittings from a disused mosque to a new one under construction in a populous place. In the words of an Ibādhi: 'we are taught that, from a squat lowly mosque, screened from our eyes there continues up from its foundations a mighty pillar of holiness through the seven heavens.'

Geographically the Ibādhis are not found continuously over large areas even in 'Omān. Thus, in the Dhāhira district, west of the northern ranges and south of Sharja, the Daru are Ibādhis but the other beduin are orthodox Sunnis; and in the southern borderlands, north of Masīra island, the Yal Wahiba are a nomad Ibādhi tribe forming a wedge between a Wahhabi tribe to the north and a block of Shafe'i (Sunni) tribes to the south and west.

The Jews

The Jews of south-west Arabia, whose physical characteristics, history, and dress are mentioned in the appropriate places, keep their religious observances strictly. They have their own schools and synagogues, though the latter must, in the Yemen at any rate, be low, modest buildings, not vying with the mosques. The height of Jewish houses may not exceed two stories. In the highland cities and villages of the Yemen and the Western Aden Protectorate, the Jews inhabit separate quarters, divided from the Arab quarters by walls and gates as at San'ā, or at least forming separate clusters of houses either within or without the walls. There are also some small Jewish settlements in Wahidi territory, in the western part of the Eastern Aden Protectorate; but the Hadhramaut proper remains closed to Jews, as it is a holy land, containing the tomb of the Prophet Hūd. In the Aden Protectorate Jews cannot own land, but in some districts they are exempt from taxation. Jews cannot be the subject of blood feuds.

Some highland villages are mainly Jewish, while others have few or no Jewish inhabitants. A detailed list of Jewish settlements in the north and central Yemen, published in 1934,[1] shows that the distribution of these settlements closely coincides with that of the Zeidi Moslems. The Zeidis are tolerant towards Jews, of whom few live in the lowland Shafe'i districts.

[1] No list of settlements in the southern Yemen could be obtained; Rathjens and von Wissmann, *Süd-Arabien Reise*, iii, pp. 133–136 (1934).

The Imam of the Yemen holds the Chief Rabbi or *Khakhām Bāshi* (Arabic form of the Turkish title) responsible for all Jewish taxes, thus following the old Turkish precedent of making the head of a religious community responsible for its affairs. The special laws prohibiting Jews from carrying arms or riding horses, and regulating their dress and manufacture of wine, are mentioned on p. 336. Otherwise Jews may follow any occupation, and much craftsmanship, such as fine metal-work, window-tracery, and certain kinds of embroidery, is almost entirely in their hands. Besides possessing many ancient scriptural manuscripts written in the Hebrew language and characters, they have also for more than a thousand years used Hebrew characters when writing in Arabic.[1] Their dances and other customs differ from those of the Arabs; on festal occasions bearded Jews sometimes dance together slowly and decorously, to the accompaniment of chants led by rabbis.

In modern Sa'ūdi Arabia there are no Jews. The existence of Jewish colonies in the Hejaz in pre-Islamic times may explain the tradition that the people of Kheibar were once Jews, whence *Yahūd Kheibar* was formerly a term of opprobrium. A Jewish colony exists at Aden itself, and there are small colonies at Kuweit and Bahrein. It has been said that the Beni Shameili tribe of Trucial 'Omān were originally Jews.

Religious Buildings

The word 'mosque' is derived from *masjid*, a place of prostration or prayer, the only name used for these buildings in the Koran and during the earliest centuries of Islam. But about the tenth century A.D. the term *jami'* came into use; it signifies literally 'the collector' or 'combiner', one of the names of God, and, as applied to mosques, the *masjid jami'* denotes the great mosque of a town in which the public prayers on Friday are held. A distinction has thus grown up between the *jami'* and mosques of a lesser rank, used principally for private devotion by those living near by. The great mosques of Mecca and Al Madina, however, retain the older name and are sometimes designated simply by the dual number, Al Masjidān, 'the two mosques'. A brief description of them is given with their cities on pp. 560, 563.

The development of mosque architecture was influenced by pre-Islamic buildings of several types; in south Arabia almost certainly by

---

[1] e.g. the Arabic text of Hayyim Habshush, *Travels in Yemen*, ed. S. D. Goitein (1941).

the form of the pre-Islamic temples, in more northern Islamic lands by that of early Christian basilicas. The simplest form consists of a rectangular open courtyard (sahan), surrounded by arcades (riwāq) covered by a flat roof (saqf), resting on arches (tāq) supported by columns or pillars ('āmūd, rukn) of stone or brick. On the side facing Mecca (the qibla) the arcade is broader than on the other three sides, to accommodate a large number of worshippers; this broader arcade, containing the mihrāb or niche (p. 380), is called al īwān al qibli, colloquially shortened to līwān qibli or simply līwān. Usually a mosque has only one mihrāb, an alcove in the inner surface of the wall, not as a rule marked by any projection outside the mosque, though in some cases it projects as a small apse, roofed by a half-dome. The Haram at Al Madina, however, has five mihrābs, one in the outer wall and four others built against pillars or partition walls (fig. 44); these have special historical associations, and form, as it were, separate chapels in the mosque, before which a devotee may perform his devotions on successive days or during successive weeks; the favourite one is the Mihrāb an Nabi, the Prophet's mihrāb. The only mosque with no mihrāb is the Haram at Mecca, where none is necessary, since the worshippers gaze on the Ka'ba itself; there the arcades on all four sides of the vast enclosure are of approximately equal breadth, since the worshippers all face the centre of the mosque (fig. 42).

The arches surrounding the courtyard are semicircular in some of the oldest mosques, e.g. the Great Mosque at San'ā, but pointed arches were constructed at an early date, and later the characteristic horseshoe-shaped Saracenic type was developed; those in the Haram at Al Madina are slightly horseshoe-shaped. The flat roofs were also frequently replaced wholly or in part by larger or smaller cupolas (photo. 314).

In south Arabia, at any rate, the form of early Christian churches appears to have affected the plan of the older mosques but little; for, though sculptured stones probably from Abraha's great church of San'ā are incorporated in the Great Mosque, the latter building, constructed in or very soon after the Prophet's lifetime and altered and enlarged from the eighth to the twelfth centuries, is of simple, primitive plan. Farther north, and notably where Christian architects or builders were employed, the plan of the early basilica has probably influenced that of the mosque more. By enlargement of the courtyard in front of a basilica, and reduction of the part corresponding to the body of the church, an approximation to the primitive mosque-plan is brought about. Moreover, after the conversion of St. Sophia in

Constantinople from a church to a mosque in the fifteenth century, the Turks built other mosques which were strongly influenced by the Byzantine style. In some the space corresponding to the open court is roofed by a large cupola as at St. Sophia, or other important parts of the building may be roofed by large domes. This has resulted in Arabia in the erection of the famous green dome over the Prophet's *hujra* in the Haram at Al Madina, soaring far higher than the many small cupolas roofing the colonnades; also of some almost purely Turkish buildings such as the Bakiliya and Mahdi 'Abbās mosques at San'ā, built by the Turks after their conquest of the Yemen in the sixteenth century. Several large mosques were reconstructed by the Turks at Ta'izz at the same period; and the Turks built the mosque of Ibrahim Pasha at Hofūf, which was named not after the conqueror of the first Wahhabi power in 1818, but after an earlier Turkish governor of Al Hasa. All these contrast markedly with mosques built in the native Arabian style. (Photos. 184, 185, 314, 319.)

The name 'minaret' (Ar. *manāra, manārat*; the place of light) is applied to towers built by Moslems, both for secular and religious uses. Farther east than Arabia they originated long before Islam, as watch-towers or signal-towers on caravan-routes. Even in Arabia, the numerous tall watch-towers at Hijla, north-east of Abhā ('Asīr), may be of this type; clay-built and circular, but reinforced with projecting rings of slates, they are now, from disuse under the present conditions of security, falling into ruin. When Islam spread to Mediterranean lands, towers to mosques may have been added from acquaintance with the towers of early Christian churches, the oldest of which were not bell-towers; later, galleries were added to minarets for the muedhdhins. The architectural form of early minarets is held to have been influenced also by lighthouses, notably the vanished Pharos at Alexandria.

There is no fixed number or position for minarets. In the south-western mountains small village mosques may have none; occasionally a large and imposing mosque has none, as in the Makhdabiya mosque at Ta'izz; but usually a small mosque has one minaret, while larger mosques have more. The Haram at Mecca has seven, that at Al Madina five, the Great Mosque at San'ā two. Various local styles and much diversity of ornament are exhibited by these towers. In the mosques at San'ā and other cities of the high Yemen, in particular, the minarets exhibit varying arrangements from the ground upwards, such as a quadrangular base surmounted by an octagonal stage, above which is a circular shaft topped by a projecting gallery, from which

188. *Shrines in Seiyūn*

189. *Watch-towers at Hijla in 'Asīr*

190. *Zeidi type of Minaret*
at San'ā

191. *An unusually tall*
Minaret at Tarīm

again rises a more slender octagonal stage capped by a graceful fluted cupola; and the surface of the brickwork bears intricate patterns in relief, picked out in whitewash. Some puritanical sects allow minarets to rise only a few feet above the walls, as in the mosques at Riyādh, while others forbid their erection altogether (photos. 190, 191, 325).

The 'gates' (bāb) of mosques vary greatly in number and position. In some parts of the Arab world the principal gate is a fine architectural feature (e.g. the mosque of Sultan Hasan at Cairo), but some of the most venerable mosques have many entrances, not always specially large or imposing. The Great Mosque at San'ā has nine gates normally open, with a tenth only opened for the Imam, and two others now blocked with masonry. The Haram at Mecca has twenty-four public entrances, besides certain others for special purposes. Small local mosques, however, have few doorways, or only one.

Of ornamentation it can only be said that, while the puritanical sects allow none or very little, even among the orthodox Sunnis and other bodies which permit ornament, the mosques are often plain and rough, with little ornament except round the mihrāb and the main doorway. Much depends on the building materials and the culture and prosperity of the local population. Some mosques are ornamented with calligraphic texts or conventional patterns of great beauty. The abstention from representation of human beings or animals, as tending to idolatry, finds few exceptions. In some of the older mosques of the Zeidis in San'ā, however, the minaret is capped by a metal dove, emblematic of an incident in the Hijra, when the Prophet was saved from his pursuers by the presence of a nesting dove in a cave where he had hid.

The courtyard of every mosque has a tank or fountain for ablutions. The pulpit (minbar), usually a wooden structure with a straight flight of steps, is generally in the south-east of the court; opposite to it, in large mosques, is a platform (dikka) raised on pillars and with a parapet, where at public services officials repeat the words uttered by the imam in the pulpit. The number of persons employed in the most important mosques is very large; thus, in the Haram at Al Madina, the imams, preachers, lecturers, muedhdhins, overseers, doorkeepers, sweepers, lamp-cleaners, water-carriers, and others number more than 1,000 men, a larger number than at Mecca. Though each receives a stipend from the endowment funds (waqf), many of the humbler grades pursue trades or businesses as well.

Libraries, academies, schools, and kitchens to feed the poor are often associated with mosques, and some of these institutions may be accommodated in special parts of the mosque itself. In fact the *madrasa* originated about the tenth century from private religious schools, later developed by Sunni rulers into official academies, which assumed the form of a small rectangular court surrounded by four large roofed halls, with houses for officials in the four corners. But to-day *madrasa* often denotes merely a secular school.

While ordinary folk are usually buried under low graves (*qabr*) marked by more or less rough stones, small mausoleums are built over the graves of important persons. The classical name for a mausoleum is *turba*, but as they are often surmounted by a small dome (*qubba*), the latter name is frequently used. Mausoleums of saints often become places of local pilgrimage; in the south-western highlands these shrines, frequently placed on mountain-tops and often near sacred springs, are sometimes colloquially called simply *weli*, a saint. Among the Zeidis these little buildings have no cupolas, but are flat-roofed. In some cases the word *qabr* persists, as in the case of Qabr Hūd, the tomb of the Prophet Hūd, in Wadi Hadhramaut (p. 226). Tomb-mosques originated from the practice of combining a mosque with a mausoleum, or building a mosque over an important tomb (photo. 183).

A *meshhed*, or place of witness, may be simply a walled enclosure with no part roofed in. The *Meshhed Sha'ūb* outside the walls of San'ā, where the Imam and people gather for worship at the Great Festival, and occasionally to pray for rain, is a large space surrounded by battlemented walls and with a low rectangular tower. Similar enclosures either exist, or formerly existed, outside other cities of the Yemen.[1] Small wayside places of prayer, adjacent to water-tanks, are in some cases marked only by a line of stones on the ground.

TRIBAL AND SOCIAL ORGANIZATION

Many class distinctions exist, and very numerous local differences, particularly in south Arabia, which differs widely from the north. Conditions also are changing fairly rapidly. In Sa'ūdi Arabia a centralized government has been developed during the past quarter of a century, and many places have been settled by the non-tribal Ikhwān. In the Yemen administrative changes have very recently been made, tending to obliterate the ancient tribal system, and parts of the Aden Protectorate have undergone the same process in varying

[1] For instance the enclosure outside the walls of Ta'izz shown in the right foreground of Niebuhr's panoramic view, and marked 12 on his plan; *Voyage en Arabie*, vol. i, plates lxvi, lxvii, p. 301 (1776).

192. *Ruwalla tribe in camp*

193. *The migrating tribe*

194, 195. *Camel litters*

degree. All these modern developments are dealt with in Chapter VI (Administration). Yet the basic social organization is still mainly tribal.

North Arabia

Though the following description is mostly drawn from one large tribe, the Ruwalla,[1] much will apply to others. The rank of tribal chieftain is hereditary in a particular house, but the member best suited by his mental and physical qualities is usually chosen, not necessarily the eldest (cf. the method of selection of Zeidi Imams, p. 386). Ruling houses may persist till they weaken or die out; chiefs of single tribes are not as easily overthrown as paramount chiefs of tribal confederations, whose authority may pass to another house within the confederation. A hereditary paramount chief without war-like ability may continue to direct external affairs as *sheikh al bāb* (sheikh of the gate), while the conduct of war is left to a man of courage and foresight, called *sheikh al harb* or *sheikh ash shadīd*, who may even be of different kin from the *sheikh al bāb*, and may eventually super-sede him, thereby combining the two offices again in one person.

The usual word for a tribe is *qabīla*, but *'ashīra* and other names are also used. The Ruwalla call themselves *qabīlat*, *badīdat*, or *'ashīrt ar Ruwalla*. They would not call themselves a *qaum*, though they would say that the *qaum* of a particular chief was encamped in a certain place; *jemā'a*, a collection of tribes obeying a chief's orders, and ready to hasten to his assistance, has nearly the same meaning as *qaum*.

The Ruwalla divide people in general into *hathar*, dwelling in permanent houses, and *'arab*, in movable tents. *'Arab al qabīla* are nomads of the speaker's own tribe; *'arab ad dīra* are nomads found in the borders of tilled areas, irrespective of tribe. *Hathar*, called also *ahl tīn* (dwellers in clay houses), also are divided into *qarāun* (sing. *qarwani*), who never leave their permanent dwelling, and *rā'iya* (sing. *rā'i* or *rā'u*), who, after sowing the autumn crops, move into tents and take their flocks to the steppe, returning to their houses for harvest in April or May.

The *'arab* consist of beduin and *shwāya* (or *shūyān*). As the latter own flocks of sheep and goats, they cannot go into the interior desert, since they must remain near water and in places where annuals grow;

---

[1] Much of the territory over which the Ruwalla roam lies outside Sa'ūdi Arabia, in Transjordan and Syria; but they are chosen as examples because detailed informa-tion about their organization and customs is available: see Musil, *Manners and Customs of the Rwala Bedouins* (1928).

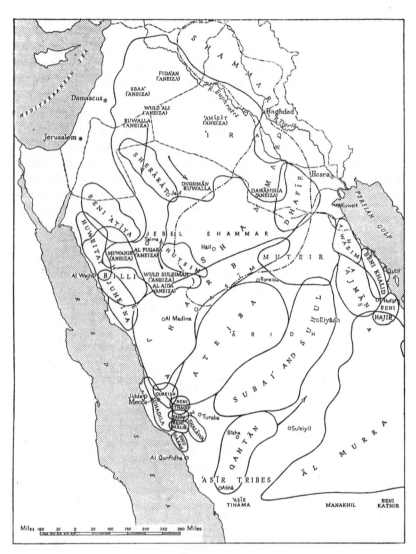

FIG. 38. *Tribal map of Sa'ūdi Arabia*

the *shwāya* are known as *ruhm ad dīra*, relatives of the people of the settled borderlands; they pay a tax (*khāwa*) to various beduin for protection, and if raiding (*ghazu*) is afoot they do not join in on a large scale.

The beduin in the restricted sense breed camels mainly if not exclusively, dwelling in the interior desert for ten months, and only migrating to its edge from about the end of June to the end of August, to provide themselves with grain, clothing, and weapons.

Under settled government the *ra'iyya* and *shwāya* tend to give up nomadic life entirely and become settled farmers. But some tribes remain true *ba'īdīn*, inhabitants of the *bādia* or great waste land; till recently, at any rate, the Ruwalla were universally acknowledged as such (photos. 192, 193).

This tribe, belonging to the northern branch of the large 'Aneiza group of tribes, exemplifies the great importance of close paternal blood relationship (*'amām*), which forms the kin or *ahl*. Much customary law depends on this; e.g. if a member of one *ahl* kills a member of another, the blood shed must be expiated by that of a member of the murderer's *ahl*. Paternal cousins are *beni al 'amm*; but rights of blood-relationship (*haqq al beni 'amm*) may, at a chief's wish, be granted to quite unrelated clans or tribes, members of which must then protect each other's neighbour (*qasīr*), guest (*dheif*), or fellow-traveller (*khawi*), even though he be an actual enemy.

Organization within the Qabīla (Tribe). The clan (and sometimes also the kin) is denoted by *āl*, a word generally meaning the same as *beni* or *ibn*, and having a wider meaning than *ahl*. A *fariq* (partition) or *ferīj* also has a wider significance than *ahl*, denoting a group of kindred descended from a common ancestor, and so having acquired the meaning of a nomad hamlet. Both *āl* and *ahl* are terms used in widely separated parts of Arabia, and in its broader sense an *ahl* is a group of distinct tribes united for mutual protection, e.g. *ahl al jebel* is sometimes applied to hill tribes, and *ahl ad dīra* to tribes who never leave settled territory. But the word, as used in a narrowly defined sense by the Ruwalla, means 'kin' in relation to an individual, so that the *ahl* of a particular man is not the same as that of his father or of his son, though the 'kins' of all these three have many members in common. A man's *ahl* includes his descendants and his forebears each to the third generation, and the descendants of these forebears also to the third generation. Descent in the male line only is recognized, and no collaterals more remote than second cousins are included. Consequently a beduin usually knows who his great-grandfather was, but nothing of his great-great-grandfather, while collaterals descended from the last named do not concern him, nor would they protect him, though they would protect his father, since members of a man's *ahl* will protect him from injustice or may suffer for his guilt.

Among the Ruwalla *ahl al beit* or *rā'iyat al beit* denotes the wife of a tent-owner (or of his brother), who has the whole tent under her control. Some tribes call the mistress of a tent *'ayla*, but this word may also indicate any family with a 'house' and hearth of its own. A Ruweili beduin in his own tent addresses his wife as *ahl al beit* or *ahl beiti*, and she addresses her husband as *rā'i al beit* or *rā'i beitana* ('lord of the house' or 'of our house'). A man's wife is not *ahl al beit* as long as he stays in his father's tent; but on the father's death, if several sons remain in the tent, it is known as the 'tent of the sons of so-and-so', or by their mother's name if she be still living.

Extent of Wanderings of Nomads in North and South Arabia. Beduin herdsmen cover great stretches of territory in their seasonal wanderings. There are, however, considerable differences between the tribes in this respect, and the roamings of particular tribes vary in extent with the rainfall in successive years. The great 'Aneiza group of tribes, regarded as the greatest beduin confederation of all Arabia, ranges over the whole steppe from the latitude of Aleppo to the Great Nafūd, and eastwards almost to Karbala. In some years certain of these tribes traverse eight degrees of latitude, spending May at their northernmost limit, and November at the southernmost. The great Beni Murra tribe of east Arabia is variously estimated to total 5,000 or even 10,000 souls; its eight sections, taken together, range from the Jafūra desert south of Hasa, between 24° and 25° N., southwards to Shanna in the Rub' al Khali, 19° N.; and from the central part of Ar Rimāl, between 50° and 51° E., westwards to Nejrān, between 44° and 45° E. One section alone, the Dimnān, roams the waterless desert from Maqainama, south of Jabrin, to Nejrān.[1] When raiding was a normal practice this tribe harried the route from Hofūf to Riyādh as far west as Kharj. These few thousand people live in an area the size of Germany, Austria, and Czechoslovakia put together, supported by water-holes sometimes covered up after use, to hide them from other beduin.

South of the Great Desert the Sei'ar, in the north-western Hadhramaut, are probably the largest purely nomadic confederation. Numbering some 1,700 armed men, they were, before the Truce of 1937, 'the wolves of south Arabia . . . a name of terror to their neighbours';

[1] Philby, *The Empty Quarter*, Appendix M, pp. 409–412 (1933).

they were elusive and wide-ranging nomads who, when outside their own territory, travelled in small numbers, by byways, and mostly at night.[1] Some of the cattle-raising tribes of south-west Arabia are, on the other hand, restricted to narrow areas and only partly nomadic; their other members are settled cultivators, and their nomadic elements travel no farther annually than some dwellers in the Alps. Entirely settled tribes in the Yemen highlands afford an even stronger contrast; some thousands of people may inhabit an area of perhaps 50 square miles. Parts of the Yemen and Hadhramaut are, indeed, over-populated in relation to the natural produce of the country, as has been seen in the recent famine.

The size of herds in proportion to the number of owners also varies widely in different tribes; e.g. while among the Murra a single individual may own several hundred camels, tribesmen of the Rashid, at the southern edge of the Great Desert, possess on an average only about five.

South Arabia

Most of the details available relate to the Aden Protectorate, but many apply also to the Yemen. The broad difference between these areas and north Arabia lies in the bulk of the population in the south-west having been, since ancient times, settled cultivators or dwellers in towns, while the areas inhabited by pure nomads are comparatively small. Distinct classes, and local variations of the social structure, are so numerous that the people are, for convenience, grouped under four heads: (a) tribal classes; (b) non-tribal influential classes including seiyids, manqads, and other townsmen; (c) subject classes; (d) mercenaries, and miscellaneous classes.

(a) *Tribal classes* include both settled tribesmen and nomadic beduin. Tribesmen, perhaps 70 per cent. of the population, include the governing class. All the ruling chiefs in the Aden Protectorate are tribesmen, though a few are descended from tribes other than those over which they now rule. With few exceptions (e.g. the 'Abdali Sultan of Lahej and the Qu'aiti Sultan of Mukalla) the chief is simply *primus inter pares*, for the tribesmen are full partners and the chief can decide nothing without their consent. Tribesmen are not bound to obey their chiefs, and in some backward areas each regards himself as his own chief. Moreover, every member of a ruling family may use the title of the head (sultan, sheikh, amir, or naqib, as the case may be) followed by his own name. Though some of the influential townsmen

[1] Ingrams, *Arabia and the Isles*, p. 189 (1942).

under section (*b*) have even wider authority than tribal chiefs, yet the tribesmen and these 'influentials' together form the local aristocracy. Settled tribesmen often own land, and those who till the soil themselves form a class of sturdy yeomen, ready to leave their farms and resort to arms when danger threatens; but unfortunately many tribesmen-landowners think manual work beneath them, and tend to oppress the subject classes whom they employ.

Some tribes are single, but many are grouped under paramount chiefs in confederations, called *zei* in the Eastern Aden Protectorate. There the principal confederations are the Seibāni, Nuwah, Hamūmi, and Shenafir; in the Western Aden Protectorate the most important are the Yāfa'i, Ja'ūd, and 'Aulaqi confederations.[1] Traces of the ancient pre-Islamic kingdoms and chieftaincies persist in the names of tribes, though these are not always the most important to-day, and some appear to have shifted from the central site of the ancient states which they represent. The Quteibi, central tribe of the Ja'ūd confederation, is held to represent Qataban; the Beni Ma'an tribe of the 'Aulaqi confederation, south of Yeshbum, near the eastern boundary of the Western Aden Protectorate, represents Ma'īn; while the Ma'afir tribe of the Yemen lowlands perpetuates the name of the 'Mapharitic' chief (p. 222). The name of the Himyarites persists in the Aden Protectorate in a group of tribes, which, though each having a distinct name of its own, all call themselves *Qabāil Hamyar*; one division, *Hamyar al Kubra*, is in Yāfa' (Western Aden Protectorate); the other, *Hamyar as Sughra*, is in Wadi Habban and Wadi Meifa'a (Eastern Aden Protectorate).

Certain tribal terms, not always corresponding with modern frontiers, are *Yemeni*, applied to certain tribes near Aden; *Jebeli*, various mountain tribes; *Mushreqi* or 'eastern', applied to an ill-defined district east of the Yemen.[2] Other terms used in south Arabia, but much farther east, are *Hinawi* and *Ghafari*, two political factions to one or other of which every tribe in the south-east owns allegiance. Superficially these seem to date from an eighteenth-century split over the succession in 'Omān, but their origin is really much deeper and may be racial. The Hinawi all claim descent from Qahtān (p. 213), while the Ghafari are non-Qahtanic stock, mainly *Ma'adi* or *Nizari*. The Sei'ar (p. 400) are reckoned as the westernmost Ghafari, while

---

[1] Most of these names do not figure in the list on pp. 361–363, since only a few are in direct treaty relations with the British Government.

[2] R. A. B. Hamilton, 'The Social Organization of the Tribes of the Aden Protectorate', *Royal Central Asian Journal*, xxx, parts 2 and 3–4 (May and Sept. 1943).'

the Āl Kathīr are Hinawi. Regional terms for the country westwards and eastwards of Dhufār are, respectively, *Ma'arab* and *Mishgas*; thus the Sei'ar and all tribes to the west are Ma'arab, although some are Ghafari and others Hinawi.

A tribe is called *qabīla* as in the north, but the names of the sub-divisions are somewhat different, namely *beit* and *fara*, corresponding roughly with clans and sections, each under its *'aqil* (elder). Primitive tribal law, which lays down rules for almost every aspect of life, and largely continues despite the attempts of such powers as the Yemen Government to supersede it by the *shar'* or Moslem law, is discussed in Chapter VI. The distinctive dress of tribesmen is described on p. 418; that they all carry arms is of itself enough to distinguish them from other classes. Only when a tribesman becomes a landowner does he tend to abandon the ancient pursuits of raiding and killing, and to seek security in ordered government.

The Mahra and associated tribes, not regarded by the Arabs as 'Arab', are mentioned on p. 376.

(*b*) *Non-tribal influential classes* have this in common, that they carry no weapons and, with few exceptions, cannot be the subject of blood feuds.

(i) *Seiyids and Sharifs.* It is sometimes said that these may be distinguished as descendants of Husein and Hasan, but no clear distinction seems to exist. The title 'sharif' is little used in south-west Arabia, the sharifs of Beihān constituting one of the few exceptions. Moreover, though women of this class are usually called *seiyida* or *sharifa* as the case may be, in the Aden Protectorate daughters of seiyids are all addressed as *sharifa*. Any legitimate child of a seiyid, even the child of an unmarried slave-mother, is either a seiyid or a sharifa. The seiyids of a large part of south-west Arabia claim descent from Seiyid Ahmed ibn 'Isa al Mohajir, who came from 'Iraq over 1,000 years ago.

In the Aden Protectorate seiyids still often act as paid arbitrators in disputes, though recently their power has lessened through the turning of the people to the newly organized Government judicature, and through the 'Irshadi movement started among Hadhrami immigrants in the East Indies. Large families of seiyids are divided into branches each under a *mansab* (p. 350), usually a recognized arbitrator, sometimes wielding more power than the chief of the tribe among whom he lives. These clans, however, are not territorial, but their members are widely dispersed in south-west Arabia; notable families thus scattered are the Āl 'Aidarūs and Āl Sheikh Bubakr.

Through their descent from the Prophet, seiyids generally rank higher than tribesmen. A tribeswoman is honoured if she marry a seiyid, but a seiyid's daughter rarely marries a tribesman and even then loses caste. Many seiyids are wealthy landowners. They expound religious learning and the *shar'*, and in the Aden Protectorate judges are chosen from them; in the Kathīri Sultanate particularly they dominate life and thought; they are largely reactionary, fearing diminution of their prestige and sources of income. After death many seiyids are regarded as saints and miracle-workers, whose shrines, guarded by their descendants, may own land and receive tithes. In San'ā and other cities of the Yemen, however, seiyids are largely idle, with little to do except attend *qāt*-parties (p. 462); their idleness results from the Imam's policy of installing his own sons in the highest administrative posts, and appointing men not of noble birth to other positions.

(ii) *Sheikhs*. This class must not be confused with ordinary tribal sheikhs, nor yet with schoolmasters and other townsmen with a certain standard of life and education who may have the title. The sheikhly class consists of clans or families among whom every member is entitled 'sheikh' or 'sheikha'. Possibly these families are successors of the priesthood of the ancient pre-Islamic religion. Well-known instances are the Bureiki Sheikhs of Shabwa, and the Ba Wazīr Sheikhs of Gheil Ba Wazīr, north-west of Shihr.

(iii) *Manqads*, a class of tribal judges, the principal members of which are hereditary, occupy a niche in the social structure, but, because of their judicial functions, are discussed in Chapter VI (p. 348).

(iv) *Townsmen*. This rather loose designation covers any tribesmen or other persons who have settled in towns and become occupied in crafts or trade. Besides this it can have special meanings, as in the Hadhramaut towns, where the townsmen are not indigenous, but mostly descended from about eighty families which migrated from 'Iraq at the same time as Seiyid Ahmed ibn 'Isa, ancestor of the local seiyids; many of these townsmen are now influential merchants. Men of this type are the chief link with the outside world, the principal taxpayers, encouraging municipal and other development, hardworking and enterprising, better educated and with a higher standard of living than most other people excepting wealthy members of the noble classes. Many small traders, artisans, and other townsmen in modest circumstances, follow hereditary callings.

(c) *Subject classes*. These may be grouped in four categories:

(i) *Ra'ya*, a word applicable in its wider sense to any class owning allegiance to a chief, though free tribesmen dislike being called ra'ya. In a narrower sense, the ra'ya in the Western Aden Protectorate and the Yemen form a distinct class of paid farm-labourers with no land or houses of their own. They are racially identical with the tribesmen but usually bear no arms and perform no military service; they may be descended from tribal sections which for some reason have lost their land. But the ra'ya have no voice in the election of their chief or other tribal affairs, and must pay taxes and obey the chief's orders. In bad cases they suffer extortion and oppression, and they tend to welcome ordered government. Besides agricultural labourers there exist merchants (*tājir*) and hereditary craftsmen (smiths, carpenters, masons, and weavers) who are ra'ya.

(ii) *Dha'if* or *dhafa*, and *heiq*; the former term is more used in the Eastern Aden Protectorate, the latter in the Western. These include small shopkeepers and artisans, wood-cutters, and drawers of water. They bear no arms and cannot be subjects of blood feuds. Their standard of living is so low, and their dependence on wealthy persons so great, that they are little better than serfs; owing to this dependence, many in the Eastern Aden Protectorate died in the famine of 1943–1944. The Qu'aiti Government is attempting to educate the children of this class.

(iii) *Negroids and negroes* have been mentioned from a racial standpoint (p. 370), but also form a distinct social stratum. The *Akhdām* are the sweeper-class in Aden itself, parts of the Western Aden Protectorate and the Yemen. The *Subiān* are also sweepers in the Eastern Aden Protectorate, but some of them, as well as the *Hajūr*, are agricultural or casual labourers, or fishermen. They have their own headmen, and their customs show a tendency towards witchcraft and phallic worship. None bear arms or are the subject of blood feuds. Their standard of living is very low, their dwellings mostly huts of brushwood (*'arish*), and they cannot eat or associate with higher classes. Scarcely any receive education, except in the Qu'aiti State. Here may also be classed the subject negro or negroid craftsmen of the towns of Nejd and the Hejaz.

(iv) *Slaves*, though clearly of the subject classes, often rise to positions of eminence; in some cases they seriously menace security as a powerful armed element. In parts of south-west Arabia they have an interest in the produce of the land on which they toil as ploughmen or water-drawers. In some cases they remain with the same family of masters for generations. All are of various negro types. Many live also in the households of important families in Sa'ūdi Arabia.

(*d*) *Classes apart from any of the foregoing*: (i) '*Askaris or Mercenary Soldiers*. In south-west Arabia these were originally tribesmen, who have lost caste by hiring themselves out to chiefs, and have become a class apart. Freed slaves often continue with their former masters as 'askaris. In the Western Aden Protectorate they enforce the collection of taxes and do other police-work, or act as bodyguards to chiefs. In the Eastern Aden Protectorate nearly all the 'askaris originated from Yāfa', whence they were brought by the Kathīris to help expel the Yemenis, but are now a powerful and sometimes turbulent body. The descendants of some have become important rulers. Many are traders or money-lenders, but now have the opportunity to join the regular gendarmerie.

(ii) *Doshans* and *Shadidhs*, though absent from the Hadhramaut States, are, in the Western Aden Protectorate and the Yemen, the minstrels of the country. They form bands of singers and dancers, either attached to particular tribes or roaming from place to place. They sing of the heroic deeds of the past, or praise important guests, or satirize enemies. A shadidh will even dare to lash his own chief and tribe with invective, if he consider their conduct pusillanimous. Here may also be classed wandering troupes of dancing-girls accompanied by male musicians.

(iii) *Jews*, forming a self-contained community, with several social strata of their own, have already been dealt with under racial and religious headings (pp. 369, 391).

DWELLINGS

Human habitations in Arabia are so diverse that it is only possible to indicate their manifold variety and stress their more outstanding types. The nomads dwell in tents, varying much in the degree of comfort which they provide; in south Arabia some nomads even live in caves or sheltered spots under the open sky. The settled inhabitants build dwellings from primitive huts of straw or brushwood to one-roomed houses of brick or stone, from which every stage exists up to the great mud-brick houses of the central Arabian oases, the stone tower-houses of the south-western highlands, the ornate mansions of the cities of the Yemen, and the skyscrapers of the Hadhramaut. Intermediate between nomads and settled inhabitants are those who live in houses during one part of the year and in tents during the remainder. Houses, moreover, are occasionally isolated, but more usually grouped in unwalled villages or towns, in the mountains often

196. Black tents in Nejd

197. Solubbi tents

198. Cave-dwelling in Wadi Dauka, 'Omān

199. *Tihama grass-hut*

200. *Mud-brick houses in Riyādh*

clustered round the castles or great fortified houses of chiefs, while the ancient cities are girt with towered and bastioned walls. As with social strata and dress, the diversity is far greater in the south, where separate valleys, ranges, and plateaux often have their own styles of building.

Tents and Nomadic Life

In a typically beduin tribe such as the Ruwalla, the famous black tents are made of strips of coarse black cloth (*shuqqa*), about 2 feet wide and from 36 to 120 feet long. Each strip is woven either of pure black goat's hair, or of a blend of cotton with a small amount of goat's hair. The weavers live in towns and villages, and the beduin buy the cloth either direct or from itinerant traders. An ordinary tent about 39 feet long by 13 feet wide, with one main pole, needs at least eight strips about 36 feet long. Besides the cloth, strips of coarse goat's hair and the poles have to be bought, as well as the ropes, which are sold by weight. In 1928 the cost of the smallest tent of heavy pure goat's hair was equivalent to nearly 30 American dollars; a new tent is needed every four or five years.[1]

A tent with one main pole is a *qatba*. Larger tents are apparently named according to the number of poles. A small tent, about 13 to 20 feet long, with no main pole but with the central part supported by four poles of equal height, is a *kharbūsh*. A still smaller tent or *tuzz* is sometimes set up for children only, when, on long summer marches, the adults sleep on the open ground; poor inhabitants of a camp, not members of the tribe, may also have to be content with a tuzz.

In making a tent, the cloth strips are sewn together with coarse goat's-hair thread by the women, a small board with a circular hole through which the pole passes being sewn in the middle. Along the edges are sewn strips of coarse goat's hair, at the end of which are leather loops for the ropes. The long, low back wall of the tent (*ruāq*) has its upper edge turned down as a hem, and a strip of inferior material sewn along its lower edge, and the shorter but higher end-walls (*ruffa*) have also pieces of lighter material attached to them. Several other parts have special names, including the ropes.

A partition hung across the tent and attached to the main pole divides the tent into the women's and men's compartments. The latter is furnished with pillows and carpets, while a rectangular or circular fire-place, about 8 inches deep, is dug so that coffee can be prepared for the men and their guests; the position of a chief's tent is

---

[1] Musil, *Manners and Customs of the Rwala Bedouins*, p. 61 (1928).

often indicated by the form of the fire-place long after the encampment has been moved.

The furnishings of the women's compartment are much more numerous, including carpets and sleeping-coverlets; sacks of grain, rice, dates, butter, salt, and coffee; spindles and looms; wooden utensils (pestles, mortars, troughs, plates, dishes, and large spoons for mixing food); copper vessels (plates, dishes, shallow pans, kettles); vessels of hide, skin, and leather, such as water-bags, buckets, and circular water-troughs sewn to a wooden framework. The women of the tribe weave the sacks and some of the carpets, tan the hides, and make the leather articles.

The male owner calls out to his sons, womenfolk, servants, and slaves the orders to pitch the tent, carry in the furniture, and dig the fire-place; but, when the tent is struck, the mistress of the house issues the orders. Tents are pitched with the back wall to windward, and in cold weather the open front is closed by a hanging wall. In hot weather the back and side walls are rolled up, and by their flapping act as fans. A tent is packed for transport by rolling it from both ends, with a pole near the top of each roll; the ropes of smaller tents are laid inside them; the nearly 100-foot ropes of large tents are tied separately. The tent is loaded on a camel with a saddle of special type (*mesāma*); women or slaves lift the load by the poles while the camel rises. The remaining poles, ropes, &c., are carried by another camel. At the head of the tribe rides the chief with his picked warriors (*salaf*) on camels, but saddled mares, tied to the camels or ridden by boys, are mounted if an enemy has to be pursued.

This brief account indicates a highly organized system of nomadic life, the main outlines of which have been unchanged for long periods, and a relatively high degree of comfort in the movable house. Other nomads, however, have a much lower standard. The gipsies (*Solubba*), who wander as tinkers among the northern beduin, being great hunters, sometimes have tents made of gazelle-skins and use horns of the oryx as pegs; they have few or no wooden utensils, but only leather ones, and use skins of asses and various wild animals in place of carpet and cushions. In south-west Arabia tents are used almost exclusively on the borders of the great sandy desert and in parts of the Mahra country, and are generally much less luxurious than those of north and central Arabia. In the Eastern Aden Protectorate many beduin live in caves or under trees; the women settle with their flocks wherever pasture can be found, build little dry stone walls as folds for the sheep and goats, and lie on the stony ground in as sheltered a spot as possible; the men join their families in these nomadic homes when not occupied in transporting goods from the coast to the interior or from town to town.

In Dhufār, the Qara tribes—though rich in camels, huge herds of cattle, and groves of frankincense trees—still build no cities, but live in the open under forest trees, or in caves or houses of hay; some caves are private property, passing from father to son. The villages of the Shahara consist of beehive-shaped straw huts, furnished with plaited reed bowls and a few pots for butter, honey, and water; larger buildings of undressed and unmortared stone are erected for the cattle in the more temperate seasons, but men and cattle shelter from summer rain and winter cold in limestone caves. The Shihuh of the Masandam peninsula in 'Omān are also troglodytes, living with their flocks either in natural caves or in artificial pits roofed with acacia-logs and earth, through which a hatchway opens to a flight of steps to the interior; these pits, called *beit al qufl* from the inordinately long door-key used, contain large water-tanks, and enable their recluse owners to disappear from sight for considerable periods.[1]

Permanent Houses

The most primitive houses fall into two categories: circular or rectangular huts of thatch, matting, or straw, and one-roomed houses of mud, brick, or stone.

Huts (*'arīsh*) in many parts of south-west Arabia are square or rectangular, with a framework of tree-trunks and branches—datepalm trunks being used in the more elaborate—and covered with palm-leaves, brushwood, matting, or any material available. In the towns of the Aden Protectorate most fishermen inhabit such dwellings as well as agricultural labourers, coolies, and other people of the poorest class; in the coastal plain and foothills of the Western Aden Protectorate some tribal villages consist almost entirely of these oneroomed houses; the floor is covered with a mat, sometimes both floor and walls are mud-plastered; there is often a small fenced compound in which cooking is done, animals are kept, and guests can stay.

Circular huts with conical roofs are found in parts of the coastal plain in Subeihi territory (e.g. Wadi Ma'ādin, about 50 miles westnorth-west of Aden) and especially in the Tihama of the Yemen and 'Asīr; thus at Jīzān the poorer folk, mostly fishermen, live in round huts with walls of *dhura*-stalks lined with clay, often 2 feet thick; the raised floor is of clay, with a hearth in which are holes of several sizes

[1] Bertram Thomas, *Alarms and Excursions in Arabia*, pp. 225–231 (1931).

for the cooking utensils; the walls are often painted with coloured arabesques and hung with mats, platters, hats, bowls, and baskets plaited by the women from dyed grass; furniture consists of couches on wooden frames, in which the seat consists of plaited dūm-palm leaves covered with mats and carpets or, in the inland districts, with sheepskins. Some groups of these huts are surrounded by zaribas of thorny brushwood, enclosing a compound in which stand huge earthenware jars used as food-stores. The aspect of these huts is very African, and their inhabitants frequently have African racial affinities. In the Subeihi coastal plain the huts of matting are more comparable with tents, being only used as sleeping-quarters, shared with goats and fowls, and furnished only with rush mats and a few cushions.

Most of the poorer people of the coastal towns of 'Omān live in oblong huts with walls constructed mainly of the midribs of date-palm leaves, and thatched roofs with projecting eaves.

In the southern Red Sea ports, in particular, huts of matting or thatch stand cheek by jowl with large houses. In the suburbs outside the walls of Hodeida several oblong straw buildings with high-pitched thatch roofs often form a single unit with one large stone house, to which they are linked by tall wickerwork fences; the whole group outwardly resembles a country house with its outbuildings.

Houses of Mud or Stone. In the south-west the smallest houses are termed *murabba'a*. Many people classed in that area as beduin, though not nomads, live in settlements composed of these primitive dwellings, consisting of one low windowless room with a single opening without a door; wooden pillars support the flat roof; the hearth is in the middle of the room, and the furniture comprises only some home-made mats, while from pegs in the walls hang garments, cooking-pots and coffee-pots; hand-mills of stone are the only other utensils. The doorway is not even always in the walls; at Suda and other villages in the highlands of 'Asīr the houses are so packed together that only the outer ones have doorways, the rest having openings only in the roof.

Houses of two or more rooms may have been developed in several ways. Some have grown piecemeal through the centuries, as, for instance, the great Government fortress at Abhā in 'Asīr, the oldest part of which is a warren of dingy chambers and staircases leading to the main reception rooms, while the newest part is a great white tower built by the Sa'ūdi Government. Generally, however, a more or less regular plan has been evolved, especially in the tall houses of the Yemen and the Hadhramaut. In the southern areas the words *beit*,

201. *Lowland type of mud-brick house. The suq at Lahej*

202. *Rough stone mountain house at Gheiman, Yemen*

204. *Stone castle at Dhāla'*

203. *Decorative houses in San'ā lining the street leading to the mosque of Al Abhar*

khalwa, or *daima* usually indicate the next stage larger than *murabba'a*; a *dar* is still larger, with two or more stories.

Much depends on the local building-material. In the wild mountains of the south-west the rectangular tower-like houses, with walls sloping inwards slightly, are built of roughly squared blocks of rock; their massive, thick walls, are often ornamented with string-courses formed by setting a row of cubical blocks diagonally; the windows and doorways, mostly small and plain, are picked out in whitewash, while some larger houses have the windows set back in round-arched recesses, unshuttered above but with a roughly carved wooden shutter beneath. The interior arrangements are described below. In some stone-built houses the walling is dry, in others cemented with mud and dung, or mud-plastered, while the plastered interiors are usually whitewashed. In coastal areas mud-brick is a commoner material, but blocks of coral-rock are also used in towns on the southern and Red Sea coasts. Thus, in Jīzān the houses of merchants and sharifs are two-storied buildings of coral, covered with stucco and in some cases decorated with raised designs. In Jidda there are tall mansions of coral-rock, with richly carved wooden window-lattices and balconies. In the central part of Hodeida, within the walls and facing the sea, stand great houses, also with carved wooden window-balconies and richly ornamented plaster-work in relief round the doorways; the ground-floors are lofty warehouses, through which the inmates pass, among bales and cases, to a staircase leading to airy and spacious rooms above.

The poorer town-dwellers on the south coast have houses of one story or more, not built for defence; in these the front ground-floor room serves as workshop or shop. Families of this class, however, sometimes live away from their workplace, in hired flats in the houses of rich merchants, consisting perhaps of only one room divided by a curtain to provide seclusion for the women.

In Abhā the houses are built of clay, with horizontal lines of projecting slates to protect the material from the heavy rains. Mud and clay are also materials very largely used in the villages and walled cities of Nejd and Al Hasa. In Riyādh, however, limestone blocks, with or without mortar, are increasingly used; palm and tamarisk also enter into house-construction. The low, but often vast, houses of these central Arabian cities 'turn their backs on the street', showing few or no windows in the outer walls, which, however, are in many cases pierced by small triangular openings in rows or geometrical groups; for the stern Wahhabi tenets forbid the elaborate ornamentation allowed by the Zeidis in the Yemen. Lime or gypsum is used for decorating the interior walls of central Arabian houses, and designs in colour are sometimes painted on woodwork; but only simple geometrical forms, particularly circles and triangles, appear to be favoured. The royal palace at Riyādh has a certain beauty derived from its simplicity and fine proportions (photo. 150).

The houses of petty chieftains or even private tribesmen in the south-west were built mainly for defence. Roof-parapets are loop-holed for rifle-fire, and there may be slits through which stones can be dropped. Doors in many cases are very low, and windows simply openings in the wall, though carved wooden or mud window-frames are often added. In mountainous districts where local rock is used, the construction is as described above. But where mud is more used, only the foundations and lower courses are stone, above which the walls are built of 'adobe', sun-dried bricks of mud mixed with straw, laid with mud plaster. But whether of stone or of mud-brick, the internal arrangement is much the same. The high thick walls keep out the heat. The house is built round a central rectangular pier, the 'arus al beit, rising from foundations to roof; round this ascends the staircase in a series of short straight flights, each doubling back on the last by a sharp bend—spiral staircases appear to be unknown; the ground floor, consisting of storerooms and stalls for cattle, has usually no windows; there is frequently a wooden gate at the bottom of the staircase, to prevent domestic animals walking up; inmates and visitors grope past trusses of fodder to the stairs, and ascend by several dark turns. The stairs, at any rate where stone is plentiful, are constructed of massive blocks, and sometimes of unequal height. In some districts the first floor is open to friends, while the women's quarters and kitchen are on the second floor; the baking of bread and some other cooking is done on the roof. In the tribal stone tower-houses of the Western Aden Protectorate and the Yemen, however, this arrangement may be varied, kitchens being provided on more than one of the upper floors. In some houses, particularly the larger houses or small castles of chieftains, the men's living-room, spacious, lofty, and well lighted, may be on the top floor. In the rougher kinds of construction these living-rooms are often provided with plain arched niches in the walls, for lamps and other objects; the roof-beams are unshaped tree-trunks, the rafters rough, but both beams and rafters are plastered and, together with the walls, whitewashed; the floor is covered with mats.

In the smaller tribal houses the whole family usually sleeps in one

205. *Mansion at Jidda. Beit Baghdadi*

206. *Mansion in Tarīm, Hadhramaut*

207. *Country house of the Imam of the Yemen in the Wadi Dhahr*

shuttered ill-ventilated room. In slightly better houses the men and women have separate rooms, where they receive visitors, and which are also used as bedrooms, the mattresses on which they sleep being rolled up and stored in closets during the day. Very poor people sleep on mats only. If the family possess a bed, this, the only piece of furniture, stands in the living-room, draped in bright materials, and is an object of admiration. Rooms are carpeted and furnished with cushions according to means. In even the poorest living-room a corner is set aside for tea and coffee making, the utensils being hung on the wall near by; in bigger houses these beverages are prepared by the servants in separate quarters. Chests or closets with shelves are used for storing clothes, among which herbs are laid (pp. 598, 601).

Richer tribesmen and chieftains have houses on the same plan, but more elaborate. The ground-floor is still given up to storerooms and cattle-stalls, but above there are more rooms, a bathroom to each floor, and more and costlier furnishings. Development of domestic architecture in the south-west progressed along two main lines, firstly, to the style of the Hadhramaut cities and second, to the much more ornate style of the cities of the Yemen.

In the Wadi Hadhramaut and its tributaries many of the lofty mud-brick houses of merchants, seiyids, and the wealthier tribesmen are barely distinguishable at a distance from the brown cliffs. But inside, the rooms are whitewashed and richly carpeted, and the walls are closely hung with ornaments and utensils of pottery and brass. In Wadi Dūʻan particularly the interiors are very elaborate. Ceilings are carried on rafters of ʻilb-wood, supported by dark stained pillars of the same wood; slats of date-palm, attractively arranged in herring-bone pattern, and laid over the rafters, support the mud floor of the story above; the doors, set in heavily carved wooden frames, are ornamented with many iron nails burnished with lead. These tall houses are divided into flats, each with its entrance leading into a small passage, and a living-room entered through a horseshoe-shaped archway, either cut in the wall or constructed of ʻilb-wood; each flat has a bathroom and a portion of the roof. (Photo. 23.)

An extreme development has been reached in Shibām, a town which grew up on a small eminence girdled by a wall, so that eventually the only direction in which to build was upwards. In recent years a committee of the townsmen has ruled that the closely packed skyscrapers must not exceed eight stories, to avoid overlooking neighbouring roofs. A new house can only be built by demolishing an old one, and the proposed positions of windows and gutters must be

passed by the committee. The foundation-walls, laid 3 feet deep and
$4\frac{1}{2}$ feet wide, are of stone mortared with a mixture of wood-ash and
lime; a goat or sheep is sacrificed on the walls when these have risen
3 feet above ground. Such a house may be nearly 100 feet high, the
thickness of the slightly sloping, unornamented walls diminishing to
less than a foot when the seventh story is reached. A building of this
type is said to last between two and three centuries, if the sanitary
arrangements are so cared for as to prevent undermining of the walls
by drainage from above. The plan of storerooms or shop on the
ground floor, guest-rooms on the first and second, and kitchens and
women's quarters higher up or at the back, still obtains. Some large
houses on the coast, built of stone or coral, reach nearly the same
height. (Photos. 349–351.)

In recent years greater security has led to the building of lower,
more spreading mansions, outside the walled cities and among date-
palm groves. The style of these houses has been copied largely from
the East Indies; the exteriors and interiors are whitewashed or colour-
washed, and intricate designs are cut in the mud-brick; the plaster
walls of the rooms are polished by rubbing with smooth pieces of flint.
Many modern devices, such as electric-light plants and refrigerators,
which were brought over the jōls on camels before motor-roads were
made, are in use. The palaces of the Sultans of Mukalla and Lahej
show Indian and European influence in their planning and architecture (photo. 343).

In the cities of the Yemen the highest degree of beauty has been
reached. The following remarks refer principally to Sanʿā, but,
allowing for slight local variations, they apply to other cities of the
high plateau as well. The walls of the ground-stories are built of
massive stone blocks, but above this they are constructed of dark
brown bricks, first sun-dried, then baked in kilns; the brickwork dis-
plays much elaborate ornamentation in relief, some of it picked out in
whitewash. On the whole the houses are less lofty than the highest
skyscrapers in the Hadhramaut, though the main building of the
Imam's palace has seven stories. More usually the houses have three,
four, or more stories, though the double series of windows in the upper
floors make the number appear greater than it is; for the living-
rooms have a lower row of plain windows, unglazed but fitted with
wooden shutters, and an upper row of arched windows, filled with
elaborate tracery and glazed in the best houses, or with thin sheets of
alabaster quarried locally. The traceried windowheads are made all in
one piece by Jewish craftsmen of very hard plaster; between the upper

210. *Door and window at Seiyūn*

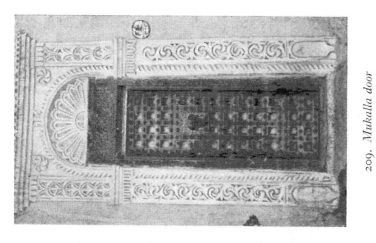

209. *Mukalla door*

208. *Door and lattice window at Hodeida*

211. *Double-traceried window of the 'Amil's guest-house at Ta'izz*

212. *Interior of a guest-house at Hāil*

and lower windows project ledges, which both shade the open lower windows and throw off the drips after rain. The massive nail-studded doors have knockers made of a thick shovel-shaped iron plate with a hinged clapper. Inside, the better living-rooms have whitewashed ceilings and walls, the latter provided with niches ornamented in plaster relief, and brackets supported by fretted plasterwork; since large spaces of wall are left bare, the effect is not marred by over-ornamentation, and the rooms, furnished with rich carpets, bright cushions, and some stained glass in the window-tracery, are very beautiful. Almost every large house has a *mifraj*, a pavilion or belvedere, ornamented in this style; in the closely built quarters this rises as an irregular addition on the flat roof, but it may be built in the garden; some houses have pavilions both on the roof and in the garden.

In 'Omān there are also large and massive buildings, contrasting with the date-thatch huts of the poor. Sifala, on the coast south-east of Muscat, for example, has a number of three-storied houses and the ruins of a five-storied house. Not far away is a great square castle with walls loopholed for muskets, telling of the former need for military preparedness.

Kitchens. The position of these, usually on upper floors, has been described. Most of the cooking is done by women, squatting or sitting on low stools. A built-up earthen block has a series of openings in which large cauldrons and other vessels can be suspended over the fire; the latter, of firewood or charcoal, needs continual fanning. Small portable charcoal burners are used for making coffee and for such cooking as is done outside the kitchen. Circular earthen bread-ovens are built on the flat house-roofs, or on the ground in the compound if the house has one; they are about $2\frac{1}{2}$ to 3 feet high and 18 inches across the top. Sticks are burned inside the oven till it is nearly red-hot, when the dough, flattened with the hand, is smeared on the inside walls, and the oven is then covered with a wooden lid. The cooks, whose hands appear insensitive to the heat, are expert at knowing the right moment to take out the bread. These remarks refer particularly to south-west Arabia, but are largely applicable to other districts.

Bathrooms and Sanitation. In north and central Arabia sanitation is still almost non-existent, even in large houses. In south-west Arabia arrangements in villages and the poorer houses generally are extremely primitive; in some place the inhabitants use the surrounding country; in others, while bathrooms may still be absent, open latrines are constructed as projecting niches in the roof-parapet or in other ways. In the tall houses described above, with at least one bathroom, or one on each upper floor, the bathroom and latrine are combined. In a corner stands a large earthenware jar of water, covered with a cloth or wooden lid; this supply also usually serves as drinking-water. The bather stands on two raised pedestals on the cement floor, and douches himself with water ladled from the jar. The latrine is a squatting-place, and the floor is so sloped that all bath-water and urine runs through a hole in the wall and pours from a projecting wooden gutter into the street, or runs down a vertical cemented groove in the outer wall of the house; the excreta drop down a walled-in shaft to a small chamber on the ground floor. When several bathrooms are built one above the other, each has its latrine in a different position, so that separate shafts can be constructed down to the ground-floor chamber. The latter can be entered through a doorway from outside the house, and cleaned out. Unfortunately this cleansing is in many places effected only at intervals of months, or not at all.

Dress

There is far greater diversity of costume in Arabia than is commonly supposed. The dress of the southern Arabs is widely different from that of the northern, and in some districts is changing rapidly under foreign influence. Tribal districts have many distinctive features, especially in the south, where different social strata, townsmen, settled cultivators, beduin and others, all have their own fashions. Among women there is, on the whole, even greater variety and more rapid change of fashion than among men.

North Arabia

As far south as the Rub' al Khali, costume is fairly uniform. The flowing garments pictured as typical Arab dress are everywhere in use. What follows is based mainly on the customs of the Ruwalla beduin of the north-west, but allowing for tribal differences among the nomads, and the greater sophistication and diversity of dress among townspeople, it may serve to exemplify the whole (photo. 213).

In male attire a long white shirt, an open flowing cloak, and a head-cloth are the characteristic features. The shirt (*thōb*), sometimes embroidered in colour round the neck, hangs to the heels; its broad sleeves end at the wrist in a lappet over a yard long, and are tied together behind the neck when the wearer is working or walking, though in riding they hàng loose. Well-to-do men wear over the shirt a garment called *zebūn*, of white linen, or partly silken black material with yellow stripes, or with stripes otherwise variegated; this reaches the ankles but is open all down the front, and its wide sleeves are much shorter than those of the shirt, and their ends may be lined with dark red and folded back. Over this is the most important article of dress, the cloak (*'aba*), made of two rectangular pieces each about 6½ feet long and nearly 2 feet wide, sewn together along their long edges; the cloak is thus a rectangle, the sides of which are folded over nearly 18 inches and sewn to the back along the top, slits being left in the fold as arm-holes; fine wool, camel's hair, and half-cotton materials may be used, and the colours are usually light grey, dark brown, or combinations of broad stripes of white, grey, and brown, each with special names. In winter a sheepskin coat (*farwa*) may be worn instead of the cloak. Over a round cap of rough wool or camel's hair (*tāziyya*) is worn a kerchief measuring over a yard square, rarely white, usually dark coloured, or woven of red and black, or patterned; this is folded in a particular manner and bound round the head with a woollen or camel's-hair cord about an inch thick (*'asāba* or *'aqal*); the Ikhwān (p. 286) wear a head-band of twisted stuff in place of the *'aqal*. Beduin in warm weather go barefoot, or tie a sole of undressed camel's hide round the big toe and the heel; herdsmen wear low thick-soled shoes of rough leather. (Photos. 160, 161, 215.)

The dress of Ruwalla women consists of a dark blue cotton shirt (*thōb aswad*), trailing on the ground, fitting close at the neck, with wide sleeves; it is tucked up in front under a broad red-and-black cotton or woollen belt. The head is wrapped in a large dark kerchief (*maqrūna*), with a smaller dark cotton kerchief (*mindīl*) folded into a narrow band and bound round the larger one. Wealthier women wear a large black-and-red shawl (*shumbar*) over the head, folded in a complicated way, as well as the kerchief. Women wear cloaks like men's, but only black or dark brown, and wealthy women wear short blue jackets (*jibba*), with narrow turned-in sleeves, or sometimes a silk kaftan, over the shirt. Beduin women go barefoot.

All women possess some jewellery, red coral necklaces, glass breast pendants, elbow-rings and bracelets, glass or copper anklets, copper ear-rings, finger-rings, and sometimes a copper ring in the right nostril. Their palms and nails, and in old women the hair also, are dyed with henna either of the Egyptian variety (*masriyya*) or the Mecca variety (*makkawiya*), the latter being considered superior. Young men and girls dye their eyelids with antimony powder (*kohl*), using a small sharp knife to apply it; this is believed to strengthen the eyesight, and men have been known to rub it even on the edges of telescopes.

While many elderly beduin men have the whole head shaved, a younger Ruwalla usually has half the back of the head up to the ears shaved, also the side whiskers and beard under the chin. Men vain of their appearance wear their front hair in plaits, two, four, six, or eight; the long plaits which are their pride have been sometimes their un-doing, since men captured in pursuit can have their hands bound behind their necks with their own plaits. A girl usually trims the front hair so that it hangs freely, but plaits the rest, on top of the head and above the ears, into braids, leaving two small pigtails tied with ribbon at the back. Nearly all women are tattooed with indigo on lips, cheeks, nose, breast, and abdomen, generally in patterns of circles and triangles. Ruwalla men and women also buy from the Solubba a belt plaited of five thin strips of gazelle leather, which they wear next the body. The Solubba or gipsies themselves are often clothed entirely in garments made of hides and pelts, except for their shepherd's cloaks, which are like those of the beduin.

South Arabia

The true beduin of the south are in dress the most primitive people in the whole peninsula. They wear only a loin-cloth, held up by a locally made broad leather belt with pouches, while a second narrower belt holds the curved dagger (*jambiya*) carried by every beduin and tribes-man. The loin-cloth was probably formerly of camel's or goat's hair; to-day it is generally of coarse unbleached calico, called *americani* because it was formerly imported from the United States, though now Britain or India are usually the sources of supply; the calico is dyed indigo and often pounded with stones or wooden hammers till it gets a sheen. Another length of indigo cloth is twisted round the waist or wrapped round the head and shoulders at night or in cold weather; or the cloth may drape half the body, crossing it diagonally, with the end brought over one shoulder. The long hair is bound round, sometimes with a piece of the rope used for tying camels' legs (the origin of the 'aqal used in the north); the hair may also be tied in a bun. The bare upper part of the body is smeared with sesame oil and indigo as a protection against both heat and cold. These beduin usually walk barefoot but possess home-made sandals of goat-hide with overhang-ing straps, the flapping of which is said to scare away snakes and scorpions. They wear silver rings, silver armlets set with cornelians,

213. *Northern beduin*

214. *A Teimani*

215. *Ikhwān dress*

216. *Southern Beduin*

217. *Zueida (Mahri) at forest village near Buzun*

218. *Yāfaʻi types*

and nearly always a cornelian amulet, set in silver, hung round the neck; this stone (*fās*) is held to have medicinal properties, such as curing snake-bite by its touch. A piece of dark cotton twisted below the knee is believed to strengthen the legs.

Tribesmen of the Qara mountains usually leave their hair wild and bushy, only bound round with a leathern thong, though sometimes the hair is tied in a bun on top. They and many Mahri tribesmen wear a single ear-ring in the right ear and a single bracelet above the right elbow (photo. 217).

Southern beduin women wear a long shapeless dress of the same dyed calico, roughly sewn, drawn in at the waist by a silver or leathern belt, or by a waist-cloth embroidered with cowries. They wind a length of cloth round the head and shoulders and in some districts wear a blue face-veil with eye-holes; otherwise they go unveiled. They wear as many anklets, bracelets, and necklaces as they can afford, and their ears, bored from end to end in babyhood, may carry six to eight ear-rings apiece. Both men and women wear the same clothes day and night for months, though new dresses are put on for the principal annual festivals.

In the *Aden Protectorate*, among more civilized tribesmen, and even petty chieftains, the loin-cloth is replaced by a coloured *futa* hanging from waist to knee, often locally woven and of many patterns, in some cases like tartans. Such men sometimes wear shirts, more often only a short white coat buttoning to the neck; peasants discard the coat during the heat of the day and toil with the upper part of the body bare. Over the leathern belt supporting the futa is a twisted girdle of coloured cloth, in which is stuck the jambiya, and behind it often a small sheath-knife for domestic use; the jambiya, though a weapon, is even more a mark of the social standing of a free tribesman. White or indigo-dyed turbans are usually worn by peasants, or, among some lowland tribes, brimless fez-shaped straw hats. Small chieftains sport turbans of many bright colours and patterns. The legs and feet are usually bare, but many tribesmen possess sandals or imported rubber-soled shoes (photo. 218).

Among seiyids, merchants, artisans, and townsmen in general dress varies more. They wear longer futas or even bright-coloured sarongs to the ankles, a shirt outside the futa and a short coat over it. The head is covered by a white crocheted cap always left on, with or without a turban. Arms are not carried, but a broad leather belt with pouches is worn. A long white nightshirt (*qamis*) is sometimes worn over the shirt and futa, especially in the Eastern Aden Protectorate.

Seiyids of the Hadhramaut, when indoors, wear sarongs inside which their shirts are tucked at the waist, but their outdoor dress is distinctive; long cream-coloured coats open in front, and high hard caps heavily embroidered with gold, while a long bright-coloured shawl is carried over the shoulder; no jambiya is carried.

In the Protectorate, women's attire has developed from simple beduin dress, but that of tribeswomen is more heavily embroidered, and many kinds of belts, of silver and other materials, are used. Women of different tribal districts have distinctive fashions. In the 'Abdali (Lahej), Haushabi, or Amiri territories brightly striped or indigo ankle-length cotton dresses, with three-quarter length full sleeves, gathered in at the waist with a wide sash tied in front (unless a silver belt is worn) are the vogue. Fadhli women wear dresses cut short in front but trailing on the ground behind. In the highlands the head-dress consists usually of a cloth dyed indigo or some other colour, worn as a cowl or a loosely bound turban. Lowland women working in the fields have home-made, broad-brimmed straw hats with high tapering crowns, worn over a head-cloth (photo. 252).

The dress of townswomen is extremely varied, with marked local features. Thus, in Wadi Dū'an their dresses are always black, with a square breast-plate of coloured patches, ankle-length, short-sleeved, with a wide square-cut neck; an orange scarf is tied under the chin, and an ordinary finger-ring worn through one nostril; out of doors a black or dark blue cloak, and a cloth over the head and face with eye-slits are worn. In Wadi 'Amd silver-embroidered dark blue dresses are in fashion, and sharifas (p. 403) wear white outdoor cloaks. In well-to-do households in Shibām, Seiyūn, and Tarīm particularly gay colours and rich materials are fashionable, though the dresses are wide and shapeless, about ankle-length in front, with a short train behind. Ornament frequently changes, sequins or heavy embroidery having given way to coloured lace, and this in turn to bands of material of contrasting colours. Shibām women out of doors wear bright blue cloaks and black head-cloths, while blue leggings are worn under the cloak but over the dress. In Seiyūn and Tarīm only sharifas wear these blue cloaks; slave women wear orange, and *meskin* (townswomen and peasants) green cloaks. In Aden itself, and in Mukalla and Shihr, which follow Aden, short-sleeved long dresses of printed silk or cotton, with black outdoor cloaks and thin black veils, are fashionable. Indian influence is apparent, and saris are worn in the household of the Sultan of Mukalla. The only undergarments are tight bodices and waist petticoats. Better-class women change into

219. *Amir of Ibb on his return*
from the mosque

220. *Son of the 'Amil of Ta'izz*
in full dress

221. *San'ā women's outdoor dress*
with enveloping shawl

222. *Slave-girls in the*
Hadhramaut

223. *Northern beduin boy with plaited hair*

224. *Hadhrami girl with green paint on chin, nose, forehead, and cheeks, and in embroidered dress*

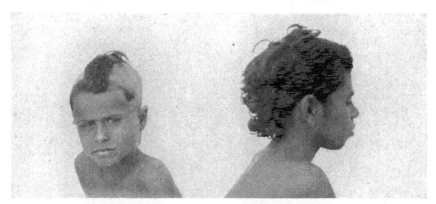

225. *Qarāwi boys. Uncircumcised boy on left*

226. *Qarāwi girls*

special dresses at night. Children follow the fashions of their elders, but very young boys are sometimes dressed as girls to deceive the evil eye.

At prayer-times in some districts special long dresses of white or orange cloth, and head-coverings, are used. Lines of women thus attired kneel and rise in unison.

Women's hair is usually arranged in numerous tiny plaits, taking a whole day to do and being undone about every fortnight. Fringes are worn in some districts, side-locks in others, though in Seiyūn an unmarried girl is not allowed side-locks. About Lahej the hair is done in two plaits covered by an embroidered bag. Tribeswomen use bright yellow face-dyes (p. 495) in some districts; in the Amiri highlands women also decorate their faces with horizontal and vertical lines and stars in black antimony powder; elsewhere the eyebrows and nostrils are dyed scarlet, or green lines are the fashion, or the face may be stained yellow in the upper half, green in the lower. *Kohl* (antimony powder) is universally used for the eyes, by men as well as women, as it is thought to strengthen—not beautify—the eyes. Henna (p. 494) is universally popular for painting designs on the hands and feet, and *khudhab*, a black paste, is also used for this purpose. Tribeswomen and beduin often have the hands and face tattooed in addition, but in better-class harems only imported cosmetics are used. The wealthier women wear gold or amber ornaments, poorer women use silver and brass. A silver anklet with bells is commonly worn on one leg by women when dancing.

The Yemen. Much of the above applies also to the Yemen proper, but local peculiarities exist. The highland cultivators in summer often wear only the white kilt and girdle, a sleeveless woollen jacket, woven in black and white patterns, over the bare body, and a white or indigo turban; in winter a shirt is sometimes worn, and a sleeveless sheepskin jacket with the rough wool turned more often inwards than outwards. Some tribes in the northern Yemen twist their hair into thick pigtails, otherwise it is worn short or hanging in ringlets to the shoulders. Tribesmen on journeys often carry over the shoulder a sack in which they sleep, closing it from within. Soldiers commonly wear indigo-dyed shirts tucked inside their girdles, white kilts, and white or indigo turbans, the latter with fringes; often swathed round the body, over the shirt, is a long white cloth. Lowlanders and townsfolk have largely adopted short white jackets, which the latter wear over striped shirts. Seiyids and men of the official classes in full dress are very brightly attired; over long white or striped shirts, with full sleeves hanging below the hands, are worn long-sleeved kaftans of various colours, such as dark or bright blue, pink, or green; a long brightly coloured or embroidered shawl must be carried, either over one shoulder or round both shoulders like a scarf, or wrapped diagonally round the body, passing under one arm and with the ends hanging over the other shoulder; a broad belt, often embroidered with gold and silver thread, girds the kaftan, and holds the jambiya, which, with elaborately ornamented sheath, is worn by every man and boy on the right side by seiyids, in the middle by other folk. Richly embroidered stiff caps (*kuffiza*) are worn by boys and men, but while young boys wear these alone, older boys and adults bind round them turbans of many colours, either tightly folded or voluminous and bulging.

Peasant women in the Yemen highlands usually have a long dark blouse hanging well below the knees, sometimes lifted by a girdle and with narrow sleeves, and trousers narrowing to the ankles; on the head a dark cloth. A most distinctive feature of women's attire is the outdoor dress of well-to-do women in San'ā and adjacent towns; the whole body is enveloped in a long, brightly coloured, printed or embroidered shawl, covering the head, hanging to the ankles, and held in with the hands; beneath this the head and face are shrouded in a long blue silken veil, printed with large diamond-shaped red rectangles each having a white inner and a black outer border, so spaced that one covers each of the wearer's eyes, producing an eerie effect (photo. 221). While men wear sandals, townswomen are shod in red or black shoes.

Jewish women are distinguished by a cowl or hood, rising to a peak at the back, bordered with silver embroidery in front, and drawn in under the chin. Rather close-fitting trousers, richly embroidered above the ankles, appear below a long dark-coloured or striped blouse. Out of doors a long shawl, dark blue or black, with a broad patterned border and coloured round patches, is worn over the hood and hangs below the waist. Jewesses, though not veiled, pull the shawl across the face at the approach of strangers. Male Jews wear small black skull-caps on their shaven crowns, and have plaited side-locks hanging to the shoulder (photo. 165). They bear no weapons, and their dress is ungirded.

FOOD

North Arabia

Milk is the staple food of the beduin. Next may be placed various cereals, dishes made from cereals and milk-products, dates, bread, and coffee; meat, whether camel, mutton, or game (gazelle and hare), is a luxury-food, eaten on occasion, and then frequently served with cooked cereals.

Camel's milk is the normal drink, on which many families live for months at a time. Butter-milk of goats and ewes is sometimes drunk, and some poorer nomads, especially the Solubba (p. 364), who have no camels, depend for milk almost entirely on goats. Beduin, in the strict sense, resort to various devices to ensure a supply of camel's milk; sometimes a weak calf is killed, the she-camel (*nāga*) is not milked for some days, and then the flow of milk is stimulated by gentle stroking of the udder, night and morning; or a calf may be killed and its mother induced to suckle another calf, so that both mother and foster-mother have milk to spare. Sometimes as many as six calves may be killed out of seven, and the surviving calf left to be nourished by the mother with least milk, while the other six have their teats enclosed in thick nets, or protected by sharp pegs from being sucked; in the morning, when a camel is to be milked, the calf is called up and the milk begins to flow; the herdsman, with the pressure of his thumb, causes the milk to spurt into a wooden vessel or a leather pouch; meanwhile, both camel and calf have to be appeased, the herdsman addressing the first by name.

A milch-camel may yield from less than one quart to over twelve quarts a day, according to the quality of the pasture and amount of good annual plants; a fertile camel gives milk for twelve months, a barren one even longer. Milk drunk warm, as freshly obtained, is called *mahaz*; or, if drunk heated, *sakhīn*; when poured into a leather bag it quickly becomes sour. Among the Ruwalla, at any rate, camel's milk is not churned but may be boiled; small cheeses made from the curds are eaten dry or stewed with bread. Owing to the salt herbs on which camels often browse, the milk may be salt and have a slightly aperient effect on strangers.

Cereals. Beduin such as the Ruwalla, before going into the inner desert, get wheat from the settled cultivators at the rate of one camel-load (nearly 3 cwt.) per person. An ordinary beduin carries an additional load for guests, while an important chief takes many loads, for his numerous guests and to relieve fellow-tribesmen who have lost their supplies through theft or otherwise. Only chiefs take flour; the womenfolk of ordinary tribesmen grind the wheat grains themselves, either with pestle and wooden mortar, or in a small mill, hewn from two pieces of basalt.

Bread is not baked during the season of abundant pasture, and only seldom at other times. In many tents it is never baked, and many women taste it rarely in their lives. Those, however, who do bake, salt the flour, add water, and knead dough in a loaf, from which they pull off pieces and knead large thin cakes; these are thrown up into the air, deftly caught and drawn out still more, till as thin as paper, when they are laid on the convex side of a bulging sheet of iron over the fire. Occasionally a large cake of dough is placed in hot ashes, and another fire is lighted above. The baking of bread in an oven, in the houses of south-west Arabia, has been described (p. 415). The Ruwalla and other tribes of the north to whom the above remarks apply prefer unleavened bread (*fatīr*); leavened bread is eaten only in the cold season, when yeast is added to a loaf made overnight and baked next morning.

Though bread is baked comparatively seldom, a porridge (*'eish*) is made from crushed wheat and boiled into a thick paste with the addition of salt. This is eaten almost daily for supper; the leavings make a cold lunch next day. On a short journey of a few days, when no tents are pitched, a little roasted wheat may be the only food carried.

The poorer Ruwalla tribesmen buy white sorghum, a millet, much cheaper than wheat (p. 475); from it they boil a porridge or bake a bread with the ground flour. The seed of the desert plant *samh* (p. 198) can take the place of cereals; different varieties of *samh*-seed are used in the preparation of porridge and other foods.

Other foods of the northern beduin include *'asīd*, a gruel made of flour and milk—the name is also widely used in south-west Arabia; *bakīla*, a paste of dates and flour; *basīsa*, a thin paste of grape-sugar and wheat-flour, for young children; *madrūsa*, a thin paste of dates, boiled wheat, and butter; *matbūkha*, dates boiled in butter; *khamei'a*, bread boiled in milk and covered with camel's suet. Locusts (*jarād*) have been an important food of the poorer nomads; first roasted, then sun-dried, they are afterwards either ground to powder or strung on threads or otherwise stored; they can be eaten thus, or food may be prepared from the ground bodies as from flour.

Salt. Tribes such as the Ruwalla prefer salt produced by evaporation in shallow pools. Salt of inferior quality is obtained from dried-up swamps; *theini* is ground rock-salt.

Among wild plants the beduin specially like the dark red fruit of the thorny *msa'* shrub; very sweet with a bitter after-taste, it is boiled to a thick syrup. They collect the sweet juice of the *rimth* shrub. The ripe fruit of the *butum* tree is dried, ground, and mixed with wheat. The stalks and tuberous parts of a number of plants are eaten raw. *Tarthūth* (p. 198) is baked or sun-dried.

Meat, as stated, is an occasional luxury, and hardly any but camel's flesh is eaten by certain tribes. Among the Ruwalla the meat, with the bones, is hacked into small pieces, boiled in a kettle with salt, and then placed in a pan and covered with *'eish*, a thick gravy being poured over the whole. *Mishwi* is salted meat, baked over the fire or in red-hot ashes. *Habīt* is meat roasted in fat and served on bread. Camel's fat, when cut up and boiled into suet, can be kept in leather bags up to three years and is preferred to butter in the hot season; it is considered a good remedy for suppurating wounds. In some districts more mutton is eaten, and in east Arabia mutton or camel may be served with rice (photo. 227).

Meals. The Ruwalla and other beduin normally eat twice a day. The main meal, supper (*'ashā*), is after sunset. Lunch (*ghada*), taken shortly before noon, consists of milk and a piece of bread, or food left over from supper the preceding day. A piece of dry bread soaked in water is thought a good 'snack'. Breakfast is unknown, except perhaps for a slight drink of milk and a morsel of bread with salt; after this nomads will travel all day without lunch, and even supper may be much reduced. Members of the family eat in the women's part of the tent. Guests partake in the men's compartment, where the host and his eldest son may sup with them; after having water poured over the right hand, those partaking kneel round the dish on the left knee, sitting back on the left heel, and eat with the right hand; pellets of *'eish* or bread are rolled, thrown into the mouth, and swallowed; everyone works inwards from the edge of the dish, hurrying to reach any pile of meat which may be in the middle, but which it is bad form to take directly; afterwards the fingers are licked and wiped against the sides of the tent.

Coffee. The preparation of coffee, the only food or drink prepared in the men's part of the tent, is a ritual, involving the use of four coffee-pots of descending size, each with a special name. The grounds from which coffee has been made for several days are put with water in the largest, and the vessel is placed on the fire. The other three are rinsed and placed ready. A handful of coffee-beans, roasted in a shallow iron pan with a long handle, is shaken into a wooden dish to cool; the beans are then pounded in a wooden mortar held between the knees. The strokes of the pestle should be measured, for by their regularity a man's musical ability may be judged. Meanwhile boiling water from the largest pot has been poured into the second, into which the freshly ground coffee is dropped and boiled over the fire; then the pot is put aside for the coffee to settle. A little beaten-up cardamom and other spices are placed in the third pot, into which the coffee is poured from the second, and again brought to the boil. Part of this decoction is poured into the smallest pot, from which a little is poured into a cup and emptied on the ground as a sacrifice for *Shādhri*, the first to boil coffee. Finally a slave or servant, having sampled the brew, pours a little—sometimes from several feet above—into each cup, handing the cups one by one to the guests, who drink slowly (photo. 228). Custom varies, but among the Ruwalla, the guest should decline the fifth cup, though he may resume drinking later.

Diet of Townsmen. The same constituents are used, but with more abundance and variety. Dishes of meat and rice may be served almost daily; more herbs and spices are used in cooking. Tea as well as coffee is drunk; mint may be added to the former, ginger and other spices to the latter. Fresh fruit, such as melons, pomegranates, apricots, and sweet citrus, is eaten when in season, and various dishes and conserves are made from dates (pp. 424, 489). The staple diet of the Arabs on the east coast used to be rice, but, with the cessation of supplies from Burma during the War of 1939–1945, they were compelled to adopt a diet of wheat, of which they at first complained. Game (bustard, gazelle, hare), truffles, and other luxuries also form part of the townsman's menu.

South Arabia

In much of the south-west, especially the Western Aden Protectorate, the only class of food abundant enough for the population is cereals, and even they are rendered unreliable by the risk of drought. The supply of milk and milk-products is poor owing to the insufficiency of good grazing, so that these important sources of protein are only 'additional' foods. Herdsmen rarely have enough milk for sale. In the towns a little goat's milk is available. In some large towns, such as Mukalla and Shihr, a few cows are privately kept by wealthy owners, and some to supply milk to the people. In the Yemen *yoghourt*, which is much eaten, is regarded medically as a first-class protein and less likely to carry typhoid and dysentery than whole milk. Cheese and locally made ghee are not abundant; but in some districts cheese is made by shaking up milk in a goatskin, and imported ghee is used lavishly in cooking in well-to-do households. Otherwise mainly vegetable fats are used, particularly oil of sesame (*jiljil*).

Cereals. Bread is usually made of the flour of *dhura* or other millets. The grain is ground, generally in a 'kneeling grindstone' (*mat-hana birk*). Water and a little salt are added gradually till the dough is formed; this is then worked with the palms of the hands into circular cakes about an inch thick, which are smeared over the inside walls of the oven, in which a fire has been lighted and allowed to die down. The oven (p. 415) is then covered till the cooks, expert at knowing the right moment before the bread falls into the ashes, remove the lid. Beduin and others without ovens simply place the dough on the ashes of a wood fire, but bread baked thus is often very heavy. Flour may also be rolled out in large thin cakes, fried in fat and then baked.

As in north Arabia, *ʿasīd* (p. 424) is a staple dish, particularly in poorer houses. But in the south-west it is a porridge made from flour of *dhura* or other millets, roughly ground and dropped bit by bit into boiling water to which a little salt has been added. The concoction, after being stirred continuously with a wooden spoon, is taken off the fire and further stirred and pressed, returned to the fire, and so on, until it is thoroughly cooked, soft and not lumpy. Then, tipped on to a plate, it is eaten with sugar and ghee; in the Hadhramaut crushed dates are added. *Haris*, a dish made with wheat and meat, crushed and boiled into a porridge in the same way as *ʿasīd*, is very popular in the Hadhramaut, eaten with sugar and ghee. *Dhura* grain may also be boiled like rice, or pounded and made into dough, which can be fermented and made into cakes.

As on the Persian Gulf coast, the War of 1939–1945 cut off the supply of imported rice. Previously rice was a staple food in wealthy households, while even in the poorest it was thought essential on festal occasions.

Dates. At the date-harvest poorer households in many districts eat little but the fresh fruit. Dried dates are a staple food of the beduin. When dates are not available they are replaced by *dūm*, the berries of the *ʿilb*-tree (p. 193), eaten fresh or, for later use, dried and pounded to a powder which is mixed with water into a paste; in drought and famine beduin and other poor people live on little else.

Fish, fresh or dried, less popular in the Western Aden Protectorate, is specially liked in the Eastern. There it is nearly always plentiful near the coast, particularly at certain seasons, when a household of four may enjoy a substantial meal for the equivalent of fourpence. The most popular fish in the interior of the Hadhramaut States is dried shark; also *hanīt* or dried *tamad*, pounded and cooked with a sauce of ghee and onions. Small *ʿaid*, called *wazif* when dried, usually plentiful and cheap, are eaten by the poorest classes, but chiefly used as fodder for camels, donkeys, and other animals. The

failure of the catch of these small fish was a factor in the recent
Hadhramaut famine, since it lessened the food for direct human consumption and also reduced the food-supply for pack animals carrying
food inland. Large freshwater fish, a species of barbel, are caught by
Jews in the Wadi Khārid, north-east of San'ā, and sold in the markets
of the city. (Photos. 230, 283, 284.)

In the Aden Protectorate *chickens and eggs* are usually only eaten
by the well-to-do, while poor people raise hens only for sale. Far too
little attention is paid to *vegetables*, though carrots and radishes,
including the giant radish, are eaten raw, and onions and chillies are
popular in cooking. *Fruit* would be popular if more were available,
as witnessed by the demand in Aden for bananas, pawpaws, mangoes,
and other fruit from the plantations of Lahej. In the fertile highlands
of the Yemen much fruit is eaten, especially apricots, peaches, pomegranates, figs, and grapes, as well as citrus and tropical fruits grown
at lower altitudes; fruit-cultivation is discussed in more detail in
Chapter IX (Agriculture). *Spices* and condiments, pepper, powdered
chillies, cloves, cardamom, &c., are much used in cooking. In Socotra
millets are the staple food, with fish on the coast. Vegetables, fruit,
and meat are rather more generally eaten than on the mainland.

Coffee and other Beverages. The commonest drink in the south-
west is *qishr*, made from the outer husks of the coffee-bean, either
roasted and ground or boiled without preparation. Usually unsweetened but flavoured with ginger, it is considered nourishing
for babies and a stimulant for adults. While coffee made from the
bean itself is, in many poorer households, only drunk on special
occasions, coffee-making is a social ritual, differing in detail from
northern practice. In some districts a traveller, on entering a house,
offers a handful of beans to his host. When coffee is prepared for
visitors, this is done by a member of the family in front of the guests
in poorer houses, but in wealthier homes a servant prepares it outside
the reception room, into which it is carried and handed round. In
the harems of the Eastern Aden Protectorate an old female servant
presides over the apparatus in a corner; she roasts the beans and husks
on a charcoal burner, handing round some roasted beans on a plaited
tray so that guests may enjoy the aroma and take a few beans to chew;
the rest is boiled up with ginger, cardamom, cinnamon, and sometimes with sugar. Usually two cups are offered and taken, after which
the visitor should leave. While in north Arabia and 'Omān the cup
is not filled, in the south-west—in the Aden Protectorate at least—
it is filled to the brim. At large gatherings an incense-burner and

227. *Northern beduin dish of lamb boiled with butter-milk and served with rice*

228. *Coffee-slave roasting mocha-beans in iron ladle*

230. *The Suq at Tarīm. Salt, sugar, ginger, coffee-berries, and dried fish on sale*

229. *Charcoal-seller in Tarīm*

rose-water are passed round after coffee. According to Landberg, coffee in south Arabia is sometimes called *shadhili* after Abu al Hasan ash Shadhili, said to have first introduced it; while the early morning cup (*bōst* or *sahīh*) is accompanied by the recital of a special *Fatihat al Qahwa* (cf. the ritual pouring of coffee on the ground by the northern beduin, pp. 425–426).

In the Hadhramaut *tea*, a very popular beverage, of which Javanese brands are best liked, is made in imported samovars and served in glasses with much sugar but no milk. Its preparation has also become a ritual, so that every well-to-do household needs several outfits, each including several small china tea-pots, glasses, trays, spoons, charcoal tongs, and sugar-cutters, for before 1939 the sugar was imported from Java in solid cones. In other parts of the Aden Protectorate tea, flavoured with cardamom, is drunk with milk and sugar.

Nebidh, the drink made from the sap of dūm-palms, and probably of other palm-trees, is popular in some parts of south-west Arabia, while *'araq*, the spirit distilled from dates, is drunk by the less strict on the coast of the Hejaz.

FUEL

Wood, charcoal, and dried camel-dung are the principal kinds of fuel. Among the nomads of north Arabia both dry roots and stems of various plants (*hatab*) and camel-dung are used; the wood of *ghadha* (p. 198) is thought the best, as it smokes little, gives out great heat, and forms embers which glow for several hours; dry *shīh* (p. 197) is the poorest, as it blazes up and crackles but does not form hot embers; fuel in the desert is collected by slaves and women. In the Rub' al Khali *abal* (*Calligonum*, called *artā* in Nejd, p. 197) is the best fuel available. In the oases of central Arabia many kinds of wood are used, but date-palm wood, even if it can be spared, is too pungent—'vinegar to the teeth and smoke to the eyes'. In the settled districts of the south-west acacia is readily available, and quantities are brought into San'ā and other cities as firewood; the long-thorned *samr*-acacia supplies much firewood in the Hadhramaut. Trees such as the *'ilb*, in request as timber, are probably less used for fuel.

Charcoal is much in demand for placing on the tobacco in pipes and for preparing coffee, but little is known about the plants used; in north Arabia charcoal-burners make it from the desert vegetation and bring it into the cities. Doughty mentions 'the light castor-oil wood' as used in the preparation of charcoal for gunpowder at Kheibar;

the *'ushar*-tree (*Calotropis*) is used for charcoal in gunpowder in south Arabia.

Camel-dung (*jalla*) in the Yemen highlands, and probably elsewhere, is made into flat round cakes which are laid out in regular rows to dry in the sun for fuel (photos. 29, 232).

SOCIAL CUSTOMS

Great diversity exists, in different parts of Arabia, in the customs and ceremonies associated with common events such as marriage, birth, and death. In describing selected examples of these usages, the rough division between north and south Arabia cannot always be observed as much as in some preceding sections; the method followed under most heads is to outline the usage in one district, and to compare those of other districts more briefly. The headings are (i) marriage, divorce, and seclusion; (ii) birth and upbringing of children; (iii) rites attending circumcision; (iv) salutations, hospitality, greeting and farewell ceremonies; (v) funeral customs.

Marriage, Divorce, and Seclusion

Marriage. Though a man's right to take up to four wives is not disputed, so long as he obeys the recognized rules, yet probably comparatively few have as many as four wives at a time. Probably most, especially poorer people and beduin, have only one wife at a time, especially if she bear children. It is accepted that two or more wives do not always live happily together, for, among wealthy seiyids in the south-west, a man marrying a second wife should provide a separate house for her, while many nomadic beduin avoid as far as possible having more than one wife in a tent. In less well-to-do households of the south-west, where two wives is a common number, each has her own room. Occasionally a wife threatens to leave her husband should he take a second, but from fear of public opinion she rarely does so. Strange cases arise, as when a man whose wife is childless consults both her and her mother on the choice of a second wife; but when this is decided the first wife takes offence, returns to her family, and must be coaxed back again with presents equal to those given her when she first married him.

Concubinage with slave-women is fairly common in many parts of Arabia. Elderly spinsters are not entirely unknown, but their lot is not happy as, in the secluded classes, they must remain in purdah all their lives, seeing only female relatives and intimate friends. Though

231. *Negro slave making black bread in the Tihama*

232. *Women bringing camel-dung for fuel into Sanʿā*

233. *Slave dance in Dhufār*

234. *Exorcism of sickness from a cow in Dhufār with incense*

young divorced women usually remarry, some older ones are left without support, often as poor dependants in rich households.

Local and tribal custom varies greatly. The following details, relating primarily to south-west Arabia and especially the Hadhramaut, may be much more widely applicable. In towns and villages the *shar'* code is generally followed. First marriages usually take place at 16 or 17 for boys and 14, 13, or even younger, for girls. Among these town and village people marriages are always arranged by the parents or other relatives; a girl normally grows up in pretended, if not real, ignorance of her marriage until the very day, though cousins (between whom marriages are commonly arranged) grow up knowing what is intended. Moreover, while a man may marry into any social class, a woman is not favourably regarded if she marries beneath her.

Three principal events in arranging a marriage are (i) *khutba*, (ii) *daf'a* and *mahr*, and (iii) *'aqd*. The *khutba* consists of the father or other male relative of the prospective bridegroom asking for the girl's hand from her father or guardian. No celebrations mark this stage, but, if the girl's relatives consent, the bridegroom must bring the *daf'a*, namely money paid for the bride, and presents for her; the money, varying from a few dollars to about $500 according to the family's circumstances and local custom, is intended for the bride but often taken by her father; the presents generally include an outdoor cloak, embroidered slippers, a goat for slaughtering, and a pound or so of incense. At the same time the amount of the *mahr* is decided, a sum varying as widely as the *daf'a*, and payable in instalments to the woman if she is divorced, while if her husband dies she receives the *mahr* and one-sixth of his estate besides. The *'aqd* is the marriage contract, enacted generally before a *qadhi*, though a layman can act as *katib* (scribe), and in the desert a handshake suffices. The *'aqd* may be signed months before the marriage or even the same day.

Though a virgin is asked at the *'aqd* if she will marry the man, she dare not refuse and the custom is a polite fiction; but a widow or divorced woman is consulted at the earlier stage of *khutba*. Moreover a man marrying a slave must enter into an *'aqd* to ensure the legitimacy of his children, for, though children by his own slave are legitimate with or without an *'aqd*, his children by a slave-woman not his own are illegitimate without an *'aqd*, however much he may recognize them.

When arrangements are concluded, an evening party of women is held in the bride's house. As the bride enters the room a woman enfolds her completely in a shawl or cloak; she sits surrounded by veiled, cloaked unmarried girl-friends, while the guests dance and sing to an orchestra of drums.

The following morning the ceremony called *Mafraq* (parting) is attended by many more guests. Hired women again play drums, while the guests clap their hands and utter shrill cries round the bride. The latter, still entirely cloaked, is supported and fanned by two women. An elderly female relative or friend, who must, to bring good luck, have been married only once, attends her throughout; this woman, the *makadia* or *haria*, at length uncovers the top of the bride's head and, with a silver-pointed cosmetic-stick, parts her hair and draws a red line down the centre. The bride is taken to the bathroom to wash and put on new clothes. Ceremonies and rejoicings, including a lunch, continue all day; in the afternoon the bride, again cloaked, is given presents of money and clothes, while the guests continue dancing and singing till tired out.

The mode of preparing the bride to meet her husband for the first time varies greatly according to local fashions. Her hands, arms, feet, and sometimes her face, are lightly painted with henna or a black substance (*khadab*), the patterns being often delicate. Her hair may be dressed into many tiny plaits and side curls; in the main Wadi Hadhramaut the hair is covered with a large wig, on top of which is set a gold-embroidered crown. All the gold ornaments of her family—necklaces, bracelets, ear-rings, anklets, and amulets—are called into use. The bride is perfumed and her new clothes, which should be green, are censed. Strongly scented flowers, and gold coins and other ornaments, may be twined in her hair.

Meanwhile separate parties of both men and women take place in the bridegroom's home, and the marriage contract (*'aqd*) is enacted. The bridegroom and male relatives go to the bride's home on the 'night of the entrance' (*Leilat ad Dukhula*); entering the women's quarters, where the guests remain veiled, the bridegroom strokes the bride's head and face through the shawl enveloping her (a ceremony called *Mus-ha*, wiping). He and the other men then return to the bridegroom's house, followed at once by the bride, her female relations (excepting her mother), and her attendant. A modern well-to-do bride may go by car, but in most places she walks, or rides a camel or donkey. She is escorted to her room by her mother-in-law and other women, to an accompaniment of drums, shrill cries, singing, and hand-clapping. The bridegroom gives the bride a money-present before seeing her face, but in better-class houses this has become a token. The *makadia* remains with her during seven days, while she is confined to her quarters.

One more day completes the ceremonies with the celebration of the *Subhia* (morning), when a party, attended by the bride's mother, is given in the harem of the bridegroom's house; the bride's face is only thinly veiled, and she is given jewellery, clothes, and money. Finally a party is held on the seventh day, when she appears before the other women unveiled and dressed in her finest clothes, and takes part in the dancing.

If a man marry a second wife who is a virgin, similar ceremonies take place at the girl's home, but in the man's household their extent depends on the attitude of the first wife. The marriage of a man with a divorced woman or widow is usually conducted much more quietly.

Among the poor contact between the sexes is freer, love-matches are more common, and polygamy is not rare. Women are an economic asset, instead of an extravagance as among the wealthy. Thus, poor women usually increase the family income by working on the land, fetching and selling firewood and water, or making baskets, mats, and other things; some seek domestic work, and may even be the mainstay of their families. Wives of beduin in south-west Arabia tend the flocks, spin and weave, and have often no home-expenses, but roam the country-side, with their families, seeking pasture.

At Mecca it probably is still the prerogative of a young man's mother or other female relative, having decided on a suitable girl, with his consent to propose the marriage to her parents or guardians. Delicate negotiations follow and, on the day of promulgation of the contract, the bridegroom and his friends partake of a feast in the house of the bride's parents. In the latter part of the ceremonies, when the bridegroom goes to the bride's house, he unveils her face; otherwise these ceremonies, and the escorting of the bride to her husband's house, are much the same as described above.[1]

Among the *northern beduin* the marriage customs of such a tribe as the Ruwalla differ greatly from those recounted. While every able man is expected to marry and increase his kin (*ahl*), and there is no veiling or other barrier to free social intercourse between boys and girls, yet there are numerous limitations to a young man's choice of a wife. The 'forbidden degrees' include not only such persons as the divorced wife of a man's father or of his son, but even a daughter of his father's divorced wife by another man. Nor will the Ruwalla

[1] Eldon Rutter, *The Holy Cities of Arabia*, vol. ii, pp. 67–69 (1928).

allow their sons or daughters to marry into certain tribes considered inferior for various reasons; nor may they marry offspring of Solubba (gipsies), blacksmiths and other mechanics living in their camps; such persons are said to have no genealogy, and they marry new-comers from towns or other tribes, regardless of social status. More-over there are degrees even among the unquestionably free Arabs; for instance the 'Aneiza tribes consider themselves superior and dislike intermarriage with others. Even protected tribes, living with their protectors not as strangers but as neighbours (*qusara*), and hiring themselves out as free servants (*fedawiyya*), though quite honourable, may not intermarry with their protectors.

The rights of kinsmen (*beni al 'amm*, p. 399) are also strict; under ancient tribal law a girl should marry the nearest young male relative (*ibn al 'amm*) permitted by custom, generally a son of her father's cousin, or, if the latter has no sons and her grandfather had no brothers, the nearest descendant of her great-grandfather. Even. the kinsman does not claim her himself, his consent to her marriage is necessary. His claim is only void when the girl's father gives her in exchange for a new wife. If her father dies and the kinsman claims her, the girl may plead with him for freedom to choose her own hus-band, but he cannot be forced to grant this. Should he refuse, she and the man she has chosen can flee to the protection of a powerful chief of another tribe, but will then live in danger of vengeance from the kinsman, who may kill her without liability for compensation, and may kill the man with liability for only half the customary blood-money.

Within these limits, boys and girls who, from twelve years old upwards, are brought together by mutual inclination are free to marry. The boy may visit the girl in her tent, talk to her, and help her with her work. A young man who has thus fallen in love will woo the girl in highly poetical terms. He confides his desire to an older male friend, who discreetly finds out whether the prospective bridegroom's father objects, since it is bad form for a son to ask his own father directly. If the father be willing he goes with some prominent man to the girl's father and opens negotiations. The con-sent of the girl's father and of the *ibn al 'amm* having been given, the amount of the dowry is fixed by the latter; the dowry or *siyāq*—a word also used for the value put on a mare—is usually a she-camel or two and a mare; one camel, the *ba'ir al kū* or 'elbow-camel', goes to the bride's mother for having nursed her (leaning on the elbow in so doing).

The wedding itself, a simple affair, follows immediately. A she-camel is killed in front of the bridegroom's tent in the morning as a wedding-sacrifice (*dhabīhat al 'ars*). Towards evening a small round tent is pitched and furnished by women near by, or poor people may only partition a corner of their own tent. Near sunset some of the bridegroom's female relatives bring the bride to this tent, where the bridegroom later joins her. Some of the slaughtered camel is served for supper in the bridal tent, the rest of the meat is given to kinsfolk and friends. There is no party or dancing. Next day the bride receives a gift from her father-in-law, then she joins the other women in her husband's tent, but is excused work for seven days (a widow or divorced woman remarrying is excused work for three days). The bridegroom works as usual, but buys his wife a trousseau of dresses, blankets, and rugs.

A Ruweili after his first marriage stays with his wife a week, but a man already married divides his time between the two wives. As many marriages are due to real inclination, the man in many cases desires no other marriage, especially if the wife bears sons. Even if he marries other wives, he usually has only one woman in a tent; but if a second wife be introduced, against the wish of the first, the two usually settle down amicably together, devoting themselves to the husband for a day and a night in turn. A man really attached to his wife will, with his sons and servants, help her in pitching and striking the tent, loading the camels, fetching water and fuel, and buying provisions—labours which otherwise she must perform alone. In cooking, sewing, weaving bags and saddle-ornaments of camel's hair, and similar tasks, the husband cannot help.

Divorce. According to common opinion a man should divorce his wife if one becomes disagreeable to the other, but he need give no reason, even though the wife beg on her knees to be kept. Many men only divorce their wives from a whim; or, in the case of chiefs, from the political motive of wishing to marry the daughters of other powerful chiefs, whom they divorce in turn after a short period, even if a mother or expectant, thus never having more than one wife at a time. A divorced woman may remarry her former husband three times, but at the second remarriage her family may ask a new dowry. A man wishing to part finally from his wife can exclaim 'Thou art divorced three times'. Besides keeping her trousseau, a divorced woman is given by her husband a camel and pack-saddle; she keeps her children till they are seven years old, when they return to their father. No secret is made if a married woman falls in love, and a magnanimous husband will free her without asking for return of the dowry he gave. As the tribesmen fear disputes about paternity, a divorced woman must not remarry till it is certain whether or not she will bear a child by her former husband; unless she is undoubtedly an expectant mother, when she may remarry at once, since no question of the child's paternity is presumed. The penalties for unchastity are so severe that an unmarried expectant mother may even kill herself rather than risk being slain by her father or brother. The kin (*ahl*) will not allow an unmarried mother to stay with them, as her child would be without kin or protection in the clan. A man accusing a woman of unchastity without adequate proof was formerly, at any rate, liable to loss of a hand. The above remarks apply to the Ruwalla beduin, but variations of tribal custom in north and south are not fully known. Among townspeople divorce is supposed to follow the code laid down in the *shar'*.

Among the Qara and other tribes of Dhufār, customs are much freer. The most expensive bride may cost twenty cows. Marriage is legalized by a qadhi, but a man can dismiss his wife with a parting gift of half a cow. A woman can also divorce her husband, but must return half her marriage gift. A man usually has only one wife, or at most two, at a time; but if he marry a young second wife, he will pacify the older woman with a gift equal to the new bride's portion. Thus women become rich, and possession of property by man and wife independently is approved. Owing to the freedom enjoyed by women, illegitimacy is almost unknown; in the rare cases of transgression a girl is turned out of her tribe, but not killed by a male relative as would happen in 'Omān proper. Among these tribes the father of a boy about to marry for the first time speaks not only to her father but often to the girl herself and her mother, praising his son; also the rights of the *ibn al 'amm* are here insisted on only by the Mahra tribes. In some sections of these last, and the Manahil, a man takes his mother's name, e.g. Muhammad ibn Maryam. The Manahil, Hamūmi, and some other southern tribes are almost entirely monogamous, and a man proposes marriage to the woman direct.[1]

Seclusion. Many women grow up in strict seclusion, not only from men other than their husbands, but in some cases from girls also. The degree of seclusion varies widely in different social strata and districts. In many tribes women are as free as men, going unveiled and talking freely to men; this applies not only to nomad beduin, but

[1] Bertram Thomas, *Arabia Felix*, pp. 95–99; W. H. Ingrams, *Arabia and the Isles*, p. 319 (footnote).

to many of the poorer classes among the settled cultivators. Among townsfolk strict seclusion is enforced, especially among the well-to-do. Even so, a man may usually see any closely related woman with whom marriage would be impossible; but he may not see, for instance, his brother's wife, even if he and she grew up together as children. Stratagems are adopted for getting round these rules; e.g. a young girl and boy may be married and almost immediately divorced, so that the boy becomes related to the girl's mother, who can then visit the boy's mother without restraint, even if the boy be in the room.

As soon as a girl is put in purdah she can only be seen by her close female relatives. She is cut off from the society of her unmarried girl friends, or can only take part in women's social diversions veiled and wrapped in her outdoor cloak. This seclusion may be due to fear that women would speak unfavourably of the girl's charms and lessen her matrimonial opportunities. These remarks apply specially to the Aden Protectorate, where girls are sometimes married as young as nine or ten, to relieve them from the inconvenience of strict seclusion.

Birth and Upbringing of Children

Every woman hopes to bear children, and, should she be childless, will take medicines, visit the tombs of saints to pray, and wear charms; if she continue barren, the husband will take another wife. In childbirth most women depend on the help of relatives or of a hired midwife, whose methods are usually traditional and insanitary. The poorest women may give birth under any slight cover in the open, and at once return to their normal work. Among such northern beduin as the Ruwalla no midwives are employed; a case is recorded of a woman giving birth while riding in the litter on a camel, which she never ceased to guide, while at the end of the journey she helped pitch the tent as usual.

Among the customs associated with childbirth the following relate mainly to well-to-do families in certain parts of the Aden Protectorate. A new-born infant is washed and dosed with castor-oil; a finger smeared with honey and oil is placed in its mouth to raise the palate and make the child speak clearly (*tarfi'a*, raising); the palate may be rubbed with pounded date, and in the Dathina (Lower 'Aulaqi country) a local holy man rubs the child's mouth with his saliva or with oil to make the devil fly away (*tahnik*, rubbing). The child is wrapped in swathing bands with arms and legs drawn out straight, and the face painted with black markings as a safeguard against the evil eye. A mother not quickly regaining strength is poulticed on the back with a mixture of oil, gum, myrrh, and other vegetable products. On the seventh day a party is given for the relatives; a piece of cloth with a sacred inscription is tied round the child's head, and its forehead, nostrils, cheeks, and chin are blackened with *hisha* as a precaution against the evil eye, while the grandfather or another male relative, taking the infant, whispers 'God is most great' several times into his ear and calls him by the name chosen; in some districts the name is that of a powerful tribal chief, who takes the child under his protection. No visitor may see the child for forty days, or among wealthy seiyids even up to two years. A mother may feed her baby up to two or three years (e.g. in Fadhli or Subeihi territories), though naturally goat's milk and other food must be added. Among wealthy seiyids a mother rarely nurses her own child, but poor women carry their babies to the fields in portable cradles or in baskets slung over one shoulder by a strap. In poor families infants are rarely washed but sometimes smeared with oil or, among the beduin, with indigo.

A Meccan father will invite a number of his and his wife's male relatives to the naming ceremony, usually just after sunset. The infant, brightly dressed and lying on an embroidered cushion, is laid with its head pointing towards the Ka'ba. The *adhān* ('God is most great') and the *iqāma* ('I testify that there is no god besides Allah'), the first two formulas cried from the mosques by the muedhdhins, are repeated three times into the child's ears by the father, after which he says 'I name thee M.', and the child is thus formally made a Moslem. The visitors place small coins beneath the cushion, and the father, knocking a pestle on a mortar, is answered with loud cries of joy (*zaghārīt*) by the women upstairs.[1]

Among the Ruwalla no animals are sacrificed nor celebrations held at the birth of a boy or girl, though near relatives congratulate the father on the birth of a boy. According to ancient tribal custom the child is bathed in camel's urine and rubbed with salt for seven days after birth. Some time later, all the women of the camp are invited to a dinner by the female relatives. Every relative gives the child something, for instance a young camel, which remains its property. The mother alone, in this tribe, names the child, in many cases from some circumstance attending its birth, such as *Matar* (rain) for a son born during a rainstorm, or *Zā'l* (anger) for the son of a mother angry at her husband's ill-treatment. A child may be named after a beast or a plant. Boys and girls remain with their mother till their seventh

---

[1] Eldon Rutter, *The Holy Cities of Arabia*, vol. ii, chap. 4 (1928).

year, helping with the lighter work and going to the father only for an occasional talk. Older boys squat with the men round the fire, learning songs and poems, and to shoot while still very young. Boys are never idle; when not working they play games, all tending to harden them and sharpen their wits. The most dangerous game, *shāra*, consists in two hostile parties slinging stones at one another, from which wounds, loss of an eye, or even death, may result; in the last case, the blood-price has to be paid by the kin of the boy who inflicted the fatal injury. In another game, *hājiya*, a pit is dug and inside it a smaller pit; a stone ball laid on the edge of the larger pit must be knocked into it by a larger stone ball thrown from a distance, and must roll into the small inner pit; the winning team ride back to the throwing-point on the backs of the losers, whom they liberally cuff and kick.

Among many townsfolk boys have usually learned to pray correctly, to recite parts of the Koran, and to answer a simple catechism, by the age of six or seven. But in the towns and villages of south-west Arabia children play round the house with little attention paid to them, except in wealthy families which can afford special servants for their children; at six or seven the boys may go to a mosque-school, and girls may be taught to read the Koran at home, but many girls and some boys are not even taught this much. A mother tends to spoil her children and control them too little, but even so they are well-behaved and respectful in their father's presence. Meccan children are usually very submissive to their elders in general, though little boys of poorer families may be extremely rebellious towards their mothers.

In parts of south-west Arabia many curious customs obtain. At Aden a child losing a first tooth must throw it towards the sun, saying, 'Oh eye of the sun, take the tooth of the ass and give me the teeth of a gazelle!' Young boys often have their heads shaved excepting tufts on top, in front, or at the side (photo. 225); in some tribes boys still wearing these tufts are safe from being killed in tribal war. A woman long childless, or who has lost her sons, may vow to her saint (*weli*) that, if she bear a son, she will shave his head thus for seven or eight years; at the end of the period, she gives a party and has the carefully kept hair-cuttings weighed against money to be given to the poor. A girl's head may be shaved at about nine years old, to make her hair grow better. A girl reaching marriageable age must count the beams in an upper room, and count certain gold coins, and dip her hand into a bag of rice, each seven times, and these rites must be performed for seven days; she must also drink boiled milk into which two drops of ghee, or some money, has been put. Hair-combings in general should be kept, as bad luck may follow if they are thrown away; moreover, persons so careless as to throw away their nail-parings will have to pick them all up with their eyelashes at the Resurrection.

Young girls of the Qara mountains have their heads shaven in alternate stripes, excepting a brow fringe, till betrothal at thirteen or fourteen, after which the hair may grow freely.

Rites attending Circumcision

Circumcision of male children is universal, and that of girls is widely practised, though tribal custom varies, and practice differs between tribesmen and townsfolk. Among the northern beduin, the most detailed information again relates to the Ruwalla, among whom boys are circumcised between their third and seventh year, usually in late April or May (the season *as seif*), on a day just before or after the middle of the lunar month. Two days earlier, the girls from the whole camp decorate the main pole of the father's tent with ostrich feathers and red handkerchiefs. After sunset the whole youth of both sexes assembles, the young men forming a semicircle towards the tent, where a great fire burns. An adult girl (*hāshi*) with face veiled and holding a sharp sword, stands between the youths and the fire; the young men clap their hands, stamp, rock their bodies backwards and forwards, and to right and left; accelerating their movements, they touch the girl, who pretends to defend herself; when exhausted, the men rest and the girl runs away; other hāshis succeed her, and the dance ends only at sunrise, being repeated the following night. On the third morning the father sacrifices a camel before the tent, and a great dinner is made of its meat with *'eish*, when anyone may enter and eat his fill. Afterwards the father performs the act on the boy, who is dressed in black, to the accompaniment of loud rejoicings by the women, and a mock battle of youths on horseback outside the tent. Later, the boy is dressed in white and given presents, clothing, young camels, and weapons.[1] In some tribes the girls dance in a ring, before the dance of the young men described.[2] The Solubba (gipsies), who formerly heeded the customs of Islam little, now practise circum-cision.[3] The postponement of the rite till early manhood, as a test

[1] Musil, *Manners and Customs of the Rwala Bedouins*, pp. 244–246 (1928).
[2] Doughty, *Arabia Deserta*, vol. i, chap. 12.
[3] Philby, *Arabia of the Wahhabis*, p. 369.

of fortitude, as in certain tribes in the mountains of southern 'Asīr, where circumcision is 'a most barbarous, exhausting ideal', is held to be a relic of pre-Islamic religion, and is disapproved by the Sa'ūdi government.[1] The rite is also performed with less festivity than formerly among the townsfolk of Sa'ūdi Arabia, owing to the Wahhabi regime; the age of the boys may be six or seven. In the households of south-west Arabia male infants of twenty to forty days are circumcised, usually by the local barber, while the father sacrifices a goat or sheep; but in delicate children it may be left till seven or eight years.

Circumcision of infant girls is the practice of the Āl Murra and some other tribes just north of the Rub' al Khali, as well as of some northern tribes. The Manasir, of the Persian Gulf coast, are said to circumcise young adult women. Many other tribes and many townsfolk do not circumcise women at all. Cases occur in Aden but probably not in the Aden Protectorate.

In the Qara tribes of Dhufār the rite is very important, but, as in many other ways, these peoples differ so widely from the Arabs that a separate origin for the custom is suggested. Girls are circumcised on the day of their birth, males not till they reach adolescence; with the Mahra, indeed, the rite was formerly postponed till the eve of a man's marriage. When a boy of about fifteen is to undergo the rite, he sits on a rock amid a large crowd of men and women, holding in his hand a blunted sword, which he throws in the air and catches again by its blade. Before him sits the circumciser, an old man of good position; behind the boy stands an unveiled virgin, generally his sister or cousin, holding a sword which she raises and lowers vertically, striking the blade with her left palm. Immediately after the act, the boy must run round the crowd of people, raising and lowering his sword; his manliness being judged by his apparent oblivion to pain.[2]

Salutations, Hospitality, and Greeting and Farewell Ceremonies

Only a few examples of the varied usages under these heads can be given. Among many of the northern beduin a salutation returned, even by a child, is a guarantee of safety, as the kin of the person returning the greeting will then protect the traveller. But adult beduin do not return a greeting as quickly as a child, but wait to find out more about the traveller or travellers. The greetings are considerably more than the ordinary *salām 'aleikum, wa 'aleikum as salām* (peace on you,

[1] Philby, *Geographical Journal*, vol. xcii, p. 18 (July, 1938).
[2] Bertram Thomas, *Arabia Felix*, pp. 71, 72.

and on you peace), consisting of a series of formal questions and answers, including inquiries about the health of the traveller and his sons, followed by others regarding destination and origin.

Travellers passing a camp are questioned by the people, even if they do not wish to stop; water is often begged from them by herdsmen, but usually refused unless fresh camel's milk is given in return. A traveller, wishing to halt and enter a tent, approaches it from the rear, halting by the men's quarters. When he has been scrutinized through chinks in the tent, a servant takes his baggage and fetters his camel, and he enters. If he is held in esteem, all rise; the host and guest kiss each other on both cheeks, each with his hands on the other's shoulders. The guest then greets each person in turn with the ordinary 'peace on you'. Many households may compete to induce a traveller to enter their tent; but a well-provisioned traveller may express the wish to be, not a guest, but a neighbour, camping beside a tent, the owner of which becomes temporarily his protector, helping him to unload and load.

Hospitality to travellers usually lasts three days and one-third; a day for salutations (*salām*), the second for entertainment (*ta'ām*), the third for discussion (*kalām*); the third part of the fourth day is reckoned from sunset till the appearance of the morning star, between which time and sunrise the guest should leave. For a further three and one-third days the host will protect his late guest from fellow-tribesmen, to a distance of nearly a hundred miles; even if the guest visits other tents during that period, his first host is still responsible, and must right him if wronged, or put him under the protection of a chief strong enough to do so.

In the mountainous south-west, certain tribes, especially the 'Aulaqis of the Aden Protectorate, perform a peculiar greeting ceremony called *mōqab*. The men of a settlement parade in a long line with their chief men in the centre. A drum is beaten and shots of salutation are exchanged with the approaching visitors, who dismount, form a similar line, and then advance to about 50 yards from the 'home side'. The men of the settlement now advance, usually holding hands in couples and uttering war-cries; the column moves in wheels and circles, presenting intentionally a snake-like appearance, with the chief men now in front (unless some chiefs are not disposed to welcome the visitors). A tribesman chants verses composed by himself, at first alone, but later the first and second halves are taken up in chorus by the front and rear parts respectively of the wheeling column. The visitors judge from the words sung whether they are welcome or not; if unwelcome, they deploy and disperse; if welcome, they then perform the same ceremonies. Next, the chief men of both sides advance and meet midway between the two lines, greeting each other, in two single files, silently, by clasping right hands, slapping them together, and each giving the other's hand a gesture between a sniff and a kiss; in this handclasp it is thought indecent to grasp the thumb, as Yemenis and Somalis do. The question 'Any news?' is at first answered by a flat denial, but, the ceremony being ended, news is exchanged normally. This 'Aulaqi ceremony is usually conducted in a dignified manner, with long monotonous chant, though some tribes perform it at an ungainly run.[1]

The Shihuh of 'Omān perform a farewell ceremony (*nadaba* or *qubqub*), in which a dozen men stand in a close circle with heads bowed inwards. In the centre a sheikh, after certain gestures with his arms, utters a curious howl, ascending and descending nearly an octave. The other men break in at intervals with a staccato barking, while the remaining tribesmen perform a frenzied dance, throwing their swords into the air and catching them with naked hands.[2]

In the Western Aden Protectorate tribal dances, doubtless of pagan origin, are performed by men and boys alone, or by girls alone. In Haushabi territory, girls form a semicircle, with arms round each other, and move up and down bending their knees rhythmically to the accompaniment of a drum. In the Yemen highlands, at weddings and other festivities, men and boys, their turbans decorated with sprigs of sweet basil or other plants, dance slowly round in a circle, each pirouetting as he advances to drum-accompaniment; each holds his dagger aloft, with point downwards. The Imam and other high persons are preceded in the streets by bodyguards of soldiers, who dance with uplifted daggers as they move forward, uttering shrill songs in chorus.

The tribesmen of the Qara mountains use a peculiar chant (*danadon*) in their welcoming ceremonies, in which improvised 'heroic' couplets are sung, and men dance with drawn swords. Their girls also sing openly in chorus.[3]

Funeral Customs

The first part of what follows refers particularly to the Aden Protectorate, but much of it may be applicable to townsfolk and

[1] Hon. R. A. B. Hamilton, *Man*, vol. xlii, no. 44 (July–Aug. 1942).
[2] Bertram Thomas, *Alarms and Excursions in Arabia*, p. 228 (1931).
[3] Id., *Arabia Felix*, pp. 53, 76 (1932).

settled inhabitants in other parts. Verses from the Koran are read when a man is dying, and the creed is quietly pronounced at the moment of death, accompanied by the dropping of a little water into the dying person's mouth. The family weep round the body till a man arrives to prepare it for burial, when most or all of them withdraw. The body, after being washed, is clothed in a long shirt (*kafan*) of white cotton material, censed and scented, and a length of cloth is bound round the head, and wound round the body from head to foot, with henna between the folds. The body, on a wooden mat-covered bier, draped with a coloured cloth, is carried by four men to the mosque, but in the streets others, perhaps chance passers-by, relieve the bearers for short distances. Many will assemble at the mosque to pray for a well-known man, but only a few for the poor. At the cemetery the grave has an overhung cavity excavated in one side, in which the body is laid, so that when filling the grave the earth does not fall on it. The body is laid on its side and a near relative, descending, unwinds the face-wrappings and places the right hand under the head. At Mecca, where special ceremonies prevail, the body is laid in a hollow, undercut in the bottom of one side of a vertical shaft; at Riyādh it is laid, covered with palm fronds, at the bottom of an inner groove (*lahad*), some 4 feet from ground-level.[1]

At a rich man's funeral bread and dates are distributed to the poor at the graveside; thereafter, a paid chanter, in a brushwood shelter, recites the Koran at various times for seven days and nights, after which a meal of dates and rice is given to poor people. For three nights the male relatives and friends of the deceased gather at the mosque to pray, read the Koran, and drink coffee, while incense and rosewater are used on the last night. Poor people dispense with many of these customs.

After a rich man's death his widow receives visits of condolence for three or four days; washed and clothed in white, with white head-veil and seated on a white-covered mattress, she holds a rosary and weeps, while the visitors throughout the day weep loudly. On the fourth day the mattress is folded up. In districts where women smoke hookahs, they must abstain during the first two days, but on the third morning a hookah is carried in ceremonially, preceded by a woman calling out the dead husband's name. The guests are entertained to meals on the third and fourth days. A widow, poor or rich, may not remarry for at least four months and ten days. But, whereas

[1] Eldon Rutter, *The Holy Cities of Arabia*, vol. ii, p. 77; Philby, *Arabia of the Wahhabis*, p. 53.

poor widows dressed in black continue their work immediately after the husband's death, well-to-do women may not exchange their white 'widow's weeds' for black, nor oil their heads, till the period of mourning has expired, and may not wear ornaments for a year. During the four months and ten days the widow is visited daily by a female Koran-reader, and on Fridays the readings are attended by friends.

When a woman dies, her male relatives attend the funeral but show no outward sign of mourning; close female relatives, however, wear a black cotton head-veil and abstain from wearing ornaments for from forty to sixty days, when an entertainment called *Fat-hat al Arba'in* (or *as Sittin*, as the case may be) is held. Infants are buried by their menfolk without observance of mourning, but for an older child women may wear black cotton head-veils indoors for a short period. The four days' mourning as described above are kept for any member of a family (except a very young child), but the white dress is reserved for widows.

Among the northern beduin such as the Ruwalla, dead bodies are avoided as much as possible, and fellahīn are hired from a settlement if within reach; these carry the body, wrapped in the shirt worn in life, or enshrouded in linen, on a mule to the grave, which is deeper for a woman than for a man. A stone is put under the head and the body laid on the right side, facing south; two stones are placed above a man's grave, one above a woman's. In the inner desert only two to four people attend the funeral; a woman never follows a dead man, and a dead woman is buried only by women. The body is carried on staves or ropes, wrapped in an 'aba, and buried perhaps only 8 or 10 inches deep. Neither the staves nor grave-digging mattock may be brought into the tent afterwards. Water, if it can be spared, is poured over the grave so that the dead may not thirst. Only the nearest female relatives are allowed to utter one quiet lamentation in the camp, but outside they tear their dresses at the breast, scratch their faces, throw dust over themselves, weep, and wind white bands round their heads. For three nights no greeting is given to the next of kin, but towards the third evening a camel, sheep, or goat is sacrificed (*habāta*) at the spot where the person died, but outside his tent, which is removed a short distance and placed as though falling down; no one is invited to the feast, but whoever wishes comes and eats. No leavings, nor even the utensils, may be taken inside the tent. In some tribes, e.g. the Mawāhib of Harrat al 'Uweiridh, a tent-pole is set up at the head of a woman's grave.[1]

[1] Doughty, *Arabia Deserta*, vol. i, chap. 16.

On the next holiday the nearest relative loads a fat she-camel with provisions and whatever a man needs, or with dresses and carpets for a woman, and, invoking the dead person three times, kills the animal, sprinkles the blood to the four quarters of the compass, salts the meat and either gives it away or cooks it outside the tent; all the objects packed on the camel should also strictly be given away. Three days after the sacrifice a piece of the fat is melted and poured over porridge, and the three stones on which the kettle stood are smeared, with an invocation that the fire burning the dead person's soul may be cooled. Similarly a man passing near the grave of one dear to him will take a pebble off, exclaiming that he does this to lighten his friend's soul.

These tribesmen say that every man and beast has a soul (*nasam*, *nafas*, *rūh*), breathed into its nostrils by God at the moment of birth, and some individuals appear to believe in reincarnation. The souls, even of animals, will probably go to paradise or hell with man. A dead man is sometimes said to be suspended in the air above his grave, with his soul floating above his head, till the *habāta* sacrifice, after which he rests quietly in his grave, and his soul departs, none knows whither.

Among the Qara tribes the blood-sacrifice and burnt-offering survive; half a man's estate, namely his cows, is sacrificed for the state of his soul; one cow, or two, may be slaughtered over the grave immediately after the burial; two nights later another cow, and from a fortnight to three months later the main sacrifice of ten to twenty cows, these later sacrifices taking place not at the grave but the place where the man lived. As relatives and friends sacrifice still more cows, all the members of a tribal section may carry away large portions of raw meat, while one cow is roasted as a feast for them and for visitors from other tribes.

African influence seems evident in Dhufār, where, when a negro slave dies, an evil spirit is thought to enter the grave, and drums and devil-dances are used to drive it away, a practice shocking to strict Ibādhis from 'Omān.[1]

[1] Bertram Thomas, *Arabia Felix*, pp. 29, 55.

CHAPTER VIII

PUBLIC HEALTH AND DISEASE

CERTAIN aspects of the public health of Arabia, which have in the past been subjects of international concern, arose from the facilities offered by the annual pilgrimages to the holy places of Islam for the interchange of infections, notably cholera. Since several cholera pandemics originated thus, the conditions under which the pilgrimages were made naturally had world-wide repercussions. With the spread of modern preventive methods and the development of public health services, it may be hoped that these events belong to the past. It therefore seems advisable to divide this chapter into two main parts: a résumé of 'Diseases met in Arabia to-day', and an account of 'Public Health in Sa'ūdi Arabia with special reference to the pilgrimage'.

DISEASES MET IN ARABIA TO-DAY

These are discussed seriatim in the order of the table below. The list is not exhaustive; but, so far as epidemic diseases go, the only ones omitted which have (so far as can be ascertained) occurred during the last ten years are plague, cerebrospinal meningitis, and rabies. Their occurrence is probably sufficiently sporadic to excuse their omission.

1. Smallpox.
2. Louse-borne fevers: (a) relapsing fever, (b) typhus.
3. Infections borne by mosquitoes and sandflies: (a) malaria, (b) filariasis, (c) leishmaniasis.
4. Helminth infections: (a) schistosomiasis, (b) guinea-worm, (c) intestinal worms.
5. The Granulomata: (a) treponematosis, (b) tuberculosis, (c) leprosy.
6. Intestinal infections: (a) enteric fevers, (b) dysenteries.
7. Eye disease: (a) general, (b) trachoma.
8. Nutritional diseases: (a) general, (b) diseases of teeth, (c) ulcers, (d) vesical calculus.
9. Mycetoma.
10. Herniae.
11. Addiction to qāt.
12. Diseases of children.
13. Malignant disease.

1. *Smallpox*

Smallpox is endemic throughout Arabia. Burton (1855) stated:

'The Judari, or smallpox, appears to be indigenous to the countries bordering upon the Red Sea; we read of it there in the earliest works of the Arabs, and even to the present day, it sometimes sweeps through Arabia and the Somali country with desolating violence. In the town of *El Medinah* it is fatal to children, many of whom, however, are in these days inoculated: amongst the Bedouins old men die of it, but adults are rarely victims, either in the city or in the desert. The nurse closes up the room during the day, and carefully excludes the night-air, believing that, as the disease is "hot", a breath of wind would kill the patient. During the hours of darkness, a lighted candle or lamp is always placed by the side of the bed, or the sufferer would die of madness, brought on by evil spirits or fright. Sheep's-wool is burnt in the sick-room, as death would follow the inhaling of any perfume.'

Some patients appear to have survived this treatment for we are told that 'On the 21st day the patient is washed with salt and tepid water'.

The primitive form of smallpox inoculation referred to by Burton is still practised in the Yemen. The material is taken from the pustules of a smallpox patient, and scratched with a thorn into the outer surface of the leg of the person to be inoculated, below the knee. The practice had been introduced in the Hejaz only a generation before Burton's visit. The introduction of modern vaccination into Arabia has not yet suppressed the older procedure. In the winter of 1942–3 cases of smallpox were reported from the Wadi Ma'ādin in the Subeihi country, Western Aden Protectorate. These were found to be cases of varioloid. A local man had gone to a village in the Yemen, where smallpox was prevalent, and had collected pus from smallpox lesions. This he brought back in a cartridge case and for a fee of one anna proceeded to vaccinate the community.

Smallpox seems always to be present in Arabia. In 1944 and 1945 there has been a considerable outbreak in the Western Aden Protectorate. In Sa'ūdi Arabia large-scale epidemics of smallpox have been less frequent of recent years. The weekly sanitary bulletin of the Hejaz reported numerous cases in 1934–5. In only 2 of the 34 bulletins published that year were no cases or deaths from smallpox reported, the greatest numbers being 25 cases and 20 deaths during a week in December. Very commonly only fatal cases are reported. The year 1936–7 was almost free from smallpox in the Hejaz. The Public Health Administration of the Hejaz (p. 470) does a certain amount of vaccination.

As a cause of blindness in Arabia smallpox is second in importance only to trachoma.

2. *Louse-borne Fevers*

The lack of any reference to louse-borne infections in the pilgrimage quarantine reports before 1939 is most interesting. Both relapsing fever and typhus would seem to be fairly recent arrivals in Arabia.

(*a*) *Relapsing fever*, first reported about 1935 from the mountainous districts of the Western Aden Protectorate near the Yemen frontier, was naturally supposed to be tick-borne. Relapsing fever carried by ticks occurs in Somaliland and camel-ticks are plentiful in Arabia; the tick *Ornithodorus moubata* has not, however, been discovered in south Arabia, though *O. savignyi* is common. The whole epidemiology of relapsing fever in south Arabia confirms the opinion that it is there carried by lice. Though this disease has only been accurately observed in south Arabia during the last ten years, many cases were seen by the British Medical Mission (p. 305) in San'ā between 1939 and 1943, though Dr. Emilio Dubbiosi of the Italian Mission stated in 1937 that he had seen cases even before that date. But these earlier cases were sporadic; the first proved outbreak occurred in the prison at San'ā in 1939, in which year typhus also occurred in the capital. In 1941, 93 cases of relapsing fever and 6 of typhus were admitted to the wards of the British Medical Mission. In 1942 relapsing fever decreased while typhus increased; only 44 cases of the former, but 143 of the latter, were admitted to the same wards.

(*b*) *Typhus.* The facts of the first known outbreak in south-west Arabia have recently become available.[1] The first outbreak of both typhus and relapsing fever occurred in 1939 at San'ā among hostages held by the Yemen Government in the prison of the citadel; these were mostly boys under 12, living uncared for in an extremely filthy and overcrowded state. Early in 1939 a few patients, admitted to the wards of the British Medical Mission, showed symptoms believed to be after-effects of typhus. Later in 1939 some cases with typical rash occurred. In 1940, despite a rush of cases, the disease was still mainly confined to the prison. The outbreak of typhus followed that of relapsing fever, a sequence noted also in the later outbreaks. Early in 1941 measures for disinfesting the prison were suggested to the Yemen Government, but instead the boys were sent to the public

---

[1] In a report by Dr. P. W. R. Petrie entitled 'Typhus in Western Aden Protectorate: a review of the position at the end of July, 1944', received through the Colonial Office.

baths, where they spread typhus to boys from an orphanage school. Relapsing fever and typhus then spread to the army and the whole city. Outbreaks with high death-rate occurred in surrounding villages, and the provincial cities of 'Amrān, Dhamār, Yarīm, and Ta'izz were successively involved. In San'ā during 1941 some households had six or seven cases with three or four deaths. According to custom, the boy hostages were sent home and replaced by relatives every six months (p. 338), thereby spreading infection still more. A severe fresh outbreak took place early in 1942, and typhus raged till early in 1944. In the summer of 1944 a lull followed, not wholly explained by the season, for no pause mitigated the pestilence in the summers of 1942 and 1943.

Conditions were aggravated by the severe famine (p. 304), resulting from failure of the rains in 1942 and the wholesale export of grain, due to soaring prices in adjacent countries. By March 1943 thousands of people from the Tihama crowded the highland cities, sleeping huddled together in the streets. To relapsing fever and typhus was added dysentery and, despite relief measures by the Yemen Government, hundreds died. In July, August, and September 1943 over 500 winding sheets per month were issued free in San'ā alone for persons who died destitute.

In 1943 typhus spread to the Jewish quarter in San'ā, hitherto free from all but sporadic cases. At the same time parties of Jews began to emigrate via Aden to Palestine (p. 304). The Aden Government at length perforce insisted on the emigrants remaining in a camp at Lahej, till they could be drafted in parties to ships. Typhus spread to Aden Colony and Protectorate. The first case ever notified there occurred in January 1944, the sufferer being a Jewish agent from Aden who periodically visited the Lahej camp.

Vigorous action by the Aden medical authorities comprised restriction of movement of all Yemenis, Jew or Arab, in the Colony and Protectorate; prohibition of entry into the Protectorate of any more Jews from the Yemen; notification of all cases, and daily returns; and isolation of some 1,600 Jewish emigrants in a camp with improvised hospital at Fiyūsh, where the inmates were shaved and scrubbed, and their clothes sterilized or burned. By 31 January 1944 the 'first wave', responsible for 15 cases and 2 deaths, was over. Though recrudescences of relapsing fever, coinciding with reinfestation by lice, occurred in the camp in February, there were no more cases of typhus.

But in widely distant parts of the Western Protectorate outbreaks began in February and March 1944—at Dhāla', whither infection may have been carried by Jews illegally entering the country, and in 'Alawi and Subeihi territories, where it probably spread along normal trade-routes from the Yemen. At Dhāla', where relapsing fever again pre-ceded typhus, one-third of the people were thought to have died in a few months; the Amir of Dhāla' stated that 41 persons out of his household of 130 died of typhus.

A military *cordon sanitaire* and sanitary squads were instituted. Recent methods of louse-control, including mass disinfestation by dusting with new insecticides, and vaccination of personnel exposed to infection, were recommended. When experts summoned from overseas arrived in April 1944 the 'second wave' was already receding; other diseases, together with prevalent malnutrition, were held by them partly responsible for the high death-rate. But before concerted action could be taken on their advice, a 'third wave' had broken in Lower Yāfa'i territory.

Action was concentrated against this new focus. The people of whole villages were dusted with AL. 63, of which some 600 lb. were used. Local 'dusters' were trained. Ruling chiefs were instructed to re-dust their people after seven days' interval, and to dust all travellers passing through their territories.

In June 1944 an organization was set up to prevent more strin-gently the entry of fresh infection from the Yemen and to eradicate the foci in the Western Aden Protectorate. Regular dusting stations were established on the main trade-routes. A new outbreak at Dhubiyāt in Amiri territory had to be combated. Plans, including provision of a still more powerful new insecticide (secret), were laid in anticipation of more virulent outbreaks in the winter of 1944-5.

The Eastern Aden Protectorate, though seriously afflicted by the famine,[1] seems so far to have escaped the typhus epidemic.

3. *Infections borne by Mosquitoes and Sandflies*

(a) *Malaria* is probably the most important cause of sickness throughout Arabia. Reports of the Administration of Health and Public Assistance of Sa'ūdi Arabia state that it is met with nearly everywhere throughout the kingdom in all its forms, benign and malignant. Recrudescences are frequent after heavy rains. Paul W. Harrison (1940) refers to the widespread endemicity and hyper-endemicity of malaria throughout 'Omān and adjacent territory; he reports the presence of all three varieties of malaria parasite in Muscat

[1] H. Ingrams, 'The Hadhramaut in Time of War', *Geographical Journal*, vol. cv, pp. 18-20 (1945).

itself and in Sohār, about 120 miles north-west of Muscat; in Sifala, on the coast south-east of Muscat, two very distinct types of the disease need study—one accompanied by only slight fever but with marked enlargement of the spleen, the other accompanied by high fever with chills but little or no splenic enlargement.[1] Petrie and Seal (1940)[2] in their medical survey of the Western Aden Protectorate found malaria nearly everywhere. There was very little in the highlands above 6,000 feet and in certain dry coastal districts. In the wadis which are dry for most of the year there is moderate endemicity, with splenic index of from 10 to 25 per cent. In areas within a few miles of perennial streams the endemicity was high, with splenic index of from 25 to 50 per cent. Quite close to such perennial streams hyperendemic malaria was found with splenic index above 50 per cent. A similar state of affairs probably exists throughout adjacent territory. In the Bahrein Islands malaria is an important cause of sickness (Afridi and Majid, 1938); in the town of Al Manāma malaria was responsible for a quarter of the cases treated at the hospital; the splenic index was 38·9 per cent.

Burton (1855) writing of the Northern Hejaz stated 'in the summer, quotidian and tertian fevers . . . are not uncommon, and if accompanied by vomitings, they are frequently fatal. The attack generally begins with the Naffazah, or cold fit, and is followed by El Hummah, the hot stage.' The description obviously applies to malaria.

Information regarding the anopheline mosquitoes responsible for transmission of malaria in Arabia is scanty.[3] In Aden Colony *Anopheles culicifacies*, a mosquito responsible for malaria transmission over large parts of India and in Ceylon, is the commonest species, but according to Petrie and Seal it is not found in the Western Aden Protectorate. There they found five species, *Anopheles gambiae, A. d'thali (dhali), A. pretoriensis, A. macmahoni, and A. rupicolus,* all African, the last three rare.

Anopheles gambiae was the most prevalent, being found in every area from which anophelines were identified, and breeding in pools and streams, in the weedy edges of which many larvae were found, as well as in shallow wells and irrigation channels; while in the high plateaux up to 6,000 feet rain-puddles form an additional habitat. This species is probably the only, certainly the most important, vector of malaria in the Western Aden Protectorate, and probably occurs

[1] Paul W. Harrison, *Doctor in Arabia*, pp. 160, 225 (1943).
[2] Dr. P. W. R. Petrie and Dr. K. S. Seal, *A Medical Survey of the Western Aden Protectorate, 1939–40* (printed for use by the Colonial Office).
[3] P. A. Buxton, 'The Anopheles of Arabia', *Trans. R. Soc. Tropical Medicine*, Dec. 1944.

throughout south-west Arabia. Perhaps the most redoubtable malaria vector in the world, it is responsible for very much of that in tropical Africa, and appears to be the only transmitter in British and Italian Somaliland. It is very common and widespread in Eritrea, breeding as high as 8,000 feet, and here, too, the most important malaria vector. Its extreme northern limit is near the Egyptian border in the Anglo-Egyptian Sudan.

In east Arabia the anopheline fauna would appear to be Asiatic rather than African. It is not known which species of *Anopheles* occur in 'Omān, but a malaria-survey of parts of the Bahrein Islands carried out by Afridi and Majid (1938) revealed the presence of *Anopheles stephensi, A. fluviatilis, A. culicifacies, A. pulcherrimus*, and *A. sergenti. A. stephensi*, the most prevalent and apparently the only species infected with malaria, was found breeding in agricultural drains, seepage pools, and shallow domestic wells, though larvae were not found in water appreciably saline.

In the north of Arabia one would expect the anopheline fauna to resemble that of Egypt, Palestine, and Transjordan. In Palestine *A. bifurcatus, A. maculipennis* var. *elutus, A. superpictus*, and *A. sergenti* are important vectors. *A. bifurcatus* is a domestic species breeding in wells and cisterns; it is responsible for nearly all the urban malaria of Palestine. *A. elutus* is the chief rural vector; it breeds in stagnant pools, wells, swamps, and reservoirs overgrown with algae, types of breeding-place less common in Arabia. *A. superpictus* breeds in eddies and backwaters of fairly rapid streams, and in the pools left in the watercourses of hill streams. *A. sergenti*, which most commonly breeds in very slowly moving streams and in seepages under rocks and pebbles, is possibly an important vector in north-west Arabia as well as Palestine.

(*b*) *Filariasis.* Cases of elephantiasis, chylous ascites, chyluria, and lymph scortum are met with in south Arabia.

An interesting condition called *blue skin disease* is thought by some experts (e.g. Dr. Affara and Dr. Smith at the Keith-Falconer Mission Hospital, Sheikh 'Othman, 1941) to be a form of filariasis. Hesitation has been felt about giving this definite clinical entity any recognized name, so that given by the late Dr. John C. Young of the Mission Hospital is adopted. The Arabs call it *sauda*, emphasizing a black rather than a blue coloration. The skin in fact becomes blue-black in the regions affected, most often the legs, especially the shin and inner side of the thigh, the affection being frequently symmetrical in the two limbs. The affected parts are very itchy and slightly scaly, rough and thickened, while an outstanding symptom is enlargement of the groin-glands. Arab sufferers, believing these enlarged glands to be the origin of the disease, often ask to have them removed. Beduin treatment consists in biting these glands through the skin, so that they are broken into small masses.[1]

(c) *Leishmaniasis.* Both the visceral and cutaneous forms of leish-maniasis have occasionally been reported from Arabia, but there is no information regarding the extent of their prevalence. The visceral form, kala azar, caused by *Leishmania donovani*, is transmitted by sandflies; cases have been reported from the Yemen and the Hadhra-maut. The cutaneous form of the disease, oriental sore, caused by *L. tropica* is (in view of its great prevalence in 'Iraq) probably much more frequent than kala azar. Recent work by Russian investigators has shown that cutaneous leishmaniasis is essentially a disease of lower mammals, communicable to man. In the desert regions of Middle Asia naturally infected wild rodents, especially the gerbil (*Rhombomys opimus*), serve as reservoir hosts of *L. tropica*, which is transmitted to man by sandflies breeding in the burrows of these rodents. It is possible that a somewhat similar state of affairs exists in Arabia. Several cases of oriental sore have been reported from south Arabia.

4. *Helminth Infections*

(a) *Schistosomiasis*, or bilharziasis, is a disease caused by the invasion of the body by a trematode worm. Two forms occur in Arabia, the urinary form caused by *Schistosoma haematobium*, and the intestinal form caused by *S. mansoni*. The adult worms live in the patient's veins; *S. haematobium* frequently in the veins of the bladder; *S. mansoni* usually in the veins of the rectum. The eggs of the worms leave the body of the human host in urine or faeces. If the embryos escaping from the eggs gain access to water containing certain species of fresh-water snail, their further development takes place within the snail's body. Having attained a certain stage of develop-ment they leave the snail's body and are capable of penetrating human skin with which they may come in contact. Bathing, paddling, or washing in infected water may result in infection.

In 1940, 30 cases of schistosomiasis were treated in the Civil Hospital at Aden; 12 of these patients came from the Yemen. Petrie and Seal found schistosomiasis in several places in the Western Aden Protectorate, for the most part at altitudes above 2,000 feet. Most

[1] Petrie and Seal, *A Medical Survey of the Western Aden Protectorate, 1939–40* (cited above).

cases were found on the plateau-top of Jebel Jihāf, which is above 7,000 feet. They made collections of fresh-water snails from many infected localities, but none of the species in their collections are the usual intermediate hosts of the parasite. *Melanoides tuberculata*, however, occurs widely in the area and has been suspected as a carrier in Nyasaland. *Bulinus truncatus* has also been found in south Arabia, though hitherto not in the districts where bilharziasis occurs. Further investigations are required.

Schistosomiasis occurs in Egypt, Palestine, and 'Iraq, so it is probable that the disease has a wide distribution in Arabia. So far, the places from which most cases are seen are Zabīd (Yemen), Jebel Jihāf (Western Aden Protectorate), and 'Azzān and Tarīm (both in the Eastern Aden Protectorate).

(*b*) *Guinea Worm.* This disease has been associated with Arabia from time immemorial. Plutarch (150 B.C.) stated that people on the Red Sea littoral had a disease which resembled the exit of small snakes from the skin, not an inapt description. The name of the guinea-worm, *Dracunculus medinensis* (Linnaeus, 1758), is derived from Al Madina; it was called *Vena medinensis* by Velsch in 1674. It appears to be fairly common throughout Arabia, but no longer specially so in Al Madina. Burton (1855) stated: 'The *Filaria medinensis*, locally called 'Farantit', is no longer common at the place which gave it its European name. At Yambu, however, the people suffer much from the Vena appearing in the legs. The complaint is treated here as in India and Abyssinia; when the tumour bursts, and the worm shows, it is extracted by being gradually wound round a splinter of wood.'

The female guinea-worm though less than 2 mm. in breadth may be a yard long. It generally lies in connective tissue between the muscles or under the skin, coming to the surface of the skin generally on the leg or foot. Intermittently it discharges countless embryos which display activity if discharged into water, where they may live for several days. If the water contains certain minute crustaceans (Cyclops) the guinea-worm larvae invade them, and human infection is contracted by swallowing water containing infected cyclops. The resulting disease is rarely serious if no attempts are made to extract the worm before parturition is complete. If the worm snaps during premature attempts at extraction, the escape of the uterine contents may cause violent inflammation.

Cases of guinea-worm have been frequently treated at the Aden Civil and Mission Hospitals, the patients coming from the Western Aden Protectorate.

(c) *Intestinal Worms.* Infestation of the intestine, especially by round-worm (*Ascaris lumbricoides*), is common in Arabia. During famine relief work in the Hadhramaut in 1944, 150 out of 300 children examined were infected with *Ascaris.* In some areas tape-worm (*Taenia saginata*) is also common. Cases of hydatid cyst have been reported from both the Western Aden Protectorate and the Yemen. In recent years hook-worm disease has been reported in the Western Aden Protectorate. In a recent examination at the R.A.F. Hospital, Aden, of some 3,000 Arabs applying for work in which they would have to handle food, the following carriers of diseases were detected: amoebiasis, 14; schistosomiasis, 17; *Ascaris lumbricoides*, 41; lambiliasis, 78; the tape-worm *Hymenolepis nana*, 36; hook-worm, 15.

5. *The Granulomata*

(a) *Treponematosis.* Syphilis, yaws, and a third treponematosis, *bejel*, have all been recorded from Arabia.

Syphilis is much commoner than had formerly been supposed. The storied strict code of the beduin in matters of sexual morality is far from universal. In any case a code allowing polygamy, easy divorce, and frequent remarriage will not, even if strictly kept, prevent the ordinary spread of syphilis. The *balūsh* disease of Beihān, previously thought to be the same as the *bejel* of north Arabia, is almost certainly syphilis; that it is accepted as a matter of course and without shame is but the natural result of the disease approaching saturation point in the population. It is rare for the central nervous system to be involved in any form of treponematosis in Arabia, but blindness from optic atrophy occurs. The commonest symptoms in untreated cases are large, foul, painless ulcers; perforation of the palate; collapse of the bridge of the nose and bowing of the tibiae. Such cases respond very quickly to treatment so far as clinical cure is concerned. Unfortunately syphilis is often acquired in Arabia in childhood; boys of 6 to 8, victims of sodomy, are frequently sufferers; a girl of 3 was the youngest case to come under the care of the British Medical Mission at San'ā.

Yaws. In the Western Aden Protectorate, Yemen, and Hejaz cases of goundou, gangosa, and juxta-articular nodes are seen. One case of florid yaws has been described from San'ā. Many patients from Zabīd in the Yemen, who come to the Mission Hospital at Sheikh 'Othman, are believed to be suffering from yaws, while a doctor from the Dutch East Indies (Dr. Ma'amun ar Rashid, in charge of Netherlands medical work in Mecca) considers the cases seen in the Hejaz to be the same form of yaws as in his own country. Patients often suffer from perforation of the palate and ulceration of the nose. As in the case of syphilis, they respond very quickly to treatment so far as clinical cure goes.

Bejel is a form of non-venereal syphilis endemic among the Arabs. Full descriptions have been published of the disease as it occurs among the beduin of the Upper Euphrates, and it has been reported among the Arabs on the Tigris below Mosul. It occurs in south Arabia, notably in the lowlands of the Yemen about Zabīd, and in 'Omān, and is probably widespread among the beduin of Arabia. The causative organisms of bejel are indistinguishable from *Spirochaeta pallida*, the cause of syphilis, but its clinical features differ considerably from those of syphilis as known in the west. Bejel is a disease of childhood, two-thirds of the cases being contracted before the patient is adult. While, however, the possibility of its being a clinical entity cannot be dismissed, the fact of its being a childhood disease is not enough to distinguish it from syphilis, the latter being (as stated) all too common among children in Arabia. The beduin do not associate bejel with sexual infection and speak of it without shame. Bejel is spread by contagion: the early lesions are very infective. Fondling and kissing an infected infant, the lack of hygiene generally, and the use of eating and drinking utensils in common, are ways in which infection is spread. Bejel does not appear to cause either sterility or miscarriage, and congenital bejel has never been reported. On the whole the disease would appear to have closer affinities to yaws than to syphilis, some observers believing the two to be identical. Bejel is very amenable to treatment.

According to Dr. P. W. Harrison moral standards are extremely low, and gonorrhoea is excessively common, in 'Omān. Venereal diseases are likewise common in Aden.

(*b*) *Tuberculosis.* References to the high prevalence of tuberculosis in Sa'ūdi Arabia, especially among women and children of the poor classes, are made in reports of the Health and Public Assistance Administration of the Kingdom. Petrie and Seal noted a prevalence of about 14 per 1,000 among an unselected population examined during their medical survey of the Western Aden Protectorate. Insanitary habits, especially promiscuous spitting; the crowding together of people in ill-ventilated rooms at *qāt*-parties where spitting is part of the regular ritual (p. 462); small, very poorly ventilated and over-crowded sleeping-rooms; under-nourishment, the confined conditions of the harem and the veils of the women, are contributory causes sufficient to explain a high incidence of tuberculosis.

(c) *Leprosy*. Though a few cases may be found in almost any part of Arabia, it is in the Yemen and the Aden Protectorate that definite foci of infection have been found. The British Medical Mission, recently in San'ā, had some twenty patients in their leper ward; the principal foci in the Yemen appear to be 'Udein, Ibb, Jibla, Madinat al Abīd, and Zabīd; in the Western Aden Protectorate there are several foci, while Wadi Dū'an has been mentioned in the Eastern Protectorate. In Dhufār also there appear to be foci, but in the Sultanate of 'Omān, as a whole, leprosy, according to P. W. Harrison, appears to have been common in the past, but it has been almost wiped out. Next to Dibai, south-west of Shārja, is a little village which is the leper asylum for the entire Pirate Coast; once a week the lepers may enter the towns and beg. Most of the patients were old burned-out cases; new cases were very rarely seen. Recent increased immigration from Baluchistan has, however, brought in many new cases.

The pale-skinned Arab, when infected, usually suffers from the nervous or anaesthetic type of leprosy, whereas the negroid Arab more usually suffers from the nodular type.

Two words indicate leprosy in Arabia; *jadham*, specially referring to the stage of the disease characterized by mutilation, e.g. loss of fingers or toes; and *baras*, denoting depigmentation of the skin, and therefore including some non-leprous conditions, such as leucoderma. It is therefore interesting to note that Burton (1855) does not appear to have noticed lepers in his travels. He says: 'the only description of leprosy known in El Hejaz is that called "baras": it appears in white patches on the skin, seldom attacks any but the poorer classes, and is considered incurable.' This may or may not have been leprosy.

6. *Intestinal Infections*

(a) *Enteric fevers* are endemic throughout Arabia, and small epidemic outbreaks appear to be common.

(b) *Dysenteries*. Dysentery in the Hejaz is reported to have a very low case-mortality rate, but a tendency to become chronic. Unprotected water-supplies, the absence of any sanitary method of excreta disposal, flies, and dust are more than sufficient to explain a high incidence of intestinal infections. P. W. Harrison refers to the importance of diarrhoea and dysentery in the causation of the very high infant mortality rates of 'Omān. Burton (1855) said that in the Hejaz 'dysenteries frequently occur in the fruit season, when the greedy Arabs devour all manner of unripe peaches, grapes and pomegranates'.

Among some 29,000 cases of sickness seen at the Sheikh 'Othman Mission Hospital during four years were 297 cases of dysentery with 22 deaths. Most of the patients at this hospital come from outside the colony. Cases were until recently thought to be almost entirely bacillary, but, with improved laboratory technique, the medical officers both in the Civil Hospital at Aden and in the Mission Hospital at Sheikh 'Othman now consider amoebic dysentery to be quite prevalent in the Colony and Protectorate of Aden; cases are also reported by Audisio from the Italian Laboratory at San'ā. In view of these facts, and the prevalence of the amoeba (*Entamoeba histolytica*) in 'Iraq, amoebic dysentery is probably widespread in Arabia.

Cholera is dealt with on pp. 471–472.

7. Eye Diseases

(a) *General*. About 8 per cent. of patients at general hospitals in south Arabia attend for some form of eye disease. Acute conjunctivitis is common and is usually due to Koch Weeks bacillus or to Pneumococcus, but purulent gonococcal conjunctivitis is not rare and is one of the causes of blindness. Results of treatment with sulphapyridine have been dramatically good. Senile cataract is, as in most sun-scorched countries, very common; in the recent survey of the Western Aden Protectorate the rate in populations over 45 years old was found to be 33 per cent.

(b) *Trachoma* is one of the major scourges of Arabia. An examination of the eyes of 100 unselected schoolboys in Aden revealed 70 suffering from trachoma. An examination of some 600 schoolboys in San'ā showed the trachoma incidence to be over 80 per cent. (Petrie and Seal). The trachoma incidence in Hodeida and other towns of the Yemen, both on the coast and in the mountains, is high. Petrie and Seal found trachoma everywhere in their survey of the Western Aden Protectorate, the incidence being specially high in the Fadhli and 'Abdali areas. Petrie has also reported that in San'ā the Jews are somewhat less prone to trachoma than the Arabs, probably because the houses and markets in the Jewish quarter are cleaner and less infested with flies; while the habit of darkening the eyelashes with powdered antimony, sometimes taken from a common vessel and applied with a metal instrument for common use, may also render the Arabs more subject; about 80 per cent. of the Jews and 90 per cent. of the Arabs in San'ā are afflicted with trachoma.[1] P. W. Harrison (1940) wrote:

[1] P. W. R. Petrie, 'Some Experiences in South Arabia', *Journ. Trop. Medicine and Hygiene*, December 1939, pp. 357–360.

'Throughout 'Omān the blind number thousands. . . . Trachoma is the usual cause. It is terribly common and, if neglected, it can cause complete blindness. . . . On our recent trip to Sifala we operated on over a hundred eyelids which were being curved inwards by their chronic trachoma.' The treatment of trachoma is slow and tedious and most patients weary of it long before cure has been effected.

8. Nutritional Diseases

(a) General. In the Yemen adult rickets in women (osteomalacia) accounts for many cases of badly obstructed labour, vesico-vaginal fistula, and death in childbirth. The Medical Survey carried out by Petrie and Seal in the Western Aden Protectorate revealed faulty feeding everywhere except in one small area. In some places the diet was almost incredibly poor; in the hills there was a serious lack of first-class proteins in the food; vitamins were deficient nearly everywhere. The incidence of rickets was very high, spongy gums and gingivitis were much in evidence, and cases of night blindness were seen. Dietetic deficiencies are probably responsible for the excessive prevalence of skin diseases, including Yemen ulcer and septic spots. Though generalizations for Arabia as a whole cannot be based on the results of so limited a survey as this, yet the conditions found in the Aden hinterland are not very exceptional. In 'Omān, also, underfeeding and poverty are largely responsible for the low standard of health.

(b) Diseases of Teeth. Writing of 'Omān, P. W. Harrison records that while caries of the teeth is rare among the beduin, whose teeth are proverbially well preserved—doubtless owing to their milk diet— pyorrhoea unfortunately is not rare.

(c) Ulcers. Skin diseases are extremely common in Arabia; among them ulcers, for which parts of Arabia have long been notorious, call for chief notice. Burton wrote:

'Ulcers are common in El Hejaz, as indeed all over Arabia. We read of them in ancient times. In A.D. 504 (? 540), the poet and warrior, Amr el Kays ('Imru al Qeis), died of this dreadful disease, and it is related that when Mohammed Abu Si Mohammed, in A.H. 132, conquered Yemen with an army from El Hejaz, he found the people suffering from sloughing and mortifying sores, so terrible to look upon that he ordered the sufferers to be burnt alive. Fortunately for the patients, the conqueror died suddenly before his inhuman mandate was executed. These sores here (in El Hejaz), as in Yemen, are worst when upon the shin bones; they then eat deep into the leg, and the patient dies of fever and gangrene. . . . There is no cure but rest, a generous diet and change of air.'

In Burton's time a distinction was made between the Hejaz *nasur* and the *jurh el Yemeni* or Yemen ulcer, but the conditions appear to have been very similar (in modern medical Arabic, however, *nasur* means a fistula, especially in the anus). Burton's reference in 1855 to the importance of a generous diet in the treatment of these ulcers is interesting, as several recent contributions to medical literature have stressed the importance of dietetic deficiency, and a lack of vitamins B or C, or both, in the causation of tropical ulcers. Such ulcers are most common among the underpaid, undernourished, and overworked members of the community. Trauma, dirt, and lack of care are the immediate causes. Petrie and Seal found Yemen ulcer to be a very common cause of disability in the Western Aden Protectorate. P. W. Harrison describes how high in importance the treatment of ulcers ranks among the activities of the Mission Hospital in Muttreh, near Muscat.

(b) *Vesical Calculus.* Stone in the bladder is very common in Arabia and 'cutting for stone' was one of the standard operations of the old Arab surgeons. In India McCarrison has shown that vesical calculus is frequently due to a deficiency of vitamin B, particularly where a certain grain is the staple food. Bilharzia is another cause of formation of stone; sections of bladder stones have shown a nucleus of eggs of Bilharzia. Many patients suffering from stone come from Zabīd (Yemen).

9. *Mycetoma (Madura Foot)*

A disease akin to actinomycosis is common in south Arabia; cases have been reported from 'Omān to the Western Aden Protectorate. The condition is said to affect especially those who trample muddy clay, for instance, in making bricks which are afterwards sun-dried. The causative fungus is thought to enter the skin through a small abrasion made by a sharp object, such as a thorn in the mud. Thus the disease occurs most commonly in the foot, but may attack other parts of the body. Its progress is slow; as the fungus spreads along the lines of least resistance, first under the skin and then between the muscles, the foot swells into irregular lumps, from each of which an 'eye', much like that of a potato, may develop. These 'eyes' discharge pus and shot-like grains, usually black but in some cases red or white, typical of the disease. Though treatment with bismuth and iodides, and also local injections of tincture of iodine, have been tried, the safest treatment and surest cure is still radical excision by operation. If neglected the disease spreads slowly, destroying tendons, muscles, and bones in its progress. An untreated patient finally dies of toxic exhaustion.

10. *Herniae*

Hernia, very common throughout Arabia, is usually inguinal in type, and the patients are generally men. Harrison, who has done much work on the subject in 'Omān, considers that hard laborious work does not cause these herniae so much as weakening of the skeletal structures with age.[1] When neglected the herniae in some cases attain the size of a football. Beduin treatment consists of cautery, and the scars left by this, combined with the great size of the hernia, often render the surgeon's work difficult. Inevitably some herniae strangulate, and some patients reach hospital too late.

11. *Addiction to Qāt*

The culture of *qāt* (*Catha edulis*) is described on pp. 492–493. The habit of chewing the young leaves, leaf-buds, and tender shoots, which has so largely taken possession of the people of south-west Arabia, is a noxious form of drug-addiction. In the cities of the Yemen the practice is universal, except perhaps among the poorest people; it also obtains widely in Aden and in parts of the Aden Protectorate.

In San'ā and other cities every house has at least one *qāt*-chewing room, and in many cases a second for the women. In the better houses a beautiful pavilion or *mifraj*, on the roof or in the garden, is used for this purpose (p. 415). Seiyids and other wealthy people hold large chewing-parties, often repeated day after day among the same persons. These parties are usually preceded by lunch and coffee; chewing begins about two o'clock in the afternoon and, for those who only work in the morning or do no work at all, it lasts till eight o'clock; even the times of prayer are altered to avoid interrupting the party, the noon and afternoon prayers being said together before the party begins, while the sunset and evening prayers are said together after it ends.

As many as from twenty to forty persons may be crowded into an ill-ventilated room. Windows and doors are shut and several hubble-bubble pipes are lit. The participants sit round the walls, each with a bundle of *qāt* and a spittoon in front of him. When a man has chewed for some time, swallowing only the juice of the plant, his cheeks become uncomfortably distended with a green paste of chewed leaves

[1] Paul W. Harrison, *Doctor in Arabia*, pp. 144, 192, 225 (1943).

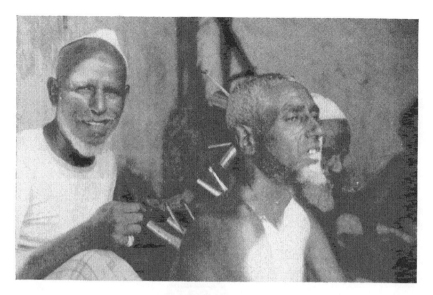

235. *Bleeding with metal cups at Mukalla*

236. *Bleeding with cows' horns*

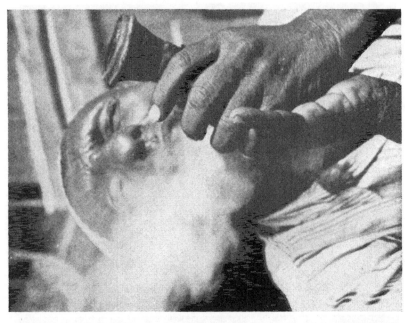

238. *A hashīsh smoker*

237. *Bunches of qāt leaves*

(the Yemenis speak of 'storing' rather than chewing or eating *qāt*); this paste is then ejected, with the aid of a finger, into the spittoon. The man then drinks noisily from a cruse of water, swilling out the mouth and also often swallowing water to assuage thirst; he then begins to chew again. During the afternoon the stale atmosphere becomes even more vitiated, and the participants break into a sweat, without which the party is not thought successful.

These parties are for the most part silent. A feeling of contentment supervenes, though the addicts claim varied and sometimes contradictory properties for the drug. Most, however, agree that it produces wakefulness and mental alertness. Europeans have found that the leaves have a rather bitter but not unpleasant taste, and that the only effect noted after occasional chewing was slight insomnia.[1] Certain alkaloids which have been isolated from the plant stimulate the brain and spinal chord, but may in large doses cause paralysis.

Qāt-chewing produces no staggering gait, though some of the addict's symptoms simulate alcoholic intoxication. An addict at the height of his bout is (in Dr. Petrie's words) a 'wild-looking, dull-witted, gaping automaton with glassy eyes'. Chronic addicts are usually very thin and of poor muscular development; deprived of the drug, they become restless, irritable, and useless for work. Whether, however, *qāt* by itself causes definite chronic nervous disorders may be disputed; for instance other causes, including the climate and high altitude, have been held partly responsible for the neurasthenia common in San'ā. At any rate, the teeth and gums of addicts become very foul through constant storage of chewed leaves; constipation, and perhaps also cirrhosis of the liver, are after-effects, while the habit has been said to result in impotence. Social results of *qāt*-chewing are waste of time, money, and land, the last because the *qāt*-trade is so profitable that vines and coffee-trees have been uprooted and *qāt* planted instead.[2]

12. *Diseases of Children*

Whooping-cough and chicken-pox are very common. Measles occurs in some areas, and outbreaks of anterior poliomyelitis have occurred in the Yemen and in both the Western and Eastern Aden Protectorates. Diphtheria and scarlet-fever seem to be rare.

[1] Wyman Bury, *Arabia Infelix*, p. 153 (1915).
[2] Among many writings on *qāt*, see C. Moser, 'The Flower of Paradise', *Nat. Geogr. Mag.* xxxii, pp. 173–186 (1917); P. W. R. Petrie, 'Some Experiences in South Arabia', *Journ. Trop. Med. and Hygiene*, p. 360 (Dec. 1939); C. E. Sage, 'Catha edulis', *Pharmaceutical Journal*, cliii, p. 128 (1944).

13. *Malignant Disease*

Both carcinoma and sarcoma occur in Arabia, but according to most of the reports available these conditions seem to be less common than in the West.

PUBLIC HEALTH IN SA'ŪDI ARABIA WITH SPECIAL REFERENCE TO THE PILGRIMAGE

As remarked (p. 447), the annual pilgrimages in the past provided opportunities all too good for the spread of epidemic diseases, particularly cholera. Between 1831 and 1912, twenty-seven cholera epidemics of varying degrees of severity were connected with the pilgrimage. An extension of infection from Mecca was responsible for the first of the English cholera epidemics of 1865 and 1866. A formidable widespread epidemic of cholera in 1893 originated in the pilgrimage.

Such catastrophes were not unmitigated disasters. The present generation owes much to past epidemics, which stimulated medical research as nothing else could. The threat of cholera was chiefly responsible for the provision of safe water-supplies and much improved sanitary standards in many lands. Recurring epidemics fostered, or rather made imperative, international collaboration. Most of a long series of international sanitary conferences were more or less concerned with the health dangers of the Mecca pilgrimage—conferences held at Paris 1851 and 1859, Constantinople 1866, Vienna 1874, Washington 1881, Rome 1885, Venice 1892, Paris 1894. The last dealt with sanitary regulation of the pilgrimage and quarantine measures in the Persian Gulf. The international sanitary conventions of 1903, 1912, and 1926 were all concerned, *inter alia*, with the pilgrimage.

The interesting history of early attempts to lessen the public health dangers of the pilgrimage cannot be fully discussed here. The incompleteness of knowledge of the epidemiology of the scourges against which protection was sought nullified some of the early efforts. Brief reference should be made, however, to two quasi-international organizations which have played, and one of which still plays, an important role in the control of pilgrim traffic. These are the Constantinople Superior Board of Health and the Conseil Sanitaire Maritime et Quarantenaire d'Égypte.

The *Constantinople Superior Board of Health*, under the old Turkish Empire administered largely by the foreign consulates in Constantinople, was formed in 1838 and had a chequered career. At one time it maintained a sanitary service at all the chief ports of the Black Sea and on the coast of Asia Minor; in the Red Sea, specially for the pilgrimage to Mecca; and on the Turko-Persian frontier, specially concerned with the pilgrimage to the Shi'a holy places. It had a staff of numerous Levantine medical officers and large funds; quarantine dues were high in the Near East. The action of the Board was largely regulated by successive international conventions. It ceased to function at the outbreak of the war of 1914–1918, and was liquidated under the Treaty of Lausanne (1923), a process completed in 1927.

The *Conseil Sanitaire Maritime et Quarantenaire d'Égypte* or *Egyptian Quarantine Board*, with headquarters at Alexandria, is financed by quarantine dues and by the Egyptian Government. Its responsibilities include the protection of the Egyptian frontiers from invasion by infectious disease, the sanitary control of shipping passing northward through the Suez Canal, and measures concerning the Mecca pilgrimage and pilgrim ships. The Board consists of the consular representatives of certain powers, its executive work being directed by the President, a position occupied for many years by a succession of British doctors. The authority of the Board has been recognized by successive international conventions. The International Sanitary Convention of 1926 entrusted it with the preparation of an annual report on the general sanitary control of the pilgrimage; the reports are well produced, well documented, sometimes illustrated, and contain much valuable information. Separate sections of these reports deal with the movement of pilgrims from Egypt and via Egypt; prevalence of disease in the Hejaz before and during the pilgrimage; happenings in the Tor quarantine station, through which north-bound returning pilgrims by sea pass, including laboratory and hospital reports; the pilgrim traffic from the south through the quarantine station on Kamarān island; and information about the pilgrimage (including special measures taken) in Algeria, French and Italian Somaliland, the French mandated states in the Levant, 'Iraq, Morocco, Palestine, the Sudan, Tangier, Transjordan, and Tunisia. Recent reports give ample evidence of vigilant health control.

As instances of the nature and magnitude of the health problems involved, certain facts and figures extracted from the report of the 1937 pilgrimage may be given. The attendance was large; about 100,000 pilgrims took part.[1] Of these 49,954 arrived by sea; 48,878

---

[1] The number of pilgrims taking part in previous years were: 1933, 50,000; 1934, 60,000; 1935, 80,000.

disembarked at Jidda, 719 at Yenbo', 156 at Al Līth, and 201 at Al Qunfidha. Pilgrims arriving at the last two ports came in sailing-craft. These sea-borne pilgrims came from many countries, in some of which the prevalence of pestilential diseases is high. The greatest numbers came from: British India and Malaya 10,588; Egypt 10,226; Java 9,381; north African countries 3,707; Afghanistan 1,756; Sudan 1,658; Syria 1,414; Bokhara, Turkistan, and China 1,312; Somaliland 1,214. Though the religious ceremonies did not begin till 20 February 1937, the first pilgrim ship arrived in Jidda on 2 October 1936. Some pilgrims thus spend as much as five or six months in the country. Pilgrim ships arriving from the south with an aggregate of 24,003 pilgrims passed by the Kamarān Quarantine Station (p. 469).

Land-routes have become increasingly important since the automobile began to displace the camel as means of transport, though the camel has by no means yet been entirely supplanted.

Land-routes from the south. A relatively small number of pilgrims travel on foot or by camel from the Yemen via the Tihama (coastal plain) to Al Līth and thence by several routes to Mecca. But the main pilgrim route from Yemen is along the mountainous track from San'ā via 'Amrān and Sa'da to Tāif. No caravan traversed this route in 1937, but in 1935 a caravan of some 10,000 pilgrims, reinforced along the route, arrived in Tāif.

Land-route from the east. Pilgrims from the Persian Gulf and 'Omān, Qatar, Al Hasa and Al Qatīf travel via Riyādh to Tāif and thence to Mecca (p. 524). Motor traffic along this route was authorized in 1934 but does not appear to have much developed.

Land-routes from the north. (1) A certain number of Egyptian and Palestinian pilgrims still follow the ancient caravan route along the eastern shore of the Red Sea to Yenbo' and thence to Al Madina.

(2) More numerous pilgrims travel via Ma'an (in Transjordan), which they reach by railway, motor-car, camel, or on foot. At Ma'an they obtain passports from the police and are medically inspected, vaccinated, and inoculated against cholera. They also obtain sufficient food to last them till Al Madina. From Ma'an most travel on camels, a few in cars, to the frontier post at Qal'at al Mudauwara (4 hours by car, 3 days by camel, 4 to 6 days on foot). From Mudauwara the journey to Al Madina, over 400 miles by camel or on foot, occupies about 18 days. In 1937, 347 pilgrims travelled by this route, and 13 from Ma'an via 'Aqaba. The old Hejaz railway which took this route has long been derelict south of Ma'an (p. 521).

(3) The motor-route Baghdad–Najaf–Hāil–Al Madina was inaugurated in 1934–5. This journey, estimated at over 900 miles, occupies 6 to 7 days by car, but the time could be reduced almost by half if the Arabian part of the road were better constructed. The Governments of 'Iraq and Sa'ūdi Arabia are responsible respectively for the upkeep of the parts of the road in their own territory. Information is sent 3 days in advance of the departure of caravans of cars. Petrol, oil, and accessories are stocked at Najaf, Hāil, and Al Madina. Permission was given for a medical officer of the 'Iraqi Health Service to be stationed at Hāil during the season, with vaccines and drugs. In 1935, the first year after its inauguration, 386 pilgrims used this route; in 1937 the number rose to 1,189.

Motor-cars each year replace more and more the old methods of transport. During the 1937 pilgrimage about 700 cars and lorries were circulating in the Hejaz, a number quite insufficient to meet the demand, though steps were being taken to increase the supply. An aeroplane flew twice daily from Jidda to Mecca and back, carrying in all 105 pilgrims. This innovation was considered to have justified further development of air transport (p. 525).

The measures which the countries interested have bound themselves to observe include: medical inspection of pilgrims before their departure and their vaccination against smallpox and cholera (several countries give anti-typhoid inoculation as well); enforcement of detailed regulations regarding sanitary and other installations in all ships engaged in the pilgrim traffic; inspection of pilgrim ships entering the Red Sea from the south at Kamarān island, where there is a well-equipped quarantine station maintained (by agreement, 1926) jointly by the Governments of British India and the Netherlands East Indies; provision of sanitary passports for pilgrims travelling by land-routes, and intercommunication between the authorities concerned so as to regulate and minimize repetition of medical measures at successive frontiers; and examination of pilgrims returning by sea northwards at the quarantine station of Tor, in Sinai.

The International Sanitary Convention (1926) made the Office International d'Hygiène Publique in Paris responsible for the co-ordination of the sanitary control of the pilgrimage; a standing Quarantine Commission was set up for this purpose.

How formidable is the task of making adequate medical and sanitary provision for those attending the pilgrimage is exemplified by a brief outline of events in 1937. One hundred thousand pilgrims were present, and the religious ceremonies began on 20 February. On the

18th pilgrims on camels, on other animals, or on foot began to leave
Mecca for 'Arafa, followed on the 19th by pilgrims in cars. The first
day of the ceremonies passed without undue incident. Water was
abundant. All the medical missions (*see below*) were represented in
'Arafa, as well as the Sa'ūdi Arabian Health Service, of which nearly
all the members are mobilized yearly at the pilgrimage, only the
medical officers of Al Madina and Riyādh and the Director of the
Jidda Quarantine Station remaining at their posts. Only two deaths
occurred on that day, both from 'ordinary diseases'. After sunset on
20 February all the pilgrims began to leave 'Arafa for Muzdalfa,
where they spent some hours (part of the ceremony) before going on
to Mina, where the majority spent three days under canvas. The
general health was good, water and food were sufficient, and the
principal roads were frequently watered. Moreover, some torrential
rain fell and the weather was relatively cold. The Sa'ūdi Health
Department had established a small hospital at Mina, where deaths
among the pilgrims during the three days of their sojourn were 10, 5,
and 7 respectively, all ascribed to 'ordinary diseases' or old age.
At the end of the third day began the return to Mecca, where the
ceremonies were completed. The pilgrims then waited in Mecca for
the King's permission to go either to Al Madina or to Jidda. At the
end of the pilgrimage the authorities had 'no public health incidents to
report'. There was neither cholera, plague, smallpox, nor typhus. A
certain number of cases of mild influenza occurred, and cases of
malaria and dysentery had been treated by the dispensaries of different
medical missions. Small epidemics of chicken-pox broke out in
Mecca and in Jidda, while Massawa reported three cases of smallpox
among returned pilgrims. (Photos. 239, 240.)

After the pilgrimage 40,295 pilgrims embarked at Jidda, and 4,868
at Yenbo'.

The foreign medical missions rendering aid to the pilgrims were:

Egyptian: 3 doctors, including the doctor of the legation, 6 sick
attendants, 1 pharmacist with 2 assistants. Their dispensaries
were stationed at Mecca, Jidda, and Al Madina.

Indian: 2 doctors including the doctor attached to the British
legation, and 2 pharmacists; dispensaries.

Javanese: 1 doctor resident in Mecca and a pharmacist.

Algerian: 2 doctors and a travelling dispensary arrived with pilgrims
on board ship and left with them.

Afghan: 1 doctor with small dispensary for the pilgrim season only.

Russian: 1 doctor at the legation; dispensary at Jidda being installed.

Kamarān island (pp. 135–137), where pilgrim ships from the south call, has a well-equipped quarantine station, since 1926 maintained jointly by the Governments of India and of the Netherlands East Indies. Each of these Governments appoints a medical officer who, alternately, acts as Director or Deputy Director, respectively, during the pilgrim season. Before 1926 Britain was responsible for Kamarān. Since 1927 sanitary conditions on pilgrim ships have been much more satisfactory than before; facilities for isolation of cases of infectious sickness exist in nearly all vessels. All pilgrims are protected by vaccination against cholera and smallpox, consequently there has been less work for the quarantine station. All ships, pilgrims, and crews are inspected, and the few who are sick can go to hospital in Kamarān if they wish. Ships are detained as little time as possible. The last occasion on which all the pilgrims in a ship had to be disembarked and detained was in 1919; 4 cases of cholera on board were the cause, and the ship was detained 6 days.

During the 1936–7 season, 24,002 pilgrims passed by Kamarān. Their health was excellent; 20 deaths and 2 births had taken place on the ships during their voyages. A European member of the crew of one ship was landed, suffering from typhoid fever. A case of measles was found in another ship; 2 cases of chicken-pox in another. Not a single pilgrim had to be disembarked for disinfection during the season; only once before in the history of Kamarān has such freedom from infection been experienced.

At *Tor* (Sinai) the large, well-equipped quarantine station organized and run by the Egyptian Quarantine Board (p. 465) plays an important role in preventing epidemic disease. All pilgrims returning by the northward sea-route must pass through the station; but pilgrim ships can now run alongside quays, which much facilitate the landing of pilgrims and the transport of their effects to the disinfecting plant. Good accommodation is provided for all pilgrims, with special accommodation for cabin passengers, an adequate and safe water-supply, hospitals, and a well-equipped laboratory. Improvements are constantly being made.

During the ten years from 1928 to 1937, 147,626 pilgrims passed through Tor, including 83,698 Egyptians. During the first three of these years the numbers were very large, e.g. 29,358 in 1929. Thereafter the economic depression caused a marked decline, so that only 4,898 pilgrims passed through in 1933. Subsequently the numbers increased to 16,730 in 1937. With the exception of 1930 and 1931 all these pilgrimages were free from dangerous epidemic disease and were declared *net*. In such circumstances vessels carrying pilgrims for destinations other than Egypt are allowed to pass through the Suez Canal in quarantine after inspection of the ship and individual medical inspection of the pilgrims. The 1930 pilgrimage was declared *brut*, on account of cholera, since bacteriological examination of the excreta of the first batch of pilgrims had revealed the presence of a cholera 'carrier'. Consequently all pilgrims *en route* for Egypt were kept 8 days in Tor, and those for other destinations 5 days. The occurrence that year of a case of cholera among pilgrims returning to Massawa further justified the precautions taken. Up to 1930 the Egyptian Quarantine Board had only the alternatives, under the Convention, of declaring the pilgrimage either *net* or *brut*; but the experience of 1930 led to a modification, so that after 1931 the Board could declare a pilgrimage *suspect* if the declaration was based on bacteriological findings alone, without occurrence of clinical cases. This third choice would not entail the long detention of pilgrims at Tor, if they were shown to be free from infection. The 1931 pilgrimage was in fact, *suspect*.

Not a single case of the 'convention diseases', plague, cholera, small-pox, typhus, and yellow fever, occurred at Tor among the pilgrims during the ten years. Admissions to hospital totalled 1,494, including 339 surgical cases; 156 of these patients died. From 1928 to 1931 dysentery and malaria were predominant causes of sickness. In the later years the pilgrimages took place in cooler weather; dysentery and malaria became less common, while bronchitis and pneumonia became more frequent. It is noteworthy that typhus is not mentioned in pilgrimage medical history up to 1939 (p. 449).

In 1937 returning pilgrims began to arrive at Tor on 4 March. The camp was closed on 10 April. Later arrivals, few in number, under-went the regulation quarantine procedure at the Lazaret at 'Ayūn Musa, Suez.

Some information concerning the activities of the Administration of Health and Public Assistance in Sa'ūdi Arabia appears in the annual pilgrimage reports of the Egyptian Quarantine Board. In theory at any rate the responsibilities of the Administration cover the whole of the vast kingdom, some 927,000 square miles with a population of several millions (p. 2). In practice its effective control appears to be limited to the more important centres of population. In the report for 1934 it is recorded that the Administration had instituted two schools for midwives, one at Mecca, the other at Jidda. The Society for Medical Relief, which had been formed during the war against the

239. *Pilgrims embarking at Jidda*

240. *Pilgrims in camp at Mina near Mecca*

Yemen, subsequently built a hospital at Tāif. The Administration had installed a sanitary post at Al Arid, nearly 5 miles east of Al Madina, on the pilgrim motor-route from Baghdad. It had decided to create dispensaries at Nejrān on the Yemen frontier and at Jauf, where malaria was reported to be very prevalent. An asylum for 200 old people had been opened in Mecca.

The Administration attempts to control the illegal practice of medicine and the traffic in narcotic drugs. Weekly publication of a bulletin recording the incidence of infectious diseases in the Hejaz is attempted. Though these bulletins in fact appear intermittently and are far from complete, it appears from them that smallpox is persistently endemic but that epidemics have been infrequent in recent years, since more general vaccination is bringing it under control (p. 448). Dysentery is very prevalent, cases being reported at all seasons, though the case-mortality rate according to published returns is not high. Typhoid fever is common. Epidemics of measles, whooping-cough, and chicken-pox are frequently reported. Puerperal fever is 'always endemic' and most cases end fatally. Tuberculosis is widespread, especially among the women and children of the poorer classes; the report for 1937 gave an average of 12 new cases reported each week, with a mortality rate of 30 per cent.

Cholera. The important part played by the pilgrimage in past years in the almost world-wide dissemination of cholera has been mentioned. The pilgrim traffic from the East, notably India, the most important endemic home of cholera in the world, sufficiently explained the frequency of epidemics in the Hejaz. Burton (1855) stated: '*El Medinah* has been visited four times by the Rih el Asfar, or Cholera Morbus, which is said to have committed great ravages, sometimes carrying off whole households. In the Rahmat el Kabirah (the "Great Mercy"), as the worst attack is piously called, whenever a man vomited he was abandoned to his fate; before that he was treated with mint, lime-juice, and copious draughts of coffee.' The Hejaz certainly paid dearly for its privilege of being the custodian of the holy places of Islam.

Since the discovery of the causative organism of cholera, the cholera vibrio or 'comma bacillus', by Robert Koch in 1883, much light has been shed on the epidemiology of the dread disease, but important problems still await solution. It is not clear why the disease should be endemic in only a limited part of the tropics and why vast tropical regions should happily have remained free, despite conditions apparently most favourable to its dissemination.

Anti-cholera vaccination has presumably contributed much to the absence of epidemic cholera from recent pilgrimages. The International Sanitary Convention of 1926 made this vaccination compulsory for all intending pilgrims, though it had been enforced by the Government of the Netherlands East Indies several years previously. From 1919 onwards pilgrims from these lands were inoculated with a typhoid-cholera vaccine and vaccinated against smallpox before departure, precautions to which there was no opposition. The dramatic disappearance of cholera from the Netherlands East Indies in 1920 was generally believed to result from the preceding mass anti-cholera vaccination campaign throughout the islands.

The existence of vibrios, morphologically indistinguishable from the true cholera vibrio, which are sometimes harboured and excreted by healthy persons, and by people suffering from other diseases, has much complicated the task of cholera control. In 1905 M. A. Ruffer isolated vibrios from patients at Tor who were not suffering from cholera. Much literature has been devoted to these and other cholera-like vibrios, only distinguishable by their biological reactions. Some observers have claimed that, in particular conditions, certain of these vibrios may acquire all the characteristics of the true cholera vibrio. But the consensus of present expert opinion appears to be that the cholera-like vibrios, including the Tor vibrio, are of little, if any, pathological importance. Opinion concerning the importance of the role played by healthy and convalescent carriers of the cholera vibrio in the spread of the disease is not unanimous.

CHAPTER IX

AGRICULTURE

THE presence or absence of water is the most important single factor in Arabian agriculture. Much of the country remains desert or steppe, fit only as grazing for the camels of the nomadic beduin, not because the soil is deficient in mineral salts but because water is lacking. In some places this has been overcome by irrigation (pp. 34–37).

In the scattered oases of the deserts and steppes, date-palms occupy nine-tenths of the agricultural land. In the Hadhramaut as a whole they are still the most important crop, but in the coastal areas of the Qu'aiti State the famous Hamūmi tobacco is the principal product. A few coconuts are grown, as a garden-crop for rich owners, at Lahej and near the coast in the Qu'aiti State, principally for the 'milk' and for eating while the flesh is soft; farther east, in Dhufār, they grow more luxuriantly. The south-western highlands, with more regular rainfall, have an elaborate ancient system of terraced fields on the steep slopes, where coffee flourishes at altitudes between 4,000 and about 6,500 feet, and *qāt* between 4,500 and 8,000 feet, while the broad stretches of highly cultivated land on the plateaux are ploughed and sown with wheat, barley, *dhura* (*Sorghum*), beans, and pulses, grown usually without irrigation.

For certain crops the land is irrigated. Thus, onions are grown in the south-western highlands in irrigated fields between 7,000 and 8,000 feet; maize, tomatoes, mustard (*khardal*, a mauve-flowered kind) at about 4,500 feet near Ta'izz (Yemen) and (in the case of tomatoes) higher; wheat may be seen, in watered fields close to San'ā (nearly 8,000 feet), in green ear before the end of February, while most of the surrounding plain is bare, dry, and undergoing winter ploughing.

Other products of ancient culture in Arabia are citron (mentioned by Theophrastus, about 300 B.C.), grapes, gingelly (*Sesamum indicum*), indigo, madder, saf-flower (*Carthamus tinctorius*), sugar, and formerly the opium poppy (mentioned in the sixteenth century by the Chinese writer Li Shi-Chen). But many areas once irrigated by water from the great works of antiquity, now in ruins (p. 36), have long been sterile.

Some of the varieties cultivated may be of interest to plant breeders, since the propagation of agriculturally valuable strains of cultivated plants is leading to wholesale extermination of local varieties almost everywhere except in primitive countries. A local variety, not commercially remunerative, may possess valuable qualities such as early cropping or resistance to disease.

REGIONAL AGRICULTURE

Till quite recently modern writers have given little systematic description of farming in Arabia. But in March 1943 the United States Agricultural Mission to Sa'ūdi Arabia issued a full report,[1] and in 1944 appeared an important account entitled 'Dry farming methods in the Aden Protectorate',[2] much of which is also applicable to farming in the Yemen highlands. These two rough divisions of Arabia are here briefly considered separately.

Sa'ūdi Arabia

A full account of the findings of the United States Mission which covered over 10,000 miles during its investigations, May–December, 1942, cannot be given. The report is cited in matters of detail several times below. But some examples will indicate the amount of land under cultivation in several of the provinces of the vast kingdom.

Al Hasa. In the Al Qatīf area 9,000 acres are cultivated at present, and an additional 3,000 can be reclaimed through draining of swamps and irrigation by artesian wells. In and about Hofūf 27,000 acres are cultivated (of which 25,000 acres are given up to date-palms), and 5,000 more acres can be irrigated by drainage-water in winter and from wells in summer; the soil is deep and exceptionally good; suitable for dates, wheat, barley, lucerne, vegetables, and fruits. In Jabrīn oasis about 7,500 acres are cultivated (photo. 30).

Nejd. Several districts were investigated, the most important being Kharj, at an average elevation of 1,360 feet. Here 2,500 acres are irrigated, and another 1,000 acres are being brought under irrigation, while it is planned to reclaim a further large tract. Most of the water is drawn from two great pits, 400 feet deep. The principal crops

---

[1] Under the names of K. S. Twitchell (Chief of Mission), A. L. Wathen, and J. G. Hamilton.

[2] By B. J. Hartley, Director of Agriculture, Aden Protectorate, in *Proceedings of Conference on Middle East Agricultural Development* (Middle East Supply Centre, Agricultural Report No. 6, pp. 37–45, Cairo, 1944).

241. *Ploughing the terraces after the dhura harvest in autumn*

242. *Terraced dhura cultivation, Jebel Jihāf*

243. *Building earthen dikes before irrigation at Dhāla'*

244. *Building a deflector-dam in the Hadhramaut*

are dates, lucerne, wheat, and *dhura* (*Sorghum*); minor crops include barley, pomegranates, citrus, melons, and many vegetables. Experimental testing of varieties of several of these crops, and also of cotton, peaches, apricots, and grapes, is being carried out.

The Hejaz. Areas such as Wadi Fātima, Wadi Hamdh and its tributaries, and Kheibar are considered. In some, e.g. the Wadi Hamdh system, many *ithil* (tamarisk) trees grow, and their number may be increased for fuel and timber, while date-palms could be planted in groups between groups of *ithil*. At Turaba the soil is good, but the date-palms, badly neglected by their beduin owners, should be better cultivated, and fruit-trees and vegetables planted among them. Near Tāif the available water is efficiently used, and no great increase in acreage can be made. In the coastal districts of Al Līth, Al Qunfidha, and Hali, all cultivable areas are productive only after floods, but good yields of millets (*dhura* and *dukhn*) are obtained; the growing of wheat, lucerne, vegetables, and fruit-trees would be possible if wells were sunk.

'Asīr. In the district of Bīsha the date-palms are well cared for and the dates excellent; an area of 1,000 acres south and east of the town would produce fine wheat and many other crops. At Nejrān (average elevation 4,000 ft.) date-palms grow well, but they are seedlings and poorly cultivated (p. 486); the soil and climate are suitable for all field crops, grapes, citrus, cotton, and sugar-cane. The Tihama and lowland districts of Sabya, Abu 'Arīsh, &c., are cultivated by flood irrigation only, producing wonderfully fine crops of *dhura* and *dukhn*. The high country (6,000 to 8,000 ft.) about Abhā, Khamīs Musheit, and adjacent districts is well terraced and cultivated, and its agriculture is best considered with that of the Yemen and Aden Protectorate.

The South-western Highlands (*the Aden Protectorate, the Yemen, and part of 'Asīr*)

In this region the comparatively dense population has by immense labour and skill made intensive farming possible in mountainous country, much of which would elsewhere serve only for grazing. Over a period extending back 3,000 to 4,000 years a dry-farming system has been developed based on conservation of soil and moisture. Only by this intensive cultivation can the people maintain their numbers on the land.

The soil is conserved by the elaborate system of terracing, while the fields depend for moisture not only on the rain falling directly

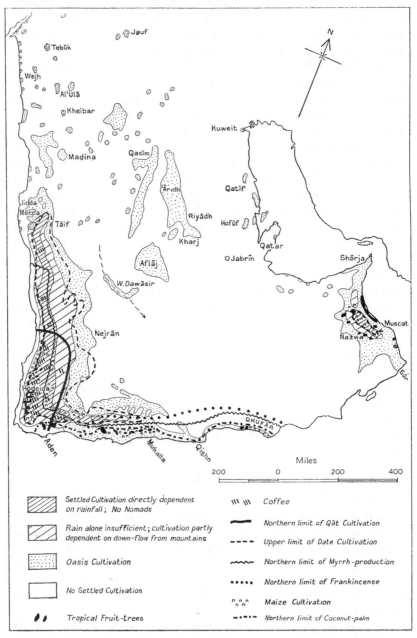

FIG. 39. *Areas and Limits of Cultivation*

on them, but on collection and control of the water running off
uncultivated slopes, carrying with it humus and fertilizing agents
derived from the excreta of grazing animals; in this dry farming the
'run-off' from surrounding areas must equal from five to ten times
the area under cultivation. The topmost terraces on steep mountain
slopes are so narrow as to be cultivated only by hand. On the easier
middle slopes the field-terraces are broader and supported by
ancient massive stone walls; to these fields the rain-water from bare
unterraced slopes is led by an intricate system of channels, often
cemented, and descending from terrace to terrace. Still lower, the
cultivators rely mainly on controlled flood-water; land bordering
wadis is carefully terraced and bunded for basin irrigation; flooded
torrents are led down between stone-faced walls and deflected by
structures of stone and brushwood into furrows which serve the land.
Below the mountains the water from the large wadi systems is
deflected to inundate the alluvial plains. (Photos. 241, 242.)

The field-terraces in mountainous districts are erected with great
toil, and severe punishments are prescribed for their neglect. Soil
is often carried from a distance, though carts and other wheeled
vehicles are non-existent. Sloping fields are unknown, low terraces
being constructed even where the incline is slight, as on the plateau
round San'ā.

On the ancient terraces the soil, though derived from many
geological formations, has become fairly uniform over wide areas.
It is usually rather deep and light, containing much silt.

In the Western Aden Protectorate the rainfall averages about
2 inches a year on the coast, about 7 inches in the better districts of
the middle altitudes, and about 12 inches at altitudes above 5,000 feet
(the much higher averages mentioned in Chapter IV, p. 178, refer to
districts of the western Yemen, in some cases above cultivation level).
Therefore, even with this elaborate system of water-conservation,
crops can only be produced without supplementary irrigation from
wells in the wetter western areas. Wells or cisterns are, indeed, found
in most districts. Devices for irrigation have been described in
Chapter II.

The pressure of population results in farms having a small average
size, e.g. about 10 acres in much of the Aden Protectorate. Most
larger farms have at least a small part under irrigation, for security
against the adverse seasons which befall every few years. Therefore
small irrigated fields of cereals, onions, and other crops are seen in
the winter months, surrounded by dry fields of stubbles.

Tillage, Implements, &c. The highland farmers have simple but effective methods; some of those described are used also in other parts of Arabia. In any field large enough for a plough to be turned the land is ploughed with primitive wooden ploughs, in which an iron-capped spike is driven simply forward, but there is no curved ploughshare to turn the soil. Or the soil is laboriously turned by a team of three men following the plough with a heavy shovel, of which one wields the handle while the other two men hold cords attached to the blade (photo. 247). In mountainous districts, e.g. the Amiri highlands, women sometimes follow the ploughman, breaking the clods with wooden mattocks, in which the shorter limb, capped with an iron spike, is bent at an acute angle to the handle. The soil of fields too narrow for ploughing is turned solely with mattocks, particularly valuable for soil-stirring in such places, where a hoe would easily be broken against the stony terrace-sides. No harrow is used, but several stirrings of the soil, with plough or mattock, before sowing, reduce it to a fineness adequate for the crops sown.

For levelling and consolidating the soil, an apparatus of boards dragged by a yoke of oxen or other beasts is used, the driver standing on the boards. An implement of the same type effectively piles up small banks of earth round the fields before irrigation, but the driver walks behind, guiding the boards with a pole (photos. 243, 248).

In the vineyards the soil is trenched to a depth of 5 or 6 feet with great long-bladed mattocks, in which the curved blade or spike is nearly at right angles to the handle, a heavy toil, since spades are unknown.

Crops grown on these terraced mountain-sides and on the plateaux are (apart from coffee, *qāt*, and certain fruit-trees, discussed on p. 484) mainly varieties of *dhura* (*Sorghum*), chosen largely for its high yield of fodder as well as grain. *Dukhn* (*Pennisetum*) is a strong second favourite below 6,000 feet. Wheat, barley, and mustard are summer rainfall crops. Wheat is grown as a winter crop in certain irrigated areas.

In most of the crops mentioned the grain is sown through a funnel and tube, a most efficient way, as the seed is run in behind the plough at whatever depth is demanded by the varying conditions of moisture in the layers of soil. But with summer rainfall crops, this device is only used for wheat, and then only when the moisture has gone into the deeper layers of soil. Otherwise the farmer sows on newly ploughed moist land; the seed is scattered in the furrow behind the

245. *Oxen drawing from a well for irrigation at Dhāla‘*

246. *Directing the water from the hide-bucket into an irrigation channel*

247. *Men turning soil with a hand-shovel behind the plough, near Sanʿā*

248. *Crushing the clods in Wadi ʿAdīm, Eastern Aden Protectorate*

plough and roughly harrowed in by a small bush trailed on a rope alongside the plough.

Cultivation of the young crops begins with hand weeding, and later the rows are earthed up. The cultivation and reaping of *dhura* is dealt with below (p. 480). Wheat and barley are reaped by men, boys, and girls who grasp handfuls of the stems and saw them through with a sickle, or in some districts these crops may be torn up by the roots. The grain is threshed with flails in the form of curved un-jointed sticks, and winnowing consists in tossing or pouring the grain and chaff from a shallow pan or other receptacle, when the chaff is blown away (photos. 251, 252).

Manuring, Alternate Cropping, and Crop Rotation. The manure of livestock is carefully conserved. That of sheep and goats is excellent for dry farming, but is usually insufficient in quantity, and is therefore used mostly on irrigated land.

The value of alternate cropping is fully understood. Land may be left fallow for a season, and the rainfall of two seasons conserved, but only wealthy farmers can follow this plan regularly. Others harvest crops whenever there is moisture enough, trying to do justice to the soil by manuring. If the spring rains (*matar as seif*) are insufficient, the land will lie fallow till the late summer rainfall (*matar al kharīf*), when the summer rainfall crops are sown.

Old local systems of mixed and overlapping rotations exist (or existed) in parts of the Eastern Aden Protectorate. The most popular was: lucerne two years, followed by millet, and tobacco the fourth year, or, if tobacco was not sown, another variety of millet. In some villages the rotation was simply tobacco, millet, and sesame the third year. In the Wadi Maseila the fields are constantly changed, a certain part of the wadi-bed being cultivated one year, then left, while another part is cultivated next season. Maize, tobacco, and coconuts are probably comparatively recent introductions. In Socotra agriculture is almost unknown.

Fodder and Forage. The extreme care with which the stems and leaves of *dhura* are conserved is mentioned on p. 481, and the use of date-stones, green dates, &c., as fodder on p. 489. Wild forage plants are mentioned under 'camels' (p. 510), and some cultivated species are listed in Appendix D (p. 594).

Reckoning of Seasons. Arab countrymen, whether nomad beduin or settled cultivators, divide the year in several ways quite distinct from the official Moslem calendar. These systems are discussed in Appendix E (pp. 603 ff.).

CEREAL CROPS

Millet

The principal cereal, at any rate in the south, is *dhura*. Grown in the south-west from near sea-level to over 9,000 feet, it is seen chiefly above 5,000, and is a characteristic plant of the highlands. Many varieties are used; in the Aden Protectorate those with red or parti-coloured grain are popular in the western districts, buff- or yellow-seeded types are commonest in the highlands, while varieties with small white seeds are grown in the eastern districts. In the lowland Tihama a single sowing may yield several crops in the year; plough-ing begins as soon as the spring rains set in, and the seed is sown directly after, by drilling through a bamboo tube; the crop is 10 feet high in June and harvested in July (photo. 250). In some interior oases also, such as Nejrān, as many as four crops are harvested from a single sowing; this is possible because some cultivated *Sorghums* develop adventitious buds, which function as independent plants, at the base of the parent stems. This 'ratooning' is also practised with success in some districts of the Aden Protectorate, especially lowland areas with good deep soil; the crop is cut to within about 6 inches of the ground, but it is little use to allow more than one ratoon (new shoot) to grow on a plant, except for fodder.

In south-west Arabia many local methods of cultivating *dhura* exist. The most detailed account available[1] refers to the 'Audhali highlands of the Western Aden Protectorate, between 6,500 and 7,500 feet above sea-level, where about one-quarter of the land is permanently irrigated from springs and wells, but the remainder is dependent on dry farming. The soil, derived from granite, is ploughed in October to break the stubble; the butts (stumps) of the *dhura* plants are then carefully hand-collected for fuel. Between November and March the land is ploughed at least twice—ploughed and cross-ploughed on wide terraces, while on narrow terraces it is ploughed diagonally or subjected to simple ridge-splitting. Next, all is made ready for tapping any run-off from surrounding uncultivated areas during the rains of March and April, and after each rain or accretion of run-off the land is again ploughed. The farmer will go on plough-ing at night rather than let the surface dry and cake, as conservation of moisture and aeration of the soil are essential at this season.

If enough moisture is conserved the farmer usually sows his *dhura* in the hot dry interval between the (north-east) spring and

[1] B. J. Hartley, op. cit., 1944.

(south-west) summer rains; commonly only one variety is sown, or perhaps two, on the terraces, the plough being so set that the seed is run into the moist soil layers about 4 inches deep. Ten to fifteen pounds of seed are sown per acre, in rows 1½ to 2 feet apart; dry-land farmers in some districts prefer a rate below ten pounds per acre, but over thirty pounds is favoured for sowing such varieties as *seif*, the best known fodder-variety in the western parts of the Aden Protectorate. When the supply of moisture has been specially good, the *dhura* may be interplanted with cow-peas (*Vigna sinensis*); these are always used as an under-crop on irrigated land, at the rate of 1 to 2 lb. of seed per acre, mixed with the *dhura* seed and sown through the same drill.

Early growth is slow, as the nights are cold on the high plateaux even during the hot spell in May; but dry weather during the first month is necessary, for wet land cannot be ploughed without burying the young plants, while if left the soil cakes and hardens. At the first *kharif* rains in July the *dhura* should be 1½ to 2 feet high, enough for a plough to be run between the rows to earth up the plants. Such inter-cultivation may be effected again after later falls of rain, till the crop is 3 feet high and its leaves shade the ground.

The temperature falls during the rains of July and August, but rises again as the second hot period in September approaches. Rain when the grain-cobs are forming is most beneficial. During the growth of the crop, weeds which have escaped the plough are removed by hand, also overcrowded plants and heads showing smut, but all such material is collected for feeding stock.

When the *dhura* grain is in the doughy stage the cow-pea pods are harvested and the plants pulled up; next, the *dhura* leaves are stripped and bundled in small sheaves for fodder. Finally the *dhura* stems are cut off a few inches above the ground and carried to the threshing-floor, usually an ancient one paved with granite. After threshing (p. 479) the grain is stored in pits hollowed out of the rock. The stems are carefully stored for fodder. Nothing is wasted; in many cases the stalks are twisted into wads and fed to cattle by hand.

Though no crop is likely to compete with *dhura* in food and fodder-value, some introductions have recently been made in the Aden Protectorate, notably that of Quinoa or Inca wheat (*Chenopodium Quinoa*), a frost-resisting plant of the high Andes. It is too early to judge results.

In the Upper 'Aulaqi country and the Dahr plateau, north of the Kaur ranges, *dhura* is also sown in May and ripens in three months, but in the Dathina and elsewhere south of the Kaur it is sown in October and harvested about four months later.[1] In the Amiri highlands (Western Aden Protectorate) and on the high plateaux of the Yemen, there is usually only one crop in the year, sown in spring; in mid-September the plateau around Dhālaʻ, 4,800 feet, and the terraced fields on the steep slopes of Jebel Jihāf up to over 7,000 feet, are covered with tall green *dhura*; in late September, after the end of the summer rains, gangs of men and boys hand-pick the cobs of grain for threshing; afterwards the tall stems are sawn off with a sickle a few inches above the ground and either used as green fodder or tied in bundles which are piled in conical stacks to dry, and later used as dry fodder or litter. Some fields are then ploughed up immediately, but in many places the stubbles are left till winter, even as late as January and February.[2] Querns of various patterns are used for grinding the grain.

On the ʻAudhali plateau the average yield of *dhura* is 400 to 600 lb. per acre, which may be compared with 400 lb. for wheat and barley, and 150 lb. for mustard.

Dhura is also grown in the Nejd oases; in Wadi Fātima (Mecca) it is (or was) sown on the same fields after the reaping of the early wheat and barley harvest.[3]

Dukhn or 'bulrush-millet' (in Aden Colony called by its Hindi name, *bajri*), a low plant, 2 or 3 feet high, with a long compact cob of grain, is grown (in the south-west) in the Tihama and the foot-hills below 4,000 feet. In the Aden Protectorate *dukhn* is sown by drilling or is 'spot'-planted, and is generally considered to need less water than other tropical cereals. It is usually sown in early summer and ripens in about four months. The grain is ground in hand-mills and the flour made into slightly sweet bread, which is rather dearer than that made from *dhura*.

Among the other millets mentioned in Appendix D (p. 595), *Panicum miliaceum* (broomcorn millet) and *Eleusine* are, in the Eastern Aden Protectorate, sown in small plots and transplanted later.

Teff (*Eragrostis abyssinica*), the crop so characteristic of the Ethiopian highlands, is called *tahaf* in the Aden Protectorate, where its distribution is peculiar. It is apparently not grown west of Aden. It is grown in the coastal district of Abyan, nearly 30 miles north-east of Aden, on land irrigated from wells, by people from districts such

[1] Wyman Bury, *The Land of Uz*, p. 310 (1911).
[2] Scott, *In the High Yemen*, p. 49 (1942).
[3] Doughty, *Arabia Deserta*, vol. ii, chap. 18.

249. *Wheat and barley laid out on a threshing-floor of bare rock to dry*

250. *Harvesting dhura at Jebel Jihāf*

251. *Threshing with an unjointed flail*

252. *Women winnowing millet in the Hadhramaut*

as Wadi Hajr, much farther east, and also by the local farmers when the conditions of rainfall demand a quic.. ..owing crop; in the latter case the seed is cast into the flooded land without previous cultivation of the soil. Near the coasts of Wahidi territory and the Hajr province of the Eastern Protectorate it is similarly grown; tribal insecurity is here a factor, as the crop is quickly sown on the flooded land, needs no cultivation, and is quickly harvested. In the middle altitudes, *tahaf* is grown in the upper Wadi Hajr at about 2,500 feet, and about Beihān at some 4,000 feet, on ground watered from wells. It is said also to be used as a catch-crop up to nearly 5,000 feet on the *jōls*.

Wheat and Barley

Above the middle altitudes of the south-western highlands, wheat and barley compete with dhura as important cereal crops. Though these are in some districts mainly summer rainfall crops (p. 479), the times of sowing are very irregular even in the same district, and are also much affected by differences of altitude. For instance, about Manākha (Yemen) barley is sown in early spring and wheat somewhat later, both being harvested after about three months.[1] Elsewhere barley may be sown in October, November, or February, and harvested in May or September. In Upper 'Aulaqi country wheat is sown in January and harvested after four months. In parts of the Yemen it is sown in February and harvested in May, or sown in June and reaped in September, or sown in October–November and reaped at the end of February (as on irrigated land near San'ā, where it is in ear in February, while most of the surrounding plain is bare). On Jebel Jihāf (Western Aden Protectorate) wheat and barley are reaped in September, the method of harvesting being described on p. 479. The wheat is sometimes seriously affected by rust. The species and varieties cultivated are mentioned on p. 595; some Arabian wheat is 'small-grained . . . yet sweet and good'.[2]

In districts where 'occult precipitation' in the form of mists is common, as on the north-eastern edge of the great escarpment of the 'Audhali plateau, farmers conserve the summer rainfall by frequent ploughings, and sow wheat, with a drill, deep in the soil in December, three months after the last rains. The grain germinates on the moisture conserved below the mulched surface, the growth

---

[1] Wyman Bury, *Arabia Infelix*, p. 109 (1915).
[2] Doughty, *Arabia Deserta*, vol. i, chap. 10.

being helped by the winter mists (*gheim*, p. 179). Rain in March and April benefits the crop, but is not essential.[1]

Farther north, wheat and barley are grown at much lower altitudes; in the oases of Nejd, at about 2,000 feet; harvest here takes place in early summer or spring—in Teima, for instance, in April.

Maize and Rice

Maize is a favourite crop of the lowlands and middle altitudes in the south-west, wherever a good supply of permanent water is at hand. It is harvested about three months after sowing, and as a rule it ripens evenly, though south Arabian varieties tend to carry three or four cobs on a stem. In parts of the Yemen it is called *rūmi* 'Roman' (i.e. from Constantinople), probably in allusion to its having been introduced during the Turkish occupation.

Rice, the consumption of which is large, is mostly imported, but is grown locally, notably in the oases of Al Hasa, where the plentiful supply of water from the warm springs renders its cultivation possible with an elaborate system of irrigation.

FRUIT AND VEGETABLES

At high elevations many temperate fruit-trees are cultivated. In the Yemen apricot, peach, plum, pear, pomegranate, walnut, quince, fig, and grape-vine grow at altitudes between 6,500 and 8,000 feet, and some small apricot trees may be seen as high as 9,000 feet. In the Aden Protectorate peaches of a clingstone variety, figs from a semi-wild tree, and grapes are grown and relished locally on the 'Audhali plateau; there also a selection of South African varieties of fruit-trees was established in 1939 on a demonstration plot at Mukeiras, with the result that certain varieties of apricot and plum proved suitable, and local farmers have been persuaded to purchase further consignments. Elsewhere temperate fruits are scarce or absent even in high districts where they would flourish. Apricot, cherry, walnut, fig, and vine are cultivated to some extent in the mountains of 'Omān (p. 592). In south Arabia fruits of tropical and warm temperate lands flourish from low to moderate altitudes; for instance, mango, tamarind, custard-apple, sugar-cane, pawpaw, banana, sweet-limes and other citrus fruits are grown in favourable situations in the south-western part of the Aden Protectorate and

[1] B. J. Hartley, op. cit.

the Yemen, from Lahej oasis, only about 400 feet above sea-level, to 6,000, or even in some cases over 7,000 feet (photo. 255).

The small fruits (*dōm*) of the *nebq*, *sidr*, or *'ilb* tree (*Zizyphus Spina-Christi*) are eaten in some districts. This tree grows from near sea-level to over 7,000 feet in the south-west. The stones are cracked and the small nuts (called *halil* or *kabasis* in the Hadhramaut, *qussei* in Aden) are eaten. In the Eastern Aden Protectorate the fruits are dried and pounded with their stones; the resulting mixture (*hati*) is sometimes stored, and is a common food of the local beduin. The fresh leaves are important fodder for goats and camels, and the *'ilb* is grown for both fodder and shade in the coffee-plantations of Lower Yāfa'. The dried leaves also form a valuable fodder (called *ligin* or *ghussa*), often soaked in water with a mixture of sesame-cake and pounded date-stones, and thus fed to stock needing special treatment. The tree is important as timber, especially in the tributaries of the Wadi Hadhramaut and the steppe country between this and the sea. In the Koran it is written that the *nebq* trees of Paradise have no thorns, and this is literally true of some cultivated examples.

Production of vegetables was much increased in Aden Colony and Protectorate during the War of 1939–1945. Sufficient vegetables of European type were grown in the lowland districts of Lahej and Abyan to supply the Colony and some of the shipping. In summer the same districts produce melons and tropical vegetables, while those of temperate type have been grown in a special area at 7,000 feet on the 'Audhali plateau; local farmers deliver about 2 tons per day to Government buyers at Laudar, whence the vegetables are taken to Aden in ten hours or less. Two crops of potatoes in the year were successfully grown on the 'Audhali plateau, between late February and the end of October; the colder months are less suitable, and frost may cause damage. A small, round, white variety is grown in parts of the Yemen, for local consumption and for overland export to Aden. The sweet potato (*Ipomoea batatas; batata, sukar ukunde*) is grown in many parts of the Protectorate, such as Wadi Tiban and its tributaries, where a good supply of water (not brackish) is present. Tomatoes are grown fairly extensively in parts of the Yemen, for instance on irrigated land near Ta'izz (4,500 ft.) and at higher altitudes near San'ā.

Farther north, products of temperate countries are grown at lower altitudes. Thus, in the irrigated gardens surrounding the cities of central Nejd, besides the prevailing date-palms, the peach, grape, fig, pomegranate, apricot, and lemon are cultivated, as well as tomato, egg-fruit (*beidhinjān*), pumpkin, and melon; in some places egg-plants are grown in rows along the sides of the irrigation channels; while melon is much in request as a dish with which to break the day's fast at sunset, when Ramadhan falls in the summer.[1]

Almonds produce satisfactory yields in Sa'ūdi Arabia at elevations of 6,500 feet and over, but all the trees are seedlings, which results in variability in the size and quality of the nuts, while lack of treatment of maladies results in shortness of life of the trees. Remedies have been suggested.[2] Camel-sticks (*mish'ab*) are of almond-wood; Muhammad used an almond stick; compare Aaron's rod, which blossomed and bore almonds (*Numbers*, chap. xvii).

The seasons of flowering and fruit vary widely according to latitude, elevation, &c. In San'ā and its environs apricot-trees blossom about the end of January, and in sheltered situations are loaded with ripening fruit in mid-February; quince and pomegranate flower a little later than apricot; fig-trees break into leaf early in February; walnut-trees remain bare the latest (photos. 260, 261).[3] In central and northern Arabia fruit may be available, according to situation, at least from July to September; thus, peaches and grapes ripen at Riyādh early in July; figs and peaches are plentiful at 'Aneiza in late August; peaches and pomegranates, also at 'Aneiza, in late September.[4]

DATE-PALM

(*Phoenix dactylifera;* Arabic, *tamra*, plur. *tamr*, the fruit; *nakhl*, a date-palm, plur. *nakhil*, a palm-grove)

Dates are probably the most important food-crop of Arabia. They also hold a high place in 'Iraq, of which they form the most reliable agricultural export,[5] but the following remarks apply specially to Arabia proper. Here date-palms are estimated to occupy 90 per cent. of the agricultural land in the oases of the deserts and steppes below about 2,200 feet; in the south-western highlands a line can be drawn at this altitude round a large block of country where they are not grown. They do, however, flourish in places at higher altitudes, e.g. Wadi Nejrān, about 4,000 feet, where, however, the fruit is poor in quality, due largely to the trees being seedlings; and the

[1] Philby, *Arabia of the Wahhabis*, pp. 6, 14, 288, 292, &c. (1928).
[2] Twitchell, op. cit., p. 29.
[3] Scott, *In the High Yemen*, p. 143.
[4] Philby, *Arabia of the Wahhabis*, pp. 25, 162, 301.
[5] *Handbook of Iraq* (B.R. 524), pp. 457–459 (1944).

253. *Tamarisk plantations and lucerne at Gheiman*

254. *Lucerne, roses, prickly pear, and apricot trees at San'ā*

255. *Banana plantation at Al Huseini, 3 miles north of Lahej*

257. *Fertilizing date-palms in the Hadhramaut*

256. *Palms at Tebūk oasis, northern Hejaz*

broad valley of Turib in 'Asīr, about 5,700 feet, where again the fruit is very inferior though the palms grow excellently;[1] possibly better fruit could be obtained at the higher altitudes, given more care in culture and the selection of varieties. The palms also occupy considerable areas of the narrow coastal plains of the south-west and south, and in 'Omān. In normal times, when rice and millet are available in the markets of the coast-towns, the people of the Wadi Hadhramaut and its tributaries store a large part of their date-crop, only consuming the entire crop fresh, and even importing extra dates, in seasons when drought in the flood-irrigated areas causes a serious reduction in the yield; some varieties of fine flavour are stored apart, in large earthen vessels, while others are mixed with the commonly stored type (*hamra*); two varieties (*shubshuba* and *umshok*), grown in the main wadi between Tarīm and Seiyūn, are preferred for eating fresh.

Since palms grown from seed do not reproduce the special characteristics of their parents, propagation is effected by detaching offshoots from palms of recognized merit and 2 to 3 years old. Male and female flowers are borne on separate trees (the male plants being readily distinguishable by their sturdy aspect and larger number of closely packed leaves), but offshoots are taken only from female trees. If a young palm be denuded of all its offshoots at once, it produces no more, hence it is customary to leave at least one offshoot on each plant.

The offshoots are planted in holes about a yard square and approximately the same depth. Young palms are placed 12 to 30 feet apart, or even farther if such crops as lucerne are to be grown beneath the trees. According to some Arab writers one-third of the soil dug out is removed, while ashes are mixed with the remainder. No manure is added, but a handful of stones may be put under the young plant, which is banked up with the loose soil. On the other hand, the growers of the *fardh* variety of dates in 'Omān work into the soil a donkey load of well-rotted manure for each tree twice a year. But generally manure is applied in autumn, so that it is absorbed by the soil before the growing-period in spring. There is no evidence that occasional irrigation with brine benefits the trees, though this was advocated by old Arab writers. On the coast fish-manure is sometimes used.

Irrigation is the principal factor in culture, though palms can also be grown without it, as at Al Madina. Irrigation from the hot springs

[1] K. S. Twitchell, *Rep. U.S. Agricultural Mission to Sa'udi Arabia*, pp. 17, 18 (1943).

of Al Hasa leads to early ripening. In some districts, e.g. parts of 'Omān, water is conveyed several miles to the date gardens through cement conduits.

Date-palms bear fruit intermittently; the older trees tend to rest every other year. Since very few male trees are grown, artificial pollination of the numerous female trees is necessary. This has been practised since many centuries B.C. (at least in 'Iraq, where it is shown in Assyrian sculptures); it is correctly described by Theophrastus and by medieval Arab writers. When the brush of male flowers, covered by its spathe, has reached maturity (a condition indicated by its scent, and a faint rustling produced by pressure with the fingers), it is cut down and split open. One or two sprigs of male flowers, after lying twenty-four hours in a basket, are inserted into a cluster of female flowers which has newly burst its spathe; or a spathe not quite ready may be split and the male flowers inserted. To avoid possible damp, the middle of the day is chosen. Pollen of certain other species of palm appears to be effective, though the Arabs believe that the male flowers used directly influence the quality and quantity of the fruit (photo. 257).

The usual flowering season is March to April, but blossoms may be found from February to June. While the peak period of the harvest is usually August, dates ripen in some districts much earlier. At Al Madina they appear at the beginning of June, while the main harvest is a month later. At Riyādh dates are in the unripe, but just eatable, stage called *laun* in late July; afterwards they pass through the half-and-half stage called *bisr*, to the nearly final stage for fresh dates, *ratab*.[1] The early ripening in Al Hasa has been mentioned. They reach the markets of 'Omān about mid-May and continue till mid-November. Very numerous named varieties exist, e.g. 116 have been recorded from the neighbourhood of Al Madina alone. The Arabs consider the *khalasi* of Hofūf and the *fardh* of 'Omān among the best.[2]

Dates are often picked while still green, boiled for an hour or more, and sun-dried for eight to ten days; these *khalal mat būkh*,

[1] Philby, *Arabia of the Wahhabis*, p. 45 (1928).

[2] For varieties of dates found in Arabia see Flügel, *Zeitschrift Deutsch. Morgenl. Ges.* xvi, pp. 686–687 (1862); E. Bonavia, *The Future of the Date-Palm in India*, pp. 35–65 (Calcutta, 1885; includes the Persian Gulf and translations of the names used at Muscat); Dowson, *Date Cultivation in 'Iraq*, i, pp. 70–75 (1921; gives a list of Arabian varieties, as well as those in 'Iraq, &c.). G. Schweinfurth's *Arabische Pflanzennamen* (1912) contains a vocabulary of terms used in date cultivation.

crisp and of nutty flavour, keep over a year. Unripe dates may also be pickled in vinegar. Fresh dates may be baked with butter, or chopped up and boiled with milk, onions, and flour. A paste, *madquqa*, of stoned dates ground up with gingelly oil is spread on bread. In the Persian Gulf a date jam is called *mu'asal*, and sweet cakes are made of dates ground up and fried in oil mixed with flour boiled in milk. Young male spathes are ground up to make bread, or eaten as a salad, or boiled with lemon peel. An unfermented liquor, called *nabidh* like other palm-liquors, and made by letting water poured on fresh dates stand overnight, has been drunk since the time of Muhammad.[1] In Bahrein tara-water, made from fresh spathes, is used in making sherbet.[2] Date-stones are (or were) steeped, ground, and sold as fodder for camels in barren lowland parts of the Hejaz.[3] In Bahrein green dates (*salang*) are used as fodder for donkeys and cattle, or, boiled with ground date-stones and fish-bones, made into cakes for milch cows.[4]

Statistics of the yield for Arabia are not available. Over 40 years ago it was estimated that the number of palms owned by individuals in the Hadhramaut—by no means the greatest date-producing district, as stated (p. 473)—varied from 10 to 3,000 trees, while numbers from 100 to 500 were frequent.[5] In 'Omān 90 per cent. of the population is dependent on date cultivation, and over a million rupees' worth of dates were exported in 1938–1939. Many 'Omāni Arab owners are, however, allowing themselves to be ousted by Baluchis.

Other uses. The leaves are used for thatch; the leaflets of tender unfolding leaves are made into matting and baskets, certain varieties being preferred. The wood is used in timber construction. In 'Omān a large proportion of the people live in huts made of the leaves or their midribs, the latter sometimes called 'date-sticks'; these are also used in some places in the construction of boats called *shasha*. The pith is edible, and the fibre used in rope-making.

Diseases of date-palms. The date-palm scale-insect (*Parlatoria blanchardi*) is widespread, but normally held in check by parasitic

---

[1] Burton, *Pilgrimage to El-Medinah and Meccah*, ii, p. 201 (1855).

[2] For other methods of preparation see E. Bonavia, *The Date Palm in India*, &c., pp. 49 sqq. (1885); A. R. Hakim, 'Supplementary Notes on Care and Culture of Date Trees,' Appendix B to Part III of *Rep. Administration Gulf Political Residency for 1883–4*, pp. 39–43 (1884).

[3] Doughty, *Arabia Deserta*, vol. ii, chap. 7.

[4] Bent, *Southern Arabia*, p. 19 (1900).

[5] W. Hein, 'Beitrag zur Statistik Südarabiens', *Mitt. Geograph. Ges. Wien.* xlvi, p. 248 (1903).

insects. A 'red spider' (not a true spider, but an acarine) is a serious pest, rendering whole clusters of fruit unfit for human consumption. The *majnūn*, or 'mad', disease is caused by a stoppage of growth, resulting in the strangling of the young leaves by the old.

COFFEE

Coffea arabica, so far as is known, is the only species grown in Arabia; at any rate it is the only kind exported from Arabia or Ethiopia, but coffee of other species, e.g. *C. robusta* (*Bukobensis*), is imported in the husk from east Africa into Arabia.

Coffee (Arabic: *bunn* means the tree, sometimes also the beverage; *qāhwa*, usually the beverage extracted from the berry; *qishr*, the husk and the beverage extracted therefrom) is not indigenous in Arabia. It is believed to have been introduced from Abyssinia. According to tradition, slips of both coffee and *qāt* were planted at 'Udein ('the two twigs') in the Yemen in pre-Islamic times, but neither plant is mentioned in the Koran. Another report attributes the introduction of coffee to one Jemal ad Dīn Abu 'Abdullah adh Dhubani, Mufti of Aden, as late as 1454. When abstinence from alcoholic drinks was generally enforced under Islam, the use of coffee gained ground, and it was designated *qāhwa*, a word formerly applied to intoxicants. From Arabia the drinking of coffee spread rapidly through the Muslim world and later to Europe; Father Anthony de Montserrate drank it in Dhufār in 1557, and by 1650 it had reached England. Attempts were made to check the spread of the habit, as when the beverage was publicly condemned at Mecca in 1511 by an assembly of lawyers and physicians, and when a fanatical mob wrecked the coffee-houses of Cairo in 1613.

In Arabia coffee is grown principally in the Yemen, throughout the length of the country from north to south; it flourishes on the steep slopes of the valleys in the western escarpment, usually at altitudes between 4,000 and 6,500 feet, though in places it may be grown at nearly 8,000 feet. The mountainous Haraz district, west of Manākha, and the upper parts of Wadi Siham and Wadi 'Ānis, to the south and east, produce the best quality (photo. 259); varieties such as *'ānisi* are named from their districts. Much is exported, from the northern districts through Hodeida, from the southern through Ta'izz and Aden. The port of Mocha, which formerly gave its name to coffee grown far inland, is completely decayed (photo. 142).

258. *Onion beds in Dhamār*

259. *Mocha coffee growing on terraces below ʿAtāra, west of Manākha*

260. *Apricot tree and young qāt bushes, Hadda, near San'ā, January*

261. *Bare walnut trees at Hadda in January*

Smaller areas of production exist in 'Asīr and the Aden Protector-ate. But the total amount is insufficient for consumption in Arabia and for export; some imported as well as local coffee is used in the Yemen by those wealthy enough to drink coffee made from the bean. The precious local product is reserved mainly for export, while poorer people drink only *qishr*, extracted from the husks.[1] In Niebuhr's time (1763) little real coffee was drunk in the Yemen, being considered heating, while *qishr* was esteemed by rich and poor alike.

In the Yemen the trees are planted (like other crops in the moun-tains) on terraced fields, the stone faces of which may rise 20 feet or more according to the steepness of the ground, and may exceed in height the width of the fields. Fruit intended for sowing is plucked and sun-dried on house-tops, till the husk opens and can be removed without injury to the 'bean'. The beans are sown, usually from October to December, by pressing each separately on to a manured seed-bed, damped and smoothed down, and then covering them with several inches of loose fine soil. The seed-beds, artificially shaded, are watered every few days, and the seedlings appear in about a month. After a period varying from six weeks to four months or more, they are transplanted, being set wide apart in rows on well-manured ground, with a depression at the base of each seedling to catch surface-water. Newly transplanted seedlings need shading and watering till established. The trees reach maturity in five years, attaining a height of 8 to 15 feet, but they do not bear profitably after twenty years. New trees can also be produced by layering suckers of mature trees. Coffee-trees are usually shaded by rows of large trees, *Ficus*, *Dobera*, tamarind, &c., and many plantations are irrigated in the dry season. The time of harvest varies greatly with altitude and the situation of individual trees; the berries on a single tree may ripen at different times according to the amount of sun falling on them; thus, an eighteenth-century observer stated the main harvest to be in May, while a recent observer recorded that it is principally in autumn.[2] The beans (*safi*) are separated from the husk by a hand-mill so spaced as to rub off the husk without injuring the bean, and are then cleaned, sorted according to colour and size, and made up in packages of plant-fibres.

[1] For methods of preparation of *qishr* see Manzoni, *El Yemen*, p. 9 (1884).
[2] J. De La Roque, 'An Account of the Coffee-tree and its Fruit,' in *A Voyage to Arabia* . . . pp. 217 sqq. (English translations, 1726, 1730); Wyman Bury, *Arabia Infelix*, p. 112 (1915).

In the Western Aden Protectorate coffee is grown in the western part of the mountains of Yāfaʻ and in the territory of the Radhfān confederation, immediately to the south-west. In the best districts of Yāfaʻ, at from 5,000 to 5,500 feet, the main harvest is in April and May. Up to 1938 some 50 tons were exported to Paris and New York, where, marketed as Yāfaʻ coffee, it commanded high prices; but since that date it has only been traded internally, particularly overland to the eastern parts of the Protectorate. In this local trade the fine dried 'cherry' of Yāfaʻ is most esteemed; except in the farthest eastern parts of the Protectorate the whole 'cherry' is pounded and, after roasting, boiled with powdered ginger or, in times of scarcity, with black pepper; sometimes the beverage is sweetened with honey. But in the Mahri Sultanate (including Socotra), where ʻOmāni influence is strong among the coastal population, coffee is made in the ordinary Arabian manner from the bean alone, and is served unsweetened.

QĀT (CATHA EDULIS)

This shrub or small tree belongs to the same Order (Celastraceae) as the English spindle-tree, and has elliptic toothed leaves about as large as those of a plum, but thicker and dark shining green, and cymes of small white flowers in the leaf-axils. Like coffee, it is traditionally supposed to have been introduced from Ethiopia, where it grows wild, and is said to have been brought in 1430 to Hodeida by one Sheikh Ibrahim Abu Zahrein ('father of the two flowers'). Qāt is cultivated in small plantations, either on terraced fields or, on more level ground, in walled gardens. It flourishes at altitudes between 4,000 and 8,000 feet, particularly on Jebel Sabir south of Taʻizz and the mountains to the north; in the mountains west of Sanʻā, and on level ground at ʻAsr, Wadi Dhahr, and elsewhere near Sanʻā (photo. 260). A few plantations of young trees may be seen in the Aden Protectorate, near Dhāláʻ. In some districts ground formerly devoted to coffee or vines is now unfortunately given up to qāt. Normally qāt is not allowed to set seeds but is propagated by cuttings. The cultivator usually floods his field till the soil is saturated, then covers it with excreta of goats, &c., and leaves it for a few days, after which the cuttings are planted in rows of shallow holes 4 to 6 feet apart. They are protected from livestock by barriers of thorn or watched by trained dogs. In a year they should be 2 feet high and ready for the first plucking, though the young trees are in some cases left several years. When the shoots are plucked, a few are allowed to remain for plucking the following year, such *qāt mubarra* being thought inferior. Three crops are said to be taken from each plant in a year, the shoots of the second crop (*qāt mathani*) being considered best. The trees reach a height varying from 5 to 12 feet. The top generally dies when the plant is about 16 years old; the stem is then cut off about a foot above the ground and suckers spring from the stumps.

Sprigs, 6 inches or more long, of the young leaves are tied in bundles, wrapped in grass to keep them fresh during transport to the centres of consumption. Varieties such as *ta'izzi* and *sabiri* take their names from particular places; the two named are worth 8 to 12 annas a bundle in Aden, while inferior varieties cost only 4 to 7 annas. The difference is probably due to the greater rainfall in places such as Jebel Sabir, for plants sent from there to less favoured localities produce only foliage of an inferior quality. The costliness of good *qāt* is due to the demand for its being fresh; *qāt* transported by camel from the Yemen to Aden arrives at Lahej on the third morning, whence it is sent to Aden by motor transport.

In south-west Arabia, where *qāt* is used by a very large proportion of the population, the leaves are normally chewed, only the juice being swallowed; when the cheek becomes distended, the green paste of chewed leaves is spat out into a cuspidor, while the mouth is rinsed with water, draughts of which are also drunk periodically.[1] Occasionally an infusion is made from the dried leaves. The effects on the addicts are described in Chapter VIII (p. 462).

OTHER CROPS

Grape-vines

South Arabia and Socotra were both known to classical writers as wine-producing countries, though production has doubtless declined since the time of Muhammad, who (for example) ordered the destruction of the vineyards of Tāif. Grapes are now grown on the high tableland of the Yemen, especially at Raudha and elsewhere north of San'ā, though good vineyards have been uprooted and replaced by *qāt*; the vines are still bare in February, when some other fruit-trees are in full bloom or early leaf; wine is made by the Jews of the Yemen.

Vines also flourish in the mountains of 'Omān, where wine is

[1] Dr. P. W. R. Petrie, 'Some Experiences in South Arabia,' *Journal of Tropical Medicine and Hygiene*, Dec. 1, 1939, p. 360.

made, and in many oases of the northern parts of Arabia, such as Al Hasa; Al Madina, where the best variety, *sharifi*, produces a long white grape; 'Aneiza, where grapes ripen at the end of June;[1] Riyādh, where ripe grapes are plentiful early in July;[2] and Teima, where vines are grown as trellis-plants beside the wells.

Tobacco

An important crop principally in the Eastern Aden Protectorate, where the chief centre of production of the Hamūmi variety is Gheil Ba Wazīr (p. 580), north-west of Shihr; here seedlings are grown in nursery beds round the wells of Al Quf, the beds being divided into patches 3 or 4 feet square and the seed sown very close; when the seedlings are about 4 inches high they are moved to Al Harth and planted in rows a foot apart, in beds of a size depending on the amount of water; each bed, *mutr* (plur. *mutīra*), is surrounded by a ridge to keep in the irrigation water. Tobacco cultivation also receives much attention in some districts south-west of Mukalla, where the seed is sown on plots heavily manured with sheep dung mixed with fine earth. The plants are ripe for cutting in four or five months according to season and district, the terminal buds being topped after all the leaves have been formed.[3]

Several Arabic names are used; apparently *tutun aswad* (black tobacco, the word *tutun* being Turkish) is restricted to *Nicotiana Tabacum*, with pink or white flowers (small plantations of which occur in the Amiri highlands, Western Aden Protectorate, between 4,500 and 5,600 ft.), while *tunbāk* is applied to the yellow-flowered *N. glauca*. A third species, the green-flowered *N. rustica* (*tutun belledi*), occurs in Sinai and the Yemen. The term *dukhān*, literally 'smoke', is also used.

Plants yielding Dyes

The following deserve mention: (1) Henna (*Lawsonia inermis*, Arabic *hinnā*), a plant of the same Order (Lythraceae) to which the English purple loose-strife belongs, is widely cultivated and may be indigenous. In Hebrew it was *copher*, translated 'camphire' in the Authorized, but 'henna' in the Revised, version of the Bible (*Song of Solomon*, i. 14, iv. 13). The stem and leaves are pounded with oil into a fine paste, which is smeared on the nails, leaving a permanent

---

[1] Doughty, *Arabia Deserta*, vol. ii, chap. 15.
[2] Philby, *Arabia of the Wahhabis*, chap. i.
[3] W. H. Ingrams, *Report on the Hadhramaut*, pp. 50, 51 (1937).

brown-red stain, or used to dye the hair and beard red; in the latter case a second staining with indigo produces a black colour. (2) *Indigo*, much used in south-west Arabia for dyeing turban-cloths and other garments, and in some tribes the body itself, is represented by wild and cultivated species. The dye is obtained from *Indigofera articulata* (*hawir*), the true indigo (*I. tinctoria*, Ar. *nīl*) being less usual in Arabia. A plant of a different Order, *Polygala tinctoria*, may be used as a substitute, while a kind called green indigo (*nīl akhdar*) is used for decorating interiors. The species of wild *Indigofera*, low grey-foliaged broom-like bushes, are common near rivers in the south-western mountains, 2,000 to 5,000 feet. Cultivated indigo needs considerable moisture, but is sown in high parts of the Aden Protectorate and may be cut in about two months.[1] (3) Safflower or bastard saffron (*Carthamus tinctorius*; Arabic *'usfur*, the flowers; the plant is called *khirriya* in the towns and *samna* by the beduin[2]), a Composite, possibly a native of Arabia, is cultivated for the flowers, which are used both as a dye and in cooking; women stain their faces yellow with the dye, in which in ancient Egypt the grave-clothes of mummies were steeped. (4) *Waras* or *ās* (*Flemingia rhodocarpa*), a leguminous plant yielding an orange dye and also used as a cosmetic and a remedy for headaches, is cultivated in the Yemen and Yāfa' (Western Aden Protectorate). (5) *Madder* (*fuwa*): a species is cultivated in Arabia, but it is uncertain whether this is the European *Rubia tinctoria*[3] or the Indian *R. cordifolia*.

CROP PESTS: THE DESERT LOCUST

Though a few insect pests have been mentioned above, the study of insect pests and fungus or other diseases of Arabian crops is so little advanced that only the desert locust is discussed in some detail. This immemorial scourge constitutes a major problem affecting the whole Middle East; it is the enemy against which organized international campaigns are being directed, and in the centre of operations lies Arabia. Events indeed are moving so rapidly that no final account can be given.

The desert locust (*Schistocerca gregaria*), the locust of the Bible, the first naming and description of which in modern scientific terms is due to Forskål, the naturalist member of Niebuhr's expedition of

[1] Wyman Bury, *The Land of Uz*, p. 310 (1911).
[2] Philby, *The Heart of Arabia*, vol. i, p. 343 (1922).
[3] In 'Iraq called *rīnās*.

1763, is one of a number of species of large grasshoppers which occasionally develop gregarious habits. In the swarming phase they differ in colour and structure from individuals of the same species in the solitary phase so much that the two phases have in the past been named and described as separate species. Though the cause of the change from the solitary to the gregarious phase is still being investigated, it is known that an important factor in this change is the overcrowding which sometimes occurs, as when a season with plentiful vegetation causes the solitary locusts to increase, and a dry season following forces them to crowd into smaller areas; the swarming migratory phase is then produced. In hot countries, when the soil is moist enough, the eggs, laid in it in cylindrical masses several times a year, may hatch in three weeks or less; the young locusts, feeding voraciously on green vegetation and moulting periodically, reach the winged adult stage in less than six weeks from the time of hatching. The immature 'hopper' stages, unable to fly, are the most vulnerable; the hoppers move relentlessly across country in masses, in some cases several square miles in extent and composed of many millions of individuals. Once the winged adult stage is reached, flying swarms (which may measure 200 square miles or more) cover enormous distances, depending on weather conditions. In the case of the desert locust, narrow seas such as the Red Sea and Persian Gulf are no barrier whatever, and the whole region from Africa to India forms one migration area. Swarms bred during the summer monsoon in India move in autumn to southern Persia and Arabia, while swarms bred in Africa also migrate to Arabia.

In north Africa the Romans used to attack locusts in the hopper stage, beating them with branches and so driving them into prepared trenches. A modification of this method is still used, but many new methods are employed, including fire, smoke-screens, flame-throwers, and especially poisoned bait and sprays; while the 'dusting' of swarms of winged adults, settled on vegetation, with poison in the form of fine powder, sprayed from aeroplanes, is being tried. In the case of bait, poisons must be sought which are deadly to the locusts but harmless to man and to livestock; while, since a single campaign in one country may require 1,000 tons of bait, methods of transport, and plenty of water (which in arid countries may have to be carried long distances) for mixing the bait, are very important.

An outbreak of swarms of the desert locust, beginning in 1925, had by 1929–1930 become very serious both in western Asia and in British territories in Africa. Moreover, in 1930 Sinai and the Sudan were heavily invaded. In Sinai over 2,500 soldiers fought the locusts with flame-guns and poisoned bait. In the Sudan immense damage was done, but a model anti-locust organization was set up, which has since served to train experts for other areas. The energetic action taken by Britain, the attempts at international co-operation in the years before 1939, and the eventual establishment of the Anti-Locust Research Centre in London, cannot be fully described here. From information received from over forty countries it appeared that all outbreaks could be traced to a few particular areas where the locusts bred undisturbed. Such is a strip of the Red Sea coastal belt in the Sudan, 200 miles long and 10 to 12 miles broad, with good winter rains; every eleven or twelve years these rains are so heavy as to cause exceptional growth of vegetation, with consequent increase of locusts and overcrowding, resulting in swarms. It was planned internationally to keep such areas under permanent observation and to prevent any tendency in the solitary locusts to form incipient swarms; but these plans were perforce postponed because the locust breeding-grounds were mainly near the Red Sea and therefore inaccessible during the early part of the War of 1939–1945.

Other plans were, however, made by the British Departments concerned, the Middle East Supply Centre becoming the co-ordinating agency. Anti-locust campaigns were organized in Persia, Arabia, and elsewhere for the spring of 1943. Small units, sent to the Trucial Coast, returned satisfied that locust control is possible in Arabia, provided that ample mechanized transport of special desert types is forthcoming. Meanwhile a Palestine Government Mission patrolled the northern Nafūd. An Egyptian Government Mission based on Jidda destroyed quantities of hoppers. International conferences on locust control, held in Cairo and Tehran in July 1943, had as one result the planning by the British Middle East Anti-Locust Unit of a full-scale offensive in Sa'ūdi Arabia for 1943–1944, comprising over 350 vehicles and nearly 1,000 personnel under ten locust officers, British, American, Egyptian, Sudanese, Palestinian, and Indian. King Ibn Sa'ūd and his Government gave every facility. Over 50,000 square miles were found to be infested with hoppers, but by the use of 1,200 tons of bait these were destroyed over some 16,000 square miles, so that only a few small swarms flew in the spring of 1944 from Arabia to Persia and India. Arabia is still in the foreground of these activities, reports received late in 1944 suggesting that an even worse infestation might be expected in 1945.

By the use of poison bait the Government of Aden prevented serious damage by 'hoppers' in the Protectorate in 1943 and 1944. Quantities of adult locusts are collected for food, especially by villagers in highland districts, who capture them at night, when news is received of a swarm having settled; but 'hoppers' are not usually eaten except in the eastern districts. The inhabitants seem to know the places where 'hoppers' will hatch after an invasion, for instance the flat and rather bushy Dathina country. Above 6,000 feet the cultivators do not fear damage from locally hatched 'hoppers', but they fear flying adults and also 'hoppers' which climb thousands of feet from hatching-grounds below.

The Imam of the Yemen at first denied entry to anti-locust workers, but in 1944 he allowed an instructor of the Aden Protectorate Agricultural Department to instruct soldiers in the use of bran poison-bait, while in 1945 some Yemenis were sent to the Sudan for training. It is hoped that the Yemeni Government will consent to a planned system of control, which may be assisted by the projected formation of an Agricultural Council by the Arab Union.

DOMESTIC ANIMALS

Camels, horses, mules, and donkeys are ridden by various sections of the population; excepting the horse, these are all used also as pack animals and, together with cattle, for drawing ploughs and other agricultural implements, and for raising water from wells. In varying degrees also sheep, goats, and cattle are reared for meat; cows, camels, sheep, and goats for their milk; camels, sheep, and goats for their hair or wool. Poultry, dogs, and cats must be added to the list of domestic animals.

Cattle

Arabian cattle are mostly small and humped, but those in Socotra, and on the mainland in the Qara mountains and Jebel Qamr (immediately to the south-west), are straight-backed. The two latter breeds, though used as dairy not draught animals, are distinct, but probably related (as their owners are); the Socotran cattle are smaller and lighter, while those kept by the Qara tribesmen and the eastern Mahra of Jebel Qamr tend to develop a layer of fat round the withers, as some African breeds do. Every man and woman of the pastoral Qara keeps some cattle, a person possessing twenty being counted prosperous, while very rich people have up to over 100. Most bull-calves are slaughtered for food. Each cow has a name inherited from its mother, and the herdsmen claim to recognize every animal, even one lost among a strange herd.

The humped cattle have a general resemblance to those of eastern Africa and south-east Asia, but their origin and date of introduction into Arabia are uncertain. In much of south Arabia they are used for agricultural work and raising water almost to the exclusion of camels and donkeys (photo. 245). In the Western Protectorate highlands they are reared in sufficient numbers, but loss from drought and disease has compelled farmers, even in fertile lowland districts, to buy *Sharabi* oxen in their place; the latter, from Sharab and neighbouring districts of the southern Yemen, are long-legged and speedy in working on light lowland soils. The Amiri breed of the Dhāla' highlands, valuable for both draught and dairy purposes, has recently been used on Government irrigation works; some head were moved to the Hadhramaut famine zone, and others were imported by the British Military Administration into Eritrea in 1943 and 1944. Mating of Amiri cows with selected Indian Sahiwal bulls has been undertaken at the Aden Military Dairy Farm.

Though camel- and horse-breeding are more characteristic of the north, yet cattle are kept in every settled part of Arabia, at least in villages and towns, where each household usually possesses a few cows, which are driven into the courtyard or ground floor of the house at night. These cows are kept not only for milking; in many places, e.g. Shaqra, 'Aneiza, and Boreida in central Arabia, and Al 'Ulā in the north-west, cows draw water from the wells, though on the whole less commonly than camels and donkeys. There is some local variation in breed; for instance, Wusheiqir, north of Shaqra, has a particularly sturdy breed, and kine are there more commonly used than other animals for water-raising.[1] The local breed in Bahrein island, though small, is highly reputed for its milk;[2] the feeding of milch kine in Bahrein on cakes made of green dates boiled with fishbones, &c., has been mentioned (p. 489). Cow's milk was esteemed medicinal in Doughty's time.[3]

Horses

Horse-breeding as an industry has greatly declined in Arabia in recent years. The horse had been rendered largely useless for tribal

---

[1] Philby, *Arabia of the Wahhabis*, p. 122.
[2] *Handbook of Arabia*, p. 314.
[3] *Arabia Deserta*, vol. ii, chap. 5.

warfare by the introduction of modern fire-arms, even before the enforcement of internal peace in Sa'ūdi Arabia and elsewhere had made it unnecessary for this purpose. Even such tribes as the warlike Murra of eastern Arabia have largely ceased to breed horses.[1] With the increase of motor transport, riding and the maintenance of studs has become a hobby of wealthy people. In Sa'ūdi Arabia, however, the tribesmen can muster mare-mounted regiments when called on, though the horse's inability to stand prolonged thirst results in cavalry having less staying power than camelry. As an example of the number of mounted personal retainers, Ibn Sa'ūd in 1918 had a bodyguard of 300 mounted men.[2] The Yemeni army also includes *sowaris* (cavalrymen), while on ceremonial occasions officers of infantry regiments are mounted, and cavalry escorts accompany great personages. In Sa'ūdi Arabia horses are used for coursing hares and hunting gazelles with *salūqi* greyhounds, and for hawking so far as it is still practised. Organized horse-racing is not carried on, though horses are sometimes reared with a view to speed.

Horses are bred principally by the beduin tribes of north and central Arabia, among whom the Muteir, Beni Khālid, Dhafir, Shammar, and 'Aneiza tribes, as well as the Murra and others, are (or have been) renowned horse-breeders. In the Yemen the city of Dhamār had a like renown. But in south-west Arabia to-day the best horses are found in the desert-border districts east of the Yemen, i.e. Jauf, Marib, and, particularly, Beihān, the people of which favour only two strains, *kubeishi* and *mu'ali*, and regard as inferior the horses of the high plateaux, a type which they call *jebeli* or *khamsi*. In the Hadhramaut states horses are limited to a very few kept by the leading rulers; in the Sultanate of 'Omān and in Trucial 'Omān also they are very few.

The famous studs maintained by Arab rulers in the cities of central Arabia, such as that of Muhammad ibn Rashid seen at Hāil by Lady Anne Blunt in 1881,[3] are constantly recruited from the beduin tribes outside, though some breeding is also carried on in the cities. The best pasture is found after the spring rains in the sandy nafūds, on which some horses from the cities are sent out to graze; the stony deserts are too poor, while in the oases only garden produce and green corn, grown for this purpose in spring, and dry barley or wheat at other times, are available.

---

[1] Philby, *The Empty Quarter*, p. 43 (1933).
[2] Philby, *Arabia of the Wahhabis*, p. 296 (1928).
[3] *A Pilgrimage to Nejd*, vol. ii, chap. 12 (1881).

But the high steppes, 2,000–3,000 feet above sea-level, produce finer horses than those bred in the oases. Those of the deserts and steppes, though frequently lacking adequate food and water, are unequalled in endurance of hunger, thirst, and cold; though often emaciated, they speedily recover condition under a spell of good feeding. During the regular yearly tribal migrations a mare and her foal may cover 2,000 miles or more. Such horses walk fast, with a light long pace, owing to being trained to walk beside camels. They are never ridden for long journeys, but for visits to neighbouring camps or in tribal warfare. On festal occasions, such as defiling before a chief, the beduin hold their mares up short so that they leap forward, rise on the hind legs, back, and leap forward again, a performance called *hedheba*. On an average Arab horses live eight to twelve years longer than European; cases are known of an Arab stallion begetting offspring at 32, and a mare foaling regularly up to 35.

Though pure breeding is almost a lost art in Arabia, the beduin will not use horses other than of Arab descent. The preservation of the pure blood has been largely due to persons outside Arabia. Even if the 'Markham Arabian', imported into England by James I, and the horses shipped from the East by Cromwell, be disregarded, the descendants of 'Manak' are well known. This famous stallion, believed to have been of Mu'niqi type (*see below*), was shipped to England in 1705 by Mr. Darley, British Consul at Aleppo, who acquired the horse from the Fid'an section of the 'Aneiza during one of their enforced migrations northwards. It is claimed that English thoroughbred race-horses can all be traced back to Manak (ancestor of Eclipse) and a very few other famous oriental horses.

Nearly two centuries later, Lady Anne Blunt took steps to preserve the pure Arab blood, even then contaminated through careless breeding by the beduin. She established studs in England and in Egypt; the Egyptian stud was dispersed after her death in 1917, but some of the best of her English stud were sent to carry on the race in the United States.

The points of the best pure Arab horses are: head fairly short, wide, with pyramidal skull, bulging forehead, and profile below the orbits concave; nostrils large, thin, wide open, set diagonally; lower lip firm, small, drawn back; eyes very large; ears small, rather short, inward pointing (some beduin tribes, e.g. the Ruwalla, tie the ears of a filly together to train them). The likeness of the head in the most beautiful strains to the horses' heads in the finest classical

Greek sculpture has been remarked. The neck is arched, chest deep, back short but wide, muscles of croup strong; thighs muscular, legs light. The long tail of fine hairs is carried high, in a perfect arch. Average height 14¾ hands. The skin (bare round the eyes) is black, but the short, fine, silky coat never darker than dark brown. Greys (*asfar*, often turning white at 8 or 9 years), flea-bitten greys (*rummani*), dark chestnuts (*ashqar*), numerous bays (*ahmar*), and other colours occur, but roan and piebald, like black, are absent. Beduin use additional names to denote colours; the Ruwalla, who associate the speed of mares with their colours, consider a light yellow mare (*shakra*), the swiftest but not the most enduring, the latter quality pertaining to bay mares (*hamra*).[1]

Of thoroughbreds ('pure', *asīl*, plur. *asāyel*), as opposed to 'common' (*kadīsh*, plur. *kudsh*), traditionally five strains exist, supposed to be descended from the first five mares, *al Khamsa*, chosen and named by the Prophet; namely the *kuheilān*, *'ubbayān*, *saqlāwi*, *hamdāni*, and *hadbān* strains. But from modern study it appears that some twenty strains and more than 200 sub-strains are all reducible to three main types: *kuheilān*, strong and muscular, ideal cavalry horses, mostly greys; *saqlāwi*, the most beautiful and refined of all Arabian horses; and *mu'niqi*, the swiftest, lean, taller, with long lines. When pure breeding within the same strain is impossible, *kuheilān* and *saqlāwi* may be crossed, but the *mu'niqi* race-horse type should not be mated with the others if the characteristic Arabian strength, endurance, beauty, and gentleness are desired.[2]

Since the beduin ride mares only, and stallions are not gelded, many large clans have only a single stud horse. Among the Ruwalla this stallion is kept outside the camp, with head covered with a nose-bag except at watering, lest he chance to see a mare. Only two mares are brought to the stallion in a day, morning and evening. If a mare give birth to a filly, a cause of rejoicing, she is wrapped in blankets, kept in the tent on cold nights, often better fed than her owner and his family, and neither saddled nor ridden for a year, lest her milk be affected. Besides the mare's milk, a filly is given camel's milk morning and evening. On the other hand, many young stallions are killed, especially in a bad season, when a shortage of camel's milk for the mares and fillies is feared. For when pasture is poor mares also are given camel's milk, besides dates and barley; 300–500 lb. of barley is a year's ration. When fresh milk is absent, *marīsi*,

---

[1] Musil, *Manners and Customs of the Rwala Bedouins*, chap. xii (1928).
[2] C. R. Raswan, *The Black Tents of Arabia*, Appendix A, pp. 213–239 (1935).

262. *Types of Arab horses: (top) Kuheilān, for strength; (middle) Saqlāwi, for beauty; (bottom) Mu'niqi, for speed*

263. *Sheep in the northern steppes*

264. *Sheep and goats in the south-west*

a beverage made by rubbing dried milk (*iqt*) in water, is used. Among the beduin a young mare is never broken in, but grows up with the women and children, the latter soon beginning to sit on her back.

A mare and her offspring are often the common property of two or more beduin. Complicated rules exist concerning the sale of mares, and recovery of captured mares and their foals. A man's mare is cared for by his womenfolk and slaves; his wife saddles the mare, gives her water carried from the well, and keeps the key of the fetters when the forelegs are chained. The beduin ride without whip or spurs; often without bit or reins, using only a nose-band and a single halter. Frequently they ride also without stirrups or saddle. Stirrups (*rukb*), often considered a positive danger in battle, are shaped among the northern tribes so that the whole foot is put into the iron, resting on a broad metal plate; but in the south-west the narrow iron is grasped by the big toe only, as in Abyssinia. The bit, if used, is a tightly fitting curb or ring-bit with a short rein attached. Most horses are shod, even on the desert sand; a few are only hind-shod; the shoes are thin and flat, with a small hole in the middle. In parts of the south-west, e.g. the Aden Protectorate, horses are not shod at all.

A mare is *faras* (plur. *farsān*, rarely used); a stallion *husān* (plur. *husn*); plural for horses collectively, *kheil*. Among the Ruwalla (and probably other beduin) a mare after foaling is *rarūs*; a mare up to her tenth year *mohra*, after her twenty-first year *'awda*; a stallion over twenty is *'awd*; special names exist for fillies in every year from the first to seventh. *Faris* signifies a cavalier, especially a young man who brings home alone a captured mare from the enemy's camp; *akheil*, a horse-dealer, especially from central Arabia, who buys horses from the northern beduin for sale in Syria, Egypt, Hejaz, Yemen, Hasa, &c.[1]

Donkeys and Mules

Donkeys abound in almost every part of Arabia, in the mountains, the oases, among the desert nomads, and even on such islands as Bahrein. The ass (as Doughty wrote) is, except for needing drink every second day, a beast of the desert hardly less than the camel, sweating little and eating even such plants as the colocynth gourd

---

[1] Besides the works cited, other information will be found in W. Tweedie, *The Arabian Horse, His Country and People* (1894); C. Guarmani, *Northern Nejd* (1917, transl. from original Italian edition of 1866); Baroness Wentworth (J. A. D. Blunt-Lytton), *The Authentic Arabian Horse* (1945), and earlier works.

(pp. 505, 597). Donkeys are ridden and used as pack animals; also in many places harnessed with kine and camels to the wells. Among renowned breeds must be mentioned that of Al Hasa, where about one-quarter of the many thousands are large white asses, famous for their excellent temperament and speed. In the 'Asīr Tihama big white asses are also ridden, while beasts of a small grey breed carry burdens. In the mountains of the Western Aden Protectorate almost all the donkeys are small and usually grey, but some are good riding animals, excellent at picking their way along mountain tracks in daylight or darkness. The gipsy Solubba of north and central Arabia (p. 368), having neither camels nor horses, rely solely on donkeys, on which they even hunt; their best breed consists of large white asses almost as powerful as mules. Ass-geldings were used by the Solubba even in Doughty's day, while castration appears to be still more widely practised now.[1]

In Sa'ūdi Arabia the large white Hasa donkeys, crossed with good mares, produce excellent, though small, mules. In the Yemen highlands mules are very numerous, though usually not large, and their absence from the Aden Protectorate, especially the mountainous districts immediately south of the Yemen frontier, is noteworthy. They appear to be also few or absent in 'Asīr.

Neither the flesh nor milk of the ass is lawful food for Moslems; with regard to horse-flesh the position is uncertain, for the Prophet did not specifically forbid its use.

Sheep and Goats

(General term for sheep, *ghanam*; *kharūf* usually signifies a young male sheep, *talī* (plur. *tulyān*) a male lamb; *na'ja*, a ewe; *rōkhal* (plur. *rokhāl*) may mean a young female sheep or goat; ordinarily a goat is *ma'z*. General terms for the 'small cattle', sheep and goats, among the northern beduin are *ghanam* or *dubbush*.)

These are numerous in almost every part of Arabia, in every type of country, in the Tihama and the interior oases, in deserts at the season of spring pasturage, in the mountains and harras; goats, at any rate, on scantily populated islands off the coast, and pasturing in the densely wooded mountains of 'Asīr. Both sheep and goats are used as milch animals, also for meat and for their wool or hair; some persons of substance, however, own no milch sheep or goats, but rear these animals simply for meat.[2] In Sa'ūdi Arabia

---

[1] *Report of the U.S. Agricultural Mission to Sa'udi Arabia*, p. 43 (1943).
[2] Philby, *Arabia of the Wahhabis*, p. 64.

the development of two distinct breeds of goat has been recently recommended;[1] one for persons who are also sheep-owners and who want a maximum production of milk in their goats; this breed of goat need not have hair long enough for shearing, as the owners can select and develop their sheep for the fleece alone; but another breed of goat is wanted for people who depend on goats for hair and meat as well as milk. At present the best milk-producing goats are on the side of Saʿūdi Arabia near the Red Sea.

Among the nomads, goats and sheep often pasture in mixed flocks, though certain tribes or clans breed either sheep or goats exclusively. Some clans of the ʿAteiba breed only sheep,[2] and Doughty saw a great flock of sheep (mostly black fleeces) without goats among the Harb beduin.[3] Goats predominate, or are kept without any sheep, in the poorest sorts of country, as on the western harras; goat's milk is the nomad's sustenance, and the goat (like the ass) is said to eat even the colocynth gourd.[4] In the north-west a Sherāri beduin hunter will wander with his tiny tent, solitary but for his wife, one camel, and a few goats. The Solubba rear both sheep and goats.

In the towns of the central oases, e.g. the Washm district of Nejd, goats and sheep are sent out to graze under hireling shepherds during the day, and driven into the ground-floor rooms of the houses at night, the owners quickly sorting out their respective animals. In Washm fleeces are both white and black, but in some districts only black sheep are seen. Sheep may be driven long distances to pasture and watered only at rather long intervals. North-east of Majmaʿa (northern Nejd) they are watered at Dijani, then marched through the cool night some 12 miles to Jadhma, the nearest strip of Dahana desert, where they graze during the day, to be driven back during the second night, reaching the wells of Dijani again at dawn.[5]

On the mainland, sheep of all breeds have broad tails loaded with fat, but in Socotra a breed with long narrow tail exists. Most south Arabian varieties (and the Socotran breed just mentioned) have long drooping ears, but on the ʿAudhali plateau and in the neighbouring north-eastern Yemen is found a small, hardy, 'earless' breed (i.e. with no protuberance of the ears); these highland sheep, generally

[1] Rep. U.S. Agric. Mission to Saʿudi Arabia, p. 42 (1943).
[2] Handbook of Arabia, vol. i, p. 68 (1916).
[3] Arabia Deserta, vol. ii, chap. 9.
[4] Doughty, op. cit., vol. i, chaps. 5, 15.
[5] Philby, Arabia of the Wahhabis, pp. 358–359.

with creamy-white or chocolate-brown fleece, furnish milk, meat, wool, and manure. Another 'earless' breed, like the highland breed but for lack of wool, is found in the steppe-country below the Kaur escarpment. In other parts of the Aden Protectorate sheep are usually long-eared, with short hair coats, frequently dark chocolate-brown in the west, while black sheep are often seen in the east. A small white mountain breed is reared in the Hejaz.

Black-haired goats are common on the plateau of the north-eastern Yemen, less numerous on the 'Audhali plateau, and reappear on the limestone steppes farther east. In Socotra goats of a fine breed, yielding hair, meat, and milk, are kept. In Aden Colony there are several thousand milch goats of various types; those locally bred are often partly of Indian blood, but many are imported from the Protectorate, especially from Subeihi territory.

Parti-coloured sheep and goats are seen in some districts, but many tribes prefer dark self-coloured animals, as being easier to conceal from thieves. In the south-western highlands generally, goats greatly outnumber sheep below about 6,500 feet. In 'Omān sheep are less numerous than goats, being most abundant among the beduin of hilly districts. In north and central Arabia ewes lamb once a year, at the time of spring pasturage, though goats may bear young out of season. In south Arabia the lambing season is usually early summer, one lamb being the average, though in some high districts with good pasture ewes bear two lambs. The sickness and death of sheep is sometimes put down to their having eaten much sharp sand with the minute desert herbage.[1] No regular time is observed for shearing, which in Sa'ūdi Arabia is wastefully done with a knife, whence the use of shears has been recently recommended; in the Aden Protectorate shears are already used.

Camels

(Arabic general term, *jamal*, plur. *jimāl*, *ajmāl*; a riding camel is *dhalūl*, plur. *dhulul*; a milch camel without calf, *mish* (plur. *misuh*), with calf in attendance, *khalfa*; many other words are used, such as *q'aud*, a young camel; *būkra*, a riding camel with her first calf; *nāga*, a female camel; *howwār*, *howwāra*, a yearling camel calf, male or female; and special names for two- and three-year-olds, and other ages up to at least eight years.)[2]

Camels are used throughout Arabia, in every kind of country,

[1] Doughty, *Arabia Deserta*, vol. i, chap. 15.
[2] Ibid., Index and Glossary.

265. *Camel-herds in the hills of Midian*

266. *Riding-camels (dhalūls) and young*

267. *Beehive in a house-wall in the Hadhramaut*

268. *Beehives near Dhāla', Western Aden Protectorate*

though in the high mountains of the south-west their place is taken by mules for riding purposes and partly for transport of goods. The riding camel (*dhalūl*) is almost always female, the pack camel usually male (in the deserts of Egypt and Libya apparently only the male is ridden). Camels are also used as draught animals, raising water from wells either alone or in teams (often mixed with other animals); in Aden (the Colony proper) and at Hodeida they are harnessed to carts; in San'ā they turn primitive oil-mills, walking round and round, blindfolded, in deep cellars.[1] Herds of milch-camels (*mish*) are kept solely for their milk in many parts; camel's hair is also used in making saddle-bags and other articles; and the meat is sometimes in request.

Though camels may live forty to fifty years, and are trained to carry loads from the third year, they do not work regularly till the sixth; they usually cease work after 25, unless worn out many years before as is frequently the case. They are bred in most districts for local needs, but the principal camel-breeders are the Ruwalla beduin and other 'Aneiza tribes in the north; the Shammar, 'Ateiba, Qahtān, and Dawāsir in the centre; the Muteir, 'Ajmān, Dhafir, and Murra in the east. The period of gestation is thirteen months, but ten or eleven months is allowed before the female is next mated, otherwise the stock deteriorates.[2] A female can be mated in her sixth year, the season being usually December or January, so that the calf is born the following February or March twelve months. The calf is fed on milk only for a considerable time, e.g. among the Ruwalla for ninety days.[3] In some herds of milch camels, when two females calve about the same time one calf is killed, and the survivor has both mother and foster-mother.[4] When nomads migrate, new-born calves are carried with the children, &c., on burden-camels. Pregnant camels need watching, to prevent them eating noxious plants, or wandering away to give birth in some lonely spot where the calf would fall a prey to wild beasts.

In south-west Arabia, riding-camels famous for speed are bred in the sultanate of Lahej. Farther east, good steppe-camels are bred in Dathina and neighbouring tribal territories, and numbers are sold to tribes employed in caravan-traffic on routes leading north-east from Aden. The Manahil, north of Wadi Hadhramaut, and the

[1] Rathjens and Wissmann, *Südarabien-Reise*, vol. iii, p. 148, fig. 66 (1934).
[2] Philby, *The Heart of Arabia*, vol. i, p. 130.
[3] Musil, *Manners and Customs of the Rwala Bedouins*, chap. xi.
[4] Philby, *Arabia of the Wahhabis*, p. 54.

Mahra farther east, supply camels for the big fairs and pilgrimages at local shrines; the pilgrimage at Qabr Hūd may involve a week's, and the fair at Meshhed three days', dealing in livestock. Wastage in these arid eastern districts is very great. In the wooded valleys of Dhufār, milch camels are kept only in small groups; the males bred there carry frankincense from the mountains to the coast, returning laden with sardines for cattle-fodder.

Breeds and Varieties. Size and colour vary greatly. Camels of the southern beduin tribes are in many cases blackish, while the northern tribes prefer dun-coloured strains, considering the black camels to be of uncertain temper and often savage. Thus, Muteir camels are mainly black or dark brown, those of the Shammar fawn or white, while in Al Qasīm, among a single clan of the Harb, black and white are the prevailing colours.[1] In the north, 'white she-camels are the pride of every clan'; a clan generally owns a herd of such white beasts, none of which is ever sold; captured white camels are (or were) added till the number reaches 100, when a new herd is started.[2] White camels were held in this high esteem even in the days of raiding, although they were dangerously conspicuous. In the Yemen, caravans of small sand-coloured camels from the eastern desert may be seen on their way to the cities of the highlands, contrasting strongly with the great shaggy, rather dark beasts of the mountain breed.[3] The camels of the Mecca district are small, while in 'Omān there exists a breed so small as to have given rise to a saying that in central Arabia the camel is first cousin to an elephant but in 'Omān to a mouse.

In the best breeds as much attention is paid to the 'points' as in the case of horses. A good female camel should have small pointed ears, bright eyes, a hard erect arched neck, muscular shoulders, small hoofs, and bulging, well-covered hips. Such are the main points in the judgement of the Ruwalla beduin in the north-west, who consider the best breeds the *sharāriya, huteimiya, tihiya,* and *'omāniya,* named from their places of origin, i.e. the Sherārāt and Huteim tribes, the Tih plateau in Sinai (p. 44), and 'Omān. In the more central districts four pure breeds are recognized: the shaggy camels bred in the north by the 'Aneiza and Huweitāt, called *hurr*; the *'arqiyya* of Bīsha and Nejrān, a whitish beast, unable to endure

---

[1] Philby, *Arabia of the Wahhabis*, pp. 308, 366.

[2] Musil, *Manners and Customs of the Rwala Bedouins*, chap. xi, and *Northern Hejaz*, p. 37.

[3] Scott, *In the High Yemen*, p. 109.

cold; the *dara'iya*, a yellowish or light brown camel from the south, towards the Hadhramaut; and the *'omāniya*, dun-coloured, lightly built and very swift. Pure-bred camels of these strains are said to be unmistakable to experts. The Manasir tribes on the coast of Al Hasa have riding camels of a very good light-coloured breed called *'usaifir*. Even within a famous breed such as the *'omāniya* there are various strains; camels bred for constant work in the sands of the great southern desert are called *ramliyat* (from *raml*, sand) and are more lightly built than those of the steppe.[1]

Speed, Endurance, &c. A camel caravan does not usually travel more than about 2½ to 3 miles an hour, so that, without night marching and with moderately light loads, 25 to 30 miles in a day's journey of some 9 hours is good progress. The average of over 40 miles a day, or 270 miles in 6 full days, accomplished by Philby when travelling westwards from Neifa across the Rub' al Khali in March 1932, would have been very good going even under easier conditions.[2] The size of a camel may affect its speed; e.g. an *'omāniya* taking 89 paces a minute was outwalked by a great shaggy white Shammar camel which took only 88 paces.[3] Records of great distances covered at high speed should generally be accepted with caution if the evidence be solely that of Arab witnesses, who are prone to exaggerate. Nevertheless many great feats of endurance have been authenticated. A riding-camel given to Nolde by Ibn Rashid covered 62½ miles one night between 10 p.m. and 5 a.m., though it had traversed 30 miles the day before and covered another 30 the day following. With relays, central Arabian camels traversed more than 400 miles between Basra and Riyādh in 3 days, an average of 135 miles a day.[4] On desert routes, a load of 330 lb. is an average burden, though as much as 400 lb. (or even 600 with exceptional animals) may be carried. The nature of the ground is an important factor. Sharp gravel or *harra*-country will cut the sole-pads of sand-bred beasts to ribbons. Such wounds are patched by sewing on to the sole strips of leather (or, in modern times, rubber, if available).

On the whole the female is more enduring than the male, persisting longer without abundant pasture or water, especially in the mating season, when males are often easily exhausted. At the time of spring

[1] Philby, *The Empty Quarter*, p. 11.
[2] Ibid., p. 343.
[3] Philby, *Arabia of the Wahhabis*, p. 370.
[4] *Handbook of Arabia*, vol. ii, p. 15 (1917).

pasture camels will go more than two months without drinking, deriving enough moisture from the fresh vegetation. Even in winter they can pass a full week waterless without discomfort; camels driven off to drink after only four days' travelling (but cool days) from Dulaiqiya in Al Hasa, early in January, 1932, for the most part spurned the proffered water.[1] In summer they must normally drink at intervals of three days, though a good riding camel carrying only its rider will subsist a day or so longer. Beduin consider that after an exceptionally exhausting march a camel needs several months' rest.

Fodder, Grazing. Among the nomads grazing camels pick their food where they can, browsing even on thorny acacia and tamarisk. Camels will eat various bitter and saline herbs collectively called *hamudh* (consisting of *ghadha, dhumrān, 'arād, shinān, suwwād,* and *rimdh*[2]), which sometimes engender excessive thirst. 'Omāniya camels apparently eat certain species of *Artemisia* called *ādhir,* which in northern Nejd are spurned by camels and considered poisonous to them. *Harmal (Rhazya stricta),* a plant marking desert watercourses, appears to be definitely poisonous. *Nussi* grass (*nasī*, p. 198) forms very highly prized pasture, especially in the Nafūds in spring. In settled districts camels may be fed with green stalks of millet; at the draw-wells of San'ā and other cities, where they and other beasts descend and ascend the inclined planes from dawn to dark, or even all night on moonlight nights, they are fed at intervals with bunches of green fodder and carrots. In central Arabia, at any rate, camels let out to graze are termed *'azib,* those in the spring desert pastures, *jazu.* They usually sit down and chew the cud for two or three hours from about midday. It is sometimes necessary to bind their jaws to prevent excessive grazing, or the surplus fat may cause breakage of the hump, resulting in death.[3] In some beduin tribes each herdsman has his special song, sung to prevent beasts straying from the herd when returning to the encampment at sunset; strayed camels easily lose themselves, running in all directions and apparently lacking any sense of finding their own herd. The boys who keep the camels and other beasts working hour after hour at the draw-wells of San'ā have also their special songs. The old-established practice of some tribes is to carry food for camels on desert journeys; several balls

---

[1] Philby, *The Empty Quarter,* p. 46.
[2] The first two are *Arthrocnemon fruticosum* and *Traganum nudatum* respectively; *suwwād* is probably *Suaeda;* the identity of the others is uncertain.
[3] Musil, *Northern Hejaz,* p. 28.

of *alej* (a mixture of millet and coarse flour), the size of a man's fist, may be given to each camel at night. In other parts of Arabia balls of dates with their stones, or crushed date stones, are fed to camels. In the Eastern Aden Protectorate dried and partly cured fish is used as fodder for camels and other animals.[1]

Harness, &c. The usual Arabian camel-bridle (*khitāma*) consists of a single rope of wool attached by a short chain to a ring in the head-stall, a band of leather round the animal's nose held in position by a strip of leather passing behind the ears. A short rope ('*aqal* or *rasan*) round the neck is used to hobble one of the camel's legs during halts.[2] The various forms of saddles and their ornaments and the elaborate litters used by different tribes cannot be described fully here.[3] In 'Omān saddles called *haulani* are used, much lighter than the ponderous structures of central Arabia; these southern saddles are set well back towards the camel's rump, with only small wooden vices gripping the hump fore and aft; the riders depend entirely on balance, frequently squatting or kneeling, sitting on the upturned soles of their own feet.[4]

Diseases. The many ailments of camels are said (among the northern beduin) to be largely forms of inflammation of the bowels and joints. The principal method of cure is by burning the affected part with a hot iron, in some cases a specified number of times; but many of the diseases are considered incurable. Complaints such as blistering, due to a badly fitting saddle, or laceration of the feet by sharp stones in camels accustomed only to sand, heal naturally with rest and good feeding.[5]

Poultry

In many districts the domestic fowls are very small, often of bantam size. Suggestions for improving the breed in Sa'ūdi Arabia have recently been made.[6] In the south-western highlands, introduced breeds succeed at altitudes above 4,000 feet, if well fed. White Leg-horns have proved less suitable owing to the young birds being too easily seen by birds of prey. But Rhode Island Reds, established on

---

[1] For local names of fodder plants in the southern deserts, see Bertram Thomas, *Arabia Felix*, p. 200, note 1 (1932).

[2] Philby, *Arabia of the Wahhabis*, p. 68.

[3] See, for instance, illustrations in Musil, *Manners and Customs of the Rwala Bedouins*, and photos. 194, 195 in this volume.

[4] Philby, *The Empty Quarter*, pp. 29, 59.

[5] List of diseases in Musil, *Manners and Customs of the Rwala Bedouins*.

[6] Twitchell, *Rep. U.S. Agric. Mission to Sa'udi Arabia*, p. 44 (1943).

the 'Audhali plateau in 1939, have been spread to neighbouring high districts of the Yemen. Below 4,000 feet the local strains withstand the heat and diseases better than imported breeds. Large quantities of eggs are exported from the Yemen to Aden by Gawaza tribes-men who purchase them from villagers near Mafālis, just over the frontier some sixty miles north-west of Aden; packed in tamarisk foliage, in empty kerosene cases, the eggs travel better by camel than can be expected from motor-transport on the existing mountain and desert tracks.

Both chickens and eggs are important elements in Arabian diet, though some local communities, such as the Kheiābara (negro villagers of Kheibar), will not eat their chickens, but only the eggs.[1]

Dogs, Cats

In much of north and central Arabia hare-coursing with *salūqi* (*slūgi*) greyhounds is the common sport of the country; in Doughty's words the beduin greyhounds were 'light with hunger, and very swift to course the hare; and by these the gazelle fawn is taken'.[2] In most parts of Arabia the ordinary dogs of towns, villages, and beduin encampments are fox- or jackal-like animals, yellowish, reddish, or black, of a type very widespread in the East. Though often starved and poorly treated (to cite the same classic, the 'starve-ling hounds' of the beduin would greedily swallow locusts), they are not always so. In some districts they are well treated and make good watch-dogs, though in the towns they usually keep their own quarters. Among the beduin the dogs do not go out with the grazing flocks, but remain to guard the encampment. Doughty remarked on the absence of town dogs in Teima. The best breeds appear to be the great shaggy dogs of the Billi (Baluwī) tribesmen in the Tihama north of Yenbo', and a large black breed which produces excellent watch-dogs in 'Asīr.[3]

In south-west Arabia domestic cats are much like the Abyssinian variety, lean and small headed, with sharply pointed nose and ears, but quite tractable in disposition.[4] Doughty remarked on the absence of cats in the villages of Nejd, but Philby records the presence of small numbers in Riyādh.[5] Doughty noted the existence of cats at Hāil and Kheibar.

---

[1] Doughty, *Arabia Deserta*, vol. ii, chap. 7.
[2] Ibid., vol. i, chap. 12.
[3] *Handbook of Arabia*, vol. i, p. 136 (1916).
[4] Scott, *In the High Yemen*, p. 71.
[5] *Arabia of the Wahhabis*, p. 45.

HONEY AND BEE-KEEPING

In north and central Arabia, particularly in rocky places, wild honey is collected. Doughty wrote of a woman at Kheibar buying wild honey from the beduin in order to sop girdle-cakes in a mixture of honey and butter; honey, mixed with butter, milk, or oil, being considered a most strengthening diet, conducing to longevity. Apparently in Doughty's time bees were kept by Christians in the limestone valleys east of the Red Sea, but the honey was 'savourless'.[1] In Nejd it is regarded as highly dangerous to eat musk melons on top of honey.[2]

In the south-west beehives consist of hollow logs[3] or earthenware cylinders, lying horizontally in tiers. For example, in the Amiri highlands (Western Aden Protectorate) batteries of nearly twenty hives may be seen, sometimes enclosed in a building with three rough-stone walls roofed with brushwood, the fourth side left open so that the ends of the hives are exposed. Such a group recalls the much larger batteries used since ancient times in Egypt. Most of this highland honey ('asal zubdi) is light-coloured and sets hard; it is stored in gourds, in which a small opening is made by neatly cutting out a piece of the rind, afterwards used as a stopper.[4] (Photo. 268.)

Horizontal earthenware cylinders are also used as hives in the Hadhramaut, in some districts of which, however, the depredations of the blue-cheeked bee-eater (*Merops persicus*) are so severe that it is considered impossible to produce honey on a commercial scale. The honey of Jardan (south of Shabwa) has great local repute, but is not produced in large quantities; old honey of this district and Markha is very dark and thick. In many eastern districts of the Aden Protectorate honey is extracted from the comb and stored in skins; droughts in these districts often cause great loss to bee-keepers, who have to replenish stocks from distant areas. (Photo. 267.)

In Wadi Dū'an honey-production is a real industry.[5] The hives, inserted into the walls of houses, consist of circular sections about a foot in diameter, additional sections being added when the hive is full. Two crops are taken annually, that of June, July, and August, when the 'ilb trees (*Zizyphus Spina-Christi*) are in blossom, being considered the best; while that of the winter crop (November

[1] Doughty, *Arabia Deserta*, vol. i, chap. 1; vol. ii, chap. 4.
[2] Philby, *Arabia of the Wahhabis*, pp. 44–45.
[3] Wyman Bury, *Arabia Infelix*, p. 44.
[4] Scott, *In the High Yemen*, pp. 58–59.
[5] Ingrams, *Report on the Hadhramaut*, pp. 52–54.

to March), when the bees collect largely from the *qarmala* bush, is thought very heating. If much rain falls during April and May the bees make a black honey called *helb*, which they consume themselves. When swarming occurs, the bee-owner rolls a mat into the shape of a hive, closes one end, and sprinkles the inside with perfume; he takes the queen from the swarm with his fingers and places her in a small cage, which he puts in the rolled mat; an assistant beats a metal tray, and the swarming bees follow the queen into the mat, which is carried to a hive, into which the caged queen is put and followed by the bees. A crop may be collected in 12 to 20 days (new sections being fitted to the hive) and 30 to 40 lb. of honey are collected at each crop. The bees are smoked out from behind and the honey, in comb or liquid, is packed in tins. Some years ago the total annual production was 90,000 to 100,000 lb. The dark golden-brown honey is highly renowned in south Arabia (among the few Europeans who try it, as well as among the Arabs) and in the East Indies. But on analysis in England it was regarded unfavourably from a commercial standpoint, partly owing to a special aromatic smell and taste. This is due probably to its peculiar chemical composition, which suggests that it is of a 'honeydew' type, i.e. not originating solely from floral nectar, but largely from the secretions of the leaves of certain plants or from the secretions of insects.

CHAPTER X

ECONOMIC GEOGRAPHY

SA'ŪDI ARABIA

MINERALS

K NOWLEDGE of the mineral resources of Sa'ūdi Arabia is extremely scanty, but the chief minerals at present being exploited are petroleum, gold, rock-salt, and gypsum.

Petroleum

In 1933 King Ibn Sa'ūd granted to the Standard Oil Company of California a concession agreement to explore for, prospect for, and to produce petroleum within the kingdom of Sa'ūdi Arabia. The agreement covered most of the eastern part of the country. The company, known as the California Arabia Standard Oil Company, or Aramco, after performing much exploratory and geological work throughout the area of the agreement, announced the production of oil in commercial quantities in March 1938 from the Dammam field in the province of Al Hasa, about 5 miles inland from Al Khobar on the Persian Gulf opposite Bahrein island. By the end of 1944 thirty-eight wells had been drilled, resulting in the discovery of two more productive fields, at Abqaiq and Abu Hadriya, which with the Dammam field have an estimated productive capacity of 140,000 barrels per day. The producing wells at Abqaiq and Abu Hadriya have been shut in, awaiting the development of transport facilities. The Dammam field supplies the refinery of the Bahrein Petroleum Company, Ltd., an associated company on Bahrein island, with 37,500 barrels of crude oil per day, as well as meeting the requirements of Aramco's refinery at Ras Tannūra (3,000 barrels per day). The Ras Tannūra refinery is connected by a 10-inch pipe-line with the Dammam field, about 40 miles away. It produces kerosene, fuel oil, and gasoline, and supplies the requirements of the Sa'ūdi Arabian Government as well as those of Aramco's operations. A new refinery with a capacity of 50,000 barrels per day was under construction at Ras Tannūra in 1944, and additional pipe-lines were to be constructed from the Dammam field. Crude oil from the Dammam field is transported to Bahrein island by a combination of pipe-lines and barges, but a pipe-line, under construction in 1944, from the Dammam field to the Bahrein refinery would allow the transport of 60,000 barrels per day.

The company employs about 850 Americans and over 8,000 Sa'ūdi Arabian nationals. Operating headquarters are at the large, well-planned permanent camp at Dhahrān on the Dammam field. Here, besides houses, recreational facilities are provided for all employees, and there are two hospitals, one for Americans and one for Arabs, and a school. The temporary housing facilities, which included tents, made necessary by the active construction programme at Ras Tannūra, are now being replaced by permanent houses, and a hospital is to be built. Schools have also been established at Al Khobar and Jebel, which with that at Dhahrān have a total enrolment of 200 students.

There were no deep-water port facilities on the Persian Gulf coast when the company began operations. But a rock-filled pier 2,700 feet long has been constructed at Al Khobar in water deep enough for all but sea-going steamers. The deep-water channels leading to Al Khobar have been marked with permanent daylight beacons, and the pier has complete freight-handling facilities and offices for Sa'ūdi Arabian customs and immigration officials. From a small fishing-village of thatched huts, with a population of a few score, Al Khobar has become a rapidly growing town, with permanent masonry buildings and a population of about 1,000.

The best deep-water harbour on the Persian Gulf coast of Sa'ūdi Arabia is under construction at Ras Tannūra. There is a rock-filled and steel pier with freight-handling facilities, to which cargoes are carried by lighter. A deep-water wharf to load oil and receive freight from sea-going vessels up to 4-feet draught at low tide was under construction in 1944. This will allow four large ships to dock simultaneously. Already the port facilities provided by Aramco on this part of the Persian Gulf coast have become quite important to the economy of eastern Sa'ūdi Arabia, particularly in alleviating critical shortages of food and petroleum caused by the war.

There seems now to be no doubt that this oilfield is likely to be one of the finest in the world. Its reserves, estimated on a basis of present development and limited drilling, are given as 2,083,000,000 barrels, against a world total of 51,549,000,000 barrels. (Compare, from the same source, U.S.A. 20,064,000,000 barrels; East Indies, 1,250,000,000; Russia, 5,735,000,000; Venezuela, 5,600,000,000; Persia, 5,500,000,000.) It is obvious that it is one of the most important influences on the economic development of Sa'ūdi Arabia, for in the first place the income will enable the Government to undertake enterprises which in a comparatively short time may result in significant economic changes. The royalties had already reached a figure of £500,000 a year by 1939. Also the company are interested in further-ing the development of the country even beyond the limits of their own enterprise. For example, incentive has been given to the growth of contract building construction, and a number of reliable contractors are now doing work on a lump-sum contract basis for the Government. The company has also helped the Government with the development of irrigation and water wells. Besides an engineering and geological report on the Al Kharj irrigation project of central Nejd, assistance in construction and operation was given by the company. Wells have been drilled in Jidda, Riyādh, 'Aneiza, Wadi al Hani, and other places, that of Wadi al Hani opening up two main routes between Nejd and the Persian Gulf, hitherto impossible for camels in summer due to shortage of water. Further, the nucleus of a general road system has been developed in the province of Al Hasa, and special motor equip-ment has been provided for use in desert areas which would other-wise be inaccessible for lack of roads. An airport has been built at Dhahrān.

Further possibilities for petroleum production in Sa'ūdi Arabia are indicated by reports of oilfields in the Hejaz and 'Asīr, though nothing is yet known of their extent. Near Dhaba, about 25 miles north of Al Wejh, the presence of an oilfield is suspected from the visible seepage along this part of the coast.

Gold

The Sa'ūdi Arabian Mining Syndicate Ltd., largely with American staff and capital, but with a considerable proportion of British capital, has undertaken the exploitation of an old gold-mine at Mahd adh Dhahab (app. 41° E., 23° 30' N.) between Mecca and Al Madina. This company is likely to have success, for although operations have been hindered by the war, the spoil from the old mine has proved valuable, and a new vein has been discovered below. It is believed to be the Beni Sulaim mine which the Prophet Muhammad gave as reward to his henchman Bilal ibn al Harith. This and other gold-mines were at the height of their development at the time of King Solomon, and were worked as late as the tenth century, declining with Europe's stability and purchasing power.

Salt and *gypsum* deposits are widespread in Sa'ūdi Arabia and are used almost entirely to supply local needs. There are three main sources of salt: by evaporation from sea-water, as at Al Wejh, where it is used for salting fish for export; from deposits of rock-salt as at Teima, at Birk (70 miles south of Al Qunfidha), Abu 'Arīsh (70 miles north of Luheiya), at Jīzān, and Madhāya (between Jīzān and Meidi) on the 'Asīr coast; and from the salt-pans of the interior, e.g. at Faidha (44° 50′ E., 25° 30′ N.) between Shaqra and Mudhnib, the large salt-pan of Mamlaha 'Aushaziya 8 miles north of Mudhnib, where there is a solid block of pure white salt 12 to 18 inches deep and 6–7 miles long, from which the people of Sirr, Mudhnib, and 'Aushaziya draw supplies without payment, and the Shiqqa pan near Qara'a, north-west of Boreida, said to be of even better quality, which supplies the bazaars of 'Aneiza and Boreida. The Jīzān salt-mine is worked by the Government. The salt is blasted out of the pit and packed in 80-lb. bags for sale in the interior of 'Asīr. Some 30–50 bags per day are produced here, equivalent to about 500 camel loads per month. Gypsum is used locally, being burned to make lime, and the location of the numerous deposits is so far unrecorded. Philby frequently refers to beds of gypsum encountered in his travels, e.g. near Barra, between Shaqra and Riyādh, and at the south end of As Sirr.

INDUSTRIES

Manufactures are practically non-existent in Sa'ūdi Arabia, apart from the oil refinery at Ras Tannūra. Domestic crafts include weaving for the production of cloaks ('abās), some of which are exported, but most industries, such as the tanning of hides and the manufacture of clarified butter, are concerned with agricultural produce, and have already been dealt with in Chapter VII. Dhow-building is carried on at the smaller ports on the Red Sea coast, for instance, Al Wejh makes sanbūqs (smacks) and exports charcoal produced inland.

Fishing is another occupation on both the Red Sea and Persian Gulf coasts, but no statistics are available and detailed information is lacking.

COMMERCE AND FINANCE

Foreign trade is of slight importance, a fact which is only too evident from the primitive harbours and general lack of port facilities. But it is necessary to import food and textiles. Thus the chief imports are rice, sugar, tea, grain, and flour, and textile goods which originally came from India but more recently from Japan. The grain comes chiefly from India and 'Iraq (46,500 metric tons from India, 8,814 from 'Iraq in 1939). Vegetables, grain, and tobacco are imported from Egypt. All machinery and transport material is imported. Exports are almost negligible, consisting of livestock, hides and skins, dates, some pearls, and gum arabic. The development of motor transport in India, Syria, and Egypt has reduced the export of camels and horses to those countries. In 1943 imports from the United Kingdom were valued at only £128,000, while exports to the United Kingdom in 1939 were valued at £23,241.

The principal source of revenue until recently was, directly and indirectly, the annual pilgrimage, which not only produced the fees paid by pilgrims but greatly swelled the customs revenue from goods imported mainly for their benefit. In good years, with an average influx of 100,000 visitors from abroad, the combined pilgrimage and customs revenue regularly reached a total of some £5 millions a year, to which land and other internal taxes may have added about half a million. The slump of 1931 reduced the pilgrimage and, consequently, the annual revenue by at least two-thirds of the old figure; and there has been no substantial recovery since then. On the contrary, the outbreak of war in 1939 set back the clock once more, and for some years the pilgrimage has been a negligible quantity. It was therefore fortunate for Sa'ūdi Arabia that this period of financial depression has been marked by the development of a new and substantial source of revenue, namely oil (p. 515). The war, however, checked further development of these resources, though the limitation imposed on production at the beginning is now being reconsidered. More recently the pilgrimage of 1944 has also shown welcome signs of revival, which should be maintained. It is, however, improbable that the total revenue of the country in any year since 1939 has reached £2 millions; but since 1940 the Government has received the benefit of some substantial assistance from the British Government as well as from the Lease-Lend administration, a sum of about £7 millions in all during the past four years. In addition it has been able to overdraw on its account with the oil company against the security of its royalties. The financial situation may therefore be regarded as reasonably favourable in view of future oil and pilgrimage prospects, while it is also hoped that the gold-mine now being operated by an Anglo-American company, though temporarily closed down for reasons arising out of the war, may soon begin to produce revenue for the Government. It may be noted that the national debt mentioned above

(p. 326) does not include the overdraft with the oil company, much less the grants-in-aid from Britain or on Lease-Lend account.

So much for the revenue situation. No budget for income and expenditure is published by the Government. But it may be said that, apart from the Civil List and the salaries of government employees of all kinds, the heaviest single item of expenditure is motor transport, which is becoming increasingly important in the Arabia of to-day. The normal annual expenditure on this account probably averages about £500,000. Army equipment of all sorts accounts for another substantial sum, while the necessity of maintaining communications in so large a country calls for considerable expenditure on the establishment and maintenance of wireless stations. The Health Department, particularly that part of it which caters for the pilgrimage, provides another substantial item, while the X-ray installation at Riyādh is reputed to be as elaborate as any in the Middle East. Great attention is paid by the Government to the development of the higher flights of medical technique but, so far as the country generally is concerned, that is done at the expense of the ordinary people, for whose medical care no provision is made apart from the hospitals and dispensaries maintained in a few of the bigger towns—Mecca, Al Madina, Jidda, Tāif, Riyādh, and Hofūf. Arabia has not yet developed the class of general practitioner who is prepared to devote himself to the care of the villages and tribes. Education does not at present figure very prominently in the state budget, and most of its current expenditure is for teaching personnel and scholarships, &c. Roads and other public works are also minor items in the budget, for Arabia is perhaps fortunate in having so little water that motor traffic can operate almost anywhere without let or hindrance.

Currency

In theory the English gold sovereign is the basis of the currency. A new silver currency, the riyal, weighing 24·055 grammes, 830 fine, replaced the Turkish Mejidie currency in 1928, with 10 riyals to £1 (gold) at par. In 1936 the riyal began to be replaced by one of 11·664 grammes, 916·6 fine, with the new par at 20 to £1 (gold). In 1940 it was declared equal in value to the Indian rupee, which it equalled in size, weight, and fineness. But in September 1944 the riyal was quoted at 44 to £1 (gold). Subdivisions of the riyal are first into 11 qursh miri (*guerches* on postage stamps), each of which contains 2 qursh darij. The qursh darij and its halves and quarters are nickel coins.

COMMUNICATIONS

With a few exceptions, it is physically possible to travel practically anywhere in Sa'ūdi Arabia without undue hardship, despite the lack of railways and of motor-roads, and to attempt a detailed account of desert tracks in a country of this size and nature would serve no useful purpose here. The future obviously lies with the development of motor transport, perhaps too of aviation, partly because of the growing realization of Arabia's geographical position fostered by ideals of Arab unity in a shrinking world, and partly as a result of the oil company's operations.

The Hejaz Railway

The only railway line which has been laid in Sa'ūdi Arabia is the southern part of the old single-track Hejaz railway (gauge 105 cm.) from Damascus to Al Madina. Funds were raised for its construction at the end of the nineteenth century in the Ottoman Empire by public subscription and a special stamp tax. The line was begun in 1900, opened to Ma'an in September 1904, and completed to Al Madina four years later. All the reconnaissance and laying of the line was done by Turkish engineers, with the exception of one German engineer named Meisner.

Ostensibly built for the pilgrim traffic, it had considerable political significance, since it enabled Sultan 'Abdul Hamid to assert himself more forcibly at Mecca. During the War of 1914–1918 it served as the sole line of communications between the Turkish troops in Al Madina and their base in Syria—a line that was difficult to maintain and extremely vulnerable to interruption both in Transjordan and the northern Hejaz (p. 294). By the end of the war many bridges had been demolished and the permanent way had suffered severely. Though the line through Transjordan to Amman and the branch from Deraa on the Syrian frontier through Samakh to Haifa in Palestine were rapidly made good, the section between Amman and Ma'an was only restored after security was re-established in Transjordan. Meanwhile the line from Ma'an to Al Madina remained abandoned and became derelict. During the War of 1939–1945 some of the rails in Transjordan south of Ma'an were removed for use on the extension of the Amman–Ma'an line to Nakb Shtar, 25 miles from Ma'an, on the way to 'Aqaba.[1]

Route. South of Ma'an the line followed the old pilgrim route fairly

[1] For a description of the existing Hejaz line to Ma'an in Transjordan see *Palestine and Transjordan*, B.R. 514, pp. 508–513.

closely throughout. It crossed the present Sa'ūdi Arabian boundary 2 miles south of the Transjordan frontier post and old railway station of Qal'at al Mudauwara, and then traversed the open desert of sand and stones at the eastern foot of the mountain barrier of Midian, crossing a number of watercourses, usually dry, draining eastwards into the depression of Al Mehteteb, north-east of Tebūk. This oasis of Tebūk is the first settlement of importance and has a fine grove of palms and a good water-supply from wells. It can be reached fairly easily by road from Muweilih on the Red Sea coast, a distance of about 115 miles.

After crossing the Wadi Ithl (17½ miles south-east of Tebūk), the line climbed steadily between limestone hills, entered a narrow sandstone gorge, tunnelled through a rocky spur, and with sharp bends descended the Wadi al Hamas to Khamīs. Qal'at al Mu'adhdham was an important station on the line generally with a good water-supply; it is much frequented by various beduin tribes (Beni 'Atiya, Billi, Aida, Shammar, Fuqara, and Sherārāt), and from it Hāil has been reached by motor in one day, though the distance is 300 miles.

After Qal'at al Mu'adhdham the line entered the bare broken sandstone foothills of Jebel 'Uweiridh. Beyond Dār al Hamra a watershed (3,752 ft.) was crossed into the Wadi Abu Tāqah, the down gradient being about 1 in 70. Here trains were often liable to be blocked or derailed by sand blown across the track. The country is even more broken after Abu Tāqah, with red sandstone rocks eroded into fantastic shapes by wind (photos. 104, 105, 269). There is little water, and there are few trees and bushes on the descent to the plain of Madāin Sālih (Al Hijr).

Madāin Sālih has a long history and was once on the southern frontier of the Nabataeans and an important post on the ancient caravan route (p. 231). There are many interesting Nabataean tombs and inscriptions near by (photo. 135), but Al 'Ulā, about 22 miles farther on, is more important to-day (p. 573). Some of the well-water is purgative, but the subsoil water is generally good and much used for cultivation. There are two or three alternative tracks from Al Wejh on the Red Sea coast to Al 'Ulā, varying in distance from 120 to 150 miles.

Few details are available of the country passed through by the railway south of Al 'Ulā. The line in this section was laid out and built by Turkish engineers and Arab labour without the assistance of Meisner, and was reported to be so bad even before 1914 that trains had to crawl at an average speed of under 10 miles an hour. The station at Al Madina was well built with seventeen stone buildings south-west of the town and had a number of sidings (fig. 43).

269. *The old Hejaz railway in the narrow pass of Abu Tāqah, north of Madāin Sālih. Formerly trains were often stopped or derailed by sand*

270. *Ri al Ahurar post on the Mecca–Jidda road*

271. *Weaving a mat in the Yemen*

272. *Drying bricks in the sun, San'ā*

A list of stations on the line between Maʿan and Al Madina is given below:

Miles from Maʿan	Station	Height (in feet)
0	MAʿAN	3,435
9·9	GHADR AL HAJJ	3,273
17·4	BIR ASH SHEDĪYAH	3,236
34·3	ʿAQABAT AL HEJĀZĪYAH	3,740
38·1	BATN AL GHŪL	3,700
44·3	WADI RUTM	3,222
54·5	TELL SHAHM (TELL ASH SHAHIM)	2,765
60·6	RAMLAH	2,619
70·2	QALʿAT AL MUDAUWARA	2,385
72·2	(Boundary of Saʿūdi Arabia)	..
84·2	QALʿAT AL AHMAR	2,469
92·9	DHĀT AL HAJJ (ZĀT AL HAJJ)	..
107·5	BIR HURMAS	2,054
121·5	HAZM	2,126
135·8	AL MEHTETEB	2,200
144·8	TEBŪK	2,249
162·2	WADI ITHL	2,743
177·1	DĀR AL HAJJ	2,944
183·9	MUSTABGHAH	3,084
187·0	QALʿAT AL AKHDAR	2,870
189·5	MAQSADAT AD DUNYA	..
200·1	KHAMĪS	2,898
215·0	DIZĀD	3,143
229·3	QALʿAT AL MUʿADHDHAM	3,185
239·9	KHISHM AZ ZANAH	3,233
261·6	DĀR AL HAMRA	3,585
276·5	MATALI	3,743
285·2	ABU TĀQAH	3,139
292·7	MUSHIM	..
308·2	MADĀIN SĀLIH	2,538
317·5	WADI AL HASHĪSH	..
330·0	AL ʿULĀ	2,213
342·8	BEDAʿI	1,956
351·1	MESHHED	2,194
358·5	SEIL MATARA	1,924
367·9	QALʿAT AZ ZUMURRUD	2,301
375·5	BIR JEDĪD	2,301
386·7	TOWEIRA	2,171
402·7	MUDURIJ	1,475
413·5	HADĪYAH	1,264
427·4	JEDAHA	1,479
438·1	ABUL NAʿIM	1,527
448·0	ISTABAL ʿANTAR	1,719
460·3	BUWEIR	1,508
472·5	BIR NASĪF	1,583
482·1	BOWĀT	1,859
494·9	HAFĪRAH	1,861
506·7	MUHEID	2,243
515·9	AL MADINA	2,096

Motor-tracks and Pilgrim-routes

There is a total of about 9,000 miles of good motor track, and this could be considerably increased with little expenditure. The chief physical obstacles are the sand-dunes and the areas of volcanic rock, the Harras. Floods in the wadis might cause a delay of twenty-four hours, but this could be obviated by bridges. The only metalled road is from Jidda to the gold-mine, which was completed by Egyptian engineers, but the whole journey from Jidda to Riyādh, by continuing beyond this road across the natural surface of the desert, has been done in a saloon car in thirty-six hours.

The general pattern of the roads is simple. The one main transcontinental route, from Jidda through Mecca and Riyādh to Dhahrān on the Persian Gulf, a distance of 850 miles, is linked with a secondary transcontinental route along the Northern Frontier posts from Amman to Basra through the Jauf depression by three north–south tracks. One, hardly used, goes from Jauf through the Hejaz to Mecca. The second goes south through Hāil, 'Aneiza, Boreida, Zilfi, and Marrāt to Riyādh, and the third from Hafr through Qaryat al Ilya to Jubeil, then south to Dhahrān. The Pilgrims' road (p. 467) runs diagonally across the country from Najaf in 'Iraq, crossing the frontier at Al Jumaima, passing west of Līna, then south-west through Hāil to meet the Hejaz link-road between Mecca and Al Madina just south of the gold-mine. In its northern section this route is known as the Darb Zobeida, for it was put into repair and given water cisterns by the Empress Zobeida in the eighth century. Recently it has been opened up for motor traffic by the 'Iraqi Government, and the section in Arabia has been improved by King Ibn Sa'ūd. On all these routes the Government maintains petrol-filling stations at the forts and citadels, and supplies of food and water are normally available for those who have authority to travel. In addition to these, supplementing the general pattern of routes, there is the track along the Red Sea coast with its transverse connexions from the ports through the highland rim to the interior, the old pilgrim track from Ma'an followed by the Hejaz railway to Al Madina, and the route south-east from Mecca, through Tāif, Turaba, Bīsha, Hamdha, and Mikhlāf, then west to the coast at Jīzān or on into the Yemen. In and around the chief ports roads have recently been improved so that motor-cars and light motor transport can make considerable journeys both inland and along the coast. It is possible to travel by motor along the coastal track from Jīzān through Jidda, Rābigh, Yenbo', and Al Wejh to Muweilih, with connexions inland from Rābigh and

Yenbo' to Al Madina.   Further details of pilgrim routes are given
on pp. 466, 467.

Aviation

At present there is no commercial aviation in Sa'ūdi Arabia, and
apart from the fortnightly calls of B.O.A.C. at Jidda on the Red Sea
route between Cairo and Aden, the nearest point of connexion with an
external air route is Bahrein island on the B.O.A.C. route to India,
which from Basra passes along the Hasa coast to Sharja in Trucial
'Omān.   But the Government is reported to be enthusiastic, and
allowed the Misr Airways of Egypt to establish a service in January
1936 between Jidda and Mecca to serve the pilgrimage.   After an
accident this was abandoned in 1938.   There are small landing-grounds
at Yenbo' and Al Wejh on the Red Sea coast, besides the airfield at
Dhahrān on the Persian Gulf coast, and at Tāif and Boaib (25 miles
NNE. of Riyādh) in the interior.

Telegraph, Telephone, Wireless, and Postal Services

Such services as there are in Sa'ūdi Arabia are primarily for keeping
order and are very limited in development.   Telegraphs are almost
non-existent, the telephone system is rudimentary, postal services are
unreliable, but the Government depends on wireless which is maintained at the chief centres and is adequate for its purpose.

The Government owns the whole telephone network, and in 1936
there were 854 subscribers, of which Mecca had 450, Jidda 254, Tāif,
Al Madina, and Riyādh 50 each.   There are stations at all these centres,
Mecca, Tāif, and Riyādh having automatic exchanges in addition.   At
Dhahrān and Ras Tannūra the California Arabia Standard Oil com-
pany have their own installations.

The wireless system centres round the two capitals, Mecca and
Riyādh, and the main link is between the two.   This is of special
importance because the King is at Riyādh for most of the year, while
the Foreign Office and other government offices are at Mecca.   The
other stations fall into two groups—those in Hejaz controlled by
Mecca, and those in Nejd controlled by Riyādh.   External links work
to Syria, 'Iraq, Yemen, and occasionally to Port Sudan.   Most of the
stations in Hejaz can work direct to Mecca, but some in the north still
using a spark transmitter work in a local group which is passed to
Mecca through Dhaba or Al Wejh.   In the south the stations at Jidda,
Zafīr, and Al Qunfidha work direct to Riyādh.   There has been considerable development in recent years, and high-frequency apparatus

is gradually replacing that of medium frequency. In 1942 there were stations at Abhā, Boreida, Qatīf, Dhaba, Hofūf, Mikhlāf, Jīzān, Mecca, Dawadimi, Al Līth, Jidda, Al Qunfidha, Hāil, Al Madina, Riyādh, Al 'Ulā, Qaraiya, Sakāka, Tebūk, Tāif, Al Wejh, Yenbo', Al Jubeil, Al 'Oqeir, and Majma'a. The Government also has several mobile wireless trucks. Experiments in 1939 with radio-telephony were not very successful as the Arab operators were incompetent, but in June of that year King Ibn Sa'ūd opened a link between Mecca and Riyādh. The California Arabia Oil Company has wireless stations at Dhahrān, Ras Tannūra, Buqeiq, and Jidda, and maintains a two-way wireless service with San Francisco. And the Sa'ūdi Arabian Mining Syndicate operates its own stations at Jidda and Mahd adh Dhahab.

Sa'ūdi Arabia became a member of the International Postal Union in 1927, but in 1939 only the post offices at Mecca, Al Madina, Jidda, and Yenbo' could handle all the operations specified by international conventions. The other post offices deal only with ordinary and registered mail. These are at Al Wejh, Dhaba, Umm Lejj, Al 'Ulā, Rābigh, Tebūk, Tāif, Al Līth, Al Qunfidha, Zafīr, all in Hejaz; Shammar, Wadi Sirhan, Riyādh, Hāil, Boreida, and Jauf in Nejd; Hofūf, Al 'Oqeir, Jubeil, Al Qatīf in the eastern provinces; and Jīzān, Abhā, and Nejrān in the south. The only daily deliveries are between Jidda and Mecca, Mecca and Tāif, Hofūf and Al 'Oqeir, and by boat between Al 'Oqeir and Bahrein island. Twice a week the Mecca–Al Madina service takes place by way of Jidda and Rābigh, and twice a month there is a motor delivery between Mecca and Riyādh.

YEMEN

MINERALS

Very little is known of the mineral resources of the Yemen, and such information as is available indicates that no important minerals have yet been discovered. The highlands may contain a little gold, despite Niebuhr's conviction that there was no gold in the country. Ansaldi has reported the presence of alluvial clays containing specks of gold to the west and north of San'ā, and the Jewish guide from San'ā who accompanied Halévy on his explorations in 1870 left an account of gold-mines which he examined. Small amounts of brittle iron are found throughout the country, and the beduin collect it for San'ā merchants. The rocks of the Haraz region (p. 358) are rich in

273. *Sawing timber in the Yemen*

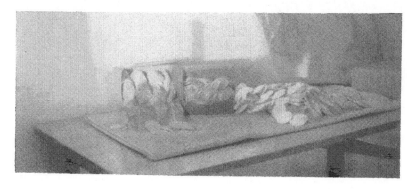

274. *Maria Theresa dollars, current in south-west Arabia*

275. *Lime-kiln at Hodeida*

276. *Suq as Sabt ('Saturday market'). A country marke nurth of Ibb*

copper pyrites and native copper, and a bituminous schist rich in hydrocarbons is found in the Beni Germūz region (north-east of San'ā), Kaukaban (p. 358), and Khoban (p. 360). Beds of rock-salt are worked at As Salīf (p. 135), Luheiya, and in the Beni Germūz and Marib regions. The As Salīf deposit is said to be very rich, and to contain 3,000,000 tons of reserves. Sulphur is obtained from Jebel Hadda, east of Dhamār, and according to a recent report brown coal also; the Jewish match-makers obtain the material for their trade from this source. Probably it is the same sulphur deposit which Niebuhr mentioned as being exploited when he visited the Yemen in 1763. Chalk and gypsum are plentiful, as in Sa'ūdi Arabia, and the alabaster found near Jebel al Gherās in the Beni Hasheish region (p. 357) is used for making the opaque windows (*qamar*) of houses in San'ā. This is due to the Yemeni belief that the rays of the setting sun are harmful, so that the west-facing windows must not be of glass. Alabaster gives a moonlight effect, hence the name (p. 135).

INDUSTRIES

Manufacturing in the Yemen is confined almost entirely to the handicraft stage, for domestic use. All the metal-working for domestic utensils and implements, and for ornaments, is in the hands of Jews. But the textile industry, chiefly the weaving of coarse cotton cloth striped with various colours, is an old-established one. The shawls of Zabīd and Beit al Faqīh are famous. Hodeida too has its colony of weavers, and there are many others scattered throughout the country. Dyeing is done with locally produced vegetable colours or with imported dyes from Europe. Indigo is cultivated for this purpose round Zabīd and Beit al Faqīh (p. 495). Hides are dressed and tanned and make sandals at Hodeida, Zabīd, and Beit al Faqīh, and in the interior where it is colder, boots are made from sheepskins. The only factory of any consequence in the Yemen is the munitions plant at San'ā, which is chiefly concerned with reloading expended cartridges and putting old rifles into commission. It is said to be capable of turning out four cases of 1,000 cartridges per day. Dhow-building is carried out on the beach south of Hodeida. For this the hard and durable acacia wood from the interior is used for the stem and stern posts and for the ribs and knees. The planking is obtained from the Malabar coast. The Yemen dhow or *sanbūq* is small, about 50 feet long and sharp-prowed, taking about three months to build. These are used as lighters, and a few larger ones are built for sea-going purposes. Fishing is a profitable occupation, and is carried out chiefly from boats.

COMMERCE AND FINANCE

Few details are available, but it is probable that the foreign trade of the Yemen exceeds that of the rest of Arabia. The greater part of all finished goods are imported, as well as a considerable proportion of foodstuffs. Thus cereals, rice from India, dates from 'Iraq, cotton piece goods, yarn, petroleum, iron and steel goods, silk, and general stores are the chief imports. Despite the local textile industry, most of the cotton and all the wool and silk fabrics are imported from Japan, Syria, India, and Europe. The chief exports are hides and skins, and coffee, transported either by camel caravan or by dhows from Hodeida to Aden for transhipment. In 1938 coffee shipments were valued at 723,715 dollars, of which 202,166 dollars' worth went to U.S.A. The rest went to Italy, France, and Egypt.

Finance, apart from the details given on p. 333, is completely unorganized. Barter is common, and the Moslem prejudice against usury has discouraged the development of banking and credit.

CURRENCY

The basis of the currency is the riyal or Maria-Theresa dollar. These silver coins, originally *thaler*, of which the word 'dollar' is a corruption, were manufactured in Europe and exported to the countries which still use them as the unit of currency. Their value fluctuates considerably from day to day. The small currency is minted locally, and consists of the *buqsha*, 40 of which equal one riyal. The buqsha and half-buqsha are copper coins about the size of a penny and half-penny respectively. Small silver pieces are worth 2, 4, and 10 buqshas, the last being the equivalent of a quarter-dollar. The *buqsha* appears on Yemeni postage stamps as *bogsha* or *bogchah* (plur. *bogshas* or *bogaches*).

COMMUNICATIONS

There are no railways, and no roads in the modern sense in the Yemen. The chief means of transport are by mule, donkey, or camel, and only with difficulty and in parts can the tracks be used by motor vehicles. A so-called motor-road was constructed by American engineers in 1930 from Hodeida to San'ā, but this is a single track 12 feet wide, much of it along steep and precipitous mountain sides, and it is neither metalled nor paved. The gradient is suitable for cars and

*277. Old road and new motor track near the pass of Naqil Isla,
between Hodeida and San'ā*

278. The motor road up to the Dhāla' pass

279. Windmills near Sheikh ʻOthman salt-works

280. Salt-works near Sheikh ʻOthman from the air

light trucks, and the journey of about 160 miles can be made in 13 hours by car, 24 hours by truck. The main tracks are (i) along the Tihama from Meidi in the north, through Luheiya, deviating inland to Zeidīya and back to the coast at Hodeida; then inland again through Beit al Faqīh and Zabīd, through Mocha and on to Sheikh Saʿīd on the Bab al Mandeb peninsula. (ii) The old highland route from Sanʿā to Aden, through Dhamār, Yarīm, Ibb, Seiyāni, and Taʿizz, or the more direct route from Yarīm across the frontier at Qaʿtaba. (iii) The route from Taʿizz to the coast at Mocha. The greater part of these three routes is passable, though difficult for cars.

There is no aviation in the Yemen; all flying has been forbidden as the result of an accident which involved a member of the Royal House. Telegraphs were first installed under the Turks, and link the ports with each other and with the interior. The chief lines are: Mocha–Hodeida–As Salīf–Luheiya–Meidi, with a short cable between As Salīf and Kamarān island; a double line, one for the State and one for local messages between Sanʿā and Hodeida, with an intermediate station at Sūq al Khamīs; Sanʿā–Dhamār–Yarīm–Ibb–Taʿizz–Mocha; Mocha–Sheikh Saʿīd, whence there is a cable to Perim island. The only telegraph communication with the outside world is from Hodeida to Assab in Eritrea. No telephones are known to be used in the Yemen, and there is only one wireless station at Sanʿā. The postal service is undependable, though the Yemen belongs to the International Postal Union.

ADEN COLONY

MINERALS AND INDUSTRIES

Salt, evaporated from sea-water, is the only mineral produced in Aden Colony. The first salt-works were constructed by an Italian firm in 1885. These, at Sheikh ʿOthman, are now known as the Aden Salt Works. In 1909 salt-works were started by a Bombay firm; in 1923 another Indian firm began work, and in 1927 the Little Aden Salt Industrial Company started operations. By 1937 these four companies were working a total area of over 4,000 acres. Most of the salt exported goes to India. The total export in 1937 was 230,379 tons out of a total production of 355,166 tons. The Government have the monopoly of salt for local consumption and have licensed some pits to Arabs at Sheikh ʿOthman.

Before the war of 1939–1945 Aden produced over half the total

A 4836   M m

Colonial Empire salt, and over 5 per cent. of the total Empire output. But during the war production has declined, largely owing to the loss of the Japanese market and the falling-off in exports to India. The pits have been operated chiefly to keep them in working order and to avoid local unemployment. Towards the end of 1941 ships calling at Aden began to buy salt for ballast, and in 1943, 70,000 tons were sold for this purpose, out of a total production of 199,236 tons.

The high and uniform temperature, low rainfall, and strong winds at Aden are favourable for a high rate of evaporation. Other geographical advantages are the shallow lagoons yielding a brine higher in salt content than that of the open sea, and the clayey soil which forms an impervious bottom to the lagoons. Brine is admitted through sluice gates either from the lagoons or from the open sea, and after preliminary treatment is run into storage tanks, from which it is taken as required into the crystallizing pans. These are worked on a two-months' rotation system, to ensure regular deliveries. The density of the brine is tested daily, and after two months the salt crust in the pans is broken up with sharp spades, leaving about one inch of salt in the pan so that all the salt removed is clean. Heaps of salt are left to dry, and when dry the salt is either stacked or removed to the crushing mills (photo. 280). Rapid transportation is ensured by tramways at each of the works, and the Aden Salt Works uses conveyer belts for loading into barges. Otherwise loading is done by hand.

The chief industries are dhow-building, soap manufacturing, dyeing, cigarette making, and fishing.

Dhow-building is carried on at Ma'ala, chiefly by Hadhrami merchants who have settled in Aden. The industry is of great antiquity, possibly dating back to the ninth century B.C. in early Sabaean times (p. 220). The dhows of to-day are much the same as those of the Phoenicians, except that the tools used in their construction have become more efficient through the centuries, and that sometimes they are fitted with motor-engines. Teak imported from the Malabar coast is used for planking; but the ribs are made from the branches of large thorn-bushes which grow on the Arabian coast and are brought in by coasting dhows. Wooden plugs are used in place of screws, and to avoid joining or hewing out particular shapes from solid wood, pieces are sought which naturally have the necessary size and form. The nails are of iron, manufactured in primitive smithies on the beach at Ma'ala. First the ribs are set up and joined to the keel, with cross beams connecting the tops. Then hand-sawn planks are laid, first on the inside and later on the outside, the interstices being filled with rope and tar. A covering of gypsum from Mukalla or Shihr, ground in a camel press and mixed with oil, is then applied, and carvers decorate the part above the waterline with designs to suit the owner's taste. The deck is then partly planked over and a central mast mounted. Most of the dhows except the small ones are built on stocks, and roofs of matting or awnings are mounted to protect the woodwork from the sun's heat and to give shade to the builders. Dhows of all shapes and sizes are built at Ma'ala. The sanbūq or smack, of 20–50 tons burthen, evolved to suit the conditions of the inhospitable Arabian coast—shelterless and subject to sudden squalls, practically without estuaries, creeks, or inlets—has a broad beam, shallow draught, and keel-less bottom so that it can be beached easily. The buggalow may be up to 350 tons burthen and is usually two-masted, a decked vessel built for sea-going purposes. The dhow-building yards of Ma'ala produce about seven dhows a year (photo. 282). Sails and ropes for hawsers and fenders are also made at Ma'ala.

The soap factory, set up in 1932, is also at Ma'ala. The process involves boiling coco-nut oil, and the daily output of 50 cases each containing 200 cakes is sold locally or exported to ports on the Red Sea.

Dyeing employs about 200 persons, in three factories and several small businesses. The cigarette industry is carried on by Jews and Greeks, using Egyptian tobacco.

Fishing is an important occupation in Aden Colony. Trawls are forbidden and the size of nets limited, but no licence is required. The nets are of the stationary, circular throwing, and drag types, and a special net operated from two boats is used during the monsoon. Drag nets are used from the shore. The chief edible fish are shark, barracuda, horse-mackerel, sea-perch, dolphins, small tunny, rock-cod, soles, and mullet. Crabs and crawfish are available throughout the year, oysters in winter. Surplus catches are salted for export, and some shark is dried. Pearl-diving, both in Aden harbour and around Perim island, requires a licence.

COMMERCE

Economic activity in Aden is dominated by the transit trade and by the function of the port as a coaling and oil-fuelling station. Indeed, its modern prosperity depends on its fuelling activities, for it is nearer than any other large port on the main eastern trade route to the Anglo-Iranian Oil Company's refining centre at Abadan on the

Persian Gulf. This has given favourable rates for oil supplies, and by so inducing ships to call for fuel has increased the transit trade. During the War of 1939–1945 trade with countries outside the sterling bloc almost ceased, owing to lack of shipping space and foreign exchange control. The chief imports in 1938, in order of value, were oils, piece goods, grain and pulse, hides and skins, coffee, tobacco, sugar, fruits and vegetables, vehicles, and spices. The chief sources of imports in order of importance were India, the United Kingdom, 'Iraq, Japan, and the Yemen. The chief exports in the same year were piece-goods, hides and skins, grain and pulse, coffee, salt, tobacco, sugar, spices, and gums and resins. These went mostly to the Yemen, Jibuti, British Somaliland, the Hadhramaut ports, France, and U.S.A. Between 1937 and 1938 there was a slight decrease in both imports and exports for seaborne trade, though for the four previous years both had been steadily increasing. Imports are normally nearly twice as great in value as exports. Land-borne trade is only of minor importance, but again imports usually exceed exports. In 1938 the value of total land-borne trade was 1,78,27,377 rupees compared with 55,52,95,073 rupees for sea-borne trade.

Gums and resins are perhaps the most characteristically Arabian items of trade at Aden and a short account would not be out of place here.

Myrrh

As stated in Chapter IV (p. 204), most myrrh now reaching the market is from Somaliland. Indian traders at Aden recognize three main types; the names as printed are conventional spellings of those used by Indian traders in Aden and Bombay, and modifications of these names exist in many Indian languages:

(i) *Heerabol*, the myrrh of pharmacy (though now rare and little used), obtained mainly from the *didin*[1] tree of Somaliland (*Commiphora myrrha*), a tree also found in Arabia, where it was first discovered at Mur, in the Tihama east of Luheiya. This product, said to be entirely scentless, is distinguishable chemically by its petrol-ether extract giving a violet flocculent precipitate when treated with bromine vapour. Oil of myrrh is distilled from heerabol.

(ii) *Bissabol*, 'sweet myrrh' or 'perfumed bdellium', now obtained from the *haddi*[2] tree of Somaliland (*Commiphora erythraea* var. *glabrescens*), has a more oily appearance and does not react to bromine

---

[1] Drake-Brockman, *British Somaliland*, pp. 301–323 (1912).
[2] Ibid.

281. *Aden frankincense shed*

282. *Boat-building at Maʿala, Aden*

283. *Pile of fish outside a store-shed at Mukalla*

284. *Mukalla shark-vendor*

vapour; but, when a few drops of its petrol-ether extract are mixed with glacial acetic acid and placed over concentrated sulphuric acid, a rose-red colour appears at the zone of contact (a green colour appears when a like test is made with heerabol). Bissabol has been mainly exported to India and China for scenting joss-sticks. Most recent authors believe it to have been the *mōr* of the Bible, used for scenting clothes or beds (*Psalm* xlv. 8; *Proverbs* vii. 17), as a perfume (*Song of Solomon* iii. 6), and for embalming the dead (*St. John* xix. 39). On the other hand, the Hebrew *lōt*, translated 'myrrh' in *Genesis* xxxvii. 25, xliii. 11, was probably *ladanum*, the fragrant resinous exudation of certain species of *Cistus*.

(iii) *Meetiya*, sometimes called 'Hadhramaut myrrh', used to be sent from Mukalla to Aden. The tree said to be its source was identified (from specimens collected by Bent in Wadi Hadira and Wadi 'Adīm, both running into Wadi Hadhramaut from the south) as *Commiphora opobalsamum* (p. 204), locally *timdud*. This resin is usually styled 'balsam of Mecca' or 'balm of Gilead', but the latter name is now applied by the perfume industry to the resins of quite different trees, including the balsam-fir of Canada; *meetiya*, in fact, smells like pine-resin. It is more oily than the foregoing kinds, and tastes somewhat like lemon.

To these may be added a dark red-brown myrrh from the Yemen, called *Hodeida Jebeli*, which does not give the characteristic reaction of heerabol with bromine, and is reputed strongly aromatic and very bitter; also *mukul*, produced in Dhufār, where more than one species of *Commiphora* occurs.

Imports of myrrh to Aden in 1920[1] (about which time experts visited Qa'taba to improve the yield of the trees) were, in hundred-weights:

	1913–14	*1918–19*	*1919–20*	*1920–1*
From Arabia	2,811	7,043	3,409	5,507
From Somaliland	19,445	15,149	15,451	11,607

Gum Arabic

This is the product of several species of Acacia. The best quality, white in colour, is produced by *Acacia senegal* (Arabic, *qarad*). *Samāj*, a reddish gum of good quality, is produced by the *talh* tree (*Acacia seyal*). The resin of *A. fasciculata* (*seyāl*) and that of *A. scorpioides* (*sānt*) are also collected. The chief commercial source of these gums is now the Sudan, where they are more carefully collected

[1] See *Journ. R. Soc. Arts*, lxx, p. 782 (1922).

and graded than in Arabia. However, 85 cwt. (valued at 2,636 rupees) of gum were imported into Aden from south Arabian ports in 1930–1, and a considerable amount is imported from Somaliland. In Arabia gum is sometimes chewed. The word 'gum' is probably derived from ancient Egyptian *qami* through Coptic *komē*; gum Arabic is believed to have been known to the ancient Egyptians[1] and to have become known in Europe in the 14th century. A bacterial infection like that attacking the cherry tree, rather than a fungus, is the probable cause of the exudation of gum.

CURRENCY AND FINANCE

The monetary unit is the Indian rupee, legal tender for any amount. Half and quarter rupees are silver coins, 4-anna, 2-anna, and 1-anna pieces are nickel, the quarter anna (pice) and 1/12th anna (pie) are bronze. These subsidiary coins are legal tender up to one rupee. Indian currency notes of 5, 10, 50, and 100 rupees are also in circulation. A lakh of rupees is 100,000, usually written 1,00,000; a crore is 100 lakhs (1,00,00,000).

Revenue and Expenditure

The colony's main source of revenue is income tax, for there are no customs duties except for drugs, intoxicating liquors, and perfumed spirits. The only other tax of importance is that on salt produced locally (p. 529). Since the inauguration of the colony in 1937, the financial year is counted from 1 April to 31 March, and budgets are produced annually. The estimates for 1938–9 were as follows:

Revenue	*Rs.*	*Expenditure*	*Rs.*
Duties, taxes, and licences.	9,60,000	Recurrent . . .	16,09,000
Fees and receipts for Government Services .	1,20,000	Extraordinary. . .	1,34,000
Contributions and Reimbursements . . .	3,94,000		
Posts and telephones .	4,00,000		
Miscellaneous . . .	16,000		
	18,90,000		17,43,000

The Extraordinary expenditure is entirely for public works.

[1] H. S. Blunt, *Gum Arabic*, &c. (1926); V. Loret, *La Flore Pharaonique*, 2nd ed., p. 84 (1892).

COMMUNICATIONS

All transport in the colony is by road or sea, the latter consisting only of the carriage of salt and building materials from Little Aden to Ma'ala and Tawahi. In 1938, of a total of 52 miles of main road, 19 were surfaced with water-bound macadam, 18½ with bituminous macadam, and 14½ were unmetalled. Most of the macadam road was in Aden town. The harbour has flying-boat facilities. There is no internal telegraph system, but Aden is an important junction for external telegraphs. The Red Sea cables branch out from Aden to Bombay, Colombo, the Seychelles, and Zanzibar, telegrams from the west being retransmitted from Aden for India, the Far East, and south and east Africa. Aden is in touch with all parts of the world through Cable and Wireless Ltd. The government telephone exchange has a capacity of 200 subscribers. There are post offices at Steamer Point, Camp, and Khormaksar, with sub-offices on Kamarān island, at Mukalla, and Seiyūn. Until 1 April 1937 Aden was included in the Indian postal system, but since that date it has had a separate postal administration with its own issue of stamps.

THE ADEN PROTECTORATE

MINERALS

None of the mineral resources known to exist in the Aden Protectorate are of great value, and none are as yet exploited. Thin lignite beds and oil shales in the Mukalla district are the most likely to receive attention, particularly if, as in the region of Jebel ad Da'liya and Neifa in Wadi Hajr, the lignite could be used for distilling the oil shales. But difficulties of labour and transport, added to the inaccessibility of many of the deposits, have so far proved too great for resources which are at best of doubtful economic value. From the presence of bitumen, bituminous sandstone, oil shales, and rock-salt impregnated with bituminous materials it seems possible that petroleum may be found at Sidara. Other minerals reported in the Protectorate are haematite, copper, manganese, bauxite, alum, potassium nitrate, and gypsum.[1]

INDUSTRIES

Manufacturing industries are few, and are mostly concerned with agricultural products. Mukalla has a large factory for the extraction

[1] O. H. Little, *The Geography and Geology of Makalla* (Cairo, 1925).

of simsim oil from sesame seed, using camel presses. Hides from the interior are tanned in Mukalla and skins in Shibām, but these are only for use in the Protectorate. East of Mukalla, in Seiyūn and Tarīm, and in many other places, lime is burnt in kilns, for use as plaster in the interior of houses. There is some dyeing, weaving, and mat-making, Shihr in particular being renowned for its weaving. Many places have potteries, and at Gheil Ba Wazīr, Shihr, and Mukalla silver ware is produced. Fishing is an important occupation along the coast, dried fish and fish oil being among the chief exports. Dried fish is sold for human consumption, fodder, and manure. Fish-curing methods are primitive, and as a sanitary measure the drying grounds and godowns have been removed from Mukalla itself. A great deal of dried shark is produced and sold in Mukalla, and sharks' fins (*rīsh*) are exported as a delicacy to China (photos. 283, 284).

COMMERCE AND FINANCE

Although the Protectorate does not live by foreign trade as Aden does, foreign trade is of great importance in a country so poor in economic resources. Nearly all the trade is by sea, but Shibām is the chief centre for land-borne trade. To it come a variety of agricultural products, including coffee berries from Yāfa' and San'ā, and raisins and almonds from San'ā. Some fire-arms and ammunition come in from Nejrān and the Yemen, for distribution in the Hadhramaut. Nearly all the imports of the Protectorate come from Aden, though the chief primary sources are the British Empire (mainly India) and Japan. In 1935 the ports of the Arabian Sea, almost all in the Hadhra-maut, were Aden's fourth most important customer. The chief imports are dates (from 'Omān and 'Iraq), flour, rice, sheep and goats, piece-goods, sesame, millet, and kerosene. Some manufactured goods such as fire-arms and ammunition, automobiles and gasoline engines for pumping water and driving electric-light plants are supplied by Europe. The chief exports are tobacco (*hamūmi*), honey, and fish products. Nearly all the tobacco goes to Aden, and a little to the Red Sea ports. Most of the honey goes to Java. Invisible imports and exports play a far more important part than in most countries. The emigrant Hadhramis normally send back large sums of money from Singapore and the Dutch East Indies, from East Africa and India, hence the serious consequences of the war for the economy of the Protectorate.

As distinct from its individual states, the Protectorate has no revenue of its own. Expenditure on Protectorate services comes from the British taxpayer, and in the last ten years this has increased from £20,000 to £200,000.

Finance is entirely in the hands of the merchants and is dependent on the overseas trade connexions. Indian and the more important Arab merchants deal in drafts on Bombay, sold in Mukalla for cash ordinarily without commission. But if money is scarce locally a small commission is charged. Dollars move freely to the interior, and if the exchange is good return to Mukalla. Dollars are exported from Mukalla to Aden when the exchange is favourable, but are brought in if there is a shortage in Mukalla or the dollar is cheaper in Aden. In Mukalla dollars are usually worth more than in Aden, sometimes equal, but never less. A few Arabs obtain their wealth from interest (10%) on mortgages, and in Shibām 5 per cent. interest is charged on borrowed money, though these transactions have to be disguised to agree with Moslem precepts against usury.

CURRENCY

The basis of the currency, as in the Yemen, is the rupee and Maria-Theresa dollar (p. 528). In November 1934 these were practically equal in value, but the rate varies considerably and rapidly. Small change is largely British Indian, with a few Mukalla pice, some Italian lire from Somaliland, and a little Javanese money. Usually, any known money will be exchanged.

COMMUNICATIONS

There are no railways in the Protectorate, but there was formerly a metre-gauge railway from Aden to just beyond Lahej, owned and operated by the military authorities. The rolling-stock, coal-burning locomotives, passenger, animal and freight cars, and a few oil-driven passenger cars, came from India, and were laid up at Aden in 1936.

The camel and the ass are still the chief means of transport, and are likely to remain important in caravan traffic whatever improvements or additions to existing tracks are made. A number of motor vehicles are in use, chiefly cars, but it is interesting to note that when these are destined for use in the interior they are dismantled on arrival and carried inland at the rate of 12 camels to one car.

The most important road in the Western Protectorate goes from Aden through Lahej, Nobat Dukeim, As Sawda, over the Khureiba pass at above 5,000 feet to Dhāla', then across the frontier into the Yemen (photo. 278). In places only a track, it is negotiable for motor vehicles, and has been important when British troops have had to keep order among the border tribes. There is a coastal track from Aden west to Sheikh Sa'īd and east into the Eastern Protectorate, with a branch from Shuqra inland to Laudar.

In the Eastern Protectorate the general pattern of tracks is simple. There is a coastal route from Fūwa through Mukalla and Shihr to Al Qarn with an alternative route farther inland between Shuheir and Shihr, through Gheil Ba Wazīr, Hibs, and Tabāla. Then there is the route down Wadi Hadhramaut in the interior, from Henin through Qatn, Shibām, Seiyūn, Tarīm, and 'Einat to Qasm. This has branches south from Henin to Hureidha, from Qatn through Haura and Meshhed to Hajarein, and is linked to the coastal route by a recently completed motor-road from Tarīm to Shihr. The motor-road is, however, in very bad condition, and only possible for cars with great wear and tear on the tyres. These main tracks are all used by cars regularly, and it is possible to reach Qabr Hūd, beyond Qasm down the Wadi Hadhramaut, by this means. Cars are also said to have reached Husn al 'Abr from Shibām at the other end of the Wadi Hadhramaut route. There is no commercial aviation in the Protectorate, but the R.A.F. maintain a number of landing-grounds on the coast and in the interior.

Telegraphs and telephones too are lacking, and there is only one wireless station, at Mukalla, connected with Cable and Wireless Ltd. There is no postal service, but letters are distributed from Shihr and Mukalla by special agents. Mukalla and Seiyūn have sub-offices of Aden Colony, and mails are picked up by the R.A.F. from Seiyūn and flown to Aden.

CHAPTER XI

PORTS AND TOWNS

SOME details are given in this chapter of the principal ports and inland towns which fall within the limits laid down in Chapter I. Of the ports, which are described first, only those of the Arabian coast are dealt with, those of the African coast having been given their general setting in Chapter III. No rule has been followed in the selection of the smaller towns for description, and lack of recent information has curtailed the list.

PORTS

THE ports fall into two groups: those of the Arabian coast of the Red Sea, described in order from north to south, and those of the south coast of Arabia, described from west to east. Four only are of importance: Jidda, Hodeida, Aden, and Mukalla, the chief ports of the Hejaz, the Yemen, the Aden hinterland, and the Hadhramaut respectively, and of these Aden stands out as the only major port and as an important refuelling station on the trade-route between East and West. Mileages are only rough estimates.

RED SEA PORTS OF ARABIA

WEJH (26° 13′ N., 36° 27′ E.). Qunfidha prov., Sa'ūdi Arabia

The harbour is formed by a small rectangular sherm, roughly alined north-east, bordered by reefs inside but with an easy entrance (fig. 23). The channel has an even width of 250–300 yards and is about 600 yards long, but shallows rapidly from 10–12 fathoms in the entrance to less than a fathom when half-way past the town, which stretches along the north-west shore of the inlet. The landing-place, which is at the south-east corner of the town, is obstructed by the ruins of two stone piers; there is a depth of 2 fathoms of water within 20 yards of the shore here, and shallow water 2–4 feet deep extends beyond along the inner half of the water-front. Though Wejh is a comfortable and commodious anchorage for small craft and dhows, there is mooring space for only a single ship of any size in the entrance of the sherm.

There is little recent information about the town, which is about one-quarter of a mile long and less in breadth. The houses are mostly of stone, and the population of some 2,000 depends largely on the caravan trade to Mecca. Water comes from a bad condenser or from brackish wells. The district is the territory of the Billi tribe.

During the war of 1914–1918 Wejh was captured in 1917 from the Turkish garrison by a landing-party of British seamen and of Arabs, after a naval bombardment which caused considerable damage (p. 294). At the same time a large force of Arab troops and tribesmen, under the leadership of Amir Feisal and accompanied by T. E. Lawrence, marched upon the town in a politically spectacular and militarily useless fashion, arriving after its capture (photo. 148).

Communications. Tracks to 'Aqaba (270 miles), Al 'Ulā (130), Al Madina (265), and Yenbo' (190). Landing-ground and wireless station.

YENBO' (24° 04′ N., 38° 02′ E.). Qunfidha prov., Sa'ūdi Arabia

Yenbo' al Bahar, the port of Al Madina, and the second port of Sa'ūdi Arabia in importance, is on the north shore of a southward-facing bay about 5,000 yards wide (fig. 22). This bay is filled with coral banks on the seaward side, but between the reef and the shore there is a deep narrow sherm entered from the south-west by a passage 250 yards wide and at first alined north-east. Deep water close outside shallows to 8–10 fathoms in the entrance and 3–6 fathoms within the inlet, which hugs the shore fairly closely. The anchorage, which is about 300 yards off the town about 1 mile inside the entrance, has depths of 3–4 fathoms shallowing to 1 fathom alongside the town quay. Beyond the town the inlet turns from north-east to east and continues to offer anchorage in 3–4 fathoms for another 1,000 yards. Though a relatively unencumbered harbour, Yenbo' is difficult to leave during north-west winds (photos. 286, 287).

Nine miles to the north-west is another Sherm Yenbo', a fine natural harbour which lacks a port and habitations.

The town, about which there is little recent information, is built on coral and faces a flat desert inland. It is of irregular shape, about 1,200 yards in length along the shore and 400–600 yards wide, and is protected by a dilapidated wall on the landward side and by marshes on its flanks. It contains in crumbling houses of limestone and coral a population of about 3,000, mostly of the Juheina tribe, whose head-quarters are to the north-east of the town at Yenbo' an Nakhal. This population is doubled or trebled during the pilgrim season; some 5,000 pilgrims came in 1938 and 2,600 in 1939. Pilgrims store bulky property in Yenbo' during their visit to Al Madina. The bazaar is

285. *Wejh*

286. *Yenboʻ, the port for Al Madina*

287. *Yenboʻ, from the sea*

288. *Jidda. Quarantine wharf from the boat-channel*

289. *Jidda. The main market*

well supplied, and water comes from cisterns and wells or from a condensing plant. The maritime trade of Yenbo' includes the export of dates, hides, and camels, and the import of textiles, coffee, and grain.

Yenbo' al Bahar has waxed and waned with the prosperity of Al Madina. During the war of 1914–1918 it was one of the first bases used for arming the Arab revolt, but nearly fell to a Turkish attack in 1917, when the presence of a monitor and of H.M.S. *Dufferin* in the anchorage caused the Turks to turn back.

Communications. Motorable tracks to Wejh (190 miles), Al Madina (130), Jidda (210). Landing-ground. Wireless.

Rābigh (22° 45' N., 39° 00' E.). Qunfidha prov., Sa'ūdi Arabia

Rābigh derives its importance from the conjunction of its sheltered harbour with a supply of water which has made it a necessary stage of the caravan route between Mecca and Al Madina, which approaches the coast for this reason. The harbour is a cruciform sherm, entered between two headlands by an unencumbered channel, alined northeast, which has 16–18 fathoms of water and is 300–400 yards wide (fig. 21). Inside, the channel continues unencumbered for about 2,200 yards with a general width of 400 yards, though the 'arms' of the sherm, which are short and narrow and alined north-west and southeast, effect a brief widening of the anchorage to 1,200 or 1,600 yards. This anchorage is completely sheltered from prevailing winds and can also be entered or left under sail during north-westerly winds. To the south-east of the deep channel the sherm contains a mass of confused reefs about 2,000 yards wide in shallow water, but on the north-west the shore is closer and at the head of the channel deep water approaches the land, from which a landing-pier juts out on the west or right bank of the mouth of the Wadi Rābigh. Cargo is landed by a few local craft, and there is a customs-house.

Rābigh 'town' is a group of hamlets in a scattered but extensive oasis of palm-groves, 2 or 3 miles north of the landing-place and to the east of the Wadi Rābigh. It is the headquarters of the Zobeid section of the Harb tribe, and contains a shrine which attracts Moslem pilgrims. No recent information is available. In 1916 the town was one of the first ports to be used for the arming of the Arab revolt.

Water is available at the landing-place, apparently from wells and reservoirs on a low coralline plateau west of the Wadi Rābigh and approached by a ruined causeway which crosses an arm of the inshore marshes.

Communications. Motorable track to Al Madina (150 miles) and Mecca (120).

JIDDA (21° 29′ N., 39° 11′ E.). Qunfidha prov., Sa'ūdi Arabia

The town lies towards the northern end of a westward-facing bay, so encumbered with reefs that only the proximity of Mecca, 55 miles distant, for which it is the principal port of entry, could have made so difficult a harbour important even on the Arabian coast. Between three main lines of reefs, alined from north to south, there are a commodious outer and an inner anchorage which are entered by channels penetrating the reefs by narrow 'gateways'. The outer anchorage, $2\frac{1}{2}$ sea-miles off shore, has 5–19 fathoms of water and the inner anchorage, $1\frac{1}{4}$ sea-miles off shore, has 4–6 fathoms. From the inner anchorage a shallow boat-channel, marked by beacons and with less than 3 feet in the season of low water, leads to the quarantine quay. This concrete quay, variously reported as 35 and 100 yards long, with 3–4 feet of water alongside, has no equipment and is used by pilgrims (photo. 288). The Government jetty, with 5 feet of water alongside, is used for government stores. Half the local establishment of 300 *sambuqs* of about 12 tons burden are usually available for the transhipment of cargo. There are storage sheds of unknown capacity.

About $1\frac{1}{2}$ miles north of the town a jetty 1,500 yards long has been built by the Sa'ūdi Arabian Mining Syndicate along a coral reef out into the inner anchorage. One ship of 12 feet draught can use this jetty, which is equipped with 2 cranes (5 and 15 tons), a pipe-line, a lorry track, and a decauville railway connecting to the shore establishments of the Syndicate.

The capacity of the port is estimated at 300–500 tons daily.

The Town. The impressive town, which faces the sea on the west and is flanked by a lagoon on the north-west and a marsh on the south-east, is a quadrilateral measuring about 900–1,000 yards from north to south and 800–900 yards from east to west; it is surrounded by a wall of coralline rock faced with mud brick and 10–12 feet high, with a broad roughly surfaced road inside. There are a water-gate, three main landward gates, named after Mecca, Al Madina, and the Sharif, and several posterns. The houses, mostly built of coralline rock, are three, four, or occasionally five stories high and have window bays built outwards and fitted with wooden lattices to catch the breezes. Foundations, however, are bad and houses are liable to collapse. There are some open squares, and the streets, though narrow, are kept fairly clean by sweeping. Sanitation is by cess-pits, and the water-supply comes from condensers and also from a conduit which brings water from two wells at Wazariya, 7 miles to the south-east. Lighting is generally by oil or petrol, but there are private electrical plants in the royal palace and in the foreign consulates. The large *suq* is clean and prosperous (photos. 205, 288, 289).

Public and commercial buildings, more numerous than usual, include a civil hospital, two banks (Misr and Netherlands Trading Society), police station and prison, offices of the Sa'ūdi Navy and of the Ministry of Foreign Affairs. There were before 1940 nine foreign missions, either consulates or legations, including British, Dutch, Italian, French, Soviet, Turkish, Egyptian, 'Iraqi, and Persian. Most of these were located in the north-west corner of the town.

Close outside the town on the north are the old Turkish barracks, the Green Palace, and a shrine known as Eve's Tomb. The establishments of the Sa'ūdi Arabian Mining Syndicate—offices, stores, workshops, and living quarters—lie 1½ miles to the north-west beyond Manguba lagoon. South of the town near the Sharif gate is a large Nigerian village. Another large village called Kandara is 1½ miles east of the Madina gate, adjoining a landing-ground.

On two islands in the bay there are quarantine stations with compounds of stone houses and one small hospital, but these are seldom used.

The population is extremely mixed, though roughly divided equally between Arab-speaking and African elements, with a minority of Indians and Persians and a number of individual Greeks and Levantines. Numbers are variously estimated at 15,000 and 30,000, though the latter figure (1935) possibly includes the seasonal influx of about 10,000 pilgrims. The town lives by pilgrim traffic, mining royalties, and import trade in foodstuffs mainly destined for Mecca. There is little or no export trade, and no crafts or industries except boat-building and the recently established activities of the Sa'ūdi Arabian Mining Syndicate, which has its base here. Professional beggars and destitute pilgrims endeavouring to earn their passage home are common in the town. The replacement of camel by motor transport to Mecca has brought a few small garages into being with a complement of about 50 drivers and 25 mechanics.

History. The importance of Jidda dates from the foundation of the Arab Moslem power, when the town became the sea exit of the capital of a world empire. Though the seat of empire was soon transferred from Mecca elsewhere, Jidda retained a large share in the profitable spice trade of the Red Sea which had passed increasingly under Arab control after the rise of Islam (pp. 251–2). It was only gradually after the Portuguese circumnavigation of Africa that Jidda ceased to be a commercial entrepot of importance and was reduced to the status of a pilgrim port. Direct attempts by the Portuguese in the sixteenth century to seize Jidda or to blockade its trade, failed (p. 259). As a part of the domain of the Sharif of Mecca Jidda fell under Turkish sovereignty in 1517. When visited by Niebuhr in 1761 the town was in a more ruinous condition that it is to-day. The products of the customs tariff were shared between the Sharif and the Ottoman Sultan; the rate was 10 per cent. for all comers except the English, who then monopolized the European trade of Jidda and enjoyed a remission of 2 per cent. Between 1806 and 1811 the Turks were driven out by the Wahhabis, who were expelled in turn by Muhammad 'Ali of Egypt (p. 267). After 1840 Turkish authority was restored and lasted until a joint Arab and British assault drove the Turks out in 1916. In 1925 after the Sa'ūdi-Hejaz war Jidda was incorporated in the Sa'ūdi kingdom.

Communications. Motorable track to Mecca. Landing-grounds.

QUNFIDHA (19° 8′ N., 41° 04′ E.). Qunfidha prov., Sa'ūdi Arabia

Qunfidha, which serves as the port of the 'Asīr town of Abhā, is at the southern end of a westward-facing bay, formed between a low peninsula on the north and a short rounded headland on the south. The inner anchorage, with 5–6 fathoms 1,000–1,600 yards off shore and 2–3 fathoms close in to the town, is protected from the west by coral reefs which project north-west from the southern headland for about a mile. The northern peninsula is also continued by reefs which encumber the bay. The channel through these reefs to the inner anchorage and the town is much blocked by wrecks. There is an islet half a mile south-west of the town on the east side of an off-shore reef.

There is little recent information about the town, which is described as a small walled town with not more than 2,000 inhabitants and consisting chiefly of huts with mosques, a bazaar, and the reputation for the best water on the coast. This is brought 2½ miles from Hafeir. Grain is grown in the neighbourhood. The former history of Qunfidha is little known. In 1761 when visited by Niebuhr it was a sizeable town and was held by a governor of the Sharif of Mecca, who resided on the islet mentioned above and exacted tolls from vessels carrying coffee between the ports of the Yemen and Jidda.

290. *A street in Jidda*

291. *Jidda bazaar looking north*

292. *Jīzān from the inland side*

293. *Meidi. The market-place*

Communications. Coastal track north-west to Jidda (210 miles) and south-east to Jīzān (200). Track inland to Abhā (150).

JĪZĀN (16° 54′ N., 42° 29′ E.). Jīzān prov., Sa'ūdi Arabia

The port consists of an open anchorage for large vessels, in 3–6 fathoms 1–2 miles off shore, and an inner anchorage within the reefs which infest this open coast, approached by a narrow boat-channel. The small town lies at the north-west end of a brief projection of the coast, 14 miles south-east of Ras Turfā, and covers a narrow strip of low ground backed by hills 150–200 feet high. It is said to be a pleasant town of pointed straw huts and square flat-roofed brick houses. Inside, there is a small mosque and a large walled compound containing buildings used as a palace. Outside, there is a citadel or fort partly in the ancient Yemeni style, tall, with deep walls and narrow windows, and used as a guest-house. There is also a modern Arab fort on the hill behind the town. The inhabitants, who numbered 6,000 in 1921, are occupied either in local pearl fisheries or in trade, dealing in locally produced salt and in the cereals grown in the highlands as well as in maritime commerce. (Photo. 292.)

Jīzān is an ancient town, reputed to have been founded before the Moslem era, and connected by some with the homeland of the Syrian Ghassānids in late Roman times (p. 232). After the rise of Islam it acquired as a local saint the Sheikh Hasan, a grandson of the more important coffee-saint, Sheikh Shadhili of Mocha. In the eighteenth century it shared in the coffee-trade of Yemen, but was independent of the Imam. In 1834 visitors described it as a small place of 400 inhabitants. From 1914 to 1916, as one of the few Tihama ports left open to trade during the blockade, it prospered greatly (p. 291), and after 1918 as the coastal capital of the Idrisi of 'Asīr this prosperity continued. But after 1932 it was absorbed into the kingdom of Sa'ūdi Arabia (p. 302).

Communications. Coastal track north to As Sabya (25 miles) and south to Meidi (45). Track inland to Sa'da (75).

MEIDI (16° 19′ N., 42° 45′ E.). Ta'izz princip., Yemen

The actual port of Meidi is in the inlet called Mersa Bagla about 2 miles to the north-north-west of the village. There is a small harbour for dhows with a pier and custom-house on the southern shore. The coastal waters in the vicinity are impeded by shoals and by the coastal reef, which near Meidi is about a mile off shore. Meidi itself stands on a hill close to the shore and is a large village of conical huts with a few houses of mud or stone, a fort, and a bazaar (photo. 293). Of some importance during the war of 1914–1918, it was one of the few ports left open to shipping, and afterwards a centre of contraband trade, particularly in guns and slaves, which was fostered at the expense of Hodeida. The pressing of sesame seed for oil is a local industry. Formerly a port of 'Asīr, it is now part of the Yemen (p. 302).

Communications. Caravan routes inland to Sa'da (85 miles) and San'ā (145). Motorable tracks along the coastal plain north to Jīzān (45) and south to Luheiya (45).

LUHEIYA (15° 42′ N., 42° 41′ E.). Ta'izz princip., Yemen

Luheiya is a small town at the northern end of a narrow and shallow bay formed between the mainland and a coral reef and bordered by mangrove swamps. The bay is continued northwards past the town by a narrow boat-channel; small craft may moor at the entrance to this channel, but large vessels lie about 4 miles south-west of the town in an open roadstead between the mainland and an islet called Urmek. Trade with Jidda, Hodeida, and Aden is of some importance, coffee being exported and cereals imported.

The town, about 1 mile long from north to south and one-quarter of a mile wide, lies on low ground, which is sometimes liable to flooding, between the shore and a line of hills which rise to 110 feet and are crowned by a ruined fort. There are a few houses of stone, but most of the 5,000 inhabitants (1917) live in huts built of mudbrick, and there is a large mosque. *Water*, scarce and brackish, is brought by channels from wells at Atan, 4 miles to the north-east.

The town has existed since the middle of the fifteenth century, and its foundation is connected by tradition with the local Moslem saint Sheikh Salei, around whose cell and later tomb the original settlement is supposed to have grown up. The descendants of the Sheikh were still regarded as a holy family at the end of the eighteenth century. At that time the town, walled and fortified with twelve towers, was already in Turkish hands. During the war of 1914–1918 it was vainly attacked by the Idrisi of 'Asīr and bombarded by British naval vessels in 1915, but in 1918 it yielded to a second assault. After the war it was held by the Idrisi of 'Asīr for a time, but was recovered by the Imam of Yemen in 1925, who retained it after his defeat in the war with Ibn Sa'ūd in 1934 (p. 302).

Communications. Coastal track and telegraph north to Meidi (45 miles) and south to Hodeida (75).

294. *Hodeida. The Boat-harbour*

295. *Scene in Hodeida. Bales of hides in foreground*

296. *Hodeida. Unloading cargo from dhows at the water-front*

297. *Hodeida. East gate of the walled city: entrance to market*

HODEIDA (14° 48′ N., 42° 57′ E.). Hodeida princip., Yemen

Though the chief port of the Yemen coast, Hodeida 'harbour' is an open anchorage off a straight shoreline, which derives but slight protection from shoals off Ras Mujāmilla. There is also a small artificial boat-harbour of limited usefulness, made by two projecting moles and a breakwater. This has silted so much that loaded lighters cannot berth alongside the short quays and light boats can barely do so at low water. Dhows anchor just outside the boat harbour and unload by portage, while large ships anchor in the roads 1½ miles off shore and are unloaded by dhows, of which 40–50 are usually available. There is no port equipment, and capacity is estimated at 100–150 tons daily (photos. 294, 296).

To the north of Hodeida town a long spit with an average width of 400 yards extends for 6 miles and terminates in Ras Katib, enclosing the Khor Katib between the spit and the mainland. This khor is a confused system of lagoons and reefs, but at its northern end there is sheltered and unencumbered anchorage between the mainland and Ras Katib with depths of 4–5 fathoms.

The winds from October to April cause heavy swell and render boatwork in the roadstead difficult.

Hodeida town stretches along the shore for 1,400 yards and is about 400 yards wide. There is a walled inner town and scattered outer suburbs. Within the walls houses are tall, large, rectangular, and built of stone. The bazaars and many of the other alleys are roofed over. In the outer town straw huts mingle with large stone houses and are often linked with them into compounds by wicker fences. Many of the stone houses are richly ornamented with carved woodwork or plasterwork patterned with geometrical designs or interlaced and wavy lines. Open spaces in the outer town serve as storage areas and are piled with bales of skins and bags of coffee or imported rice, the principal objects of trade. The town population, said to number 30,000, is very mixed and contains many Indian and negroid elements, Somalis, and Eritreans, as well as Arabs. (Photos. 90, 295, 297.)

The town has a Yemeni governor and a British political agent. The law-court and municipal office are in a building near the south end of the sea front next to the government rest-house, and near by is the prison. A small clinic was kept by an Italian doctor in 1940. Three Red Sea shipping firms have establishments at Hodeida. *Water* from local wells is brackish; a better supply is brought from a distance.

History. Hodeida grew in importance after the second Turkish conquest of the Yemen in 1849 (p. 272), when it became the chief

Turkish base and port of entry for the Yemen and attracted such part of the trade of Mocha as was not diverted to Aden. By 1914 the total value of its trade exceeded £1,000,000. After 1906 the Turks planned the building of a deep-water harbour behind Ras Katib and laid 5 miles of metre-gauge railway track along the spit. The project was abandoned after the bombardment of Hodeida by Italian ships during the Italo-Turkish war of 1912 had destroyed much of the material. In 1918 Hodeida was bombarded and occupied by the British, who handed it over to the Idrisi of 'Asīr in 1921. His government proved unpopular, and the Imam of Yemen recovered the port in 1925. Later it was occupied during the Sa'ūdi-Yemen war of 1934 by Sa'ūdi troops who travelled in lorries from Jidda, but the peace treaty restored it again to the Yemen (pp. 301–2). Until 1940 Hodeida was a centre of Italian intrigues in the Yemen (pp. 305–7).

Communications. Motorable track and telegraph to San'ā (13 hours by car, 24 by lorry). Coastal track and telegraph north to Luheiya (75 miles). Site for landing-ground north of the town.

MOCHA (13° 19′ N., 43° 15′ E.). Ta'izz princip., Yemen

Mocha, now a decayed port of Yemen, faces west on the shore of a shallow bay between two headlands, and is situated in an arid plain relieved by scattered palm-trees mainly to the south of the town. There is unprotected anchorage for large vessels about $1\frac{1}{2}$ miles off shore in depths up to 4 fathoms, and small craft find anchorage in 7–10 feet within the bay one-quarter of a mile off the town. The water-front of Mocha is encumbered by flats and shoals except at the southern end, where a channel with 3 feet of water leads south past the town wall into the Khor Umbaya lagoon.

The town is about half a mile long and one-quarter wide (photo. 142). Formerly walled, it is now in a state of general decay. Many of its stone houses are ruined and abandoned, and part of the present population of 1,000 which includes Arabs, Somalis, and Jews, lives outside the town. Streets are narrow, but some of the mosques are still impressive with their lofty minarets, particularly the tomb of Sheikh Shadhili within and that of Sheikh al Amudi outside the town. Good *water* is brought by conduit 27 miles south from Musa.

History. The foundation of Mocha in the fourteenth century is connected with the life of the Moslem saint Sheikh Shadhili, who is supposed by one account to have introduced the drinking of coffee into Arabia. The port became the principal export centre for coffee

298. *Aden. Crater town*

299. *Aden. Ma'ala front from the east*

300. *Aden. The Crescent, Tawahi*

301. *Western end of Aden peninsula seen eastwards from the air. Steamer Point and Post Office pier in right foreground; Tawahi in centre; Ma'ala in distance*

and a general emporium of trade with San'ā, Mecca, Cairo, Alexandria, and India. It was visited by many Europeans in the seventeenth and eighteenth centuries, including the Englishmen Jourdain and William Revett in 1609, who reported its buildings as 'very much ruinated for want of repairing', despite its commercial importance (pp. 262-3). Exports other than coffee then included aloes, myrrh, incense, senna, ivory, mother-of-pearl, and gold. The most valuable imports were crude metals—iron, steel, and lead—guns and textiles. This trade was shared by the Dutch and English East India companies after 1600, and in the early eighteenth century by the French, one of whose vessels bombarded Mocha in 1737 in order to compel the settlement of their accounts (p. 265). By 1763 the English company had ousted their European rivals, although they only sent one ship every other year to Mocha. The development of Aden in the nineteenth century, however, killed the trade of Mocha, which also lost ground heavily to Hodeida, and between 1824 and 1884 the population fell from 20,000 to 1,500.

Politically, it was early in the hands of the Turks, who used it as a base against the Portuguese in the sixteenth century. But in 1609 they kept a garrison of only 40 men in the town, and vacated it in 1636. They did not regain possession until 1849, but held it thereafter until the war of 1914-1918.

Communications. Track and telegraph to Hodeida (125 miles). Track to Aden (170).

PORTS OF THE SOUTH COAST

ADEN (12° 46′ N., 45° 00′ E.). British Crown Colony. Banks. Hospitals. Hotels. Clubs. Airfields.

Aden harbour is formed by two volcanic peninsulas, Aden or Jebel Shamsan and Little Aden or Jebel Ihsan, which are connected northwards by short necks to the low sandy shore of the mainland. The two have a general similarity. Both are irregular ovals in shape with sides scalloped by deep bays, Aden measuring about 5 miles long from east to west and 2-2½ miles wide from north to south, and Little Aden about 6 miles long and 3 miles wide. The Little Aden isthmus to the mainland is short and broad, that of Aden is longer and narrower. In either case the embayments of the sea between peninsula and mainland are partly cut off from the main central bay by sandy spits, and end as shallow tidal lakes and marshes to east and west. The volcanic forms are better preserved on Aden than on Little

Aden, where the crater rim is broken down into a group of hills separated by deep gullies. On Little Aden these hills rise to 1,135 feet (346 m.) in Jebel Al Muzalqam in the centre of the peninsula and to 700 feet (213 m.) in Jebel Ihsan at the inner or eastern extremity. Aden is loftier and more rugged with the principal heights in the centre, where Jebel Shamsan rises to 1,800 feet (549 m.); towards the inner or western end Amen Khal and Al Aineh reach 1,000 and 750 feet (306 and 228 m.). All these hills are scarred by gullies draining directly to the sea or down the interior slopes, Wadi Tawela which drains the crater of Aden being the largest. The peninsulas are bare of vegetation except for sparse shrubs and bulbs in some of the gullies, and on Little Aden the only human habitations are two fishing-villages, Bandar Sheikh and Bandar Ghadir, on the south-eastern bays, and a third, Bandar Fuqum, in the western-most bay. (Photos. 91–94.)

The mainland shore is formed by the sandy plain of the Tihama, covered with maritime scrub and scattered groups of *dūm*-palms, and the isthmuses are similar. About half-way between the two there is the delta of the Wadi Kabir with seasonal cultivation along its course, and three-quarters of a mile from the sea the village and oasis of Hiswa stands on its left bank.

The Port. Aden harbour is divided by the sandy spit mentioned above into the main bay, which has depths from 3 to 5 fathoms, and a smaller eastern area on the north side of Aden peninsula with depths of 1–2 fathoms. The two are connected by a channel 400 yards wide along the north-west end of the peninsula which is dredged to depths of 30–36 feet. The actual division into an Outer and an Inner Harbour is, however, artificial, since the Inner Harbour is defined by an arbitrary line to the west of the spit and includes part of the main bay.

The port consists of anchorages in the Outer and Inner Harbour and of lighter wharves and jetties along the north-western shore from Steamer Point to Ras Hejaf and farther east at Ma'ala (fig. 40). There are no quays at which large vessels can berth, and all handling of goods and coal is done by lighters and small craft. There are mooring buoys for about 20 large vessels in the dredged channel and room for more vessels to moor themselves in the main bay between the two peninsulas. The dhow harbour and quays for native craft are at Ma'ala, where there is the largest of the commercial wharves. Details of the main jetties, all of stone construction, are given in the follow-ing table, which however omits many small wharves between Abkari

302. Aden. Main bazaar in Crater town

303. Aden tanks. View towards Crater town

304. Aden. Tunnel through Mansuri hills connecting Crater with the isthmus

305. Main Pass, between Crater and Ma'ala

pier and Ras Hejaf, in which sector the coal wharves are mostly located.

Name	Length in ft.	Depth of water in ft.
Pilot Pier . . .	130	5–5½
Post Office Pier . .	92	6–10
Prince of Wales Pier .	60	6–8
Abkari Jetty . .	40	2–8
Ma'ala Jetty . .	2,000	4–6

There are six *oil berths* in the main anchorage linked by pipe-line to the tank farms in Ma'ala plain, the rate of intake being up to 500 tons an hour. There is also a supply service by oil lighters which fuel at a petroleum jetty at Ma'ala.

Cranage is confined to Ma'ala jetty (3 cranes of 1½–5 tons), to some small cranes on private wharves, and to a 25-ton floating crane. *Warehouse* accommodation is ample, including 18 or 20 sheds mostly ranging from 60 × 25 ft. to 162 × 30 ft. *Oil storage* in Admiralty and A.I.O.C. tanks totals about 500,000 tons of various fuels.

Repair facilities include a small private floating-dock (230 ft. long lifting 1,400 tons overall) and four Admiralty slip-ways for small craft of 2½–5 feet draught. The Port Trust workshops equipped for the repair of harbour craft include foundry, fitting, boiler, blacksmith, and carpentry shops.

Commerce and Industry. Aden is a free port and charges are levied only for actual services such as wharf dues; there are no customs dues except on liquor, drugs, and salt. Its present great prosperity depends upon its position as a coaling and oiling station, but there is also a considerable entrepot trade, of which a great part is carried by sailing dhows, with southern Arabia, the Somali coast, and India. The entire supply of food and firing for the settlements is imported mainly by sea but also by caravan from the interior. In 1939, the last normal year, 2,079 large vessels of 8,650,411 tons total called at Aden; 1,310 of them were British. Also 1,456 small craft of 76,963 tons total used the port. The value of the 1939 trade in rupees was, for imports, 6,23,12,746, and for exports 3,43,41,168.

There is no local industry except the building of dhows, the extraction of salt from extensive pans round Sheikh 'Othman, the unhusking of coffee berries, and the making of cigarettes in the bazaars (p. 530).

The Towns. The settlements on Aden peninsula are somewhat widely separated. The oldest is 'Crater', on the east side of the peninsula and facing Front Bay through the broken rim of the volcanic crater from which it takes its name. On the west some 4 miles distant is Tawahi, which includes the port and commercial area of Steamer Point and residential suburbs to the south. On the northern coast between Tawahi and Crater is Maʻala, an extensive settlement around the dhow harbour. Towards the northern end of the isthmus there are numerous military and air establishments at Khormaksar, and on the mainland beyond there is the town of Sheikh ʻOthman. The inhabitants are mostly Arabs with a large Somali element at Maʻala; the population of Crater is about 20,000, that of Tawahi about 10,000.

Crater, though called the old town, has nearly all been built since the British occupation. It is laid out with military regularity, and its houses, squat, whitewashed cubes of mud-brick or stone, are set in square blocks. There are barracks, bazaars, mosques, and churches. Places of interest are limited to the mosque of ʻEidarus, patron saint of Aden, a Hindu temple, a Parsi funeral tower, and the ancient water tanks, of pre-Islamic origin, set at the upper end of the town. Thirteen of these, repaired in 1856, could hold 8,000,000 gallons of water, which was obtained by careful damming and management of the Wadi Tawela gullies, since even a slight shower produces a considerable spate. But the present water-supply is drawn by pipe from boreholes at Sheikh ʻOthman. (Photos. 92, 298, 302, 303.)

Tawahi, the business quarter, is more modern than Crater, and its stone houses have two or three stories. Here there are the offices of the Port Trust, shipping, banking, and commercial establishments, government buildings, military headquarters, hotels, clubs, hospitals, and churches for Europeans. Barrack Hill contains most of the military offices; the Aden Secretariat is near the Prince of Wales Pier, and the residence of the Governor is in the south-western outskirts near Ras Tarshain. There are various sports clubs connected with the Services, and a bathing-pool in Gold Mohur bay. (Photos. 300, 301.)

Maʻala, with its Arab and Somali quarters, and its dhow-building yards, has the least of European influence. There is a large residential area of stone houses and mud huts.

Sheikh ʻOthman, on the mainland, notorious for its brothels, is a small Arab town laid out with the monotonous regularity of Crater and intended to house the surplus population of Aden peninsula. It is clean and well kept with a large bazaar and several mosques, and also the buildings of the Keith-Falconer medical mission of the Church of Scotland. It stands in an oasis and has shady public gardens and good water. It is the headquarters of the Aden Protectorate Levies and of the Aden Government Guards (p. 352). There is a large airfield with several hangars.

These settlements are connected by a road which traverses the crater rim by the impressive 'main pass' between Ma'ala and Crater. There is a direct road from Ma'ala to Sheikh 'Othman, while a link from Crater to the Isthmus tunnels through the crater rim to reach Khormaksar (photos. 304, 305).

History. An account has been given in Chapter V of the importance of Aden as a port in ancient and Islamic times, and of the British occupation in 1834 and the subsequent development of the Settlements. Here a few notes are added on the history of the port itself.

After the British occupation the usual anchorage was in Holkat bay until 1850, when Aden was declared a free port. Between 1850 and 1880 coal wharves were built on the foreshore of the present Inner Harbour, and in 1862 a floating light was placed, on an old brig, at the entrance to the Inner Harbour. The opening of the Suez Canal in 1869 increased the value of Aden as a coaling station and rendered it desirable that the harbour should be dredged uniformly with the depth of the canal. This task was taken over from the Bombay Government by a Port Trust formed in 1888, and by 1901 an area of 163 acres had been dredged to provide six berths with depths of 26 feet. Meanwhile Post Office Pier had been built to accommodate mail barges (1876) and Ma'ala Wharf acquired (1869) and extended. Lights on Ras Marshag and Elephant's Back were first placed in 1886 and 1911 (photos. 93, 94).

Demands by the Chamber of Commerce (first established 1886) for the increase of lighter wharfage and the further deepening of the harbour led to a commission of inquiry, which recommended instead the construction of deep-water piers for large vessels. These proposals were not carried out. Instead a dredging contract was placed and completed between 1905 and 1910 which provided for two deep berths of 33–34 feet; the spoil was used to reclaim 15 acres of the bay on which Port Trust and other offices were built. Prince of Wales pier was built in 1905 and the engineering workshops were extended; also a sea wall was built on the sandy spit to give added protection to the Inner Harbour. After 1914 the need for oiling berths arose and three were completed by 1926. In 1928 a fresh dredging scheme was undertaken which resulted in the accommodation available in 1939. Large tank farms were built for the Admiralty and the A.I.O.C., and the number of oil berths was increased.

Communications. From Sheikh 'Othman there is a motor-road to Lahej. There are cables to Bombay, Zanzibar, and Suez, and the R.A.F. has airfields.

MUKALLA (14° 31′ N., 49° 08′ E.). Eastern Aden Protectorate

Mukalla, the capital of the Sultan of Shihr and Mukalla, is a coastal town with an open anchorage in the bight between Fūwa and the great headland which comprises Ras Marbat, Ras Kodar, and Ras Mukalla. The anchorage is on the west side of a level promontory about 1,000 yards long from north to south and 500–700 yards wide, on which the oldest part of Mukalla town is built. East of the promontory the coast is cliffed, but to the west there is a narrow stretch of level ground immediately backed by the steep slopes of Jebel Qarat (1,300 ft.). Farther west this strip continues as a raised beach of sand. (Photos. 98, 306–309.)

Though the port is second in importance to Aden for south-west Arabia the anchorage cannot be used from June to August (except for landing in the early morning) during the south-west monsoon; the anchorage at Ras Burūm is then used instead. There are no reefs or other encumbrances, and the water deepens rapidly from 6 to 30 fathoms 2 miles off shore. Large vessels usually anchor a mile off shore and unload goods by dhow at the landing-place. Small craft use the more sheltered anchorage close in shore in the bay west of the promontory and at high water can unload directly on to the Customs Wharf. This, with a minimum of 6 feet of water alongside, projects at the north-west corner of the promontory and affords an open space about 30 yards wide backed by sheds or godowns; there are steps down to the water for embarkation.

The town consists of Al Bilad on the promontory and the newer quarters which stretch behind it to east and west along the coastal strip and climb the lowest slopes of Jebel Qarat. Al Bilad is separated by the open space of the cemetery from Haft al 'Abīd, the poorest quarter stretching eastward, and from Haft al Hara, which stretches westward from the cemetery to a recently built mosque. Beyond this is the most modern part of the town, called Bara as Sida, containing some of the finest buildings and planned with wide and motorable roads parallel to and at right angles to the sea front. Bara as Sida ends at the town wall, which reaches from the steep flank of Jebel Qarat to the sea and is pierced by a single gate of Indian design. There is a motor-road from the landing-place, through the narrow, crowded bazaars, and along the sea front to this gate.

Houses generally are in the fine Hadhrami style, built of stone with four or five stories, but interspersed in the older quarters with many huts of mud or matting. In Al Bilad the seven-storied Kasādi palace, now used as government offices, dominates the quarter. The Sultan's newest palace is in Bara as Sida immediately within the wall by the gate, and behind is an older palace now used as the official guest-house.

Beyond the wall there is a broad level space called Therib, formed by the mouth of a wadi and used as an encampment for the numerous camel caravans which visit Mukalla. On the far side of the wadi there is the Subian village or suburb called Sherij Bā Salam.

The town, walled only on the west, is elsewhere protected by the steep cliffs of Jebel Qarat. Since this has a flattened top there are four small defensive towers on the escarpment which used to be manned in times of beduin raids. To the east the narrow approach between the mountains and the sea needs no artificial defence. *Water* is piped from a reservoir at Al Baqrein behind Jebel Qarat, which is filled from the sources of the Wadi Wasit; the supply is reckoned at 4,500 gallons an hour. An electric lighting plant supplies the Sultan's palace and guest-house and also an erratic system of street lighting in Bara as Sida.

The town contains the offices of the Sultan's administration and the residence of a British political officer, and for social services has a dispensary and three schools, two of the government and one of an Indian Christian mission. The population, estimated at 10,000 in 1931, contains not only Arabs but numerous Indian traders from British India, Somalis and other east Africans from as far south as Zanzibar, some Jews, Persians, and an occasional stray Levantine Greek. The Arabs include an aristocratic class of Seiyids, townsmen working as traders, artisans and labourers, and tribesmen concerned with the organization of caravans. The negroes are largely of servile origin, and there are also the despised Subiān (p. 370), who perform menial tasks, hewing wood and drawing water, and are not allowed to live inside the town.

Trade and Industry. The town's wealth depends mainly on commerce, fishing, and shipbuilding. Commerce with Aden, Bombay, the Persian Gulf and Red Sea ports, Somaliland, and Zanzibar, is carried mainly by dhows but also by steamers calling monthly. Exports are chiefly tobacco, skins, dates, wheat, honey, gums, and limestone, and imports are mainly foodstuffs, textiles, hardware, other domestic goods, and petroleum. Fishing is extensive, either shore fishing with circular cast-nets or inshore fishing from small boats carrying a single lateen. Large quantities of small fish are taken, dried for food, fodder, and fertilizer, and exported inland by caravan. Sea slugs, dried shark, and shark fins for China are local specialities. As for manufactures, in the shipbuilding yards situated on the shore north of the landing-place dhows of up to 50 and 100 tons and even of 400 tons burden are built. Fish oil is made, and vegetable oil is pressed from seeds. A fine lime is produced by local quarries, and bazaar trades include the making of curved daggers and silver scabbards, and of large coloured baskets for the Aden market.

History. Mukalla, though first mentioned in the thirteenth century, seems to have been of little importance in ancient and early Islamic times, when Cana and Aden monopolized the incense trade of the Hadhramaut. Generally the port has been of subsidiary importance, and in the eighteenth century Shihr seems to have predominated over Mukalla, which in the nineteenth became one object of the struggles between the ruling families of the Kathīris, Kasādis, and Qu'aitis (p. 277). Attempts by the Turks to establish a foreign overlordship in 1850 and 1867 failed, and between 1876 and 1888 the Qu'aiti with British support secured full control of Mukalla, which they have retained since then. A British political agent was installed at Mukalla as Resident Adviser to the Qu'aiti Sultan in 1937 (p. 309).

Communications. There is a motorable track to Gheil Ba Wazīr (30 miles) and Shihr (50 miles); in 1935 there were 30 cars and 50 light trucks in Mukalla. R.A.F. airfield at Fūwa. Seaplane landing area in the east bay.

GAZETTEER OF INLAND TOWNS

Though striking architectural styles have been developed, there has been little or no planning of towns. In the more densely populated districts most of the townsmen and villagers live in conditions of squalor and overcrowding; prevention of the last, with adequate ventilation of houses and sanitation are, indeed, crying needs. In many feudal tribal areas, particularly in the south-west, villages and small towns have assumed a nearly uniform plan; the tribesmen's houses are crowded round the castle of the chieftain; there is at least one mosque, and usually a saint's tomb near by, the site of an annual fair. Such places have few shops and craftsmen; sometimes the huts inhabited by serfs form a special quarter. In certain of the larger towns, particularly in the Hadhramaut states, extreme contrasts are afforded by the immense palatial homes of the wealthy adjacent to the squalid dwellings of the poor. The oasis towns of the north have often grown up from the most important hamlet of many within the oasis, and have been walled.

The walled cities display more evidence of planning, but vary considerably in layout, in the number and position of their gates, and of the bastions

306. *Mukalla sea-front*

307. *Mukalla harbour*

308. *Mukalla westwards from the air*

309. *Mukalla eastwards from the air*

in their walls. Country houses and other buildings have now arisen outside the walls of most cities. The curious narrow-waisted form of San'ā origi-nated through the building, outside the walls on the west, of garden-suburbs which were still unwalled in the mid-eighteenth century, but were later walled in (fig. 46).

The following notes of some of the larger inland towns have been com-piled from sources of varying reliability and date. Some of the information may therefore be inaccurate and certain important features may have been omitted. The towns are arranged in three groups—Sa'ūdi Arabia, the Yemen, and the Aden Protectorate—alphabetically, except that the two holy cities of Mecca and Al Madina are placed first. All figures for geo-graphical position, height, population, and especially mileage are estimates and must be treated with suspicion. Some alternate spellings used by different writers are given in brackets.

I. SA'ŪDI ARABIA

MECCA. 21° 25' N., 39° 48' E.; alt. 1,970 feet. Population 80,000. Capital of Sa'ūdi Arabia and of the Hejaz.

Mecca lies in a valley, rather more than half a mile wide, between steep rocky hills rising in places to nearly 2,000 feet above it. The valley slopes from north to south. There is a break in the hills to the west through which runs the road to Jidda. The city and an area round it, marked by boundary pillars, is sacred ground and may be entered only by Moslems. The city walls, which were incomplete, no longer exist, but the names of the gates survive.

The centre of Mecca and of Islam is the Great Mosque (Al Haram). Surrounding it are the bazaars, including the crowded Al Mas'ā with the sacred hills, As Safā and Al Marwa, at either end (fig. 41), the drapery and perfume market (As Suweiqa, No. 22 on plan), the slave market (Sūq al 'Abīd), and the 'Little Market' (Sūq as Saghīr, No. 13), which is often swept by flood; some of these floods have been disastrous (p. 25). The grain market (Sūq al Habb, No. 20) and fruit market (Al Halaqa) are near the north gate. Muhammad was born in a house east of the Mas'ā (No. 25). The mosque built on its site, the house of his first wife Khadija, where his daughter Fatima was born, the domes in the cemetery Al Ma'lā, and those of other shrines were damaged by the Wahhabis.

King Husein built his palace in Al Ghazza (No. 26); Ibn Sa'ūd's new palace, with garden and pillared audience hall, is farther north in the Mu'ābda quarter. Near it is the new wireless station. The old Turkish quarter, Al Jiyād, south-east of the Haram, contains a fortress (Qal'a Jiyād, No. 2), some fine houses, the modern hospital, and the Ministry of Finance. But the town has developed most on its western side along the road to Jidda. Here the street called Ash Shubeiqa (No. 9) is now thickly popu-lated, mainly by Central Asian, Indian, and East Indian guides for pilgrims;

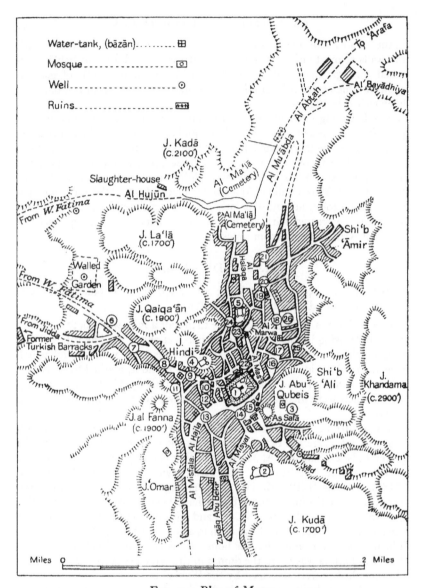

Water-tank, (bāzān)..........⊞

Mosque_____ ⊡

Well_____ ⊙

Ruins_____ ⊞⊞

J. Kadā
(c.2100)

Slaughter-house

Al Hujūn

From W. Fātima

J. La'lā
(c.1700)

Al Ma'lā
(Cemetery)

Al Ma'lā
(Cemetery)

Shi'b
'Āmir

Walled
Garden

From W. Fātima

J. Qaiqa'ān
(c.1900)

From Jidda

Former
Turkish Barracks

J.
Hindi

Al
Marwa

Shi'b
'Ali

J.
Khandama
(c.2900)

J. Abu
Qubeis

As Safa

J. al Fanna
(c.1900)

J. Omar

J. Kudā
(c.1700)

Miles 0   1   2 Miles

FIG. 41. *Plan of Mecca*

Heights in feet above the central valley are approximate

1. Al Haram	10. Donkey-drivers' inn	19. Al Jaudharīya
2. Qal'a Jiyād	11. Graveyard	20. Sūq al Habb
3. Masjid Bilāl	12. Zuqāq as Suwaq	21. Al Ma'lā
4. Qal'a Jebel Hindi	13. Sūq as Saghir	22. As Suweiqa
5. Qal'a Filfil	14. Al Hamīdīya	23. Al Qarāra
6. Sheikh Mahmūd	15. Egyptian kitchen	24. Al Falq
7. Jarwal	16. Al Qashāshīya	25. Prophet's birthplace
8. Hārat al Bab	17. Sūq al Leil	26. Former Sharif's palace
9. Ash Shubeiqa	18. Al Ghazza	

and Jarwal (No. 7), perhaps the most extensive quarter of all, is largely occupied by the offices and garages of motor-transport companies. It is here that pilgrims arrive by bus from Jidda; immigrants from west and central Africa live in this quarter, mostly in hovels. The camp for Syrian pilgrims lies north-west of Mecca, that for those from the Yemen outside the south gate. (Photos. 1, 149, 310, 311.)

The main streets of the city are fairly wide and were unpaved until recently, but Ibn Sa'ūd is known to have ordered that the Mas'ā should be paved. One or two bazaars are roofed. The better houses are built of fine dark grey granite, many being of three or four stories. Besides the buildings already mentioned, Mecca contains a police headquarters, Court house and other government offices, a new hotel, and many hostels for pilgrims. Though King Husein introduced electric light into the Haram, the streets are probably still lit only by oil lamps fixed to the corners of the houses, at long intervals, and only during the first and last weeks of the lunar month.

The *Haram* (No. 1) comprises a quadrangle measuring about 650 feet by 520, enclosed by a wall and buildings (fig. 42). There are twenty-four gates. Among the buildings is the Madrasa, intended as lodgings for students and teachers, but now let to wealthy pilgrims. The central court is surrounded by pillared arcades and seven minarets. In the centre is the Ka'ba, with the well of Zemzem and other sacred objects described below.

The *Ka'ba* or *Beit Allah*, successor to the Ka'ba of pagan times (p. 235), is about 40 feet long, 33 feet broad, and 50 feet high to the top of the parapet surrounding the roof (photo. 312). Massively built of fine Meccan granite, with marble roof supported on beams and three wooden columns, its entrance door, of carved wood heavily plated with silver, is placed in the north-east wall near the south-east corner, nearly 7 feet above the ground. Since pre-Islamic times the key has been kept by the Sheikh of the Beni Sheiba family, who reaches the door by portable ladder. Daylight only enters when the embroidered green 'Veil of the Door' is drawn aside. Inside, the floor is paved and the walls are lined with marble, above which is a sculptured frieze. In the south-west wall is the Prophet's prayer-niche; in the north-east corner a door called Bab at Tauba (Gate of Repentance) leads to the roof which is forbidden to pilgrims. The walls, but not the roof, are draped outside with the black *Kiswa*, embroidered with Koranic texts in gold. The Kiswa is renewed yearly at the pilgrimage; since 1928 it has been provided by King Ibn Sa'ūd; previously for a long period it was sent by the ruler of Egypt and, still earlier, sometimes by the Imam of the Yemen. This 'clothing' of the Ka'ba is said to date back to about A.D. 390, but was afterwards consecrated as an Islamic rite by Muhammad. The venerable 'Black Stone', really dark brown and probably a meteorite, an idol in pagan times, is now set in a heavy silver mounting nearly 2 feet high and $2\frac{1}{2}$ feet wide, built into the south-east corner and facing nearly due east. Its exposed surface, about 10 inches in diameter and 5 feet above the ground, can conveniently be kissed.

The Ka'ba stands on a raised marble pavement, Al Matāf (the place of *tawāf*, circumambulation); on this, north-west of the Ka'ba, is Al Hateim, a semicircular wall nearly 5 feet thick and slightly less in height, enclosing

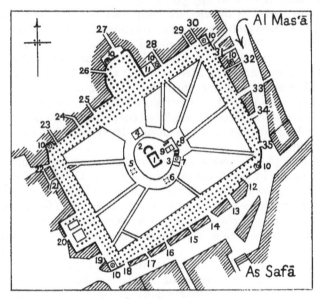

FIG. 42. *The Haram of Mecca*

1. Ka'ba	13. Bab al Baghla	25. Bab al Bāsita
2. Al Hateim	14. Bab as Safā	26. Bab al Qutbi
3. Al Matāf	15. Bab ar Rahma	27. Bab az Ziyāda
4. Al Maqām al Hanīfi	16. Bab Jiyād	28. Bab al Mahkama
5. Al Maqām al Māliki	17. Bab Ajlān	29. Bab al Madrasa
6. Al Maqām al Hanbali	18. Bab Umm Hāni	30. Bab ad Dureiba
7. Zemzem	19. Bab al Widā	31. Bab as Salām
8. Bab Beni Sheiba	20. Bab Ibrahim	32. Bab Qāit Bey
9. Maqām Ibrahim	21. Bab al Dāūdīya	33. Bab an Nabi
10. Minarets	22. Bab al 'Umra	34. Bab al Abbās
11. Law Court	23. Bab 'Amr ibn al 'Ās	35. Bab 'Ali
12. Bab Bāzān	24. Bab az Zamāmiya	

a space called *Al Hijr Isma'īl* (Ishmael's flight), reputed to have enclosed the graves of Hagar and Ishmael.

Other objects include a stone arch, the Bab Beni Sheiba, through which pilgrims step on to an outer granite pavement surrounding Al Matāf; a covered building of two compartments over the well Zemzem, on the roof of which the chief muedhdhin chants the calls to prayer, which are then taken up by the muedhdhins in the seven surrounding minarets; and the *Maqām Ibrahim* (Abraham's standing-place), with domed roof supported on pillars, covering a framework draped in green silk, which conceals *Al Hajar al As'ad*, the stone on which Abraham stood when rebuilding the

310. *Mecca. One of the Gates*

311. *Mecca. General view from the north*

312. *Mecca. The Haram with Qal'a Jiyād (Qasr Ajyad) on hill behind*

313. *Al Madina. General view*

Ka'ba. The imam of the Shafe'i school stands behind the Maqām Ibrahim when conducting the service; the other three orthodox schools (p. 384) have their own maqāms, that of the Hanafis being a small pavilion raised on pillars, those of the Mālikis and Hanbalis being merely little pyramidal roofs supported on columns; the imams of the four rites lead the services in rotation. The pointed roof of the beautiful marble pulpit given by the Ottoman Sultan Suleiman the Magnificent in the sixteenth century is nearly as high as the Ka'ba.

Water-supply. Water is brought from springs at Jebel 'Arafa by conduit which runs underground through the city, and is tapped at intervals by well-pits.

Communications. Tracks to Al Madina (c. 300 miles), Riyādh (555), Tāif (70), Hodeida (585), Jidda (55). Posts daily to Jidda and Tāif, twice weekly to Al Madina and Rābigh, twice monthly to Riyādh. Wireless station. Telegraph and telephone to Jidda and Tāif.

AL MADINA (Medina). 24° 33′ N., 39° 52′ E.; alt. 2,100 feet. (Railway, 2,096 feet). Population 20,000.

The city lies on the western side of its oasis of date-plantations and cultivated fields which is fed by water draining the hills to the east. The core of the city is the old town with its walls and gates; on the south and south-west an outer wall encloses the newer town; beyond the walls are residential suburbs, the northern and western outskirts having been favoured in the past by wealthy Turks. Both inner and outer walls are pierced by gates and are named on the plan (fig. 43). From the Bab al Masri in the west side of the inner wall the principal street, the cobbled As Suq, runs east to the Bab as Salām in the south-west corner of the Mosque of the Prophet, the heart of the old town, and thence eastwards to the Bab al Jum'a (or Bab al Bakia). The oldest quarter of the town, Harat al Bakia, lies between the Mosque and the Jum'a Gate; here many streets are so narrow that pedestrians can only pass by turning sideways, but throughout the old town the streets are narrow and only in part paved. Most houses are built of granite or basalt blocks; many of the better mansions have pillared halls opening on to bathing-pools; some are of three or four stories. But considerably more than half the city area is included in the 'new town', between the two walls. At the northern end of this area is the suburb of Manākha, where in the open space known as Barr al Manākha, caravans —and now motor-buses—arrive to deposit pilgrims. Around it are the government offices, mansions, hotels, lesser mosques, and garages. To the north-west is the suburb of Al Wajha, separated by a shallow wadi from Al Anbarīya; the latter was formerly the business and warehouse quarter and now contains garages for the growing motor-traffic. The broad street leading from the railway station towards the police headquarters, municipal office, and the Bab al Masri is flanked by the old Turkish barracks, a public kitchen for the poor, the governor's house, and private mansions. The

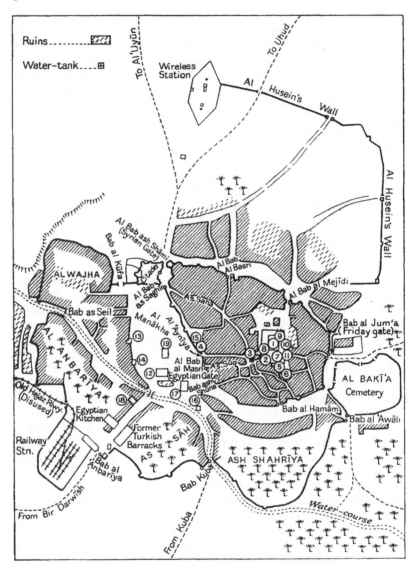

FIG. 43. *The Plan of Al Madina*

1. Al Haram	8. Bab ar Rahma	14. Masjid Abu Bekr
2. Bab as Salām	9. Bab al Mejīdi	15. Masjid Mālik ibn Anas
3. Al Balāt	10. Bab an Nisā	16. Masjid 'Omar
4. Zuqāq Mālik ibn Anas	11. Bab Jibrīl	17. Police Headquarters
5. 'Omar's garden	12. Masjid al Ghanama	18. House of the Governor
6. Library of 'Ārif Hikmat	13. Masjid 'Ali	19. Municipal Office
7. The Prophet's Hujra		

vegetable and livestock markets are held in the new town outside the Bab
ash Shūna, and the grain market outside the Bab al Masri. On the south
of the old town are the suburban districts of As Sāh and Ash Shahrīya, the
latter containing palm-groves with mud-brick houses and camel-yards.

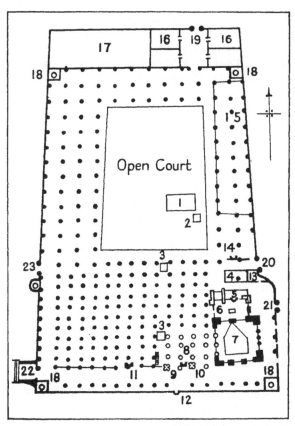

FIG. 44. *The Haram of Al Madina*

1. Fatima's orchard	9. Pulpit	17. Storerooms
2. Well	10. Mihrāb an Nabi	18. Minarets
3. Platforms	11. Mihrāb as Suleimānīya	19. Bab al Mejīdi
4. Platform of the Aghas	12. Mihrāb 'Othman	20. Bab an Nisā
5. Mihrāb al Mutahajjad	13. Storeroom	21. Bab Jibrīl
6. Tomb of Fatima	14. Mihrāb	22. Bab as Salām
7. The Prophet's Hujra	15. Women's praying place	23. Bab ar Rahma
8. The Raudha	16. Koran schools	

The *Haram* or Mosque of the Prophet consists of a quadrangle, 500 feet
long from north to south and over 300 feet broad, its open court surrounded
by colonnades and its walls hemmed in on all sides by houses and narrow
lanes (fig. 44). In the court are the Prophet's well and some palms said to
have been planted by Fatima, whose tomb is near by. Muhammad, who

died in June 632, is buried in the Hujra, originally the house of his wife 'Ayesha, which stood outside the first mosque. The Hujra, a five-sided enclosure covered by a black pall, under a lofty green dome in the south-east corner of the mosque, contains also the reputed tombs of Abu Bekr and 'Omar. Between 1848 and 1860 much of the mosque was rebuilt.

Water-supply. Water in Al Madina is plentiful, and comes for distribution by underground conduits from 'Ain Zarqa, a spring near the village of Kuba. Nearly every house also has a well in its courtyard.

Communications. Tracks to Hāil (275 miles), Mecca (300), Jidda (240), Yenbo' (130), Wejh (265). Wireless station. Post and telegraph offices.

ABHĀ (Ibha, Ebha). 18° 00' N., 42° 30' E.; alt. 7,500 feet. District H.Q., 'Asīr al Sirat province.

Abhā, a small town on the right bank of the Wadi Abhā or Wadi Bīsha, is built round a large market-place dominated by a fortress. The Amir resides in the fortress which contains the government offices, barracks, wireless station, hospital, and a great white tower built by the Sa'ūdi Government (p. 410). Abhā includes four villages: Manāzir, Muqābil, Khish'a, and Qarā, the first-named being the largest.

The houses are built entirely of clay but reinforced to withstand the rainfall of these parts by rings of slates set horizontally in the clay and projecting outwards. A masonry bridge of several arches spans the river-bed, which is fertile and fed by springs. The town is surrounded by derelict forts, and the mountains rise about 2,000 feet above it on the north-west.

Communications. Tracks to Tāif (320 miles), Bīsha (155), Sabya (75). Wireless station. Post office.

ABU 'ARĪSH. 17° 00' N., 42° 48' E.; alt. 850 feet. Population 7,500. District H.Q., Jīzān province.

Abu 'Arīsh was formerly the capital of the principality of 'Asīr (p. 256), and lies in the best-known district of the Tihama. Most of its houses are of stone. Water is abundant and cultivation plentiful. Tracks to Sabya (17 miles), Sa'da (55), Jīzān (20).

'ANEIZA ('Unaiza, 'Oneizah). 26° 09' N., 44° 10' E.; alt. 2,050 feet. Population 15,000. District H.Q., Qasīm province.

The oasis of 'Aneiza comprises gardens and several hamlets in a great sandy basin 2 miles from the Wadi ar Rima, the whole enclosed by a dilapidated wall. The principal settlement forming the town is enclosed by an interior wall. It is straggling, with a maze of crooked streets narrowed by the upper stories of houses. In the centre is an open space (Majlis), with shops on all sides and the narrow alleys of the bazaar radiating from it. The chief mosque, with tapering minaret, stands beside the Majlis, and about a dozen other minarets are scattered about the town and suburbs.

314. *Al Madina. The Great Mosque; the green dome over Muhammad's tomb on the left*

315. *Al Madina. Interior of the Great Mosque*

316. *The town of 'Aneiza*

317. *Governor's residence in Wadi Dawāsir, between the towns of Dām and Mishrif*

Date-palms, cornland, vegetable gardens, orchards, and fields of lucerne supply the needs of the population. The best water comes from the Khureijiya grove about a quarter of a mile outside the south gate. Two sandhills within the walls command a wide view of the surrounding country.

Communications. Tracks to Boreida (20 miles), Mecca (470).

ARTAWIYA. 26° 32′ N., 45° 24′ E. Population 10,000. District H.Q., Sudeir province.

Artawiya was founded by Muteir and Harb tribesmen in 1912 as the first Ikhwān colony (p. 286), and no European has yet entered its walls. The wells were formerly an important halting-place on the route between Zilfi (42 miles) and Kuweit (280).

BĪSHA. 19° 55′ N., 43° 15′ E. Unattached district H.Q., Al Madina province.

Bīsha is an agricultural district oasis (*balda*) comprising a number of villages in the valley of the same name, about 240 miles east-south-east of Mecca. The chief settlements are Raushan, Naji, and Junaina. The oasis is noted for its dates, the gardens being watered by a stream flowing north-east to join the Wadi Dawāsir. Its breed of camel known as 'arqiyya is notable. Tracks to Abhā (155 miles), Tāif (220), Sa'da (270).

BOREIDA (Buraida). 26° 20′ N., 44° 09′ E.; alt. 1,913 feet. Population 20,000. Capital of Qasīm province.

Boreida covers an oblong area of about 180 acres and stands on the top and south-west slope of a sandy ridge about 7 miles from the Wadi ar Rima. It is entirely surrounded by a wall, 2 feet thick and from 15 to 20 feet high, surmounted by a fringe of stepped pinnacles.

Most of the area within the walls is built over, but there is an open camping-ground in the north-east or Jarada quarter where camels are auctioned. Much of the town is laid out in rectangular blocks, the two principal buildings being the fortress of Qasr Mahanna and the Great Mosque. The Qasr stands by the camping-ground and is used by the King on visits; the Great Mosque, with tapering minaret, is in the centre of the town. There are about a dozen other mosques. There are said to be 300 shops. The bazaars extend on both sides of the Great Mosque and include the smiths' quarter, grass-market, and meat-market amongst others.

There are no gardens inside the walls, but date-plantations extend for about 3 miles towards the Wadi ar Rima. The area is generally healthy because of altitude and sandy site, but the water, derived from a group of wells at Saqa'a, at the foot of the eastern slope, has a disagreeable taste. Boreida is engaged in the caravan trade between Mecca and 'Iraq.

Communications. Tracks to Kuweit (375 miles), Riyādh (235), Mecca (480), Al Madina (330), Hāil (160), Jauf (? 410). Wireless station. Post office.

DĀM. 20° 30′ N., 44° 33′ E.; alt. 2,385 feet. Population 3,000. Wadi Dawāsir province.

Dām is the chief town in the Wadi Dawāsir oasis and stands on an eminence on the south bank of the wadi, being about 500 yards each way and nearly square in shape. Its houses are of mud-brick and the town wall mostly ruined. There is no general bazaar, but there are a number of scattered market booths. The best building is a fort-like mansion, the Qasr Husaiyin, owned by a local sheikh. The Amir, who is assisted by qadhi and council, lives beyond the west wall in the Qasr Barzan, which was completed in 1917. Two disused forts lie on the south and west of the town. The inhabitants belong to the Rujbān clan of the Dawāsir tribe.

Communications. Tracks to Bīsha (100 miles), Sa'da (? 350), Tāif (300), Riyādh (360).

DILAM. 23° 58′ N., 47° 12′ E.; alt. 1,360 feet. Population 8,000. Capital of Kharj province.

The town, or *hilla*, takes its name from the oasis and is enclosed by a wall. It contains a fort, Jami' and other mosques, markets and shops, and spacious well-built houses.

GHATGHAT. 24° 28′ N., 46° 18′ E. Population 8,000. Kharj province.

A new town built by Ikhwān of the 'Ateiba tribe on the site of an ancient capital of the kingdom of Yamāma (p. 233), some miles to the west of Muzahimiya, on the edge of the Nafūd Jau.

HĀIL. 27° 32′ N., 41° 58′ E.; alt. 3,180 feet. Population 5,000. Capital of Jebel Shammar province.

Hāil lies in the middle of a plain about 9 miles wide. The greyish-red granite cliffs of Jebel Ajja (Aya) rise to a maximum height of 1,500 feet above the plain on the west and are pierced at one point (Ria Akhdar) by an entrance so narrow that it can be closed by gates (photo. 48). The low range of Jebel Fittij rises about 6 miles to the east. North of the town the plain is interrupted by small basalt ridges of Jebel Salmā which make the town stuffy in summer. Hāil was the capital of the Rashidi Amirate during the nineteenth and early twentieth century, when it outrivalled Riyādh and is said to have had a population of 20,000. It fell to Ibn Sa'ūd in 1921 (p. 297).

The town is surrounded by a 15-foot wall, built by 'Abdul 'Aziz ibn Rashid (p. 283) of mud-brick, from 3 to 4 miles in circumference, with round towers and five gates. Within are the Amir's castle, the Great Mosque, and the market. Houses are of sun-dried brick, some having upper stories and towers. Much land inside the walls is planted with figs, wheat, and other crops. There is cultivation outside also, and walled

318. *Hāil. Qasr and mosque*

319. *Hofūf. Ibrahim Pasha mosque*

320. Hofūf. Suq al Khamīs. Wall of Kut quarter on right

321. Jauf. Street and minaret

plantations of dates, wheat, pomegranates, oranges, sweet lemons, apricots, and apples. The summer palace of Muhammad ibn Rashid, Amir of Hāil from 1872 to 1897, adjoins the Madina gate on the south-east.

Water is drawn by camels from wells about 90 feet deep; that in the northern part of the town is slightly salt. Rice and other grain are imported from 'Iraq and India.

Communications. Tracks to Najaf ('Iraq) (380 miles), Teima (235), Jauf (270), Kheibar (230), Al Madina (275), Boreida (160). Wireless station. Post office.

HOFŪF. 25° 23′ N., 49° 30′ E.; alt. 475 feet. Population 30,000. Capital of Hasa (or Ahsa) province.

Hofūf, taken by Ibn Sa'ūd from the Turks in 1914, lies outside western Arabia, but is included here as it is a provincial capital and the largest town in Sa'ūdi Arabia. It is the centre of the oasis of Al Ahsa ('murmuring'), so called from its perennial streams fed by many springs.

The town within its walls is divided into three quarters, Na'athil, Rifa', and Kut ('fort'), occupied respectively by artisans, merchants, and the professional classes. Kut was fortified and made self-contained by the Turks and now includes the headquarters of the provincial government, fort, and the fine mosque of Ibrahim Pasha (p. 394), a Turkish governor of the province. The mosque is a blend of Byzantine and Saracenic archi-tecture and has been described as the most beautiful in central and eastern Arabia. The Rifa' quarter includes the Suq al Khamīs, where a market is held every Thursday attended by the greater part of the population of the surrounding district, perhaps numbering nearly 100,000. Na'athil is the more lowly quarter with slums inhabited by artisans engaged in brass-work, leatherwork, saddlery, and other crafts. Salihiya, a suburb outside the south-eastern wall, is of comparatively recent growth. Many of the merchants have branches or agents in Bahrein, Basra, and Bombay through whom they exchange the products of Arabia with those of the outside world.

Water from wells in Kut and Na'athil is sweet, but most of those in Rifa' and all in Salihiya are slightly brackish. Some of the springs which feed the perennial streams of the oasis are warm or sulphurous, others cool or cold and sweet.

Al Mubarraz is a town only 2 miles north of Hofūf, surrounded by a ruined wall with two gates, one on the north, the other on the south. As in Hofūf, its buildings are largely of stone; it has narrow, crooked streets, contains about 1,800 houses, and holds some 9,500 inhabitants. Its market is on Friday. Both Hofūf and Al Mubarraz are noted for their learning and for the study of the literary and religious sciences and arts.

Communications. Tracks to Qatīf (110 miles), 'Oqeir (50), Dohah (180), Riyādh (200), Kuweit (345). Wireless station. Post and telegraph offices.

JAUF (Al Jauf, Jauf al 'Amr). 29° 55′ N., 39° 33′ E.; alt. 2,030 feet.
Population 10,000. District H.Q., Juba (Jauf) province.

Jauf comprises the group of hamlets in an oasis south-east of the
southern end of the Wadi Sirhan and near the northern edge of the
Great Nafūd. It contains two stone castles and some round brick
towers, and is noted for its dates. Water from wells is plentiful.
Tracks to Hāil (270 miles), Ma'an (Hejaz railway) (260), 'Aqaba (335).
Post office.

KHAMĪS MUSHEIT. 18° 08′ N., 42° 47′ E.; alt. 7,000 feet. District
H.Q., 'Asīr al Sirat province.

Khamīs Musheit lies among hills to the south of the Wadi Bīsha. It is
a flourishing town and marketing centre for dates, but too high for their
cultivation. Water is abundant and good. Tracks to Abhā (20 miles),
Bīsha (135), Tāif (300).

KHEIBAR. 25° 42′ N., 39° 30′ E.; alt. 2,800 feet. Population 2,500.
District H.Q., Al Madina province.

Kheibar lies in a rather unhealthy oasis in the Wadi Zeidīya. The houses
cluster at the foot of a steep flat-topped basalt rock which is crowned by
the ancient citadel of Al Hisn. The town, little more than a large village,
is said to have been founded by Jewish refugees in the time of Nebuchadnezzar. It has been likened to an African village. The landholders are
beduin, but most of the cultivators who raise the crops of date and
millet are negroid. Water is derived from springs, many slightly
sulphurous.

Communications. Tracks to Hadīyah (derelict Hejaz railway) (50 miles),
Hāil (230), Al 'Ulā (105).

KHURMA. 21° 52′ N., 42° 02′ E.; alt. 3,650 feet. Population 4,000.
Unattached district H.Q., Al Madina province.

Khurma lies on a branch of the Wadi Subai' and comprises several
straggling and unwalled groups of mud-brick houses, occasionally two-
storied. The population includes Ashraf and Subai' landholders, about
3,000 negro freeman-cultivators, and some 50 merchants from Shaqra,
'Aneiza, and other places, who have made Khurma a kind of clearing-
centre for trade between Nejd and the Hejaz. The beduin landholders
arrive for the date-harvest, and the population at that season may reach
10,000. Khurma was a bone of contention between King Husein of the
Hejaz and Ibn Sa'ūd in 1918 and 1919 (p. 296).

Water of excellent quality is abundant a few feet below the ground in
the higher fields and is also obtainable anywhere just below the surface in
the sandy wadi-bed.

Communications. Tracks to Riyādh (380 miles), and Tāif (120).

LEILA. 22° 15′ N., 46° 43′ E.; alt. 1,750 feet. Population 4,000. Capital of Aflāj province.

Leila, or Ghusiba, is the only town in the Aflāj province. Within its walls is the Amir's castle (Qasr ash Shuyukh) and a bazaar with about forty-three shops. Among its inhabitants are about 400 sharifs. Leila oasis measures about a mile from east to west and half a mile from north to south; it grows corn and dates.

Communications. Tracks to Riyādh (180 miles), Dām (205).

NEJRĀN. 17° 23′ N., 44° 22′ E.; alt. *c.* 4,000 feet. Population 10,000. Capital of Nejrān province.

Nejrān is an extremely fertile oasis settlement fed by the Wadi Nejrān (Marwan) not far from the north-eastern corner of the Yemen. It lies in a great valley-basin filled with palm-groves and corn-lands and bounded on either side by lofty granite cliffs. Just above the oasis the river enters the basin through a gorge, while below the oasis the waters escape through another gorge between rock-walls barely 20 feet apart. The settlement is neither a true town nor a group of hamlets. Three clans inhabit it, and the houses are mostly fort-like mansions spread among the oasis, mostly detached from, though within musket-shot of, their neighbours. Only occasionally a group of a few such strongholds are enclosed together within a wall, and the whole layout reflects the strife and feuds which existed between the clans before the Sa'ūdi Government brought them security and peace.

The oasis is of considerable historical interest, and in ancient times was a pillar of civilization. The ruins of the island city of Ukhdud ('the ditch'), including a magnificent castle and moat, the remains of ancient dams and rock-hewn channels testify to the existence of a city which survived almost to the Islamic period. As the seat of a Christian bishopric it is said to have been destroyed by one of the later Himyaritic kings who had accepted Judaism, because it refused to follow suit. The Koran preserves the tradition of the extermination of the Christians of Ukhdud, a name now found attached to a neighbouring hill, but the present name is even older, for it occurs both in Himyaritic inscriptions and in Strabo's account of the expedition of Aelius Gallus (p. 223). There is a small settlement of Jews living in the oasis at the present day.

Water is plentiful and good throughout the basin. Tracks to Sa'da (60 miles), Bīsha (220). Post office.

QAFĀR (Qifār). 27° 25′ N., 41° 55′ E.; alt. 3,300 feet. Population 3,000. Jebel Shammar province.

Qafār lies in a valley south-west of Hāil under the slopes of Jebel Ajja, and next to Hāil is the most important town in the province. Its oasis has more palms than that of Hāil and is inhabited by the Beni Tamim. Tracks to Hāil (10 miles), Teima (230), Kheibar (190), Al Madina (250).

RIYĀDH. 24° 40′ N., 46° 41′ E.; alt. 1,920 feet. Population 30,000. Capital of 'Āridh province.

Riyādh is a walled town lying in a green hollow surrounded by date-groves, which approach the walls closely on the west. Its importance lay in its commanding position on the main route between Hasa (Hofūf) and Mecca, and in its role as a route-centre in southern Nejd. In 1821 Riyādh

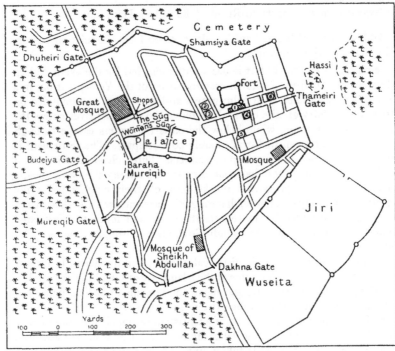

FIG. 45. *Plan of Riyādh*

1. Masjid al Qasr
2. Beit Ajnān
3. Old palace
4. School
5. Shilhub
6. 'Abdullah Quseiba

became the Sa'ūdi capital (p. 269) and the chief centre for the revival of Wahhabism after its recovery by 'Abdul 'Aziz ibn Sa'ūd from the Rashidi amirs in January 1902. It is now the capital of the viceroyalty of Nejd and the headquarters of the Crown Prince as Amir Nejd (pp. 320–1).

The royal palace lies in the centre of the town with the Great Mosque, devoid of ornament, near it (fig. 45; photos. 150, 324, 325). A large open space outside the palace walls is used for public prayers. The Shamsiya gardens and house of the king's sister Nura are outside the city on the north. From the Thameiri gate in the east wall a wide street with two-storied houses leads to the car park, and outside the south wall are the government garage and wireless station. The poorer quarter lies between

322. *Riyādh from the south*

323. *Walls of Riyādh and Hasa Gate*

324. *Riyādh. Great Cemetery*

325. *Riyādh. The Great Mosque*

326. *Riyādh. Interior of the Great Mosque*

the south-east wall and the palace. There is a market just inside the west gate. The king has a country palace at Budeiya (Badiya) in the Wadi Hanīfa, 5 miles to the west of the town; the race-course is 2 miles east of the Thameiri Gate.

Communications. Tracks to Kuweit (400 miles), Hofūf (200), 'Oqeir (250), San'ā (820), Mecca (555), Hāil (390). Wireless. Telephone between the king's country house, the government buildings, and the palace. Post office, with service to Mecca twice a month. Garages.

SABYA (As Sabya, Sabiya). 17° 14' N., 42° 40' E.; alt. *c.* 650 feet. Population 10,000. District H.Q., Jīzān province.

Once the Idrisi capital (p. 289), now only a district headquarters, Sabya faces the coastal plain of the Tihama. The old town consists of beehive huts built of clay and straw with raised clay floors. The newer part contains some stone-faced houses, including the former two-storied palace and fort, the latter restored by the present government since 1932. There are a fine mosque, many wells, and extensive fields of millet.

Communications. Tracks to Abhā (75 miles), Abu 'Arīsh (17), Hodeida (210), Jīzān (25).

SHAQRA. 25° 15' N., 45° 20' E.; alt. 2,250 feet. Population 10,000. Capital of Washm province.

Shaqra is a fair-sized town which in the nineteenth century had a considerable trade with India, 'Iraq, and Syria. Its gardens are small in relation to the extent of the town, the walls and towers of which have been ruinous since its siege by Muhammad ibn Rashid in 1891 (p. 270). Shaqra still has a bazaar with about fifty shops, and some well-built houses, but the centre of the town is greatly congested; as a Nejdi trade-centre it is said to rank after 'Aneiza and Boreida. Dates, citron, and figs are plentiful, but the grapes are poor.

Water, from wells 60–70 feet deep, is clear, but is said to be not very good. Tracks to Boreida (120 miles), Riyādh (120).

SULEIYIL. 20° 28' N., 45° 28' E.; alt. 1,975 feet. Population 2,000. District H.Q., Wadi Dawāsir province.

Suleiyil oasis, some 50 miles east of Dām, is at the sandy confluence of the Wadi Dawāsir and Sha'ib Majma'; it is about 2 miles long by a quarter of a mile wide. The settlement is composed of five villages, Far'a, Sabha (or al Muhammad), Dahlā, Al Hanash, and Āl Suwailam, each with perhaps 300 inhabitants, and there are many huts scattered about the oasis, and some castles among the palm plantations on the left bank of the Sha'ib Majma'. The amir resides at Al Hanash. The population of 2,000 given for the whole oasis includes some freed negro slaves, formerly pearl-fishermen, but does not include the nomadic Arabs who come to the oasis at the date-harvest to lay in supplies.

Wheat and dates grown are sufficient for local needs; fruit and some cotton are also grown. Irrigation is partly by flood-water, partly from wells. Tracks to Dām (50 miles), Leila (155).

TĀIF. 21° 17′ N., 40° 22′ E.; alt. 6,165 feet. Population 5,000. Unattached district H.Q., Qunfidha province.

Tāif lies on a sandy plateau surrounded by hills and is, as it was in the Prophet's time, a summer hill-station for officials from Mecca; its climate is much cooler than that of Mecca, the variations of temperature being extreme, and abundant rain falling in autumn. The town is enclosed within a wall of stones and mud, built by the orders of King Husein, and having bastions at the corners and gates; it is oblong in shape, with the longer sides facing north-east and south-west. There are three gates: two in the south-west wall, Bab ar Rī' and Bab ibn 'Abbās, and one in the north-east wall, Bab Shūbra or Bab as Seil, through which passes the Mecca road. Most of the houses are of stone. The Turkish-built barracks, surrounded by a stone wall, occupies nearly a quarter of the town area on the west. The mosque of Ibn 'Abbās, with open court surrounded by cloisters, is between the two gates in the south part of the town. Two domes, which formerly surmounted the tombs of 'Abdullah ibn 'Abbās and one of the Prophet's infant children, were demolished by the Wahhabis in 1923, when they sacked the town and massacred about 300 inhabitants (p. 299). The citadel, strongly built but now dilapidated, is on rising ground inside the wall on the south. The pre-Islamic fetish of Al Lāt, outside the Bab ibn 'Abbās, is a shapeless mass of granite (p. 235).

The suburb of Qarwa lies close to the former Turkish barracks, and many of the officers had houses there. The summer residences of prominent Meccans, including the Sheibi, hereditary keeper of the keys of the Ka'ba (p. 559), are in the suburb of As Salāma, a village of well-built stone houses about a mile south of Tāif; 3 miles beyond it to the south is the village of Al Mathrā, amid orchards and cultivated fields at the foot of the mountains.

Vineyards, orchards, and vegetable-gardens outside the walls are extensive; pomegranates, lemons, apricots, and quinces are grown, but not dates, because of the cold. Tāif is famous for its vines and its roses from which attar is distilled at Mecca.

Water derived from springs, wells, and brooks is good.

Communications. Tracks to Mecca (70 miles), Bīsha (220), 'Abhā (320). Wireless station. Post office with daily service to Mecca. Telephone to Mecca. Inn accommodation is available.

TEIMA. 27° 38′ N., 38° 51′ E.; alt. 3,400 feet. Population 2,500. District H.Q., Jebel Shammar province.

The oases of Teima lie near the northern border of the Hejaz about 25 miles west of the edge of the Great Nafūd. The principal oasis is Haddaj,

327. *Tāif. Ibn 'Abbās mosque and south-east side of the town from the south*

328. *Tāif. Eastern section of the town from the north*

329. *Zilfi. The Suq*

330. *Dhamār from the air*

named after its famous wells (p. 37), and is circular in shape, lying in a depression in the plain at 3,400 feet. The oasis is surrounded by dilapidated mud-walls with towers; the houses, mud-built and generally two-storied, stand in walled gardens. The Great Mosque is in the east of the settlement, and the stone fort of Qasr Zellum north-west of the oasis. Two smaller oases lie south-east of Haddaj and north-west of the fort. The population are mostly of the Wuld Suleiman. Date-palms, wheat, barley, dhura, tobacco, and several kinds of fruit are grown, the dates being among the best kinds; rock salt is dug from beds in the neighbourhood. The products of the oases are sold to nomads and exchanged with goods from Baghdad and the Persian Gulf brought by traders from Jebel Shammar. There are no shops.

Teima has a good and healthy climate. The water from the Haddaj wells, though inexhaustible, is not very palatable.

Communications. Tracks to Hāil (235 miles), Qal'at al Mu'adhdham (55), Ma'an (310).

AL 'ULĀ (El 'Ala). 26° 37' N., 38° 13' E.; alt. 2,210 feet. Population 3,000. District H.Q., Al Madina province.

Al 'Ulā is a large oasis, 2 miles from its station on the derelict Hejaz railway. The oasis has a length of about 3 miles, but the town itself is only 600 yards long, walled on the south-west side. Houses are of stone, but streets narrow and congested. There is no bazaar. The date-gardens are irrigated by tepid and sulphurous water, but that of underground canals in Manshīyah gardens is reported good. This centre is a source of date-supply for beduin of north-west Arabia and there is some traffic in corn and imported rice.

Communications. Tracks to Ma'an (330 miles), Al Madina (185), Wejh (130). Wireless station. Post office.

ZILFI. 26° 11' N., 44° 51' E. Population 4,000. District H.Q., Sudeir province.

Zilfi comprises two villages, Zilfi Shamaliya the main settlement, and 'Aqda or Zilfi Janubiya. They stand on a plain and are surrounded by walls, about 16 feet high, with three towers about 10 feet higher. The north-east part is ruined; a few of the houses are two-storied. The population is about evenly divided between the two villages. Tracks to Boreida (55 miles), Kuweit (320), Riyādh (200).

II. THE YEMEN

BĀJIL. 14° 58' N., 43° 15' E. Population *c.* 3,000. Qadha H.Q., Hodeida principality.

A lowland town at an altitude of several hundred feet near the inner edge of the Tihama, about 30 miles inland from Hodeida; an important stopping-place between Hodeida and San'ā, whether by Manākha or by the motor-road through Madinat al Abīd, branching south-east at 'Obal.

BEIT AL FAQĪH. 14° 30′ N., 43° 17′ E.; alt. *c.* 600 feet. Population *c.* 5,000. Qadha H.Q., Hodeida principality.

A lowland town and ancient seat of learning, once famous for its weaving and dyeing. The citadel lies on the north side, and, in Niebuhr's time, presented an imposing appearance. Tracks to Hodeida (33 miles), Zabīd (25), Mocha (90).

DHAMĀR. 14° 31′ N., 44° 28′ E.; alt. *c.* 7,500–8,000 feet. Population 5,000. Qadha H.Q., San'ā principality.

This unwalled town lies on a fertile plain between the recent volcano of Haidar al Lissi, which rises to over 10,000 feet, 8 miles to the east, and the old crater of Jebel Qariat Yafa', nearly 9,000 feet high, 4 miles to the west. It was the seat of an ancient Zeidi university and a centre of the highland horse-breeding industry. The old 'Central' liwa or Amirate of Dhamār has now been abolished and its districts have been incorporated in the 'principalities' of San'ā and Ibb (pp. 331, 357).

Most of the buildings are of mud-brick, plastered over, but there are some tall stone-built houses, as well as mosques with minarets, square mosque-tombs with cupolas but no towers, and two public baths. The principal mosque and the government offices are in the large square in the centre of the town. Particularly when approached from the south, over an expanse of black harra, the city is seen to comprise two parts, separated by a broad stretch of irrigated market-gardens (photo. 330). The vast cemetery lies to the north.

Communications. Tracks to San'ā (66 miles), Yarīm (23), Ta'izz (108).

HAIS. 13° 58′ N., 43° 32′ E.; alt. *c.* 1,200 feet. Zabīd qadha, Hodeida principality.

A town on the lowland route from Hodeida to Ta'izz. Its potteries have been noted for several centuries; the rough reddish ware, often partly glazed and with coloured designs, is exported as far as Aden. The name is pronounced so as nearly to rhyme with the English words 'rye is'. Hodeida (80 miles), Ta'izz (45).

IBB. 13° 58′ N., 44° 12′ E.; alt. *c.* 6,700 feet. Population *c.* 4,000. Capital of principality.

Ibb, formerly the seat of an Amir, is a highland city of very striking appearance, standing on a spur of Jebel Shemahe. Its walls, mosques, and tall houses are of stone. The streets are narrow and unpaved, and, except for the market-place, the space within the walls is built upon. The west side of the city stands on level ground, artificially built up and supported

332. *Ibb. Principal Gate*

331. *Ibb. South Gate*

333. *The walls of Ibb*

334. *Jibla, a few miles south of Ibb*

by a wall, with large curved buttresses broadening towards the base. The principal gate, flanked by circular towers, is on this side, approached by a stone-paved incline and with a sharp bend in the entry. There is also a small unfortified gate in an angle of the south wall (photos. 331–333). Mosques number about sixty, mostly low inconspicuous buildings; only two large ones have single minarets, that of the Jami' Masjid being a circular tower with designs picked out in white, and the other being octagonal, whitewashed, and with a roofed gallery just below the top.

On the plateau to the east water is brought from the mountain by a long curving aqueduct, 10 feet high or more near the city, and pierced by a series of arches separated by stretches of blank wall. The water feeds a tank supplying one of the large mosques, and is also raised thence, by a pulley-apparatus erected on a lofty wall, to a higher level, for distribution to the city.

The ancient town of Jibla, capital and burial-place of the eleventh-century Suleihid princess Saiyida (p. 248), lies a few miles to the south, and west of the road from Ta'izz (photo. 334).

Communications. Tracks to Dhamār (55 miles) and San'ā (120), Ta'izz (36), Zabīd (75). Telegraph office.

MANĀKHA. 15° 00' N., 43° 45' E.; alt. *c.* 7,600 feet. Population *c.* 7,000. Haraz qadha, San'ā principality.

A fortified town and former Turkish post with substantial buildings, perched on a narrow ridge precipitous on one side. The track to it on both sides is zigzagged and steep. Manākha has figured much in the history of the Yemen, as, for example, during the Turkish advance from Hodeida to relieve San'ā during the Arab risings of 1891, 1904–5, and 1911; but its importance has declined now that most traffic from Hodeida to San'ā is by motor through Madinat al Abīd. It has good water. Tracks to Hodeida (*c.* 100 miles), San'ā (72).

QA'TABA. 13° 50' N., 44° 43' E.; alt. over 4,000 feet. Population *c.* 1,500. Qadha H.Q., Ibb principality.

A small frontier town on the routes converging from Aden, i.e. that by Al Khureiba pass and that by Dhāla', from which Qa'taba is distant about 12 miles round the eastern flank of Jebel Jihāf.

SA'DA. 16° 50' N., 43° 37' E.; alt. 7,000 feet. Qadha H.Q., San'ā principality.

The town of Sa'da, as yet unvisited by European travellers, is the burial-place of Al Hādī Yahya, the first Imam of the Zeidis of the Yemen, of the Rassid line which reigned here between the tenth and fourteenth centuries (p. 247). In more modern times it was the capital of a liwa under an Amir, but in the recent reorganization the liwa was divided up between the principalities of Ta'izz and San'ā (pp. 332, 357–9), Sa'da itself being

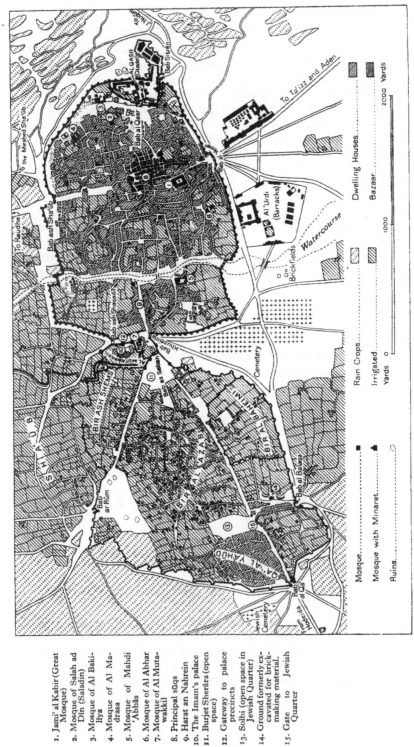

FIG. 46. *Plan of San'ā*

1. Jami' al Kabir (Great Mosque)
2. Mosque of Salah ad Din (Saladin)
3. Mosque of Al Bakiliya
4. Mosque of Al Madrasa
5. Mosque of Mahdi 'Abbās
6. Mosque of Al Abhar
7. Mosque of Al Mutawakkil
8. Principal sūqs
9. Harat an Nahrein
10. The Imam's palace
11. Burjet Sherāra (open space)
12. Gateway to palace precincts
13. Solbi (open space in Jewish Quarter)
14. Ground formerly excavated for brickmaking material.
15. Gate to Jewish Quarter

335. *San'ā. Bir al 'Azab in foreground; Jebel Nuqūm in distance*

336. *San'ā. Harat an Nahrein*

directly under San'ā. In past centuries Sa'da was famous for its leather, and probably still is; another local manufacture is stoneware vessels said to give an agreeable flavour to food stored in them.[1] Tracks to Jīzān (75 miles), San'ā (115).

SAN'Ā. 15° 22' N., 44° 12' E.; alt. between 7,500 and 7,900 feet. Population 40,000. Capital of the Yemen.

San'ā, the seat of the Zeidi Imams since the sixteenth century, headquarters of the former liwa and of the modern principality of San'ā, is one of the largest and most venerated cities in Arabia. It lies on a plain at the west foot of Jebel Nuqūm. The resemblance of its ground to a figure-of-eight, about 2½ miles from east to west and up to three-quarters of a mile from north to south, is due to its being composed of two parts (fig. 46): (a) the old walled Arab city on the east, and (b) certain garden suburbs, together with the Jewish quarter, formerly unwalled, but later surrounded by a wall. The walled-in precincts of the palace, *Bustān al Mutawakkil 'alā Allah* ('Garden of the Relier on God'), in which the royal palace rears its seven stories, lie in the narrow isthmus uniting the two halves.

The Arab city is partly on the site of the pre-Islamic stronghold, Ghumdan. The citadel is raised on a spur of Jebel Nuqūm at the east end. The walls of sun-dried brick rise to between 20 and 30 feet, with numerous semicircular bastions (totalling 128, including the circular towers flanking the gates). Near its western end the Arab city is traversed from north to south by a broad watercourse, dry except in times of flood. West of this lies much garden-ground; east of it, almost the whole space is occupied by massive houses of several stories, separated by narrow streets and a maze of still narrower, sharp-turning lanes, with occasional small open spaces. A broad street of shops, Harat an Nahrein, extends from the western wall to the watercourse, but the *suqs* properly speaking are centrally situated east of the latter (photos. 335–338).

The western division contains more modern (partly Turkish) official and private houses enclosed in gardens, walled market-gardens without houses, and the Imam's hospital. The walls are less massive with far fewer bastions. The greater part consists of three quarters named after springs, Bir ash Shems, Bir al 'Azab, and Bir al Baheimi, the last enclosed in walls of its own; all these contain numerous deep draw-wells, which (with a brook running from the north through the palace-precincts) provide the copious water-supply (photo. 29). At the extreme west end is the Jewish quarter, shut off at night by closed gates.

San'ā can be entered from the country by seven gates, or eight if the entrance through the citadel be included; two are respectively north and south of the Arab city (the southern one, Bab al Yemen, of Turkish construction, being the most imposing of all); two lie north and south of the narrow isthmus; while the western division has three gates. The Arab city

[1] Hayyim Habshush, *Travels in Yemen*, p. 57 (1941).

A 4836

P p

opens into the western division by the Bab as Sabah ('gate of the morning'), leading on to the parade-ground or Burjet Sherara.

The mosques, numbering about forty-four, are all except six in the Arab city. The Great Mosque, incorporating remains of pre-Islamic buildings, is an oblong with little external ornament, measuring 214 by 197 feet, with a small domed ka'ba in the court (photo. 182); extensions to the original fabric were made from the eighth to the twelfth century, and the twin white minarets were completed about 1261. Twenty-two other mosques have a single minaret apiece; these towers, in some cases surmounted by an emblematic metal dove, are richly ornamented in the Zeidi style, to which the flat-roofed smaller mosques conform. Certain larger ones, such as Al Bakiliya, built under Turkish influence, have large cupolas (photo. 184).

Outside the Arab city, to the north-east lies the Meshhed Sha'ūb, a vast walled and battlemented enclosure where the Imam and people pray on the annual festivals. The barracks and landing-ground lie to the south. Jebel Nuqūm is crowned by a triangular fort of uncertain age. Raudha, a town containing some large country houses, and renowned for its vineyards, lies 5 miles to the north.

Communications. San'ā is about 160 miles by motor from Hodeida via Madinat al Abīd, and 288 from Aden via Yarīm, Ibb, and Ta'izz. Post and telegraph offices. Landing-ground.

TA'IZZ. 13° 35' N., 44° 02' E.; alt. 4,500 feet. Population 3,000. Capital of principality.

This beautiful though somewhat decayed city, capital of the former southern liwa and now of the principality governed by the Crown Prince, lies at the northern foot of Jebel Sabir (9,800 ft.), which forms its southern rampart. The city is roughly quadrilateral and its north, east, and curved west sides are enclosed by walls fortified with towers and pierced by two arched gateways, Bab al Kabir and Bab Sheikh Musa, at either end of the eastern sector of the north wall; other former gates are now blocked.

Many of the houses have three or four stories, with much external ornament and traceried upper windows, but there is much waste space within the city walls. The market is small; Mocha being a decayed port, the trade of Ta'izz is mostly by motor-lorry with Aden. The road to the governor's principal residence, Dar an Nasr ('house of victory'), perched on a spur 1,500 feet above the city, has many hairpin bends. There is at least one government guest-house (*Beit adh Dhuyūf*) within the city, and another in the eastern suburb of Al 'Urdi, where there are barracks and the lower residence of the governor.

The Eiyubid dynasty, founded at Ta'izz in the late twelfth century by Tūrān Shah, was succeeded in the thirteenth by the Rasulids, who later gave place to the Tahirids, under whom (15th century) many colleges were founded, predecessors of the modern schools. Though some of the mosques were founded by the Rasulids, all the principal ones were rebuilt

337. *San'ā. The Suq*

338. *San'ā. Bab al Yemen*

339. *Ta'izz. Citadel hill behind*

340. *Ta'izz. View north from the guest-house*

during the Turkish dominion in the sixteenth or early seventeenth century; glistening white, they display a local variation of the Turkish style, characterized by series of recessed alcoves, one above the other, in the minarets. The Jami' Masjid (Al Muzaffarīya), centrally situated, has several large cupolas but only one minaret; Ash Sharifīya has one large dome and twin minarets (photo. 185); Al Makhdabīya has ten smaller cupolas but no minaret. Among many smaller religious buildings is the sixteenth-century mausoleum of Husein Pasha. The ruined city of Thabad, resort of twelfth-century Suleihid princes, lies to the east in a wadi of Jebel Sabir. The lofty minaret of the ancient mosque of Janadīya rises from the plain about 12 miles north-east (photo. 183).

The climate is agreeable, with cool nights, but malaria is prevalent. Water is conveyed by many plaster-lined channels from Jebel Sabir, and stored in tanks.

Communications. Tracks to Yarīm (80 miles), Mocha (66), Aden (128) (motor-track via Wadi Natīd). Telegraph to San'ā.

YARĪM. 14° 17′ N., 44° 26′ E.; alt. *c.* 9,000 feet. Population 4,000. Qadha H.Q., Ibb principality.

The plateau of Yarīm is dominated on the south-west by Jebel Sumara, rising to 10,000 feet. The town is approached, after descending from the Sumara pass, across Qa' al Haqal, a plain devoted to cereal crops, west of which rises Jebel Zafar, where the ruins of the Himyaritic capital (p. 222) are said to be still visible. Though Yarīm, backed to the north by low rocky hills, has been described as strongly walled and provided with gates, this is not to-day apparent on the same scale as at Ta'izz or San'ā, and the city, when approached from the south, looks largely open; nor did Niebuhr (1763) mention walls; but there is a fortified gateway on the east or south-east, and a gate opening to the north. The castle surmounting a detached crag, where the 'Dola' (governor) resided in Niebuhr's time, appears to be now ruinous. The present government building (*Hakūma*) is a large structure of several stories, with a courtyard; it contains the office of the 'amil, the telegraph office, and guest-rooms. Some other large, lofty houses are built in the San'ā style, with stone lower parts and upper stories of sun-dried brick. There is one tall minaret, cylindrical and ornamented with brickwork designs in relief. But on the whole the town seems poor, though several springs and tanks are situated within a mile or two. Forskål, the pupil of Linnaeus and naturalist of Niebuhr's party, died at Yarīm in July 1763, but his grave is unknown.

Communications. Yarīm is on the main road south of San'ā (80 miles) and Dhamār (23); to Qa'taba (42) and Aden (135); Ta'izz (80). Telegraph to San'ā and Ta'izz.

ZABĪD. 14° 10′ N., 43° 18′ E.; alt. 900 feet. Population 8,000. Qadha H.Q., Hodeida principality.

Zabīd was founded early in the ninth century as the capital of the Ziyadids, who ruled all the Tihama, and even more widely, till overthrown by Tūrān Shah about 1174; the latter transferred the Eiyubid capital to Ta'izz, which he thought healthier (pp. 247-8). Under the Turks before 1918 Zabīd was the residence of a Qaimmaqam. The city, built on the north bank of the Wadi Zabīd, is walled. Al Khazraji (died early 15th century) described it as circular, with walls, bastions, and four gates, opening respectively north, east, south, and west; Niebuhr (1763) found the walls ruinous and the only remaining fortification a small citadel; recently the city has been described as strongly walled and quadrilateral, with the four gates as stated above. Zabīd was famous as a centre of learning even before the time of Al Khazraji, and, till recently at any rate, it boasted a university and college of Sunnis of the Shafe'i school, housed in the Great Mosque, also several other large mosques and many smaller ones. The bazaar, considered by Manzoni (1884) the finest in the Yemen, is well stocked with local produce. The weaving and dyeing industries have declined. The old Islamic town of Jerahi lies a few miles south-east, on the road to Hais.

Communications. Tracks to Beit al Faqīh (25 miles); Ta'izz (75). Telegraph to Hodeida and Mocha.

III. ADEN PROTECTORATE

DHĀLA'. 13° 41' N., 44° 45' E.; alt. 5,200 feet. Population 2,400. Western Aden Protectorate.

Dhāla' is the seat of the Amir of Dhāla', whose castle stands on a small rocky hill at the head of a wide valley. The town lies on the road from Aden to the Yemen at the foot of the northern slope of the hill, a compact collection of square, storied houses with thick walls of dark coloured stone. The streets are narrow, the town is unwalled. The principal mosque with one short minaret stands on the north side. A skin-curing industry is carried on. A weekly market is held. There is a Jewish quarter and a good deal of cultivation in the country round; also a government rest-house and a guard's post in the neighbourhood. For its occupation by the Turks in 1873, see p. 275.

Many tracks; Aden, 80 miles. The small landing-ground is 3 miles to the north.

GHEIL BA WAZĪR. 14° 47' N., 49° 20' E.; alt. 360 feet. Population 6,000. Mukalla province, Qu'aiti State, Eastern Aden Protectorate.

A well-built walled town, the centre of the Hamūmi tobacco industry (p. 494). The Mukalla Government maintains an experimental farm as there is a good water-supply from springs in the neighbourhood; the place is renowned for its well-diggers. Tracks to Shihr (20 miles), Mukalla (30), Tarīm (140).

341. *Gheil Ba Wazīr*

342. *Dhāla‘ from the castle hill. Lower slopes of Jebel Jihāf behind*

343. *Lahej. Sultan's palace from the air*

344. *Lahej. Street-scene*

HAUTA (Wadi Hadhramaut), 15° 50' N., 48° 27' E.; *see* Qatn.

LAHEJ. 13° 03' N., 44° 52' E.; alt. 400 feet. Population 15,000. Capital of 'Abdali Sultanate, Western Aden Protectorate.

A mud-built town standing in a large oasis of date-palms and millet-fields. Streets are narrow and irregular; houses mostly of one story, but some have two or three, and a few four or five. There are covered bazaars, one being set aside for metal-workers, and a large market; also an open space where camels are unloaded, and a car park. The old and the new palaces of H.H. the Sultan of Lahej face a large parade-ground. Much cultivation in the neighbourhood, and new methods are being applied. Mosquitoes are bad. Water is obtained from the Wadi Tiban. Tracks to Aden (25 miles), Mocha (130), San'ā (205).

LAUDAR (Lodar). 13° 52' N., 45° 53 ' E.; alt. 3,200 feet. Population (estimate) over 6,000. Capital of the 'Audhali tribal confederation, Western Aden Protectorate.

An unwalled town, the seat of the 'Audhali Sultan, and an important trade-centre with agricultural land about it. Market on Wednesdays. Landing-ground on the outskirts. Tracks to Shuqra (45 miles), Aden (100), Nisāb (70), San'ā (175).

MUSEIMĪR. 13° 27' N., 44° 37' E.; alt. *c.* 3,000 feet. Capital of the Haushabi tribal area, Western Aden Protectorate.

Museimīr, the seat of the Haushabi Sultan, stands on the left bank of the Wadi Tiban and looks north to the Jebel Warwah and west to the mountains of the Subeihi country. It is a mere collection of huts dominated by the storied palace, which is roughly built of stone but somewhat ruinous. The approach from Lahej is guarded by the hill-top fortress of Al 'Anad.

A perennial stream in the Wadi Tiban irrigates maize fields. A school has recently been established. A centre of caravan tracks: Ta'izz (50 miles), Lahej (35), Aden (60).

NISĀB (Ansāb). 14° 30' N., 46° 30' E.; alt. 3,650 feet. Population 4,000. Capital of the Upper 'Aulaqi tribal district, Western Aden Protectorate.

An unwalled town, with residence of the Naqib, representative of the Upper 'Aulaqi Sultan, whose seat is at Medāq. The mosque of Sidi Muhammad is a fine building. Iron is said to be worked by local smiths; indigo and cotton are grown. Tracks to Shuqra (115 miles), Yeshbum (35), Mukalla (200).

QATN (Hautat al Qatn[1]). 15° 50' N., 48° 27' E.; alt. *c.* 2,500 feet. Population 2,000. Shibām province, Qu'aiti State, Eastern Aden Protectorate.

[1] Hauta (=sanctuary) on some maps.

A walled town in the centre of a good agricultural area, producing a special variety of date known as *Hajar*. It has good wells. Landing-ground near the town. Tracks to Shibām (15 miles), Tarīm (50), Mukalla (145), Shihr (160).

SEIYŪN.[1] 15° 57′ N., 48° 47′ E.; alt. *c.* 2,300 feet. Population 20,000. Capital of Kathīri State, Eastern Aden Protectorate.

Seiyūn is a walled town at the foot of Jebel Seiyūn containing some 1,500 mud-brick houses, often with delicate decoration and whitewashed parapets, many mosques, the Kathīri Sultan's palace (photo. 348), and an ancient religious academy (*rubat*). The streets are dusty and broad. There are a number of palm-groves and cornfields on its outskirts and the many-storied mansions of the wealthy stand in their own gardens. In normal times there are close ties between Seiyūn and both Malaya and Java. For the history of Seiyūn and the Kathīri State, see pp. 277-9, 309.

Tracks to Mukalla (175 miles), Shihr (180), Shibām (15), Tarīm (25). The landing-ground is no longer serviceable because of drifting sand. Wireless station. Post office (pp. 343, 538).

SHIBĀM. 15° 56′ N., 48° 37′ E.; alt. 2,500 feet. Population 7,000. Capital of Shibām province, Qu'aiti State, Eastern Aden Protectorate.

The Qu'aiti town of Shibām, probably the most spectacular in Arabia, stands on a small eminence at a strategic junction of routes in the Wadi Hadhramaut. By local tradition it is the successor to Shabwa, and there are certainly traces of Himyaritic times in the wadis to north and south. It is walled, and being unable to expand outwards has, like New York, grown upwards (p. 413). Of the houses, said to number about 500, many have six or seven stories, though they appear to have as many as fourteen, because of their recessed exterior decoration (photo. 350). Some of the mansions belong to wealthy merchants with East Indian trade connexions. Streets are very narrow.

Shibām is an important market town and a commercial centre (p. 536). Outside are extensive palm-groves, but these have suffered severely from prolonged drought from 1941 to 1944. Tracks to Seiyūn (15 miles), Tarīm (40), Shihr (150), Mukalla (160). Post agency. The landing-ground just north-east of the town is no longer serviceable.

TARĪM. 16° 02′ N., 49° 00′ E.; alt. 2,200 feet. Population 15,000. Kathīri State, Eastern Aden Protectorate.

The second town of the Kathīri State, a centre of religious teaching, is built on a slope at the foot of cliffs on the north side of the Wadi Hadh-ramaut, and a small stream, the Kheilah, runs through it. It is surrounded on all sides by the Āl Tamim, who are a Qu'aiti tribe. The walls, pierced by five gates and defended by twenty-five forts, enclose an area sufficient

[1] Incorrectly Sewun.

345. *Seiyūn from the palace roof*

346. *Seiyūn from the air*

347. *Houses in Seiyūn*

348. *The Kathīri Sultan's palace in Seiyūn*

349. *Shibām from the air looking east*

350. *Shibām from the Wadi Hadhramaut*

351. *Shibām, inside the Gate*

352. *Tarīm, from the air*

to hold over 2,000 houses and extensive gardens. 'Aidid is a wealthy suburb. All the houses are mud-built, but rich Seiyids with East Indian connexions own imposing mansions, fitted up with such modern conveniences as electric light and fans, telephones, ice-plants, and bathrooms and shower-baths with running water (photo. 206). Mosques are said to number 300, the elegant balconied minaret of one being the tallest in the Hadhramaut (photo. 191). The principal mosque adjoins the market square; there is an ancient religious academy (*rubat*). Within the city is an enclosure with a few houses inhabited by the Seiyids of Al Haddad, who are independent of the Kathīri Sultan.

Water is said to be good, but the drainage system is open. Tracks to Seiyūn (25 miles), Shibām (40), Mukalla (200). Post agency. There is a small landing-ground at Gharaf, 5 miles to the south-west.

YESHBUM. 14° 20′ N., 46° 52′ E. Upper 'Aulaqi tribal district, Western Aden Protectorate.

A walled town and trade centre, the headquarters of the Upper 'Aulaqi Sheikh. Its honey, which is exported, is famous throughout south-west Arabia. Tracks to Nisāb (35 miles), Ahwar (75).

APPENDIX A

DEEP INLETS (SHERMS) IN THE RED SEA

DEEP inlets of very similar form occur on the African and Arabian coasts. Owing to some sections of coast being still incompletely surveyed, it is often difficult to tell from existing charts whether an inlet is a true *sherm* or merely a shallow lagoon. Deep branching channels may be present beneath a shallow lagoon, as at Rābigh, described on page 70. About sixty inlets are classed as having the true sherm-formation, as follows:

(1) *The African Coast* (*north to south*). From the harbour of Quseir to Ras Benas, these inlets are few and far between, consisting only of Sherm Medamer, Mersa Mubarak, and Sherm ash Sheikh. South of Ras Benas, in Foul Bay, are several curiously shaped inlets, but from Ras Benas to Cape 'Elba only two may be regarded with certainty as sherms, the large branching Mersa Sha'ab, and Mersa Haleib, an anchorage lying between an islet with a crescentic southern shore and the mainland coast, which here trends north-west to south-east.

Between Cape 'Elba and Ras Rawāya is a series of eleven sherms close together, many of them beautifully formed and typical: Mersa Bela, Khor al Mar'ōb, Mersa Ribda (Eeles Cove), Khor Abu Assel, Mersa Masdud, Mersa Hamsayat, Mersa Wassa, Khor Abu Fanādīr, Sherm Abu Amara ('Abu Emma'), Khor Dhu Lawa (Khor Delweih), and Khor Shin'āb.

South of Ras Rawāya, about level with the southern end of the long island of Mukawwar, lies Khor Inkeifal (Munkafal), then a gap of about 36 miles till Mersa Arakiyai is reached. Then within another 36 miles between this inlet and Port Sudan are several inlets, of which at least four are regarded as true sherms: Mersa Fijja, Khor Bolonai, Khor Lokiai, Mersa Gwiyai. Next to the south is Port Sudan (fig. 15), and between it and Suākin several small bays and indentations, some having the designation 'mersa' but not apparently the typical structure. South of Suākin (fig. 16), Mersa Sheikh Ibrāhīm may be regarded as a true example, as may be the large, deep and branching Khor Nawarat, not far from the Eritrean frontier; some other inlets are called 'mersa', but may not have the typical structure. This name is scarcely found, and inlets of any kind are much fewer, south of the Eritrean frontier.

Some 26 sherms have thus been enumerated on the African coast, where they are most plentiful in the second quarter of the length of the Red Sea from its northern end.

(ii) *The Arabian Coast* (*north to south*). Sherms begin farther north than on the African coast, the northernmost being located between Maqsūr island and the mainland, just south of latitude 28° N. Southward follow Sherm Yahar, Sherm Jubba, Sherm Zubair, Sherm Qafafa, four inlets in the mainland (the first two having a most remarkable T-shaped configuration), then Sherm Na'mān, between Na'mān island and the mainland, a little north of latitude 27° N. Between this place and Ras Abu Madd lie Sherm Dumeigh, Sherm 'Antar, Sherm Wejh (harbour of Al Wejh); Sherm Habban and Sherm Minaibara (both about level with Marduna island). South of Ras Abu Madd follow another Sherm Habban, Sherm Hassey, and Sherm al Khor; then the large, narrow, irregularly branching Sherm Yenbo', some way north-west of Yenbo' harbour itself. Farther south, Sherm Bureiqa (north of Cape Abyadh), Sherm Kharrar (just south of 23° N.), and Rābigh harbour; several long inlets roughly parallel to the coast north of Cape Hātiba; and Sherm Ubhar, a deep long narrow inlet between this point and Jidda.

South of Jidda a long stretch of coast shows no inlets, nor do the names *Sherm* or *Mersa* occur. A very long inlet, Al Sharifa, parallel to the coast immediately north-west of Al Līth, is shut in by a long narrow island, Jezirat Qishrān, with a narrow opening to the sea at either end, but it has not the structure of a sherm.

In the southernmost division of the Red Sea, south of Al Qunfidha, are a number of inlets designated *khor*, some of which apparently have the peculiar structure under consideration, notably Khor Nohud, Khor al Birq, Khor al Wasm, Khor Makra, and Khor 'Itwad. This last lies some way north of the Farasān islands. Level with these islands are Khor al Wahla, a long and very narrow inlet without branches, and Mersa Bagla, a sharply defined, broadly oval bight. Inlets are much less numerous farther south, but possibly the large northward-facing anchorage north of Hodeida, east of Ras Katib, has the structure of a true sherm.

Among the Farasān islands the following inlets, or passages between islands, are almost certainly sherms: Khor Maadi between Great and Little Farasān islands; Khor Segīd, an oval inlet cutting into Little Farasān on the east; Al Qabr or Khor Hasayif, penetrating Great Farasān from the west and bending northward; and the long funnel which nearly bisects Dumsuk island from the north.

This enumeration of some 34 sherms by no means exhausts the indentations on the Arabian coast. There are other places designated *sherm* (or more rarely *mersa*), and some large bays designated *ghubba*, but they do not appear to have the typical structure of true sherms.

APPENDIX B

LIST OF THE EARLIER CALIPHS
(with the dates of their accession)

Abu Bekr	632
'Omar I	634
'Othman	644
'Ali	656
Hasan	661

(Omeiyads)		(Abbasids)	
Mu'āwiya I	661	Abul 'Abbas al Saffāh	750
Yazīd I	680	Abu Ja'far al Mansur	754
Mu'āwiya II	683	Al Mahdi	775
Marwān I	683	Al Hadi	785
'Abdul Malik	685	Harun ar Rashid	786
Al Walīd I	705	Al Amin	809
Suleiman	715	Al Mamūn	813
'Omar II	717	Al Mu'tasim	833
Yazīd II	720	Al Wāthiq	842
Hisham	724	Al Mutawakkil	847
Al Walīd II	743	Al Muntasir	861
Yazīd III	744	Al Musta'in	862
Ibrahim	744	Al Mu'tazz	866
Marwān II	744	Al Muhtadi	869
		Al Mu'tamid	870

APPENDIX C

THE 'AUDHALI TREATY

THE following is a free translation giving the substance of a treaty, based on tribal customary law ('*urf*), made between the 'Audhali tribesmen and their own Sultan.

Private settlement of disputes

(1) Any dispute may be settled by a voluntary peacemaker, without fee. He shall separate the parties, and whoever resists shall incur the customary penalty. After a week's interval he shall proceed to a settlement. If a tribesman involved in the dispute demands to see the record of the customary law, no order of the Sultan can prevent him.

Arrest and trial of offenders

(2) (a) An accused tribesman who is tried by the Sultan shall be judged by customary law. The summons shall be a thread from the fringe of the Sultan's kilt. Should the accused fail to appear within three days he shall incur a fine of one dollar; provided that in case of sickness or absence such period shall run from the date of his recovery or return. He shall also be liable to arrest but may be released upon giving up his dagger as bail for his appearance in Court. In default of arrest, or of appearance after having given bail, his ox shall be attached until he surrender.

Compensation for bloodshed

(b) A wound shall be kept under observation for the period of one year and the Sultan shall order a just compensation according to the nature of the wound. No compensation shall be paid for a trivial injury.

The Sultan's dues

(3) (a) The Sultan shall be entitled to receive hospitality when he requires it, and 'coffee money' [usually a sheep] on the occasion of a marriage or circumcision in his family, or on the 'demise of the crown'. He is also entitled to free entertainment, or a sheep in lieu thereof, when he visits a *locus*, e.g. in connexion with a boundary dispute.

> [*Note*. In all the Semitic desert countries, stones, or cairns, are used as landmarks. Jacob and Laban erected such a landmark as a reminder that there was to be no trespass beyond the limit thus marked out (*Genesis* xxxi. 45 ff.). The sacredness of landmarks was enforced by a curse on the remover of them (*Deuteronomy* xxvii. 17), and such removal was regarded as a peculiarly wicked action (*Hosea* v. 10; *Job* xxiv. 2). Doughty, in *Arabia Deserta*, refers to 'heaps of witness'.]

Debts due to the Sultan

(*b*) A debtor to the Sultan, whose field has been sequestrated, may release it by pawning his person or his ox, and he may release his ox by pawning his rifle.

Liability of shepherd

(4) (*a*) If a shepherd throw stones, to keep his flock from straying, he is liable in compensation to the owner only if he hit and kill a sheep at the rear of the flock.

Sequestration of stock

(*b*) Neither cattle nor the camels which are used in irrigation shall be attached during the breeding-season.

Garrisoning of Laudar

(5) The Bijeiris shall supply two-thirds of the garrison of Laudar and the Tuheifis one-third. The garrison shall be exempt from legal process and from market dues on purchases but shall pay market dues of one-eighth of the price on sales.

Tribal feuds

(6) (*a*) Feuds between the tribes of the 'Audhali confederation shall be settled by the tribesmen. The Sultan shall not intervene unless to impose a year's truce on the application of one of the tribes. No tribesman may enter the market-place of a hostile tribe unless he be weak or poor. If he has already entered he may not be harmed at the Sunday market but shall depart on Monday.

'Protected persons'

(*b*) The Sultan may grant or refuse permission to 'protected persons' to remain in the district. A 'protected person' is a stranger who lives under the patronage and protection of a tribesman of upright character. The patron may intercede with the Sultan on behalf of his protégé, and the matter shall be decided according to customary law.

Debtors

(7) A tribesman summoned for debt shall be allowed a week's delay. Failing payment within the week he shall pay 30 riyāls to the Sultan (or 15 riyāls to a member of the Sultan's house) as Court fees.

(8) Tribesmen shall pay to the naqib one load of red grain, and, for each ox owned by the tribesman, half a measure of corn and one scoop of millet.

Officers' fees

(9) A guard shall receive a fee of half a.riyāl for an arrest or the attachment of an ox, unless the defendant give up a rifle or dagger as bail for his

appearance in Court. Nothing shall be payable (except *ex gratia*) for his services on missions connected with disputes about irrigation rights or boundary marks, or to investigate complaints.

Fines for breaches of the peace

(10) The fine for a breach of the peace is payable to the person who separated the parties, or, failing this, to the Sultan.

Liability of camel-driver

(11) A camel-driver who uses a stick over a yard and a half long to drive the camel which works a well shall be responsible if the beast die.

Upkeep of well

(12) The Bijeiris shall be responsible for two-thirds of the upkeep of the well of Am Shubibiyah, and the Tuheifis for one-third. Any dispute between them shall be punishable with a fine of 70 cattle.

Offences committed on the Thira road

(13) Whoever is guilty of homicide on the Thira road [an ancient track, formerly paved, dating from pre-Islamic times, up the Kaur range beyond Al Kubeida] shall pay a fine of 70 cattle, and whosoever is guilty of theft on the said road shall pay four times the value of the stolen goods and four cows for sacrifice.

[*Note.* The cows are sacrificed on the scene of the theft and the flesh distributed to the poor. Such customs are almost certainly relics of pre-Islamic rites.]

Fines in kind

(14) If cattle stray off the road into crops the penalty is the fine of an ox; and the penalty for breaking into a house is also an ox.

Maintenance of post

(15) Two-thirds of the cost of entertainment at the post of Am Rasas shall be borne by the Bijeiris, and one-third by the Tuheifis.

Exemption of a Seiyid family

(16) The house of 'Omar ibn Ahmed al Jifri shall be exempt from payment of tithes, entertainment charges, and market dues.

[*Note*: The ancestor of this house, of whom there are many in the Hadhramaut, settled in the 'Audhali country at Al Kubeida. The case is a good example of the privileged position of Seiyids, who frequently act as professional peace-makers.]

This is the table of the customary law. Any amendment shall have reference to this document.

APPENDIX D

PLANTS OF ECONOMIC IMPORTANCE

1. *Trees and Shrubs*

Tamarisk (*ithil, tarfa*): several species of *Tamarix* occur in Arabia; *ithil* is usually *T. aphylla, tarfa* is applied to the smaller species, especially *T. mannifera*. Timber (of *T. macrocarpa* and others) used in building houses and boats, and for making bowls; also (in Aden Protectorate) for plough-stocks, yokes, and poles, while the green branches, twigs, and dried foliage are the favourite brushwood used in house-building, and in the stone and brushwood walls constructed to divert flood-water; foliage is also used to stiffen sun-dried bricks. Camels browse on tamarisk.

Acacia: several species are widespread, but Arabic names are not consistently applied; *samr* is usually *A. spirocarpa*; *talh* usually *A. Seyal*, characteristic of the Hejaz and used in shipbuilding on the Red Sea coast; *sānt* usually *A. scorpioides*; *qaradh* is *A. senegal* (leaves used for tanning); '*asaq* is *A. Asak*, common in Tihama and Hadhramaut; *dhub* is *A. mellifera*; *khereb* is *A. Edgeworthii*, common about Aden; *herut* is *A. etbaica*; *seyāl* usually *A. fasciculata*; '*urfut* is *A. orfota* (stated by Niebuhr to prevent camels' milk souring); *salīm* usually *A. flava*. In the Aden Protectorate the seeds of *samr* are eaten in times of famine. The widespread destruction, within 100 miles of Aden, of acacias to supply the colony with charcoal, has greatly reduced the various species forming the most important 'browse' for camels and goats from sea-level to 6,000 feet. Hollow thorns of some species, perforated by insects, produce a whistling sound.

Willows (*gharab*): reported from north-west of Riyādh, from near Kuweit, and from parts of the Yemen (San'ā, Ta'izz), but nowhere common. *Salix acmophylla* occurs in north-west Arabia.

Poplars (*quāq*): less common, but known from central Arabia and Sinai. *Populus nivea*, *P. graeca*, and *P. euphratica* are recorded from Sinai, where the name *safsāf* is used, though this more usually means the Egyptian willow, *Salix subserrata*. The trees mentioned in *Psalm* cxxxvii. 2 ('by the waters of Babylon') may have been *Populus euphratica*, common on the banks of the Euphrates, but not the weeping willow (*Salix babylonica, safsāf rūmi*), which despite its botanical name is really a native of China.

Socotran box: *Buxus Hildebrandtii* (Socoteri *methaye* or *metayne*), locally abundant in Socotra; the very hard wood might be a substitute for 'lignum vitae', if the small diameter of the stems, rarely more than a few inches, did not make its use impracticable for many purposes, though pulley-blocks for sailing-craft are made of it. The tree is said to grow also in the Qara mountains, and to be used for making threshing-sticks and heavy sticks pointed at both ends which are thrown as weapons.[1]

Oak (*mallūl*): collected in Midian by Burton; the species is *Quercus infectoria*, on which are found the galls known commercially as 'Aleppo' or 'Mecca' galls, caused by the egg-laying of the gall-wasp *Cynips gallae-tinctoriae*.

Cypress: in the cities of the high Yemen, probably introduced by the Turks.

Juniper: in mountainous districts. Burton recorded large trees of *Juniperus phoenicea* (' halibeh') at 4,000 feet in Midian. Unidentified species occur in the southern Hejaz, 'Asīr, and the Yemen, at altitudes above 6,000 feet. *J. macropoda* occurs in the mountains of 'Omān.

Eucalyptus (*khamé, galiptūs*): occasionally planted in the Yemen.

Wild Jujube (*Zizyphus Spina-Christi*, Ar. *'ilb*): see p. 485.

Mimusops Schimperi (Ar. *lebakh*): a large tree, the fruit of which may have been the 'persea' of Pliny and Theophrastus, and that mentioned in Egyptian records from the Eighteenth Dynasty onwards.

Balanites aegyptiaca: the hard wood of the *helej* is used for making domestic utensils; the tree also yields resin. In Egypt the fruit-stones have been found in Twelfth Dynasty tombs. The tree serves as fodder for camels and goats in the Aden Protectorate.

Mangroves: see pp. 193–197. Abūl 'Abbās an Nabāti states that the resin of the white mangrove (*Avicennia marina*; Ar. *shūra*) is a remedy for toothache, but that its fruit causes dizziness if eaten.

Ariata (*Conocarpus erectus*): reaches a height of 50 to 70 feet in parts of south Arabia; leaves dried for fodder; timber also probably used.

Tree- and bush-euphorbias: in the south-western highlands the arborescent *'amaq* (*Euphorbia Ammak*) is used to form hedges. The latex of these cactus-like plants, highly irritant to the human skin, contains some rubber, but is too resinous to be of value. A drastic purgative is prepared from the dwarf *E. officinalis*, which grows at the highest altitudes.

Prickly pear (*Opuntia decumana*; Ar. *balas turki*, 'Turkish fig'): this American plant, the only member of the true cactus order seen in Arabia, is used to form hedges in the south-western highlands, up to nearly 8,000 feet; fruit edible.

Bēn tree, *Moringa peregrina*: the seeds yield an oil used by watchmakers, and locally in Arabia as an unguent.

Wild figs: the *taulaq* (*Ficus vasta*) or 'Arabian banian' is a colossal tree with many secondary trunks. Other large species are the *vuda* (*F. populifolia*) and the *tha'b* (*F. salicifolia*).

Dūm-palm (*Hyphaene thebaica*): the branched *dūm, sār,* or *tāfi* has several uses; sweet pericarp of the fruits commonly eaten, buttons made

[1] Bertram Thomas, *Arabia Felix*, p. 68 (1932).

from the hard inner wall; the drink *nabidh* is procured from the tree; the leaves, called *sāf*, are made into mats, baskets, string, &c.; the wood resists decay and is used in building.

Other palms: a many-stemmed shrubby wild date (*Phoenix reclinata*) grows in the valleys of the south-western highlands from 2,000 to 5,000 feet; fan-leaved *nataq* palms, 40 to 50 feet high, in Wadi Hajr; and a dwarf palm (*ghadaf*), perhaps a species of *Nannorhops*, in 'Omān. For date-palm, *see* pp. 486–490.

Bead tree (*Melia Azedarach*): a tree with lilac-like flowers, planted in streets.

Portia tree (*Thespesia populnea*): a common strand-tree of the warmer . parts of the Old World, with mallow-like flowers and leaves like those of poplar, is planted in some places.

Baobab (*Adansonia digitata*, locally called *istanbuli*): occasionally planted in south Arabia; though rare in the Aden Protectorate.

Gold mohur: this name is applied to the 'flamboyant' tree (*Delonix regia*) with brilliant scarlet flowers and long flat pods, cultivated for ornamental purposes; also to a related wild species with white flowers. The Hindustani name *gulmūr*, 'peacock flower', became corrupted to 'gold mohur', formerly an Indian coin.

2. *Fruit Trees and Shrubs*

These, including some mentioned on pp. 484–487 and others less commonly grown, are apple (*tuffāha*), pear (*kummathrā, 'anbarūd*), quince (*safarjal*), guava (*jawāfa;* uncommon), apricot (*barqūq, mishmish*), peach (*firsik*; south-western highlands and 'Omān), plum (*anjās*; south-western highlands), cherry (*qerāsiā*; south-western highlands and 'Omān, rare). Besides the wild '*ilb* (*Zizyphus Spina-Christi*), the lotus plum or cultivated jujube (*Z. Jujuba*, Ar. *arj* or *'annab*), with large oblong fruit, is sometimes grown; it is not native of Arabia; and is supposed to have been the sole food of the lotus-eaters. Pomegranate (*Punica Granatum*, Ar. *rummāna*), sweet and sour kinds known (possibly the Socotran *P. protopunica* is the ancestral form).

Citrus fruits already grown in Arabia include sweet orange (*bortugala* (= Portugal) *hali*; at Hofūf especially), bitter or Seville orange (*tūbbai, tibba'*), sweet lime (*līm hali*), sour lime (*līm hāmidh*), lemon (*līmūn*; less common), citron (*utruj, turunj*; perhaps the 'apples' of Arabia Felix mentioned by Virgil, *Georgics*, ii. 126), mandarin orange (*Yusuf effendi*; grown at Lahej), and pummelo or shaddock (*līmūn hindī*; grown in the Bātina, 'Omān). Wild oranges (*tenage* in Socoteri) found in Socotra are not believed to be indigenous. Grapefruit, orange, and tangerine orange trees have been planted at Tāif. Suggestions for improved culture of citrus have been made.[1]

Grapes (*'anab*), raisins (*zabīb*): among many local varieties *al bayādh* (pl.

[1] K. S. Twitchell, *Rep. U.S. Agric. Mission to Sa'udi Arabia*, pp. 29, 30 (1943).

of *abyadh*, white), a seedless grape, is much esteemed in the Yemen; *beidh al hamām* ('pigeon's eggs') and *asābi' zeinab* ('Zenobia's fingers') are also white; *atrāf al 'adhāra* ('virgins' glances') is a black variety; *zeitūn* (literally 'an olive') is red. The vine is called *kaul* (plur. *akwāl*) or *habla* in the Yemen. 'Kissmisses' are small seedless raisins exported from Muscat.

Figs (*tīn*): common fig (*Ficus carica*), probably indigenous; sycamore fig (*F. sycomorus, balas, suqum*), fruit edible, believed to have been the 'sycamore' of the Bible. Some wild species also have edible fruits.

Mulberry (*tūt, tukkī*): the black mulberry, *Morus nigra*, is called also *habūn al mulūk* ('beloved of kings'?); the white mulberry, *M. alba*, is cultivated in Sinai.

Date palm: *see* pp. 486–490.

Tamarind (*Tamarindus indica*): *tamr hindī*, 'Indian date', is an Egyptian name; in Arabia it is often called *humar hindī*, from the red seeds.

Carob (*Ceratonia siliqua; kharruba*): cultivated in the south-western highlands; seeds the original carat weight of jewellers; the name is little changed from that of ancient Assyria.

Sebestens (in Egypt *mukhayt*; elsewhere *dabq*): a name applied to the edible fruit of several species of *Cordia*-trees, often confused. *C. Myxa*, from which wine is said by Pliny to have been made in Syria, is the one usually cultivated in Arabia; *C. crenata* is the *mukhayt el rūmi* of Egyptian gardens; another species grows in Abyssinia, and a fourth (*C. obliqua*) is the 'sebesten' of India (from Persian *sapistān*, 'dog's nipples').

Olive (*Olea europea; zeitūn*[1]): cultivated in parts of north-west Arabia and 'Omān. The wild olive (*O. chrysophylla; 'athum*) may be the ancestor of the cultivated tree; the black streak in the wood of the latter is said in Arab folk-lore to be a sign of mourning for the Prophet.

Tropical fruits: besides those mentioned, the following are grown in parts of south Arabia, mainly at low elevations, though in the Yemen banana and pawpaw are grown at 4,500 feet at Ta'izz; banana (*Musa paradisiaca; mauz*), pawpaw (*Carica Papaya; fefai*), custard apple (*Anona squamosa; khirmish* or *safarjal hindī*, 'Indian quince'), mango (*Mangifera indica; mankū*, or in the Yemen '*anbā*), jak-fruit (*Artocarpus integra*; Hindustani *kathal*). Lahej oasis in the south-west, and the coastal plain or Bātina of 'Omān, are among the principal localities for these fruits.

Wild edible fruits: *see* under '*ilb* tree (p. 485) and under 'Miscellaneous' (p. 600).

3. Nut-trees and Shrubs

Almonds: besides the true almond, *lauz kabir* (p. 486), the so-called Indian almond (*Terminalia Catappa; badām*), a large tree with broad clustered leaves, is cultivated in the south, partly for shade (as at Lahej),

---

[1] *zeitūn* is also applied to the guava about Aden.

partly for its edible nuts, resembling true almonds. Caju-nuts (*lauz hindī* or *hilb al 'azīz*), the seed of *Anacardium occidentale*, curved and almond-like, are imported.

Walnut (*jauz*): cultivated in Sinai, the Yemen, and the mountains of 'Omān.

Areca- or betel-nut (*Areca catechu; faufal*): occasionally cultivated in the Yemen and the Bātina of 'Omān. Both the nut and the vine yielding betel pan leaf (*Piper Betle*) are grown by the Ba Hassan tribe in a small wadi at some altitude in the Qu'aiti State, and are exported to Mukalla and other coastal settlements of the Eastern Aden Protectorate.

Coconut (*jauz hindī*, 'Indian walnut', or *jauz narjīl*): planted on the southern coast, especially in Dhufār (*see* p. 473). Small numbers in coastal gardens of the Eastern Aden Protectorate, and at Lahej and Aden.

Pistachio nut (*Pistacia vera; fistiq*); other species of *Pistacia*, the Tere- binth (*Pistacia Terebinthus; batam*), and the lentisc or mastic (*P. Lentiscus, mustakā*) occur in northern Arabia.

4. *Forage Plants, other than Native Species*

Lucerne or alfalfa (*Medicago sativa; qadb*): widespread in cultivation; grown in the south-west from sea-level to over 9,000 feet, wherever permanent irrigation exists, and at moderate altitudes in central and northern Arabia; according to Philby, also called *barsim*, a name usually applied to *Trifolium alexandrinum*.

Bitter vetch (*Vicia Ervilia*): cultivated in north-west Arabia; the Syrian name *kersenneh* is derived from a Sanskrit word meaning black.

Wild fodder plants: *see* under 'Camels' (p. 509). Other important fodders include varieties of *Sorghum* grown specially, and either fed to stock green or dried and stored; also hay of *tahaf* (*Eragrostis abyssinica*, p. 482), harvested before the plant seeds; and cowpea vines (p. 481), fed green or dried with the *dhura* leaves among which they grow.

5. *Pulses, Cereals*

Beans, peas, &c., include: broad bean (*Vicia Faba; fūl, bāql*); chick-pea or common gram (*Cicer arietinum; hamas*, also *nakhī* at Kuweit); pigeon-pea or dhal (*Cajanus Cajan; qishta*, at Aden called *tūrai*), cul- tivated in the Yemen and Aden Protectorate, and in oases farther north; lentil (*Lens culinaris; 'adas, bilsin*); green gram (*Phaseolus aureus; qusheri*); black gram (*Phaseolus Mungo; māsh, dizur aswad*), imported to Aden from India; *qatn* (*Phaseolus aconitifolius*), cultivated in the Yemen; chickling vetch (*Lathyrus sativus; jalbān*); fenugreek (*Trigonella foenum-graecum; hilbe* or, in the Yemen, *fussa*, served as a paste with salt and pepper). Chick-peas are not grown in the Aden Protectorate, but imported from India and Ethiopia, and used with bran and oilcake as concentrated feed for livestock and horses.

Fig-marigold (*Mesembryanthemum Forskahlei; samh*) covers large areas of stony desert in northern Hejaz. Fruits are gathered in bags, which are then beaten to separate the seeds; the flour is made into bread or into puddings with dates.

Sesame, gingelly (*Sesamum indicum; simsim*): oil (*salīt*) extracted from the seeds (*jiljilān*) by crushing in camel-mills.[1] In the Aden Protectorate the oil is very important, and oilcake is used as food for stock, and eaten by the people in times of scarcity.

Wheat (*burr, hinta, qamh*): *Triticum aestivum* and *T. durum* (macaroni wheat), both cultivated; the latter is possibly a descendant of a wild wheat, *T. dicoccoides*, found in Transjordan.

Barley (*sha'īr*): several species and varieties, among them *Hordeum vulgare*, and including the wild 'devil's barley', *sha'īr iblīs*.

Oats (*shūfān*): *Avena sativa* var. *abyssinica* is reported from the Yemen.

Millet: (1) *dhura* (in Socotra, *makedhīra*), several species and varieties of *Sorghum*, with grain red, yellow, or white, large or small, are grown, including *S. cernuum* var. *yemense*, *S. subglabrescens* var. *rubrocentrum* (*kubri*) and var. *arabicum* (*gia 'aidi*), *S. caffrorum* varieties *albida* (*ahnessi*), *usorum* (*gendab ahmar*), and *bicolor* (*gherb*); called *jowārī* at Aden. (2) *Dukhn, &c.*: *Pennisetum glaucum* (or *typhoides*), bulrush millet, is *dukhn* proper, though the name (said to be from *dukhān*, smoke, and to refer to the smoky aspect of the grain) may be sometimes used for *Panicum miliaceum*, broomcorn millet, or for *Eleusine*. *Pennisetum dichotomum*, foxtail millet, is called *thummām*, and *P. spicatum* (in Kuweit) *ilm* or *ulm*. *Eleusine coracana*, kurakkan or ragi in India, &c., is *keneb;* this last name and *msebeli* are used in the Eastern Aden Protectorate for Italian millet[2] (*Setaria italica*). In the Protectorate as a whole, *Sorghum* is called *dhura* in some highland districts, but elsewhere farmers use local names for the different varieties; general terms for the grain are *habb* and *ta'am*, while the Hindi name *jowārī* is used by merchants in Aden. *Pennisetum* is called *msebeli* instead of *dukhn* in Wadi Hadhramaut and adjoining districts, while *dukhn* is there applied to *Panicum miliaceum*, which is termed *siyal* in the Western Protectorate. These examples show how confusing is the usage of local names. *Eragrostis abyssinica* (p. 482) is *tahaf*.

Maize (*Zea Mays*): called *rūmī, hindī*, or *dhura shamīya*, i.e. 'Syrian millet'.

Rice (*Oryza sativa, ruz*): largely imported, also grown locally (p. 484).

6. *Industrial plants*

Cotton (*qutun*): despite small scale of cultivation (p. 475), several species occur. *Gossypium Stocksii*, the wild cotton of Dhufār, is indigenous. *G. arboreum* ('*otb*) is the species usually grown, and probably the one mentioned by Theophrastus (*Hist. Plant*, lib. iv, chap. 9)

[1] See Rathjens and Wissmann, *Südarabien-Reise*, iii, pp. 148–149, fig. 66 (1934).
[2] Ingrams, *Report on the Hadhramaut*, p. 55 (1937).

as cultivated in the island of Tylos (Bahrein) about 350 B.C. Races of *G. Nanking* are known from the Eastern Aden Protectorate; *G. barbadense* (*leked*), the species from which Egyptian long staple cotton is derived, has been introduced.

Hemp: plants yielding hemp-fibres include *Sansevieria Ehrenbergii* (*sēleb*, the fibre of which resembles bowstring-hemp (*S. zeylanica*), *dēnaq*, *haraq*), which is used in Nubia and Egypt for making ropes. Sunn-hemp (*Crotalaria juncea*) and Deccan or ambari hemp (*Hibiscus cannabinus*) have been cultivated in the Yemen.

Flax (*Linum usitatissimum*): has been tried experimentally.

Sugar-cane (*Saccharum officinarum; qasab as sukkar*; also called *qand*, a word of Persian origin); grown on a small scale, in Lahej oasis, &c.

Plants yielding dyes: *see* text, pp. 494–495. It may be added that the red dye of *waras* (*Flemingia rhodocarpa*) is yielded by a beautiful red powder covering the seed-capsules, and a black dye called *khudab* is made in the Aden Protectorate from an unnamed succulent growing at high altitudes.

Plants yielding gums and resins: *see* text, pp. 203–205.

7. *Medicinal Plants*

Aloes: *see* text, p. 208.

Hashish (*Cannabis indica*, hemp, an annual herb; Ar. *hashīsh*, literally 'grass'): in Arabia, though not eaten by respectable people, those who indulge eat it mixed with honey, sugar, and nutmeg: in Egypt it is smoked. The sale of hashish was forbidden in Aden a few years ago.

Opium poppy (*Papaver somniferum; afiūn*, or *khash-khāsh*, rattle, the latter name referring to the dry heads): formerly cultivated in the Yemen highlands. It has been reported as grown in parts of Upper Yāfa'; the seed is given to children to make them sleep, and is used as an ingredient of *sambusa* pastries. In Aden itself the sale of opium was forbidden a few years ago.

Castor oil (*Ricinus communis; tobsha'*, *khirwa'*; the oil, *dihn khirwa*, or at Aden called *salīt az zeit*, literally 'olive oil'): seeds used medicinally or as source of oil for lighting; light wood of large plants used for making charcoal.[1]

Camel grass (*Cymbopogon Schoenanthus; sakhbar*): this, the 'herba schoenanthi' of pharmacists, was known to the Greek physician Dioscorides late in the first century A.D.

Senna (*sunā*): the well-known purgative. *Cassia angustifolia* is usually known in Europe as Indian senna, wherever grown, while *C. Senna*, called Alexandrian senna, is considered superior. A third species, *C. italica*, '*ashreq*, is used in local medicine.

Datura (*Datura Metel; benj*) was the *jauz mēthel* of medieval Arab writers on medical subjects.

[1] Doughty, *Arabia Deserta*, vol. ii, chap. 6.

Colocynth (*Colocynthis vulgaris; handhal*): the seeds, from which an oil is prepared, are used in Arab medicine as a purgative and for expelling worms. Principal commercial source now the Sudan.

Withania somnifera (in the Yemen *'ubab*): a plant of the family Solanaceae used in native medicine (sometimes with garlic, in treatment of snake-bite).[1]

Chamomile: *Matricaria aurea, bābūnaj* (said to be from a place in 'Iraq); another Composite, *Achillea fragrantissima, qeisūn*, is used medicinally and perhaps in other ways, like ordinary chamomile.

Arabian wormwood (*Artemisia judaica; ba 'eythirān*) was formerly cultivated and exported, according to Forskål. The Arabic name is sometimes used for *A. herba-alba*, more properly called *shīh*.

Salvia nudicaulis (*daru*): formerly exported by the Dutch merchants of Mocha.

Wild rue (*shadhāb*): *Ruta chalepensis* and possibly other species.

Other plants used medicinally are mentioned under 'Miscellaneous' (p. 600).

8. Aromatic Plants

Anise (*Pimpinella Anisum; ānīsūn*).

Ajowan (*Ammi copticum; zamūtā*).

Coriander (*Coriandrum sativum; kabzare*): cultivated.

Dill (*Anethum graveolens; shibith, halwa*): used for flavouring; seeds sprinkled on dates in Al Hasa.

Fennel (*Foeniculum officinale; shamār*).

Cummin (*Cuminum cyminum; kammūn*): seeds used in the same way as caraway seeds, but the latter (*Carum carvi; karawiya*) are also used, being imported.

Black cummin: this name is sometimes applied to *Nigella sativa* (*quhta, shūnīz, habba sauda* or 'black seed'): seeds sprinkled on certain kinds of bread (and used in Europe for adulterating pepper); believed to have been the plant (Hebrew, *ketzach*) translated 'fitches' in the Bible (*Isaiah* xxviii. 25, 27), where it is explained that the small seed of fitches and cummin is not threshed with a sharp threshing-instrument or crushed out under a wheel, but beaten with a staff.

Rose (*ward*): rose-water (*mai ward*) is produced locally in the Shaibi country, Western Aden Protectorate, where acres are covered with straggling bushes. The species is *Rosa damascena*, damask rose, as in India—not *R. centifolia*, cabbage rose, as in Bulgaria. In Doughty's time at any rate 'attar of roses' was distilled by Indians at Mecca from roses grown at Tāif.[2]

Jasmine: *Jasminum Sambac* is cultivated, and *J. officinale* (*sherkhāt*)

---

[1] According to Hayyim Habshush, *Travels in Yemen* (in 1870), ed. S. D. Goitein (1941).

[2] *Arabia Deserta*, vol. ii, chap. 18.

grows wild, in the Yemen highlands and in the Qara mountains; an oil is extracted from the flowers.

Orris root (*Iris florentina; dahāq*): mountains of the Yemen (p. 202).

Screw-pine (*Pandanus tectorius;*[1] *kādhī*; in the Yemen, '*aūdh adh dhīb*, 'wolf's wood'): introduced from India, now a characteristic plant in the south-west, in tropical oases such as Lahej and the valleys up to 2,000 feet; the fragrant flower-heads are (or were) worn with sweet basil in men's turbans on festal occasions. Only male plants are found in Arabia.

Sweet basil (*Ocimum Basilicum; habaq*; in the Aden Protectorate known as *shokr*): cultivated for perfume, medicine, and as a kitchen herb; in the Yemen sprigs are stuck in men's turbans at marriages and other festivities; pieces are laid among clothes in chests (*see also* p. 601). Other species cultivated are *O. gratissimum* (*habaqbaq*) and *O. Vaalae* (*uāle*).

Thyme (*zatar*) is cultivated: *Thymus Serpyllum* and *T. Musilii* both appear to be used.

Marjoram (*Origanum Majorana; bardaqūsh*).

Lavender (*Lavandula vera; khūzamā*): other species grow wild in the south-western mountains.

Mint (*na‘nā‘, no‘z, fautenāq*): various species of *Mentha* are cultivated for use as febrifuge or cardiac medicines, to flavour tea and coffee, and as the source of a syrup.

Peppermint (*Mentha piperita; na‘nā filfil*): cultivated. Doughty[2] mentions peppermint growing in dry *seil*-beds at ‘Aneiza, near Tāif, and elsewhere. In the first case the seed had been brought from a distance, and the plant was considered medicinal.

(For frankincense, myrrh, &c., *see* pp. 203, 532.)

9. *Vegetables*

Garden peas (*Pisum sativum; bizāliya, ‘atar*).

French beans (*Phaseolus vulgaris; fasūliya, lūbī*).

Runner beans (*Phaseolus multiflorus; lūbī ahmar*, 'red lubiya'): one of the few plants which twine from right to left.

Lablab bean (*Dolichos Lablab; kisht, lūbiyā*).

Cowpeas (*Vigna sinensis; dijr*), cultivated in southern Arabia (pp. 481, 594).

Sword bean (*Canavalia gladiata; fūl hindī*).

Ladies' fingers, okra (*Hibiscus esculentus; bāmia*).

Tomato (*Lycopersicum esculentum; tamātīs*); in the Yemen (p. 485).

Egg-plant, aubergine, or brinjal (*Solanum Melongena; beidhinjān*) (p. 486).

Chillies and pepper: two kinds of chillies occur, *Capsicum annuum* (*bustas*), the source of cayenne pepper, and *C. frutescens* (*dhir filfil*), the paprika.

---

[1] Called *Pandanus odoratissimus* in some books on Arabian travel.

[2] *Arabia Deserta*, vol. ii, chaps. 14, 16, 17.

Cucumber (*Cucumis sativus; khiyār, qiththā*): several varieties. In the Amiri highlands, Western Aden Protectorate, small vessels, 2–3 inches long, are said to be made from the ripe yellow fruits of another species, *C. prophetarum*.[1]

Loofah (*Luffa aegyptiaca; tūrīā*); name derived from Arabic *lūf*.

Bottle-gourd (*Lagenaria siceraria; dubbādībba*).

Water melon (*Colocynthis Citrullus; habhab, batīkh*): there is also a small yellow melon, with yellow flesh and black seeds, like a water melon. Some local melons are rather tasteless, as in parts of Al Qasīm (Sa'ūdi Arabia), where a sweeter variety called *fureiduni*, originally imported from Az Zubeir near Basra, is also grown.[2]

Musk or sweet melon (*Cucumis Melo; yaqtīn, kherir*, also in 'Iraq *batīkh*; the wild form *smitt*): also much grown, slices of water and musk melons being sometimes served together, at any rate in Al Qasīm.[3]

Pumpkin (*Cucurbita maxima; qara'*).

Marrow (*Cucurbita Pepo; qara' kosa*): grown in Sinai.

Beetroot (*Beta vulgaris; banjar, shawandar*).

Carrot (*Daucus Carota; jazar*).

Radish (*Raphanus sativus; fijl*).

Ginger (*Zingiber officinale; zanjabīl*): grown in coffee plantations (sometimes used for flavouring coffee).

Potato (*Solanum tuberosum; findāl, batāta*, the latter also applied to the sweet potato, *Ipomoea Batatas*); for both vegetables, see p. 485.

Taro (*Colocasia esculenta; sanj, kurkum*): tuber edible.

Artichoke (*Cynara Scolymus; kharshuf*, also *ardī shauki* from which the English name is probably derived): the true artichoke, with edible bracts surrounding the thistle-like flower-head. The cardoon (*Cynara cardunculus; shūk al hamīr*, 'donkeys' thorn') also occurs.

Edible campanula (*Campanula edulis; khubz al 'uqāb*): grows in the south-western mountains, above 7,000 feet; the thick roots were, and probably still are, eaten; related to the rampion, formerly cultivated for this purpose in England.

Jew's mallow (species of *Corchorus*): *C. olitorius* (*malukhiya*), a common vegetable in Egypt, Sudan, Syria, &c., is also grown in Arabia; in south Arabia *C. antichorus* is known as *saghrab*.[4] The English name originates from *Job* xxx. 4, where the Hebrew *mallūach* is translated 'mallows' in the Authorized Version (though the Revisers substituted 'salt-wort'). In India another species of *Corchorus*, an annual about 10 feet high, furnishes jute-fibre.

[1] This statement, hitherto unpublished, is based on specimens and information obtained by the British Museum (Natural History) Expedition in October 1937.
[2] Philby, *Arabia of the Wahhabis*, p. 295.
[3] Philby, op. cit., p. 256.
[4] Freya Stark, *A Winter in Arabia*, Appendix i, p. 317 (1940).

Onions (*Allium Cepa; buslī istanbūlī, buslī turkī* or collectively *basal*, plur. of *basla*, a bulb); garlic (*Allium sativum, thūm*); leek (*Allium Porrum; karāt* or *basal 'arabī*), the wild parent of which, *A. ampeloprasum, basal al 'afrīt,* occurs in southern Palestine; shallot (*A. ascalonicum,* first seen by the Crusaders at Ashkelon; *buol*). See also p. 473.

Agati (*Sesbania grandiflora; seseban*): a leguminous plant, cultivated in parts of the Tihama.

Asparagus (*Asparagus officinalis; sūf al hirr,* cat's hair): cultivated in the coffee districts.

Celery (*Apium graveolens; karafs*).

Parsley (*Petroselinum crispum; baqdūnīs,* a corruption of the Turkish name *maghdūnos,* Macedonian).

Cabbage (*Brassica oleracea; lahāna*) and cauliflower (*qarnabīt*), both cultivated in parts of the Yemen.

Mustard: a field mustard with purple flowers (a variety of *Brassica campestris; khardal*) is cultivated in the Yemen as an oil seed; Indian or brown mustard (*B. juncea*) also occurs.

Garden cress (*Lepidium sativum; half, habb reshād*).

Lettuce (*Lactuca sativa; hiss*).

Spinach (*Spinacia oleracea; sbanak,* both this and the English name being probably derived from a Persian root); also spinach beet (*siliq*). Certain plants of quite a different family are used in the same way, e.g. *Amaranthus oleraceus, shedēb hindī,* and *A. chlorostachys* and *A. mangostanus,* both known as *dadh.*

10. *Miscellaneous*

Saltbush (*Suaeda monoica; 'asal*): the coastal plant from which the Yemen Arabs formerly made potash (*hutam* or *dulūk*), a dilute solution of which was used for washing clothes before the introduction of soap.

Solanum coagulans (*bēkamān*): said by Forskål to have been used for turning sour the milk of asses.

Calotropis procera (*'ushar,* pregnancy): a bush or small tree with glaucousgrey leaves; in the south-western highlands characteristic of the foothills; the silky floss packing the inflated seed-vessels has many uses, like kapok; the plant yields *sūkkar al 'ushar,* a tapioca-like substance sometimes used as a substitute for flour. In parts of south-west Arabia the plant is used in the manufacture of gunpowder.

Fish poison: several species of leguminous plants of the genus *Tephrosia* (*dhafar*) are widely used in Africa and tropical America as well as Arabia. In the latter country the practice was recorded by Niebuhr, and more recently by the Yemeni Jew Hayyim Habshush, that the black seeds are used to narcotize fish.[1]

Tinder: the pith of a plant of the Asclepiad family, *Leptadenia pyrotechnica* (*markh*), is used by some Arabs when making fire by rubbing

[1] See Scott, *In the High Yemen,* p. 238, Note C (1942).

sticks together; the hard wood used is that of a tree, *Cordia Gharaf*. Another species of *Leptadenia*, *L. arborea* (*qorenna*), has a fruit which is edible when cooked.

Bulbs (*basla*, plur. *basal*): besides onions and other cultivated bulbs (p. 600), many bulbous plants grow wild, and the bulbs of some are used: *basla al rubah*, baboon bulb (*Pancratium maximum*), *basla al hanash*, snake bulb (*Haemanthus arabicus*); '*asansal* (*Colchicum Szovitsii*, related to the English meadow saffron); the little Aden lily (*Littonia minor*) and the yellow 'shum-shum' lily (*Albuca Yerburyi*); species of *Iris* (four in number), and of *Gladiolus*, *Crinum*, *Ixiolirion*, *Bulbine*, *Dipcadi*, *Kniphofia* and *Scilla*. An asphodel, *Asphodelus tenuifolius* (*barwaq*) is one of the plants used by the beduin in making brick cheese (*īqt*).

Rakh (*Salvadora persica*): the frayed wood of this shrub is a favourite with the beduin for tooth-brushes. The fresh fruit (*mashg*) and dried fruit (*berīr*) are eaten, while a decoction of the bark is believed to be a tonic; in the Western Aden Protectorate the fresh fruit is called *mered*, and the crushed leaves are applied as poultices to wounds. Forskål stated that the crushed leaves were used with fruits of *Cocculus pendulus* (*kebāth*) as a remedy for the tumours caused by the guinea-worm (*Filaria medinensis*) (p. 455). Camels readily eat *rakh*, but smell unpleasantly afterwards.

Kebāth, also *lebakh al jebel*, *turakh* (*Cocculus pendulus*, mentioned above): a liquor called *khamr al majnūn* was, according to Forskål, prepared from this plant.

Caralluma: in this genus of the Asclepiad order, *C. dentata* (*dra't al kalb*) and *C. quadrangularis* (*gholak*, a name also applied to some euphorbias) are small cactus-like plants with edible stems and fruits, though the flowers smell like carrion.

Carissa edulis (*la'dh*): a wild shrub with edible fruit.

Cassytha filiformis (*shubbota*): a parasitic plant resembling dodder; berries edible, tasting rather like pepper.

Capers: *Capparis galeata* (*lasaf*), *C. decidua* (*sodad*), and *C. spinosa* (*kabar*, '*alas*) have edible flowers and fruits. Formerly pilgrims to Sinai lived for forty days on caper-berries at Hammam Fara'ūn. The capers of commerce, produce of *C. spinosa*, are pickled in France and Italy. *C. galeata* is eaten by camels, and the leaves of *C. spinosa* are pounded to scrape the hair off water-skins.[1]

Preventive against clothes'-moths: the leaves of *Cleome brachycarpa* (*khuzām*), a spider-wort, are sold in Aden market to put with clothes as protection against moth; flowers of white melilot (*Melilotus alba*, *remān*) are laid among clothes for their fragrance; and *see under* 'Sweet basil' (p. 598).

Tarthūth, *zubb al ardh*, *masrūr* (*Cynomorium coccineum*): the stems,

[1] Freya Stark, *A Winter in Arabia*, Appendix I, p. 317 (1940).

peeled and sun-dried, have a flavour recalling both turnip and potato;
or they may be pounded into a flour and made into balls with soured
milk; *see* pp. 198, 199.

Camel-thorn (*Alhagi maurorum*; '*āqūl* at Kuweit and in 'Iraq, though
this name is elsewhere applied to other leguminous trees; also *shok
shibram*): a honey-like sap appears on the leaves in hot weather,
hardening into brown drops; this product is exported from Persia,
and called 'manna', though distinct from that of the Bible (p. 201).

NOTE: references to other useful Arabian plants appear in many books;
see especially Appendix I to Freya Stark's *A Winter in Arabia* (1940).

THE ARAB COUNTRYMAN'S DIVISION OF THE YEAR INTO SEASONS, AND HIS WEATHER-LORE, ETC.

THE official Moslem lunar year, with its retrocession of any given day in a lunar month, 10, 11, or 12 days[1] in each solar year, is not used in reckoning the seasons for pastoral and agricultural purposes. Both beduin nomads and settled cultivators have their own divisions of the year into seasons, guiding themselves largely by the stars. Sailors in the Red Sea have also their peculiar way of reckoning, to which brief allusion is made below.

North-west Arabia

Since the climate differs in several parts of the peninsula, the year is differently divided into seasons. Among certain beduin tribes of north Arabia, for example the Ruwalla,[2] it is regarded as consisting of five seasons, beginning in October, namely *sferi, shitā, rabī', seif,* and *qeiz. Sferi* corresponds to the season of autumnal rains (*al wasm*). *Shitā,* the winter, consists of two halves, the first lasting from about the beginning of December to late January, the second continuing till about the beginning of March; the transition may be abrupt, woollen coats being discarded on 21 January. *Rabī'* (the period of plenty) is indefinite, depending on rainfall; it may begin as late as March; or (according to some tribes) it may occasionally begin in November, when the first grasses spring up, and last till April; or, again, in some years there is no *rabī'* at all; the word cannot, therefore, strictly be translated 'spring'. If rain is plentiful in *seif* (early summer) and again in autumn (the *wasmi* rains), perennial plants flower the following February or March; but if *seif* is dry, these plants make poor pasture in spring and do not flower till *qeiz* (late summer).

The rains are divided by the northern beduin into *al wasm, ash shitāwi, as smāk,* and *as seifi,* corresponding approximately to the first four of the above seasons (the fifth, *al qeiz,* having normally no rain). By some tribes these are subdivided into periods of days corresponding to the appearance of particular stars. Thus, among the Ruwalla in the north-west, the year begins early in October with the first heavy rain following the appearance of *Sheil* (more correctly *Suheil,* Canopus), which is followed by *Thureiya* (the Pleiades) and *Jauza* (Gemini). These periods, called *ash sheilāwi, ath thureiyi,* and *al jauzāwi* respectively, cover about three months, October–December, and together comprise the rains of *as sferi* or *al wasm.* When Canopus appears the nomads leave the borders of

---

[1] The lunar year is shorter than the solar by just over 10 days and 21 hours.

[2] Almost all the information given about north Arabia is from A. Musil, *Manners and Customs of the Rwala Bedouins,* chap. i (1928), and the spelling of the Arabic terms is little altered from Musil's representation of the tribal dialect.

settled districts and wander into the desert in search of the new pasture which will spring up, being also careful to move their camps from dry river-beds which may now be swept by autumnal floods. This period is followed by the star *Ash Sha'era* (Sirius), whose reign lasts forty nights, corresponding approximately to the season of winter rains (*ash shitāwi*), ending about 20 February. After Sirius the ruler for fifty nights is *As Smāk* (Arcturus), the period of spring rains (identical in part with *rabī'*, but not entirely, since *rabī'* is variable and in certain years non-existent). About mid-April the reign of the stars ends, as summer (*seif*) then begins and lasts till about the beginning of June, being followed by the four dry months of *al qeiz*, till early October. Most ordinary beduin know no other way of dividing the year.

If the earlier autumnal rains, *ash sheilāwi* and *ath thureiyi*, are copious, grasses and other annuals reach full growth and camels have fresh pasturage before winter (*ash shitā*) sets in. Most important of all is *ath thureiyi*, which, with the still later *jauzāwi* rains, assures the growth of both annuals and woody plants and banishes fear of hunger. The spring rains (*as smāk*) will not by themselves assure abundant pasturage, unless the ground has previously been soaked by autumn rain.

The hottest weather, *hamm al quleiben*, occurs in late summer (*al qeiz*); the next hottest spell, *hamm ash sheil*, just before the rise of Suheil (Canopus) early in October. In *ash shitā*, the winter, the time of greatest cold, called *al marba 'aniya* (possibly an alternative form for *arba'iniya*, the forty days), is from about 11 December to 20 January; in the Syrian Hamād, in Al Wadiyān, Al Hisma, and other northern districts, including the Nafūd, the ground is often covered with white frost (*halīt*), trees and bushes being white with hoar-frost (*jelīd*). Snowfalls (*felejat ad dunyā*) occur annually, but usually the large flakes (*thuweirāt*) do not lie more than a day (though in northern Syria losses in sheep and goats befall their owners). Cold nights do not begin to be relieved by occasional warm ones till about mid-February; in the weeks following the *marba 'aniya* the nights are still so cold that men and animals suffer, so the beduin subdivide this period into the *sab'a semm* ('seven nights of poison'), the *sab'a dem* ('seven nights of blood', when the noses of camels bleed from the cold), and the *yesīr ad desem w'lā yesīr*, the time when the fat (of camels) increases and decreases; still later is the *bard* (*barid*) *at tawīlein* ('cold of the two giants', so called because the air, though warm close to the heated ground, still cools off a few feet above, whereby the camel and the date-palm still suffer much from cold).

The dew (*tall, tofal, nida*), plentiful throughout the year, and on which vegetation in many districts depends for its existence, is believed by the beduin to be sent by the moon to refresh grasses and annuals generally (*'ushb*), and woody plants (*shajar*).

Hail sometimes falls, with or without rain, and the stones (*halūb*) may be large enough to wound or even kill a young camel.

A light wind is *hāwa* or *habūb*, a strong one *salf*. The west wind, the most frequent, rising in summer regularly about two hours after noon and tempering the heat, is called *barrad* or *da'dā'i*. The north wind, *ash shamāli*, blowing much in winter and dispersing cloud, is called *as salaita*; but south winds, *adh zhibli* (= *al qibli*), also blow in winter at times, to the delight of the nomads, as they bring rain (*as siqaiye*, 'that which gives drink'). The east wind, *ash sherzhi* (*sharqī*), said to be always followed by the west, usually blows only for three or four days, but at the end of *as smāk* (the spring rains) and of *al qeiz* (late summer) it may blow very strongly for seven days as an exceedingly hot dry *simūm* (a prolonged *khamsīn*), which women and children could not endure were it to blow longer. No one, however, dares curse the wind, as all winds are from God.

A moonless winter night with brilliant stars and icy-cold north-west wind (locally *an nachbe*, for *an nakbā*) is called *jird*; a night with stiff, cold west wind, *shalta*; a warm cloudless night, *qamra zerīzh* (? 'black moon'); a warm cloudy night, *zalma delqes*; a dark rainy night, *ghadrā* ('thick darkness').

Rain is believed to be caused by the new moon, which sucks up tiny drops from the great sea (the Mediterranean), places them in symmetrical rows, and forms therefrom thin clouds, *gheim*. These mists form in the far west, whither Allah sends an angel on the appearance of the star Canopus above the horizon in autumn, when the beduin sorely need both water and pasture. The angel compels the mists to cluster into thick clouds, which he drives eastwards before him on his camel, till they discharge rain on the territories of the Ruwalla and other beduin. Any cloud which resists is beaten by the angel with his camel-stick into thunder and lightning (*yer'aj*), when the frightened cloud gives up all its water and disappears. Much other lore exists concerning clouds and rain.

South-west Arabia

Some of the more general terms are used in other parts of Arabia as well; for instance, *gheim* is applied to the wet mist which in winter lies thick on the Kaur ranges of the south-west from dusk till about 9 a.m. (though a more general term for mist in the Aden Protectorate is *madhūra*, while dew, which is often very heavy, is called *nedwa*). Apart from this, the whole of the above relates to northern districts, with no summer monsoon rains.

In the south-west the settled cultivators in particular use the solar year, dividing the seasons largely by the stars, especially the Pleiades, the Ox, the dog-star (Sirius), Arcturus, Orion, and Gemini.[1] But the climate is different, particularly in the south-western highlands, where the *matar as seif* (spring or early summer rains) and *matar al kharīf* (late summer rains) figure largely. According to Rossi,[2] on the Yemen plateau about

[1] Wyman Bury, *Arabia Infelix*, pp. 109, 110, and other writers.
[2] *L'Arabo parlato a San'a* (1930).

San'ā four principal agricultural seasons are recognized: *jiyād*, the harvest of late winter; *dithā*, the harvest of spring and summer; *'allām*, the rainy season (corresponding to *matar al kharīf*); and *sorāb*, the autumn harvest. But in parts of the Yemen Tihama these seasons are reduced to three, *seif*, *kharīf*, and *'aqb*, corresponding respectively to the summer, autumn, and winter harvests.

Most cultivators in the Western Aden Protectorate divide the year into three seasons, approximately as follows: *seif*, roughly amounting to March, April, May, and June, the season when crops depend on such rains as may fall at the end of the NE. monsoon; *kharīf*, that is July, August, September, and October, the time of the SW. monsoon; and *shitā*, November, December, January, and February, when no monsoon rain is expected, but at rare intervals storms from the sea may bring a few inches of rain to districts within about 40 miles of the coast. Though much of the country is under controlled irrigation, failure to observe the correct times may easily result in loss from unfavourable climatic conditions, pests, and diseases.

The following two examples show the close attention paid to particular astronomical phenomena in this part of Arabia. (i) *The Plough*: the seven stars of the Great Bear are carefully watched in the season of summer rains (*kharīf*); in the coastal districts of the Western Aden Protectorate great attention is paid to times of sowing crops, especially varieties of *Sorghum*, within the period that these seven stars, observed just before dawn, are above the horizon; when all seven stars are 'up' together, the planting-season is considered over till the following March, no matter what be the state of the irrigation-water supply. (ii) *The Sun*: above 6,000 feet, where temperature becomes of paramount importance in the growing of tropical or subtropical crops, especially *Sorghum*, the 'Audhalis and other tribes of the plateau (either in the north-eastern Yemen or the adjacent parts of the Aden Protectorate) observe the passage of the sun. When it is seen through a hole in a roof to be overhead in early summer, the cultivator will plant his *Sorghum* and expect it to grow quickly in the hot, dry weather.

It appears that in Subeihi territory, west of Aden, the solar months are called *shuhūr an nujūm* ('the months of the stars'). The calendar there used is sometimes termed the Coptic Calendar but, though the months may begin and end on the same dates, their names, though apparently not used by the tribes surrounding the Subeihi, are those used by the Syrian Christians (whereas the Coptic Christians use entirely distinct names, of different origin). The names, from January to December, are *kānūn ath thānī, shubāt, ādhār, nīsān, mabkar, hazīrān, tammūz, āb, eilūl, tishrīn al auwal, tishrīn ath thānī, kānūn al auwal; mabkar* (May) may be a local form for the more usual *eiyār*. This calendar is also used in the Sultanate of Lahej, where it is said to have been introduced after the Turkish occupation of 1915–1918; in that district at any rate (and probably wherever this calendar is used), the first day of each month is the 14th of the corresponding month in the Gregorian Calendar, e.g. 1st *kānūn ath thānī* falls on 14 January, and so on—probably an indication that the Gregorian correction has not been adopted, but that the Julian reckoning is still used, as among the Christians of Ethiopia.

In the Eastern Aden Protectorate 40 days of extreme heat, the *arba'- iniya*, are expected from 4 May onwards, before the monsoon season, and another hot period of 8 days is looked for later in the year.

The Lunar Mansions

According to Landberg[1] an ancient system used in the Dathina, south of the Kaur al 'Audhilla, resembles and also differs in some ways from the systems used in the north. The year is divided into four seasons (*faqal*, plur. *aqfāl*), each of which is subdivided into seven shorter periods, making twenty-eight in all, each distinguished by a particular star or constellation; some of these stars are thought lucky or the reverse for certain undertakings. Each of the twenty-eight periods lasts 13 days, except the first period of the fourth season, which lasts 14 days, so that the year totals 365 days. The first season, *seif* (summer), dominated by *Al Iklīl* (Scorpio), begins about 21 April; the second, *kharīf*, begins about 21 July, its star being *As Suheil* (Canopus); the third, *shitā*, presided over by *Ath Thureiya* (Pleiades), begins on 21 October; the fourth season, *rabī'*, begins on 21 January with *Al Jabha* (certain stars of Leo). The first star of each season, called *abu*, 'father', of the season, is said always to rise on a Friday at daybreak.

From more recent information it is evident that a similar division of the year into twenty-eight periods is in common use over the districts from Upper Yāfa' to Lower 'Aulaqi, and as far east as the eastern districts of the Hadhramaut. It is clearly a form of the 'Lunar Mansions', which are widely used in the East. For example, here the First Mansion of the Spring, *Geminorum*, begins on 31 December; its Arabic name, *Al Hana'*, means the star-shaped mark on a camel's neck caused by branding with a red-hot iron; all the seasons of the year will begin on the same day of the week as the first day of this Mansion. Few Arabs in the Aden Protectorate to-day, however, claim to be able to recognize the stars of the Mansions.[2]

Nautical Reckonings

The following paragraphs deal with systems of reckoning used by sailors or by landsmen in certain maritime districts.

[1] *Glossaire Datinois*, vol. ii, pp. 1092–1110 (1920).
[2] A table, at present unpublished, has been compiled by Mr. B. J. Hartley, Agricultural Adviser to the Aden Protectorate, from information given by Seiyid Muhammad ibn Hashim, a local Arab with a knowledge of astronomy, and from A. M. H. Samaha, *Arabic Names of Stars*, Helwan Observatory, Bulletin 39, Cairo, 1944 (Egyptian Ministry of Public Works).

During the SW. monsoon the current, setting towards India, is called *hindi*; during the NE. wind the current sets strongly to the west, and is then deflected north-westwards at the strait of Bab al Mandeb, whence it is termed *shami* (northern). Sailors and fishermen note the changes in temperature of the water and current, and the presence of weed and phosphorescence, before the change in the wind makes itself felt. During the SW. monsoon season also, when northerly winds (*shamāl*) periodically blow, landsmen in sandy coastal districts, such as those of Subeihi territory (or, in the Eastern Protectorate, Wadi Hajr), move inland to higher altitudes, to escape the dust-storms and wind.

The *Nehruz Calendar*, a cycle of 260 days, is spoken of by Arab sailors from the Persian Gulf, who visit the Aden Protectorate, as beginning on 18 September, *Al Fargh al Muqaddam*, The Leader (the same day and almost the same Arabic name as that of the 21st Lunar Mansion, *Pegasi*). From this date the days are counted during the sailing season, when long passages are made on the Trade Winds. From 6 June (beginning of the 13th Lunar Mansion, *Scorpionis*, Arabic *Al Qalb al Aqrab*) to 17 September (end of the 20th Lunar Mansion, *Aquarii*, in Arabic *Al Khiba*) the days are not counted, as the mariner then careens and refits his ships, purchases a shipment of dates (which are then being harvested), and rests with his crew.

According to Klunzinger, Egyptian sailors in the Red Sea divide the year into twelve periods of very unequal length, dominated by certain stars and characteristic types of weather. Their calendar has many peculiarities, such as the first period beginning about 20 February, a day called 'the little sun', on which no captain will sail, but waits for strong winds at the end of the period, while the second period begins with 'the great sun' (the vernal equinox), and consists of 30 to 40 days of high tides and gusty weather; the third period, from the *dufūn ath Thureiya* (setting of the Pleiades), comprises the *arba'iniyat as seif* or 40 days of summer. These examples must suffice. This calendar appears to correspond in some ways with the systems outlined above, but also presents many differences.[1]

The recurrence of certain numbers of days, particularly 40, in these systems of reckoning, is noteworthy. In Egypt many places are called Arba'in (forty) a name supposed to refer to the Companions of the Prophet; while the old camel route from Asyut to El Fasher (Darfur) is called the Darb al Arba'in, a name believed to indicate the number of days' journey between the two places.[2] It cannot here be stated whether any common ground exists for these allusions to the number forty (cf. *Exodus* xxiv. 18; *Matt.* iv. 2; *Acts* i. 3; etc).

[1] C. B. Klunzinger, *Upper Egypt*, pp. 301–302 (1878).
[2] G. W. Murray, 'The Road to Chephren's Quarries', *Geographical Journal*, vol. xciv, pp. 97, 112 (August 1939).

APPENDIX F

SOCOTRA

SOCOTRA is the largest and most easterly island of an archipelago lying some 120 miles from the coast of Africa, nearly opposite the eastern horn which terminates in Cape Gardafui, under the 12th parallel N. latitude. The principal other islands are the Brothers, frequently called the Sisters by the older navigators, consisting of two islets, Semha and Darzi, slightly to the southward; and 'Abd al Kuri, the second in size and nearest to Africa. The Brothers as well as 'Abd al Kuri are surrounded by banks covered by only 10 to 30 fathoms of water. The former bank is united to that on which stands Socotra, but from 'Abd al Kuri it is separated by a valley of 100 fathoms, while 'Abd al Kuri is cut off from the extensive projecting shelf of Gardafui by a narrow trough several hundred fathoms deep. The summits of the larger islands are now known to be among the land surfaces of the globe which have longest, if not always, held their heads above the sea, their sculptured peaks and pinnacles attesting to the waste and wear they have so long endured. They have been mute witnesses, probably since earliest Palaeozoic times, of the drowning of many lands around them, and of the uplifting from the ocean of mighty ranges on the two continents towards which they now look, and of which in their wonderful vicissitudes they have formed a part (photos. 353, 354).[1]

Socotra is some 75 miles long from east to west and has an average breadth of 20 miles. The whole island is mountainous along its axis; the highest peaks of granite protrude from the limestone plateaux and are deeply scored with torrent-beds, which in places may cross a stretch of boulder-strewn plain before reaching the sea. The eastern half of the island is dominated by the Haggier range, reaching over 4,000 feet, and it is in this region that the most favourable conditions of rainfall and vegetation are found. West of this range drier conditions prevail on the limestone plateaux which cover the higher parts of the island, until granite again appears in the far west (fig. 47).

Of the plains below the mountain scarps, that of the southern coast extends as a narrow plain some 30 miles long between the limestone hills and the sea. On the northern coast the plain behind Hadibu, the principal port and seat of Government, is a boulder-strewn area of some 12 square miles surrounded by spurs of the Haggier. Farther west and inland of the fishing settlements of Mouri, Deham, and Goba', lies the main northern coastal plain, covering some 50 square miles.

Climate. The climate is torrid, though tempered somewhat by the NE. monsoon, which brings rain in the cool season from November to March, and later the hot season is relieved in June, July, and August by the

---

[1] *The Natural History of Socotra and 'Abd al Kuri,* chap. i, pp. 16, 17 (1903).

high winds of the SW. monsoon. The most unpleasant season is May, when great heat and humidity characterize the period of calm airs between the monsoons.

The following figures for one rainfall station established at the R.A.F. station west of Kathub (Qatub), on the northern coastal plain, indicate the nature of the rainfall to be expected in the drier parts of the island. At the higher altitudes, and particularly on the Haggier range, the rainfall may be expected to be very much greater, while above 2,000 feet cloud and mist and occult precipitation are factors responsible for the existence of the moist highland zone, the most productive and attractive part of the island.

Rainfall at Kathub (Socotra)

Month	1943		1944		1945	
	mm.	in.	mm.	in.	mm.	in.
Jan. . .	0·01*	0·001*	4·8	0·19	3·6	0·14
Feb. . .	0·1	0·04	2·1	0·07	3·5	0·14
Mar. .	0·01	0·001	31·4	1·24	nil	nil
Apr. . .	0·01	0·001	0·01	0·001	nil	nil
May . .	0·01	0·001	nil	nil	4·3	0·17
June . .	nil	nil	nil	nil	91·0	3·58
July . .	nil	nil	0·6	0·02	0·01	0·001
Aug. . .	0·01	0·001	nil	nil	nil	nil
Sept. .	3·2	0·13	nil	nil	4·0	0·16
Oct. . .	3·8	0·15	4·1	0·16	21·3	0·84
Nov. .	89·6	3·53	60·2	2·37	5·5	0·22
Dec. . .	75·2	2·96	76·6	3·02	—	—
Year . .	171·9	6·81	179·8	7·07	[133·2]†	[5·25]†

* The figures 0·01 millimetres and 0·001 inches indicate only a trace of rainfall which was immeasurable.

† The totals for 1945 are exclusive of December, when no recordings were made.

Vegetation (see pp. 207, 208). The Socotran flora is rich and interesting. Since 1834 a succession of botanists has established the relationship between the vegetation of the island and that of Africa, of the opposite Asiatic mainland, and of East Indian regions. From an economic standpoint the vegetation suffices to support the meagre pastoral existence of some 3,000–4,000 nomads, who graze upwards of 16,000 sheep and goats, 1,000 cattle, and 800 camels over the island;[1] it also affords a means of livelihood to those who collect bush-products such as the resin of the dragon's-blood, frankincense, and the juice of the once famous Socotran aloes (photos. 125–128).

Water-supplies. The general aridity below the highland zone, and the high proportion of deeply scored slopes, favour rapid run-off. The moist highlands of the uppermost Haggier, where a sponge of vegetation, mostly permanent grass, retards run-off, give rise to many springs the waters of which descend through deep gorges to the lower arid zones. After rain

[1] Major Spencer-Cook, *Report on Population and Livestock* (1943).

these gorges carry spates, which can quickly increase from small perennial streams to impassable torrents. The short distance between the mountains and the sea causes the valuable precipitation to be quickly carried off the island. Domestic water-supplies give little difficulty, as there are no large communities to be supplied. At Hadibu, the largest settlement, shallow wells are sunk in almost every house-compound, and the water drawn is used for domestic purposes and for the hand-watering of vegetable crops. The use of animal-power for raising water for irrigation is not understood by the Socotrans, but in the mountains a few patches of ground are irrigated from springs by gravity.

In general the limestone areas are deficient in surface water-supplies and underground sources have not so far been explored with modern appliances and methods. But in places good local supplies exist even in the limestone areas, as for instance at Kathub, where a local well supplied the many thousands of gallons needed daily by the R.A.F. station and Aden Levy garrison in the last two years of the war of 1939–1945.

Historical and Political. The long history of Socotra fades back into mythology, which cannot be fully discussed. One suggested derivation of the name is from the Sanskrit *Dvipa Sukhādhāra*, 'Isle of the Abode of Bliss', but the theory that this was corrupted into *Suq al Katra*, 'market of the exudations', is untenable on philological grounds. Socotra has been identified with the Panchaia of Virgil, with which was connected the story of the Phoenix, lying down to die in a perfumed nest of cinnamon and frankincense sprigs. A connexion is also suggested with Castor and Pollux, the Dioscuri, twin sons of Jupiter and Leda, whence the Roman name *Dioscoridis Insula* may have arisen. To this day the Arabs call the dragon's-blood *dam al akhwein*, 'the blood of the two brothers'.[1]

Iskuduru, one of a list of countries conquered by Darius on an inscription at Persepolis, is believed to have been Socotra.[2] The island was apparently visited, along with the Land of Punt, by the ancient Egyptians, to obtain frankincense and myrrh by the direct sea-route (pp. 214–15). The writer of the *Periplus* referred to Socotra as containing (1st century A.D.) a mixed Greek-speaking population trading, especially in turtle-shell of high quality, with Arabia and India; while Cosmas Indicopleustes, visiting it in the sixth century, thought that the Greek-speaking people had been placed in 'Dioscorides' by the Ptolemies. Traders from Mūza (Arabian Red Sea coast) and Barygaza (Gulf of Cambay) visited the island for turtle-shell. As far back as the tenth century it was a noted haunt of pirates from Cutch and Gujerat. Marco Polo, among other writers, described the harpooning of whales round its coasts, for ambergris and sperm-oil.

The Socotrans, to-day Moslems, were for centuries Christians (p. 228), though it is uncertain to what Church they belonged. The explorers Bent believed them to have been Monophysites, converted during the times of

[1] Harold F. Jacob, *Kings of Arabia*, chap. xv (1923).
[2] Theodore Bent and Mrs. Bent, *Southern Arabia*, chap. xxix (1900).

Ethiopian domination in south-west Arabia, and stated that crosses and
other symbols, still to be seen inscribed on flat rock, are of Ethiopic form.
Marco Polo, however, apparently took the people to be Nestorians, subject
to their patriarch in Asia. This view is perhaps borne out by the Jesuit missionary, S. Francis Xavier, who, visiting Socotra after 1541 and describing
the then debased forms of Christian worship, recorded the great veneration
of the Socotrans for Saint Thomas, which would seem to link them with
the Nestorians of south India. The last traces of active Christianity were
seen by a Carmelite missionary, PadreVincenzo, in the seventeenth century.

In later times the island became a calling-place for the early European
voyagers to India, previous to 'laying' before the monsoon for the Malabar
coast.

The islands have long formed part of the domains of the Mahri Sultan
of Qishn and Socotra (p. 363). Socotra was occupied by a British force,
following an agreement with the Sultan in 1834, for about five years, while
the Government of India was negotiating the purchase of the island as a
coaling-station. The expedition proved disastrous; several members of an
advance party of the Royal Indian Marine, on landing, were drowned in the
surf, while malaria later took a heavy toll. Negotiations, still in progress
when Aden was captured in 1839, broke down, and the survivors left
Socotra. In 1876, however, the Sultan agreed not to alienate any part of his
possessions except to the British, and in 1886 he accepted a Protectorate
Treaty (p. 276). All the islands then became part of the Aden Protectorate,
dealt with from India through the Resident at Aden, till the transfer of the
Protectorate to the Colonial Office in 1937. The Sultan, whose capital is
Hadibu, rules with the help of his Wazir, and of headmen appointed from
the coastal settlements and the pastoral clans of the interior. Law is upheld
by about a score of men, recruited mainly from the Sultan's slaves and
armed with rifles. Tribal law is followed for the most part, but the Sultan
occasionally enforces the *shar'*, even as far as amputation of the hand for
persistent thefts of livestock. Apart from a small Government stipend, the
Sultan's revenue is derived mainly from taxes on imports and exports and
a tribute of one-tenth on local produce entering the trading settlements.
The Sultan also keeps livestock and engages in trade as opportunity offers.

The *population* of the island, said to be between 6,000 and 8,000, is
divided equally between those living in permanent coastal settlements and
the nomadic pastoral people, who move on a system of rotational grazing.
In the coastal settlements a small number of immigrant Arabs, mostly
traders, is found; also many negroes, particularly at Hadibu, where the
Sultan's slaves are numerous. The rest of the people are Socoteri, a name
covering the ancient population and their descendants, as well as numbers
of immigrants, sometimes from shipwrecks, in many cases 'left behind' and
'turned Socoteri' by their own choice. Generally the people are primitive;
slim, brown-skinned, and timid, and, unlike their neighbours on the African
and Arabian shores, without fire-arms, spears, bows, or other destructive

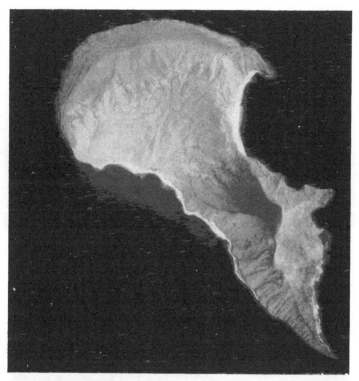

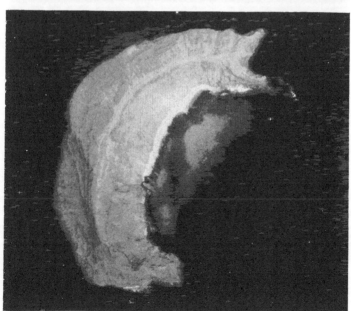

353, 354. *The Socotran Brothers, from the air*

355. *The Kuria Muria island of Sūda with Hallānīya behind, seen eastwards from the air*

356. *Tilted limestone strata on the northern coast of Hallānīya*

357. *Jezirat Ghardhawāt, Kuria Muria*

weapons. The Socoteri language is allied to the South Arabian languages used by the Mahra, Qara, and Shahara (p. 374). Like the tribes of the Qara mountains, most of the people would no doubt be classified by modern anthropologists as Veddoid (p. 368).

Communication with the outside world is maintained by sailing-vessels. A Socoteri trader will usually maintain one large, one small, and two medium-sized dhows, which carry goods from Socotra and return with maize, rice, millet, and consignments of trade goods. In normal times maize from Mombasa and dates from the Persian Gulf form the staple diet and voyages are arranged at the appropriate seasons. For trade goods and rice the Socoteri dhows visit Aden and the larger vessels may make the voyage to Bombay. During the SW. monsoon there is no attempt at trade to or from the island.

Socotra has only one good anchorage and well-protected landing-beach, that of Hadibu. Others which can be used are Kathub (Qatub) and the beaches of Mouri, Deham, and Goba', all on the north coast. Kallansiya (Qalansiya) at the north-west corner of the island, has a sheltered bay but the shore is rocky and shallow; while at the eastern tip, west-north-west of Ras Momi, shelter can be found for small craft and for the landing of cargo in small parcels portable in the canoes used by the fisherfolk. The southern coast has only two small settlements with a total population of 38. In April 1944 the people on the south coast were without canoes or other craft and could only communicate with other settlements overland.

Tracks passable for laden camels link up the coastal settlements, and the track from Kallansiya to Kathub jetty was motorable in 1943; but movement of caravans across the mountainous inland areas is only attempted on a few routes. Only a little traffic is carried on pack animals to the interior and across the island, for the requirements of the pastoral people are remarkably small, and when migrating they generally carry their belongings, consisting of a few cooking-pots, goat's-hair coverlets, and small stores of grain or dates, on their backs. Foot-paths used by herdsmen are frequent, but often indistinct or overgrown. Once off these paths the traveller soon gets into difficulties with thickets of the Socotran Box, and with massive pieces of limestone impeding progress in valleys which, from a distance, look easily passable.

The mustering of camels required for transport is not easy, though, since the occupation of the island by a garrison, the needs of travellers have been better understood by the people, who have earned high and steady wages in the latter years of the war of 1939–1945, by hiring out their beasts. The Socotran camel relies on the natural browse and grazing for his upkeep. Like all camels bred in mountain-areas he is sure-footed, but not accustomed to carry heavy loads or to traverse the long distances required of camels in south Arabia.

Though donkeys are used, the good service of this animal for riding and pack-work is not appreciated by the Socotrans to the same extent as in south Arabia. There are no horses in Socotra at present, but Sir Thomas Roe, in his account of his visit to the island in 1612, records that 'the Sultan came down to the shore with about 300 men. . . . He was a-horseback, as well as two of his chief servants.' Sir Thomas noted a more curious means of transport when he saw 'the savage people . . . the ancientest natives of the place, riding about on buffaloes'.

The first *landing-ground for aircraft* was established on Hadibu plain in 1940, but on the entry of Italy into the war it was found expedient to render the landing-strip unserviceable. It was repaired in May 1941, and in 1942 was replaced by a much larger landing-ground on the northern coastal plain, some 2 miles west of Kathub. This landing-ground was used by planes operating against enemy submarines in the Gulf of Aden.

Economy of the Coastal Population. The coastal villages, inhabited by people very mixed racially, consist mainly of one-storied houses of rough stone or coral-rag. The best are plastered and whitewashed inside, with well-constructed flat roofs, but the poorer dwellings are circular or oblong, with high-pitched roofs of palm-leaves. Garden-crops, where present, include sweet-potatoes, pumpkins, beans, and tobacco. Groves of inferior date-palms are maintained, the water-supply being partly direct rainfall, partly the natural flow of springs and flood-water. A few poultry, sheep, and goats are usually present about the larger settlements, where the people also weave goat's-hair and cotton-thread coverlets for local use and for export.

But in normal times almost all the coastal people are part-time or whole-time fishermen, while on the north coasts they also engage in pearl-fishing and collect ambergris. Even in 1944, when many persons were getting work with the occupation force and the Air Ministry Works Directorate, over 1,840 people out of the 3,000 to 4,000 inhabiting the coastal settlements claimed to be dependent on fishing for a livelihood; 1,770 of these lived in eighteen settlements along the north coast; south-west of Kallansiya and along the whole south coast, the total population was reckoned to be less than 130 persons, of whom 73 were fishermen. The coastal community then owned 338 canoes and 6 row-boats.[1]

Shark, tunny, king-fish, and bonito are taken by trolling and by set-nets and harpoons; while many smaller kinds, excellent as food, are caught inshore by means of fish-pots, traps, cast-nets, seine-nets, and hand-lines. Shark, the most important fish, and king-fish are dried for export, the salt used in their preparation being brought from Nait, on the south coast. Tunny and bonito are smoke-dried. Small species are eaten fresh. The coasts also abound with oysters and other shellfish, and quantities of clams, limpets, and sea-urchins are consumed by the fisherfolk. Turtles also are eaten, on 'Abd al Kuri so abundantly that the people have been called 'chelonophagi'.

Most north-coast fishermen are part-time pearl-divers. The best pearling-

[1] Capt. H. L. Flower, *Report on Fisheries* (April, 1944).

grounds lie off the villages of Goba' and Deham. The divers sell pearls and shell to local traders, or to buyers who bring cash, grain, and dates from Arabia in exchange. Aden is the usual market for shell.

The weakness of the fishing industry is its dependence on imports for the maintenance of craft and for tackle. Canoes and timber come from Malabar; cotton sheeting, cotton yarn, hemp fibre, wire traces, swivels, and hooks are all imported from Aden or India. In 1943 and 1944 the fishing-community suffered hardship through lack of such goods and the high price of any available supplies.

Economy of the Pastoral Socotrans. The nomads of the interior, mainly dependent on stock-keeping, were reckoned in 1944 at between 3,000 and 4,000 people, owning about 17,000 cattle, sheep, and goats, and 800 camels. The people's sustenance is chiefly flesh and milk. To buy imported goods they sell ghee made from the milk of cattle and goats, goat's hair, and occasionally a head of livestock. They also collect the resin of the dragon's-blood tree, the juice of aloes (p. 208), and some frankincense; and they capture the civet to obtain the secretion used in perfumery. These products are usually bartered to traders for grain and cloth. The pastoral people grow tobacco and the cereal *Eleusine* on a few small irrigated field-terraces, and have an interest in groves of dates of inferior quality in the better-watered valleys.

Pastoral society is organized, under the headmen responsible to the Sultan, in tribes, clans, and families. Tribal, family, and individual rights over land are recognized, and there is a system of rotation of grazing, particularly between highlands and lowlands.

Reference has been made (pp. 498, 505, 506) to the domestic animals owned by the pastoral tribes. It may be added that the small unhumped cattle (*Bos taurus*), numbering about 1,000 head, belong to families with grazing rights in the moist highland zone, whither the cattle are taken in dry weather. The fine goats, yielding milk, meat, and hair, flourish best below the moist zone; much of the island is only suitable for goats, many of which have run wild in the hills, though claimants to ownership appear whenever a wild goat is killed. The sheep, not a fat-tailed breed like those of the adjacent parts of Africa and Arabia, but long-tailed, yielding only a poor hair-fleece, and altogether like a degenerate breed of European sheep, are found mostly on the coastal plains, grazing in small flocks. Camels are kept in the drier parts of the island. A race of the ass, which has become wild, was considered by the joint Expedition of the British and Liverpool Museums (1898–9) to be allied to the Upper Nubian race (*Equus asinus africanus*).

APPENDIX G

THE KURIA MURIA ISLANDS

THIS archipelago (p. 340) lies in Kuria Muria Bay, off the coast of 'Omān. The islands, five in number, extend about 45 miles from west to east, and are some 25 miles south of the mainland. The most westerly, Hāsikīya (Haski), only about 20 miles east of Hāsik on the mainland, is more than a mile long, with two peaks some 400 feet high, but without water or vegetation, occupied only by flocks of pelicans and other birds. Next to the east is As Sūda (Soda or Suweidīya), the second largest island, some three miles long and composed of granite, rising to about 1,300 feet, with a supply of water, usually brackish; As Sūda was once inhabited but long since deserted, the people having migrated to Al Hallānīya. This latter, the third island from the west, is the largest of the group and now the only one with permanent human inhabitants; it is eight miles long and 23 in circumference, composed mainly of metamorphic rocks, but with a huge tabular mass of limestone and other sedimentary rocks rising to over 1,500 feet, forming a peak with a high plateau to the west of it; the island has a scanty vegetation of maritime shrubs, tamarisks, and acacias; water is found everywhere near the surface, but is generally brackish. The fourth island to the east, Jebelīya (Jiblīya, Kiblia), twelve miles from Al Hallānīya, is a limestone peak over 500 feet high, about two miles long by one mile broad, quite waterless and inhabited only by sea-birds; a few tombs indicate that it formerly had human inhabitants. The fifth island, Ghardhawāt (Gharzaut, Karzawīt, or, in old Portuguese writings 'Rodondo'), lies out of line with the rest, north-east of Al Hallānīya; it is a red granite peak over 200 feet high. Hāsikīya and Jebelīya formerly had thick deposits of guano. (Photos. 355–357).

Geologically the islands are of much interest. Like Masīra island, far to the north-east, they stand on the edge of the submerged Arabian continental shelf. The Kuria Muria granites are believed to correspond with those of Socotra and with the granitic mass of the Seychelles. The sandstone formation, mainly horizontal in the eastern part of the archipelago, is, with the overlying limestone strata, much tilted upwards at the west end of Al Hallānīya, the extreme western end of which (as well as the adjacent island of As Sūda) is composed of granite; the slopes of this granite, which is intrusive into the sandstone, have been traced down the submerged continental slope to a depth of at least 4,500 feet. The stratified sandstone must have formerly extended farther east and south-east, which, with other evidence, has been taken to indicate that extensive scarp faulting has occurred along this part of the coast.[1]

[1] J. D. Wiseman and R. B. Seymour Sewell, 'The floor of the Arabian Sea', *Geological Magazine*, vol. lxxiv, pp. 219–30 (May 1937).

Historical. Older Arab geographers called the islands Khuryān Muryān (conventionalized to Kuria Muria or, in old Portuguese writings, Curia Muria), but in recent times they have been called Jazāir Beni Ghalfān, after a head of that house named Sheikh Sa'īd ibn 'Omar ibn Ghalfān; he, having failed in an attempt to seize Marbāt in Dhufār, retired temporarily to Al Hallānīya and, on returning to the mainland, kept possession of the islands, which his descendants occasionally visited to exact tribute (when Col. Miles visited Al Hallānīya in 1883, out of less than 40 inhabitants, two women of the Beni Ghalfān were considered 'queens').[1] The first-century writer of the *Periplus* referred to the islands as seven, and called them 'Zenobian', a name considered to be a Hellenized form of the Arabic Beni Zenāb or Genāb, a tribe who possessed the neighbouring coast;[2] the 'Beni Geneba' of Wellsted, and 'Jenefa tribe' of Bent, are other forms of the name. The islands lay near the frontier between the kingdom of the Parthians and that of the Hadhramaut, in which latter the writer of the *Periplus* stated the islands to be included (p. 224).

The chronicler Idrīsī, who died in 1164, recorded that the islanders, then politically under Shihr, lived very poorly in winter, but made a moderate livelihood in the sailing season by voyages to 'Omān, Aden, and the Yemen; with the last they traded turtle shell and occasionally very fine amber. The islands, discovered to Europeans by Albuquerque in 1503, figured in the movements of the Portuguese in those regions. Later they passed to the Sultan of Muscat, who, after the French had several times tried to get possession of the guano, ceded the islands to Britain by deed of gift on 14 July 1854. Between 1855 and 1860 some 200,000 tons of guano were removed from Hāsikīya and Jebelīya; the archipelago often presented a busy scene, as many as 52 ships being present on one occasion. A cable-station of the Red Sea and Karachi Telegraph Company was established at Al Hallānīya in 1861, but abandoned the following year on failure of the cable. A signal station of the Eastern Telegraph Company was established later. As explained on p. 340, though technically part of Aden Colony, the islands are, because of their remoteness and inaccessibility, left to the supervision of the British Resident in the Persian Gulf.

The population is now about 100. In former days it may have been larger, and, as stated above, certain islands, now deserted, were inhabited. Miles records that in 1818 a pirate squadron from Ras al Khaima sacked the settlement on Al Hallānīya, carrying off women and children. On his visit to that island in 1883, the 36 inhabitants, consisting of five men, eleven children, and 20 women (including the two Beni Ghalfān women mentioned above), were living in primitive round or oval huts, about six feet in diameter and three to four feet high, of unmortared stones, with scanty mat roofs laid over sticks and fish-bones. At certain seasons the islanders

[1] For much historical and other information, see S. B. Miles, 'The countries and tribes of the Persian Gulf', vol. ii, pp. 351, 495–7, 548–9 (1919).

[2] W. H. Schoff, 'The Periplus of the Erythraean Sea', pp. 35, 144–6 (1912).

betook themselves to caves. They lived on fish, shellfish, and goat's milk, occasionally exchanging dried fish for dates and rice from passing ships. They fished entirely with hooks, being without boats or nets. Only their headman spoke Arabic, the rest Mahri. Between 200 and 300 goats roamed the island, some quite wild, others attended by the women and children. Bent, who passed the islands at night in December 1894, recorded that their inhabitants, the Jenefa tribesmen, swam on inflated skins in pursuit of sharks.[1]

[1] 'Southern Arabia', p. 230 (1900).

APPENDIX H

AUTHORSHIP, AUTHORITIES, AND MAPS

AUTHORSHIP

THIS volume has been written mainly by Dr. Hugh Scott, F.R.S., of the British Museum (Natural History), and by Professor Kenneth Mason and Miss Mary Marshall, of the School of Geography, Oxford University, assisted by Miss Frances Pickard-Cambridge. Contributions have been made by Messrs. A. H. G. Alston, C. F. Beckingham, L. C. W. Bonacina, Brian J. Hartley, Dr. P. W. R. Petrie, Mr. H. St. J. B. Philby, Miss M. V. Seton Williams, and Dr. Norman White. Assistance has also been received from Sir Bernard Reilly, K.C.M.G., Colonel Gerald de Gaury, Colonel the Hon. R. A. B. Hamilton, Dr. J. V. Harrison, Mr. W. H. Ingrams, Mrs. W. H. Ingrams, Miss Rahima 'Ali Ja'far, Dr. Laurence Lockhart, Dr. R. B. Serjeant, Mr. A. N. Sherwin White, and Mr. E. Gardiner Smith.

Among many whose photographs have been used are Dr. Scott, Mr. Philby, Mr. Bertram Thomas, Mr. E. B. Britton, Mr. and Mrs. Ingrams, Herr Robert Deutsch, Colonel M. C. Lake, Colonel the Hon. M. T. Boscawen, Sqdn.-Leader A. R. M. Rickards, Colonel G. E. Leachman, Mr. Douglas Carruthers, Miss Gertrude Bell, Major R. E. Cheesman, Mr. H. J. L. Beadnell, Mr. Carl Raswan, Mr. Norman Lewis, Miss Freya Stark, and Miss G. Caton-Thompson. A number of photographs have also been supplied by the Admiralty, the War Office, the Royal Air Force, and by the Royal Geographical Society.

Maps and diagrams, with the exception of the coloured map at the end, have been drawn under the direction of Mr. K. W. Hartland.

AUTHORITIES

Knowledge of Arabia has still to be drawn largely from books and articles on travel and exploration which, though valuable, rarely deal exhaustively with any one subject. No attempt is therefore made here to give a complete bibliography of Arabia, nor even to cite all the books and articles which have been examined. A few published bibliographies, some of the most useful books of general reference, and the works of the more important travellers and writers are given below. Many of these last have also been used in several chapters and they are not repeated among the short lists on special chapters which follow.

Much unpublished material has been incorporated in the book, especially in Chapters VI, VII, VIII, and IX, most of which has been freely supplied by certain of those named above.

To save space the following initial abbreviations are used: *J.R.G.S.* (Journal of the Royal Geographical Society); *G.J.* (Geographical Journal); *J.R.C.A.S.* (Journal of the Royal Central Asian Society); *J.R.A.S.* (Journal of the Royal Asiatic Society). The dates given in brackets are those of publication. The place of publication is given only when outside Great Britain.

1. Bibliographies

(*a*) *General*

HOGARTH, D. G.: *The Penetration of Arabia* (1904); short lists after each of first 13 chapters.

KIERNAN, R. H.: *The Unveiling of Arabia* (1937); short list, 341–343.

LESCH, W.: Arabien, *Mitteilungen geograph. Gesellschaft München*, 1931; extensive list.

(*b*) *Sa'ūdi Arabia*

CARRUTHERS, D.: *Arabian Adventure to the Great Nafūd* (1935); short list.

GAURY, G. DE: *J.R.C.A.S.* xxxi. 315–320 (1944).

(*c*) *South-west Arabia*

HUNTER, F. M.: *An Account of the British Settlement of Aden* (1877), App. A (197–202).

PLAYFAIR, R. L.: *A History of Arabia Felix or Yemen* (Bombay, 1859).

SCHMIDT, W.: *Das südwestliche Arabien* (Halle, 1913); long list of books and chronological list of travellers.

(*d*) *Under preparation*

SERJEANT, DR. R. B.: a comprehensive list of some thousands of works on all subjects relating to 'Asīr, the Yemen, Aden Protectorate, and Dhufār.

MACRO, ERIC: a general list of works (at present some 2,000) relating to the Arabian peninsula as a whole.

2. Books of General Reference (with bibliographies)

The Encyclopaedia of Islam: a dictionary of the geography, ethnography, and biography of the Muhammadan peoples (by many leading orientalists; Leyden and London, 1913–).

VON WISSMANN, H.: *Arabien*, in F. KLUTE, *Handbuch der geographischen Wissenschaft*, pp. 178–211 (n.d., but *c.* 1936).

BLANCHARD, R.: *Géographie Universelle*, vol. viii, chap. vi (Paris, 1929).

Handbook of Arabia: (compiled by Naval Intelligence Division of the Admiralty), 2 vols. (1916, 1917).

Oriente Moderno, from about 1920 to 1940 contains many articles on political and other matters in Arabia.

3. GENERAL WORKS AND TRAVELS

ALBUQUERQUE, AFFONSO D': *Commentaries* (Hakluyt Series, 1877).

BEADNELL, H. J. L.: *The Wilderness of Sinai* (1927).

BENT, J. T.: *Southern Arabia* (1900); *G.J.* iv. 315 (1894); vi. 109 (1895).

BLUNT, LADY ANNE: *A Pilgrimage to Nejd*, 2 vols. (1881).

BURCHARDT, H.: see MITTWOCH, E.: *Aus dem Jemen: Hermann Burchardt's letzte Reise durch Südarabien* (Leipzig, 1926).

BURCKHARDT, J. L.: *Travels in Arabia* (1829); *Notes on the Bedouins and Wahabys* (1830-1831).

BURTON, SIR RICHARD F.: *A Pilgrimage to Al-Madinah and Meccah*, 2 vols. (1855); *The Gold Mines of Midian* (1878); *The Land of Midian (Revisited)* (1879); *Report upon the Minerals of Midian* (1879).

BURY, G. WYMAN: *The Land of Uz* (1911); *Arabia Infelix* (1915); *Pan-Islam* (1919).

CARRUTHERS, D.: *Arabian Adventure to the Great Nafūd* (1935); *G.J.* lix. 401 (1922).

CATON-THOMPSON, G.: *The Tombs and Moon Temple of Hureidha* (Hadhramaut) (1944); *J.R.C.A.S.* xxvi. 79–92 (1939); *G.J.*, xciii. 18–38 (1939).

CHEESMAN, R. E.: *In Unknown Arabia* (1926).

COX, SIR PERCY Z.: *G.J.* lxvi. 193–227 (1925).

DEFLERS, A.: *Voyage au Yemen* (Paris, 1889).

DOUGHTY, C. M.: *Travels in Arabia Deserta*, 2 vols. (1888): new ed. in 1 vol. (1926).

EUTING, J.: *Tagbuch einer Reise in Inner-Arabien* (Leyden, 1896, 1924).

FORBES, ROSITA: *G.J.* lxii. 271–278 (1923).

GAURY, G. DE: *Field Notes on Sa'udi Arabia* (Air Ministry Pub. 1936); *J.R.C.A.S.* xxxi. 40–47 (1944); *G.J.* cvi. 152 (1945).

GIBB, H. A. R.: *The Travels of Ibn Battuta*, 1325-1354 (1929).

GLASER, E.: *Skizze der Geschichte und Geographie Arabiens von den ältesten Zeiten bis zum Propheten Muhammad* (Berlin, 1900); also other works.

GUARMANI, C.: *Il Neged settentrionale* (Jerusalem, 1866; trans. as *Northern Nejd*, 1917, 1938).

HAINES, S. B.: *J.R.G.S.* ix. 125–156 (1839); xv. 104–160 (1845).

HAMILTON, HON. R. A. B.: *J.R.C.A.S.* xxix. 239–248 (1942); xxx. 269–274 (1943). *G.J.* c. 107–123 (1942); ci. 110–117 (1943). *Man,* xlii. no. 44 (1942).

HARRIS, W. B.: *A Journey through the Yemen* (1893).

HARRISON, P. W.: *The Arab at Home* (1925); *Doctor in Arabia* (1943).

HALÉVY, J.: *Journal Asiatique,* xix. 5–98, 129–266, 489–547 (Paris, 1872). *Bull. Soc. de Géog.* vi. 5–31, 249–273, 581–606; xiii. 466–479.

HAYYIM HABSHUSH (guide to Halévy): *Travels in Yemen* (in Arabic) (Jerusalem, 1941).

HITTI, P.: *History of the Arabs* (1937).

HOLT, A. L.: *G.J.* lxii. 259–271 (1923).

HUBER, C.: *Journal d'un Voyage en Arabie* (Paris, 1891).

HURGRONJE, J. SNOUCK: *Mekka,* 2 vols. (The Hague, 1888–1889) (transl. as *Mekka in the latter part of the nineteenth century,* 1 vol. (1931)).

HUZAYYIN, S. A.: *Arabia and the Far East* (Soc. Royale de Géog. d'Égypte, Cairo, 1942).

INGRAMS, W. H.: *Arabia and the Isles* (1942). *A Report on the Social, Economic, and Political Condition of the Hadhramaut* (Colonial no. 123 (1937)). *G.J.* lxxxviii. 524–551 (1936); xcii. 289–312 (1938); cv, 1–29 (1945). *J.R.C.A.S.* xxiii. 378 ff. (1936); xxxii. 135–155 (1945); xxxiii. 58–69 (1946). *J.R.A.S.* (1945) 169–185 (Burton Memorial Lecture).

INGRAMS, DOREEN (MRS. W. H.): *G.J.* xcviii. 121–134 (1941); cv. 1–29, (1945).

JACOB, HAROLD F.: *Kings of Arabia* (1923).

JOURDAIN, JOHN: *Journal,* 1608–1617 (ed. by SIR WILLIAM FOSTER, Hakluyt Soc., 2nd Series, no. 16, 1905).

JULLIEN (*née* PLOWDEN), JOAN M. C.: *Once in Sinai: the Record of a Solitary Venture* (1940); *J.R.C.A.S.* xxix. 222–234 (1942).

KAY, H. C.: *Yaman, its Early Medieval History* (1892).

KEANE, J. S.: *Six Months in the Hejaz* (1887).

LEACHMAN, G. E.: *G.J.* xliii. 500–520 (1914).

LEES, G. M.: *G.J.* lxxi. 441–470 (1928). *Quart. J. Geol. Soc. Lond.,* pp. 585 ff. (1928). *J.R.C.A.S.* xxxiii. 47–69 (1946).

LEWIS, N.: *Sand and Sea in Arabia* (1938).

MANZONI, R.: *El Yemen: tre Anni nell' Arabia Felice* (1884).

MILES, S. B.: *The Countries and Tribes of the Persian Gulf,* 2 vols. (1919). *J.R.G.S.* xli. 210–245 (1871). *G.J.* vii. 522–537 (1896); xviii. 465–498 (1901); xxxvi. 159–178, 405–425 (1910).

MOSER, C.: (Socotra). *Nat. Geog. Mag.,* no. 33, 266 ff. (1918).

MUSIL, ALOIS: (American Geog. Soc. Oriental Explor.): *Northern Hejaz* (1926); *Arabia Deserta* (1927); *Northern Nejd* (1928); *Manners and Customs of the Rwala Bedouins* (1928). Other works include: *In the Arabian Desert* (1931); *Nord-Arabien* (Vienna, 1909).

NALLINO, M.: *L'Arabia Saudiana* (Rome, 1938).

NEWCOMBE, S. F.: *J.R.C.A.S.* xxxi. 158–164 (1944).

NICHOLSON, R. A.: *Literary History of the Arabs* (2nd ed. 1930).

NIEBUHR, C.: *Beschreibung von Arabien* (Copenhagen, 1772; French transl. *Description de l'Arabie* (1774)); *Reisebeschreibung nach Arabien*, &c., 2 vols. (Copenhagen, 1774; French transl. *Voyage en Arabie* (1776, 1780)).

NOLDE, E.: *Reise in Innerarabien* (Brunswick, 1895).

PHILBY, H. ST. J. B.: *The Heart of Arabia*, 2 vols. (1922); *Arabia of the Wahhabis* (1928); *Arabia* (1930); *The Empty Quarter* (1933); *Sheba's Daughters* (1939); *A Pilgrim in Arabia* (limited ed. 1943; pop. illustrated ed. 1946); *Arabian Highlands* (in the press).

—— *G.J.:* (Southern Najd) lv. 161 ff. (1920); (Persian Gulf to Red Sea) lvi. 446 ff. (1920); (Jauf and Northern Desert) lxii. 241 ff. (1923); (Rub' al Khali) lxxxi. 1 ff. (1933); (Land of Sheba) xcii. 1 ff., 107 ff. (1938).

—— *J.R.C.A.S.:* (Highways of Central Arabia) vii. 112 ff. (1920); (Recent History of the Hijaz) xii. 332 ff. (1925); (Triumph of the Wahhabis) xiii. 293 ff. (1926); (Survey of Wahhabi Arabia) xvi. 468 ff. (1929); (Rub' al Khali) xix. 569 ff. (1932); (Mecca and Medina) xx. 504 ff. (1933).

—— *International Affairs:* (Arabia To-day) xiv. 619 ff. (1935).

PITTS, JOSEPH (of Exon): *A True and Faithful Account of the Religion and Manners of the Mohammetans, &c.* (Exeter, 1704).

RASWAN, C.: *The Black Tents of Arabia* (1935); *Geog. Review*, xx. 494–502 (1930).

RATHJENS, C., and VON WISSMANN, H.: *Südarabien-Reise*, 3 vols. (Hamburg University, 1931–1934), and other works.

REILLY, SIR BERNARD R.: *J.R.C.A.S.* xxviii. 132–145 (1941).

RIHANI, A.: *Ibn Sa'ud of Arabia, his People and his Land* (1928); *Around the Coasts of Arabia* (1930); *Arabian Peak and Desert* (1930).

ROQUE, J. DE LA: *Voyage dans l'Arabie Heureuse* (Amsterdam, 1716; Engl. transl. 1726, 1730, &c.).

RUTTER, ELDON: *The Holy Cities of Arabia*, 2 vols. (1930).

SADLIER, G. F.: *Diary of a Journey across Arabia* (Bombay Govt. Rec. 1866).

SCHOFF, W. H.: *The Periplus of the Erythraean Sea* (transl. and annot., New York, 1912).

SCOTT, HUGH: *In the High Yemen* (1942). *G.J.* xciii. 97–125 (139). *J.R.C.A.S.* xxvii. 21–44 (1940); xxviii. 146–151 (1941).

STARK, FREYA: *The Southern Gates of Arabia* (1936); *A Winter in Arabia* (1940); *Seen in the Hadhramaut* (1938). *G.J.* lxxxvii. 113–126 (1936); xcii. 1–17 (1939).

THOMAS, BERTRAM: *Alarms and Excursions in Arabia* (1931); *Arabia Felix* (1932); *The Arabs* (1937); *G.J.* lxxviii. 209–242 (1931); *Proc. Brit. Acad.* xxiii. 231–331 (1937); *J.R.C.A.S.* xviii (1931), xx (1933).

VARTHEMA, LUDOVICO DI: *Travels* (1503) (Hakluyt Soc., ed. by J. W. JONES and G. P. BADGER, 1863).

WAHBA, H. E. SHEIKH HAFIZ: *J.R.C.A.S.* xvi. 468 ff. (1929).

WALLIN, G. A.: *J.R.G.S.* xx. 293–344 (1850); xxiv. 115–207 (1854).

WASI', 'Abd al: *Tarīkh al Yemen* (Cairo, 1928).

WAVELL, A. J. B.: *A Modern Pilgrim in Mecca and a Siege in Sanaa* (1912).

WELLSTED, J. R.: *Travels in Arabia*, 2 vols. (1838). *J.R.G.S.* (Socotra) v. 129–229 (1835); vii. 102–113 (1837).

WERDECKER, JOSEF: *Bull. Soc. Roy. Géog. d'Égypte*, xx. 1–160 (1939).

WILSON, SIR A. T.: *The Persian Gulf* (1928).

WISSMANN, H. VON: see under Rathjens.

WREDE, A. VON: *Reise in Hadhramaut* (Brunswick, 1870).

ZWEMER, S. M.: *Arabia, the Cradle of Islam* (1900).

4. CLIMATE AND VEGETATION (*short list*)

Admiralty Pilots: Red Sea and Gulf of Aden (8th ed. 1932); *Persian Gulf* (9th ed. 1942). With meteorological tables.

DAKING, C. W. G.: (Kamarān I.) *Quart. Journ. R. Met. Soc.* lxviii (1932).

HANN, JULIUS VON: *Handbuch der Klimatologie*, B. ii, iii (1910–1911), and other papers.

RANGE, PAUL: (Sinai) *Meteorol. Zeitschrift*, xxxiv. (1917).

AUCHER-ÉLOY, P. M. R.: *Relations des Voyages en Orient de 1830 à 1838* ii. 364–563 (Paris, 1843).

BLATTER, E.: *Rec. Bot. Survey of India*, viii (1919–1923); (Aden) vii (1914).

SCHWARTZ, O.: *Mitteil. Inst. allgemein. Botanik Hamburg*, x (1939). Comprehensive list of flora south of the Tropic.

SCHWEINFURTH, G.: *Verhandl. Ges. Erdkunde Berlin*, xviii. 531–550 (1891); *Bull. Herb. Boissier* ii. App. 2, 1–113 (1894), and iv. App. 2, 115–266 (1896); *Engler Bot. Jahrb.* v. 40–49 (1884).

5. HISTORY (*short list*)

AL KHAZRAJI: *Pearl Strings: A History of the Resuli Dynasty of Yemen* (transl. SIR J. REDHOUSE: Gibb Memorial Series, i (1906); ii (1907)).

JAUSSEN et SAVIGNAC, PÈRES: *Mission Archéologique en Arabie*, 4 vols. (Paris, 1914–1922).

KAMMERER, A.: *La Mer Rouge, l'Abyssinie et l'Arabie depuis l'Antiquité* 2 vols. (Cairo, 1929–1935).

LANE, E.: *Arabian Society in the Middle Ages* (ed. Stanley Lane-Poole, 1883).

LAWRENCE, T. E., and WOOLLEY, L.: *The Wilderness of Zin* (2nd ed. 1936).

LYALL, SIR C.: *The Muallaqat. A Commentary on Ten Ancient Arabic Poems* (Calcutta, 1894); *Ancient Arabian Poetry* (1885).

MOBERG, A.: *Book of the Himyarites* (1920–1924).

NIELSEN, DITLEF: *Handbuch der Altarabischen Altertumskunde* (Copenhagen and Paris, 1927).

O'LEARY, LACY: *Arabia before Muhammad* (1927).

ROSTOVTZEFF, M.: *Caravan Cities* (1932).

WARMINGTON, E. H.: *Commerce between the Roman Empire and India* (1928).

6. PUBLIC HEALTH AND DISEASE (*short list*)

BUXTON, P. A.: *Trans. R. Soc. Trop. Med.* (Dec. 1944).

PETRIE, P. W. R., and SEAL, K. S.: *A Medical Survey of the Western Aden Protectorate, 1939–40* (for the Colonial Office).

7. AGRICULTURE (*short list*)

HARTLEY, B. J.: *Dry Farming Methods in the Aden Protectorate* (1944).

TWITCHELL, K. S. (and others): *Report of the United States Agricultural Mission to Sa'udi Arabia* (1943).

(Extensive use has also been made of works cited in the general list and in technical works.)

MAPS

There are few reliable maps of Arabia or of the Red Sea coasts. The Aden Colony, Sinai, and parts of the Aden Protectorate alone are based on survey and in places supplemented by air-photographs, but maps of the rest are only compiled from travellers' route-maps and reports. The most useful maps are those of the International 1 : M series (3 (*a*) (*b*) (*c*) below), but even these are incomplete and leave large gaps in south-central Arabia and on the Red Sea coast of Africa.

The following maps have been consulted in the preparation of this book:

1. *Scale 1:4,000,000*

   (*a*) Europe, Asia, and Africa (G.S.G.S. 2957). Sheets *Persian Gulf* and *Gulf of Aden* (1934). Coloured and layered. Parts of the two sheets have been published as a single map of the whole of Arabia and the Red Sea.

   (*b*) Bartholomew's *The Middle East*. Coloured and layered. International boundaries are out of date.

2. *Scale 1:2,000,000*

   (*a*) Southern Asia (Survey of India, 1934). *SE. Arabia* (G.S.G.S. 4340). Contoured in metres.

   (*b*) Asia (Arabia) (512 Field Survey Coy. R.E., 1943). *SE. Arabia*, and *Gulf of Aden*. Coloured and layered with air information added.

(c) Africa (G.S.G.S. 2871). *Sudan* (1943), *Upper Egypt* (1943), *Egypt* (1942). Ground/Air style, covering Red Sea and coasts, Sinai Peninsula, Gulfs of Suez and 'Aqaba, and Africa roughly east of Nile valley.

3. *Scale 1:1,000,000*

(a) Carte Internationale (Asia, G.S.G.S. 2555). Sheets ND. 38 (Aden), ND. 39 (Mukalla), parts of NE. 37 and 38 (Kunfida), NF. 37 (Mecca), NF. 38 (Laila), NG. 37 (Medina), NG. 38 (Riyadh), NG. 39 (Hofuf), NG. 40 (Bandar Abbas), NH. 36 (Cairo), NH. 37 (Al Jauf), NH. 38 (Basra), NH. 39 (Bushire). Six sheets covering south-central Arabia have not yet been published. Several editions are available in the standard 'International' layered style of all but the Mukalla, Kunfida, and Mecca sheets which have only first or second editions unlayered. Later editions of most of the others are in Army/Air style, layered in purple and grey. Though compiled from the best available sources the relief is unreliable.

(b) Carte Internationale (Africa, G.S.G.S. 2465). Sheets NF. 36 (Wadi Halfa), NG. 36 (Aswan); available in Army/Air style (ed. 1943). Generally reliable.

(c) Carte Internationale (compiled by Instituto Geografico Militare, 1934–1936). Sheets ND. 37 (Asmara), NE. 37 (Nacfa). The best map available of these areas.

(d) Africa Orientale Italiana (compiled by the Touring Club Italiano). Sheets 1–8, 10, 11 cover Eritrea. Hachured hill features.

(e) A.A.F. Aeronautical Charts (compiled by U.S. Army Air Force). The Arabian sheets are generalized compilations from existing maps and less informative than the Carte Internationale.

4. *Scale 1:500,000*

(a) 'Iraq Desert frontier (G.S.G.S. 3954). Sheets *Rutba, Wadi-al-Ubaiyidh, Ash-Shabicha, Salman-Busaiya, Basra-Kuwait*. Detail on Arabian side is less reliable than on the 'Iraq side of the boundary and is compiled from the reports and route-surveys of Alois Musil and other travellers.

(b) Egypt (G.S.G.S 4084). Sheets 2 (Cairo), 3 (North Sinai), 5 (Asyūt), 6 (South Sinai). Sheets 2 and 6 by 512 Field Survey Company R.E., 1942, layered (contours at 100 metres). Sheets 3 and 5 by Survey of Egypt, 1937–1938, unlayered.

5. *Scale 1:253,440* (1 inch = 4 miles)

(a) SW. Arabia (G.S.G.S. 3108). 'Maunsell's sheets': 1 (Taiz), 2 (Sanaa), 3 (Saada), 4 (Ebha), 5 (Wadi Shehran), 6 (Kunfida), 7 (Wadi Bishe), 8 (Mecca), 9 (Taif). Compiled from available sources, Turkish and other, early in the 1914–1918 war, and of little use to-day.

(b) Aden Protectorate (G.S.G.S. 3892 and 3997). 2 sheets, the first covering Bab al Mandeb to Wadi Hasan from surveys in 1891–1894 and 1901–1904, the second from Wadi Hasan to Wadi Ahwar compiled from air-photographs taken in 1933–1934. Both are coloured; the earlier has hachures, the later form-lines at 200 feet.

6. *Scale 1:250,000*

Sinai Peninsula (G.S.G.S. 2761). Sheets 1 (Port Said), 2 (Rafa), 3 (Suez), 4 (Akaba). Fourth ed. 1941, except Sheet 3 which is first ed. 1915 with road revision 1936. Coloured and contoured (100 feet). Parts reduced from surveys 1908–1914, supplemented by compilation.

7. *Scale 1:126,720* (1 inch = 2 miles)

Aden (G.S.G.S. 3879). 10 published sheets, originally by Survey of India, 1917. Coloured, with form-lines.

8. *Scale 1:100,000*

(a) North Sinai (G.S.G.S. 4208). 18 sheets, by Department of Survey and Mines, Egypt, 1935–1939. W.O. edition 1941. Coloured and hachured.

(b) Egypt. Eastern Desert, Sheet 2 (Suez), by Survey of Egypt 1936. Coloured and hachured.

9. *Scale 1:31,680* (2 inches = 1 mile)

Aden Peninsula (G.S.G.S. 3893). Original by General Staff, India, 1917.

10. *Scale 1:25,000*

Aden and Little Aden (E.A.F. 1591, 1592). 2 sheets based on triangulation, air-photo control, and interpretation by 36 N.Z. Survey Battery 1942, with corrections by H.Q. Aden. Coloured and contoured at 25 metres.

11. *Scale 1:15,840* (4 inches = 1 mile)

Perim Island (G.S.G.S. 3894). Original by Survey of India, 1917. Contoured in brown at 25 feet, otherwise in black.

INDEX

Additional references may also be given under the alternative names which are sometimes shown in brackets. To save space the first words of composite names have not been repeated; thus 'Abd al Wasi' is found under 'Abd al Kuri, and Abu Bekr under Abu 'Ail. The only abbreviations used are A.C. (Aden Colony), A.P. (Aden Protectorate), Hadhr. (Hadhramaut), S.A. (Sa'ūdi Arabia), and Y. (Yemen). The index should be used in conjunction with the Table of Contents at the beginning of the volume, which is fully paged.

Abādhis, see Ibādhis.
'Abādilah House, 282.
'Abbās, Al, 242.
Abbasids, 8, 242–6, 250, 267, 586.
'Abd, al Kuri island, 208, 210, 614; al Qadir peninsula, 117–18; al Qeis tribe, 244; al Wahhāb ibn Tahir, 249; al Wasi', 21.
'Abdali, Sultanate, 345, 361; Sultans, 256, 274–5, 291, 342, 361, 401.
'Abdalis, 420, 459.
'Abdul, 'Aziz ibn 'Abdurrahmān ibn Sa'ūd, see Ibn Sa'ūd; 'Aziz ibn Muhammad ibn Rashid, 270, 283–5, 566; 'Aziz ibn Muhammad ibn Sa'ūd, 266–7; Hamid II, Sultan, 286–7, 521; Ilah, 282; Malik, 25, 586; Muttalib ibn Ghālib, 271, 282; Wahid, 309.
'Abdullah, 235; (Amir of Transjordan), 281–3, 287, 292–4, 296–8, 301; al 'Amri, Qadhi, 330; al Hasan, Sheikh, 322; al Wazir, Seiyid, 331; ibn 'Abbās, 572; ibn 'Ali, 244; ibn az Zubeir, 243; ibn Feisal ibn Sa'ūd, 269–70; ibn Ibādh al Murri al Tamīmi, 390; ibn Ja'far al Kathīr, 277; ibn Meimūn, 244; ibn Mit'ab ibn Rashid, 297; ibn Muhammad ibn 'Aun, 271, 282; ibn Rashid, 269; ibn Sa'ūd, 267–8; Pasha, 274, 287; Suleiman, Sheikh, 321.
Abdulqadūs al Wazir, Seiyid, 331.
Abdur, Jebel, 119–20.
'Abdurrahman, 242.
'Abdurrahmān ibn Feisal ibn Sa'ūd, 270, 284.
Abeilat island, 124.
Abhā, 564; administration, 356; agriculture, 475; communications, 526, 564; history, 289; houses, 411, 564; Wadi, 564.
ablution, 380, 390, 395.
Abqaiq oilfield, 515.
Abrad, Wadi, 31.
Abraha, 229, 234, 393.
Abraham, 560.
Abramus, see Abraha.
'Abs tribe, 231.
Abu, 'Ail, 59; al Hasan ash Shadhili, see Shadhili; Amara, Sherm, 584;

'Arīsh, 355, 475, 518, 564, Sharifs, 256, 271, 289; Assel, Khor, 584; Baka, Ras, 87; Baqara, 384; Bekr, 237, 239, 379, 384, 390, 564, 586; Berima, 44; Dāra, Ras, 108; Diraj, Ras, 86; Durba, 80; Emma, Sherm, 584; Fanādir, Khor, 109, 584; Gurdi, Jebel, 105; Hadriya oilfield, 515; Hajar, Ras, 103; Hanīfa, 384; Hāshim Muhammad, 244, 282; Hurghada, 89, 100; Ja'far al Mansur, 586; Kasha, 93–4; Madd, Ras, 129; Massarib, Ras, 126–7; Mingar, 99; Mokhadig, Mersa, 101; Nuqta, 271; Ramlah, 92; Rimāthi, 99; Sa'id, 244; Shagara, Ras (Rawāya), 109–10, 584; Sha'r al Qibli, Jebel, 88; Sōma, Ras, 101; Tahir, 244; Tāqah, 522–3; Tiyur, Jebel, 104; Zenima, 79–80; Zereibat, 128.
Abul, 'Abbas al Saffāh, 586; Dufuf, 51; Futuh, 244; Na'im, 523.
Abyadh, Jebel, 13; Ras, 129; Wadi al, 40.
Abyan oasis, 23, 36, 482, 485.
Abyssinia, geology, 16–17, 19–20; history, 228–30, 256–7, 259, 261, 265, 281; name, 228.
Abyssinian, highlands, 20, 97–8, 202–3; occupations, 229–30.
Abyssinians, history, 222, 229, 246, 249–50, 252.
Achaemenids, 216.
'Ad, descendants of, 220, 227.
Adabiya, bay, 85; Cape, 85.
Adago Berai, 118.
'Adal, state, 250.
'Adali tribe, 250.
Adam, Guillaume, 253, 256.
Addis Ababa, roads, 115, 122, 125–6.
Aden, 8, 539, 549–53; administration, 8, 309, 339–40, 553; centenary, 309; Chamber of Commerce, 553; climate, 154, 158, 163–4, 166, 172, 175, 180–1; communications, 143–4, 529, 535, 537–8, 553; earthquakes, 21; exports, 490, 532, 551; faults, 12, 18, 52, 60, 86, 98, 141; frankincense, 206; frontier, 275–6; Government, 305, 309–

556; industries, 536; people, 420, 426; Sultan, 309, 342, 363; water, 150.

Shihuh people, 179, 409, 443.

Shilling, Andrew, 263.

Shin'āb, Jebel, 109; Khor, 69, 109, 584.

Shiqqa salt-pan, 518.

shrines, 396, 404, 557.

Shuheir, road, 150, 538.

Shukheir, Ras, 87–8.

Shukri al Quwatli, 300.

Shuqeiq, 133, 356.

Shuqra, 145, 361, 538.

Shurta (police), 328.

Shurwein, Ras, 151.

Sibila, battle, 301.

Sidara, 24, 535.

Sifala, 179, 415, 452, 460.

Sig, Wadi, 44.

Siham, Wadi, 185, 490.

Sikait, Jebel, 104.

silk trade, 229, 252.

Silveira, Eitor da, 260.

simsim oil, 536, 595.

Sin (moon-god), 214, 216, 225–6.

Sinafir (Sanafīr) island, 95.

Sinai, 2, 43–7; agriculture, 494, 594, 599; camels, 508; climate, 153, 157, 164, 169, 175, 181–2, 188–92; coasts, 62–3, 75, 77–84; drainage, 24, 26–7, 43, 77; geology,16; history, 213–14, 217–18, 232; locusts, 496–7; name, 214; people, 366; springs, 33, 44–5; tracks, 77, 79–81; vegetation, 200–1, 590.

Sinan Pasha, 255.

'singing sands', 42, 50–1, 81.

Sinn Bisher, Jebel, 79.

siqaya (wayside reservoirs), 35.

Sira island, 263, 274.

Sirhan, Wadi, 15, 27, 39–40, 96, 198, 270, 300, 315, 526.

Sirr, 355, 518.

Sirra, Wadi, 28–9, 48.

Sirwah, 220, 226.

Sisters (Brothers) islets, 609.

Siyāl islands, 108.

skin diseases, 460.

sky-goddess, 214.

skyscrapers, Hadhr., 1, 4, 406, 413–14, 582.

slave trade, slaves, 271, 276, 278, 284, 300, 312, 335, 351–3, 366, 370, 405–6.

Sleyb, *see* Solubba.

Small Strait, 139.

smallpox, 307, 448–9, 467–9, 471–2.

Smith, Dr., 453.

smoking, 381, 383, 385, 390.

smuggling, 328.

snow, 153, 182, 186, 604.

soap factory, 531.

Soares de Albergaria, Lopo, 260.

social, customs, 430–46; organization, 396–406.

Society for Medical Relief, 470–1.

Socoteri language, 613.

Socotra, 609–15; administration, 345, 363, 612; agriculture, 479, 493, 614–15; climate, 609–10; coasts, 65, 609; history, 224, 228, 244, 253, 259, 262, 274, 277, 307, 612; livestock, 498, 505–6, 613, 615; people, 365, 428, 614–15; Sultanate, 274, 276, 309, 343, 363, 612; vegetation, 207–8, 590, 592, 610.

Soda island, 616.

sodium, 121.

Sodre, 259.

Sohār, malaria, 452.

Sokkari, Jebel, 104.

solar radiation, 174–5.

Solomon, 217, 517.

Solubba, 364, 368, 408, 418, 423, 434, 440, 504–5.

Somaliland, 16, 204–6, 250, 308, 532–4.

Somalis, 276, 366, 371, 547–8, 552, 555.

Soncino, Raimondo di, 257.

Sorghum, *see* dhura.

South Arabian, kingdoms, 218–25; languages, 372–7, 613; Marginal Elevation, 53–5.

south coast, 141–52, 195–6.

south-eastern trough, 49–51.

southern desert, 49–51.

south-west Arabia, history, 246–9, 290–1.

south-western highlands, agriculture, 473, 475–9; climate, 184–8; livestock, 506, 511; vegetation, 201–5, 591–2; *see also* 'Asīr highlands *and* Yemen highlands.

Soviet political mission, 543.

spices, 214–15, 217, 221, 251, 258, 261–2, 428.

spirits, 236.

springs, 33–4, 38, 49, 56; hot, 6, 21, 24, 32, 52, 79, 146, 150; sacred, 226, 235, 265, 396.

squalls, 158–9.

Standard Oil Company, 515.

Stark, Freya, 196.

statues, pre-Islamic, 227.

Steamer Point, 535, 550, 552.

steppes, 3.

Stone Age cultures, 213.

Storrs, Ronald, 292, 295.

Stotzingen, Baron von, 291.

Strabo, 220–2.

structure, 12–16.

Suākin, 107, 112; al Qadim ('Aidhāb), 108; archipelago, 97, 113; history, 112, 249–50, 260, 279; island, 112; roads, 112, 114; sherm, 68–9; water, 112.

T - #0070 - 270225 - C0 - 234/156/46 - PB - 9780415653213 - Gloss Lamination